India: Industrialisation in a Reforming Economy

Professor K.L. Krishna

India: Industrialisation in a Reforming Economy

ESSAYS FOR K L KRISHNA

Editors:
Suresh D Tendulkar
Arup Mitra
K Narayanan
Deb Kusum Das

Academic Foundation
NEW DELHI

First published in 2006
by
ACADEMIC FOUNDATION
4772-73 / 23 Bharat Ram Road, (23 Ansari Road),
Darya Ganj, New Delhi - 110 002 (India).
Phones : 23245001 / 02 / 03 / 04.
Fax : +91-11-23245005.
E-mail : academic@vsnl.com
www.academicfoundation.com

India: Industrialisation in a Reforming Economy
— Essays for K.L. Krishna
Editors :
Suresh D. Tendulkar, Arup Mitra,
K. Narayanan, Deb Kusum Das.

ISBN 81-7188-488-1

Designed and typeset by Italics India, New Delhi.
Printed and bound in India.

CONTENTS

...Contd. ...

Part 2

Urbanisation, Employment and Infrastructural Issues for Indian Industries

Part 3

Trade and Indian Industrialisation

Part 4

MNC and Technology Transfer in Indian Industries

...CONTD. ...

Part 5

Indian Industry and Environment

Contributors to the Volume

C. RANGARAJAN

Chairman, Prime Minister's Economic Advisory Council

BISHWANATH GOLDAR

Professor, Institute of Economic Growth, Delhi, India

SUBHASH C. RAY

Professor, Department of Economics,
University of Connecticut, USA

ZHANG PING

Fraud Risk Manager, e-bay, 2211 North First St,
San Jose CA 95131, USA

T.A. BHAVANI

Reader, Institute of Economic Growth, Delhi, India

ANITA KUMARI

Sir Ratan Tata Fellow,
Institute of Economic Growth, Delhi, India

ABDUL AZEEZ E.

Researcher, Faculty of Economics,
University of Groningen, The Netherlands

EDWIN S. MILLS

Professor, Emeritus of Real Estate and Finance, Kellog School of Management, Northwestern University, USA

ARUP MITRA

Professor, Institute of Economic Growth, Delhi, India

PRASAD SANKAR BHATTACHARYA

Graduate Student, Florida International University, Miami, USA

SURESH D. TENDULKAR

Honorary Professor, Delhi School of Economics, University of Delhi, India

K. LAL

Researcher, UNU-INTECH, Institute for New Technologies, Masstricht, The Netherlands

SANJEEVAN KAPSHE

Professor, Railway Staff College, Vadodara, India

ISHER JUDGE AHLUWALIA

Chairperson, Board of Trustees, IFPRI, Washington, USA

HIRANYA MUKHOPADHYAY

Economist, Asian Development Bank, New Delhi, India

DEB KUSUM DAS

Reader, Department of Economics, Ramjas College, University of Delhi, India

Saikat Sinha Roy

Fellow, Research and Information System for Developing Countries (RIS), New Delhi, India

V.N. Balasubramanyam

Emeritus Professor of Economics, Department of Economics, Lancaster University Management School, UK

David Sapsford

Edward Gonner, Professor of Applied Economics, Management School, University of Liverpool, UK

Nagesh Kumar

Director General, Research and Information System for Developing Countries (RIS), New Delhi, India

Aradhana Agarwal

Reader, Department of Business Economics, University of Delhi, India

K. Narayanan

Associate Professor, Department of Humanities and Social Sciences, Indian Institute of Technology-Bombay (Mumbai), India

Neelam Singh

Reader, Department of Economics, Lady Shriram College, University of Delhi, India

K.U. Umakrishnan

Research Associate, National Institute of Bank Management, Pune, India

U. Sankar

Honorary Professor, Madras School of Economics, Chennai, India

M.N. Murty

Professor, Institute of Economic Growth, Delhi, India

Surender Kumar

Associate Professor, TERI School of Advanced Studies, New Delhi, India

Smita Misra

Senior Environmental Specialist, World Bank, New Delhi, India

Simanti Banerjee

Economist, National Institute of Public Finance and Policy, New Delhi, India

Sarmila Banerjee

Professor, Department of Economics, Calcutta University, India

Acknowledgments

We owe our thanks to many institutions and individuals from whom we derived enormous support in bringing out this volume. In particular, we would like to thank V.N. Pandit, Aditya Bhattacharjea, T.C.A. Anant, Partha Sen, B.N. Goldar and Isher Ahluwalia in organising a conference in honour of Professor K.L. Krishna, in which many of the articles included in this volume were presented. Besides them, a large number of students and well-wishers of Professor Krishna helped us in all possible ways to make this volume a reality.

We would like to thank the entire support staff of Centre for Development Economics, Delhi School of Economics and especially Jai Mohan Pandit, without whose untiring efforts this volume would not have been complete. We owe special gratitude to Prashant Jha for excellent research assistance.

We gratefully acknowledge the financial support received from the Export-Import Bank of India, Housing and Urban Development Corporation Ltd., Industrial Development Bank of India, Infrastructure Development Finance Company Ltd., ITC Ltd., Planning Commision, Government of India and State Bank of Hyderabad.

Finally, we thank the team at Academic Foundation for preparing the manuscript for publication at a very short notice, and in particular Uma Kapila who in fact has been a student of Prof. Krishna.

— *Editors*

Professor K.L. Krishna: A Tribute

Professor Kosaraju Leela Krishna, or KL to everyone who has known him, retired from the Delhi School of Economics on August 14, 2000, a little over 42 years since he joined the School, first as a statistician and shortly thereafter as Lecturer in Economic Statistics. In 1963 KL proceeded to the University of Chicago to pursue his doctoral studies with Professor Zvi Griliches. His three-year stay at Chicago was followed by a year's stint at the Brookings Institute on a fellowship. With hindsight it would now appear that his return to the School in 1967 could not have been timed better. For, this was the time when econometrics had become an indispensable tool for research in almost all areas of applied economics and a prominent component of academic curricula at all leading institutions. Professor A.L. Nagar who had joined the School a few years earlier was already working on the frontiers of econometric theory with some of his students. These new research explorations were enormously bolstered by KL's efforts to stimulate research in and teaching of applied econometrics. His contribution to both of these areas over the ensuing three decades has been overwhelming.

It would indeed be no exaggeration to say that KL's impact on both applied research and teaching of econometrics has been a countrywide phenomenon rather than being confined to Delhi. The fact that he saw a successful completion of over 40 Ph.D & M.Phil dissertations, covering almost all important branches of economics, is indeed impressive. But equally, or even more than this, one is amazed at the number of researchers outside doctoral programmes and spread over different parts of the country and even abroad whose work has got enormously enriched by the guidance, encouragement and patient listening that they received from KL. No wonder he stands out to be a role model as a "Teacher", with a capital T. For, it has indeed been much more than mere competent and authoritative imparting of skills to scholars and students. The exemplary humility, dignity and understanding with which KL treated his students and fellow scholars has stood out as the hallmark of his personality. The fact that KL resisted the usual temptations to take up teaching and/or research assignments abroad bears testimony to his commitment to the scholars he was working with, and of course to the School. During his long career it is only once that he agreed to teach for a year at Monash University, Australia in the mid-seventies. It is, therefore, not surprising that KL was happy to continue teaching at the School till the end of the summer semester of 2000-01 well beyond the day of his formal retirement.

The academic and professional world in which KL took his last bow as member of the department, could not but be more different from the one that he first entered more than four decades back. Yet remarkably, he remains as active within the profession and relevant to it today as when he joined it, and this bespeaks a rare and special ability to keep abreast of fast emerging new developments in econometric techniques and applications, the hallmark of the Teacher *par excellence*. Another facet of KL's commitment to the promotion of scholarship has been his devoted decade-long founder-editorship of the *Journal of Quantitative Economics*, the journal of the Indian Econometric Society. The Andhra Pradesh Association of Economists and the Indian Econometric Society have indeed raised their own prestige by electing KL as their President in 1991 and 1996 respectively.

Joseph Schumpeter is said to have remarked in his twilight years that his life would have been worth living if he had been able to make a difference to the lives of at least a few of his students. Professor Krishna has made a significant difference to the lives not only of the innumerable number of Master's degree students that he taught during the four decades of distinguished teaching, but also to the large body of research scholars and colleagues at the Delhi School of Economics and elsewhere. All the editors of this volume, who share the fortune of being the students of K.L. Krishna, wish him a long, healthy and intellectually active retired life. We are sure a large number of his other students, colleagues and friends would join us in this humble tribute to our Teacher.

— *Editors*

Introduction

Industry is rightly regarded a leading sector in economic growth because of its intensity in reproducible tangible capital, scale economies and greater amenability to rapid technological changes. This volume contains a set of papers on Indian industrialisation in the context of market-enhancing and trade-liberalising reforms that have been taking place. These reforms have enabled the Indian economy to come out of the low growth equilibrium – what the late Professor Raj Krishna called "the Hindu rate of growth". Since 1980, the Indian economy has been one of the top ten fastest-growing economies among the developing countries. The papers in this volume attempt to throw light on the various facets of this remarkable transformation of the Indian economy with reference to industrialisation, an area of major interest to Professor K.L. Krishna, to whom the volume is presented on his seventieth birthday.

In the lead paper, Rangarajan traces the shifts in the industrial policy regime and reviews the industrial growth performance since independence. He deals in greater detail with more recent post-1991 period of systemic industrial sector reforms. He notes with concern the slackening of industrial growth in the second half of the 1990s following the boom in the immediate post-reform period and highlights the necessity of maintaining the continuity in economic policy to sustain the reform-led growth momentum. In this context, he rightly underlines the need for consensus among political parties and policymakers on the core elements of economic policy.

Technological change is known to be the most fundamental driver of sustained economic growth and it has historically been most marked in the industrial sector. Measurement of technological change in the industrial sector, however, has been beset with several conceptual and methodological problems. The most widely used measure, namely, total factor productivity growth (TFPG) is known to be sensitive to the (single or double) deflation of value added, the specification of two (labour and capital) or three (material input additionally) inputs, residual or production/cost-function based estimation procedure and the type of data used. The first Part deals with these important issues. In the lead paper, Goldar traces the channels through which liberalisation is expected to promote industrial productivity and input efficiency, reviews the available studies on TFPG in Indian manufacturing, and noting their conflicting nature, presents his carefully worked out estimates of TFPG using alternative specifications and deflation procedures. Contrary to the dominant view, his empirical analysis suggests that the decade of the 1980s was a period of rapid TFPG in Indian manufacturing followed by a slowdown in the 1990s (1990-97). The paper by Ray and Ping uses the technique of Data Envelopment Analysis to examine changes in levels of technical efficiency in a sample of state owned enterprises in China during their first decade of market-oriented reforms, 1980-89. In order to measure the effect of reforms on technical efficiency, they employ a Tobit regression model to conclude that reform related variables were effective in improving technical efficiency. This may offer some lessons for the Indian public sector reforms. In another paper, Kumari provides an assessment of productivity growth in the Indian engineering industries during the pre- and post- reform periods based on the company level data. She also finds that there was a decline in total factor productivity growth during the post-reform (1990-91 to 1994-95) period and that there was a negative impact of foreign equity participation on productivity growth. In the next paper, Bhavani explores the micro-level determinants of technological change in small-scale industries. The study is based on the intensive survey of small-scale garment units in Delhi. Apart from the scale being important, she finds the technological change to be induced by the need to maintain quality and timely delivery. The final paper by Azeez in this Part refutes the accepted wisdom at the 1980s that imports of capital goods were responsible for the lower rates of capacity utilisation in the Indian capital goods industries. His empirical analyses indicates the two to be complementary.

Urbanisation, an inevitable concomitant of industrialisation, industrial labour absorption and infrastructure required mostly, if not wholly for the industrial sector, constitute the theme of the next

Part. Agglomeration economies arising from urbanisation intereact with industrialisation in both positive and negative fashion. Benefits arising out of large human settlements and indivisible urban infrastructure induce firms toward faster productivity growth and higher levels of technical efficiency. However, diseconomies in the form of congestion, pollution, hikes in land and housing prices and administrative unmanageability tend to have adverse impact on quality of life. In this context, Mills brings together salient stylised facts and theories about the relationships among industrialisation, urbanisation and poverty reduction and tries to fit India into the picture. He notes that industrialisation has limited impact in reducing poverty through direct employment generation but combined with urbanisation, it promotes general economic growth that is directly instrumental in poverty reduction. He underlines the need for urban economic policy. The findings of Mills are partially confirmed in the Indian context by Mitra and Bhattacharya. Their estimated system of simultaneous equations in five endogenous variables shows that indirect employment and productivity effects of organised industrial growth have been effective in reducing poverty. They bring out the role of human capital formation in raising the productivity of the informal sector and recommend the urgent need for strengthening the linkages between the organised and the unorganised industrial segments for facilitating poverty reduction. In the context of the apprehensions regarding the possible adverse effects of liberalisation and globalisation on employment and in the background of the "jobless growth" in the Indian factory sector in the 1980s, Tendulkar shows that the post-1991 industrial policy reforms have proved favourable for factory employment growth. In the next paper, Lal reviews the structuralist policies before 1991 and pro-active economic policies since then in the context of the rapid growth of the Indian Information Technology (IT) industry in the export and domestic markets in the 1990s. He notes the inability of the existing policies to attract private foreign direct investment in the IT hardware manufacturing and suggests the need for corrective policies. In the final paper of this Part Kapshe advocates a bottom-up or micro level approach to management of infrastructure projects. In order to improve investment climate, he proposes a variant of typical Build-Operate-Transfer (BOT) contract structure that enables estimation of contingent fiscal liabilities (CFLs) arising from it. He argues that once CFLs are estimated, it is possible to mitigate them through innovative instruments that can be sold in the market to finance a particular project.

A major change in the role of international trade in the Indian development strategy and the consequent changes in trade policies have been an integral part of the ongoing process of structural adjustment and economic reforms. In the context of industrialisation, this has meant a change from import substitution-orientation of industrial policy toward an export-oriented one with greater integration with the global economy. Part 3 is devoted to these issues in the context of the Indian manufacturing sector. Ahluwalia provides an overview of policy changes and their impact on the performance indicators like growth in value added, total factor productivity and exports at a disaggregated level in the 1980s and 1990s. The next paper by Das investigates the linkage between trade policy reforms and total factor productivity growth drawing on a panel of capital and intermediate goods industries at three-digit industry classification level for the period 1980-95. Mukhopadhyay offers a theoretical macro-model assuming an open dual economy to show that a higher tariff actually pushes the domestic relative price ratio in favour of the comparatively advantaged sector. He also provides an empirical test of his result. The final paper in this Part by Sinha Ray attempts to answer a question why, despite a turnaround in the 1980s, India's manufacturing export performance remained persistently low and trace the underlying factors over the long period 1960-97. The papers in this Part highlight the fact that trade liberalisation is a major factor impacting industrial growth. However, this impact may remain muted in the face of other rigidities in the economic system such as inability to restrain fiscal and revenue deficits, persistence of overprotective labour laws and reservation of labour-intensive exportable manufacturing industries.

One other major area of economic reforms relates to foreign direct investment (FDI) which is being encouraged with a view to facilitating technology transfer that is expected to impact industrial performance. There are several contentious issues in this area relating to the role of multinational enterprises (MNEs) that are examined at the macro level of economy or industry and the micro level of a firm or company in Part 4. The lead paper by Balasubramanyam and

Sapsford covers a variety of issues relating to the determinants and efficacy of FDI in promoting growth and other related development objectives in developing countries. The main proposition in the literature indicates that FDI is a catalyst and rarely an initiator of growth. However, the catalystic role is likely to be neutralised in the absence of growth promoting factors such as human capital endowments, infrastructure facilities and effective market competition. The next paper by Kumar and Agarwal examines the impact of post- 1991 reforms on Research and Development (R&D) behaviour of MNE affiliates and local enterprises. Their analysis suggests that although average level of R&D spending has declined, increased competition due to liberalisation seems to have pushed local firms to rationalise their R&D activity by absorption of imported technology and provide a backup to their outward expansion. MNE affiliates, on the other hand, either focused on customisation of their parent's technology for local market or on exploiting the advantages of India as R&D platform for their parents. In another paper, Narayanan studies the impact of import liberalisation and technology transfer through the dual channels of FDI and the market on the international competitiveness of the Indian automobile firms in terms of their export intensity. The major finding is that, with a change in the policy regime, firms that have accomplished technological paradigm shifts through foreign equity participation by MNEs or in-house R&D efforts tend to be more competitive. In the next paper, Singh analyses the firm level determinants of R&D and intensities of technology import, export and merchandise imports to find that a higher import of technology and higher R&D spending act as complements rather than as substitutes. Similarly, greater export-orientation and R&D intensity are found to be mutually reinforcing in nature *albeit* with differences between medium and large sized firms. The final paper in this Part by Umakrishnan takes account of heterogeneity of FDI and differences in their nature and behaviour across sources to bring out significant differences in the level and determinants of technology transfer between the U.S. and the Japanese firms in India.

Recent literature in industrial development in both developed as well as developing countries have shown increased awareness of the environmental consequences of rapid industrialisation. Policy measures to promote industrialisation in newly industrialising countries have also taken into account the design of environmental policy within which one can promote adoption of clean development mechanism (CDM). The policy framework for prevention and control of pollution in India is largely based on the standards and regulation approach. The final Part in this volume is devoted to these issues in the Indian industrial context. The paper by Sankar explores various cost-effective options for internalising the externalities by means of a mix of regulatory and market-based instruments which lighten overloaded government's burden and sometimes even contribute to revenues while providing flexibility to economic agents in finding least-cost solutions for compliance of environmental regulations. He advocates the involvement of the affected parties, industry associations and communities in different stages of policy making and enforcement. Murty and Kumar provide estimates of measures of technical efficiency for alternative specification of production technology of firms and show that the estimate of technical efficiency is sensitive to whether you consider environmental services as inputs or not. This result highlights the importance of environmental resource accounting for the firms as also of estimating environmentally corrected GDP. The study by Misra of 250 small-scale factories in Nandesari Industrial Estate shows that the cost burden of water pollution abatement is much higher for small factories providing greater cost advantage to treat effluents jointly in a Common Effluent Treatment Plant (CETP). She argues that the institutional arrangement of the Common Effluent Treatment Plant is necessary to internalise the cost of eliminating the negative externalities generated by water pollution by the operation of the concerned small-scale industries. Banerjee and Banerjee's analysis suggest that in India, there exist differences in the marginal cost functions for wastewater treatment across industries, even though they employ the same technique for pollution control. Also, the pollutant specific standards (MINAS) set by the Central Pollution Control Board, sometimes vary across industries, and these differences can be successfully utilised to formulate a policy which allows trading in emissions between industries.

Industrialisation in the reforming Indian economy has been an ongoing and multi-faceted process. It is hoped that the papers in this volume would add to the understanding of important aspects of this process and constitute a fitting tribute to Professor K.L. Krishna.

1

Shifts in Industrial Policy Paradigm

C. RANGARAJAN

Given the historical developments world over, it is not surprising that growth was identified with industrialisation in all the developing economies. The Indian planners went a step further and talked of industrialisation with an emphasis on heavy industries. It was, no doubt, recognised that for the process of industrialisation to start, there has to be a transfer of resources from agriculture. That inadequate agricultural growth and insufficient availability of wage goods including food-grains could act as a restraint on industrial growth was realised only later. The industry-agriculture relationship was mainly seen in terms of agriculture making available the required raw materials. Once again, the recognition of the importance of agricultural growth and rural incomes as a source of demand for industrial goods, thereby fueling industrial growth, came later.

The process of industrialisation in India in the first four decades was governed by two considerations — import substitution and industrial licensing. Import substitution constituted a major plank of India's foreign trade policy and, therefore, of industrialisation. Planners, more or less, chose to ignore the option of foreign trade as an engine of India's economic growth. This was primarily due to the highly pessimistic view taken on the potential for export earnings. A further impetus to the inward orientation was provided by the existence of a vast domestic market. In retrospect, it is clear that the policymakers not only under-estimated the export possibilities but also the import intensity of the import substitution process itself. As a consequence, India's share of total world exports declined from 1.91 per cent in 1950 to about 0.53 per cent in 1992.

The inward looking industrialisation process did result in high rates of industrial growth between 1956 and 1966. However, several weaknesses of such a process of industrialisation soon became evident, as inefficiencies crept into the system and the economy turned into an increasingly 'high-cost' one. Over a period of time, this led to a 'technological lag' and also resulted in poor export performance.

Foreign trade policy issues became the subject of intensive discussion in early eighties. It came to be realised that a scheme of import licensing under which imports were permitted only to the extent that domestic production fell short of domestic demand irrespective of differences in cost and prices, could only lead to inefficiency. The view gained ground that a more liberal policy of imports of capital goods and technology would enable India to reap the benefits of international division of labour. The attempt, therefore, was to move away from import substitution *per se* towards efficient import substitution, so that considerations relating to cost and efficiency were incorporated in the overall policy framework. It also became increasingly clear that production for export could not be isolated from production for the home market.

Another important element in the process of industrialisation was a system of industrial licensing under which a license was required before setting up any large unit. This practice had roots in the belief that resources could be best allocated only by a planning authority and that licensing was the best way to manage limited resources. While the industrial licensing system underwent some changes in terms of threshold levels and types of products, it formed an essential part of Government policy until the end of the 80s.

Commenting on the process of industrialisation until the end of 80s, Prof. K.L. Krishna wrote: "Since independence, industrial policy in India has stressed rapid industrial growth with diversification of the industrial structure as one of the important objectives of industrialisation. There is general agreement that while India has achieved a very diversified industrial structure, her growth performance leaves much to be desired, both with regard to the magnitude of the growth rate and its stability over time. Three phases of growth have been distinguished: a phase of rapid growth from the early 1950s to the mid-1960s; a phase of deceleration from the mid-1960s to late 1970s; and a phase of revival in the late 1970s followed by rapid growth in the 1980s."

The year 1991 is an important landmark in the economic history of post Independent India. The country went through a severe economic crisis triggered by a serious balance of payments situation. The crisis was converted into an opportunity to introduce some fundamental changes in the content and approach to economic policy. The response to the crisis was to put in place a set of policies aimed at stabilisation and structural reform. While the stabilisation policies were aimed at correcting the weaknesses that had developed on the fiscal and the balance of payments fronts, the structural reforms sought to remove the rigidities that had entered into the various segments of the Indian economy. The structural reforms introduced in the early nineties broadly covered the areas of industrial licensing, foreign trade, foreign investment, exchange rate management and the financial sector. From the point of view of industrialisation, changes in the areas of licensing and foreign trade and investment had important implications. Even before the onset of reforms the problems associated with industrial licensing were well recognised. The approach document of the Eighth Plan submitted in May, 1990 had remarked: "A return to the regime of direct, indiscriminate and detailed controls in industry is clearly out of question. Past experience has shown that such control system is not effective in achieving the desired objective. Also the system is widely abused and leads to corruption, delays and insufficiency." One early step that was undertaken as part of the structural reform process was to dispense with licensing. Changes in foreign trade policy focussed on reducing the tariff rates and dismantling quantitative controls over imports. The tariff rates have been brought down in stages. Some caution in this regard becomes necessary to enable the Indian industries set behind high protective tariff walls to adjust to the changed situation. The policy towards foreign investment underwent a significant change with foreign investors given the freedom to own majority share holding over a wide spectrum of industries.

Without going into details, the common thread running through the various policy measures introduced since 1991 has been the improvement of the efficiency of the system. The regulatory mechanism involving multitudes of controls had fragmented capacity and reduced competition even in the private sector. The thrust of the New Economic Policy has been towards creating a more competitive environment in the economy as a means to improving the productivity and efficiency of the system. This is to be achieved by removing the barriers to entry and the restrictions on the growth of firms. While the Industrial Policy seeks to bring about a greater competitive environment domestically, the Trade Policy seeks to improve the international competitiveness subject to the degree of protection offered by the tariffs. Private sector is being given a larger space to operate in as much as some of the areas reserved exclusively earlier for the public sector are now allowed to private sector. In these areas, the public sector will have to compete with the private sector, even though the public sector may continue to play the dominant role. What is sought to be achieved is an improvement in the functioning of the various entities, whether they be in the private or public sector.

Judged by the standard criteria of growth rates in national income and per capita income, the Indian economy has done well since liberalisation. Between 1992-93 and 1998-99 the average annual growth rate was 6.55 per cent. This is even higher than the previous high of 6.04 per cent achieved between 1985-86 and 1989-90. Between 1992-93 and 1999-2000, there is no year in which the growth rate has been less than five per cent. The coefficient of variation of growth rate has been lower than in the 80s. The average annual per capita income growth rate between 1992-93 and 1998-99 has been 4.7 per cent as compared with a growth rate of 3.4 per cent in the eighties. There has, thus, been a significant step up in terms of the per capita income growth rate. The current account deficit has remained low and averaged only 1.3 per cent of GDP, since 1992-93.

The average growth rate of industrial production since 1992-93 has been 6.4 per cent. This is lower than the growth rate of 7.5 per cent in industrial production in the 80s. However, in terms of value added in industry, the growth rate in the 90s works-out to 6.62 per cent which is a shade higher than the growth rate of 6.55 per cent in the 80s. The distinctively higher growth rate in GDP in the 90s has been because of the sharp increase in the growth rate of services. The share of the services sector in the gross domestic product has increased by 7 percentage points in the nineties to reach 47.10 per cent in 1999-2000.

The liberalisation process has come in for criticism from two opposite ends. There are those who feel that the process has been slow and not sufficiently comprehensive. At the other end, there are critics who view the reform process as misconceived, ignoring the basic requirements of the people. While it is accepted that the growth rate in the post reform period has generally been higher, some concerns have been expressed about the slower growth rate in agriculture, lesser impact on poverty, reduction in capital expenditures of Government, lack of adequate investment in social infrastructure and growing disparities in growth rates among States. Some of these criticisms have a validity and some others do not. Some are related to the liberalisation process. Others are not. Obviously the reform process must take into account these criticisms. Reforms have not reduced the role of the state. In some areas, the role has expanded and some others, it has contracted. As has been, somewhat paradoxically, remarked "More market does not mean less government but only different government." The need for expanded state intervention in areas of education, health and sanitation cannot be underestimated. But it is only an efficient economy which will generate the necessary surplus which will enable the state to fulfil its socio-economic obligations. Efficiency and equity should not be posed as opposing considerations.

Changes in the foreign trade and foreign investment policies have altered the environment in which Indian industries have to operate. The path of transition is, no doubt, difficult. A greater integration of the Indian economy with the rest of the world is unavoidable. We must recognise that there are many countries which are knocking on the doors of the WTO to enter. It is important that the Indian industry be forward looking and get organised to compete with the rest of the world at levels of tariff comparable to those of other developing countries. Obviously, the Indian Government should be alert to ensure that Indian industries are not the victims of unfair trade practices. The safeguards available in the WTO agreement must be fully utilised to protect the interests of Indian industries. India must take a proactive stand in the next round of trade negotiations and articulate its own demands, focussing on what it wants from the global trading system, such as prohibition of unilateral trade action, establishing symmetry between the movement of capital and natural persons and zero tariffs in industrialised countries on labour intensive exports of developing countries.

There have been some concerns on the slackening of the growth of the industrial production particularly in the current year. The growth rate is still reasonable because of the utilisation of the higher capacities created earlier. The three years beginning 1994- 95 were marked by high rates of growth of industrial production. This was also the period during which the investment rate remained high. In 1998-99, which is the latest year for which data on savings and investment are available, the gross domestic savings rate had declined by 2.4 percentage points. With current account deficit as percentage of GDP remaining more or less at the same level, there has been a decline in the aggregate investment rate as well. The decline in the savings rate is highest in relation to public sector. The savings rate of the public sector which comprises both government administration and public sector enterprises is estimated at zero. In the final analysis, investment is the major driving force of growth. All investment decisions are, however, based on future prospects. Continuity of economic policy thus becomes key to sustaining expectations in the right direction. This can happen only, if there is a consensus on the core elements of the economic policy among the political parties and policymakers. Such a consensus will pave the way for the economy to achieve higher levels of investment and growth.

Part 1

Indian Industrialisation: Technical Efficiency and Total Factor Productivity

2

Productivity Growth in Indian Manufacturing in the 1980s and 1990s

BISHWANATH GOLDAR

SECTION 1

INTRODUCTION

In the 1980s, particularly in the second half, there was a gradual process of liberalisation of economic policies in India. This process gained considerable momentum from 1991, and major, far-reaching changes in industrial and trade policies were made in the 1990s. These reforms were aimed at making Indian industry more efficient, technologically up-to-date and competitive, with the expectation that efficiency improvement, technological up-gradation, and enhancement of competitiveness would enable Indian industry achieve rapid growth. Since productivity increase in Indian industries was a key object of the economic policy reforms, the success of the reforms should be judged in terms this yardstick. Accordingly, a study of productivity performance of Indian manufacturing in the 1980s and 1990s assumes significance.

It is often argued that economic liberalisation would promote industrial productivity and input-use efficiency. This is expected to occur through several channels: (a) economic liberalisation will provide to industrial firms greater and cheaper access to imported technology, capital goods, intermediate goods (embodying advanced technology) and global capital, and all these will enable the firms improve their productivity performance, (b) by relaxing various constraints on input-use and technology choices, and investment decisions of industrial firms, economic liberalisation will create conditions conducive to productivity growth, (c) the increased competitive pressure (both domestic and foreign) on industrial units in a liberalised policy regime will force them to be more efficient in the use of resources (which can be achieved through better organisation of production, improved managerial efficiency, more effective utilisation of labour, better capacity utilisation, etc.), (d) the increased competitive pressure coupled with expanded opportunities for importing technology and capital goods will bring greater technological dynamism in industrial firms, and (e) inasmuch as the business environment permits more efficient firms to grow and compete out inefficient firms, the average level of efficiency of various industries would improve. Another possible channel through which economic liberalisation may lead to improved industrial productivity is that a more realistic exchange rate associated with economic liberalisation, and other favourable conditions in the economy would enable industrial firms compete more effectively in export markets. This would allow them to increase their sales and reap economies of scale with concomitant gains in productivity. Going by all these arguments, one should expect a significant growth in industrial productivity in India in the 1980s and 1990s, especially in the decade of nineties when the reforms were much more substantial.

While the arguments given above may appear quite persuasive, it needs to be pointed out that economic theory does not lead us to unambiguous conclusions on the effect of trade liberalisation and increased competition on industrial productivity and efficiency (Srivastava, 2000). The theoretical basis for expecting a large positive effect of economic reforms on industrial productivity is not strong; nor is there a strong empirical basis for taking such a view (Balakrishnan, Pushpangadan and Suresh Babu, 2000; Balakrishnan and Pushpangadan, 1998). Thus, the effect of economic reforms on industrial productivity in India is largely an empirical question.

The object of this paper is (1) to review the available studies on productivity growth in Indian manufacturing in the 1980s and 1990s,[1] and (2) present some new estimates of productivity growth for this period. The motivation for making a fresh set of productivity estimates has come mostly from the fact that the earlier studies have reached sharply conflicting conclusions on the rate of productivity growth achieved by Indian manufacturing in the 1980s. Also, there are some deficiencies in the deflators used in these studies for

1. The literature on productivity growth in Indian industry has been reviewed earlier by Balakrishnan and Pushpangadan (1998) and Goldar and Mitra (1999).

correcting time-series data on output and intermediate inputs for price changes. An attempt is therefore made in the new productivity estimates to improve on the deflators.

SECTION 2

EARLIER STUDIES

There have been quite a few studies on total factor productivity (TFP) growth in Indian industry. Some notable, but relatively older studies are Banerji (1975), Hashim and Dadi (1973), Ahluwalia (1985) and Goldar (1986). The time periods covered in these studies do not go beyond 1979, and the studies are therefore not of interest for this paper since the focus here is on the productivity performance in the 1980s and later.

Among the studies, which have presented estimates of TFP growth in Indian industry for the post-1980 period, Ahluwalia (1991) is an important one. Ahluwalia's study was based on data drawn from the *Annual Survey of Industries* (ASI),[2] which is also the principal data source of most other studies on productivity growth in Indian industry. Ahluwalia found a marked increase in the growth rate of TFP in Indian manufacturing in the period 1980-81 to 1985-86 (3.4 per cent per annum) as compared with the period 1965 to 1979-80 (-0.3 per cent per annum) (Table 2.1). Her estimates of the translog production function using pooled cross-section and time-series data also showed a marked improvement in the rate of TFP growth from 1982-83. She attributed this observed "turnaround" in productivity growth in Indian manufacturing in the 1980s to liberalisation of economic policies.

Similar results have been reported in some other studies. A study on productivity growth was carried out by the Industrial Credit and Investment Corporation of India (ICICI, 1994) for companies to which it provided assistance. The growth rate of TFP was estimated as -2.7 per cent per annum for the 1970s, -0.9 per cent per annum for the period 1982-83 to 1986-87 and 2.1 per cent per annum for the period 1987-88 to 1991-92. In a more recent study, carried out by Gangopadhyay and Wadhwa (1998), TFP estimates have been

2. The *Annual Survey of Industries* covers only the registered (or organised) manufacturing sector (i.e. the factories employing 10 workers with power or 20 or more workers without power).

Table 2.1

Growth Rate of Total Factor Productivity in Indian Manufacturing: Some Estimates

Author	*Method*	*Period*	*Growth Rate (per cent per annum)*
Ahluwalia	VASD	1965-79	-0.3
		1980-85	3.4
Gangopadhyay and Wadhwa	VASD	1974-80	1.17
		1981-85	5.44
		1986-90	5.01
		1991-93	3.88
Balakrishnan and Pushpangadan	VASD	1970-79	0.02
		1980-88	2.02
	VADD	1970-79	5
		1980-88	-1
Dholakia and Dholakia	VADD	1970-80	0.56
		1980-88	2.86
Rao	VASD	1973-80	-0.2
		1981-92	2.1
	VADD	1973-80	4.6
		1981-92	-2.2
	GOF	1973-80	5.5
		1981-92	-2.2
Pradhan and Barik	GOF	1972-81	3.06
		1982-92	-1.23
Mitra	VADD (Production Function)	1976-84	0.76
		1985-92	5.57
Trivedi, Prakash and Sinate	VASD	1973-80	1.04
		1980-90	3.60
		1990-97	1.97
	VADD	1973-80	2.00
		1980-90	7.63
		1990-97	3.76
	GOF	1973-80	0.57
		1980-90	1.66
		1990-97	0.95

Note: VASD = single deflated value added; VADD = double deflated value added. GOF = gross output function.

made for aggregate manufacturing and various two-digit industries. The study has used ASI data for estimating output, inputs, and productivity. The estimates of TFP growth rate for aggregate manufacturing are 1.17 per cent per annum for the period 1974-80, 5.44 per cent per annum for 1981-85 and 5.01 per cent per annum for 1986-90. For the period, 1991-93, the estimated growth rate of TFP is 3.88 per cent per annum. Evidently, the estimates of TFP growth reported in the two studies mentioned above support Ahluwalia's finding of acceleration in TFP growth in Indian manufacturing in the 1980s.[3]

Balakrishnan and Pushpangadan (1994) have challenged Ahluwalia's finding of a "turnaround" in productivity growth in Indian manufacturing in the 1980s. They have seriously questioned the use of single deflation procedure for the measurement of real output. By using double-deflated value added, instead of single-deflated value added, they have shown that TFP growth rate in Indian manufacturing in the 1980s was not any higher (rather it was lower) than that during the 1970s (Table 2.1).[4]

Balakrishnan and Pushpangadan (hereafter B-P) have pointed out that the price index of materials input used in manufacturing as a ratio of the price index of manufactured articles increased sharply in the 1970s, and there was a marked decline in the relative price of materials in the 1980s. They have argued that the use of single-deflated value added is inappropriate in such a situation, as it does not correctly measure the growth in output.[5] When they derived TFP estimates from single-deflated value added, a "turn around" in productivity growth could be confirmed. But, when TFP was derived from a more appropriate measure of real value added, *viz.* double-deflated value added, the growth rate of TFP for the 1980s turned out to be much lower than that in the 1970s. Instead of acceleration

3. Goldar (1992) found a marked increase in the growth rate of TFP in Indian manufacturing after 1975. While the growth rate was 0.3 per cent per annum during 1964-75, it was much higher at 2.1 per cent per annum during the period 1975-76 to 1984-85. Goldar (1995) has reported estimates of TFP growth in the organised manufacturing sector during the period 1970-71 to 1990-91. According to these estimates, TFP in Indian manufacturing grew at the rate of 1.55 per cent per annum in the period 1970-71 to 1980-81, which rose to 3.85 per cent per annum during 1980-81 to 1985-86 and further to 5.05 per cent per annum during 1985-86 to 1990-91.

4. It should be pointed out here that in the studies of Ahluwalia (1991), ICICI (1994) and Gangopadhyay and Wadhwa (1998) single-deflated value added is used. Banerji (1975), Hashim and Dadi (1973), Goldar (1986, 1992, 1995) and Ahluwalia (1985) have also used single deflated value added. Some researchers did recognise the utility of double deflation of value added, but it was felt that it would be very difficult to deflate properly the intermediate input series.

5. This point was made earlier in Goldar (1992).

in TFP growth, the results indicated a downward trend in TFP in Indian manufacturing in the 1980s.

For constructing a price index for materials used in manufacturing, B-P have used the input-output transactions table prepared by the CSO (Central Statistical Organisation) for 1973-74. They consider 19 input groups and take the weights from the input-output table. The price indices for the 19 groups, which include agricultural products, minerals, manufactured products (except machinery and transport equipment) and electricity, are combined to form the price index for material input (including energy). The gross output series is deflated by the wholesale price index for manufactured articles, and the materials input series is deflated by the materials price index to obtain double-deflated value added.

Dholakia and Dholakia (1994) have pointed out that while the B-P study covers registered manufacturing, the input-output table is based on inputs and output for the entire manufacturing sector, i.e. it also includes unregistered manufacturing. Accordingly, they argue that the weights for the inputs groups obtained from the input-output table are incorrect. Dholakia and Dholakia have computed the right weights to be used for registered manufacturing and estimated TFP growth (based on double-deflated value added method) using those weights. Their estimate of TFP growth rate for the period 1980-81 to 1988-89 is higher than that for the period 1970-71 to 1980-81 (Table 2.1). These results are in line with Ahluwalia's findings and in sharp disagreement with the findings of B-P.

In their papers published subsequently, Balakrishnan and Pushpangadan (1995, 1996) have replied to this criticism of Dholakia and Dholakia, and shown that even if weights for registered manufacturing are used the estimated growth rate of TFP in Indian manufacturing is much lower for the 1980s than that for the 1970s. Indeed, they note that the two sets of weights are quite similar.

Rao (1996) has estimated TFP growth in Indian manufacturing for the period 1973-74 to 1992-93. In his paper, he has discussed at length various methodological issues in TFP measurement. He has argued for using the three-input framework based on the gross output function in which labour, capital and materials (including energy) are taken as three inputs. It should be noted here that the use of two-input framework for the estimation of TFP growth, which involves a value added function, requires that the production function (gross output function) be separable in material input and factor input (labour and capital). Without this condition of separability holding, the concept of value added is ill-defined and one will get a biased estimate of TFP growth if a two-input framework is used as done by B-P, Ahluwalia, Goldar and many others.

From his estimates of TFP growth, Rao (1996) has noted that the single-deflation method results in a significantly larger magnitude of error than the double-deflation method. The productivity index for manufacturing estimated by him by using the double-deflation method indicates an exponential growth of TFP of 4.6 per cent during 1973-74 to 1980-81 and -0.2 per cent during 1981-82 to 1992-93, implying a shift from positive growth to zero productivity growth during the eighties. Rao has also presented productivity estimates based on gross output function. These estimates show a pattern similar to the estimates obtained from double-deflated value added (Table 2.1). Thus, the TFP estimates made by Rao do not indicate a turnaround in TFPG in the 1980s and support the contention of B-P.

Pradhan and Barik (1998) have tested for separability of production function and found this assumption to be rejected by the data for Indian manufacturing. They accordingly argue that for estimating TFP growth in Indian manufacturing a three-input framework based on the gross output function should be used. Making use of such a framework, they have estimated TFP growth in Indian manufacturing. Their results show a decline in the rate of TFP growth in the 1980s (Table 2.1), which supports the findings of B-P and Rao.

The estimates of TFP growth in Indian manufacturing presented in the studies of B-P, Rao and Pradhan and Barik are broadly in agreement with one another. Considering these estimates of TFP, and the rightful claims of methodological superiority over the TFP estimates of Ahluwalia (1991) (which applies also to Gangopadhyay and Wadhwa, 1998), one might conclude that the estimates of productivity growth made by Ahluwalia, and Gangopadhyay and Wadhwa are incorrect (being subject to serious bias), and in reality TFP in Indian manufacturing declined during the 1980s, or at best there was a negligible growth. However, the estimates of TFP growth presented in a recent study undertaken by Trivedi, Prakash and

Sinate (2000) suggest that such conclusion is unwarranted. This study of Trivedi *et al.*, is based on ASI data and has used a methodology very similar to that used by B-P, Rao, and Pradhan and Barik. The intermediate input series has been deflated by a price index for materials (including energy) constructed from wholesale price indices for different input-output sectors and the weight taken from an input-output table, as done by B-P and others. TFP estimates have been made by using double deflated value added as well as the three-input model i.e. the gross output function. Even though the methodology applied is quite similar, the growth rates of TFP emerging from the estimates are very different. The estimated TFP growth rate in Indian manufacturing using double deflated value added is 7.63 per cent per annum for the period 1980-81 to 1990-91 as compared to only 2 per cent per annum in the period 1973-74 to 1980-81 (Table 2.1).[6] Similarly, for the three-input model, the growth rate of TFP is 1.66 per cent per annum for the period 1980-81 to 1990-91, significantly higher than the growth rate of 0.57 per cent per annum for the period 1973-74 to 1980-81. Clearly, the productivity estimates reported by Trivedi, Prakash and Sinate indicate that the 1980s was a period of rapid productivity growth in Indian manufacturing and there was an acceleration (rather than a deceleration) in TFP growth in this decade as compared to the previous decade. These results are sharply at variance with the results reported by B-P, Rao, and Pradhan and Barik, and support the position taken by Ahluwalia that there was a turnaround in productivity growth in Indian manufacturing in the 1980s.

Another recent study, which has reported an increase in the growth rate of TFP in Indian manufacturing in the 1980s, is by Mitra (1999). To study technical efficiency and TFP growth in Indian industries, he has used the methodology suggested by Cornwell, Schmidt, and Sickles (1990). He has used a two-input framework; labour and capital are taken as the two inputs, and double-deflated value added is taken as the measure of output. The econometric analysis is based on panel data, which covers 15 states and 17 two-digit industries for the period 1976-77 to 1992-93. A frontier

6. Trivedi, *et al.*, have presented the TFP indices of the years 1973-74 to 1997-98. The growth rates of TFP shown in Table 2.1 have been computed by the author by fitting a semi-log trend equation.

production function is estimated for each of the industries using state-wise, year-wise panel data. In addition, he has estimated a frontier production function for the aggregate industry across states and at the all-India level. At the all-India level, the estimate is based on data for 1976-77 to 1993-94.

Mitra has presented estimates of TFP growth for two sub-periods 1976-77 to 1984-85 and 1985-86 to 1992-93, and for the whole period 1976-77 to 1992-93. His estimates show that in four industries there has been a decline in TFP growth rate in the latter period as compared with the former in most or majority of the states. In the other 13 industries, there has been an increase in TFP growth rate in the latter period in most or majority of the states. The estimate of TFP growth rate at the aggregate level is 0.76 per cent per annum during the period 1976-77 to 1984-85 and 5.57 per cent per annum during 1985-86 to 1993-94, showing a marked acceleration in TFP growth.[7,8]

Turing now the productivity performance of Indian manufacturing in the 1990s, the estimates of TFP presented by Trivedi, Prakash and Sinate (2000) indicate that the growth rate of TFP in Indian manufacturing was positive in the 1990s, but it was lower than that in the 1980s. The estimated rate of TFP growth based on double deflated value added is 3.76 per cent per annum for the period 1990-91 to 1997-98 as compared to 7.63 per cent per annum for the period 1980-81 to 1990-91 (Table 2.1). A similar fall is there in the estimated rate of TFP growth based on single deflated value added (from 3.60 per cent per annum to 1.97 per cent per annum) and that based on the three-input model (from 1.66 per cent per annum to 0.95 per cent per annum). It may be noted here that the TFP estimates of Gangopadhyay and Wadhwa (1998) also indicate a fall in the growth rate of TFP in Indian manufacturing in the 1990s. They report a growth rate of TFP of 3.88 per cent per annum during 1991-92 to 1993-94 as against a growth rate of over five per cent per annum during the 1980s.

7. Srivastava (1996) has used company level data (drawn from the Reserve Bank of India) for analysing productivity growth in Indian industry. The period covered in the analysis is 1980-81 to 1989-90. Production function estimates (based on three-input Cobb-Douglas and Translog specifications) made by him indicate a significant improvement in TFP growth rate in the period 1985-89 as against 1980-84.

8. Das (1998) has carefully estimated TFP growth at three-digit industry level using a three-input framework for the period 1980-81 to 1993-94. In 45 out of 76 industries covered in the study, the rate of TFP growth for the period 1985-86 to 1993-94 is found to be higher than that for the period 1980-81 to 1985-86.

The finding that there was a marked fall in the growth rate of TFP in Indian manufacturing in the 1990s as compared with the 1980s is corroborated by empirical results reported in two other recent studies, Balakrishnan, Pushpangadan and Suresh Babu (2000) and Srivastava (2000). Both the studies are based on company level data (private sector, public limited companies). Srivastava has done a careful and detailed econometric analysis of productivity growth and technical efficiency in manufacturing firms in India using data for about three thousand companies for the period 1980-81 to 1996-97. Productivity analysis has been carried by using both the growth accountancy approach and the production function approach. In addition, estimates of technical efficiency have been obtained using a frontier production function. The results obtained in the study clearly point to a decline in the rate of productivity growth in Indian manufacturing in the 1990s as compared with the 1980s.

Balakrishnan *et al.*, (2000) have used for their analysis data for about 2300 firms registered with the Bombay Stock Exchange. The period covered for the analysis is 1988-89 to 1997-98. Following Hall (1988), they have used a model that yields both an estimate of price-marginal cost ratio and an estimate of productivity. Their results suggest a worsening of productivity growth in the manufacturing sector in the 1990s.[9]

SECTION 3

SOME METHODOLOGICAL ISSUES

The main methodological issue to be highlighted here is that if one uses double deflated value added as a measure of output, then the computed growth rate of real value added (and hence of total factor productivity) is not invariant to the choice of the base year of the price indices. A shift in the base year of price indices of output and materials, say from 1970-71 to 1981-82, may lead to a substantial change in the estimated growth rate of productivity. This point comes out clearly from a comparison of the TFP indices presented by B-P in their 1994 and 1995 papers. For the period 1980-81 to 1988-89, one set of estimates (which use price indices

9. Krishna and Mitra (1998) have reported a statistically significant increase in productivity growth in the post-1991 period in four industries chosen by them for study. However, Balakrishnan *et al.*, (2000) express reservations about the construction of variable in that study.

with 1970-71 base) give a growth rate of TFP of –0.11 per cent per annum, while the other set of estimates (which use price indices with 1981-82 base) give a growth rate of 3.91 per cent per annum (Table 2.2).[10] While in one case the growth rate of TFP is found to have declined sharply in the 1980s, in other case there is an increase.

Since the construction of intermediate input price index requires taking a weighted average of price indices of different input-output sectors, the choice of base year of the price indices affects also the results of productivity estimates based on the three-input model. This probably explains why the estimates of productivity growth obtained in the study of Trivedi, Prakash and Sinate differ so much from the estimates reported in the studies of Rao, and Pradhan and Barik. Trivedi *et al.*, use price indices with 1981-82 as base while the other two studies use price indices with 1970-71 as base.

It is reasonable to argue that while making estimate of productivity growth for the 1980s the price indices with base 1981-82 should be preferred over the price indices with base 1970-71. Accordingly, going by the estimates made by B-P as well as Trivedi, Prakash and Sinate, shown in Table 2.2, it may be concluded that there was a significant growth in TFP in Indian manufacturing in the 1980s.

Another methodological issue is whether it is right to use the index number of wholesale prices for "manufactured articles" for deflating gross output of the manufacturing sector. In the studies of B-P, Rao, Pradhan and Barik and Trivedi *et al.*, this has been done. It should be noted that the official series on wholesale price index for manufactured articles is based on value added weights. On the other hand, gross output as reported in ASI is simply the addition of gross output of different industries. The underlying weights for different industries are obviously quite different. An industry coming at a later stage of processing may have small value added but high value of production. It will have a small weight in the price index for manufactured articles, but a relatively larger weight in the gross value of production for aggregate manufacturing reported in ASI.

Questions can be raised also about the use of wholesale price indices for deflating industrial consumption of energy reported in

10. These growth rates are estimated by fitting a semi-log trend equation to the TFP indices reported by B-P in their 1994 paper (Table 2.2, last column) and their 1995 paper (Table 2.1, first column).

ASI. The wholesale price index for petroleum products is not right for deflating expenses on petroleum products consumed by industries because the index gives a large weight to kerosene, petrol and HSD, while from the viewpoint of industries it is the prices of naphtha and fuel oil/LSHS which are important.

Table 2.2

Base of Price Indices and Estimates of TFP Growth Rate in Manufacturing

	Balakrishnan and Pushpangadan			*Trivedi et al.*	
	Single Deflated	*Double Deflated*	*Double Deflated*	*Single Deflated*	*Double Deflated*
Base year of price index	1970-71	1970-71	1981-82	1981-82	1981-82
Period	1980-81 to 1988-89	1980-81 to 1988-89	1980-81 to 1988-89	1980-81 to 1990-91	1980-81 to 1990-91
Growth rate of TFP (% p.a.)	2.42	–0.11	3.91	3.60	7.63
Growth rate of value added (% p.a.)	6.94	5.94	9.95	About 7	About 11

Note: Trivedi *et al.*, (2000) do not report the series on value added. The growth rate of labour productivity (value added per employee) is used to compute the underlying growth rate of real value added. Similarly, in the case of the TFP estimates made by Balakrishnan and Pushpangadan, the growth rate of total input is computed from the reported growth rates in value added and TFP. This is then used to work back the growth rate of value added for the TFP estimates that use the price index with 1981-82 as base.

SECTION 4

NEW ESTIMATES OF TFP GROWTH

Available estimates of TFP growth in Indian manufacturing in the 1980s and 1990s have been reviewed in the previous section. This section presents a fresh set of estimates of TFP growth in manufacturing industries covering the period 1981-82 to 1997-98.[11] Estimates of productivity growth are presented both for aggregate (registered) manufacturing and for various two-digit industries.

11. These are preliminary estimates of TFP growth rate made in an on-going research project on 'Productivity Growth in Indian Manufacturing' being carried out by the author along with Ms. Anita Kumari.

TFP Estimation Method

A three-input framework is used for the TFP estimates presented in the paper. Such a framework has been used earlier in the studies of Rao (1996), and Pradhan and Barik (1998) (also in Trivedi *et al.*, 2000), and arguments have been given in its favour. The growth accountancy equation used for making the estimates of TFP growth is as follows:

$$TFPG = G_Q - (S_L \times G_L + S_K \times G_K + S_M \times G_M),\ S_L + S_K + S_M = 1.$$

TFPG is the growth rate of total factor productivity. G_Q is the growth rate of gross output, G_L and G_K are the growth rates of labour and capital input, and G_M is the growth rate of intermediate (materials and energy) input. S_L, S_K and S_M are the income shares of the three inputs in gross output.

Estimates of TFP growth rate have been made for two sub-periods, 1981-82 to 1989-90 and 1990-91 to 1997-98, and for the entire period 1981-82 to 1997-98. For each period, growth rates of gross output, intermediate input, labour input and capital input are computed by fitting a semi-log trend equation. The average income share of labour is computed by dividing total emoluments by gross output (both at current prices) for each year and then taking an average. The share of intermediate input is computed in a similar way. Given the shares of labour and intermediate input, the share of capital is obtained as the residual.

TFP estimation at the aggregate manufacturing level has been done also by using the two-input framework to facilitate comparison with estimates presented in the earlier studies. In this case, real gross value added (computed by both single and double deflation procedures) is taken as the measure of output. Labour and capital are taken as the two inputs. Let G_Y be the growth rate of real value added, G_L and G_K be the growth rates of labour and capital input, and S_L be the average share of labour in value added, then the growth rate of TFP denoted by TFPG is computed as:

$$TFPG = G_Y - [S_L \times G_L + (1 - S_L) \times G_K]$$

The share of labour for each year is computed by dividing total emoluments by gross value added (both at current prices) and then the period average is taken.

Data Sources

Basic source of data used for the productivity estimates is the *Annual Survey of Industries* (Central Statistical Organisation, Government of India), which has been the principal data source in most earlier studies on industrial productivity. For making price corrections to the reported data on gross output and intermediate input, suitable deflators have been constructed with the help of the official series on wholesale price indices *(Index Number of Wholesale Prices* in India, prepared by the Office of the Economic Advisor, Ministry of Industry). These have been taken from the official publications and the publications of the Centre for Monitoring Indian Economy. For a few specific items, other sources of data have been used (mentioned later) to construct price indices for those items. The construction of deflator for intermediate input requires that the price indices for various categories of items be combined using appropriate weights (representing their shares in intermediate input cost). For this purpose, the weights have been taken from an input-output table for 1989-90. This input-output table has been prepared by the Central Statistical Organisation (CSO). For constructing capital input series for manufacturing industries, estimates of net fixed capital stock (for the benchmark year) and gross fixed capital formation (for different years) made by the CSO have been taken from the *National Accounts Statistics* (NAS).

Construction of Variables

Labour: Total number of persons engaged in industrial units is taken as the measure of labour input. This is reported in ASI. For the recent issues, it is reported under the head "persons engaged"; for earlier issues, it is reported under the head "number of employees".

Capital: Gross fixed assets at 1980-81 prices is taken as the measure of capital input. This has been computed in the following way:

(a) Aggregate manufacturing sector. An estimate of net fixed capital stock for the registered manufacturing sector for end March 1971 (benchmark) is taken from NAS.[12] This is

12. Note that while the productivity estimates are made for the period 1981-82 to 1997-98, the capital series is built from 1970-71. The purpose in building the capital series from an earlier year is that the pre-1971 assets would form only a part of the capital stock of 1981-82 and hence any error in the estimation of the benchmark capital stock will be rendered relatively small.

multiplied by a gross-net factor to get an estimate of gross fixed capital stock for the year 1970-71. The ratio of gross to net fixed assets in medium and large public limited companies (as reported in *Reserve Bank of India Bulletin*) was 1.86 in 1970-71. Thus, the net fixed capital stock for registered manufacturing for the benchmark year, reported in NAS, is multiplied by 1.86 to get an estimate of gross fixed capital stock for the benchmark year. To build the capital series from the benchmark capital stock estimate, the perpetual inventory method is used. Thus, gross investment in fixed assets in registered manufacturing in 1971-72 is added to the benchmark capital estimate (1970-71) to obtain the capital stock estimate for the next year, i.e. end March 1972. In this manner, the entire capital series is built. The gross fixed investment series is taken from NAS (the series on gross fixed capital formation at constant prices for registered manufacturing). In preparing the time series on capital stock, it is important to allow for discarding of assets (Goldar, 1992). The rate of discarding has been taken as 2.6 per cent per annum (based on some estimates available from a study undertaken by Chaturvedi and Baghchi, 1985).

(b) Two-digit industries. The benchmark estimate of gross fixed capital stock made for registered manufacturing for 1970-71 is distributed among various two-digit industries in proportion to the fixed capital stock (net) of these industries reported in ASI, 1970-71. This provides the benchmark capital stock estimates for individual two-digit industries. Then, for each industry and for each year, the gross investment at current prices are computed, taking the difference in the book-value of fixed capital assets reported in ASI and depreciation.[13] For each year, gross investment in fixed capital assets is available for the registered manufacturing sector from NAS. This is distributed among the two digit industries in proportion to the gross investment (at current prices) computed from

13. Gross investment in year t denoted by I(t) is computed as $I(t)=B(t)-B(t-1)+D(t)$, where B(t) is the book-value of fixed assets in year t and D(t) is depreciation of fixed assets in year t, both as reported in ASI.

ASI data. In this manner, the real fixed investment is obtained for each two-digit industry for each year, from 1971-72 to 1997-98. Then, following the perpetual inventory method, the time series on fixed capital stock has been constructed for all the two-digit industries. In this case again, the rate of discarding is taken as 2.6 per cent per annum, to be consistent with the capital series for aggregate manufacturing.

Output, intermediate input and value added: Time series data on gross output and cost of intermediate inputs have been deflated by suitable deflators (base 1981-82=100) to measure real output and real intermediate input. The latter has been subtracted from the former to obtain real value added by the double deflation procedure. To obtain real value added by the single deflation procedure, the value-added series has been deflated directly by a suitable price index. Needless to say that the construction of deflators for gross output and intermediate inputs is crucial for the proper measurement of output. The procedure followed for constructing the deflators is described below:

(1) In the first step, price indices have been formed for each of the 99 sectors of the 1989-90 input-output table, belonging to agriculture, mining, manufacturing, and electricity.[14] For some sectors, the available wholesale price index series could be used directly. In some other cases, the available category-wise price indices have been combined to form the price index for the relevant input-output sector.[15] For three sectors, the wholesale price index series did not seem appropriate for forming deflators of intermediate input. In these cases, other sources of data have been used. Thus, for crude oil, data on domestic prices of crude oil have been taken from *Petroleum and Natural Gas Statistics* and a price index has been formed. Similarly, a price index for electricity used in industries has been formed using data on electricity tariff paid by industries. For petroleum products (as

14. The input-output table for 1989-90 has 115 sectors of which 99 belong to agriculture, mining, manufacturing and electricity.

15. In a number of cases, no suitable price index was available. So, some approximation has become necessary, and the best price index among the available ones has been applied.

inputs to industries), the prices of naphtha and fuel oil/ LSHS have been considered. The fact that fertiliser units have been paying a lower price than other industries has been taken into account in preparing price indices of petroleum products as inputs to industry. Three price indices have been formed for this purpose: one for consumption of petroleum products in fertiliser plants, one for petrochemical units, and one for other industries.

(2) For each input-output sector engaged in manufacturing (66 sectors), a price index for intermediate inputs has then been formed. This is done by taking a weighted average of price indices of the 99 sectors (discussed in (1) above). The column for the relevant sector in the Absorption Matrix provides the weights used.

(3) The input-output sectors have been mapped into the two-industry classification of ASI. To work out the price indices for the two-digit industries, weighted averages of the price indices of the constituent input-output sectors have been taken. For combining the intermediate input price indices of different constituent sectors, the expenditures on intermediate inputs are used as weights. For deriving a price index for gross output of a two-digit industry from the output price indices of the input-output sectors, the weights used are the gross output of the constituent sectors. For deriving a price index for deflating value added (for the single deflation procedure), the output price indices of the constituent sectors are combined according to the value added of the different sectors.

TFP Estimates

Estimates of TFP growth in the manufacturing sector are shown in Table 2.3. Growth rates are presented for the periods 1981-82 to 1989-90 and 1990-91 to 1997-98, and for the entire period 1981-82 to 1997-98. Estimates of TFP growth based on the study of Trivedi *et al.*, (2000) are also shown in the Table for comparison. The two sets of estimates are quite similar.

It is seen from the Table 2.3 that the estimated growth rate of TFP for the period 1981-82 to 1989-90 is 8.97 per cent per annum when double deflated value added method is used, and it is 2.13 per cent per annum when the three-input framework is used. Evidently, the TFP estimates indicate a significant growth in TFP in Indian manufacturing in the 1980s. Also, there is a clear indication of a fall in the rate of growth of TFP in the 1990s as compared to the growth rate in the 1980s. This finding is in agreement with the TFP estimates of Trivedi *et al.*, (2000), and Gangopadhyay and Wadhwa (1998), as well as the results of econometric analysis presented by Srivastava (2000) and Balakrishnan, Pushpangadan and Suresh Babu (2000). For the entire period 1981-82 to 1997-99, the growth rate of TFP in manufacturing is estimated at 5.8 per cent per annum using the double deflated value added method, and 1.49 per cent per annum using the three-input framework.

Table 2.3

TFP Growth in Indian Manufacturing, 1981-82 to 1997-98

Method	*TFP Growth Rate (per cent per annum)*	
	This Study	*Trivedi et al. (2000)*
Single deflated value added		
1981-82 to 1989-90	4.52	3.10
1990-91 to 1997-98	1.86	1.97
1981-82 to 1997-98	3.36	2.64
Double deflated value added		
1981-82 to 1989-90	8.97	6.83
1990-91 to 1997-98	2.92	3.76
1981-82 to 1997-98	5.79	4.34
Gross output function (three input model)		
1981-82 to 1989-90	2.13	1.58
1990-91 to 1997-98	0.90	0.95
1981-82 to 1997-98	1.49	1.00

TFP estimates for two-digit industries are shown in Table 2.4. The estimated growth rate of TFP for the period 1981-82 to 1989-90 is positive for fourteen out of the seventeen groups. For the period 1990-91 to 1997-98, the growth rate of TFP is positive for eleven groups out of seventeen. In most cases, the growth rate for the latter period is relatively lower (11 out of 17 groups). This is consistent with the finding of a decrease in the growth rate of TFP in the 1990s as compared to the 1980s at the aggregate manufacturing level.

Trivedi *et al.*, (2000) have presented TFP estimates for five major industrial groups, namely textiles, metals and metal products, machinery and transport equipment, chemicals and chemical products, and leather and leather products. For textiles and chemicals, the growth rate of TFP is lower in the 1990s compared to the 1980s. For metals and metal products, and leather and leather products, the growth rate is higher in the 1990s. For machinery and transport equipment, no significant change in TFP growth rate is indicated. The estimates of TFP growth presented in Table 2.4 are broadly in agreement with the TFP estimates of Trivedi *et al.*, for industry groups.

Table 2.4

Estimates of TFP Growth Rates, Two-digit Industries, 1981-82 to 1997-98

NIC Code	*Description*	*Growth Rate of TFP (per cent per annum)*		
		1981-89	*1990-97*	*1981-97*
20-21	Food products	1.62	0.57	0.66
22	Beverage & tobacco	-0.45	-1.48	-1.09
23	Cotton textiles	1.83	-1.80	1.03
24	Wool, silk and manmade fibre textiles	2.95	1.68	2.80
25	Jute textiles	0.27	0.50	0.38
26	Textile products	0.40	-2.28	0.53
27	Wood, wood products, furniture	3.17	-9.77	-2.45
28	Paper, paper products, printing and publishing	-0.83	1.16	-0.19
29	Leather, leather products	-0.85	1.77	0.16
30	Chemicals, chemical products	2.99	0.93	2.55
31	Rubber, plastic, petroleum and coal products	4.41	-1.52	1.36
32	Non-metallic mineral products	3.12	-0.89	1.80
33	Basic metals and alloys	0.63	2.68	1.48
34	Metal products	0.98	2.33	0.40
35+36 +39	Machinery	2.54	1.61	1.85
37	Transport equipment	1.50	3.15	2.11
38	Other manufacturing	7.32	3.82	6.00
All	Manufacturing sector	2.13	0.90	1.49

Based on his analysis of productivity growth for various industry groups, Srivastava (2000) reports that the growth rate of TFP decreased in the 1990s relative to the 1980s in food products and beverages, non-metallic mineral products, tobacco products, wood and wood products, and machinery and equipment, while the rate of TFP growth went up in the 1990s in basic metals and alloys, fabricated metal products, paper and paper products, publishing and printing, leather and leather products, and rubber and plastic products. For textiles, chemicals and motor vehicles, the evidence is mixed. However, for textiles, the evidence is on balance indicative of a fall in productivity performance, and for transport equipment an increase in TFP growth is indicated. It would be noticed that the TFP growth rates presented in Table 2.4 show a pattern considerably in agreement with the pattern reported by Srivastava in his study.

SECTION 5
CONCLUSION

Estimates of productivity growth presented in the studies of Banerji (1975), Goldar (1986), and Ahluwalia (1985) indicated that in the first three decades of planned industrialisation in India (1950s through 1970s), the performance of Indian industry has been rather poor in terms of the rate of productivity growth achieved. The estimates made for a later period showed better productivity performance. Ahluwalia (1991) found a marked rise in the growth rate of TFP (total factor productivity) in Indian manufacturing in the period 1980-81 to 1985-86 (3.4 per cent per annum) as compared with the period 1965 to 1979 (-0.3 per cent per annum). A marked increase in the rate of TFP growth in Indian manufacturing in the 1980s has been reported also by Gangopadhyay and Wadhwa (1998) (from about 1.2 per cent per annum during 1974-80 to over 5 per cent per annum during 1981-1990).

Balakrishnan and Pushpangadan (1994, 1995, 1996), Rao (1996) and Pradhan and Barik (1998) have questioned the use of single deflated value added for measuring TFP. Since Ahluwalia (1991) and Gangopadhyay and Wadhwa (1998) have used the single deflation procedure in their studies, serious doubts arise about the validity of their findings. B-P, Rao and Pradhan and Barik have applied estimation methods that are free from biases in single deflated value added and have arrived at very different estimates of TFP growth for the 1980s. The results reported in these studies give an impression that (1) there was a marked fall in the growth rate of TFP in Indian manufacturing in the 1980s as compared to the 1970s, and (2) the growth rate of TFP in the 1980s was negative (or, if not negative, there was negligible growth in TFP in the 1980s).

This paper has shown that the finding of B-P of a deceleration in TFP growth in the 1980s is essentially due to the choice of base year of price index. When they use price indices with base 1981-82=100, rather than the price indices with base 1970-71=100, their estimates of TFP also show a significant increase in TFP in the 1980s. This is in conformity with the results reported in a recent productivity study by Trivedi *et al.,* (2000). A new set of estimates of productivity for Indian manufacturing industries presented in this paper also show a significant increase in TFP in Indian manufacturing in the 1980s. The growth of TFP based on double deflated value added is found to be in the range of six to nine per cent per annum, which is obviously quite high. This is in sharp contrast to the finding of a downward trend in TFP for the 1980s in the studies of B-P, Rao and Pradhan and Barik.

Another major finding of the analysis is that there was a marked fall in the growth rate of TFP in Indian manufacturing in the 1990s as compared to the 1980s. This is corroborated by the TFP estimates presented in the studies of Trivedi *et al.,* (2000), Srivastava (2000) and Balakrishnan, Pushpangadan and Suresh Babu (2000).

Why TFP growth in Indian manufacturing decelerated in the 1990s is an important question to be investigated. Since there was a spurt in investment activity in the 1990s in response to economic reforms, there was possibly an immediate adverse effect on productivity due to gestation lags. If this is the main cause of deceleration in productivity growth, one would expect the growth rate of productivity to pick up in the coming years.

Another possible line of argument is that there was considerable potential for productivity improvement in the beginning of the 1980s (for example, an overhung of employment existing by the end of the 1970s), and this potential could be used for attaining a rapid growth in productivity. And, as this source of productivity enhancement got increasingly exhausted, it became difficult to maintain a rapid growth in productivity in the 1990s.

References

Ahluwalia, I.J. (1985). *Industrial Growth in India*, Delhi: Oxford University Press.

————. (1991). *Productivity and Growth in Indian Manufacturing*, Delhi: Oxford University Press.

Banerji, A. (1975). *Capital Intensity and Productivity in Indian Industry*, Delhi: MacMillan.

Balakrishnan, P. and K. Pushpangadan (1994). "Total Factor Productivity Growth in Manufacturing Industry: A Fresh Look," *Economic and Political Weekly*, July 13.

————. (1995). "Total Factor Productivity Growth in Manufacturing Industry," *Economic and Political Weekly*, March 4.

————. (1996). "TFPG in Manufacturing Industry," *Economic and Political Weekly*, February 17.

————. (1998). "What Do We Know about Productivity Growth in Indian Industry," *Economic and Political Weekly*, August 15-22.

Balakrishnan, P., K. Pushpangadan and M. Suresh Babu (2000). "Trade Liberalisation and Productivity Growth in Manufacturing: Evidence from Firm-level Panel Data," *Economic and Political Weekly*, October 7.

Chaturvedi, D.N. and A. Bagchi (1985). "Age Structure of Fixed Capital in the Indian Economy, 1970-71 to 1980-81," *Journal of Income and Wealth*, 7(1). January, pp. 82-103.

Cornwell, C., P. Schmidt, and R.C. Sickles (1990). "Production Frontiers with Cross-Sectional and Time-Series Variation in Efficiency Levels," *Journal of Econometrics*, Vol.46, pp.185-200.

Das, D.K. (1998). "Trade Liberalisation and Productivity Growth: A Disaggregated Analysis of Indian Manufacturing Sectors," *Working Paper, No.* E/200/98, Institute of Economic Growth, Delhi.

Dholakia, B.H. and R.H. Dholakia (1994). "Total Factor Productivity Growth in Indian Manufacturing," *Economic and Political Weekly*, July 13.

Gangopadhyay, S. and W. Wadhwa (1998). "Economic Reforms and Labour," *Economic and Political Weekly*, May 30.

Goldar, B.N. (1986). *Productivity Growth in Indian Industry*, Delhi: Allied Publishers.

Goldar, B. (1992). "Productivity and Factor Use Efficiency in Indian Industry," in A. Ghosh *et al.*, (eds), *Indian Industrialisation: Structure and Policy Issues*, Delhi: Oxford University Press.

————. (1995) "Technology Acquisition and Productivity Growth: A Study of Industrial Firms in India," *Working Paper No.* E/172/95, Institute of Economic Growth, Delhi.

Goldar, B. and A. Mitra (1999). "Total Factor Productivity Growth in Indian Industry: A Review of Studies," Paper presented at a conference organised by the Indian Association for Research in Income and Wealth.

Hall, R. (1988). "The Relation Between Price and Marginal Cost in US Industry," *Journal of Political Economy*, 96, pp. 921-47.

Hashim, S.R. and M.M. Dadi (1973). *Capital-output Relations in Indian Manufacturing (1946-64)*, Baroda: M.S. University of Baroda.

ICICI (1994). Productivity in Indian Manufacturing: Private Corporate Sector, 1971-72 to 1991-92, Industrial Credit and Investment Corporation of India, Bombay.

Krishna, P. and D. Mitra (1998). "Trade Liberalisation, Market Discipline and Productivity Growth: New Evidence from India," *Journal of Development Economics*, Vol. 56, pp. 451-76.

Mitra, A. (1999). "Total Factor Productivity Growth and Technical Efficiency in Indian Industries," *Economic and Political Weekly*, July 31.

Pradhan, G. and K. Barik (1998). "Fluctuating Total Factor Productivity in India; Evidence from Selected Polluting Industries," *Economic and Political Weekly*, February 28.

Srivastava, V. (1996). *Liberalisation, Productivity and Competition: A Panel Study of Indian Manufacturing*, Delhi: Oxford University Press.

————. (2000). "The Impact of India's Economic Reforms on Industrial Productivity, Efficiency and Competitiveness" (Report of a project sponsored by the Industrial Development Bank of India), National Council of Applied Economic Research, New Delhi.

Trivedi, P., Prakash, A. and D. Sinate (2000). "Productivity in Major Manufacturing Industries in India: 1973-74 to 1997-98" Development Research Group Study No. 20, Department of Economic Analysis and Policy, Reserve Bank of India, Mumbai.

3

Technical Efficiency of State Owned Enterprises in China (1980-1989)

An Assessment of the Economic Reforms

SUBHASH C. RAY
ZHANG PING

SECTION 1
INTRODUCTION

The economic reforms launched by the post-Mao leadership in China mark the formal closure of a turbulent era in the history of the Peoples' Republic that started with the outbreak of the Cultural Revolution and ended in the eventual arrest and overthrow of the Gang of Four a decade later. Introduced gradually and phased in over years, the industrial reforms drastically relaxed the rigid bureaucratic control over the various state-owned enterprises (SOEs). Under the new regime, the enterprises were granted significantly greater autonomy allowing them to retain a share of profits and to sell above-plan output directly to buyers in an emerging market. The reforms increased the share of bonuses in the total compensation paid to employees. These reforms also permitted the SOEs to make appropriate use of material incentives in order to increase technical efficiency and productivity.

In this paper, we use data envelopment analysis (DEA) to examine changes in levels of technical efficiency over time in a sample of SOEs during 1980-1989. The data set comes from a survey of activities of 769 SOEs in four provinces during 1980-1989, containing 321 quantitive variables and a questionnaire answered by the managers of these enterprises. It is a comprehensive firm-level data set at on the Chinese SOEs and has been used previously to analyse different aspects of the SOEs applying different techniques., Li (1997) estimates a nonlinear production function; Liu and Liu

(1996) estimate a stochastic production function; Groves *et al.,* (1994, 1995) analyse the managerial incentives of the SOEs; and Shirley and Xu (1998) analyse the effectiveness of managerial contract system

Our paper adds to the literature in this area by obtaining measures of technical efficiency of individual SOEs over years and by identifying how different aspects of the reforms have affected efficiency. We find that technical efficiency, as a whole, improved in the 1980s in these SOEs, a result that is consistent with recent studies. Improvement in efficiency was not steady over years, however. During the years 1980-1986, when the economy grew at a fast pace, technical efficiency tended to be low. This matches the general impression about the Chinese practice of resource utilisation during that period. That is, in the first half of the 1980s, China utilised resources extensively rather than intensively. A structural change occurred in 1987 in the state-owned industrial sector. As noted in Hay *et al.,* (1994), the SOEs stepped-up cost-cutting efforts in the late-1980s. Thus, in 1988, even though the economy grew at a fast pace, technical efficiency not only did not decline, but actually improved. Our results show a large increase in technical efficiency in 1989 as well, a result at odds with many studies that show a decline in TFP in 1989.

Further, we find evidence that fluctuation in technical efficiency in various industries is closely related to the level of competition and entry by new firms. In the 1980s, China gradually lifted the barriers to entry for non-state-owned enterprises into sectors that were previously monopolised by the SOEs. Industries like textile, metallurgy, and food, which were more competitive and experienced entry by many new firms, exhibit greater fluctuation in technical efficiency when compared to other industries. Technical efficiency in textile dropped dramatically in 1985 when competition intensified. In metallurgy, technical efficiency peaked in 1983, then declined steadily and never recovered during this period. Food industry saw ups and downs over the whole period.

In order to measure the effect of the reforms on technical efficiency, we estimate a Tobit regression model, using the technical efficiency score as the dependent variable and a set of reform variables and firm attributes as regressors. We find that specific aspects of the reforms were very effective in improving technical efficiency.

The rest of this paper is organised as follows. Section 2 notes the main highlights of the reforms. The nonparametric methodology of DEA is briefly explained in section 3. Section 4 describes the data and construction of variables and reports the empirical findings – first the technical efficiency measures obtained from DEA and subsequently the second stage Tobit regression results. Section 5 concludes.

SECTION 2

THE REFORMS

Two key components of the Marxian "Materialistic Conception of History" are the forces of production and the relations of production. The forces of production correspond to the available productive resources along with technical knowledge and productivity. The relations of production, on the other hand, are defined by the ownership distribution of property and determine how the output is distributed. In the Maoist strategy of development, the primary emphasis was on the relations of production. The underlying assumption is that once private property rights are eliminated through socialisation of industry and collectivisation of agriculture, productivity would automatically rise to higher levels. In the economic policy debate that took place during the Great Leap Forward, opponents of this Maoist point of view, who were accused of "economism", argued that the basic contradiction faced by the nation was one of economic backwardness and low levels of productivity and efficiency associated with underdevelopment of the forces of production. In fact, they proposed numerous reforms that emphasised division of labour, specialisation, greater individual responsibility, and material incentives. In many ways, they anticipated the post-Mao economic reforms. In that sense, introduction of these reforms represents a shift of emphasis from the relations to the forces of production within Marxian dialectics.

Prior to the reforms, SOEs in China were trapped in a cobweb of regulation and control enforced by several layers of government. An important aspect of the reforms was to simplify the bureaucracy by eliminating most of direct government control and transferring considerable decision-making authority to the managers of the enterprise. Economic management in a Soviet-style command system is material balance planning that involves an output plan for individual producers, a supply plan for transfer of resources between producers, and a schedule of material use that earmarks inputs for outputs. Clearly, this implies detailed micro management by a central authority far removed from the actual production facilities. At the enterprise level, the party secretary outranked the factory manager. Even when the party boss did not issue direct orders, the manager had to seek his agreement in matters of management of production and administrative work.

China kicked-off the economic reforms with a fundamental change in development strategy in 1978, shifting away from a heavy industry oriented strategy. Development of agriculture and light industry gained much higher priority. Investment in agriculture and light industry was increased while investment in heavy industry was cut. Meanwhile, advanced equipments were imported to upgrade the technology at the SOEs

In the early-1980s, the Chinese Government further consolidated the control of the SOEs through devolution of proprietary rights to municipal governments continuing a trend started during the Cultural Revolution. In 1985, many SOEs were administered by municipal governments. The functionary departments of both the central government and local governments gave up direct control over most SOEs. Under the fiscal contract system effective since 1980, the responsibilities of municipal governments to their superiors mainly were to hand over a portion of fiscal revenue fixed in the fiscal contracts. Thus, municipal governments became the *de facto* owners of most SOEs. In fact, each local government became a conglomerate and an active player in the market. Thus, market competition intensified dramatically.

To manage numerous SOEs in various industries, municipal governments tried various methods. One of them was the managerial contract system where SOEs and government negotiate and sign three- to five-year contracts. Under such contracts, the firms must deliver the contracted profit regardless of performance. The director had responsibility for decision-making. Firms retained profits only when the target was exceeded. The success of the household land contract system in agriculture inspired and popularised this system. Not long after its inception in 1985, the managerial contract system was widely accepted and became the dominant relationship between government and SOEs during 1986-1993.[1]

An alternative to the contract management system is the director responsibility system where the director of the firm controls business operations while the party committee provides the political education of the employees. This system provided for substantially higher remuneration for the director compared to the workers.

Inside the SOEs, the government reformed the rigid wage system, allowing the SOEs to pay bonus to the workers. During 1978-1985, the SOEs were allowed to pay a portion of retained profit as bonus according to certain rules set by the government. Under the managerial contract system starting in 1986, the bonus was linked to the performance of the firm, and was stipulated by their firm's contract with the government. Studies suggest that the bonus system was the most effective component of the reform.

The success of agricultural reform not only freed a great number of farmers from land, but also generated initial capital funds for the rural enterprises for industrialisation. With no support from the state, these town and village enterprises (TVEs) circumvented the plan system to purchase raw materials and equipment, and to market their products. The government finally reformed the price system after the emergence of TVEs which broke the monopoly of the SOEs in the second half of 1980s. The market mechanism played an increasingly important role within the system of planning. Every planned good had a plan price and a market price. Meanwhile, the SOEs sold their output beyond quota at market price. Initially, a large gap between the high and volatile market price and a suppressed planned price led to severe corruption. To address this problem, the government adjusted the plan prices upwards in 1987, thereby narrowing the gap. At the same time, intense competition and abundant supply also helped to close the gap. By 1993, the dual price system was eliminated ending the economy of shortage.

Together these reforms drastically altered the operating environment of the SOEs, creating new opportunities for improving

1. Several studies evaluate the effectiveness of the managerial contract system in improving productivity (Groves 1994, 1995, Zhuang and Xu 1996, Shirley and Xu 1998).

productivity and efficiency and allowing a greater role for individual initiatives. We employ the nonparametric method of data envelopment analysis explained in the next section to examine if, and to what extent, the reforms helped to raise productivity.

SECTION 3

THE METHODOLOGY OF DATA ENVELOPMENT ANALYSIS

Technical efficiency of a firm can be measured by the ratio of its actual output to the maximum output producible from its observed input bundle defined by the frontier production function. In parametric models, one specifies an explicit functional form for the frontier and econometrically estimates the parameters using sample data for inputs and output. Hence the validity of the derived technical efficiency measures depends critically on the appropriateness of the functional form specified. The method of DEA introduced by Charnes, Cooper and Rhodes (CCR) (1978) and further generalised by Banker, Charnes, and Cooper (BCC) (1984) provides a non-parametric alternative to parametric frontier production function analysis. In DEA, one makes only a few fairly weak assumptions about the underlying production technology. In particular, no functional specification is necessary. Based on these assumptions, a production frontier is empirically constructed using mathematical programming methods from observed input-output data of sample firms.

Consider an industry producing a scalar output, y, from bundles of m inputs, $x=(x_1,x_2,\ldots,x_m)$. Let (x^j, y^j) be the observed input-output bundle of firm j ($j= 1,2,\ldots, n$). The technology is defined by the production possibility set

$$T=\{(x, y): y \text{ can be produced from } x\}.$$

An input-output combination (x^0, y^0) is feasible if and only if $(x^0, y^0) \in T$.

We make the following assumptions about the technology:

(1) All observed input-output combinations are feasible. Thus, $(x^j, y^j) \in T$ ($j = 1,2,\ldots,n$).

(2) The production possibility set, T, is convex. Hence, if $(x^1, y^1) \in T$ and $(x^2, y^2) \in T$, then

$$(\lambda x^1+(1-\lambda)x^2, \lambda y^1+(1-\lambda)y^2) \in T,\ 0\leq\lambda\leq 1.$$

In other words, weighted averages of feasible input-output combinations are also feasible.

(3) Inputs are freely disposable. Hence, if $(x^0, y^0) \in T$ and $x^1 \geq x^0$, then $(x^1, y^0) \in T$. This rules out negative marginal productivity of inputs.

(4) Output is freely disposable. Hence, if $(x^0, y^0) \in T$ and $y^1 \leq y^0$, then $(x^0, y^1) \in T$

Varian (1984) pointed out that the smallest set satisfying assumptions (1)-(4) is;

$$S = \left\{ (x, y) : x \geq \sum_{j=1}^{n} \lambda_j x^j ; y \leq \sum_{j=1}^{n} \lambda_j y^j ; \sum_{j=1}^{n} \lambda_j = 1 ; \lambda_j \geq 0 ; j = 1, 2, \ldots, n \right\}$$

Let $\bar{x} = \sum_{j=1}^{n} \lambda_j x^j, \bar{y} = \sum_{j=1}^{n} \lambda_j y^j ; \sum_{j=1}^{n} \lambda_j = 1 ; \lambda_j \geq 0$. By virtue of convexity

$\{x, y\}$ is feasible.

Then, for any $x \geq x, (x, y)$ is feasible. Finally, for any $y \leq y, (x, y)$ is also feasible.

Technical efficiency of any firm producing output y^0 from input x^0 is $1/\varphi*$, where

$$\varphi^* = \max\ \varphi : (x^0, \varphi y^0) \in S.$$

Note that this is an output-oriented measure of efficiency. Alternatively, one could use an input-oriented approach, where efficiency lies in conserving inputs while producing the observed output quantity. In the present study, like Zheng *et al.*, (1998), we select an output-oriented efficiency measure, because the Chinese SOEs during the 1980s were more inclined towards expanding output than towards cutting cost.[2]

Thus, for any observed firm *t*, we solve the following linear programming problem:

$$\text{Max } \phi_t \qquad t \in (1, \ldots, N) \qquad \ldots(1)$$

$$\text{s.t } \sum_{n=1}^{N} \lambda_n x_{nj} \leq x_{tj} \qquad j = 1, \ldots, J \qquad n = 1, \ldots, N \qquad \ldots(2)$$

---

2. Hay *et al.*, (1994) find that in late-1980s, the SOEs paid closer attention to cost reduction.

$$\sum_{n=1}^{N} \lambda_n y_n \geq \phi_t y_t \qquad ...(3)$$

$$\sum_{n=1}^{N} \lambda_n = 1 \qquad ...(4)$$

$$\lambda_n \geq 0 \qquad ...(5)$$

This BCC model allows increasing, constant, or diminishing returns to scale along the frontier of the production possibility set at different levels of inputs.

SECTION 4

THE EMPIRICAL ANALYSIS

Data Construction

Our panel data come from a survey of activities of 769 SOEs in four provinces (Jiangsu, Jilin, Shanxi,, and Sichuan) that was carried out by the Chinese Academy of Social Science in 1990. For each SOE, there are 10 annual observations for 321 quantitative variables over 1980-1989 and a questionnaire completed by managers of these firms. In essence, the survey consists of a set of accounting statements including profit statements, production and sales statements, personal and wage statements, and balance sheets, in which each element can be checked against others.

We consider a single-output, 4-input technology for the firms under investigation. The inputs included are: (a) labour, (b) capital, (c) materials, and (d) energy. The input-output variables are defined as follows.

We use gross industrial output in constant 1989 price, rather than value added. The firm-specific deflator comes from the variable "output in 1980 constant price". Productive labour includes production workers and apprentices, and purchasing and marketing personnel. Management and technical personnel were regarded as non-production workers and were excluded. Gross capital-in-use measures productive capital. Though the data are available, we do not use net capital-in-use, because the depreciation rates applied were arbitrary and would not accurately reflect the extent of capital consumption. Because our efficiency measures are based on yearly cross-section data, if the rate of capacity utilisation within any one year is assumed to be equal across all firms in any particular industry, use of gross capital in-use would not affect relative efficiency measures. Raw materials are measured by deflating the expenditure on materials by a material input price index. We construct the firm-specific composite price index for raw materials, using quantity and price information of two main input materials available in the survey. The energy input quantity equals the expenditure on energy divided by an energy price index The survey does not give price information for energy. We use the energy price information available in *China Statistical Yearbook 1998*. Because during 1980-1989, the central government still set price for energy across the country, firm-specific prices of energy were not needed.

Our construction of key variables takes into account the existence of a "dual track" price system. Coexistence of a "plan price" side by side with a "market price" for planned goods required careful construction of a composite price index for each firm, because the portion of materials purchased from market and the portion of output sold to market varied from firm to firm. Availability of detailed price information of materials in the survey enabled us to construct the composite firm-specific price indexes for both output and raw materials. Following Li (1997), we measure both output and raw materials in constant 1989 composite prices. In order to calculate the deflator for capital, we use the information in the questionnaire about inflation rates for equipment estimated by the managers. The deflator, thus, is firm specific rather than aggregate like the one used in Li (1997). This is justified on two grounds. First, because almost all the firms in the survey were established before 1980, their capacity was mainly expanded by upgrading their equipment, rather than constructing new buildings. Changes in buildings prices had little effect on the value of their capital. Second, prices of building materials and wages of construction workers varied greatly across regions, mainly because of great variation in prices of locally producced building materials. A single aggregate price for all firms in each year is a rough approximation and would be inappropriate.

DEA Results

For measurement of technical efficiency, the observations were cross classified by year and industry group. A BCC DEA model was solved for each firm in any year with reference to the relevant cross section data for that specific industry. Table 3.1 reports the technical efficiency for each of eight industries[3] averaged over firms. Overall, the paper industry ranks highest with a mean efficiency of 92 per cent, followed by an average efficiency of 82 per cent in the building material industry, while the textile industry scored the lowest with a mean of 52 per cent. Both electrical equipment and food industries have average technical efficiency of about 74 per cent.

Table 3.1

Mean Technical Efficiency by Industry and Year

Year	Chemical	Textile	Electrical	Food	Machine	Metals	Paper	Building mat.
1980	0.4770	0.4776	0.6782	0.7025	0.5302	0.8375	0.8935	0.7822
1981	0.6733	0.5053	0.7202	0.7477	0.5734	0.8950	0.9589	0.7835
1982	0.6675	0.4602	0.7307	0.6845	0.6110	0.9191	0.9260	0.7735
1983	0.6631	0.3172	0.7071	0.7674	0.6362	0.8106	0.8829	0.7784
1984	0.6879	0.5988	0.7321	0.7195	0.6568	0.8533	0.9425	0.7711
1985	0.7082	0.4047	0.7194	0.7573	0.6687	0.7356	0.9545	0.8119
1986	0.7218	0.4795	0.7079	0.6967	0.6545	0.7265	0.9399	0.8178
1987	0.5332	0.5985	0.7110	0.7088	0.6747	0.7091	0.9339	0.8677
1988	0.7631	0.6738	0.8023	0.8459	0.6282	0.6975	0.9063	0.9043
1989	0.7656	0.6913	0.8531	0.8129	0.7757	0.6958	0.9332	0.9387
Mean	0.6654	0.5224	0.7385	0.7461	0.6424	0.7848	0.9273	0.8235
Annual growth	2.28%	1.78%	1.11%	0.7%	1.84%	-0.89%	0.21%	0.88%

Source: calculated by authors.

Considerable variation exists in annual rates of growth in technical efficiency across industries. Chemicals had the lowest average efficiency in 1980, and experienced the highest average annual growth rate of 2.3 per cent. Textiles and machine manufacturing had annual growth rates of over 1.75 per cent while electrical equipment also improved in efficiency at an annual rate of over 1 per

3. We regroup the firms from the 24 three digit industries into eight categories. Food industry includes food, beverage, and feed manufacture. Textile industry includes textile, apparel and leather, fur and other clothing manufacture. Paper industry includes paper and its product, cultural and teaching product manufacture, printing, and crafts. Chemical industry includes chemicals, pharmaceuticals, synthetic fibres, and rubber and plastic industry. Building material industry includes building material and other non-metal products industry. Metal industry includes non-ferrous metals and other non-metal minerals. Machinery industry includes machine and transport equipment manufacturing. Electric equipment industry includes electronic equipment, communication equipment, and meteorological equipment manufacturing.

cent. Food paper, and building materials experienced only marginal growth in technical efficiency. Metal industry is the only one that experienced decline. The industries with lower efficiency in 1980 generally gained more than those with higher efficiency in the 1980. There is, thus, some evidence of convergence in technical efficiency across industries over the 1980s.

Figure 3.1 shows the trends in technical efficiency for each of the eight industries over the sample years. A notable feature is the large fluctuation in technical efficiency in the textile industry during 1982-1987. The textile industry is relatively labour-intensive and requires less capital compared to the other industries. After 1978, the central government encouraged local governments to build new textile enterprises in order to increase employment.[4] Several years later, township governments began to found town and village enterprises (TVEs) in textiles and metal processing. The SOEs in the textile industry negatively affected by the new competition and only gradually restructured and recovered. Similarly, a downward trend is found in the technical efficiency in metallurgy that fluctuated during 1983-1985. The food industry also experienced ups and downs over most years.

Figure 3.1

Technical Efficiency 1980–1989

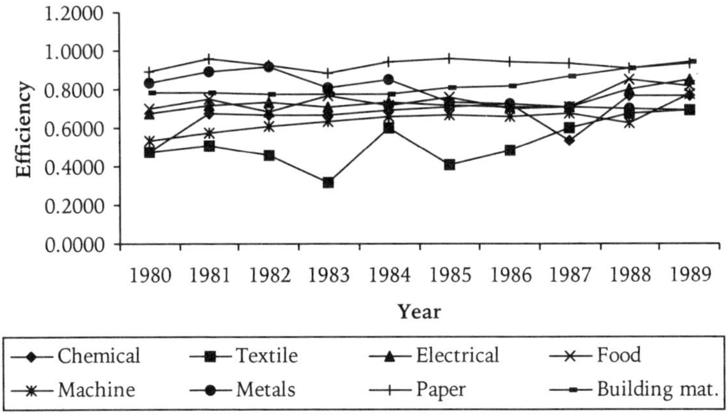

Source: Based on Table 3.1.

4. There were two major sources of employment pressure. One was from the millions of people ready to join the labour force; the other was from the millions who were sent to countryside under Mao's re-education policy and were returning back to city.

Competition from TVEs had an effect on the efficiency of SOEs. Because the textile industry has lower barriers to entry, it was the first to witness entry by TVEs. Faced with this new competition, the SOEs in this industry went through some initial adjustment, which lowered their technical efficiency. They improved their technical efficiency only gradually. On the other hand, in the metal industry, the SOEs did not recover from the negative effects of competition during the survey period.

The two studies most directly comparable with ours are Liu and Liu (1996) and Zheng, Liu, and Bigsten (1998). Liu and Liu measured technical efficiency from an estimated stochastic frontier production function using the same survey data set. Except for food and chemicals, their measures of technical efficiency are generally lower than ours. Moreover, they find evidence of productivity decline in textiles and productivity growth in metals, directly contrasting our findings. Also, their results show quite different patterns of the changes in technical efficiency over years.

Several possible factors may explain these differences. First, their reference technology is specified as a stochastic Cobb Douglas production frontier while we use a non-parametric frontier. In general, DEA measures of efficiency are higher than stochastic frontier measures obtained from the same data. Second, they use value added rather than gross output. Also, their measure of capital differs from ours. Nevertheless, despite specific differences in results both studies conclude that technical efficiency was higher in most industries in the later half of the 1980s.

Zheng, Liu, and Bigsten (1998), use DEA to examine difference in technical efficiency of firms by ownership structure. They pool SOEs, collectively owned enterprises (COEs), and TVEs and analyse the data for 1986-90. Their measure of average technical efficiency for SOEs across all industries covered and over their entire sample period is 0.77, comparable to what would be obtained from our DEA results for the same time period. Their coverage of industries is somewhat different from ours, however. When we look into specific industries, results do differ. For textiles, their average of 82 per cent efficiency is understandably higher than our comparable average of about 62 per cent because they include the COEs and TVEs, which are more efficient than the SOEs. Similar differences emerge for metals. For electricals and chemicals the two studies obtain comparable levels of mean efficiency. For paper, their overall measure of 82 per cent for all types of firms is lower than our average of over 90 per cent for the comparable period (1986-89) for SOEs alone.

Findings from the Tobit Regression

In non-parametric studies of efficiency using DEA, it is common practice to estimate a second stage regression model explaining variation in the measured efficiency scores in terms of a number of relevant environmental variables that affect the performance of a firm. Given that the technical efficiency measures are bounded from above at unity, we estimate a Tobit regression for limited dependent variables instead of the usual regression.

We specify a regression model including a number of explanatory variables pertaining to different aspects of the economic reforms along with a number of other relevant variables. Our objective is to determine whether the economic reform led to any improvement in the level of technical efficiency in the SOEs, as expected, and, if so, which specific aspects of the reforms had a significant effect on efficiency.

We treat the technical efficiency score as the dependent variable and a number of SOEs' attributes and reform policy variables as regressors. The explanatory variables can be broadly categorised as those related to (a) different aspects of the reforms directly or indirectly, (b) technology, (c) attributes of the firm, and (d) fixed effects related to time and geographical location.

The variables directly related to the reforms included: (i) the bonus-wage ratio, (ii) the type of management control, and (iii) the tax ratio. Variables indirectly related to the reforms include: (i) the level of government owning the enterprise, and (ii) the ratio of output and input prices. The technology variables include (i) capital per worker, and (ii) ratio of non-production to production workers. The attributes included are (i) firm size, and (ii) its industrial classification.

The bonus to wage ratio *(BWR)*, measured by the ratio of bonus to the fixed wage paid to workers, is often regarded as the most crucial of the reform variables and captures the incentive effect directly. We also include a squared term to capture possibly non-linear effects.

The SOEs in the sample can be broadly grouped into four different categories according to the type of management control: (a) director-responsibility, (b) contract responsibility, (c) a combined category of share, leasing, or asset-management responsibility, and (d) old style bureaucratic control. We include three dummy variables for different types of management control: DC-Contract for contract responsibility, DC-nochange for old style management, and DC-Combined for the mixed category. The director-responsibility system was treated as the reference category.

The tax ratio *(TRATIO)*, defined as a ratio of total tax liability over value-added, captures the effect of taxes on technical efficiency. Total tax liability includes turnover tax and income tax. We treat profit remittance to the government before 1984 as a tax liability of firms, because, no enterprise income tax existed across China before 1984. Comparison over years would be misleading if we consider only the income tax that came into existence after the 1984 reforms. Furthermore, the contract system implemented gradually after 1986 also contracts the overall tax liability including income tax and turnover tax.

The SOEs are by definition government owned. Ownership of individual enterprises is, however, vested at different levels of government in the political hierarchy . These range from a ministry of the central government at the national level down to a local county government within a city. McAffee and McMillan (1991) argue that informational distortions increase as information moves up a hierarchy. Also, the closer is the ultimate decision-maker to the production floor the more effective are the incentives to the workers. But, at the same time, in the case of a firm that is owned by the local government, there may be political considerations against downsizing or closing an inefficient enterprise. We treat the county government as the reference category and include specific dummy variables for the central government (DG-Central), the provincial government (DG-Provincial), and the city government (DG-City).

The market power of a firm is usually measured by its mark-up ratio, (i.e., the ratio of price to marginal cost). Unfortunately, in our case, the marginal cost is not observable. We, therefore, following Li

(1997), use the ratio of output price to input price *(ROPIP)* as a proxy measure of market power. Given that the reforms allowed the market to play a significant role in the operating environment of a firm, we include this variable in the model explaining changes in technical efficiency.

Among the technology variables, the capital-labour ratio *(RKL)* is included for several reasons. First, the degree of automation of the production process closely relates to the technical efficiency of a firm, because production lines determine the pace of production. Higher automation usually requires a higher capital-labour ratio. Second, workers with more capital usually work more efficiently because they can perform simpler and repeated job. We also include a quadratic term to allow non-linearity.

The other technology variable is the proportion of non-productive workers in total employment *(PNPW)*. Conventional wisdom suggests that a greater proportion of non-productive workers reflects a more unwieldy bureaucracy. Hence, it may be expected to have a negative effect on efficiency. At the same time, over the years, the SOEs have provided a range of social services to their employees and many employees work to provide these services. In defining total employment, we include only production workers and marketing personnel and exclude management and technical personnel, because it is difficult to estimate how many management and technical personnel in the SOEs work on non-production activity.

The survey groups the SOEs into three different size categories: small, medium, and large. We include two dummy variables – DS-Large and DS-Medium – for large and medium sized firms. The smallest size group is treated as the reference group.

The SOEs represent eight different industry groups as explained earlier. We treat the electrical equipment industry as the base category and include seven dummy variables for the other industries.

Apart from these explanatory variables, we include year dummy variables (with the year 1989 as base) and three region dummy variables for the provinces of Jiangsu, Jilin, and Shanxi, respectively, with Sichuan treated as the base.

Table 3.2 reports the estimated coefficients from Tobit and OLS regressions for comparison. Coefficients of the industry dummies

Table 3.2

Regression Results

Variables	Tobit Model Estimation		Tobit Model Std. Error	OLS Estimation		OLS Std. Error
DI_food	-.033760		0.02459	-0.02609		0.01935
DI_textile	-0.28982	***	0.01919	-0.25063	***	0.01523
DI_paper	0.24940	***	0.03076	0.16244	***	0.02260
DI_chemical	-0.12131	***	0.01825	-0.09765	***	0.01442
DI_building mat.	0.09727	***	0.02223	0.06061	***	0.01715
DI_metals	0.00756		0.02656	-0.00414		0.02052
DI_machine	-0.11430	***	0.01655	-0.08794	***	0.01312
DY_80	-0.15724	***	0.02674	-0.01530	***	0.02114
DY_81	-0.06290	**	0.02627	-0.07076	***	0.02071
DY_82	-0.08083	***	0.02585	-0.07979	***	0.02042
DY_83	-0.09516	***	0.02532	-0.09461	***	0.01999
DY_84	-0.09467	***	0.02167	-0.08334	***	0.01698
DY_85	-0.10743	***	0.02166	-0.09701	***	0.01699
DY_86	-0.10457	***	0.02120	-0.08973	***	0.01665
DY_87	-0.13594	***	0.02068	-0.11809	***	0.01621
DY_88	-0.07340	***	0.02047	-0.06131	***	0.01595
DS_large	-0.01996		0.01602	-0.00992		0.01251
DS_middle	-0.10217	***	0.01216	-0.07607	***	0.00954
DR_Jiangsu	0.01657		0.01268	0.01674	*	0.00999
DR_Jilin	-0.02862	**	0.01514	-0.02118	*	0.01206
DR_Shanxi	-0.06070	***	0.01383	-0.04090	***	0.01099
DG_central	-0.13598	***	0.02619	-0.10268	***	0.02075
DG_provincial	-0.10298	***	0.02610	-0.07937	***	0.02062
DG_city	-0.04520	**	0.01938	-0.03690	**	0.01520
DC_no change	-0.03287	**	0.01511	-0.02330	*	0.01203
DC_combined	0.06885	***	0.02281	0.05388	***	0.01759
DC_contract	0.03011		0.02032	0.01985		0.01577
Tax ratio	0.08783	***	0.02633	0.07862	***	0.02074
BWR	0.21367	***	0.04211	0.17300	***	0.03259
PNPW	0.01223		0.03375	0.01820		0.02574
ROPIP	0.04256	**	0.01758	0.03002	**	0.01401
BWR^2	-0.04830	**	0.01991	-0.04577	**	0.01504
RKL	0.00643	***	0.00101	0.00296	***	0.00058
RKL^2	-0.00001	***	0.00000	-0.00001	***	0.00000
Intercept	0.08834	***	0.03273	0.08278	***	0.02568

Note: 1. Other statistics: likelihood for Tobit =-1125.78; R^2 for OLS =0.2447. Total number of observations =3677, of which non-censored =2831 and censored =846

2. ***— one per cent significant; **— 5 per cent significant; *— 10 per cent significant.

3. Marginal effect of variables in Tobit = coefficient* proportion of non-sensored observations.

show considerable variation. The difference in average technical efficiency between the paper industry and textile industry is 0.4152, over 40 per cent[5] holding all other factors constant. The paper industry has the highest average efficiency, followed by construction material, electric equipment and metallurgy, machinery, chemical and textile in descending order. The difference in average levels of technical efficiency in metallurgy and machinery industries is not statistically significant.

The bonus-wage ratio *(BWR)* has the largest and positive effect on technical efficiency. This confirms Groves *et al.,* (1994) and Liu and Liu (1996). Marginally, the bonus ratio at unity can promote technical efficiency about 13 per cent. A negative sign of the quadratic term indicates a diminishing marginal effect of bonus. When the bonus ratio is at about 2.21, the effect of bonus reaches its peak. Overall, the result indicates that the bonus system provided strong incentives to workers in the 1980s.

The capital-labour ratio *(RKL)* makes large positive contributions to technical efficiency. On average, a 10,000 yuan increase in capital for each production worker can induce a 0.5 per cent increase in technical efficiency. The negative sign and small value of squared capital labour ratio indicates a slowly diminishing effect. Technical efficiency continues to increase with the capital-labour ratio up to the level of 321,000 yuan of capital per worker.

The ratio of non-production workers to production workers *(RNPW)* has no significant impact on technical efficiency. This possibly implies that the positive effects of the social services provided by the non-production workers neutralise any detrimental effects of a large bureaucracy.

The tax ratio has a large and positive effect on technical efficiency. On average, a 10 per cent increase in average tax rate promotes a 0.68 per cent increase in technical efficiency. This is at odds with conventional wisdom in a market economy. SOEs with lower tax burdens, however, generally have more restricted access to resources under government control such as cheaper loans, planned material supplies, and foreign currency. In contrast, the government offers

5. Marginal effect is calculated by the formula: coefficients*(number of non-censored observations/total number of observations).

more resources to SOEs with a higher tax burden. Until 1984, the government took most of the profits and offered SOEs grants for financing investment. Our result implies that the tax rate may be highly correlated with preferential treatment received by SOEs from the government. This, we must acknowledge, is only a speculation.

The levels of government administration of the SOEs have a great effect on technical efficiency. Coefficients of the relevant dummy variables are all statistically significant. The result shows that county government is 10.47 per cent more efficient than the central government that scores lowest. Efficiency of an SOE owned by a provincial government is only 2.5 per cent higher than that of one owned by the central government but about 4.4 per cent worse than one owned by a city government. This lends support to the conclusion of McAfee and McMillan (1991). Our results strongly suggest that decentralisation improved efficiency in the 1980s in China.

The output-material price ratio *(ROPIP)* contributes positively to technical efficiency as expected. A 10 per cent increase in the ratio on average can raise technical efficiency by 0.33 per cent. A higher output-material price ratio not only means higher profit margin for the enterprises, more bonuses, and better welfare for workers, but also means higher demand for goods produced by the SOEs. In 1980s, output price grew slower than material price in manufacture sector. Thus, the output-material price ratio actually reduces technical efficiency.

The coefficient of the dummy variable is negative and statistically significant for the middle size but not significant for the large size class. Thus, small and large SOEs do not differ in technical efficiency but the middle sized enterprises are less efficient. There are several possible explanations. The government adopted discriminatory tax and credit policies toward different sizes of firms. China's industrial policy emphasised development of large firms. Large firms, in general, paid more taxes and had easy access to credit. In contrast, small firms paid fewer taxes and had less access to credits. At the same time, large firms were under tighter government control and suffered more interference from government bureaucrats. Small firms were subject to harder budget constraints and had stronger incentives to operate efficiently. Moreover, they faced much less bureaucratic interference compared to large firms. Overall their specific advantages and disadvantages must have put the large and the small enterprises on a par. The middle-sized SOEs had much less protection than the large firms and the same time less autonomy than small firms. Even though smaller than large firms, they are large enough to cause harm to the regional economy if a medium sized firm is closed. In that sense, they are too large to fail. As a result, they had only limited freedom to enforce cost cutting measures by downsizing.

The location of the enterprises also makes a little difference on technical efficiency. The survey was carried out in four provinces, Jiangsu, Jilin, Shanxi and Sichuan. We set Sichuan as the base. The result contradicts the general perception that the coastal province Jiangsu performs better than inland province Sichuan. There are two possible causes. First the coastal province Jiangsu, next to the largest industrial city Shanghai, was a dynamic region in the 1980s. But this general perception ignores the unbalanced nature of development within Jiangsu. South Jiangsu has been one of fastest developing regions, while North Jiangsu languishes at the same development level as many inland provinces. Because the survey samples SOEs from various districts of a province, it shows the performance of the whole of Jiangsu, not merely the Southern region. Second, the survey includes a high proportion of large SOEs and Sichuan has the greatest number of large SOEs in the country. This may cause over-estimation of the average technical efficiency in Sichuan. SOEs in Jilin and Shanxi are 2.16 per cent and 4.7 per cent less efficient than in Jiangsu and Sichuan respectively. A note of caution is in order here. Shanxi is the home of coal mining industry. However, we exclude mining from our analysis due to numerous missing values. This may lead to lower estimated average technical efficiency in the province.

The coefficients of the year dummy variables trace the fluctuation in technical efficiency over years. The difference between the coefficients for adjacent years shows the change in average efficiency between those years. The year 1981 shows the greatest annual increase in technical efficiency in the 1980s, at a rate of more than 6.93 per cent, while the following two years, 1982 and 1983 show a slight decline. 1984 sees almost no gain while 1985 experiences a loss of one per cent. There is a tiny increase in 1986 and a more than 2.3 per cent decrease in 1987. The technical efficiency improves significantly in 1988 and 1989 at a rate of 4.77 per cent and 5.62 per cent, respectively. The annual average rate of improvement in technical efficiency is about 1.21 per cent, which is slightly lower than the 1.6 per cent estimated by Liu and Liu (1996).

This pattern is consistent with China's gradualist reform in the 1980s. Rawski (1996, p. 190) noted that in China "reform unfolds as a process replete with interactions among governments, enterprises, workers and consumers rather than a sequence of events in which the state makes decisions to which businesses and individuals react". When the economy overheated and technical efficiency fell, the government responded with new initiatives of reform so as to maintain macroeconomic stability and improve efficiency. At the beginning, in the early-1980s, the bonus system had impressive and quick effects as observed in Liu and Liu (1996) and Zhuang and Xu (1996), but gradually lost its effectiveness. Equalisation of bonus payments to all workers unlinked to workers' productivity was the major cause. Other reform measures also seem to be ineffective in the middle 1980s. Reforms in taxation and investment in 1984 did show some effect. But in 1985, there was a 1.2 per cent decline in technical efficiency. The government then introduced the management contract system in 1986. That seemed to be working in 1986. A dip in technical efficiency in 1987 pushed the government to popularise the contract system. The contract system seems to have been effective in 1988 and 1989.[6] Of course, we do not attribute all improvements in technical efficiency to the contract system, because various reform measures had penetrated into every facet of SOEs by the late-1980s. Nonetheless, the reforms eventually led to significant gains in technical efficiency of SOEs.

A comparison with the trend of the whole state industry sector reveals more interesting results. Figure 3.2 shows a negative relation between the output growth in the whole state industrial sector and the technical efficiency during 1981-1987. When the output grows at a rapid pace, technical efficiency declines. There appears to be a structural change, however, in 1987. In 1988 when output grows, technical efficiency increases as well, while in 1989

6. The contract system was abolished in 1994 in favour of formal and stable relationship between the government and the SOEs.

output decreases sharply, technical efficiency almost still increases. The divergence of output growth rates for the SOEs in the survey from overall mean of growth rate in state industrial sector may be associated with the fact that the survey over-represents large- and middle-sized SOEs and that the selected SOEs do not represent proportionally all industries.

Figure 3.2

Growth Rate and Technical Efficiency

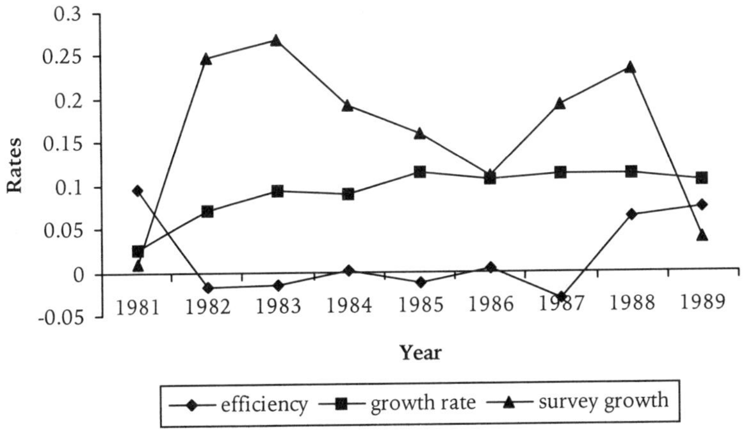

Note: Efficiency–technical efficiency of sample SOEs; growth rate–growth rate of the whole state industrial sector; survey growth–growth rate of the sample SOEs.

Figure 3.3 includes four different series showing (a) labour productivity, (b) production cost of comparable products for the whole state industry sector, (c) technical efficiency, and (d) growth of output of the sample firms. It shows that the labour productivity is positively and closely related to output growth. A comparison of the two series, technical efficiency and the cost of comparable products for the state sector, reveals that technical efficiency is closely and negatively related to cost reduction by the SOEs. When SOEs reduce cost more, their technical efficiency improves more. This relation is even more obvious in 1988 and 1989 when SOEs stepped-up their cost cutting efforts.

Figure 3.3

Comparison of Technical Efficiency, Labour Productivity, Growth Rate and Change of Cost

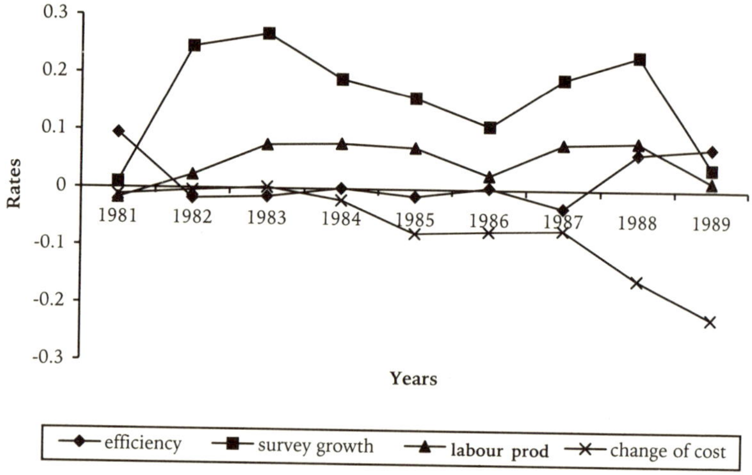

Note: Efficiency denotes technical efficiency calculated from dummy variables for years; growth rate is the growth rate of industry gross products of the state industrial sector, from *China Statistical Yearbook 1993*, p.413; survey growth is calculated from the survey data used. Change of cost is production cost of comparable products for the whole state industry sector. The survey growth appears to be more volatile.

The contract system (DC) has been quite effective in promoting technical efficiency. Firms under the contract system achieved at least 2.53 per cent higher technical efficiency. Furthermore, different contract system has different effect on technical efficiency. As expected, firms under the lease, stock, and capital management responsibility system perform better than firms under contract responsibility system. Their difference in technical efficiency is about three per cent. The contract responsibility system is statistically indifferent from factory director responsibility system. Our result is at odds with Huang and Kalirajan (1998). They find that contract system did not work. They acknowledged, however, that this might be due to their small sample size (only 67 firms).

Our results have general implications for reforms of a state industrial sector in a transition economy. First, piecemeal reform such as the introduction of the bonus system by itself can be effective over a short period, but cannot result in any sustainable improvement in technical efficiency. Second, substantial gains in technical efficiency come only after partial reforms accumulate to a critical mass. Reform measures do require certain time to take effect. Thus, we need to take a long-term view.

SECTION 5
CONCLUSIONS

In this paper, we apply DEA to examine the technical efficiency of a sample of SOEs in the 1980s. We find that technical efficiency in SOEs as a whole improved in the 1980s, but not steadily over years. The fluctuation in technical efficiency in various industries over years is closely related to competition and entry of new firms. Textile, food and metallurgy were more competitive and had entry by more new firms. These industries experienced greater fluctuation in technical efficiency than the other industries.

The Tobit regression analysis reveals how different aspects of the reforms affected levels of technical efficiency of the SOEs. The bonus system made the greatest positive contribution to improving technical efficiency. Second, various managerial contract systems made different degrees of positive contribution to technical efficiency. Among the various systems, the lease, stock, and asset management system contributed the most, while the contract management system and the factory director responsibility system are equally effective. This result confirms the serious concern about soft-budget constraint. Third, firms under the administration of a lower level government had higher technical efficiency. Fourth, middle-sized SOEs had lower technical efficiency than small- and large-sized SOEs, but the latter two size classes had the same average efficiency.

Our findings indicate that it is possible to improve technical efficiency without privatisation on a large scale and appropriate reforms can successfully improve technical efficiency of SOEs. Our study also shows that the market mechanism can function side by side with predominant state ownership of industries at least in the short run. One can only speculate if the SOEs would have functioned even more efficiently if they were privatised altogether. But, at least, the Chinese experience shows the viability of a middle ground between the chaotic reforms in the former Soviet Union and old style business-as-usual under a socialist bureaucracy.

References

Banker, R.D., A. Charnes, and W.W. Cooper (1984). "Some Models for Estimating Technical and Scale Inefficiencies in Data Envelopment Analysis." *Management Science,* 30: 9, 1984, pp 1078-1092.

Charnes, A., W.W. Cooper and E. Rhodes (1978). "Measuring the Efficiency of Decision-Making Units." *European Journal of Operation Research,* 2:6, 429-44.

Charnes, A., W. Cooper, A.Y. Lewin and L.M. Seiford (1994). "Introduction." In Charnes, A., W. Cooper, A.Y. Lewin, and Lawrence M. Seiford, eds., *Data Envelopment Analysis: Theory, Methodology and Application.* Boston/Dordrecht/London, Kluwer Academic, 3-22.

Chen, Derong (1998). *Chinese Firms between Hierarchy and Market: The Contract Management Responsibility System in China.* St. Martin Press.

Chen, K.W., Hongchang, Z. Yuxin, B. Jefferson, & T. Rawski (1988). "Productivity Change in Chinese Industry: 1953-1985." *Journal of Comparative Economics,* December, 12(4), 570-591.

Granick, David (1990). *Chinese State Enterprises: A Regional Property Rights Analysis.* Chicago and London: The University of Chicago Press.

Groves, Theodore, Yongmiao Hong, John McMillian and Barry Naughton (1994). "Autonomy and Incentives in Chinese State Enterprises." *Quarterly Journal of Economics,* February 109(1), 183-209.

————. (1995). "China's Evolving Managerial Labour Market." *Journal of Political Economy,* August 103 (4), 873-92.

Hay, Donald, Derek Morris, Guy Liu, and Shujie Yao (1994). *Economic Reform and State Owned Enterprises in China, 1979-1987.* Oxford University Press.

Huang Yiping and Kalirajan K.P. (1998). "Enterprise Reform and Technical Efficiency of China's State Owned Enterprises." *Applied Economcs* 30, 585-592.

Hussein, Athar and Zhuang, Juzhong (1996). "Pattern and Causes of Loss-Making in Chinese State Enterprises." *Working Paper,* Economic and Social Research Council, London School of Economics.

Jefferson, Gary H. (1998). "China's State Enterprises: Public Goods, Externalities, and Coase." *American Economic Review,* Vol. 88, No. 2, May, 428-432.

————. (1990). "China's Iron and Steel Industry: Sources of Enterprise Efficiency and the Impact of Reform." *Journal of Development Economics* 33: Oct. 329-55.

Jefferson, G.H., T.G. Rawski, & Y. Zheng (1992). "Growth, Efficiency, and Convergence in China's State and Collective industry." *Economic Development and Cultural Change,* 40(2), 239-266.

Jefferson, G.H., & T.G. Rawski (1994). "Enterprise Reform in Chinese Industry." *Journal of Economic Perspectives,* Spring, 47-70.

Li, Wei (1997). "The Impact of Economic Reform on the Performance of Chinese State Enterprises, 1980-1989." *Journal of Political Economy,* Vol. 105., No. 5, 1080-1106.

Liu Zinan and Guy Shaojia Liu. (1996). "The Efficiency Impact of the Chinese Industrial Reforms in the 1980's." *Journal of Comparative Economics,* 23, 237-255.

McAfee, R. Preston, and McMillan, John (1991). "Organisational Diseconomies of Scale." mineo, University of California, San Diego.

Naughton, Barry (1995). *Growing Out of the Plan: Chinese Economic Reform, 1978-1993.* Cambridge University Press.

Rawski, Thomas G. (1998). "An Overview of Chinese Industry in the 1980s." In Gary H. Jefferson and Inderjit Singh, eds. *Reform, Ownership, and Performance in Chinese Industry.*

———. (1994). "Chinese Industrial Reform: Accomplishment, Prospects, and Implications." *American Economic Review*, Papers and Proceedings, Vol. 84, No. 2.

Shirley Mary and Lixin Colin Xu. (1998). "Empirical Effects of Performance Contracts: Evidence from China." *Working Paper*, The World Bank, THE World Bank.

State Statistical Bureau (1990-1998). *China Statistical Yearbook*. China Statistical Publishing Press, issues.

Zheng Jinghai, Xiaoxuan Liu and Arne Bigsten (1998). "Ownership Structure and Determinants of Technical Efficiency: An Application of Data Envelopment Analysis to Chinese Enterprises (1986-1990)." *Journal of Comparative Economics*, 26, 465-484.

Zhuang Ju Zhong and Chenggang Xu (1996). "Profit-Sharing and Financial Performance in the Chinese State Enterprises: Evidence from Panel Data." *Economics of Planning*, 29(3), 205-22.

4

Determinants of Firm-level Technological Change in the Indian Small-scale Industries

A Case Study of Garment Industry

T.A. BHAVANI

SECTION 1

INTRODUCTION

Small-scale industries occupy an important place in the Indian economy in terms of creation of employment opportunities and hence providing a source of income to millions of people. However, it has been the general observation that majority of small-scale industries are not competitive and need to be improved in this respect. Accordingly, Government of India initiated numerous policies and programmes to improve the competitive strength of the small-scale industries with a special emphasis on the technological upgradation.[1] Despite the policy efforts of four decades, Indian small-scale units at large remained technologically backward and lacking in competitive strength.[2] In the mean time, rapid technological

1. The lack of competitive strength of small-scale industries and the need for their technological upgradation had been noted both by Mahalanobis (1963: 73) that formed as the base for the development strategy of India and by the Karve Committee (Committee on Village and Small-scale Industries, Second Five Year Plan, p. 30) which provided an immediate base to the policies on small-scale industries. The Industrial Policy Resolution 1956 adopted the same: "The aim of the State policy will be to ensure that the decentralised sector acquires sufficient vitality to be self-supporting .... The state, will, therefore, concentrate on measures designed to improve the competitive strength of the small-scale producer. For this, it is essential that the technique of production should be constantly improved and modernised....."
2. See, for example, Report of the Working Group on the SSIs for the Ninth Five Year Plan (p.73): "The fact has to be admitted that the sector has lagged behind in technological upgradation, modernisation, quality assurance, etc. This has, no doubt, affected the competitive strength of this sector *vis-à-vis* medium and large industry and the MNCs." Refer also to the Report of the Expert Committee on Small Scale Enterprises (Abid Hussain Committee), Ministry of Indistry, Government of India, New Delhi, 1997, p. 151; and Ayyar (1994: 39).

developments coupled with the on-going changes in the business environment due to liberalisation and globalisation of the economy, made technological upgradation of industrial units imperative. In this context, the study of technological change in small-scale industries[3] in India, assumes significance. This paper aims to examine the factors influencing technological change in the garment industry, which is one of the dynamic sectors of the Indian economy growing at a rate of 20 per cent per annum for the last two decades.[4]

Garments besides being a small-scale industry,[5] it plays an important role in the Indian economy both in terms of employment generation and in earning foreign exchange. The direct employment of the industry was about 0.6 million persons in 1980 and has gone up to around 2.0 million persons in 1992. The exports of garments were worth US$ 2.58 billion in 1990-91 and have risen to US$ 4.91 billion by 1997-98.[6] These exports accounted for about 9 per cent of total Indian exports in 1981-82. The share has almost doubled to 17 per cent by 1994-95.[7]

The paper is presented in six sections. The next section brings out the analytical factors that can possibly influence the technological changes in small industrial units. Section 3 briefly discusses the salient features of the Indian garments industry. For the purpose of empirical analysis, we have conducted a primary survey of garment factories located in and around Delhi. Based on the survey data, Section 4 studies the empirical relevance of the analytical factors discussed in Section 2. Section 5 deals with the estimation and interpretation of the technological change function. For the estimation purpose, we have made use of the Probit Model. The final section summarises the findings and makes concluding observations.

---

3. Conceptually 'Unit' (firm or enterprise) is different from 'industry' in the sense that the former is defined as the ownership or decision-making unit in the production of goods and services and the latter is taken to consist of all units - small and large in the production of a specified product. However, in the general context of small-scale industries they have been used synonymously.

4. NIFT (1998: 2).

5. Garments being a reserved product till very recently, the industry mainly consists of small-scale units.

6. Koshy (1997: 72).

7. Bhavani and Tendulkar (2000: 66).

SECTION 2

ANALYTICAL FRAMEWORK

The existing literature on technological change suffers severe limitations in considering the factors influencing firm-level technological changes.[8] It, thus, necessitates the development of a comprehensive analytical frame that enables one to study the firm-level changes in technologies and its determinants especially in the small-scale units. This section makes an attempt to develop such a framework following an eclectic approach. We draw on the evolutionary economics, economics of technological change, technological capabilities and organisation theories for the relevant concepts.

From the evolutionary economics, we have made use of the concepts of selection mechanism and the salient features of innovation process. Selection mechanism brings out how business environments select successful firms and how firms in turn select products and processes to get selected by the environment. Literature on technological change provides us the concept of technology and a broad set of theoretical factors that can possibly influence the technological changes. Technological capabilities literature helps us in defining the firm-level capabilities that are required to undertake and manage technological change. Finally, organisation theories enable us to locate the decision-maker and technological capabilities within the firm by providing us the basic components and structures of economic organisations.

We take firm as an economic organisation that produces a given set of goods and services for a specified market. Firm competes with many other firms that are producing similar or substitutable products in the market. Markets (product as well as factor), industry (competing firms) and other institutions such as service organisations and government policies form the business environment of the firm. The business environment of the firm changes continuously as all its elements keep changing. For instance, the product market changes as incomes, tastes and preferences change causing shifts in the demand for the specified products. The number and structure of the firms in the industry change and affect the supply of the given products. Government policies change over time shifting the demand and

8. Bhavani (2001).

supply structures of the products further. The demand and supply structures affect the price of the products and thereby profitability and commercial viability of the firms producing them. The variations in the business environment thus change the parameters of selection of successful firms in terms of the importance of different characteristics of the firms such as the type of product the firm produces and its methods of production, i.e. technology. Firms strive continuously to get selected, i.e., to maintain and to improve commercial viability through different strategies in the face of the changing environment. We treat the changes in technology as one such strategy of firms to operate effectively in the changing environment.

Somebody within the firm does the job of formulating and implementing the strategies. We refer them as 'decision makers'. Change of technology requires abilities to understand and manage technology, i.e., technological capabilities. So, we focus, for the purpose of analysis, on the three basic elements of a firm to study the unit-level technological change. They are: technology (that undergoes change), decision-maker (who undertakes change including the strategic decision making) and technological capabilities (pre-requisite for change). We elaborate on these elements in the subsequent paragraphs.

Technology is taken to include only the physical process of transformation of inputs into outputs, i.e., transformation. The transformation aspect mainly includes plant and machinery, tools, components and accessories.[9] Technological change is referred to any changes in transformation processes that are undertaken by the firm to improve its competitive strength either through cost reductions or, through quality or productivity improvements or a combination of all three.[10] Since we deal with the small-scale industrial units, technological changes mostly refer to the changes in their existing technologies either in the form of addition of or replacement by a

---

9. In the literature of technological change, technology has been defined to include both transformation and organisation methods (Dahlman and Westphal 1982). However, for the empirical analysis, all the studies have taken mainly the transformation aspect of technology only (Bos and Cole 1994: 232).

10. This is the most widely recognised purpose for which firms undertake changes in technology.

later vintage technology that has been already in practice elsewhere in the industry.[11, 12]

In order to locate the decision-maker and technological capabilities in the small-scale unit, we consider these units to have simple organisational structures with a strategic apex and an operating core. The operating core consists of all the workers involved in the basic production process like machine operation and maintenance. Their work is co-ordinated by the strategic apex through direct supervision. Strategic apex in the small units includes mainly the owner-managers. The owner-manager not only assigns the resources to different tasks as well as monitors these tasks on a day-to-day basis but also deals with the relevant outside agents like suppliers and customers on behalf of the organisation. In addition, *owner-managers* are the sole decision-makers in the small-scale units as they take all, strategic as well as administrative decisions. So, the decision-making regarding technological change depends on the owner-manager's perception of the business environment and its changes.

Equally important are the technological capabilities to relate the available technologies to the changing markets, and adapt and manage technological change. In specific terms, it requires investment, linkage and production capabilities. Investment capabilities refer to the abilities to search, select and commission a new production facility. Linkage capabilities include the abilities to transmit technology related information and skills from the relevant outside agents like customers. Production capabilities are the abilities to control and monitor as well as to operate and maintain production systems.[13] But for the capabilities to operate and maintain the production systems that are mainly located in workers, all other technological capabilities are to be possessed by the owner-manager

11. Industry, here, refers to the units producing similar products not only in India but also in other countries.

12. Consequently, we consider the addition of the same machines, tools, etc., as capacity expansion than technological change.

13. These definitions are taken from Dahlman *et al.*, (1987) and Lall (1992). Production and investment capabilities are considered by both the studies. In addition, Dahlman *et al.*, discusses innovation capabilities and Lall includes linkage capabilities. Since technological changes that can be considered innovation are an exception than a rule in the small units, we are not considering innovation capabilities in our study.

in the small-scale units. Technological capabilities are taken to be determined by the education and experience of the relevant personnel.

Following the evolutionary economics especially the principle of *ex ante* selection of technologies and products by firms and the salient features of the innovation, we consider the firm-level technological change as a deliberately initiated process of search, selection, execution and absorption.[14] To achieve change, concerned individuals/units have to seek for it, search for alternatives, i.e., to get to know the available alternative technologies in terms of cost, content, their sources and modes of acquiring them. If alternatives exist, unit has to select among the alternatives, then negotiate and acquire it. Then comes the execution which includes modification if need be, and installation of the machinery. With the execution, physical change of technology occurs. However, installation of a new machine does not automatically ensure the purpose of having it. Workers take sometime to get to know the machine and to be able to operate it smoothly. Thus, the actual process of technological change can be completed only when the acquired changes are mastered, i.e., absorbed. It is the execution followed by absorption that ensures the attainment of the purpose of change, namely, improvements in the competitive strength of the firm.

As the process of technological change can be treated as a set of distinct though related stages, we consider the factors affecting this process stage-wise. Consequently, we examine the factors initiating search, factors facilitating search, factors influencing the selection and factors affecting execution and absorption. Following the salient features of innovation that are brought out by evolutionary economists, we consider technological change as the result of the interaction of factors that are internal to the firm as well as external to it. Hence, we take the factors under these two categories.

We take market both in terms of its structure and demand as the main external factor and technological capabilities of the owner-manager as the internal factor that is responsible for initiating a search for alternative technologies by the firm. Since we are dealing with the imitator firms, it is the competitiveness of the product

14. This is a modified version of Dosi' (1988: 222) characterisation of innovation process, i.e., "search for, discovers, experimentation, development and adaptation of new products, production processes and organisational set up". We have modified it to suit the context of imitation as we are dealing with the imitator firms.

market that creates a pressure on firms to improve their technologies.[15, 16] On the other hand, rising demand for the product[17] may provide an incentive for the firms to go for technological improvements. How far a given unit acts in this direction depends on the owner-manager's perception of demand situation, market competition and its likely impact on the unit, and his/her capabilities to foresee the potential benefits of change or potential losses if not going for change. Hence, we consider the product market, owner-manager's perception of market and his/her technological capabilities especially the investment capabilities as the factors that initiate search for technological alternatives at the firm level.

A primary factor that facilitates search is the availability of information to the firm. Availability of information depends on the development of informational infrastructure of the nation like documentation centres, trade journals, consultancy organisations and the extent of dissemination of information through trade fairs, seminars etc. Widespread development of information infrastructure improves the access of small units to information and makes it easier for these units to obtain information. Equally important for gathering information is the awareness and resourcefulness of the owner-manager that depends on his/her linkage capabilities. In other words, it is the firm's access to information sources together with the linkage capabilities of the owner-manager that either facilitates or constrains the search for available alternative technologies. These factors also determine the degree of choice that a unit has in terms of technology.

Once the choice of technology is given, units need to select the technology that suits their requirements. The critical external factors that influence the selection of technology are the availability of finances, availability of complementary factors like materials and skills and relative factor prices. Availability of finances depends on unit's access to sources of finance and the cost of finance. Use of

15. Studies that went beyond innovators to include imitators argue that innovators do better when competition is restrained and imitators do better when there is aggressive competition (Elster 1983: 145). Also, see Mansfield (1961: 310).
16. Competitiveness of the market can be taken in terms of either increasing number of suppliers or, introduction of substitutes or, demanding customers or a combination of all these.
17. Demand for a product here refers to the total market demand for the product X not the demand for X produced by the given unit.

technology requires specific materials and skills and their availability in the vicinity thus becomes an important factor in influencing the selection of technology.[18] Availability of complementary skills depends on the national level (to be taken as the concerned region) technological capabilities and matters only when a unit is going for a totally new technology that is not at all related with the existing technology. The existing relative factor prices is another factor that the owner-manger may keep in mind while selecting a technology so as to choose the one that uses more of a relatively cheaper factor.

As regards the internal factors, investment capabilities that are required to evaluate the available technologies, to select one of them and finally to negotiate, have direct impact on the selection of technology. In addition, owner-manger may look for such technologies that suit their scale of operation[19] and can be put in use by the existing production capabilities.[20]

In effect, relative factor prices and availability of finance, complementary skills and materials are the important external factors, and technological capabilities, investment as well as production, and scale of operation are the internal factors that influence the selection of a technology by a firm.

At times, technological changes occur in terms of the production of additional products, i.e., product diversification. Product diversification not only changes the product composition but also brings changes in machinery and tools.

---

18. The importance of the availability of complementary skills can be seen from the following example. Ramming process is one of the many processes of metal castings. It involves ramming the sand around the model to achieve a compact mold in the form of the model. The quality of sand mold critically depends on the compactness of the casting sand. It can be done manually or by machine. In the Howrah region, the traditional region for the metal castings, the availability of skilled mold makers who are capable of achieving greater uniformity of compactness by the hand ramming method is the major reason for the limited introduction of machine ramming techniques. In other regions of India where these skills are not available locally, machine ramming is in use. Little *et al.*, (1987: 140-1).
19. The importance of scale of operation in the selection of technology can be seen in the steam generation process of the garment industry. Steam is used for pressing the garments and it can be generated through either diesel-operated boiler or electricity-operated boilers. Electricity-operated boiler is inferior to diesel-operated boiler in terms of the quality (i.e., uniformity) of the steam it generates. However, many units use it as diesel-operated boilers require certain minimum scale. This example is taken from the field notes of the author prepared during the survey.
20. The importance of the existing production capabilities is due to the 'path dependency theory' of Dosi (1988a).

Once the new technology is selected, execution and absorption of it depends on the internal production capabilities and workers/ labour. Production capabilities are required to unpack, modify if necessary, install and finally to operate and maintain the technology. Behaviour and attitudes of labour are as important as their capabilities for absorption of technology.

In sum, we consider the product market, owner-manger's perception of market, scale of operation, technological capabilities and the availability of information, finance, complementary skills and materials, relative factor prices and labour as the possible factors influencing technological change in the small-scale units.

It is important to note that although the significance of the analytical factors is discussed in the context of a specific stage in the process of technological change given their immediate relevance at this stage, the influence of some of these factors goes beyond the specified stage. For instance, the scale of operation may influence all the stages. Availability of finances may initiate the process of technological changes at times.

We further elaborate on these factors in terms of firm-level characteristics and their specific relationship with the technological change in the subsequent paragraphs.

The kind of product market a unit is serving influences the unit-level technological changes. The market can be of international (exports), domestic but national (or regional), or composed of specific customers as for the original equipment manufacturers of components in any industry, or a replacement market as in the auto component industry. These markets differ widely in terms of the degree of competition and hence influence the firms differentially to go for technological change. For instance, exporting units are likely to face more competition and stricter quality norms that push these units to improve their technology relative to the units serving the domestic market.

The owner-manager's perception of product market can be taken in terms of their views on the demand for the product, market competition and the likely impact on the concerned unit. If the owner-managers view that demand is a problem in the sense that it is stagnant or falling, they do not have an incentive to make improvements in the technologies of their plants. On the other hand, rising demand for the product induces units to go for technological upgradation. If the markets are becoming increasingly competitive in the owner-manager's view, units consider upgradation of technology to improve their competitive strength so as to maintain commercial viability. Finally, if the owner-managers consider the market changes as opportunities for growth, they go ahead with the technological changes.

Technological capabilities of the units are deduced from the formal education of the owner-managers, their experience in the relevant area and the extent of the usage of professional labour. It is argued that higher the education and experience of the owner-managers, greater is the unit's capabilities to undertake and manage technological change. The larger the proportion of professional labour, the easier it is for the unit to master the new technologies and in lesser time.

Scale of operation, if taken in terms of annual sales turnover, reflects the actual size of the market the unit is catering to and also provides an idea of the returns on its investment. Accordingly, a higher scale of operation implies a larger size of the market that ensures returns on new investments and increases the scope for exploiting indivisibilities associated with the new technologies compared to the smaller ones. Hence, larger the scale of operation of the unit greater is the possibility for it to undertake technological change.

As regards the access to information on technology, it is easier for the unit to search for and select new technologies if it has better access to information. Access to information can be taken as better if the unit is making use of multiple sources of information rather than relying on one or two sources. Alternatively, inaccessibility of information can be deduced from the concerned unit's difficulties in obtaining it. If the owner-manager finds it a problem to get information about new technologies, we take it that the concerned unit has limited access to information about technologies.

With respect to the access to finance, the greater the access the easier it is for the firms to go for technological change. Better access to finance also widens the unit's choice and makes the selection among the alternative technologies easy. Access to finance can be considered better if the unit has been obtaining credit from the financial institutions including commercial banks rather than relying solely on personal finances of the owner-managers.[21] Alternatively, whether unit's access to finance is limited or not can be deduced from the unit's problems in obtaining the credit.

The attitudes and behaviour of labour not only affect the absorption of technological changes but can also induce these changes. Attitudes of labour normally are taken in terms of their willingness to work and learn. We consider willingness to work in terms of labour delivering the product in terms of quantity, quality and in time even when the manager is away. Willingness to learn is taken in terms of working on new machines. If the labour attitudes are (negative) positive and hence (not) giving their best when the manager is away or (un) willing to work on a new machine, it is (difficult) easier for the units to master the technologies and get maximum benefits. The behaviour of labour is considered in terms of absenteeism, turnover and unionisation of the work force. While absenteeism and unionisation problems are mostly associated with the regular work force, turnover is the most common problem with the casual labour. If a unit faces labour behavioural problems, it is difficult for it to manage the technological changes. Labour problems at an extreme levels may even induce the growing units to go for technological change.

SECTION 3

INDIAN GARMENT INDUSTRY

We begin the discussion with a description of the garment production process as it enables one to understand the industry structure better. Production of garments involves a sequence of designing, pattern making, fabric processing and testing, cutting, stitching, zipping/button work and finishing. Design is a highly creative and skilled activity. Pattern making is a process in which design is translated into a pattern on a cardboard or a particular paper for different sizes and shapes. It is again a skilled job. Fabric is cut according to the given specifications by placing it on the relevant pattern marker. Before it is cut, grey fabric is processed for colour, prints, etc., and tested for things like texture and inflamability.

21. Personal finances are the only source of finances for majority of the small-scale units and one of the major sources for the other small units.

The cut pieces are stitched together as per the specifications. Once the garment is tailored, it is trimmed, checked for dimensions and then sent for finishing. Finishing involves washing, spot removing, ironing and packing. Value added activities like embroidery or sequin work are done either before or after the stitching. Of all these, stitching is the major operation both in terms of time involved and costs. Sewing machines constitute around 87 per cent of the total machinery and tailors account for 80 per cent of the employment of the industry.[22]

All the stages of production are separable allowing an industrial unit to make or sub-contract any number of operations. Stitching, the major production operation can be organised in two different ways. The whole garment is stitched either by a single operator or, through an assembly line where several operators do specific stitching each. In addition, all the production operations can be done manually or by manual-driven machines or by power-driven machines. The garment production, hence, permits numerous configurations both in terms of physical technologies and the organisations.

The Indian garment industry began in an unorganised way in the sense that scattered, small players entered the business to avail immediate gains that came in the form of external demand.[23] This character was further enhanced by the reservation of garments for exclusive production in the small-scale sector.[24] As a result, the garment industry in India is highly disintegrated and consists of disparate groups of small-scale units, which are confined to a particular small activity.[25] Notwithstanding, one finds a wide variation in the scale of operation across the exporting and non-

22. Textile Committee Report cited in Berry (1997: 3 & 7).

23. For this reason, data relating to the various aspects of the industry are almost non-existent even with the government. Whatever little information available pertains to the export sector (Khanna, 1991: 47-48). Most of the details are collected through the primary surveys conducted by individual researchers. Accordingly, details presented in this section, mostly, relate to the export segment. Limited qualitative information presented about the domestic market is collected through the author's interaction with the industry associations and individual garment factory owners.

24. The production of garments has been reserved for small-scale units officially defined in terms of ceiling limit on the original value of investment in plant and machinery. This industry was opened for large-scale units in July 1993 subject to an export obligation and a limit on the investment in plant and machinery. Recently, Government of India has de-reserved the garments industry unconditionally. *Economic Survey 2000-2001*, p. 45.

25. According to the Textile Committee Report 1991, 80 per cent of the units in the industry are tiny. Also see Khanna (1991: 77); and Koshy (1997: 1).

exporting units, and across the form of business organisation, namely, proprietary concerns, partnership firms and limited companies.[26] In a majority of the units, pattern making, cutting and finishing jobs are done in-house. Tailoring, the core production operation has, generally, been sub-contracted to numerous fabricators located in residential, commercial and industrial areas of metropolitan cities.[27] Significant activities like processing of fabric and value added activities such as embroidery, appliqué and sequin work are carried out in several non-descript and tiny units.[28] In other words, garment industry so far is constituted by numerous small-scale units, which can be taken more as organisers in the garment business than as manufacturers of garments. These units are getting specialised jobs done such as procurement of orders, procurement of materials and getting the garment made by independent tailors and earning commissions for their jobs. As the industry consists of very large number of small-scale units and there are no entry or exit barriers except reservation, the industry structure comes nearer to perfect competition.

With regard to the physical technologies, the industry by and large employs older technologies. Pattern making and finishing operations are done, mostly, manually. Though cutting machines are present, a good number of units cut the fabric using hand shears and treadle machines. Manually operated sewing machines account for 83 per cent of the sewing machines.[29]

As regards the market, the Indian garment industry serves both the international and domestic market. However, the two segments of the market are independent of each other in terms of the units serving and the nature of product. Indian garment exports are confined to few product categories of cotton base such as men's shirts and women's tops[30] and a major proportion has so far been to quota countries like USA, UK and Germany.[31]

---

26. Bhavani and Tendulkar (2000: 74 & 89).
27. Khanna (1991: 114). Fabricators are none other than a group of tailors operating independently with their own sewing machines.
28. Koshy (1997: 1).
29. Khanna (1991: 127; and Koshy (1997: 72-73).
30. 81.44 per cent of the exports in 1994 were of cotton garments. Men's shirts and women's tops together constitute 40.25 per cent in quantity and 43.48 per cent in value of total garment exports in the year 1994. See Khanna (1991: 41, 77-8); Koshy (1997: 16&83); and Ramaswamy and Gereffi (1998: 125).
31. Bhavani and Tendulkar (2000: 4).

A majority of the garment units that export, deal *indirectly* with the marketing and production of their products. This can be seen from the dominant presence of merchant exporters and fabricators in the industry. Of the 30,844 garment exporters registered with the Apparel Export Promotion Council (AEPC) by 1994, only 9.97 per cent were manufacturer exporters and the remaining 90.03 per cent were merchant exporters.[32] At the production level, as mentioned earlier, core tailoring operations are mostly sub-contracted to fabricators. The significance of the fabricators can be seen from the fact that they have 71 per cent of the total machinery and contribute an equal percentage to the total employment of the industry.[33] It indicates less control over quality, costs, time and the ability to satisfy the customers.

With respect to the domestic market, a majority of the population even in urban areas go for made-to-measure clothing. Notwithstanding, the domestic market for garments has been growing at a rate of 25 per cent per annum and was estimated as worth US$ 5 billion in 1994.[34] Wholesale dealers of the garments mostly serve this market. These dealers get the garments made by tiny fabricators after supplying them with the sample piece and fabric. Majority of them serve regional markets.

Industry is currently undergoing transformation due to the changes in the rules of international trade in textiles as well as the on-going domestic policy reforms. As per the Agreement on Textiles and Clothing (ATC), quota restrictions, imposed by the importing developed countries, on different textile products will be eliminated by the end of 2004. There would be a free-for-all situation in which a large number of exporting countries/units have to compete with each other. On the other side, India has already opened its domestic market to textile imports from the USA and EU as per its bilateral agreements. Import restrictions will be phased out for several more products by 2003.[35] The net result is severe competition for Indian garment units in the domestic as well as the export markets. Feeling the pressure of the market

32. Koshy (1997: 37).
33. Textile Committee Report 1991 cited in Berry (1997: 4&6).
34. Koshy (1997: 12).
35. WTO (1998: 146).

competitiveness, exporting units that have established themselves reasonably in the business in the sense of getting regular export orders of large size over time are going in for a full-fledged manufacturing unit. Most of the units are going for quality sewing machines imported from Japan or South Korea to the extent that their finances permitted and some of the units are recruiting professionals like textile engineers or trained fashion designers. Though at a smaller level, some of the units established in the domestic market are also slowly going in for their own manufacturing plants and raising their in-house production. Thus, the Nineties witnessed a shift from the numerous small-scale organisers in the garment business aiming at immediate commission to the development of garment manufacturing units focussing on quality improvement and cost reductions so as to establish in the market.

It must be noted that technological change in the industry primarily came through the shift away from the fabricators towards in-house production. Machines are entirely different whether tailoring is done by the fabricators or in-housed. Fabricators mainly used second hand manually operated sewing machines, whereas all the units used first hand electrically operated sewing machines, Indian or imported, for in-house production. Labour, especially tailors are hired on contract and paid on a piece rate basis even in the in-house production. The main disadvantage with the fabricators is lack of supervision that resulted in lower quality and delays in the delivery of garments. This has been controlled substantially in the in-house production through close supervision. Since the labour is hired on contract basis their behavioural problems are not found relevance for the industry. Rather it is the labour attitude that needed to be controlled closely, pushed the units to go for in-house production and hence technological change.

SECTION 4

DATA BASE AND RELEVANCE OF IDENTIFIED FACTORS

Information relating to all the characteristics that are identified in Section 2 to possibly influence technological change has been collected through the primary survey of garment units in Delhi through a questionnaire. Delhi is a recognised natural cluster of garment units[36] and one of the important centres for exporting units as well as for the units serving the domestic market.[37] The questionnaire has been structured to have 13 blocks to collect the information under different headings like general information, outputs and inputs, existing technologies, changes in the technologies over time, owner-manager's profile, market profile, sources of information about technology, sources of finance, sources of technology, selection of technology and labour problems. Some questions are categorical like 'yes' or 'no' type. Some other questions especially the questions relating to the problems like demand, information, finance and labour are on ordinal scale. Plus, quantitative data are obtained for the value of output and inputs. Reference year for the quantitative data is 1998-99. For the purpose of survey, we have followed purposive sampling given the nature of the problem.

We have done an intensive survey of 31 garment units in order to study the technological change and the factors affecting it in the garment industry. The survey includes units producing men, women and children garments. We summarise the relevant characteristics of the survey units in the subsequent paragraphs.

Factory units (17) outnumber non-factory units (14). Most of the sample units are proprietary concerns and started by educated persons. Although non-owner management is seen in some units, most of the units are owner-managed.

As regards the technological change, while 19 units of the sample reported to have changed machinery over time, the remaining 12 units have not made any such changes.

As far as the market is concerned, of the total 31 units surveyed, 22 are exporting and the remaining nine units are catering to the domestic market. As discussed earlier, we have considered owner-manger's perception of market in terms of their views about the market demand, market competitiveness and their likely impact on their unit. Almost all of them think markets are more competitive

36. Gulati (1997: 36-40).

37. Delhi, Chennai and Mumbai accounted for 84 per cent of the value of Indian garment exports in 1987 [Khanna (1991: 104)]. Delhi, Calcutta and Mumbai have a concentration of units catering to the domestic market. See the Textile Committee Report 1991 cited in Berry (1997: 3).

in the sense that the customers are demanding higher quality, lower price and timely deliveries. Little more than half of the units (17) consider market changes as opportunities for the unit. Rest of the units (14) take the market changes as threatening for their unit.

Of the total 31 surveyed units, 22 are owned and managed by people having higher education but of non-professional nature whereas the owner-managers of the remaining units are professionals. As far as the owner-manager's experience is concerned, the average experience of the sample is around 13 years with a variation of 54 per cent around the mean and within the range of two to 30 years. 13 of them have an experience that is less than or equal to 10 years. Owner-managers in 13 units have an experience that ranges between 10 to 20 years. Owner-managers of the remaining five units have more than 20 years of experience. Very few units have used professionals like merchandisers to deal with the importers and/or textile engineers to manage production systems. In majority of the units professional employees are absent.

Scale of operation is taken in terms of annual sales turnover of the unit. The mean sales turnover of our sample is around 575.57 lakh of rupees. Sales turnover of the sample units shows a variation of 134 per cent around the sample mean and within the range of 1.80 and 3032 lakh. 12 units have a sales turnover that is less than 100 lakh of rupees. Eight units have it in the range of 100 to 500 lakh of rupees. Six of the sample units fall in the range of 500 to 1000 lakh of rupees and another five units have a sales turnover that is greater than 1000 lakh of rupees.

Majority of the sample units (23) have not reported any information problems. However, good number of units surveyed (14) use only one source of information namely, trade fairs or, trade journals or, business associates.

Survey evidence relating to finance reveals that little less than half of the units (15) have used personal resources. The other half of the sample (16) borrows from the institutions like commercial banks. Otherwise, 13 units of the sample have reported that they have not had any finance problems. The remaining 18 units have reported that finance is a problem for them.

With respect to labour, 14 units have complained of having problems. Rest of the sample has not reported any labour problems.

Suppliers of machinery are the major source of technology for garment industry. All the sample units are aware of alternative machinery like Juki and Brother of Japan, Sunstar of Korea in addition to the Indian based Meritt and Singer machines. Of all the foreign machines, Juki is fairly established in the Indian garment industry. Units have gone for a foreign machine like Juki stitching machine for quality reasons. Availability of finance and the cost of machine given the lower scale of operation are some of the reasons given by the units that have not bought good machines like Juki. One finds good presence of foreign machinery in the industry though very few units have all foreign machinery. All the machines are first hand. None of the survey units consider that the availability of complementary skills and materials, and relative factor prices are important in the selection of technology. This could perhaps be due to the fact that tailoring requires a general skill of handling the sewing machines, which is relatively easily available in all the parts of India. Technology is still at a level that each machine requires a person to run and hence there is no scope for substitution. Again the machine, which embodies technology is not material specific.

SECTION 5

ESTIMATION AND INTERPRETATION OF THE SURVEY RESULTS

The survey evidence, discussed in Section 4, shows that but for the professional labour, complementary skills and materials, and relative factor prices, all other analytical factors are turned out to be relevant. Accordingly, we have specified our technological change equation as given below:

CT = *f* (MKT, OMP, TCAP, SCALE, FIN, INF, LAB) ...(1)

Where,

CT = Change in technology is taken as a binary variable with Change=1 and No change=0;

MKT = Type of market; exports=1 and domestic market=0;

OMP = Owner-manager's (OM) perception taken in terms of their opinion about Market demand, competitiveness of the markets and likely impact on their units;

TCAP = Technical capabilities taken in terms of OM's education and experience;

SCALE = Scale of operation taken in sales turnover;

FIN = Access to finance represented either by the sources of finance or, by OM's feeling of problem;

INF = Access to information about technology proxied by the number of sources of information or by OM's views of the problem;

LAB = OM's views about having labour problems.

For the purpose of estimation, we have used the Probit model as the dependent variable is binary. We have tried different specifications of the equation using alternative representatives of the specified factors. Finally, we present the equation that yields more meaningful results from the point of interpretation. Thus selected equation is given below:

$$CT = \underset{(-2.519)}{-2.0184} + \underset{(1.820)}{0.2284}\,ST + \underset{(0.595)}{0.4223}\,RSF + \underset{(1.895)}{1.2741}\,RSTI + \underset{(1.614)}{1.1295}\,LAB \quad ...(2)$$

ST = Annual sales turnover taken in '000 of rupees

RSF = Source of Finance; personal = 0, institutional =1

RSTI = Sources of technology information; single source = 0, multiple sources = 1

LAB = OM's views about labour problems; no problem = 0, problem =1

t-values given in parentheses, indicate that all the parameter estimates excepting that of the sources of finance are statistically significant and directionally consistent with *a priori* expectations. Estimated parameters are not marginal coefficients in the case of Probit model. The marginal coefficient for a given explanatory variable, x_j, in the case of Probit model is written as[38]

$$\partial E\,(Y/\,x_j)/\partial x_j = \phi(\beta'X)\beta \quad ...(3)$$

Where, j = 1, ...4 refers to individual explanatory variables, and $\phi(...)$ is the standard normal density. From (3), it is clear that the marginal coefficients are proportional to parameter estimates (β). We present marginal coefficients too for the clarity in interpretation. Likelihood ratio index (LRI) can be used to measure the goodness of fit of the equation for the models like Probit. It is measured as

38. Green (1993: 639).

$$LRI = 1 - \ln L/\ln L_0 \qquad \text{...(4)}$$

Where $\ln L$ = Unrestricted log-likelihood function.

$\ln L_0$ = Restricted log-likelihood function.

It is bounded by zero and one and increases as the fit of the model increases. So the higher values of LRI can be taken as indicative of better fit.[39] We present the marginal coefficients and LRI of the equation (2) below.

ST = 0.0632; RSF = 0.1169; RSTI = 0.3526; LAB = 0.3126; LRI = 0.5342.

Marginal coefficients of the technological equation indicate that the likelihood of change in technology increases by sales turnover, use of multiple sources of information rather a single source and the presence of labour problems in the concerned unit. The increase in the probability of having technological change is the highest for the sources of information followed by the labour problems and sales turnover.

Multiple sources of information that include customers, suppliers of machinery and internet besides trade fairs, trade journals and business associates which are used more as a single source of information, implies better access to technology information. Access to information, as discussed in Section 2, facilitates the unit's search for alternative technologies and thus creates a favourable environment for the technological change to occur. Without information about the alternative technologies such as costs, contents and sources of these technologies, it could not have been possible for the units to think about changing their technologies.

Labour problems, as mentioned earlier, primarily relates to its attitude towards quality and timely delivery of the product. Quality of the product gets adversely affected partly because of the carelessness of the labour and partly due to the second hand machinery the independent tailors operating outside the units use. Further, it affects the unit's market adversely. To control these problems, units try to get labour in-house so as to provide them with better machines and to supervise them closely. That is how the technological change occurs in the garment industry.

39. Green (1993: 651).

Larger sales turnover means larger size of the market that can ensure returns on new investments. Hence, larger sales turnover is raising the scope for the units to undertake technological change.

Statistical insignificance of the finance in determining technological change is perhaps due to the fact that institutional finance for these units mainly refers to the working capital from the banks as majority of the units depend on their personal finances (including the internal reserves of the unit) for fixed capital. At the same time, shorter production cycles of the garment industry coupled with the availability of materials like fabric on credit reduced the importance of working capital too.[40] It explains the insignificant impact of the sources of finance in determining technological change.

More surprising result is the statistical insignificance of the type of market and owner-manager's perception of market changes in explaining the unit-level technological change. One possible reason could be that there may not be qualitative change in the owner-manager's perception about the market changes over time as the industry, as discussed in Section 3, has been competitive from the beginning with numerous small players. Hence, it may not be playing the significant role of inducing technological change. As regards the type of market, although international exports market differs noticeably from the domestic market in terms of competitiveness, it is not showing any significant impact on the technological change. When included it is upsetting the other coefficients of the equation. We suppose it is due to higher degree of correlation between sales turnover and type of market. It may be noted here that the general observation has been that exporting units, as a group are quite larger compared to the units serving domestic market.[41]

SECTION 6

SUMMARY AND CONCLUDING OBSERVATIONS

In this paper, an attempt is made to identify the factors influencing the unit-level technological changes and to examine their empirical significance in the case of Indian garment industry based on the primary survey data.

40. Author's observations during the field survey.

41. See for instance, Bhavani and Tendulkar (2000: 74).

Drawing on the evolutionary economics, economics of technological change, technological capabilities literature and organisation theories, we have identified unit-level factors having influence on technological change.

Analysis of the study brings out the product market, owner-managers' perception of the product market, technological capabilities, scale of operation, availability of information, finance, complementary skills and materials, relative factor prices and labour as the factors influencing technological change in the units. These factors are further taken in terms of empirically usable characteristics and quantities. They are: type of market served; owner-managers' views about the market demand and its competitiveness; education and experience of the owner-manager, extent of the use of professional labour, sales turnover, unit's sources of information and finance; owner-manager's opinion about the availability of information, finance, skills, materials and labour attitudes.

For the purpose of analysis, we have conducted intensive survey of 31 units in and around Delhi. Survey evidence indicates that all the analytical factors are turned out to be empirically relevant except the availability of complementary skills and materials, and relative factor prices. Accordingly, the technological change function has been specified and estimated using the Probit model. Parameter estimates of the study reveal that the availability of information followed by the labour problems and sales turnover are important in determining the technological change in the garment units. In particular, multiple sources of information that include internet, customers and suppliers of machinery besides trade fairs, trade journals and business associates (that are used more as a single source of information) implies better access to information, which facilitates the change in technology. Labour problems in the industry are mainly due to the casual attitude of the tailors towards quality and timely delivery of the product. Apart from their attitudes, the second hand machinery that tailors use when operating independently is having an adverse impact on the quality of the product. To avoid these problems, units are getting tailors in-house so as to be able to motivate and supervise them closely and provide them with better machines. Higher sales turnover reflecting the larger size of the market that ensures the returns on new investment makes it worth going for technological change.

Empirical results of the study have important implications for the policies on small-scale industries. Garments industry, being reserved till recently for the small-scale sector, mainly has small-scale units. Government policies regarding the small-scale industries are creating perverse incentive to remain small by protecting small units from competition with the large-scale counterparts in combination with the numerous statutory obligations on large-scale organised units. For instance, small units producing under the specified limits of production are given excise duty exemption. If the unit grows beyond this limit it has to pay the excise duty, which is providing a positive disincentive to grow. If the unit grows it also has to face numerous labour problems such as unions that are due to the existing liberal labour legislation. Unless these policies are changed in such a way to create incentive to grow large and to provide flexibility in dealing with the labour, it is very difficult for these units to improve their competitive strength by growing large and having technological change. Equally important are the policy measures to improve the informational infrastructure so as to increase the accessibility of small units to information.

It is a part of the work done for the IDPAD Project entitled " Technological Change in Rural as compared to Urban Small-scale Industries in North India" at the Institute of Economic Growth. I am thankful to IDPAD for financing the project. I am also grateful to my gurus professors K.L. Krishna and Suresh Tendulkar for their moral support and for sparing their busy time to clear my doubts.

Reference

Ayyar, S.R. (1994). "New Emerging Challenges and Opportunities for Small and Medium Enterprises through Technological Upgradation and Better Financial Management" in Small Industry Bulletin for Asia and Pacific, No. 29, United Nations, New York, pp. 38-40.

Berry, V.K. (1997). *A Background Paper on the Technological Changes and Changes in Women's Employment in Garment Industry*. IAMR Working Paper No. 3/1997.

Bhavani, T.A. (2001). *Towards Developing An Analytical Framework To Study Technological Change In The Small Units of The Developing Nations*. Working Paper Series No. E/216/2001, Institute of Economic Growth, Delhi.

Bhavani, T.A. and Tendulkar, S.D. (2000). "Determinants of Firm-level Export Performance: A Case Study of Indian Textile Garments and Apparel Industry" in the *Journal of International Trade and Economic Development*. Vol. 10 (1, March), pp. 65-92.

Bos, Antonio and Willian, Cole (1994). "Management Systems as Technology: Japanese, US and National Firms in the Brazilian Electronic Sector" in *World Development*. Vol. 22 (2), pp. 225-236.

Dahlman, C.J., Bruce Ross-Larson and L.E. Westphal (1987). "Managing Techological Development: Lessons from the Newly Industrialising Countries" in *World Development*. Vol. 15 (6), pp. 759 - 775.

Dahlman, Carl and Larry Westphal (1982). "Technological Effort in Industrial Development" in Stewart, Frances and Jeffrey James (eds). *The Economics of New Technology in Developing Countries*. London: Pinter Publishers, pp. 105 - 137.

Dosi, G. (1988a). "Sources, Procedures, and Microeconomic Effects of Innovation" in *Research Policy*, Vol. 26, September, pp. 1120 - 1171.

Dosi, G. (1988b). "The Nature of the Innovative Process" in Dosi, G., Freeman, C., Nelson, R., Silverberg, G., and Soete, L. (Eds) (1988). *Technical Change and Economic Theory*. London: Pinter Publishers. Pp. 221 - 239.

Elster, J. (1983). *Explaining Technical Change*. Cambridge: Cambridge University Press.

Garud, R., Nayyar, P.R., and Shapira, Z.B. (eds) (1997). *Technological Innovation: Oversights and Foresights*. Cambridge: Cambridge University Press.

Gereffi, G. (1995). "Global Production Systems and Third World Development" in Stallings, B. (Ed). *Global Change and Regional Response: The New International Context of Development*. Cambridge, UK: Cambridge University Press, pp. 100-142.

Green, W.H. (1993). Econometric Analysis. New York: Macmillan.

Gulati, M. (1997). *Restructuring and Modernisation of Small Medium Enterprise Clusters in India: A Report*. UNIDO.

Hoffman, K. and H. Rush (1988). *Micro-Electronics and Clothing: The Impact of Technical Change on a Global Industry*. New York: Praeger.

Khanna, S.R. (1991). *International Trade in Textiles: MFA Quotas and a Developing Country*. New Delhi: Sage.

Koshy, D.O. (1997). *Garment Exports: Winning Strategies*. New Delhi: Prentice-Hall of India.

Lall, Sanjaya (1992). "Technological Capabilities and Industrialisation" in *World Development*, Vol. 20 (2), pp. 165 - 186.

Little, I.M.D, Mazumdar, D. and J.M. Page (1987). *Small Manufacturing Enterprise*. New York: Oxford University Press.

Mahalanobis, P.C. (1963). *The Approach of Operational Research to Planning in India*. Bombay: Asia Publishing House.

Mansfield, E. (1961). "Technical Change and the Rate of Imitation" first published in Econometric (October). Later reproduced in Rosenburg, N. (ed) (1971). *The Economics of Technological Change*. Baltimore: Penguin Books, pp. 284-316.

Meyanathan, S.D. (1994). *Managing the Restructuring in the Textile and Garment Subsector: Examples from Asia*. EDI Seminar Series. The World Bank, Washington, D.C.

Mintzberg, H. (1979). *The Structuring of Organisations*. Englewood Cliffs, N.J: Prentice-Hall.

Nelson, R.R., and Winter, S.G. (1982). *An Evolutionary Theory of Economic Change*. Cambridge, Mass.: Belknap Press of Harvard University Press.

NIFT (1998). *Indian Garment Exports: In The New Millennium*. National Institute of Fashion Technology, New Delhi.

Pepper, R. and Bhattacharya, H. (1994). "Changing Trends in Global Textile Technology and Trade" in Meyanathan, S.D. (1994). *Managing the Restructuring in the Textile and Garment Subsector: Examples from Asia*. EDI Seminar Series. The World Bank, Washington, D.C., pp. 31-58.

Raffaeli, M. (1994). "Some Considerations on the Muti-Fibre Arrangement: Past, Present and Future" in Meyanathan, S.D. (1994). *Managing the Restructuring in the Textile and Garment Subsector: Examples from Asia*. EDI Seminar Series. The World Bank, Washington, D.C., pp. 59-82.

Ramaswamy, V.K. and G. Gereffi (1998). "India's Apparel Sector in the Global Economy: Catching Up or Falling Behind." *The Economic and Political Weekly*. Vol. 33, No. 3 (January 17-23), pp. 122-130.

Saviotti, P.P. (1996). *Technological Evolution, Variety and the Economy*. Cheltenham, U.K: Edward Elgar.

Saviotti, P.P., and J.S. Metcalfe (eds). 1991. *Evolutionary Theories of Economic and Technological Change*. Paris: Harwood Academic Publishers.

Stoneman, Paul (1995). "Introduction" in Stoneman, Paul (ed). *Handbook of Economics of Innovation and Technological Change*. Oxford: Blackwell. Pp. 1 - 13.

Stoneman, Paul (ed) (1995). *Handbook of Economics of Innovation and Technological Change*. Oxford: Blackwell.

Teitel, S and L.E. Westphal (1984). "Introduction" to the Symposium on Technological Change and Industrial Development in *Journal of Development Economics*, Vol. 16, Nos. 1-2, (September - October), pp. 1-12.

Tendulkar, S.D. and T.A. Bhavani (1997). "Policy on Modern Small Scale Industries: A Case of Government Failure" in the *Indian Economic Review*, Vol. 32, No.1, January-June, pp. 39-64.

WTO (1998). *Trade Policy Review: India 1998*. Geneva: WTO.

WTO (1998). *Trade Policy Review: India*. A Report by the Secretariat.

5

Productivity Growth in Indian Engineering Industries During Pre-Reform and Post-Reform Period

An Analysis at Company Level

ANITA KUMARI

SECTION 1

INTRODUCTION

Productivity growth is a key factor in determining the growth of industries. Total factor productivity growth reflects technical progress and changes in technical efficiency. In India major economic reforms have been undertaken since July 1991 with the objective of increasing the productivity and competitiveness of the companies. The new policies have liberalised many government controls on production capacity, imported capital goods, intermediate inputs and technology. Foreign investment has also been liberalised. These reforms have made imported inputs cheaper and more accessible for companies and have exposed the companies to both domestic and international competition. These reforms have altered the economic environment in which the companies operate. The purpose of this paper is to see the impact of these reforms on productivity of engineering industry. A study of engineering industry is important as it plays a crucial role in the economic development with its close linkage with every single sector of the national economy. It is the base for growth and development in all economic sectors.

This paper seeks to analyse the productivity of engineering industry, electrical and non-electrical groups, during pre-reform and post-reform period of 1991. The study is organised as follows. First, productivity growth of Indian engineering industries at company level in the two periods is analysed. Then the factors which affect company level productivity growth are considered. An analysis of the determinants of productivity growth is useful in identifying the policy needed for improving the growth of productivity. Productivity performance of an industry is the result of many factors operating on the industry. Some of these factors may relate to the overall economic environment and some of these may be industry specific where as some of these may be company specific. We shall also examine whether impact of the factors determining productivity performance have changed substantially in the changed economic environment. In the literature the relationship between productivity growth and output growth, trade and research and development expenditure has been established. Apart from these factors productivity growth also depends on the pace at which advanced technology is acquired. The advanced technology may be acquired through direct purchase of designs or embodied in imported inputs and capital. Using our estimates of productivity growth we shall examine such a relationship for Indian engineering industries.

The scheme of the paper is as follows. Section 2 shall give the factors affecting productivity growth. Section 3 gives a review of Indian studies. Section 4 discusses the methodology. In this section we shall discuss the various methods of measurement of productivity growth. The regression function for analysing determinants of productivity growth shall also be specified in this section. The methods of estimation of specified function are also discussed here. The sources of data and construction of variables shall be given in section 5. Analysis of company level variations in productivity growth and regression results giving determinants of productivity growth shall be presented in Section 6. Finally the summary of findings are given in Section 7.

SECTION 2

FACTORS AFFECTING PRODUCTIVITY GROWTH

In the literature on productivity growth, various factors are considered to be influencing it. The most important factor influencing productivity growth is found to be output growth. Output growth permits an industry to gain from economies of scale — internal and external, technological progress and learning by doing.

Thus, a positive association is expected between output growth and productivity growth. The other key factor is technology advancement. Technological change decides, by its pace, the nature of restructuring inevitable in industry along with how fast will it grow as well as the productivity of industrial production. The technology advancement may take many forms — the flow of technology embodied in the imports of capital goods and intermediate inputs, technology transfers accompanying foreign direct investment, foreign collaborations and imports of technology against lump sum payments, technical fees, royalty etc. After the technology is imported, it is suitably modified and assimilated before it reaches the take-off stage in industrial growth. Thus advances in the technology results in the improvement of productivity. The international trade also affects productivity growth. Exports generate competitive pressure on companies which causes productivity increase. Exports also provide opportunity to learn about new technology and its application in production. On the other hand, imports permit availability of embodied technology whether in capital goods or inputs. This brings about an expansion of domestic demand and widening of the market for the company through improvement in productivity and better quality products. The exports has an effect on productivity growth through growth of demand. It enables the company to exploit the economies of scale which increases productivity growth. During the post-reform period in India various policy measures have been adopted to make trade regime more open. Import restrictions arising out of tariff and import quota have been reduced. Conditions have been made more favourable to export. This open trade regime it may be argued tends to generate greater competition, accessibility to foreign markets and also imports of better capital equipment and material input which improve productivity. These issues shall now be taken up for discussion in detail.

Productivity Growth and Output Growth

P.J. Verdoorn found a positive link between productivity growth and output growth in the inter-war period. This link is therefore known as "Verdoorn's Law" after him. The faster a company grows the more it has the opportunity to exploit the benefits of economies of scale. These are often stated as specialisation and division of labour in production, the existence of indivisibilities, the economies of increased physical dimension of some plant and economies of massed resources. Some of these economies are obtained because of technological progress while others are obtained because of specialisation either within the same industry or in the input supplying industry.

Technological progress can be either exogenous, that is external, or endogenous which is internal. If technological progress is exogenous, then the higher rate of growth of output, the higher is rate of growth in productivity. This is so because faster output growth would allow addition of new and better quality machines[1]. This will lead to higher productivity growth.

The rapid expansion of growth of output allows for the introduction of new techniques because of large scale of production. In situations where the output of company is not expanding rapidly and excess capacity is there, the expansion in the level of operations allows for the utilisation of such capacity. This results in better efficiency of factor use. Also, rapid growth of output shortens the time lag in the application of new technological advances. The new technological advances are applied to production scales and utilise better skills. This increases productivity growth. When the output growth is faster, endogenous technological progress also occurs and improvement in the methods of production takes place. Several studies, Fabricant (1942); Verdoorn (1949); Reddaway (1966); Kaldor (1967); Kendrick (1961); Kendrick (1973); Fucns (1968); Kendrick and Grossman (1980) and many other studies found a strong positive association between output growth and productivity growth.

Productivity and Technology Acquisition

The technology embodied in the imported inputs and capital goods constitute one flow of technology and the other important source of inflow of advanced technological knowledge is technology imports at arm's length i.e. direct purchases of knowledge through lump sum payments or licensing for patents, blueprints, and so on.

1. Salter (1960) and Kennedy (1971).

The lump sum payments and licensing constitute a short term, assured and risk free return to technology transfers. However, not all technologies are available at arm's length. Some may be obtainable only through majority ownership or project specific joint ventures. According to Markusen (1995, 1998), companies will be averse to unbundling and selling knowledge or products if there are important incentives for internalisation and thus companies will prefer foreign collaboration for acquiring knowledge (*see* Pack and Saggi (1997) for a general survey on technology transfer).

Thus the technology advancement through foreign collaboration is also an important means of transfer of technology. Indeed, foreign collaboration in equity seems to bring relatively efficient technologies into host country and thus increases the productivity of the host country. Foreign collaboration also provides management and organisational competence. These assets have spillover effects on the rest of the economy. The foreign collaborator puts pressure and assists the local companies to improve their technology and the product quality. Foreign collaboration also helps the host country in improving its export competitiveness by increasing productivity by improving the product quality. Because of international linkages of foreign collaborators, host country gets better access to foreign markets. Foreign collaboration also contributes to exports directly if equity investments have been made with the specific intention of sourcing parts or components from the host country to take advantage of low cost conditions there. The export expansion overcomes the demand side constraints on growth. Foreign collaboration via equity flows is considered as a long term investment since returns to foreign investor from remitted profits and dividends accrues to him after a time.

Caves' study (1974) for Australian manufacturing found that the very presence of foreign firms have a positive impact on labour productivity growth in the corresponding industries. For Canada, Globerman (1979) also confirmed that foreign firms have a positive impact on productivity growth. For Mexico, Blomstrom and Persson (1983); Kokko (1994) and Blomstrom and Wolff (1994) also found the same effect. But for Morocco, Haddad and Harrison (1993) found that foreign presence has no significant effect on labour productivity.

Productivity Growth and Research & Development Expenditure

According to Evenson and Westphall 1995, technology acquisition often amounts to adapting existing methods to local circumstances. Once the advanced technology has been acquired, the recipient company has to make efforts for adaptation and development of the technology and gain mastery over it for achieving the productivity potential of the advanced technology. Research and development (R&D) expenditure is an important part of the competitive strategy of the company as it helps in assimilation and adaptation of foreign technology and making it suitable for indigenous use. Research and development (R&D) expenditures also helps in developing new processes or new products that are different or better than those already existing. The productivity of the company will increase as R&D will change the conditions under which the company operates in markets and also if these goods are exported. Terleckyj (1974); Scherer (1982); Griliches (1984); Odagiri (1985) and Jaffe (1988); Fecher and Perelman (1989); Lichtenberg and Siegel (1991); Coe & Helpman (1993); Coe, Helpman and Hoffmaister (1995); Maury Gittleman and Edward N. Wolff (1998) and many others have studied the nexus between productivity and research and development and have revealed that advances in the technology result in the improvement of productivity growth.

Productivity Growth and Trade Policy

The role of trade in raising productivity has been extensively studied in the literature. Little, Scitovsky and Scott (1970); Bhagwati (1978); Krueger (1978); Nishimizu and Robinson (1984); Nishimizu and Page (1986); Kajiwara (1994) Kwak (1994) Osada (1994); Urata and Yokota (1994) have concluded that economies with relatively open trade regime show a better performance with respect to growth of productivity than the economies which have restrictive trade regimes.

Exports serve as a conduit for technology transfer from abroad and generate competitive pressure on companies which generates productivity. Chen and Tang (1987); Haddad (1993); Aw and Hwang (1995); Tybout and Westbrook (1995); and Aw and Batra (1998) have shown that productivity of exporting companies is more than their counterparts that sell primarily in the domestic market. The productivity improvements may also result from learning by exporting. Companies gain knowledge and expertise as a result of its experience in the export market which gives the opportunity to have access to new product designs and production methods where as the companies which operate in the domestic market do not have the access to these technical expertise. Evenson and Westphal (1995); Grossman and Helpman (1991); Rhee, Ross-larson, and Pursell (1984); World Bank (1993) and Clerides, Lach, and Tybout (1998) examined the link between productivity and exports. They hold the view that exporters learn from their contacts in the export market and as a result they adopt better production methods and achieve higher productivity. Technology may also diffuse from exporters to non-exporters in the same industry through demonstration effects, skilled worker training or expertise imparted to their local suppliers. Clerides, Lach and Tybout (1998) find that when many firms have been exporting from a particular region, all firms in that region tend to enjoy lower average costs.

The other important role of trade is technology transfer through imports. Imports permit availability of embodied technology in capital goods and inputs. The availability of embodied technology in these imported inputs and capital goods allows for a degree of specialisation in the production of goods which has an enhancing impact on the productivity growth of the company. Several studies, such as Coe and Helpman (1995); Coe, Helpman, and Hoffmaister (1997); Evenson (1995); Keller (1997, 1998a, 1998b); and Litchenberg and Van Pottelsberghe de la Potterie (1998b) have assessed that imports play an important role in transmitting foreign technology to domestic companies and increasing productivity growth.

SECTION 3
REVIEW OF INDIAN STUDIES

In India, most of the studies of productivity growth relate to the pre- and post 1985 period of liberalisation, when the reforms in the Indian industry were in the initial stage. But very few studies have covered the post-reform period of 1991 when major economic reforms were initiated in the Indian industry. We shall review here some recent studies only.

Industrial Credit and Investment Corporation of India (ICICI, 1994) carried out a study on productivity growth for companies to which it provided assistance. The study found that growth rate of TFP was 2.1 per cent per annum for the period 1987-88 to 1991-92. Gangopadhyay and Wadhwa (1998) has estimated total factor productivity (TFP) estimates for various two digit industries and aggregate manufacturing. Using ASI data the study estimated a growth rate of TFP for aggregate manufacturing as 5.01 per cent per annum for 1986-90 and 3.88 per cent per annum for 1991-93. Trivedi, Prakash and Sinate (2000) found that TFP growth rate in Indian manufacturing was 3.60 per cent per annum in the period 1980-81 to 1990-91 and 1.97 per cent per annum in the period 1990-91 to 1997-98. Balakrishnan, Pushpangadan and Suresh Babu (2000) investigated the growth of productivity in Indian manufacturing spread over five industry groups over the period 1988-89 to 1997-98. The industry groups chosen were machinery, transport equipment and parts, textiles, textile products and chemicals. These groups were chosen on the basis of the significant tariff reductions since 1991. Using CMIE database, he used the data for about 2300 firms registered with the Bombay Stock Exchange and found a significant decline in the growth rate of TFP after 1991-92. Srivastava (2000) has estimated productivity growth and technical efficiency in manufacturing firms in India for the period 1980-81 to 1996-97. Using data for about 3000 companies for the period 1980-81 to 1996-97 he found a decline in the rate of productivity growth in the 1990's as compared with the 1980's.

There is widespread evidence of association between productivity growth and various factors discussed above for a number of countries. Now we shall discuss the Indian studies to explain the association between productivity growth and various factors.

Goldar (1986a) analysed the inter industrial differences in TFP growth for 37 three digit industries of India during the period 1960-70. He found a significant positive relationship between output growth and productivity growth (partial and total). He also used other variables in his analysis of inter-industrial differences in productivity growth during the period 1960-70. Using the effective rate of protection as an indicator of trade policy his analysis revealed a negative but statistically significant link between the trade policy and TFP growth. Goldar (1986b) used a different variable to represent import substitution as an indicator of trade policy and found again a significant negative relationship between TFP growth and import substitution.

Ahluwalia (1991) attempted to explain the inter-industry differences in TFPG in 62 industry groups for the period 1960 to 1986. She regressed TFPG on output growth along with other factors like the degree of import substitution and capital intensity growth. She also tried to capture the impact of competitive pressure on productivity growth by using the variable, rate of growth of factories, along with other explanatory variables. She found output growth as a significant explanatory variable in explaining the inter-industry differences in TFPG. Growth in the number of factories is found to have a significant negative sign though a positive sign was expected *a priori*. She also found a negative relationship between Chenery measure of import substitution and TFPG.

Basant and Fikkert (1993) studied the impact of firms' R&D, technology purchase expenditures, and foreign and domestic R&D spillovers on productivity at the micro level using panel data for Indian manufacturing firms for the period 1974-75 to 1982-83 and international R&D and patent data from nine countries. He considered only the disembodied technology purchased from foreign countries acquired through licenses in the form of expenditure on foreign technical licenses in the form of lump sum payments, technical fees, royalties etc. The perpetual inventory method was used to construct the knowledge stocks generated from technology purchase and R&D. After controlling for firm-level heterogeneity through fixed effects estimation, the results indicated high private rates of return to both R&D and technology purchase. They argued that India's restrictions on technology licensing agreements may have had a substantial cost to the economy as the returns to technology purchase expenditures being much higher than those to R&D. The estimates indicated that R&D and technology purchases are substitutes for one another. This suggested that India's technology licensing regulations had their desired effect of stimulating domestic R&D. Furthermore, after controlling for firms' own R&D and technology purchase expenditures, international and domestic R&D spillovers increase productivity, the social benefits of both international and domestic R&D exceeding the private benefits. This gives opportunities to pirate foreign inventions for those Indian firms who are willing to expand their own R&D resources. Fujita (1994) evaluated the effect of liberalisation policies on productivity growth in Indian manufacturing industries for the period 1981-82 to 1987-88. He argued that increase in the share of public sector in value added usually reflects restrictions in attempts at liberalisations. He thus used this share as a proxy for trade policy and found a negative relationship between increase in share of public sector and TFP growth.

Goldar (1995) studied the relationship between technology acquisition and productivity growth for Indian industrial firms. He has done the analysis both at the aggregate level as well as at the firm level using data for 347 large industrial firms for the years 1987-88 to 1989-90. A number of variables are used to capture technology acquisition such as R&D intensity, foreign equity participation, technology import against royalty, technical fees, licensing fees and lump sum payments and capital goods import intensity along with export intensity, intermediate goods import intensity and age of the firm. His study found that in Indian industrial firms there is not any strong positive effect of the technology acquisition activities, including R&D and technology imports on productivity growth. In particular his results suggested that imports of technology contributed very little to productivity advancement, R&D and technology transfers accompanying foreign direct investment were found to have a favourable though small effect on productivity growth. Export intensity, and intermediate input import intensity were found to have a significant positive relationship with productivity growth.

Ramaswamy, K.V. (1996) pooled the data for 18 industry groups for the period 1975 to 1990 and estimated a multiple regression model with a time dummy to capture the effects of the two periods, 1974-75 to 1979-80 and 1980-81 to 1989-90. He regressed the labour productivity growth on output growth rates, net entry and capital intensity. He found that output growth has a positive effect on productivity growth. His estimates supported the hypothesis that entry in the period of industrial deregulation had a positive impact on productivity growth. He argues that it is the entry of new firms with new and improved technology and the substitution of inefficient plants by efficient plants, that leads to productivity growth. The firms that entered during this period have had presumably better access to imported raw materials and technology. The index of capital intensity is found to be insignificant in explaining labour productivity.

SECTION 4

METHODOLOGY

The previous sections have quickly reviewed the literature. In the following sections, we present the results of our analysis. We begin with a discussion on the methodology adopted, followed in the next section by discussion of data sources and variables. The empirical results are presented in section 6.

Methods of Measurement of TFPG

We start with the most commonly used approach to TFP measurement, namely that of Solow (1957). He provided an elementary way of segregating variations in output per head due to technical change from those due to changes in the availability of capital per head. Solow index of TFP is based on the Cobb-Douglas production function under the assumption of constant returns to scale, autonomous Hicks-neutral technological progress and payment to factors according to their marginal product.

The discrete method of measurement of productivity due to Solow is obtained as follows:

$$\Delta A(t)/A(t) = \Delta V(t)/V(t) - [S_L(t)(\Delta L(t)/L(t)) + S_K(t)(\Delta K(t)/K(t))]$$

where,

$\Delta V(t)/V(t)$ is rate of change of real gross value added

$\Delta L(t)/L(t)$ is rate of change of labour

$\Delta K(t)/K(t)$ is rate of change of real gross fixed capital

$S_L(t)$ is share of labour in gross value added in year t

$S_K(t)$ is share of capital in value added in year t

Thus $\Delta A(t)/A(t)$ gives the annual rates of total factor productivity growth according to Solow method.

The Translog index of technological change is based on a translog production function characterised by constant returns to scale. It allows for variable elasticity of substitution and does not require the assumption of Hicks neutrality. The Translog index is a discrete version of the continuous Divisia index and is obtained as follows:

$$\Delta P(t)/P(t) = \Delta V(t)/V(t) - \left[\overline{S_L(t)}\left(\Delta L(t)/L(t)\right) + \overline{S_K(t)}\left(\Delta L(t)/K(t)\right)\right]$$

Here $\Delta V(t)/V(t)$, $\Delta L(t)/L(t)$ and $\Delta K(t)/K(t)$ are approximated by corresponding logarithms of ratios of variables over successive years, i.e.,

$$\Delta V(t)/V(t) \sim \ln[V(t)/V(t-1)] = \ln V(t) - \ln V(t-1) = \Delta \ln V(t)$$

$$\Delta L(t)/L(t) \sim \ln[L(t)/L(t-1)] = \ln L(t) - \ln L(t-1) = \Delta \ln L(t)$$

$$\Delta K(t)/K(t) \sim \ln[K(t)/K(t-1)] = \ln K(t) - \ln K(t-1) = \Delta \ln K(t)$$

$$\overline{S_L(t)} = 1/2[S_L(t-1) + S_L(t)]$$

$$S_K(t) = 1/2[S_K(t-1) + S_K(t)]$$

$S_L(t)$ and $S_K(t)$ being shares of labour and capital in value added. $\Delta P(t)/P(t)$ is thus the translog index of total factor productivity growth.

The above methods are based on the assumptions of constant returns to scale and payments to factors according to their marginal product. The conventional methods do not distinguish between technological progress and changes in the efficiency with which existing technology is applied to production i.e., technical efficiency. Cornwell, Schmidt and Sickles (1990) suggested a model which gives the rate of growth in productivity (TFPG) as a sum of the rate of technological progress and the rate of change in technical efficiency. Assuming a Cobb-Douglas production technology with two inputs, they suggested the following model:

$$\log Y_i(t) = \alpha + \lambda t + \alpha \log L(t) + \beta \log K(t) + e_i(t) \qquad \ldots(1)$$

$$\text{and} \quad e_i(t) = v_i(t) + u_i(t)$$

where α and β are the elasticities of output with respect to labour and capital respectively, λ is the rate of technological progress, $Y_i(t)$ is the level of output of the i th company at time t and $e_i(t)$ is the error term. $e_i(t)$ is postulated as combining a random error term, $v_i(t)$ and the term associated with technical efficiency, $u_i(t)$ which is both time varying and company specific. The term $v_i(t)$ has the usual properties while $u_i(t)$ is assumed to be independent of $v_i(t)$ and non-positive.

Assuming a time varying efficiency approach, efficiency term $e_i(t)$ is estimated (from OLS residuals for each company separately) as a quadratic function of time t.

$$e_i(t) = n_{oi} + n_{1i}(t) + n_{2i}(t^2) + v_i(t)$$

where n_{ki} (k=0,1 and 2) are parameters associated with individual companies. Following the above decomposition of $e_i(t)$, the rate of growth in productivity TFPG(t) is given as

$$TFPG(t) = \lambda + (n_{1i} + 2\, n_{2i} t)$$

where λ is the rate of technological progress and $(n_{1i} + 2\, n_{2i} t)$ is the rate of technical efficiency change.

Following the approach of Cornwell *et al.*, recently applied by Yanrui (1995); Fecher and Pestieu (1993); and Krishna, K.L. and Sahota, G.S. (1991), the above model is implemented for this study in the following steps. First of all, the Cobb-Douglas production function given in equation (1) is estimated using a cross-section of pooled time series data for all the year with time dummy t which takes the value 0 for pre-reform years and value 1 for post-reform years with the residuals saved. (The Cobb Douglas production function could have been estimated separately for two periods but a single function was estimated to have the large degrees of freedom). The above model is estimated with pooled cross-sectional and time-series data using OLS. For pooling the data for different industries group panels, the standard Chow test was applied. F-ratio indicated poolability of data for different industry group panels. After pooling the data, panel data techniques of estimating the regression function for pooled cross-section and time series data using OLS were applied. The estimated value of coefficient of t is that of t for the pre-reform period and value of coefficient of t and coefficient of dummy variable and t for the post-reform period. Then, these estimated residuals are regressed against t and t^2 including a constant term separately for each company. The estimated value of coefficient of t from this equation gives an indicator of technical efficiency. Thus, the growth rate of total factor productivity for each company i is estimated as:

$TFP_i(t) = \lambda + n_{1i} + 2n_{2i}t$ for the pre-reform period, and

$TFP_i(t) = \lambda$ + coefficient of $dt + n_{1i} + 2n_{2i}t$ for the post-reform period, and

Where λ is the rate of technological progress for the pre-reform period and λ+coefficient of t and dummy for the post-reform period and $n_{1i} + 2n_{2I}t$ is the rate of technical efficiency change.

Specification of Function for Inter-Company Variations in TFPG

Based on the theoretical and empirical literature of factors affecting productivity growth discussed above we shall develop an econometric model to examine factors influencing productivity growth The postulated hypotheses regarding productivity determinants are stated below:

Function I: TFPG=f(GO)

Function II: TFPG=f(GO,MT,MMI,CGI,FE,RD,KLR,XI)

Where, TFPG is total factor productivity growth, GO is growth rate of output, MT is technology imports intensity, MMI is materials input import intensity, CGI is capital goods import intensity, FE is foreign equity participation, RD is research and development intensity, XI is export intensity, and KLR is capital intensity.

The above model is estimated with pooled cross-sectional and time-series data using OLS. First, for pooling the data for different industries group panels, the standard Chow test was applied. F-ratio indicated poolability of data for different industry group panels. After pooling the data, panel data techniques of estimating the regression function for pooled cross-section and time series data were applied.

Methodology for Panel Data Analysis

While using the panel data the consistent estimation of equation by OLS is difficult because the error terms are no longer homoskedastic. If errors are not homoskedastic OLS estimates will be consistent but inefficient. Thus the reported standard errors will be incorrect. Both the fixed effects and random effects models solve this heteroskedasticity problem, although the random effects model is more efficient. Under panel data techniques three different methods of estimation could be considered: ordinary least squares estimates (OLS), the fixed effects model (FE) or least squares dummy variables (LSDV), and the random effects model (RE). The diagnostic tests were applied so that a best statistical model could be selected among these three models. Three different test statistics are applied to choose the best statistical model. The likelihood ratio (LR) test is applied to test for the OLS model against the FE model, a large value for the LR statistic favours the use of the FE model over the OLS model. The Lagranges multiplier (LM) test is applied to test for the OLS model against the RE model, a large value for the LM statistic favours the RE model against the OLS model. The Hausman specification (HS) test is applied to test for the RE model against the FE model, a large value of the HS statistics favours the FE model over the RE model. The LIMDEP package is used for the panel data analysis of pooled cross-section and time series data. It provides the estimates based on all the three models — OLS, FE and RE.

SECTION 5

DATA AND VARIABLES

Sources of Data

The database of the Reserve Bank of India (RBI) on finances of Medium & Large Public Limited Companies are the basic source of data for this study. Different sets of data[2] were obtained from RBI for engineering companies: 1985-86 to 1987-88, 1987-88 to 1989-90, 1989-90 to 1990-91, 1990-91 to 1992-93, and 1992-93 to 1994-95. All these data sets were matched to get a common subset of companies. Finally, we were left with a subset of 44 large companies belonging to electrical and non-electrical engineering industries common in different sets. Thus, the data set used for this study covers 44 engineering companies for the years 1985-86 to 1994-95. There are 10 companies in Electrical Engineering, belonging to the following groups: Cables, Dry Cells, Electric Lamps and other Electrical Machinery, apparatus, appliances, etc. There are 34 companies in Non-Electrical Engineering, belonging to the following groups: Machine Tools, Textile Machinery and accessories and Misc. Machinery not elsewhere classified. The econometric analysis presented in the paper is based on the pooled time-series and cross-section data for the 44 companies belonging to these groups. Separate analyses have been carried out for the pre-reform (1985-86 to 1990-91) and post-reform (1991-92 to 1994-95) periods.

2. Each data set is for three years. The coverage of firms differs between the sets.

Measurement of Variables

Output

Gross value added has been taken as the measure of output. The data tapes give data on value of production, and manufacturing expenses, namely, raw materials and components consumed, stores and spares consumed, power and fuel, royalty and other manufacturing expenses. We have subtracted the sum of manufacturing expenses from value of production to get value added. This includes depreciation and therefore what we get is gross value added at current prices. This is, then, deflated by the Index number of wholesale prices for relevant product groups. Product groups given in the Index Number of Wholesale Prices are not the same as those given in the RBI. Therefore, product-wise indices of wholesale prices are regrouped to make them comparable to product groups given in the RBI. The groups of WPI used as deflator for different industry groups are given in Appendix A-5.1. Index number of wholesale prices in India for the financial years from 1985-86 to 1994-95 are taken from Index number of wholesale prices in India, Office of the Economic Advisor, Ministry of Industry, Government of India. This gives the indices at base 1981-82=100. The base of this series is converted to base 1985-86=100. This method of deflation suffers from the limitation that the same price index is used for all companies belonging to a product group which may not be appropriate since the basket of products produced by various companies belonging to a product group (say, textiles machinery) may differ.

Capital Input

Gross fixed capital stock at constant (1985-86) prices is taken as the measure of capital input. RBI tapes gives the total gross fixed assets at current prices. It consists of land, buildings, plant and machinery, capital work in progress, furniture, fixtures and office equipments and others. To estimate real gross fixed capital stock, we employ the perpetual inventory method. This requires bench-year estimates of gross fixed capital stock at 1985-86 prices and real gross investments at 1985-86 prices over successive years for the period under consideration.

Fixed investment for each year is first calculated and deflated by the capital goods price deflator of that year to get the real investment. But where the fixed investment comes out to be negative, deflator taken is the price index for benchmark year. This is so because negative fixed investment implies that some of the gross capital in bench year has been discarded (which had been estimated previously at bench year price index). The deflator used for gross fixed assets is the Index number of wholesale prices for machinery and machine tools. This is taken from Chandhok (1990). Chandhok gives two series on index number of machinery and machine tools: (1) a series from 1971-72 to 1988-89 at base 1970-71=100, and (2) a series from 1982-83 to 1988-89 at base 1981-82=100. The Wholesale price indices from 1971-72 to 1981-82 (at base 1970-71) was merged with wholesale price indices of latter series 1982-83 to 1988-89 (at base 1981-82) and then the base of the combined series was shifted to 1985-86. Once the series with 1985-86=100 is obtained, the deflator for benchmark year i.e., 1985-86 is obtained as the average of indices from 1971-72 to 1985-86 if the company was incorporated more than 15 years prior to 1985-86. But if the company was incorporated after 1972-73 (i.e. less than 15 years prior to 1985-86), the average of indices from the year of incorporation to 1985-86 is taken as the deflator for the benchmark year. Deflator for investments from 1986-87 to 1994-95 is the price index of machinery and machine tools at base 1985-86 for the corresponding year. Index number of wholesale price for the years 1989-90 to 1994-95 is taken from Index Number of Wholesale Prices in India, 1989-90, Office of the Economic Advisor, Ministry of Industry, Government of India.

Labour Input

The RBI data source does not contain data on number of workers/employees. But it provides salaries, wages and bonus for all the employees and managerial remuneration. Thus, to obtain a measure of labour/employment, we have first aggregated the salaries, wages and bonus for all the employees and managerial remuneration to get total salaries and wages, and then deflated it by the wage rate which has been obtained from ASI (Annual Survey of Industries). From ASI, we get data on total emoluments and total employees for various industry groups belonging to electrical and non-electrical engineering. The industry-wise wage rates (emoluments per employee) are computed from these data and then used as the deflator for company level salaries and wages to arrive at a measure of labour input. One difficulty we have faced in making these computations is that the industrial classification in ASI are not the same as in company finance data of RBI. Thus the industries in the ASI have been re-grouped to match it with the RBI industrial classification. The industry groups combined are given in Appendix A-5.2.

Scale of Production (GO)

Growth in real value added is taken as a variable for measuring growth of scale of production. As mentioned earlier, growth in scale of production permits adoption of new technologies which improves productivity. Expansion of scale also generates scale economies which improves productivity. Therefore, we expect a positive relationship between growth in productivity and growth in value added.

Capital Intensity (KLR)

The ratio of real gross fixed capital stock to labour is taken as a measure of capital intensity. Companies with relatively high capital intensity will be the companies with more chances of embodied technical progress (Ahluwalia, 1991). We, therefore, hypothesise that capital intensive companies attain higher rates of productivity growth.

Technology Imports (MT)

The ratio of payments for royalty, technical fees (for know how, of drawings, designs, etc.), professional and consultation fees and others to sales turnover is taken as a measure of technology imports. The import of technology brings know-how and designs etc., which enhances productivity.

Export Intensity (XI)

Export intensity is computed as the ratio of exports to sales. It is hypothesised that higher export intensity induces the companies to make efforts to be more competitive, through greater efficiency in production.

Research Intensity (RD)

Company efficiency may improve with greater research effort. The ratio of research and development expenditure to sales turnover is taken to capture the research intensity.

Intermediate Inputs Import Intensity (MMI)

Imported inputs generate value addition. Further, imported intermediate inputs may embody advanced technology. The ratio of imports of materials, spares, components, etc. to total materials is taken as a variable for intermediate inputs import intensity.

Capital Goods Import Intensity (CGI)

While technology imports constitute one means of technology inflow, the other important source of new technology is capital goods import. Imported capital goods improves technological level. The ratio of import of capital goods to fixed investment is taken as a measure of capital goods import intensity.

Foreign Equity Participation (FE)

Foreign participation in management may improve company efficiency. The share of dividends declared in foreign currency to total dividends paid is taken as a measure of foreign equity participation.

SECTION 6

EMPIRICAL RESULTS

Company Level Variations in Productivity Growth

Table 5.1 presents a comparison of mean and standard deviation of the key variables in the pre- and post-reforms period. It is interesting to note from Table 5.1 that the average growth rate of real value added in the sample firms declined in the post-reform period as compared with the pre-reform period. The fall in the growth rate was from 10.6 to 5.8 per cent per annum. A decline is observed also, to a lesser extent, in the average rates of growth of labour and capital. The fall in the growth rate of capital was from 9 per cent per annum in the pre-reform period to 7.5 per cent per annum in the post-reform period. The fall in the growth rate of employment was from 3.2 per cent per annum in the pre-reform period to 2.1 per cent per annum in the post-reform period. The average technology import intensity was higher in the post-reform period (0.92 per cent) than that in the pre-reform period (0.58 per cent). Similarly, the average R&D intensity of the firms was relatively higher in the post-reform period (0.43 per cent as against 0.15 per cent). The mean values of

Table 5.1

Averages of Variables in the Pre- and Post- Reform Period

Variable	*Pre-Reform*	*Post-Reform*
GL (% p.a.)	3.21 (12.46)	2.05 (10.78)
GK (% p.a.)	9.02 (13.2)	7.48 (15.8)
GO (% p.a.)	10.6 (21.95)	5.82 (21.42)
MT (%)	0.58 (0.87)	0.92 (1.95)
MMI (%)	24.42 (18.36)	21.9 (16.99)
CGI (%)	16.72 (75.99)	10.99 (37.05)
FE (%)	12.26 (16.18)	13.55 (17.10)
RD (%)	0.15 (0.64)	0.43 (0.53)
KLR	11.42 (11.047)	13.54 (8.31)
XI (%)	5.46 (7.85)	6.80 (8.37)

Notes: Figures in the parentheses are standard deviations

GL = growth rate of employment; GO = growth rate of output; GK = growth rate of capital; MT = technology import intensity; MMI=materials input import intensity; CGI= capital goods import intensity; FE = foreign equity participation; RD = research and development intensity; KLR= capital-labour ratio; XI= export intensity.

other variables did not differ much in the two periods. This comparison depicts that while the rate of technology acquisition has gone up in the post-reform period, this has not been accompanied by a faster growth of output. Thus the reforms seems to have constrained the growth of the large engineering firms.

Tables 5.2 and 5.3 show the productivity performance of companies at the aggregate level by all the three methods, *viz.*, Solow, Translog and cornwell method in the pre- and post-reforms period respectively. These tables bring out clearly that productivity performance of companies are varying. In the pre-reform period, though a large number of companies are recording significant growth in productivity, yet considerable number of companies show decline in productivity. At the aggregate level of all companies, total factor

Table 5.2

Productivity Performance of Companies at Aggregate Level Pre-Reform Period (1985-86 to 1990-91)

	Solow	*Translog*	*Cornwell*
Total No. of Companies	44	44	44
Average TFPG	3.18	1.97	4.70
Average Output Growth	10.60	10.60	10.60
Share of TFPG in Output Growth	30.00	18.58	44.34
No. of Companies Showing Increase in TFPG	**33**	**32**	**35**
Average TFPG	6.83	5.16	6.58
Average Output Growth	13.06	12.78	12.74
Share of TFPG in Output Growth	52.30	40.38	48.59
No. of Companies Showing Decline in TFPG	**11**	**12**	**9**
Average TFPG	-7.75	-6.54	-2.66
Average Output Growth	3.21	4.78	2.25
Total No. of Companies Showing Positive Output Growth	**40**	**40**	**40**
Average TFPG Growth	4.09	2.71	5.28
Average Output Growth	11.81	11.81	11.81
No. of Companies Showing Increase in TFP Growth	**32**	**31**	**34**
Average TFPG Growth	6.95	5.21	6.05
Average Output Growth	13.59	13.32	12.86
No. of Companies Showing Decline in TFP	**8**	**9**	**6**
Average TFPG	-7.34	-5.90	-2.96
Average Output Growth	4.69	6.61	2.34

productivity growth rate is moderate. The companies which record a fall in productivity are pulling down the aggregate productivity growth rate. If these companies are excluded, then average productivity growth rate is quite impressive. Further, productivity growth shows low contribution to output growth at aggregate level, but if companies with falling productivity are excluded as earlier, then productivity share in growth of output becomes very impressive. In the post-reform period, according to Solow and Translog method the number of companies showing decline in productivity are more than the number of companies showing increase in productivity thereby showing a decline in productivity performance at the aggregate level. However, according to the cornwell method, the

Table 5.3

Productivity Performance of Companies at Aggregate Level Post-Reform Period (1991-92 to 1994-95)

	Solow	*Translog*	*Cornwell*
Total No. of Companies	44	44	44
Average TFPG	-0.43	-1.49	3.04
Average Output Growth	5.82	5.82	5.82
Share of TFPG in Output Growth	-7.39	-25.60	52.23
No. of Companies Showing Increase in TFPG	**19**	**16**	**32**
Average TFPG	6.23	4.88	6.36
Average Output Growth	11.79	13.32	8.48
Share of TFPG in Output Growth	52.84	36.64	75.00
No. of Companies Showing Decline in TFPG	**25**	**28**	**12**
Average TFPG	-5.49	-5.14	-5.84
Average Output Growth	1.28	1.54	-1.28
No. of Companies Showing Posiive Output Growth	**34**	**34**	**34**
Average TFPG	1.83	0.79	5.25
Average Output Growth	9.50	9.50	7.60
No. of Companies Showing Increase in TFPG	**19**	**16**	**29**
Average TFP Growth	6.23	4.88	6.62
Average Output Growth	11.79	13.31	9.83
No. of Companies Showing Decline in TFPG	**15**	**18**	**5**
Average TFPG	-3.73	-2.84	-2.76
Average Output Growth	6.59	6.11	7.60

number of companies showing increase in TFPG are more than those showing decline in TFP. Therefore at the aggregate level TFPG is moderate by this method. But if we exclude the companies showing decline in productivity, the average TFPG is quite impressive. Thus in the post-reform period also the companies showing decline in TFPG are pulling down the aggregate productivity growth rate. Also productivity growth shows low contribution to output growth at the aggregate level but if the companies with falling productivity are excluded as earlier, then productivity share in growth of output increases. At the aggregate level it was also found that, according to all the methods, number of companies showing positive productivity growth has declined from pre-reform to post-reform period whereas number of companies showing decline in productivity performance has increased from pre-reform to post-reform period. Average productivity growth at the aggregate level, comprising all companies, has declined in the post-reform period as compared to the pre-reform period. It has even recorded negative growth in the post-reform period by Solow and Translog methods

The distribution of companies according to productivity performance is shown in Table 5.4. This table depicts that both in pre-reform as well as post-reform period there are quite a large number of companies showing a decline of more than 5 per cent per annum. Among the companies recording positive productivity growth, while some companies show low growth rates, several other companies record very high growth rates. A large number of companies are in the range of 0 to 5 per cent of TFPG in the pre-reform period. This number has however declined in the post-reform period.

Table 5.4

Distribution of Firms According to Total Factor Productivity Growth

	Pre-Reform			*Post-Reform*		
TFP Growth (per cent)	*Solow*	*Translog*	*Cornwell*	*Solow*	*Translog*	*Cornwell*
Below -5 per cent	8	8	1	9	10	5
-5 to <-2 per cent	1	2	4	10	10	5
-2 to <0 per cent	2	2	4	6	8	2
0 to <2 per cent	4	10	4	5	5	9
2 to <5 per cent	16	11	13	4	5	6
5 to 10 per cent	8	7	12	6	5	9
Above 10 per cent	5	4	6	4	1	8
Total No. of Companies	44	44	44	44	44	44
Annual TFP Gr. (per cent)	3.18	1.97	4.69	-0.43	-1.49	3.04

Determinants of TFPG During Pre- and Post- Reforms Period

The above analysis reveals that there are wide variations in productivity growth among companies according to all the methods. In this section we shall examine the factors which affect inter-company variations in productivity growth according to the hypothesis postulated above. This analysis shall be based on the translog index of total factor productivity which is derived from translog production function. The translog production function is a more general specification of the production function. It is a flexible functional form imposing relatively few *a priori* restrictions on the properties of the underlying technology. It allows for variable elasticity of substitution. It does not require a Hicks-neutral or a constant rate of technological change. Therefore we have used the TFPG measured by translog method in the analysis of determinants of total factor productivity growth. Chow test (Chow, G.C., 1960) was applied for homogeneity with respect to different engineering industries. Chow test confirms the homogeneity. The functions specified in the earlier section are estimated. The results are given in Tables 5.5 and 5.6.

Table 5.5

Estimates of TFPG Based on Translog Method of Measurement

Dependent Variable : TFPG

	OLS		*FE*		*RE*	
	Pre-Reform	*Post-Reform*	*Pre-Reform*	*Post-Reform*	*Pre-Reform*	*Post-Reform*
Constant	-0.0516*** (-7.319)	-0.0603*** (-8.170)			-0.0525*** (-6.25)	-0.0604*** (-8.077)
GO	0.6732*** (23.229)	0.7797*** (23.381)	0.6956*** (23.535)	0.8341*** (22.810)	0.6820*** (24.386)	0.7818*** (23.562)
LR Test	81.358*** [43]	53.268 [43]				
LM Test	7.8504*** [1]	0.0008 [1]				
HS Test	2.0243 [1]	11.571*** [1]				
R^2	0.71	0.76	0.80	0.82	0.71	0.76
No.	220	176	220	176	220	176

Note: Figures in the parentheses () are t-ratios, [] are d.f.
* Significant at 10%
** Significant at 5%
*** Significant at 1%

Table 5.5 presents the results of the function-I using the OLS, FE and RE statistical models. The estimates are based on the sample of 44 companies for the electrical and non-electrical engineering industries for both pre- and post-reform periods. This table shows that significance levels and parameter magnitudes are different in the three models. Thus we have to choose one of the three models depending on different test statistics as discussed in the methodology. In the estimates for pre-reform period, LR statistics is found to be insignificant showing that OLS is better than FE model. LM statistics is significant implying that RE model to be preferred over OLS. The HS is insignificant which further supports that RE model is better than FE model. The consideration of all the three statistics leads us to choose the RE model as the best specification in the pre-reform period. The chosen model i.e. the RE model explains about 71 per cent of the variations in productivity growth in this period.

In estimates for the post-reform period, the LR statistics is found to be insignificant indicating that OLS model is better than FE model, and LM statistics is also insignificant indicating that OLS model is even better than RE model. But the high value of HS statistics argues in favour of FE model against RE model. The consideration of all the three statistical models thus suggested that OLS is the best statistical model for the post-reform period. The chosen model, that is the OLS model, for this period explains 76 per cent of the variation in the productivity growth.

In both the pre- and post-reforms period, the coefficient of growth rate of value added is found to be positive and highly significant. This finding is consistent with "Verdoon's Law". Thus it may be argued that economies of scale have been a source of productivity growth in both the periods. Thus growth in output has provided an opportunity for employing techniques of production which are more efficient and generates higher growth in productivity. This finding is consistent with the finding of Goldar (1986) and Ahluwalia (1991) for Indian manufacturing industry. The elasticity of total factor productivity growth with output is 0.68 in the pre-reform period. However the elasticity has increased to 0.78 in the post-reform period. Hence, after reforms output growth is generating faster productivity growth.

In Table 5.6, the effect of other variables apart from the effect of growth of value of output on total factor productivity growth i.e. function-II are shown. For function-II also, we have to first choose the best statistical model from the given three models-OLS, FE and

Table 5.6

Estimates of TFPG Translog Method

Dependent Variable: TFPG

	Pre-Reform			Post-Reform		
TFP Growth (per cent)	*OLS*	*FE*	*RE*	*OLS*	*FE*	*RE*
Constant	-0.0427***		-0.0440***	-0.0504***		-0.0505***
	(-2.864)		(-2.669)	(-2.604)		(-2.458)
GO	0.6749***	0.6994***	0.6805***	0.7903***	0.8228***	0.7957***
	(22.865)	(22.439)	(23.603)	(23.486)	(22.868)	(23.843)
MT	0.6446	-0.8570	0.4549	0.5425	0.6244	0.5780
	(0.890)	(-0.701)	(0.587)	(1.475)	(1.104)	(1.530)
MMI	0.0485	0.0366	0.0497	0.1006***	0.1213	0.1030***
	(1.379)	(0.405)	(1.276)	(2.423)	(1.359)	(2.367)
CGI	0.0016	0.0035	0.0020	-0.0435**	-0.0427**	-0.0433**
	(0.192)	(0.399)	(0.250)	(-2.278)	(-2.093)	(-2.284)
FE	-0.1278***	-0.0653	-0.1221***	-0.0724*	-0.0399	-0.0737*
	(-3.160)	(-0.945)	(-2.824)	(-1.709)	(-0.455)	(-1.665)
RD	-1.7948*	0.1636	-1.5326	-0.9881	0.5068	-0.9233
	(-1.803)	(0.111)	(-1.464)	(-0.727)	(0.234)	(-0.658)
KLR	-0.0003	-0.0004	-0.0003	-0.0015*	-0.0090***	-0.0016*
	(-0.492)	(-0.294)	(-0.490)	(-1.688)	(-2.718)	(-1.694)
XI	-0.0589	0.0688	-0.0488	0.0218	0.1323	0.0241
	(-0.716)	(0.436)	(-0.549)	(0.242)	(0.742)	(0.257)
LR Test	67.352			59.525		
	[43]			[43]		
LM Test	1.2175			0.0312		
	[1]			[1]		
HS Test	8.8715			14.9269*		
	[8]			[8]		
R-Square	0.73	0.80	0.73	0.78	0.85	0.78
No. of Observations	220	220	220	176	176	176

Note: Figures in the parentheses () are t ratios, []are d. f.

* Significant at 10%

** Significant at 5%

*** Significant at 1%

RE. In the results for pre-reform period LR statistics is insignificant suggesting that OLS model is better than FE model. The LM statistics is also insignificant indicating OLS model to be even better than RE model. The insignificance of HS statistics, however, argues in favour of RE model against FE model. The consideration of the three test statistics leads us to choose the OLS as the best statistical model in the pre-reforms period. As regards the results for the post-reforms period, both the LR statistics and LM statistics are insignificant indicating that OLS model is better than both FE and

RE models. The HS statistics is statistically significant at 10 per cent level of significance suggesting that FE model is better than RE model but it is insignificant at 5 per cent level suggesting that RE model is better than FE model. But, since based on LM and LR statistics, OLS is found to be better than both RE model and FE model, it may be argued that the right model for the post-reform period is the OLS model.

Turning to the coefficients to various explanatory variables, the coefficient of capital intensity is found to be insignificant for pre-reform period. For the post-reform period, this coefficient is negative and statistically significant. This is contrary to the expected positive coefficient as the companies with relatively higher capital intensity should be the companies with greater chances of embodied technical progress and more scope for learning by doing. It may be inferred that the policies in the post-reform period encouraged companies to create more capacity which was not fully utilised causing a negative relationship to arise with TFPG. This is consistent with the finding of Ahluwalia (1991) for the Indian manufacturing industry. Ahluwalia gives two explanations for a negative relationship between capital intensity and TFPG. First, there must be certain other factors (not included in the specification of the equation) which are highly correlated with the capital-labour ratio and which have a negative effect on productivity growth. Second, the policy regime with its emphasis on discretionary licences and permits encouraged overcapitalisation.

Among the technology acquisition variables, the coefficient of capital goods import intensity is insignificant for the pre-reform period but it is negatively significant for the post-reform period. This indicates that though capital goods were imported these probably could not be optimally utilised. The imported material intensity has an insignificant coefficient in the pre-reform period where as contrary to capital goods import intensity, it has a positive and significant coefficient for the post-reform period. During the post-reform period import relaxations permitted better quality imports. These imported materials may have contributed to productivity increase either by requiring less labour/capital use for further processing and conversion into final product or by helping in the production of better quality products. The coefficient of foreign equity participation is statistically significant with a negative sign for both the periods.

Though foreign equity is supposed to generate a positive influence it is showing a negative influence in both the periods. This may be because foreign participation brings in such technologies which are very expensive and there may be a time lag in getting the positive influence. Technology acquisition through imports of technology against lump sum payments, technical fees, royalty etc. is found to have no influence in both the periods. The coefficient of research intensity is negative and significant at 10 per cent in the pre-reform period and is insignificant in the post-reform period. The negative relationship in the pre-reform period is however not very strong statistically. In this context it needs to be recognised that R&D intensity of industrial firms in India is generally very low as compared to that of the firms in the industrialised countries. This low level of R&D intensity cannot be expected to lead to a significant advancement in technology (Goldar, 1995). He found a positive but statistically insignificant relationship between TFPG and R&D intensity. Export intensity is found to be insignificant in both the periods. Though a greater export orientation was expected to be favourable to productivity growth, no favourable impact of exports was found to be there. It may be because export orientation was not yet large enough.

SECTION 7

SUMMARY OF FINDINGS

In this paper, productivity performance of companies at the aggregate level in Indian Engineering industries in the pre- and post-reforms period has been analysed. Also the factors affecting inter-company variations in productivity growth in the pre- and post-reforms period were considered. It was found that the productivity growth of companies has declined in the post-reform period as compared to the pre-reform period. Average output growth at the aggregate level has also declined in the post-reform period as compared to the pre-reform period. Even after excluding the companies showing decline in output growth, the average output growth shows a deceleration in the post-reform period. The average productivity growth of such companies has also declined, in general, between the two periods. The number of companies showing increase in productivity has declined from pre-reform to post-reform period whereas number of companies showing decline in productivity has increased from pre- to post-reform period. Thus the results indicated that the reforms had not shown any improvement in the productivity growth.

An analysis of the factors affecting productivity changes has been carried out by estimating a regression function using panel data techniques of analysis. The results indicated that growth of scale significantly generates productivity growth. Its marginal contribution has increased in the post-liberalisation period. After reforms the companies which had relatively low levels of capital intensity were having better productivity performance. More capital intensive companies had a relatively lower productivity growth. The companies having better access to imported materials had better productivity performance. On the other hand imported capital goods were not having a desired positive impact on productivity performance. The arms length purchase of technology and exports intensity have increased in after reforms. But, these appear to have had no positive effect on the productivity performance of companies in both the periods. The technology acquisition through technology transfer accompanying foreign equity participation and research and development expenditure needed for modifying and adapting imported technology was mainly showing a time lag in showing its positive influence

• This paper is a part of ongoing Ph.D. work, 'Sources of Growth in Indian Engineering Industries', under the Supervision of Prof. (Mrs.) Rashmi Agarwal, Department of Business Economics, University of Delhi and Prof. B.N.Goldar, Institute of Economic Growth, Delhi. I gratefully acknowledge their guidance.

Appendix A-5.1

Output Deflators

Industry	*RBI Group*	*WPI Group*
Cables	445	IIkb2
Dry Batteries	446	IIIkb3 (414)
Electric Lamps	447	IIIkb4 (417+418)
Other Electrical Machinery, Apparatus, Appliances, etc.	448	IIIkb
Machine Tools	449	IIIka393
Textile Machinery and Accessories	450	IIIka2 (385+386+387)
Miscellaneous Machinery n.e.s.	451	IIIka

Appendix A-5.2

Wages Deflators

Industry	*RBI Group*	*ASI Group*
Cables	445	361
Dry Batteries	446	362
Electric Lamps	447	363
Other Electrical Machinery, Apparatus, Appliances, etc.	448	36-(361+362+363)
Machine Tools	449	357
Textile Machinery and Accessories	450	353
Miscellaneous Machinery n.e.s.	451	35-(353+357)

References

Ahluwalia, I.J. (1991). *Productivity and Growth in Indian Manufacturing*, Delhi: Oxford University Press.

Aw, Bee Yan, and Amy Hwang (1995). "Productivity and the Export Market: A Firm-Level Analysis." *Journal of Development Economics* 47 (2): 313-32.

Aw, Bee Yan, and Geeta Batra (1998). "Technology, Exports, and Firm Efficiency in Taiwanese Manufacturing." *Economics of Innovation and New Technology* 7 (1): 93-113.

Balakrishnan, P., K. Pushpamgadan and M. Suresh Babu (2000). "Trade Liberalisation and Productivity Growth in Manufacturing: Evidence from Firm-Level Panel Data," *Economic and Political Weekly*, October 7.

Basant, R. and Fikkert, B. (1993). "Impact of R&D, Foreign Technology Purchase and Technology Spillovers on Indian Industrial Productivity: Some Estimates," *Working Paper No.11*, Institute for New Technologies, United Nations University Masstricht.

Bhagwati, J.N. (1978). *Foreign Trade Regimes and Economic Development: Anatomy and Consequences of Exchange Control Regimes*, Cambridge (Mass.): Ballinger.

Blomstrom, M. and Persson, H. (1983). "Foreign Investment and Spillover Efficiency in an Underdeveloped Economy: Evidence from the Mexican Manufacturing Industry," *World Development*, 11: 493-501.

Blomstrom, M. and Wolff, E. (1994). "Multinational Corporations and Productivity Convergence in Mexico." in W. Baumol, R. Nelson & E. Wolff, editors, *Convergence of Productivity: Cross-National Studies and Historical Evidence*. Oxford: Oxford University Press.

Caves, R.E. (1974). "Multinational Firms, Competition and Productivity in Host-country Markets," *Economica*, 41: 176-93.

Chandhok, H.L. and the policy group (1990). *India Data Base: The Economy (Annual Time Series Data, Vols 1&2)*, New Delhi: Living Media India Ltd.

Chen, Tain-Jy, and De-Piao Tang (1987). "Comparing Technical Efficiency between Import Substituting and Export-Oriented Foreign Firms in a Developing Country." *Journal of Development Economics* 26 (2): 277-89.

Chow, G.C. (1960). "Tests of Equality between Sets of Coefficients in Two Linear Regressions," *Econometrica*, Vol.28, No.3, pp.591-605.

Clerides, Sofronis, Saul Lach, and James Tybout (1998). "Is Learning-by-Exporting Important? Micro-Dynamic Evidence from Colombia, Mexico, and Morocco." *Quarterly Journal of Economics* 113 (August): 903-47.

Coe, D.T. and Helpman, E (1993). "International R&D Spillovers," Cambridge, Mass: *NBER Working Paper No.4444*, August

Coe, D.T. Helpman, E. and Hoffmaister, A.W. (1995). "North-South R&D Spillovers," Cambridge, *Mass: NBER Working Paper No.5048*, March.

Coe, David, and Elhanan Helpman (1995). "International R&D Spillovers," *European Economic Review* 39 (5): 214-42.

Coe, David, Elhanan Helpman, and Alexander Hoffmaister (1997). "North-South R&D Spillovers," *Economic Journal* 107 (440): 134-49.

Cornwell C., Schmidt P. and Sickles, R. C. (1990) "Production Frontiers with Cross-Sectional and Time-Series Variations in Efficiency Levels," *Journal of Econometrics* 46, 185-200.

Cuneo, P. and Mairesse, J. (1984). "Productivity and R&D at the Firm Level in French Manufacturing," in Griliches (ed.).

Evenson, R.E. and Larry Westphal (1995). "Technological Change and Technology Strategy." In Jere Behrman and T.N. Srinivasan, eds., *Handbook of Development Economics*, Vol.3, Amsterdam: North-Holland.

Evenson, R.E. and Westphal, L.E. (1994). "Technological Change and Technology Strategy," in T.N. Srinivasan and J. Behrman edited *Handbook of Development Economics*, Vol.3, North-Holland Publishing Company.

Evenson, Robert, (1995). *Industrial Productivity Growth Linkages Between OECD Countries: 1970-1990*, Department of Economics, Yale University, New Haven, Conn.

Fabricant, S.(1942). *Employment in Manufacturing, 1899-1939*, NBER.

Fecher, F. and Perelman, S. (1989). "Productivity Growth, Technological Progress and R&D in OECD Industrial Activities," in *Public Finance and Steady Economic Growth*, The Hague: International Institute of Public Finance.

Fecher, F. and Pestieau, P. (1993). "Efficiency and Competition in OECD Financial Services," in Harold O. Fried, C. A. Knox Lovell, and Shelton S. Schmidt (eds.). *The Measurement of Productive Efficiency: Techniques and Applications*, pp 374-385. New York: Oxford University Press.

Fucns, V.R. (1968). *The Service Economy*, New York: National Bureau of Economic Research.

Fujita, N. (1994). "Liberalisation Policies and Productivity in India," *The Developing Economies*, Vol.xxxii-4, December, 509-24.

Gangopadhyay, S. and W. Wadhwa (1998). "Economic Reforms and Labour," *Economic and Political Weekly*, May 30.

Globerman, S. (1979). "Foreign Direct Investment and Spillover Efficiency Benefits in Canadian Manufacturing Industries," *Canadian Journal of Economics*, 12: 42-56.

Goldar, B.N. (1986 a). *Productivity Growth in Indian Industry*, New Delhi: Allied Publishers.

———. (1986 b). "Import Substitution, Industrial Concentration and Productivity Growth in Indian Manufacturing," *Oxford Bulletin of Economic and Statistics*, Vol.48, No.2, 143-64.

———. (1995). Technology Acquisition and Productivity Growth: A Study of Industrial Firms in India,Working Paper Series No.E/172/95, IEG, New Delhi.

Griliches, Z. (ed) (1984). *R&D, Patents and Productivity*, Chicago: University of Chicago Press.

Grossman, Gene, and Elhanan Helpman (1991). *Innovation and Growth in the World Economy*. Cambridge, Mass.: MIT Press.

Haddad, M. and Harrison, A. (1993). "Are there Positive Spillovers from Direct Foreign Investment? Evidence from Panel Data for Morocco." *Journal of Development Economics*, 42: 51-74.

Haddad, Mona (1993). "How Trade Liberalization Affected Productivity in Morocco." *Policy Research Working Paper* 1096. Development Research Group, World Bank, Washington, D.C. Processed.

Handousa, H., M. Nishimizu, and J.Page (1986). "Productivity Change in Egyptian Public Sector Industry after The Opening': 1973-79," *Journal of Development Economics*, Vol.21, No.1.

ICICI (1994). *'Productivity in Indian Manufacturing: Private Corporate Sector, 1972-73 to 1991-92*, Industrial Credit and Investment Corporation of India, Bombay.

Jaffe, A.B. (1988). "Demand and Supply Influences in R&D Intensity and Productivity Growth," *Review of Economics and Statistics*, Vol.70(3), August, pp.431-37.

Jaiswal, M.C. and Thakkar, P.H. (1982). "Measuring Total Factor Productivity," *Productivity*, Vol.23, No.3, 264-74.

Kajiwara, H. (1994). "The Effects of Trade and Foreign Investment Liberalisation Policy on Productivity in the Phillippines," *The Developing Economies*, Vol.xxxii-4, 492-508.

Kaldor, N. (1967). *Strategic Factors in Economic Development*, Itcha: Cornell University Press.

Katz, J.M., (1969). *Production Functions, Foreign Investment and Growth*, Amsterdam North-Holland Publishing Company.

Keller, Wolfgang, (1997). "How Trade Patterns and Technology Flows Affect Productivity Growth," *Policy Research Working Paper* No.1831. Development Research Group, World Bank, Washington, D.C.

———. (1998a). "Are International R&D Spillovers Trade-Related? Analyzing Spillovers among Randomly Matched Trade Patterns." *European Economic Review* 42 (8): 1469-81.

———. (1998b). *Trade and the Transmission of Technology,* Department of Economics, University of Wisconsin, Madison. Processed.

Kendrick, J.W. (1961). *Productivity Trends in the United States,* New York: National Bureau of Economic Research.

———. (1973). *Postwar Productivity Trends in the United States, 1948-1969,* NBER, New York.

Kendrick, J.W., and Grossman, E.S. (1980). *Productivity in the United States,* Blatimore: Johns Hopkins University Press.

Kennedy, K.A. (1971). *Productivity and Industrial Growth,* Oxford: Claredon Press.

Kokko, A. (1994). "Technology, Market Characteristics, and Spillovers." *Journal of Development Economics,* 43 (2): 279-93.

Kokko, A., Tansini, R. and Zejan, M. (1996) "Local Technological Capabilities and Productivity Spillovers from FDI in the Uruguayan Manufacturing Sector." *Journal of Development Studies,* 32: 602-11.

Krishna, K.L. and Sahota, G.S. (1991). "Technical Efficiency in Bangladesh Manufacturing Industries," *The Bangladesh Development Studies,* Vol.XIX, Nos. 1 & 2.

Krueger, A.O. (1978). *Foreign Trade Regimes and Economic Development: Liberalization Attempts and Consequences,* Lexington Mass: Ballinger.

Krueger, A.O. and B. Tuncer (1982 b). "An Empirical Test of the Infant Industry Arguments," *American Economic Review,* Vol.72, 1142-52.

———. (1982a). "Growth of Factor Productivity in Turkish Manufacturing Industries," *Journal of Development Economics,* Vol.11, 307-326.

———. (1982). "Estimating Total Factor Productivity: Growth in a Developing Country," *World Bank Staff Working Paper* No.432.

Kwak, H.(1994). "Changing Trade Policy and Its Impact on TFP in the Republic of Korea," *The Developing Economies,* Vol.xxxii-4, 398-422.

Lichtenberg, Frank, and Bruno van Pottelsberghe de la Potterie,(1998b). "International R&D Spillovers: A Comment." *European Economic Review* 42 (8): 1483-91.

Litchenberg, F.R. (1992). "R&D Investment and International Productivity Differences," Cambridge, Mass, *NBER Working Paper No.4161,* September.

Litchenberg, F.R. and Siegel, D. (1991). "The Impact of R&D Investment on Productivity: New Evidence Using Linked R&D-LRD Data," *Economic Inquiry,* 29: 203-28.

Little, I.M.D., T. Scitovsky and M. Scott (1970). *Industry and Trade in Some Developing Countries: A Comparative Study,* London: Oxford University Press.

Markusen, James (1995). "The Boundaries of the Multinational Enterprise and the Theory of International Trade," *Journal of Economic Perspectives* 9 (1): 169-89.

———. (1998). *'Multilateral Rules on FDI: The Developing Countries Stake',* International Trade Department, World Bank, Washington, D.C. Processed.

Maury Gittleman and Edward N. Wolff (1998). "R&D Activity and Cross-country Growth Comparisons in Daniele Archibugi and Jonathan Michie, (1998). edited *Trade, Growth and Technical Change,"* Cambridge, United Kingdom, Cambridge University Press.

Nishimizu, M. and J.M. Jr. Page (1986). *'Economic Policy and Productivity Change in Industry and Agriculture: An International Comparison',* Paper presented at the VIIIth World Economic Congress of the International Association, New Delhi.

Nishimizu, M. and S. Robinson (1984). "Trade Policies and Productivity Change in Semi Industrialised Countries," *Journal of Development Economics,* Vol. 16, Nos. 1-2, Sept./ Oct.

———. (1986). "Productivity Growth in Manufacturing" in Chenery, H., S. Robinson, and S. Syrquin (ed.), *Industrialisation and Growth: A Comparative Study,* Oxford: Oxford University Press.

Odagiri, H. (1985). "Research Activity, Output Growth and Productivity Increase in Japanese Manufacturing Industries," *Research Policy,* Vol.14.

Osada, H. (1994). "Trade Liberalisation and FDI Incentives in Indonesia: The Impact on Industrial Productivity," *The Developing Economies,* Vol.xxxii-4, 479-491.

Pack, Howard, and Kamal Saggi (1997). "Inflows of Foreign Technology and Indigenous Technological Development." *Review of Development Economics* 1 (1): 81-98.

Ramaswamy, K.V. (1996). "Labour Productivity,Emplyment Growth and Industrial Structure in India: An Exploratory Hypothesis," *IGIDR, Discussion Paper No. 136,* September.

Reddaway, W.B. and Smith, A.D., (1960). "Progress in British Manufacturing Industries in the Period 1948-54," *Economic Journal.*

Reddaway, W.B. (1966). "The Post-War Scene," An Addendum, in Salter, *W.E.G., Productivity and Technical Change,* Cambridge University Press, (2nd edition).

Rhee, Yung W., Bruce Ross-Larson, and Garry Pursell (1984). *Korea's Competitive Edge: Managing the Entry into World Markets.* Baltimore, Md: Johns Hopkins University Press.

Salter, W.E.G. (1960). *Productivity and Technical Change,* Cambridge (Mass).

Scherer, F.M. (1982). "Inter-industry Technology Flows and Productivity Growth," *Review of Economics and Statistics,* Vol.64(4), November.

Solow, R.M. (1957). "Technical Change and Aggregate Production Function," *Review of Economics and Statistics,* August.

Srivastava, V. (1996) *'Liberalisation, Productivity and Competition, A Panel Study of Indian Manufacturing,* Oxford Univ. Press.

———. (2000). *The Impact of India's Economic Reforms on Industrial Productivity, Efficiency and Competitiveness* (Report of a project sponsored by the Industrial Development Bank of India), National Council of Applied Economic Research, New Delhi.

Terleckyj, N.E. (1974). *Effect of R&D on Productivity Growth of Industries: An Exploratory Study,* Washington: National Planning Association.

Trivedi, P., Prakash, A. and D. Sinate (2000). "Productivity in Major Manufacturing Industries in India: 1973-74 to 1997-98," *Development Research Group Study No. 20,* Department of Economic Analysis and Policy, Reserve Bank of India, Mumbai.

Tsao, Y. (1985). "Growth Without Productivity: Singapore Manufacturing in the 1970s," *Journal of Development Economics,* Vol.19, 25-38.

Tybout, James R., and M. Daniel Westbrook (1995). "Trade Liberalisation and Dimensions of Efficiency Change in Mexican Manufacturing Industries." *Journal of International Economics* 31 (August): 53-78.

Urata, S. and K. Yokota (1994). "Trade Liberalization and Productivity Growth in Thailand," *The Developing Economics,* Vol.xxxii-4, 444-59.

Verdoorn, J.P. (1949). *'Fattori Che Regolano lo Svilluppo Della Productivita Del Lavaro", L'Industia."*

World Bank (1993). *The East Asian Miracle: Economic Growth and Public Policy.* New York: Oxford University Press for the World Bank.

Yanrui Wu (1995) "Productivity Growth, Technological Progress, and Technical Efficiency Change in China: A Three-Sector Analysis," *Journal of Comparative Economics 21,* 207-209.

6

Domestic Capacity Utilisation and Import of Capital Goods: Substitutes or Complementary?

Evidence From Indian Capital Goods Sector

ABDUL AZEEZ E.

SECTION 1

INTRODUCTION

A new technology usually gets embodied in capital goods. Therefore import of capital goods is often considered as import of technology. However, 'while access to new knowledge is a positive factor for future growth, it should be clearly recognised that accompanied by liberalisation of imports of capital goods on a significant scale, domestic costs of production are unlikely to come down if the imports act largely as substitutes for domestic production' (Chakravarty, 1987 p.66). Following this view, the improvement in the growth of capital goods imports in India in the phase of stagnant domestic production during the eighties is often attributed to the substitution of domestic production by imports (Singh and Ghosh, 1988, Chandrashekhar, 1992). Comparing the growth rates of imports and domestic production of capital goods, Chandrasekhar concludes that the liberal policy sphere has led to increased excess capacity in the sector.[1] That is, the import liberalisation policy has affected the domestic production adversely, imposing a social cost in the form of unutilised capacity in the sector.[2]

1. "The different components of capital goods sector which had registered rather creditable growth rates during the late-1970s and early-1980s recorded a sharp fall in rates of growth to just 4.1-6.8 per cent in 1984-85 and 0.5-10 per cent in 1985-86 as compared to 6.2-14.1 per cent during 1983-84" (Chandrasekhar, 1992).
2. The basic argument is that an increase in capital goods import will cause a drop in demand for domestically produced capital goods resulting in a reduction in domestic capacity utilisation, making the domestic firms to operate at high unit cost of production.

This problem, however, is not seriously addressed since the initiation of the liberal policy reforms. With the introduction of new industrial policy in 1991, the capital goods sector has attained significant importance in terms of import liberalisation. Therefore, it is important to examine what is the current role of import of capital goods in domestic production. As is tentatively noted by Rangarajan (1995), one may also think of the possibility of having a complementary relationship between import of capital goods and the domestic capital goods. This could happen if the capital goods imports are such that they enhance the productivity of domestic capital goods.

Earlier attempts in this line agree on the fact that the imports of capital goods influence the unit cost of domestic production of capital goods. This makes it important to examine the relationship between import of capital goods and the economic capacity utilisation. Economic capacity utilisation refers to the realisation of optimal output (Cassel, 1937; Hickman, 1964).[3] The present paper is an attempt to examine the proposition that '...increased imports (of capital goods) will evolve a syndrome of lower rates of domestic capacity utilisation....' (Singh and Ghosh, 1988 p.86). For this purpose a theoretically consistent and empirically relevant capacity utilisation series is estimated and is compared with the import of capital goods in the Indian non-electrical machinery manufacturing sector over the period 1985-97.

The paper is organised in five sections. Section 2 presents briefly the importance and growth of capital goods sector over years. Section 3 presents the methodology used for estimating the economic capacity utilisation. Section 4 demonstrates a detailed analysis of the data on the import and domestic capacity utilisation, drawing attention to the accepted wisdom on substitution of capital goods import and domestic production. The paper is concluded in the final section 5.

SECTION 2

THE CAPITAL GOODS SECTOR IN INDIA

Capital goods sector, being the corner stone of industrial development, gained pivotal status in planning for industrialisation

3. Optimal output is defined as the output where the firms' short run average total cost is minimised.

in India. Since the Second Five-Year Plan, the sector has been given strategic importance in industrialising the country. In order to boost the capacity to invest and come out of external dependence, the planning design was to raise the capacity for fabricating capital goods domestically. This resulted in building up of a capital goods base for the economy[4] and in making the country largely self-sufficient in the production of capital goods (Chakravarty, 1987). As the export promotion policies were slowly initiated since mid-sixties, export of capital goods started to pick up gradually (Rath and Sahoo, 1990). However, the sector has failed to become internationally competitive despite the higher scale of production achieved over the years (Mundle and Mukhopadhyay, 1992).

The state-dominated policy within the high protective barriers has disappeared partly by the initiation of liberal policy regime in late-eighties and fully by the introduction of new industrial policy in early-nineties. The rationale for these changes were provided under the analytical underpinnings of traditional trade theory, demonstrating that free trade is the best policy under certain conditions. The sector has got further significance in the new industrial policy regime, particularly regarding import liberalisation. Most of the capital goods industries fall in the list of industries for automatic approval of foreign technology agreements and for 51 per cent foreign equity participation. It accounts for 38 pert cent of total FDI flow to the country after 1991 (Subramanian *et al.*, 1996).

The output and value added share of capital goods in total manufacturing has increased from 11 per cent in 1960 to around 19 per cent in 1997 and the sector has been growing at an annual average rate of 7 per cent over the last twenty years. Among the three major components of the capital goods sector the non-electrical machinery manufacturing[5] constitutes one-third of total output. This sector shows a similar pattern in the movement of both imports and domestic production as in aggregate capital goods sector (appendix Figure A-6.1). Therefore, being a good representation of capital goods sector, we analyse the economic capacity utilisation and its relationship with import of capital goods in this sector.

4. The sector registered its peak growth rate during the initial years of planning (during 1956-65 the growth rate in terms of net value added was 12.7).

5. This sector includes ten three-digit industries, according to ASI classification.

SECTION 3

ECONOMIC CAPACITY UTILISATION

The Concept and Measurement

Capacity Utilisation (CU) has been generally defined as the ratio of actual output to capacity or potential output. While potential output can broadly be defined as the maximum possible output given the level of inputs and technology, there is little consensus on its measurement. Most studies in the context of India are based on the engineering notion of capacity, i.e. the output that may be produced given the level of plant and machinery, using the installed capacity data. Such a measure of capacity is subject to serious criticism for lacking theoretical foundation[6]. Economists, on the other hand, recognise that potential output "is conditioned in most cases by economic circumstances and must be interpreted as being the 'optimum output' from the economic point of view". Cassel (1937) and Hickman (1964) define it as the output (Y*) at which the short run average total cost curve reaches its minimum. This definition of economic capacity, which exhibits the unit cost conditions of firms, is accepted for our study.

Estimation of optimal level of output is carried out by employing a translog short run cost function following Berndt and Hesse (1986). We assume the stock of capital available to the industry as a quasi-fixed input so that the industry attempts to minimise its variable cost of producing a given output (Y) conditional to a given size of plant (K). Assuming a translog functional form, the variable cost function can be written as,

$$\ln VC = \alpha_0 + \alpha_i \sum_{i=1}^{n} \ln P_i + \frac{1}{2} \sum_{i=1}^{n} \alpha_{ij} \ln P_i \ln P_j + \beta_Y \ln Y + \frac{1}{2}\beta_{YY} (\ln Y)^2 + \sum_{i=1}^{n} \beta_{Yi} \ln Y \ln P_i + \gamma_K \ln K + \frac{1}{2} \gamma_{KK} (\ln K)^2 + \sum_{i=1}^{n} \gamma_{Ki} \ln K \ln P_i + \gamma_{KY} \ln K \ln Y + \delta_T T + \frac{1}{2} \delta_{TT} T^2 + \sum_{i=1}^{n} \delta_{Ti} T \ln P_i + \delta_{TK} T \ln K + \delta_{TY} T \ln Y \quad ...(1)$$

6. See Christiano (1981) for a review of different measures and associated problems.

Where *VC* is the total variable cost and P_i represents the vector of variable input prices; i = labour (*L*), fuel (*F*), and material (*M*). *Y, K and T* are respectively gross output (not value added), capital stock and a time variable to capture the disembodied technical change. (See appendix for more details on data and variables).

The above equation is estimated simultaneously with the input share equations. The share equations are included in the model in order to incorporate the economic optimisation behaviour of firms. The economic measure of capacity output (Y^*) and utilisation ($CU \equiv Y/Y^*$) are defined in terms of short run average total cost (SATC) which includes both average total variable cost and average total fixed cost. The total fixed costs are defined as the expenditures on the fixed input, capital. Then the short run average total cost, SATC is $(VC/Y) + (C_k/Y)$, where C_k is the cost on capital. If Y* is defined as the minimum point on SATC, then, ∂SATC/ ∂Y* = 0, i.e.,[7]

$$\frac{\partial \, SATC}{\partial \, Y^*} = VC(\mu_Y - 1) - C_K = 01 \qquad ...(2)$$

Where μ_y and *VC* are functions of both *ln Y** and *Y** and therefore, it is not possible to obtain an analytical or closed model solution for *Y** in (2). Then the estimate of CU will be the ratio of Y to Y*.

Estimated Results

Our model gives a system of four equations, one variable cost function and three share equations, which constitute a seemingly unrelated regression model that can be used to estimate the parameters. The estimation is carried out using an iterative version of the Zellner's Seemingly Unrelated Regression Estimates (SURE) technique. The estimated coefficients of the variable cost function are presented in appendix Table A-6.1. The R-square values for the variable cost function, fuel share equation and material share equations are respectively, 0.98, 0.35 and 0.63. The imposed restrictions are tested using the Wald statistic, which follow a Chi-square distribution. The χ^2 value is significantly high (661.53). However, a cost function is well behaved only if it is concave in input prices and if its input share functions are positive. The translog function doesn't satisfy these restrictions globally and therefore we

7. See appendix for the derivation of equation.

have to confirm it at each observation. It is found that the estimated variable cost shares are positive at all observations, thereby satisfying the first order condition (or postitivity) globally. The second order condition (concavity) is satisfied if the Hessian matrix based on the parameter estimates is negative semidefinite; it is also satisfied at all observations. Hence we conclude that the cost function corresponds to a well-behaved production structure.

Table 6.1

Average Growth of Output and Net Import

Year	Non-electrical		Capital Goods	
	Output	Net-Import	Output	Net-Import
1985-90	7.07	3.10	9.49	5.73
1991-97	8.77	14.1	9.87	14.71

Source: Annual Survey of Industries, RBI currency and finance.

Figure 6.1

CU and Imports of Capital Goods

Non-Electrical Machinery, 1985-97

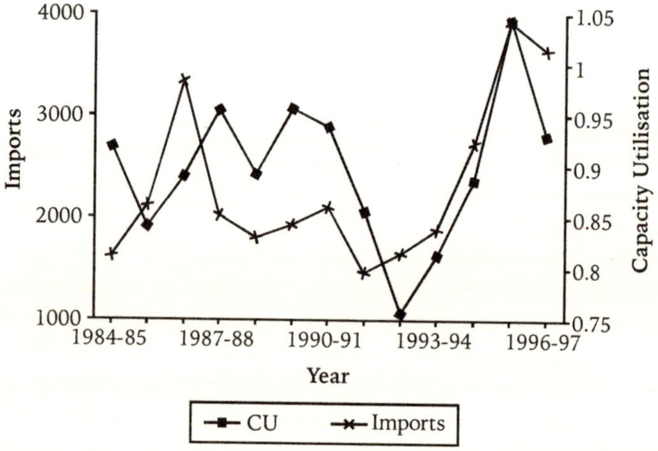

Since a closed form solution is not feasible, we use the iterative procedure for solving the equation (2) for potential output. The estimated optimal CU figures are plotted in Figure 6.1. Capacity utilisation varies between 0.75 and 1.02 over the period 1985-97 (coefficient of variation is only 7.8). The movements in the CU, however, are in accordance with the ups and downs in the economy, depending on the cost and production conditions. After a significant drop in nineties, following the general recession in the economy, the sector registered an improvement in CU after 1993. Let us now move on to the issue of relationship between these movements of economic CU and import of capital goods.

SECTION 4

IMPORT OF CAPITAL GOODS AND DOMESTIC CAPACITY UTILISATION

The prevailing view is that the import of capital goods[8] is having an adverse impact on the domestic capital goods sector due to the substitution effect (Singh and Ghosh, 1988, Chandrasekhar, 1992). However, there is a contrasting view that import of capital goods will enhance the domestic production due to the complementarity between the two. To quote Rangarajan (1995 p. 553), "Import of capital goods rose buoyantly highlighting the strong complementarity between the pattern of industrial recovery and the spurt in import demand, dispelling the traditional expectation of trade off between domestic production and imports." Let us examine these propositions empirically using the economically relevant CU ratios and import of non-electrical machinery over 1985-97.

Following the policy changes, let us divide the whole period of analysis into two - the partial liberalisation period, 1985-90 and an accelerated second phase of 1991-97. In the first phase, we do not find one to one relationship. While in the initial years they show a diverging trend, in the proceeding years they move in the same direction. Again in 1986-87, even with a significant decline in imports, the CU moves up, but after that they move in the same direction. The growth rates of imports and domestic production also do not show any divergent result. However, as the inverse movements are dominating and are more significant, one may argue that there are possibilities of substitution of domestic production by imports in the 80s. Singh and Ghosh, (1988 p.86) argues that the

8. Import of capital goods are equally important as that of domestic production for remodelling the domestic technologies.

"increased imports will involve a syndrome of lower rates of domestic capacity utilisation and lower levels of production, in which imports, by eating into the domestic market, reduce domestic production, thereby increasing per unit cost and thereby rendering domestic industry less competitive, which therefore leads to more imports". This may be valid, as we observe drop in CU in the phase of increasing imports for some years. However, this cannot be attributed solely to the liberalisation policies as the period is characterised only by partial liberalisation.

In the second period, we have a vivid picture. Following the liberal policy regime there is considerable improvement in the import of non-electrical machinery. Except the negative growth in 1991-92, which is followed by a negative growth in domestic production too, in all the five years import show a positive growth rate.

There is a clear pattern in the movement of both import and domestic CU, and thereby domestic production. In almost all the years they move in the same direction. Even if we take the growth rates of import and domestic production (Figure 6.2) the picture is the same. This implies that the import of capital goods cannot be considered as a substitute for domestic production. Rather it could be

Figure 6.2

Growth of Domestic PDN. & Imports

Non-Electrical Machinery, 1985-97

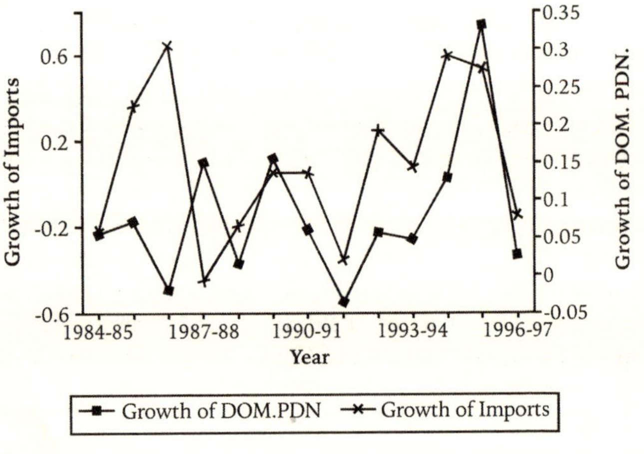

a complementary that supports and enhances the domestic firm to utilise its capacity more and thereby to increase production.

However, an important issue to be noted when considering the import of non-electrical machinery as complementary to domestic CU is the fact that this happens amidst an increasing market share of imports. The average market share of imports in total sale of non-electrical machinery in the domestic market has increased from 16 per cent in 1992 to 26 per cent in 1996 (Appendix Table A-6.2). This implies that the share of domestic output in the domestic market has come down. It may appear to be puzzling that how could the import of non-electrical machinery enhance the domestic production of the same, and at the same time increase the market share of imports. The reason could be, as in most of the earlier studies we consider only import and domestic production, ignoring the presence of exports. Export of non-electrical machinery is also increasing in recent years. Therefore, when examining the relationship between domestic capacity utilisation and import, one may have to consider the net imports. Interestingly, the evidences show the same results (Figure 6.3), reinforcing our observation that import of capital goods is complementary to domestic CU and production of non-electrical machinery. The evidences from CMIE reported companies further

Figure 6.3

CU and Net Imports of Capital Goods

Non-Electrical Machinery, 1985-97

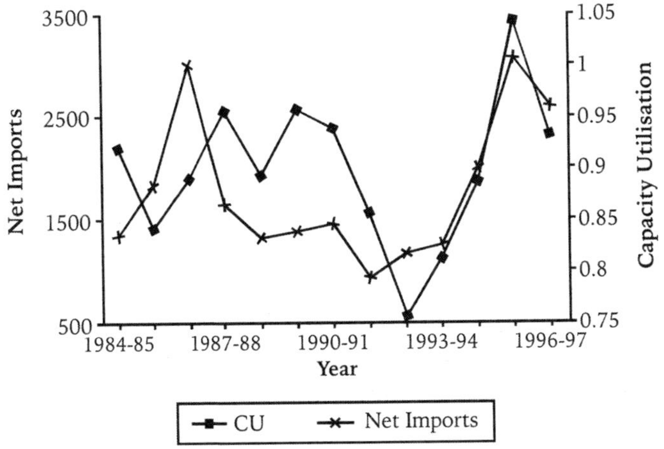

support it. It is found that the share of capital goods import in gross fixed asset of non-electrical machinery industry is increasing recently (Table 6.2). The import intensity of export is almost constant hovering around two. Thus there is a clear case to argue that utilisation of domestic capacity in non-electrical machinery producing sector is having a complementary relationship with import of capital goods.

Table 6.2

Share of Capital Goods Import in GFA and Import Intensity of Exports, Non-electrical Machinery

Year	*Share of Capital Goods in GFA*	*Import Intensity of Exports*
1992-93	18.3	1.92
1993-94	13.8	1.81
1994-95	16.9	1.79
1995-96	21.7	1.99
1996-97	26.0	1.82

Source: CMIE.

A comparison of domestic production of capital goods (not capacity utilisation) and imports, at aggregate capital goods sector (Appendix Figure A-6.1) also show the same relationship. Thus we may argue that the scenario of substitution of domestic production by imports in the eighties have given way to a complementary relationship between the two in the nineties.

SECTION 5

CONCLUSION

In the present study we made an attempt to estimate economic capacity utilisation for Indian non-electrical machinery manufacturing sector using a translog short-run cost function. This measure of CU captures the optimisation behaviour of firms associated with the minimum unit cost of production. A comparison of the estimated CU ratios with the import of capital goods shows that the capital goods imports have shifted away from a substitute, in the eighties to a complementary one, that enhance the domestic capacity utilisation in the nineties. However, the study warrants further analysis of the same at a more disaggregated level.

APPENDIX

Data and Variables

We use the time series data for the Indian non-electrical machinery manufacturing sector over 1974-96, for the estimation of cost function. However, our period of analysis is confined to 1985-97 only. The data has been collected from various issues of the Annual Survey of Industries (ASI). The variables used are the following.

Output: Gross value of output deflated by the wholesale price index for non-electrical machinery products is used. The choice of gross output measure overcomes the controversies on the method of calculation and the validity of separability assumptions for the use of value added.

Capital Stock: A perpetual inventory method is followed to construct consistent capital stock series. A benchmark estimate of capital stock for 1960 is calculated using the data from 1947 to 1960 making required adjustments for age structure. Then a perpetual inventory component is added to this benchmark estimate.

Capital Cost: The gross operating surplus after adjusting for emoluments and profits is used. Note that the sum of labour and capital cost is identically equal to gross value added at factor cost.[9]

Labour Cost and Wage Rate: The value of total emoluments is considered as the labour cost and the total emoluments divided by number of employees as the wage rate.

Price and Total Cost of Fuel: The value of total expenditure on fuel is used. For the price of fuel, we construct a composite price by combining prices of different components of total fuel consumed by the non-electrical machinery industries. The input components were grouped according to the availability of wholesale price indices and are clubbed into a single price using the appropriate weights, weights having been calculated from the input output transaction matrix, 1989-90.

---

9. However, a high gross operating surplus does not make it less profitable to employ more capital, as pointed out by Prof. J.S. Cubbin. There exists some skepticism on whether the capital cost is sufficiently exogenous or not, however, the absence of any other better data makes us to rely on this.

Price and Total Cost of Material: The value of total purchase of materials is used. For constructing the material price we follow the same procedure as in the case of fuel.

Imports and Exports: Data on exports and imports in US $ million for non-electrical machinery sector, published by Reserve Bank of India, Report on Currency and Finance is used.

Derivation of Potential Output From Cost Function

Any well-behaved variable cost function must be homogenous of degree one in prices. For the translog function this requires the following parameter restrictions:

a) $\Sigma\alpha_i = 1$, b) $\Sigma\alpha_{ij} = \Sigma\alpha_{ji} = 0$, c) $\Sigma\beta_{Yi} = 0$, d) $\Sigma\gamma_{Ki} = 0$,

For the empirical implementation it is useful to employ additional equalities that reflect economic optimising behaviour. Using Shephard's lemma, the variable cost share equation is obtained by logarithmically differentiating the variable cost equation with respect to the exogenous variable, input price P_i, given K and Y.[10]

$$\frac{\delta \ln VC}{\delta \ln P_i} = \alpha_i + \sum_{j=1}^{n} {}_j\,\alpha_{ij} \ln P_j + \beta_{Yi} \ln Y + \gamma_{Ki} \ln K + + \delta_{Ti} T = \mu_i{}^2$$

Where μ_i is the cost share of i th input.

Since the average total cost, SATC = (VC/Y) + (C_k /Y), where C_k is the cost of capital. If the potential output Y = Y* is defined at the point where SATC is minimised, then (∂SATC/∂Y*) = 0, which implies that

$$(1/Y^*)(\partial VC/\partial Y^*) - (VC/Y^{*2}) - (C_k/Y^{*2}) = 0 \qquad \text{(A)}$$

Since ∂ln VC/∂ln Y* = (∂VC/∂Y*)(Y*/VC), the required estimate of ∂VC/∂Y* is

(∂ln VC/∂ln Y*)(VC/Y*), where

$$\frac{\delta \ln VC}{\delta \ln Y^*} = \beta_Y + \beta_{YY} \ln Y^* + \sum_{i=1}^{n} {}_i\,\beta_{Yi} \ln P_i + \gamma_{KY} \ln K + \delta_{TY} T = \mu_Y{}^3$$

10. Following Shepherd's lemma, $\partial C/\partial P_i = X_i$; $\partial \ln C/\partial \ln P_i = P_i i X_i/C = \mu_i$, where Pi is the price of i-th input (X_i) and μ_i is its cost share.

Then, $(\partial VC)/(\partial Y^*) = \mu y\ (VC/Y^*)$, substituting in (A) we obtain

$(1/Y^*)\ \mu y(VC/Y^*) - (VC/Y^{*2}) - (Ck/Y^{*2}) = 0$

$= \mu y(VC/Y^{*2}) - (VC/Y^{*2}) - (Ck/Y^{*2}) = 0$

$= (VC/Y^{*2})[\mu y - 1] - (Ck/Y^{*2}) = 0$

$= VC(\mu y - 1) - Ck = 0$

Solving this equation we can obtain the optimal output (Y^*)

Appendix Table A-6.1

Seemingly Unrelated Regression Estimates for Translog Cost Function

Parameter	*Estimates*	*t-statistic*	*Parameter*	*Estimates*	*t-statistic*
α_0	-0.2041	(-8.45)	γ_{KF}	0.3067	(1.69)
α_F	0.0514	(3.24)	γ_{KM}	-0.3142	(-1.78)
α_M	0.7332	(47.10)	γ_{KY}	-11.7040	(-12.27)
α_{FF}	0.0248	(1.50)	δ_T	0.3791	(15.39)
α_{MM}	0.0581	(2.96)	δ_{TT}	-0.3215	(-20.04)
α_{FM}	0.0011	(0.02)	δ_{TF}	-0.0187	(-1.65)
β_Y	-0.6061	(-8.08)	δ_{TM}	0.0227	(2.05)
β_{YY}	6.2827	(8.15)	δ_{TK}	4.2446	(19.78)
β_{YF}	-0.0476	(-0.91)	δ_{TY}	0.3981	(7.77)
β_{YM}	0.0787	(2.52)	DW (VC)	2.31	
γ_K	-4.0313	(-11.13)	DW (μ_f)	1.91	
γ_{KK}	-49.9350	(-17.58)	DW (μ_m)	1.67	

Note: DW indicates Durbin Watson Statistic.

Appendix Table A-6.2

Market Shares of Import, Non-elect Machinery

Year⇒	*1992-93*	*1993-94*	*1994-95*	*1995-96*	*1996-97*	*1997-98*
Agri. Machinery	12.40	9.48	14.81	12.12	12.48	6.80
Tractors	0.07	0.08	0.09	0.22	0.13	0.11
Mining Machinery	38.21	59.32	62.42	52.35	65.97	75.99
Earth Moving Mach.	1.79	1.49	1.75	2.93	2.38	3.19
Construction Mach.	0.27	8.35	4.98	8.34	10.08	8.24
Material Handling	9.05	5.64	12.13	22.54	33.82	26.98
Cranes	9.51	17.04	23.36	32.25	34.45	38.85
Lifts & Escalators	0.03	0.11	0.68	0.98	5.43	9.36
Dairy Mach.	13.01	17.08	25.73	12.37	8.93	27.93
Textile Mach.	47.80	57.76	62.11	66.12	65.95	67.48
Chemical Mach.	0.00	0.00	0.00	0.00	0.00	0.00
Rubber Mach.	36.29	45.03	54.82	53.71	37.09	42.49
Plastic Mach.	29.29	44.65	62.32	77.20	68.08	73.45
Printing Mach.	43.04	59.04	69.24	83.16	73.88	87.68
Packaging Mach.	0.00	0.00	0.00	0.00	0.00	0.00
Cement Mach.	0.59	0.35	3.51	1.93	0.38	0.56
Sugar Mach.	0.00	0.08	1.50	0.17	0.00	0.01
Metallurgical Mach.	39.38	35.89	43.54	50.74	74.97	62.58
Environment Control	0.00	0.00	2.11	3.29	4.46	3.22
Machine Tools	27.13	32.44	31.96	41.21	46.43	40.55
Sewing Mach.	58.63	64.80	64.33	63.44	55.64	59.68
Drilling Eqpt.	5.90	5.99	3.53	7.93	7.28	4.93
Fire Protection Eqpt.	0.05	3.44	1.34	1.87	0.98	0.46
Motors & Generator	13.08	10.80	26.76	37.67	26.74	27.47
Average	16.06	19.95	23.88	26.36	26.48	27.83

Appendix Figure A-6.1

Net Imports

Capital Goods and Non-Elect. Machinery, 1985-97

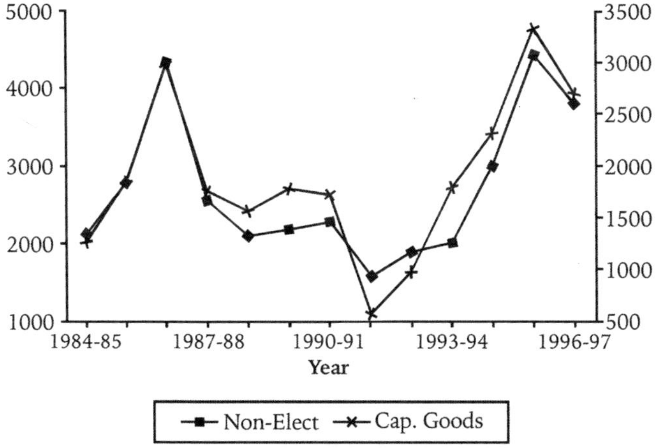

Appendix Figure A-6.2

Growth of Net Imports and Output

Capital Goods, 1985-97

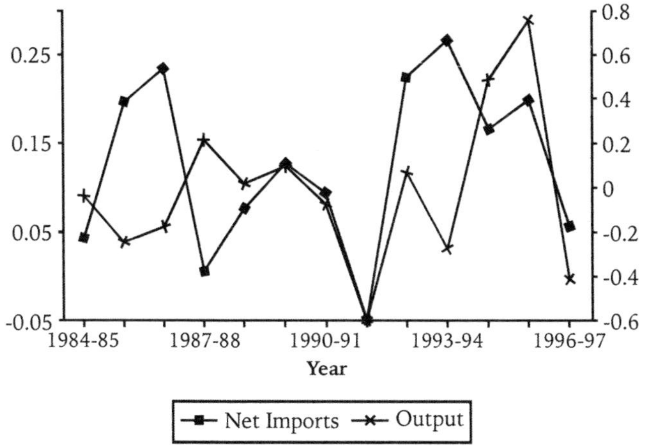

References

Berndt, E.R, and Hesse, D.M. (1986). "Measuring and Assessing Capacity Utilisation in the Manufacturing Sectors of Nine OECD Countries," *European Economic Review*, 30, pp. 961-989.

Cassel, J.M. (1937). "Excess Capacity and Monopolistic Competition," *Quarterly Journal of Economics*, 51, pp. 426-443.

Centre for Monitoring Indian Economy, (1999). *"Industry: Trends in Market Shares,"* CMIE, Mumbai.

Chakravarty, S. (1987). *"Development Planning: The Indian Experience,"* New Delhi, Oxford University Press.

Chandrashekhar, C.P. (1992). "Investment Behaviour, Economies of Scale and Efficiency in an Import-Substituting Regime: A Study of Two Industries," in Ghosh, A. *et al.*(ed), *"Indian Industrialisation, Structure and Policy Issues"*, New Delhi, Oxford University Press.

Christiano, L.J. (1981). "A Survey of Measures of Capacity Utilisation," *IMF Staff Papers*, 28, pp.144-99.

Government of India, *"Annual Survey of Industries,"* various issues.

Hickman, B.G. (1964). "On a new method of capacity estimation," *Journal of American Statistical Association,"* 59, pp. 529-549.

Klein, L.R. (1960). "Some Theoretical Issues in the Measurement of Capacity," *Econometrica*, 28(2), pp.272-86.

Mundle, Sudipto and H. Mukhopadhyay (1992). " Protecting Growth and Competitiveness: Study of Indian Capital Goods Industry," *Economic and Political Weekly*, Vol. XXVII, No. 9, February 29.

Rangarajan, C. (1995). "Prospects for Balance of Payments," *Reserve Bank of India Bulletin* June, pp. 553-56.

Rath, D., and Sahoo, A. (1990). "India's Export of Capital Good: An Evaluation," *Economic and Political Weekly*, 25, 1897-1904.

Reserve Bank of India, *Report on Currency and Finance*, various issues.

Singh, A, and Ghosh, J. (1988). "Import Liberalisation and the New Industrial Strategy: An Analysis of their Impact on Output and Employment in the Indian Economy" *Asian Employment Program Working Paper*, New Delhi.

Subramanian, K.K., *et al.*, (1996). *Foreign Collaboration under Liberalisation Policy: Pattern of FDI and Technology Transfer in Indian Industry Since 1991*, Mumbai, Reserve Bank of India, Department of Economic and Analysis and Policy"

Zellner, A. (1962). "An Efficient Method of Estimating Seemingly Unrelated Regression and Tests for Aggregation Bias," *Journal of the American Statistical Association*, 57 (298), pp.348-68.

Part 2

Urbanisation, Employment and Infrastructural Issues for Indian Industries

7

Industrialisation, Urbanisation and Poverty

EDWIN S. MILLS

SECTION 1
INTRODUCTION

This paper attempts to bring together in coherent form prominent facts and theories about the relationships among industrialisation, urbanisation and poverty reduction. I try to fit India into the story.[1]

Most census definitions of urban areas are that they are high-density collections of at least 5,000 or so residents in which most resident workers are employed in non-agricultural sectors. The rural-urban distinction is in part one of convenience. Rural densities in India and Korea exceed many urban densities in the United States. But urban densities exceed rural densities in all countries. In India and some other countries, some agricultural workers and their families live in villages, but they are unlikely to be counted as urban. Thus, relative density and sector of employment are both crucial to the urban definition.

The only advantage of high density or urban areas is proximity among diverse people and organisations. High densities permit diverse workers to be close to diverse jobs, consumers to be close to retailers, businesses to be close to trading partners, and both people and businesses to be close to local and long distance transportation and communication nodes and to government and non-profit

1. Until recently there was a danger that development economics would be predominantly about India. Not only is India the longest and best functioning democracy among developing counties, but also it is one of the world's best documented and best studied countries, and has been for a century. It is a completely open country where the worst penalty for saying or writing what one thinks is being ignored. Finally, it has the advantage to semi-literate foreigners that nearly all data and vast amounts of scholarly and other writing are available in English, the world's most imperialist language.

facilities. Large numbers of people and businesses, and both local and long distance transportation and communication nodes enable businesses to produce at large scales to take advantage of scale and scope economies. If there were no scale or scope economies or if transportation and communication were costless, there would be no urban areas. Even if there were scale and scope economies, if transportation and communication were free, then production would be geographically concentrated, but workers and consumers would live at uniform densities to avoid residential patterns that would make land values higher than necessary. In practice, the advantages of proximate locations justify land values and rents near the centres of large urban areas that may be 10 to 100 times as great as those 25 to 50 kilometers away, at or beyond the periphery of the urban area.

The interactions among scale and scope economies, proximity, land values and land uses provide a key to understanding the sizes and spatial structures or urban areas. I will try to use these interactions to understand the facts about urban development.

SECTION 2

DEMOGRAPHIC BACKGROUND

A nation's population growth equals its urban plus rural growth. Although low-income country population growth rates are still about 25 per cent greater than world rates, the demographic revolution has reduced both world and low-income country population growth rates by nearly half during the last quarter of the 20th century. India's decline in population growth rate has been about the same as that of average declines in low-income countries. A few countries are already experiencing modest population declines, and many more will, at current total fertility rates, after the worldwide bulge of women born in the 1950s and 1960s passes through childbearing ages. (*See* World Bank (2000) and Becker and Morrison in Cheshire and Mills, eds. (1999)).

Urban birth (and death) rates have long been a little lower than rural rates in most countries, but that now appears to be a minor matter. The demographic revolution has reduced both urban and rural population growth rates. The revolution has resulted from many changes, but improvement in the educations and labour force access of women appears to be prominent, generally increasing the opportunity cost of large families, as well as enabling women to become better informed about their options and improving their decision-making capabilities within families.

Urbanisation has long had at least some tendency to reduce birth rates in developing countries. Urban women have better access than rural women to education and to paid jobs, as well as to devices and instructions for birth control. The result of the demographic revolution, and of other changes, has been to reduce total and urban population growth rates and to change the part of urban growth rates that is accounted for by natural population growth. In India, natural urban population growth fell from 66 to 59 per cent of total urban population growth from 1970-1980 to 1990-1995. (*See* Becker and Morrison (1999)).

It appears not to be known to what extent, if any, recent slowing of rural/urban migration results from rising rural relative to urban incomes. It seems unlikely. More likely is a demographic effect. Much rural/urban migration is associated with education and takes place among 15-25 year olds. Lower birth rates after about 1970 must have reduced the percentage of rural people in that age range, at least in many developing countries, since the late-1980s.

Few people doubt that slower population growth is beneficial, especially in a densely populated and low-income country such as India. There are two specific effects of slower urban population growth and rural/urban migration rates that most people would regard as beneficial. First, slower urban growth rates reduce the need for rapid urban infrastructure and housing expansion. Second, many rural/urban migrants are the poorest and least well educated people in some urban areas, and slower migration presumably reduces the amount of poverty, alienation, squatting and malnutrition in urban areas. A qualification is that reduced migration is a clear benefit only if there are fewer desperate rural residents, and not if they are simply remaining in rural areas, for whatever reason. Despite the fantasies of middle class urban residents, in the United States, India and elsewhere, evidence is overwhelming that poor migrants improve their living standards and those of their children when they voluntarily migrate to urban areas. Everyone makes mistakes, but large numbers of people do not persistently behave in ways that make them worse off.

SECTION 3

INDUSTRIALISATION AND URBANISATION[2]

Industry consists of manufacturing, mining, construction and what are referred to as infrastructure or capital intensive services such as provision of gas, electricity, piped water and liquid waste disposal. In some countries, including India equipment repair is included in the industrial sector. In others, such as the United States, equipment repair is included in the service sector.

The percentage of the labour force that is in industry varies from two or three in the poorest sub-Saharan African countries to 35 or 45 in some industrialised countries. But the share is by no means monotonic in stage of development. Industry's labour force share is lower in many of the highest income countries than in some more recently industrialised countries.

Industry's labour force share is about 50 per cent greater than manufacturing's share in many countries, and manufacturing's share has fallen in many high-income countries during recent decades.

Industry's value added share is 50 to 75 per cent greater than its labour force share in many developing countries. In India, industry's value added share is more than twice its labour force share. The basic reason is of course that industry is much more capital intensive than other sectors, indicating, as does other evidence, that industrial sector production functions have substitution elasticities between capital and labour that are less than one. In addition, industrial sectors in many countries receive special government protection, resulting in wages that are higher relative to workers' opportunity costs than in other sectors, even if adjustment is made for worker qualifications.

Manufacturing and other industrial sectors primarily locate in urban areas. In all such sectors, the reasons are the same as those for all sectors: proximity to inputs and customers. In manufacturing, a diverse labour force and financial, legal and government services are important. At least factory manufacturing sells most of its outputs, and buys large amounts of its material inputs, outside the urban area where it is located. For that reason, manufacturing tends to locate near inter-urban transport nodes, often near harbours and railheads

---

2. On the subject of this section, see Mills and Mitra (1996).

or, if the inter-urban road system is adequate, in metropolitan suburbs. In the United States, manufacturing increasingly, since the 1950s, has moved not only to metropolitan suburbs but also outside metropolitan areas altogether. Manufacturing facilities can be seen strung along rural stretches of our interstate highway system. In countries such as India, where the inter-urban road system is poor, manufacturing locates nearer centres of large urban areas. Government attempts to force or induce manufacturing to locate very far from large urban areas are doomed to frustration.

Twenty or thirty years ago a remarkable number of large urban areas in developing countries had 25 to 40 per cent of their workers in manufacturing. That is no longer common, mostly because rapid productivity growth has reduced manufacturing's employment share in many countries, but also because improvements in inter-urban area transportation and communications have resulted in at least some dispersal to smaller urban areas, where land and labour costs are lower.

Arthur Lewis (1978) argued that governments should avoid locating infrastructure in large urban areas because much infrastructure capital had to be imported and high land values made infrastructure unduly expensive. The argument is without merit. Infrastructure should be located where its benefits are large relative to its costs. Although land values are high in large urban areas, infrastructure is more productive in such areas because high densities imply that costs per user are lower than in smaller places. For example, in the U.S. and many developing countries, road costs per vehicle/kilometer of travel are lower in large than in small urban areas because roads are much more intensively used in large places (World Bank (1994)).

In addition, infrastructure benefits are spatially bounded. Typically, benefits are capitalised in land values. To the extent that the investments are justified, taxes on the land values generated or fees charged to beneficiaries can finance the assets. Private or decentralised government provision can introduce an element of competition in infrastructure service provision, thus limiting the demand for infrastructure that will be paid for by people and businesses other than its beneficiaries. In the U.S., for example, the assumption by the national government of financial responsibility for most capital costs of local public transit has resulted in strong demands for such systems by local governments even though total benefits are small relative to costs. The local term is "pork barrel" expenditures. The same phenomenon exists in all countries in which local populations can influence national or provincial governments that have assumed responsibility for projects whose benefits are mostly local.

Although the worldwide correlation between per cent of employment or value added in industry or manufacturing and the per cent of population living in urban areas is substantial, the correlation between per cent employed in non-agricultural sectors and per cent urban is much higher (*See* Mills and Becker (1986)). That is hardly surprising, since virtually all non-agricultural sectors locate predominantly in urban areas in most countries. It also attests to the size and diversity of the service sector, which includes both providers of menial informal sector services and extremely well paid consultants, attorneys and other professionals, including the attendees at this conference. In the U.S. and, I suspect, most countries, service sectors are even more urbanised than industrial sectors. The reason is probably that face-to-face and related electronic communication are more important among specialised service sector firms than among industrial firms. You can invest your money halfway around the world almost as quickly as you can invest it in your hometown, but both parties to the transaction are likely to be in large urban areas in either case. In addition, electronic and face-to-face communication appear to be complementary. (*See* Gasper and Glaeser (1998)). Many business phone calls are local and between workers who also have face-to-face contact. The phenomenal growth of "business centres" in hotels which out-of-town business people visit for face-to-face communication with local workers also attests to complementarity between electronic and face-to-face communication. An enormous amount of cell phone usage appears to be between people who recently have, or shortly will, meet, for either business or social purposes. Electronic communication may contribute to the dispersal or sub-urbanisation of economic activity, but it seems unlikely that it will slow the pace of urban growth, in either low or high income countries.

It is well known that real earnings per worker in urban areas exceed those in rural areas. In developing countries, urban earnings may be two- to four times as great as rural earnings. The ratio is much lower in high income countries, and is probably not more than about 1.25 in the U.S. Several reasons have been identified for much higher urban than rural earnings in developing countries (*See* Pernia and Quibria in Cheshire and Mills (1999)). Urban workers are better educated and more skilled, and some urban sectors are simply higher productive than many agricultural and related sectors that predominate in rural areas. In addition, information flow about urban job opportunities is probably worse in developing countries. Rural-to-urban worker migration is an equilibrating process, although it is typically slow and imperfect. Urban-to-rural business migration is an equilibrating process in the U.S., but it is also slow and dependent on high quality rural transportation/communication facilities.

More subtle is the notion of agglomeration economies. There is by now persuasive evidence that an urban area's total factor productivity is an increasing function of the population or employment of the urban area. (*See* Eberts and McMillen in Cheshire and Mills (1999), and Shukla (1996)). A baker's dozen studies have been conducted with U.S. data and a few have been done with European and East Asian data.

Shukla (1996) is by far the most meticulous study that uses Indian data. Findings among studies that analyse data for urban areas of various sizes are remarkably consistent: each doubling of the population or employment of an urban area results in a 4–10 per cent increase in the urban area's total factor productivity. Commonsense suggests that the effect must dissipate for sufficiently large urban areas, but the subject has not been studied carefully. (*See* Shukla (1996)).

A related literature has analysed total factor productivity growth through time or among countries at the national or sectoral level. This subject is obviously related to the urban agglomeration literature, but the two sets of studies have proceeded independently. Indian data have been used prominently in such national or sectoral studies for at least two decades. K. L. Krishna made important early contributions to this subject (*See* Mitra (1999) for the most recent analysis and literature review). This subject is beyond the scope of this paper. I content myself with the observation that estimates with Indian data vary enormously by time period, by industrial sector and by level of aggregation. For an economy whose prominent characteristic is its stability, such variation is simply unbelievable. (*See* Becker, Williamson and Mills (1992), Hulten and Srinivasan (1999) and Mills and Mitra (1996)).

Where might agglomeration economies come from? Scale and/or scope economies of individual plants or firms is the easy answer and they are certainly part of the story. Large urban areas tend to have somewhat larger plants and firms than small urban areas, since markets for inputs and outputs are larger.

Much more complex is the notion that technology might depend on the numbers or sizes of plants in given sectors in an urban area. The phenomenon can be understood in two senses. First, a firm's total factor productivity might be greater, given its size in an urban area, the more or larger are other similar firms in the same urban area or sector. Second, a firm's total factor productivity might increase faster the more or larger are other similar firms in the same urban area. Both phenomena are suggested by the data.

Concentrations of both research and development and production among high tech electronic firms in Silicon Valley, Tsukuba, Bangalore, Pune, Hyderabad and many other centres around the world have been much written about and almost certainly illustrate both interpretations of technology and agglomeration economies.

In the U.S. and some other countries, biotech R&D and production also illustrate a close relationship between basic and applied science, engineering and production. My impression is that biotech R&D is more concentrated in a small number of high income countries than is electronic R&D, perhaps because much stronger government controls on products require very large markets for profitability. At least within the U.S., biotech R&D appears to be less regionally concentrated than electronic R&D. I do not know why.

Geographical concentration of sectors is not restricted to these prominent examples. Within large urban areas, sophisticated banking, finance, public relations and law are concentrated in small neighbourhoods. Reasons may vary from sector to sector. Lawyers may need to be near corporate, financial and property-owning and managing clients, near each other, near courts and, in Washington, near the government agencies that they interact with on behalf of clients.

Whether agglomeration economies relate to technology or other phenomena, all sources come down to the advantage of urban areas with which the paper started: proximity. If transportation and communication were free of both financial and time costs, proximity would be of no value; nobody would pay one or two orders of magnitude more to occupy downtown land than the cost of land 20 to 50 kilometers away. Thus, businesses locate near other businesses with which they interact, at least to some extent on a face-to-face basis. Furthermore, the sophisticated sectors used above to illustrate agglomeration economies employ some of any economy's most expensive workers. Both New York and Bombay illustrate this phenomenon.[3] An important reason for the concentration of high priced talent in both cities is that both are in regions that encourage private enterprise, both are major ports and both engage in complex legal, financial and logistical activities required by international trade and by the interactions between international and domestic trade.

Proximity promotes technology, as has been suggested. But directly it economises on transportation/communication costs, which are transactions costs. A sufficiently detailed set of accounts would include all transactions costs in production costs and would undoubtedly show more nearly constant total factor productivity with respect to urban sizes than existing data show. Many transactions costs are included in existing data: business shipments and communications. Time costs of commuting are missing from national income accounts. Large urban areas economise on commuting costs not so much by permitting shorter work trips, but by permitting better matches between worker abilities and employment opportunities, within normal commuting times and distances. Imperfectly correlated labour demands among sectors also permit

3. Both cities also contain large numbers of desperately poor people. In New York, the poorest are mostly blacks and Hispanics living in the outer Boroughs (Brooklyn, Queens and the Bronx) and even in northern Manhattan. In early-2000, a desperately poor and innocent Haitian immigrant was riddled with bullets at the entry to his Brooklyn apartment by New York City policemen. None were punished. U.S. police are of much higher quality than those in many countries, but I am frequently struck by the similarities between certain parts of U.S. cities and those in developing countries. One cannot go through Kennedy Airport's international arrivals without noticing similarities with such airports in developing countries: noise, confusion, armed guards, repeated demands for documents, danger to unprotected luggage, etc.

large urban areas to operate with lower unemployment rates than smaller urban areas.

Virtually all studies of agglomeration economies pertain to manufacturing sectors. But increasingly, all business sectors become more information-intensive. Information generation, processing, storage, analysis and distribution are service sector activities, so the distinction between service and manufacturing sectors becomes increasingly obscure. In many countries, certainly including India, research, development, management analysis, public relations, accounting and other functions may be performed either by the manufacturing company or by outside organisations that manufacturing firms contract with to undertake specific activities. That certainly includes computer software production (*See* Banerjee and Dufto (2000)). The close interaction and proximity among research, development and manufacturing is especially noteworthy in the electronic and biotech sectors. In many cases, interaction includes proximity to major research universities.

What about the future? There is no reason to doubt that agglomeration economies will continue to be important. The immediate implication is that governments discourage growth of urban areas at peril to overall economic development. Governments invariably think they can direct locations of business activities better than markets can. High tech sectors are especially attractive to governments because they are non-polluting and employ well paid and well educated workers. The U.S. landscape is littered with government-provided "industrial parks" that failed to attract the businesses that governments thought should be there. In fact, in the U.S. governments had almost nothing to do with development of the prominent high tech centres now scattered around the country, except to accommodate their growth. The most consistent failure is governments' efforts to attract high tech businesses to blighted locations in inner cities.

In concluding this section, it is important to emphasise that manufacturing sectors should be valued for their effects on productivity and economic growth, not for their effects on employment. In the U.S. and other high income countries, manufacturing's employment share has declined for several decades. In India, manufacturing's employment share has grown slowly at least since about 1960, but is probably even now not more than 10 per cent. Yet, the direct and indirect contribution of manufacturing to GDP and to total factor productivity growth in nearly all sectors is very great.

A simple example illustrates this proposition. Cellular phone manufacture is a small part of total employment in nearly all countries; Finland, where nearly half the world's cellular phones are made, is an exception. Yet, in one country after another, government monopoly phone services have kept phone connections in short supply and have provided inadequate service. Cellular phones have enabled businesses and consumers to circumvent conventional services, and the effect on productivity must have been great. Even in the U.S., where conventional phone services are ubiquitous, inexpensive and of high quality, cellular phones are a great convenience. Much the same is true in Northern Europe. In many other countries, they must be of much greater importance. Similar stories could be told about other modern electronic devices: photocopiers, fax machines, the personal computer and the internet.

SECTION 4

URBANISATION, INDUSTRIALISATION AND POVERTY

Until two or three centuries ago, most history was the history of attempts by armed groups of men to slaughter, plunder and rape each other's people and produce. Most of the world's great pre-1800s structures, which now attract tourists by the millions, were built on the backs of slaves and near-slaves. Much of this had little direct effect on average people, who lived close to subsistence levels regardless of which government taxed or seized surplus production. Death rates from combat were mostly modest. Those from starvation, malnutrition and disease were greater. The greatest effect was the impairment of incentives to accumulate human and physical capital and to invest in technology. The result was little or no increase in per capita income of working people.

Slaughter continued on a more deadly but more selective basis until mid-20th century. The resulting gradual improvements in people's control of governments was the industrial revolution, which started in the U.K. in the late-1600s and early-1700s and spread from there to several other countries during a couple of centuries.

Since mid-20th century, organised violence has nearly disappeared from the planet. Tropical Africa is almost the only region with traditional organised violence, with devastating consequences.[4] The result of the half century of nearly worldwide peace and of the resulting gradual increase of control of their governments by people has been dramatic increases in industrialisation, economic growth and new technology in most of Asia, much of South America and smaller parts of Africa.

The above potted history is absurdly oversimplified, but I am confident that the paucity of organised violence and the resulting ability of people to control their governments are crucial to economic growth. The deeper question, which I duck, is how the world has managed to control violence for the last 50 years. India must have much to teach the world on these issues, but my paper is not the right venue. I made the foregoing observations merely as background for discussion of the rapid spread of economic growth and poverty reduction during the second half of the 20th century.

Many countries and several international organisations publish poverty data. Both governments and private groups provide analysis of poverty data. This section relies heavily on World Bank (2000), seven Asian studies in *Asian Development Review* (1994), Pernia and Quibria in Cheshire and Mills (1999), Mills and Mitra (1996), and Pernia (1994). As in many other subjects, India provides some of the best poverty data and analysis in the developing world (*see* the paper by Mathur in *Asian Development Review* (1994). Counts of people or households below a poverty line based on income or expenditure are the most common measures. The World Bank publishes two head count indexes, for \$1 and \$2 per day of purchasing power parity. Since it matters how far below the poverty line people are, the World Bank and other organisations publish poverty gap data, showing how much money would be required to bring the poor up to the poverty line.

The World Bank poverty measures are meaningless for high income countries, and local data require careful adjustments to make

4. U.S. devastation of South-east Asia in the 1960s and 1970s defies easy explanation. The U.S. neither had nor gained any economic benefit from the slaughter. Nor did they achieve any identifiable political goal. In contrast, in the Gulf War the U.S. had classical economic motives.

them comparable (*See* Smeeding, *et al.*, (1990)). The U.S. poverty line is about $15,000 per year for a family of four, which exceeds average incomes in most countries.[5]

Three kinds of events exhaust the ways to improve living standards of the poor: general economic growth, which raises earnings of the poor and non-poor; improvements in the relative earnings of the poor, either by increases in the relative wages in their occupations or, more likely, by improvements in their educations, health or experience (human capital), which increase their earning capacity; and transfers from the non-poor to the poor.

Low income countries have neither the data, the resources nor the administrative machinery needed to transfer purchasing power to the poor, so they have wisely relied on the first two kinds of events to reduce poverty. Even high income Asian countries – Japan, Korea, Singapore, Taiwan – seem to make relatively little use of government transfers, relying instead on macro growth and on human capital accumulation among low income segments to achieve remarkably narrow measures of income inequality.

Rapid economic growth is the key to long term poverty reduction. It would be impossible to achieve Korea's low poverty incidence at the average income levels of India or the Philippines. There is still serious disagreement as to the determinants of long run macro growth among the many authors who have written on the subject. However, there is some convergence to the view that government respect for physical and human private property rights, the right of owners to retain most of the produce of their labour and property, and a semblence of monetary stability are important contributing factors (*See* Barro (1999)). Major government actions do not change rapidly in a country as large and diverse as India, but governments seem to have moved in the right directions for at least the last quarter of the 20th century.

---

5. Much has been made of the fact that the U.S. poverty incidence of about 13 per cent has hardly fallen during the prosperous 1990s. One reason is that inequality of both earnings and property income has increased. A second reason is that the U.S. poverty measure is poor. Some kinds of income are excluded. Expenditure surveys indicate that expenditure by the poor exceeds measured income by about 50 per cent. A third factor is that attempts to find measures of deprivation are mostly unsuccessful. None of the above is to deny that many people in the U.S. live chaotic and alienated lives.

Improvements in human capital appear to have been very important in poverty reduction in many Asian countries during recent decades. The evidence is dramatic reductions in poverty incidences, which appear to be beyond the likely direct effects of economic growth.

Table 7.1 shows estimates of poverty rates for four Asian countries: one set of estimates is from local studies for the long period from the 1960s or the 1970s to the late-1980s or the early-1990s; the other set of estimates is World Bank data from the late-1980s or early 1990s to the mid-1990s. World Bank GNP per capita growth data are presented for the 1985-1995 decade for comparison. All the data precede the Asian financial crises of the late-1990s.

All the data derive ultimately from local sources. The World Bank has made its GNP and poverty estimates as accurate and comparable as possible. The local estimates were presented by distinguished local experts for an Asian Development Bank study (*See* the referenced volume of the *Asian Development Review* and Pernia (1994)). Local poverty standards vary somewhat from country to country, but authors made the reported data as comparable as possible, and I believe the poverty reduction estimates are as reliable as is humanly possible. Except for India, the data in Table 7.1 are national poverty rates. Urban poverty rates are 5 or 10 percentage points lower than rural poverty rates in all countries. Every study of data for the countries in Table 7.1 shows similar declines in urban and rural poverty rates.

Urban and rural poverty rates are correlated through time, among countries and among provinces within countries.

The relationships among urban and rural poverty are undoubtedly complex (*See* Mills and Mitra (1996)). Rural-urban migration does not cure poverty any more than it causes poverty. Instead, people move from rural to urban areas when they reasonably foresee the likelihood that better living standards will result. Poor states or provinces are likely to have poor urban and rural residents, but people nevertheless migrate to urban areas when and where urban incomes, and job opportunities are better. Urban opportunities typically improve steadily relative to rural opportunities, so a steady rural-urban flow provides only a partially equilibrating mechanism.

Table 7.1

Poverty Reduction and GNP Per Capita Growth in Selected Asian Countries

Poverty Incidence

Country	*GNP Growth per year*		*Local Data*				*World Bank Data*			
	Years	*Per cent*	*Year*	*Per cent*	*Year*	*Per cent*	*Year*	*Per cent*	*Year*	*Per cent*
Bangladesh	1985-95	2.1	1973-74	60	1988-89	30	1991-92	43	1995-96	36
India	1985-95	3.2	1972-73	45	1987-88	34	1992	41	1994	39
Indonesia	1985-95	6.0	1976	40	1990	15	1987	17	1995	15
Philippines	1985-95	1.5	1961	59	1991	45	1994	41	1997	38

Sources: GNP Growth: *World Development Report 1997*, World Bank poverty estimate: *World Development Report 2000*; Local poverty incidence estimates: country papers in *Asian Development Review*, V12, N1, 1994 (local Indian estimates are urban).

Virtually all net employment growth is in urban areas in most developing countries. As was shown above, rural-urban migration is a large source of urban employment growth. Although individuals migrate to urban areas mainly because of better economic (and related educational) prospects there, increases in the percentage of employment that is in urban areas, an inexorable consequence of economic development, would not be possible without relatively unconstrained opportunities to move to urban areas.

The data presented above are in dramatic contrast with the dozens of publications that appeared in the 1970s and 1980s claiming that the poor do not benefit or do not benefit much during the early stages of economic growth (*See* Mills and Becker (1986) for a partial survey). The idea that overall income inequality increases during the early stages of economic growth and urbanisation may be partially correct and is identified with Kuznets (1955). But all the data from the mid-1970s indicate strongly that the poor benefit strongly from economic growth.

How are we to account for the dramatic reductions in poverty reported in the literature? Certainly, direct effects of economic growth are part of the answer. All the countries referenced above have experienced substantial economic growth from the 1970s to the 1990s. Productivity and real wages have increased, and jobs have been created, especially in urban areas. Poverty appears to have declined faster in countries that have grown faster (e.g. China and Indonesia). But decreases in poverty rates have been dramatic even in the two countries in Table 7.1 with the slowest GNP growth rates, Bangladesh and the Philippines.

I do not believe that the reductions in poverty rates reported in Table 7.1 can be accounted for by significant changes in the standards for measuring poverty. Of course, measures of low-income living standards improve through time. But it is not clear whether the results should be more or fewer people identified as poor. In addition, distinguished experts have worked on the available data. Finally, although all countries prefer to demonstrate progress to the world, dealing with international lending agencies is not helped if low-income countries understate their poverty problems.

It seems nearly certain that a large part of the reductions in poverty rates in the countries portrayed in Table 7.1 and in other developing countries has been the result of human capital accumulation. First, dramatic reductions in population growth and in total fertility rates have reduced the share of GNP needed to equip youth with a given stock of human capital. Second, direct evidence abounds. From 1980 to 1996, in all the countries in Table 7.1 except Indonesia, and including many others in the developing world, infant and child mortality rates fell dramatically during the same period. During about the same period, access to safe water and to sanitation improved in all four countries and in many other developing countries. (The data in this paragraph are from World Development Report 2000.) The list could go on, but other data are available for only fewer countries.

The interactions between economic growth and human capital accumulation are complex. One example must suffice. Improvements in women's educations have direct effects on economic growth because educated women are more productive in the labour force and raise higher quality children. Indirectly, better-educated women have fewer children and are likely to spend more of their adult lives in paid work (*See* Becker and Morrison in Cheshire and Mills (1999). Much of the data collection and analysis has been sponsored by the World Bank).

Industrialisation, urbanisation and poverty reduction relate to each other in several ways. I have already indicated that the distinction between modern industrial and business service sectors is increasingly vague. But it is not possible to separate business service sectors in existing data. Industrial growth depends on many factors. As industry becomes increasingly information and technology intensive, industrial growth depends increasingly on the human capital of the labour force. By and large, the urban poor lack the human capital to quality for industrial jobs. But industrialisation helps to provide the government and private resources needed to finance human capital accumulation. That process is certainly part of the human capital improvements discussed above. Also important, as industrialisation provides well paid employment for the non-poor, the poor are increasingly recruited and trained for jobs that were previously unavailable to them. We have seen this in the U.S. during the last half-decade of very full employment. Poor and both physically and mentally handicapped people have qualified for jobs they were not previously considered for. As part of the same process, relative wages of poorly paid workers have risen, for the first years in two decades. The non-poor have not been drained off by manufacturing; that sector's employment has been stagnant. Instead, non-poor workers have entered business and consumer service sectors in large numbers. People with low levels of human capital, especially those who cannot qualify for minimal computer skills, have found jobs in the same sectors, but on the bottom rungs of the employment ladder.

Much the same thing must be happening in most developing countries. During the 1980-1998 period, *World Development Report 2000* reports that GNP shares of industry and manufacturing increased only from 38 to 41 and from 27 to 29 per cent respectively in the set of low income countries. The World Bank no longer reports employment shares by sector. But given that labour productivity increases faster in industry and in manufacturing than in other sectors, the modest increases in their GNP shares reported above must imply that employment shares fell during the 18 year period in most low income countries. Thus, it is almost certainly true that industrial growth effects on poverty reduction in low-income countries are indirect and do not result from increased industrial or manufacturing sector employment.

What has all this to do with urbanisation? It has already been mentioned that in the United States some manufacturing plants have been locating on the fringes of metropolitan areas or outside metropolitan areas altogether since the 1950s. This pattern is the result mainly of our superb inter-urban highway system, but also of the small labour requirements of many manufacturing activities. Subsidiary advantages are lower taxes, weaker regulations and weaker unions. It has also been mentioned that manufacturing has been a declining share of total employment, with the result that ex-urbanisation of manufacturing has taken place while the urban share of total employment has continued to grow.

The U.S. pattern is a luxury that most developing countries cannot afford. Inter-urban transportation systems are typically slow, so locations in urban areas near related sectors, ports, railheads and large labour pools are important. For both international and inter-regional coastal trade, port cities are especially valuable. This accounts for the attraction and great sizes of Bombay, Shanghai, Hong Kong, Singapore, Jakarta, Pusan and other great Asian port cities.

Every country has its peculiar size distribution of urban areas.[6] Smaller urban areas are either more specialised in the goods and services they produce or serve smaller, typically regional, markets. The smallest urban areas are typically market towns where nearby rural residents bring agricultural and other products and buy agricultural and other inputs and most of their consumer goods and services. As economies grow, the smallest urban areas frequently shrink or disappear, mainly because an improved internal transportation system enables rural producers and consumers to

6. India and the U.S. have similar urban size distributions in several respects. Not only are New York–Los Angeles and Bombay – Calcutta the largest and second largest urban areas in their countries, but also they are respectively of similar size and are located at opposite East-west sides of the countries. Although similar in location and size, Chicago and Delhi are otherwise quite different. Delhi owes its size to being the national capital, whereas Chicago has no substantial political function. Chicago owes its location and size to its industrial sector, which in turn developed from the urban area's water access to both the Atlantic Coast and the Gulf of Mexico. Both countries have a rich size distribution of smaller urban areas.

travel to larger, although more distant, urban areas where a great variety of establishments is available.[7]

Whatever the size of the urban area, the basic reason for its existence is the advantage of proximity of diverse activities. The sizes of urban areas are limited by the sizes of the markets on which the urban area's goods and services can be profitably sold and by the availability of produced and raw material inputs. Comparative advantages of urban areas are determined by natural and produced conditions. Comparative advantages shift through time as natural conditions change, as products and production technologies change, and as the educations and skills of local workers change.

SECTION 5

GOVERNMENTS AND URBAN AREAS

Neither urban nor overall economic development can proceed rapidly unless national, provincial and local governments provide basic legal infrastructure that protects people and their rights and defines and enforces property rights and commercial law. Governments must also provide a basic and stable monetary system. National governments must relate to each other and must defend their citizens from foreign enemies and from domestic criminals. Higher levels of government must oversee the behaviour of lower levels of government.

Beyond the above, governments provide an enormous range of products and services. However, there is no "natural" list of products and services that only governments can provide efficiently. Every product or service that governments provide is also provided, often in the same jurisdiction, by private organisations. The products and services that governments provide are determined much more by political and historical circumstances than by benefits and costs in comparison with private provision. Nevertheless, during the last couple of decades there has been a substantial move to privatise provision of some products and services. Privatisation has of course been most notable in formerly communist countries, but has also

7. In prosperous U.S. farm areas it is not uncommon for several farmers to co-own a small airplane which they keep at a small local airport and use for shopping and recreational trips to a metropolitan area that may be 200 or 300 kilometers distant.

occurred in many developing countries, including India, and in East, South-east and Southern Asia. It has been much discussed in the United States, but there has been little change. The United States preaches a much better sermon to developing countries, especially through its influence on international agencies, than it practices on its home turf.[8]

Many countries, including India, have been gradually privatising heavy manufacturing. Government ownership of Indian heavy industry was influenced by local writers, but also by Harold Laski and other socialists in the U.K.[9] Transportation services are gradually being privatised and deregulated in many countries. So far, only limited progress has been made in permitting competitive private financial markets in developing countries.

Governments have indisputably important roles to play in laying out basic urban transportation and communication infrastructure patterns. Governments must design and provide for construction of urban road systems. Private companies can and do operate urban bus and jitney systems. Fixed rail commuter systems are difficult to make competitive because of their natural monopoly characteristics, although Tokyo has a complex mixture of government and private rail lines. Water supply, solid and liquid waste disposal and five protection systems are similar. Governments must assume basic planning responsibility in those sectors although various combinations of government and private construction, operation and financing are possible. Education and health care are complex combinations of government and private responsibility in most countries, although no intrinsic characteristics require government provision. In both cases, a major motivation is redistribution. Education and good health are crucial to escape poverty, and people recognise the long run benefits of the poor being provided more than they can pay for themselves.

---

8. The U.S. government has gradually deregulated financial and transportation sectors and gas and electricity distribution. But there has been little privatisation. The biggest socialist producer in the country is the Tennessee Valley Authority, and no national government has seriously proposed to privatise it. Local bus companies, which are private and competitive in some countries, are mostly owned and operated by local governments in the U.S. Solid waste collection and disposal have been privatised in some U.S. cities, with large savings where it has been accomplished without corruption.

9. It still puzzles me that India was so willing to import socialist ideology from its former colonial masters.

Whoever builds and operates urban transportation infrastructure, pricing its use is controversial. Governments in many countries badly under-price road use. Fuel taxes are a simple and efficient way to price road use by both government and private vehicles. In the U.S., a fuel tax that repays the opportunity cost of the land used for a typical urban roadway, the depreciation rate for the produced capital, and the operating costs of the road would be about 10 times the current level: a tax of about U.S. $2.50 per U.S. gallon compared with a present tax of about U.S. $0.25 per U.S. gallon.[10] An appropriate tax plus modest improvements in roadway operation would eliminate urban congestion for the foreseeable future. In the U.S., an appropriate fuel tax could replace the detested and distorting real estate tax. Many countries in Western Europe and Asia now have roughly appropriate fuel taxes. Indonesia and Peru are dramatic exceptions, with congestion levels that should be expected. In many countries, bus and fixed rail fares are also subsidised. Fixed rail subsidy may be justified if the system has excess capacity and the road system is congested, but heavily subsidised bus fares are not justified, since buses compete with cars for the same road space.

All countries regulate the uses of land. Most countries, including India, limit the conversion of land from rural to urban uses. Governments inevitably permit less conversion than is needed to accommodate urban growth without escalating house prices. The inevitable result is extremely high house prices, especially in large and rapidly growing urban areas, where house prices may be 8-12 times the annual incomes of owners. A secondary result is enormous increases in prices of land when conversion is permitted. The likely result is corruption of government officials. In India, government formerly froze rural land prices at their levels years before conversion was permitted, then purchased the land at the frozen prices when it was decided to permit conversion. Any such scheme motivates governments to permit insufficient conversion, since it increases the profit from conversion when it is permitted.[11] In Korea, land use conversion controls have been gradually relaxed since about 1990 and the result has been reductions in Seoul's relative house

10. See Mills (1998).

11. See Hannah, Kim and Mills (1993).

prices from about 10 to about 5 times annual incomes (in part the result of the financial crisis of the late-1990s). Proposals to control rural-urban land use conversion have spread rapidly in the U.S. in the last couple of years ("anti-sprawl" is the local term). Very few people understand the implications of such proposals.

Many governments especially want to limit the growth of the largest urban areas. Governments appear especially to fear the congestion in large urban areas, but neglect the fact that the appropriate policy is better user costs and infrastructure for the transportation system, not direct controls on urban growth. Governments sometimes levy special taxes on some activities in large urban areas or provide special subsidies for locating activities elsewhere. Sometimes painful direct controls are used. China formerly rationed food and other consumer goods and made ration cards valid only in urban areas where the government had approved residence. Formerly the Indonesian government employed military tactics to pick up poor people on the streets of Jakarta if they had no residence permit and transported them to smaller urban areas. In India, government has sometimes made illegal the only housing that the poor can afford in large cities. The result is either to criminalise poverty or to prevent the poor from migrating to large urban areas.

I conclude this section with a personal conjecture as to one reason that governments try to control the growth of large urban areas. In the United States, effective demands for civil rights by the black minority began only after millions had migrated to large cities by the 1950s. In Europe, demands for democratic representation of the poor were expressed in large cities in the 19th century. In the last decades of the 20th century, demands for democratic reform in China, Korea, Indonesia, the Philippines and elsewhere, were concentrated in the largest cities. In Russia, both 20th century revolutions took place in the largest cities. Likewise, the unsuccessful revolts in Eastern Europe during the communist period took place in large cities.

It appears simply to be more difficult for governments to control the assembly of people, the dissemination of information and the organisation of protests in large cities. The effect of the rapid spread of electronic communication on such activities is beyond my comprehension. But I believe that unruly students and others frighten governments of large cities. It is thought by some that fear of unruly students has motivated governments to move universities from city centres to peripheral locations in some countries.

SECTION 6

WHAT ARE APPROPRIATE GOVERNMENT POLICIES TOWARD URBAN AREAS?

My first comment is that influencing the sizes of urban areas or cities should not be among government policies. If big cities are excessively congested or polluted, the reason is either inappropriate pricing of government services, insufficiently stringent controls (or pricing) of polluting discharges or inadequate transportation or other infrastructure. Appropriate charges or fees for government services may indeed make large urban areas more expensive places to live and produce than small urban areas. If so, it is an appropriate signal to locate elsewhere.

As has been stated, responsibility for services provided in urban areas is divided among national, state or provincial, and local governments, and the private sector in arbitrary fashion in most countries. Economists typically advocate division of responsibility among levels of government and the private sector on benefit-cost grounds. If taken seriously, the result would be more services provided by private sectors. Financing of government services at the local level has the great advantage that local people pay for services from which they are the beneficiaries. If the national government finances a service provided by local government, local residents demand, through the political process, more services than are justified, since the costs are mostly borne by taxpayers elsewhere. If all government investments were determined by careful benefit-cost analysis, the entire problem would be solved. But government investments are made in a political context, which generates its own incentives, and they are not overruled by economists doing benefit-cost analysis. Local government finance of projects with local beneficiaries generates an approximation to benefit-cost analysis. If local residents know they will have to pay for projects they persuade their local government to undertake, they will presumably advocate projects whose benefits exceed their costs. Thus, local government financing and decision-making provides an approximation to market allocation, as Tiebout and half a century of local public choice analysts have appreciated.

The difficulty is that local government taxes are much more distorting than similar taxes levied by higher levels of government. Higher motor vehicle fuel taxes, which I advocated above, could not be levied by a local government because drivers would buy fuel elsewhere and travel on local roads. Any tax could in principle be levied by a higher level of government (national in the case of a motor vehicle fuel tax) and be distributed to local governments. However, it is not easy to imagine a formula for distributing the revenues from a national, or provincial, tax to local governments that would not involve distortions similar to those that result from distributing infrastructure costs from higher governments' general revenues.

User fees, in which people can consume the service only if they pay the fee, would solve the problem, but if a user fee is feasible, private provision is likely also to be feasible.

References

Asian Development Review, (1994). Vol. 12, No. 1.

Banerjee, Abhijit and Esther Duplo (2000). "Reputation Effects and the Limits of Contracting: A Study of the Indian Software Industry," *Quarterly Journal of Economics,* VCXV, N3, pp 989-1018.

Barro, Robert (1999). *Determinants of Economic Growth.* Cambridge, MA.: MIT Press.

Becker, Charles, Jeffrey Williamson and Edwin Mills (1992). *Indian Urbanization and Economic Growth Since 1960.* Baltimore, MD: Johns Hopkins University Press.

Behrman, Jere and T. N. Srinivasan (eds.) (1995). *Handbook of Development Economics,* V3A Amsterdam: Elsevier Science BU.

Cheshire, Paul and Edwin Mills (eds.) (1999). *Handbook of Regional and Urban Economics V3.* Amsterdam: Elsevier Science BU.

Gasper, Jess and Edward Glaeser (1998). "Information Technology and the Future of Cities," *Journal of Urban Economics,* Vol. 43, No. 1, pp 136-156.

Hannah, Lawrence, Kyung Hwan Kim and Edwin Mills (1993). "Land Use Controls and Housing Prices in Korea," *Urban Studies,* Vol. 30, No. l, pp 147-156.

Hulten, Charles and Sylafa Srinivasan (1999). "Indian Manufacturing Industry: Elephant or Tiger? New Evidence on the Asian Miracle." Cambridge, MA: NBER Working Paper 7441.

Kuznets, Simon (1955). "Economic Growth and Income Inequality." *American Economic Review,* Vol. 45, March, pp 1-28.

Lewis, W. Arthur (1978). *The Evolution of the International Economic Order.* Princeton, N.J.: Princeton University Press.

Mathur, Om Prakash (1994). "The State of India's Urban Poverty," *Asian Development Review,* Vol. 12, No. l. L, pp 32-67.

Mills, Edwin (1998). "Excess Commuting in the United States," *Network Infrastructure and the Urban Environments.* Berlin: Springer-Verlag in Lars Lindquist, Lars-Goran Mattson and Tschango Kim (eds.)

Mills, Edwin and Charles Becker (1986). *Studies in Indian Urban Development.* New York: Oxford University Press for the World Bank.

Mills, Edwin and Arup Mitra (1996). *Urban Development and Urban Ills.* New Delhi: Ajay Verma for Commonwealth Publishers.

Mitra, Arup (1999). "Total Factor Productivity Growth and Technical Efficiency in Indian Industries," *Economic and Political Weekly,* Vol. 34, July 31.

Pernia, Ernesto, ed. (1994). *Urban Poverty in Asia.* Hong Kong: Oxford University Press.

Shukla, Vibhooti (1996). *Urbanization and Economic Growth.* Oxford: Oxford University Press.

Smeeding, Timothy, Michael O'Higgins and Lee Rainwater eds. (1990). *Poverty, Inequality and Income Distribution in Comparative Perspective.* Washington: Urban Institute Press.

United Nations, (1994). *Human Development Report.* New York: Oxford University Press for the United Nations Development Programme.

World Bank, *World Development Report 1994.* New York: Oxford University Press.

World Bank, *World Development Report 1997.* New York: Oxford University Press.

World Bank (2000). *World Development Report 1999-2000.* New York: Oxford University Press for the World Bank.

8

Industry-Urban Nexus, Employment and Poverty

A Quantitative Assessment

ARUP MITRA
PRASAD SANKAR BHATTACHARYA

SECTION 1

INTRODUCTION

Whether it is agricultural productivity growth or a deterioration in the land-man ratio resulting in rural underemployment, in both the situations surplus labour is released from the agriculture sector and made available to the organised industry for its expansion. And industrial growth being an indispensable feature of economic development, its rate, spread and structure all are of considerable importance for the economy. Industrial growth is expected to bring in structural, and locational shifts of both value added and workforce involving an upward mobility of occupations and incomes, (Kuznets, 1966).

As non-agricultural activities generate economies of scale, producers benefit from spatial concentration, which leads to formation of large urban settlements. The nexus between industry and urban, therefore, needs to be understood in relation to the concentration of activities and population, generating productivity-augmenting effects of urbanisation and resulting in economic development through (productive) employment generation which help reduce poverty.

In analysing the theme of industry-urban nexus it would not, however, be appropriate to focus only on the organised industry. The process of ancillarisation and the growth potential of the micro enterprises, which would mainly fall into the domain of the so-called unorganised manufacturing, need to be considered in order to draw a complete profile of the relationship. Further, the rural-urban division of the unorganised manufacturing is also of great significance for analytical purposes, as agricultural growth and agro-based industries, traditional industries like handicrafts and the role that village artisans have played over the centuries in a country like India, cannot be ignored. Keeping in view these aspects, the present study is organised as follows: Section 2 analyses the growth pattern of the organised industrial sector, and Section 3 focuses on the unorganised manufacturing growth, separately in rural and urban areas. Section 4 presents the econometric exercise which involves estimation of a simultaneous equation system model integrating organised industry urbanisation, productivity in unorganised manufacturing and urban poverty. Main findings are summarised in Section 5.

SECTION 2

ORGANISED INDUSTRIAL SECTOR: BROAD PATTERNS

In this section, we analyse industry specific growth rates of output and gross value added (obtained by double deflation method), employment, wages and salaries per employee, capital-labour ratio, capital- output ratio and labour productivity over the following three sub-periods: 1976-77 to 1984-85; 1985-86 to 1990-91; and 1991-92 to 1993-94.

The growth rates for three different sub-periods have been calculated by estimating the following function:

$$\ln Y = a_0 + a_1 D_1 + a_2 D_2 + b_0 t + b_1 t D_1 + b_2 t D_2 \qquad \text{...(1)}$$

where, Y is a given variable, D_1 and D_2 are time specific dummies used for separating sub-periods 2 and 3 respectively from the period 1, t is time trend and ln stands for natural log. The growth rate for the sub-period 1 is given by b_0 whereas for the other sub-periods 2 and 3, it is given by $(b_0 + b_1)$ and $(b_0 + b_2)$ respectively.

Relative to the first sub-period, from 1976-77 to 1984-85, the industrial growth rate both in terms of output and value added accelerated during the latter half of the eighties (Table 8.1). However, as evident from Table 8.1, output growth fell at least in seven

Table 8.1

Growth Rates of Some Variables (per cent per annum)

Industry Code	Output			Gross Value Added			Employment			Wages, Salaries (per employee)		
	1976-77 to 1984-85	1985-86 to 1990-91	1991-92 to 1993-94	1976-77 to 1984-85	1985-86 to 1990-91	1991-92 to 1993-94	1976-77 to 1984-95	1985-86 to 1990-91	1991-92 to 1993-94	1976-77 to 1984-95	1985-86 to 1990-91	1991-92 to 1993-94
20-21: Food Products	3.97	10.33	2.86	19.73	3.54	7.79	-1.20	3.21	4.08	6.27	4.46	0.47
22: Beverages, Tobacco and Tobacco Products	1.11	4.13	7.29	-1.37	2.36	6.97	2.08	7.16	-0.30	2.66	-0.86	-3.14
23: Cotton Textiles	-2.32	5.87	5.89	-6.80	6.27	8.29	-1.23	-0.99	1.84	1.35	0.92	-0.52
24: Wool, Silk and Synthetic Fibres Textiles	5.52	9.43	15.08	-1.95	6.87	28.66	5.05	1.94	6.46	1.82	2.54	3.24
25: Jute, Hemp and Mesta Textiles	-0.60	0.47	-0.35	1.98	1.92	-2.29	-0.00	-0.01	-7.11	0.75	1.58	5.02
26: Textile Products	2.43	14.31	21.51	1.83	17.59	27.20	1.69	9.76	21.89	0.98	1.95	-0.91
27: Wood and Wood Prod., Furniture and Fixtures	1.17	11.81	-22.97	-5.41	2.60	15.95	-0.11	-1.29	4.58	3.02	1.97	5.59
28: Paper and Paper Products and Printing and Allied Industries	5.44	7.66	3.46	2.61	6.67	10.93	2.48	0.23	2.11	1.72	3.15	1.96
29: Leather and Leather and Fur Products	7.11	11.22	18.10	6.80	13.39	26.00	3.37	8.94	3.63	0.22	-1.10	0.48
30: Chemical and Chemical Products	13.68	10.65	7.15	22.51	15.78	9.77	20.66	1.08	5.20	4.12	1.99	2.44
31: Rubber, Plastic, Petroleum and Coal Prod.	1.47	7.87	19.36	-21.75	16.96	20.21	-13.03	5.88	7.07	-0.87	2.83	2.49

Contd...

... Table 8.1 Contd...

Industry Code	*Output*			*Gross Value Added*			*Employment*			*Wages, Salaries (per employee)*		
	1976-77 to 1984-85	*1985-86 to 1990-91*	*1991-92 to 1993-94*	*1976-77 to 1984-85*	*1985-86 to 1990-91*	*1991-92 to 1993-94*	*1976-77 to 1984-95*	*1985-86 to 1990-91*	*1991-92 to 1993-94*	*1976-77 to 1984-95*	*1985-86 to 1990-91*	*1991-92 to 1993-94*
32: Non-Metallic Mineral Products	8.22	9.59	-1.14	5.52	9.55	-3.68	4.72	0.56	-1.48	1.51	1.88	5.04
33: Basic Metal and Alloys	9.28	7.95	5.47	6.81	-0.86	20.42	3.64	0.27	2.42	1.46	2.29	14.47
34: Metal Products and Parts	4.36	10.02	10.11	4.12	-1.05	6.66	0.43	4.83	1.80	2.63	0.53	4.93
35-36: Machinery and Equipment	5.38	10.13	3.96	2.06	9.70	7.54	2.93	1.87	0.85	1.97	2.11	1.85
37: Transport Equipment and Parts	8.45	10.68	13.82	5.05	7.98	14.64	5.45	0.01	1.38	2.18	1.96	-0.05
38: Other Mfg Industries	5.89	14.41	27.50	6.73	13.65	31.46	1.17	5.16	10.33	2.02	-0.45	6.79
All Industries	5.36	9.24	8.75	2.58	9.39	12.02	1.72	1.89	2.98	2.68	1.65	3.10

Notes: (1) Growth rates of Output, Employment, and Wages corresponding to different periods have been calculated by taking the variables a function of time and time dummies as explained in the text.

(2) Since gross value added figures for industries 20-21 and 27 turned out to be negative for some of the years, the growth rates have been calculated by taking the yearly average.

Source: Based on ASI data.

industries during the post-reform period, particularly in comparison with the period of deregulation (1985-86 to 1990-91). Food products (20-21), jute textiles (25), wood and wood products (27), paper and paper products (28), chemical and chemical products (30), non-metallic mineral products (32), basic metal and alloys (33) and machinery and equipment (35-36) registered a decline in the growth rates which in fact, brought the overall industrial growth rate down to 8.75 per cent per annum during the post-reform period as compared to 9.24 per cent during its previous sub-period. Even in terms of gross value added originating from jute textiles (25), chemical and chemical products (30), non-metallic mineral products (32) and machinery and equipment (35-36) the growth rate decelerated during the early-nineties. However, as mentioned above, the third sub-period in our study is too short and, therefore, the analysis based on growth patterns can at best be suggestive. Nevertheless, the revival from the initial deceleration of the reforms seems to have been quicker in the Indian context as compared to many other countries which have also undergone structural reforms. This could be one of the reasons why the industrial output growth rate corresponding to the third period was only marginally lower than that of the second period.

The industrial growth rate subsequent to the reforms is said to be constrained by (a) the balance of payment crisis of 1991 which necessitated an import squeeze affecting availability of inputs and their costs, (b) the tight monetary policy pursued to contain inflation which affected demand and raised the cost of borrowing for the industries, and (c) a fall in investment demand due to reduction in public expenditure and investment. The slow industrial growth in the early-nineties is also attributable to inherent adjustment lags in the process of industrial restructuring, early uncertainties about the commitments to the reform policies and the lack of supplementary reforms at the sectoral and local levels (Ministry of Industry, 1996).

As mentioned above, the process of adjustment seems to have had a much shorter time span compared to international experience. From April, 1994 industrial recovery seems to have taken place, and this broad based industrial recovery is attributed to a number of factors such as cumulative success of industrial restructuring, resurgence of exports in response to trade and payment policies, declining nominal and real interest rates, cumulative efforts of tax reforms, growing public expenditure on poverty alleviation and employment generation programmes, another agricultural bumper crop, a buoyant infrastructural sector and growth confidence and improvement in investment climate due to cumulative succeess of industrial trade, financial and capital market reforms, (Ministry of Industry, 1996, 1997). From Goldar (2000) it may be noted that the gross value added growth rate during 1990-97 was only marginally lower than the growth rate observed between 1980-90.

Despite an appreciable growth of output in the industrial sector during the eighties employment growth was quite sluggish in a large numer of industries (Table 8.1). The overall employment growth in the organised industry was only 1.89 per cent per annum between 1985-86 and 1990-91. Surprisingly the employment growth over the three year period following the structural adjustment, turned out to be higher (2.98 per cent per annum). Some of the industries which recorded either a negative or a sluggish, though positive, growth rate of employment during the early-nineties are beverages, tobaco and tobacco products (22), cotton textiles (23), jute textiles (25), non-metallic mineral products (32), metal products and parts (34), machinery and equipment (35-36), and transport equipment and parts (37). The growth rate of wages and salaries per employee corresponding to all-industries, however, turned out to be marginally above (3.10 per cent per annum) the employment growth during this period. Industries which recorded a fall in the growth rate of wages and salaries per employee in this period compared to the period, 1985-86 through 1990-91, are food products (20-21), beverages (22), cotton textiles (23), textile products (26), paper and paper products (28), rubber, plastic, petroleum and coal products (31), machinery and equipment (35-36) and transport equipment and parts (37). As noted above, many of these industries also recorded an increase in employment growth in the third sub-period. On the whole, the decline in the growth rate of real wages seems to have raised the employment growth in the third period. Goldar (2000) also noted an employment growth of 2.69 per cent per annum for the period 1990-97 and the decline in the growth of wages is said to be responsible for an acceleration in the employment growth rate. Employment elasticity calculated by us elsewhere, however, does not show any sign of improvement in the nineties (Mitra, forthcoming).

Table 8.2

Average Capital-Labour, Capital-Output and Labour Productivity across Industries

Industry Code	*Capital-Labour (Rs. Per employee)*			*Capital-Output*			*Labour Productivity (Rs. Per employee)*		
	1976-77 to 1984-85	*1985-86 to 1990-91*	*1991-92 to 1993-94*	*1976-77 to 1984-85*	*1985-86 to 1990-91*	*1991-92 to 1993-94*	*1976-77 to 1984-85*	*1985-86 to 1990-91*	*1991-92 to 1993-94*
20-21	13066 (4.76)	22850 (7.51)	30667 (10.02)	0.15 (–0.41)	0.14 (0.39)	0.16 (11.24)	18330 (1.43)	36583 (11.57)	42962 (3.48)
22	4382 (–0.12)	8850 (1.42)	10556 (16.55)	0.11 (0.85)	0.20 (4.5)	0.22 (8.94)	18401 (–3.45)	18034 (–4.80)	17682 (7.27)
23	13122 (7.08)	21363 (1.49)	28239 (18.56)	0.22 (8.18)	0.26 (–5.84)	0.25 (14.52)	22108 (–5.57)	26380 (7.74)	32839 (6.45)
24	28106 (9.92)	48706 (8.00)	79081 (14.24)	0.25 (9.45)	0.30 (0.50)	0.34 (5.63)	48148 (–7.00)	48985 (4.94)	37506 (22.20)
25	4772 (3.13)	9806 (15.67)	11420 (–3.87)	0.14 (3.72)	0.23 (14.34)	0.25 (–10.64)	15844 (2.00)	18988 (2.58)	20909 (4.84)
26	10036 (4.41)	16724 (5.50)	19879 (9.02)	0.10 (3.66)	0.13 (0.95)	0.12 (9.39)	46128 (–3.52)	57794 (7.83)	73033 (5.31)
27	10202 (6.10)	15713 (9.10)	20488 (31.86)	0.23 (4.82)	0.25 (–4.00)	0.37 (59.41)	15938 (–5.65)	6121 (40.15)	–9029
28	38026 (9.00)	57281 (4.00)	63150 (11.21)	0.56 (6.04)	0.60 (–3.43)	0.57 (9.85)	26181 (0.14)	28260 (6.45)	29677 (8.83)
29	14227 (3.59)	17128 (3.18)	22613 (12.47)	0.16 (–0.14)	0.15 (0.92)	0.16 (–1.98)	23523 (3.42)	27503 (4.44)	44149 (22.36)
30	86121 (0.43)	120162 (9.16)	156988 (10.51)	0.33 (7.42)	0.38 (–0.4)	0.38 (8.57)	70795 (–8.72)	105047 (10.48)	157074 (13.14)
31	80788 (0.12)	119363 (3.16)	142043 (14.78)	0.28 (–14.38)	0.19 (1.17)	0.23 (2.49)	76965 (1.84)	121360 (14.64)	189933 (4.57)
32	26343 (7.64)	66039 (6.33)	146271 (12.91)	0.48 (4.14)	0.71 (–2.70)	0.64 (12.56)	20162 (0.80)	30918 (8.99)	70568 (–2.19)
33	93213 (2.67)	133642 (8.73)	225818 (9.09)	0.69 (–2.98)	0.64 (1.04)	0.84 (6.02)	41756 (3.17)	32945 (–1.14)	35769 (18.01)
34	16611 (4.23)	26461 (8.24)	40530 (23.41)	0.21 (0.10)	0.25 (3.05)	0.31 (15.1)	26682 (3.69)	23836 (–5.88)	26895 (4.86)
35-36	27174 (1.52)	41012 (6.01)	50911 (4.69)	0.24 (–0.93)	0.24 (–2.25)	0.25 (1.76)	52572 (–0.86)	59092 (7.84)	72416 (6.70)
37	33593 (3.28)	47194 (2.28)	53976 (10.58)	0.40 (0.29)	0.34 (–8.38)	0.29 (–1.85)	38825 (–0.40)	46641 (7.97)	42897 (13.26)
38	19776 (4.39)	33197 (7.44)	45224 (16.15)	0.25 (–0.33)	0.21 (–1.81)	0.17 (–1.03)	38639 (5.56)	85845 (8.49)	159517 (21.13)
All Ind.	31422 (4.43)	51506 (6.35)	70225 (11.32)	0.31 (0.79)	0.32 (–1.00)	0.35 (5.79)	33660 (0.86)	44350 (7.50)	61187 (9.80)

Notes: Figures in parentheses give growth rates. See notes (1) and (2) below Table 8.1.

Source: Based on ASI data.

The average capital-labour ratio has been highest during the post-reform period (Table 8.2). In fact, in most of the industries except jute textiles (25) and machinery and equipment (35) the growth rate accelerated during this period. Similarly, the capital-output ratio was also stepped-up during the early-nineties mainly because of a fall in output initially, subsequent to the reforms. The average capital-output ratio, however, fell in six of the seventeen industries, i.e., cotton textiles (23), textile products (26), paper products (28), non-metalic mineral products (32), transport equipment etc. (37) and other manufacturing industries (38). The average labour productivity defined as gross value added per employee, increased in the third sub-period compared to the second except in a few industries like beverages etc. (22), wool etc. (24), wood products (27) and transport equipment etc. (37). In terms of growth rate also a large majority of the industries reported a higher growth rate of labour productivity in the nineties compared to the second half of the eighties.

SECTION 3

UNORGANISED MANUFACTURING

Based on the NSS surveys on unorganised manufacturing for the year 1989-90 and 1994-95 we focus, in this section, on employment growth, gross value added growth and employment elasticity across industries and states. The unorganised sector has been divided into three components, namely, Own Account Manufacturing Enterprises (OAME), Non-directory Manufacturing Enterprises (NDME) and Directory Manufacturing Enterprises (DME).[1] In the rural areas in almost all the categories of units, employment declined considerably even in absolute terms during 1989-90 through 1994-95. OAMEs registered a growth rate of -1.81 per cent p.a., NDMEs -3.46 per cent

1. Enterprises registered under the Factories Act, 1948 (i.e., enterprises employing 10 or more workers using power and those employing 20 or more workers without power) and *bidi* and cigar manufacturing enterprises registered under *bidi* and cigar workers Act, 1966 are not covered in the unorganised sector. Unorganised manufacturing enterprises are divided into three categories: (a) own account manufacturing enterprises (OAME): small enterprises not employing any hired worker on a fairly regular basis, (b) non-directory manufacturing enterprises (NDME): enterprises employing 5 or less, and (c) directory manufacturing enterprises (DME): size being 6 or more but less than 10 if using power, and less than 20 if not using power.

p.a. and DMEs -2.31 per cent p.a. during the same period. The negative growth rate has been quite prominent in a large number of industries (Acharya and Mitra, 2000). Also, across states the growth rate turned out to be negative except in Assam, Bihar, Karnataka, Orissa and Uttar Pradesh. Gross value added on the other hand, remained more or less stagnant during this period. At the aggregate level, it increased only at a rate of 0.65 per cent p.a. Some of the industries like wool etc. (24), jute textiles (25), rubber, plastic, petroleum and coal products (31), non-metallic mineral products (32) and 39 recorded a high growth rate of gross value added, but their share being nominal in total value added originating from the rural areas, the overall growth rate still remained modest. Across categories like OAMEs and NDMEs gross value added growth rate was virtually zero, which pulled the overall growth rate down to 0.65 per cent p.a. Among the states, only Assam, Haryana, Karnataka, Orissa, Tamil Nadu and Uttar Pradesh registered a growth rate of at least 5 per cent p.a.. Employment elasticity in eight of the fifteen major states turned out to be negative, and also at the all-India level it was estimated at -3.07 per cent. All this tends to suggest that unorganised manufacturing in rural India, and even in the highly industrialised states did not generate employment opportunities to any significant extent. Among the rural non-farm activities, manufacturing is considered to be influenced largely by the demand-side factors. But sluggish or negative employment growth in this activity only reconfirms the absence of percolation effect of growth benefiting those located at the lower echelons of the socio-economic ladder.

In the urban areas, though the employment growth in unorganised manufacturing turned out to be positive, the magnitude was as low as 0.11 per cent p.a. Both NDMEs and DMEs registered a growth rate of 0.80 and 0.69 per cent p.a. respectively. The OAMEs, however, seem to have undergone a decline in employment during the same period (Table 8.3). Also, across states nine out of the fifteen, registered a negative employment growth (Andhra Pradesh, Haryana, Karnataka, Orissa, Punjab, Rajasthan, Tamil Nadu, West Bengal), some of which are agriculturally prosperous states and some industrialised states (Table 8.4).

Gross value added, on the other hand, increased in all categories of enterprises, though in OAMEs and DMEs the rates have been impressive somewhat. Some of the industries which recorded a negative growth rate in gross value added are manufacturing of food products (21), wool etc. (24), paper products (28), basic chemicals etc. (30), non-metalic mineral products (32), machinery etc. (35) and transport equipment etc. (37) (Table 8.5). Among states except Andhra Pradesh, Kerala, Orissa, and Rajasthan all other showed a positive growth in value added (Table 8.6).

Table 8.3

Growth Rate of Employment Across Industries: Urban Unorganised Manufacturing (1989-90 through 1994-95)

Industry Division	*OAME*	*NDME*	*DME*	*ALL*
20: Manu. of Food Products	2.10	2.19	1.95	2.10
21: Manu. of Food Products	-5.64	-3.03	-7.92	-5.44
22: Beverages etc.	-6.08	-6.72	-13.54	-6.47
23: Cotton Textiles	-11.41	-7.32	-2.94	-7.72
24: Wool etc.	-4.88	-12.69	1.00	-5.07
25: Jute etc.	-15.33	22.04	-14.56	-9.67
26: Textile Products	-4.44	1.26	12.13	3.48
27: Wood Products	1.37	5.67	0.98	2.55
28: Paper Products	-0.50	-6.86	-4.80	-4.43
29: Leather Products	6.45	12.57	11.16	9.63
30: Basic Chemicals etc.	-5.36	-2.65	-8.46	-5.96
31: Rubber etc.	-7.77	4.38	7.76	4.44
32: Non-Metallic Mineral Products	-1.24	7.65	-13.31	-4.30
33: Basic Metal etc.	23.14	2.91	-7.79	2.25
34: Metal Products etc.	-0.75	5.51	4.96	4.00
35: Machinery etc.	5.67	5.72	-11.18	-3.62
36: Machinery etc.	-2.78	-10.31	-8.66	-8.76
37: Transport Equipment etc.	6.47	5.12	-4.67	-0.95
38: Other Manu. Industries	7.64	-2.31	4.59	4.63
39: Repair of Capital Goods	-2.11	-0.63	1.13	-0.66
97: Repair Services	3.96	3.61	-0.94	3.31
99: Not recorded cases	5.14	16.36	n.a.	14.51
All	-0.69	0.80	0.69	0.11

Source: NS 45th and 51st round surveys.

Table 8.4

Growth Rate of Employment Across States: Urban Unorganised Manufacturing (1989-90 through 1994-95)

State	*OAME*	*NDME*	*DME*	*ALL*
Andhra Pradesh	-3.02	1.64	-2.04	-1.75
Assam	8.62	7.74	-7.92	5.06
Bihar	7.41	6.67	-4.50	5.55
Gujarat	11.82	-6.10	3.55	3.57
Haryana	-8.33	-0.97	-1.65	-4.20
Karnataka	-3.91	3.53	-7.96	-3.16
Kerala	-13.97	-11.15	-21.60	-15.48
Madhya Pradesh	3.51	13.03	-3.54	4.55
Maharashtra	1.66	2.34	6.64	3.89
Orissa	-3.11	-5.87	-8.21	-4.55
Punjab	0.13	-4.17	2.00	-0.93
Rajasthan	-6.77	-3.15	-14.85	-6.97
Tamil Nadu	-6.47	-0.94	0.70	-3.11
Uttar Pradesh	1.79	7.73	-1.02	2.58
West Bengal	-2.25	-0.53	3.10	-0.44
All India	**-0.69**	**0.80**	**0.97**	**0.19**

Source: NS 45th and 51st round surveys.

Table 8.5

Growth Rate of Gross Value Added Across Industries: Urban Unorganised Manufacturing (1989-90 through 1994-95)

Industry Division	*OAME*	*NDME*	*DME*	*ALL*
20: Manu. of Food Products	-1.00	3.69	1.59	1.33
21: Manu. of Food Products	-5.37	-0.07	-1.88	-2.65
22: Beverages etc.	6.14	-4.86	-15.10	2.56
23: Cotton Textiles	-6.81	-4.72	8.59	1.63
24: Wool etc.	-1.21	-19.82	-2.74	-9.14
25: Jute etc.	3.22	40.17	-24.70	4.59
26: Textile Products	-2.72	2.61	12.79	7.98
27: Wood Products	4.97	16.72	7.83	10.51
28: Paper Products	11.34	-4.36	-8.62	-4.79

Contd...

...*Table 8.5 Contd...*

Industry Division	*OAME*	*NDME*	*DME*	*ALL*
29: Leather Products	11.32	14.02	18.45	14.91
30: Basic Chemicals etc.	4.59	-10.90	-5.12	-5.09
31: Rubber etc.	6.04	8.04	4.02	5.22
32: Non-Metallic Mineral Products	2.73	2.85	-10.59	-3.43
33: Basic Metal etc.	39.62	3.50	44.77	25.67
34: Metal Products etc.	0.60	9.29	4.87	5.86
35: Machinery etc.	7.16	4.30	-14.19	-7.65
36: Machinery etc.	-2.56	-9.50	n.a.	46.49
37: Transport Equipment etc.	11.86	15.69	-8.85	-2.50
38: Other Manu. Industries	16.11	-3.67	9.51	8.92
39: Repair of Capital Goods	2.03	2.93	20.30	9.3
97: Repair Services	8.37	7.24	3.63	7.37
99: Not recorded cases	13.27	16.51	n.a.	18.11
All	5.46	1.36	4.40	3.72

Source: NS 45th and 51st round surveys.

Table 8.6

Growth Rate of Gross Value Added Across States: Urban Unorganised Manufacturing (1989-90 through 1994-95)

State	*OAME*	*NDME*	*DME*	*ALL*
Andhra Pradesh	-2.78	-1.12	-4.61	-2.67
Assam	13.17	9.44	-11.56	5.53
Bihar	8.59	3.93	-13.65	2.9
Gujarat	15.46	-22.74	21.74	1.61
Haryana	10.37	14.68	-3.51	4.34
Karnataka	1.53	7.88	-1.15	2.43
Kerala	-8.65	-6.92	-25.47	-15.72
Madhya Pradesh	8.74	30.07	10.88	16.86
Maharashtra	10.54	6.14	6.74	7.06
Orissa	3.25	-0.95	-21.81	-4.66
Punjab	7.78	-0.83	4.05	3.41
Rajasthan	2.98	2.25	-12.05	-0.41
Tamil Nadu	4.98	3.90	14.06	8.97
Uttar Pradesh	3.08	7.23	-0.86	3.01
West Bengal	2.67	4.19	0.54	2.46
All India	5.46	1.37	4.68	3.83

Source: NS 45th and 51st round surveys.

Sluggish employment growth despite a reasonably good value added growth resulted in a negligible employment elasticity. At the all-India level, corresponding to all industries, it turned out to be only 0.05; in relative sense NDMEs (0.59) performed better than OAMEs and DMEs. In some of the industrialised states like West Bengal employment elasticity has been - 0.18, and even in Maharashtra it has been well below unity, i.e., 0.55. Although unorganised manufacturing is expected to be highly labour intensive, empirical evidence does not seem to support this view. Economic reforms were expected to encourage employment in the informal/ unorganised sector; but activities within the unorganised sector which are expected to be relatively better paid — as they draw their growth momentum from the demand side factors — do not seem to have generated job opportunities on a large scale. An increasing residual absorption of labour in low productivity activities, as open unemployment may not be affordable for long, cannot be taken to suggest rapid employment growth in the economy. The organised industrial sector, as noted above, experienced a rise in employment growth in the nineties but that is due, as mentioned above, mainly to decline in real wage growth (Goldar, 2000). Besides, the employment elasticity, though calculated for a shorter period in the nineties, is not indicative of any improvement (Mitra, forthcoming).

SECTION 4

ECONOMETRIC MODELLING

In this section we suggest a simultaneous equation model, which involves five equations corresponding to the following endogenous variables: (i) URBN - urbanisation rate (percentage urban), (ii) IND - Industrialisation (percentage of organised industrial value added in total gross state domestic product), (iii) RPROD - labour productivity in rural unorganised manufacturing, (iv) UPROD - labour productivity in urban unorganised manufacturing and (v) UPOV - incidence of urban poverty. The model has been developed in the light of the following major hypotheses: (i) industrialisation[2] leads to urban growth, as spatial concentration of activities encourages rapid population (labour) inflow from the rural areas; (ii) urbanisation

2. By industrialisation we mean the expansion of organised industrial sector.

attracts industries as it creates external economies of scale and augments productivity, (iii) (organised) industrial spread enhances labour productivity in unorganised manufacturing in both rural and urban areas through inter-sectoral linkages, (iv) rural manufacturing productivity raises its urban counterpart in the unorganised sector, as better performing enterprises tend to shift to urban locations, (v) rise in industrialisation and productivity improvement in the unorganised sector reduces urban poverty.

Urbanisation (URB) is taken to be a function of industrialisation (IND), rural poverty (RPOV), infrastructure (INF) and agricultural productivity (AGVAPC). The over-urbanisation literature would suggest that rural poverty induces rapid population movement from rural to urban areas, as propensity to migrate among the poor is much higher than that among the rural non-poor (Harris and Todaro, 1970). The alternative view, however, suggests that the propensity to migrate among both rural poor and rich is modest; it is high only among those located in the middle income groups (Banerjee, 1986). So, according to the latter view, rise in rural poverty would reduce urban in-migration and hence urbanisation. Both infrastructure (percentage of gross state domestic product originating from transport, storage and communication) and agricultural productivity - agricultural value added per rural population taken as a proxy — are expected to raise urbanisation.

Apart from the productivity augmenting effects of urbanisation on industrialisation, as suggested in several studies (Mills, 1967; Mills and Mitra, 1997; Mitra, 1999), the other explanatory variables taken in equation (2) for IND are per capita income (PCI), agricultural productivity (AGVAPC) and literacy (LIT). With a rise in PCI, demand for non-food products including consumer durables and non-durables increases, which provides an impetus to industrialisation (Kuznets, 1966). Agricultural productivity (in our study, it is taken in terms of agricultural value added per rural population), however, can either raise or reduce industrialisation. Rise in agricultural productivity releases the surplus resources which can be utilised either for industrial growth or for further investment to be made in the agricultural sector itself, expected to make the region agriculturally prosperous. Hence, a negative relationship between AGVAPC and IND cannot be ruled out though a positive association between agricultural productivity and industrial growth has been suggested in the literature (Lewis, 1954).[3] Similarly, improvement in urban literacy means better quality of labour, which can be utilised in the organised industrial sector mostly located in the urban areas. But literacy can also divert people away from the blue collar jobs to white collar jobs. As firms may like to invest in regions endowed with easy supply of labour for industrial jobs, states with higher literacy may witness less industrial growth and faster growth of service oriented activities.

Both urbanisation and organised industry can have a positive effect on rural unorganised manufacturing productivity (RPROD). With rising urbanisation, rural enterprises develop access to better marketing facilities. Similarly, with a rise in industrialisation inter-sectoral linkages are said to work more prominently — demand for certain products manufactured by the small enterprises located in the rural or urban areas increases, or the supply of certain products generated by the large units as by-products and processed by the small units picks up. But urbanisation may affect negatively the performance of the rural based units if the entrepreneurs in the urban areas tend to compete with their rural counterparts. Agricultural productivity can affect rural manufacturing productivity positively if backward and forward linkages between agriculture and manufacturing in the rural areas are strong. Percentage of rural labour force engaged as agricultural wage labour (AGLAB) is a rough proxy for surplus labour in the rural areas. With a rise in AGLAB, the supply of labour to rural manufacturing goes up, which may reduce wages and encourage employment in rural manufacturing. But this would then have a dampening effect on manufacturing value added per labour, if value added does not increase at least proportionately in this sector.

In the case of urban unorganised manufacturing productivity (UPROD) its rural counterpart plays a positive role because, as mentioned above, better performing units tend to shift to the urban areas. Even if they do not shift physically, the linkages seem to grow between the small units in the rural areas and those in the urban

---

3. Krishna (1977) while showing an association between industrial cost and pricing highlights the role of agriculture in determining the wage rate in the industrial sector.

areas, with a rise in productivity in the former. Industrialisation is expected to have a positive impact on the small units, and more so in the urban areas because of their physical proximity. Development of infrastructure, in a region, however, does not essentially require physical movement of enterprises from rural to urban areas. With improvements in infrastructural growth, units located in villages, and in the rural hinterland of the big cities reap the advantages most by developing access to facilities available in the urban areas. On the other hand, small units actually located in the urban areas have to strive for space and access to resources, for, commercialisation responds promptly to infrastructure growth. Hence urban unorganised manufacturing productivity may actually fall in relation to INF. Urban literacy, not necessarily though, would possibly have a positive effect on productivity in urban unorganised manufacturing, by improving the quality of labour and its capabilities to utilise better technology more efficiently.

In the equation for urban poverty, UPROD is included expecting a negative effect. But industrialisation as defined in this paper, can raise urban poverty if in the process of industrial growth capital intensive technology is adopted largely. Among some of the rural specific variables which can influence urban poverty is the rural male work participation rate (RMWPR). With increasing work opportunities in the rural areas, urban in-migration is expected to slow down and hence the spill-over effect of rural unemployment and underemployment would get dissipated. Another variable included in this equation is the percentage of scheduled caste population in the urban areas (USC). Poverty is expected to be more prevalent among lower castes, as they have less access to economic opportunities, compared to other higher castes. However, in the process of economic development, particularly in the urban areas, the caste factor, at least ideally speaking, is likely to get blurred.

These equations have been estimated both by OLS and 2SLS (Table 8.7); results do not seem to be much different. The cross section data have been taken for two time points, the late-eighties and the mid-nineties. The reference years for all the variables are not same as information from different sources such as NSSO, NAS, and population census have been compiled for the estimation of the model.

Table 8.7

Estimates of the Structural Form of the Model: OLS and 2SLS Results Endogenous Variables

Explanatory	*URB*		*IND*		*RPROD*		*UPROD*		*UPOV*	
Variables	*OLS*	*2SLS*	*OLS*	*2SLS*	*OLS*	*2SLS*	*OLS*	*2SLS*	*OLS*	*2SLS*
Inter	1.67	1.80	14.49	15.22	659.24	561.03	-3117.7	-3113.0	132.09	136.40
	(0.29)	(0.303)	(2.86)*	(2.77)*	(1.18)	(0.95)	(-1.28)	(-1.27)	(6.04)*	(7.07)*
RPOV	-0.095	-0.109								
	(-1.15)	(-1.29)								
IND	0.78	0.96			136.58	179.20	146.61	153.78	1.63	2.22
	(4.90)*	(4.66)*			(3.34)*	(2.93)*	(2.20)*	(1.72)**	(4.70)*	(5.80)*
INF	2.32	2.08					-597.23	-523.02		
	(4.82)*	(4.00)*					(-2.48)*	(-1.94)**		
AGVAPC	0.004	0.004	-0.006	-0.007	1.17	1.23				
	(2.74)*	(2.39)*	(-4.56)*	(4.33)*	(4.58)*	(4.25)*				
URB			0.23	0.18	-19.70	-36.43				
			(2.50)*	(1.52)***	(-0.71)	(-0.96)				
PCI			0.005	0.005						
			(4.14)*	(3.87)*						
ULIT			-0.19	-0.197			102.37	84.80		
			(-2.50)*	(-2.38)*			(2.29)*	(1.82)**		
AGLAB					-31.09	-32.95				
					(-1.89)**	(1.86)**				

Contd...

...*Table 8.7 Contd*...

Explanatory Variables	*URB*		*IND*		*RPROD*		*UPROD*		*UPOV*	
	OLS	*2SLS*	*OLS*	*2SLS*	*OLS*	*2SLS*	*OLS*	*2SLS*	*OLS*	*2SLS*
RPROD							1.13	1.46		
							(4.41)*	(4.29)*		
UPROD									-0.003	-0.005
									(-4.86)*	(-6.24)*
RMWPR									-2.04	-2.19
									(-4.82)*	(-5.80)*
USC									0.47	0.67
									-1.14	(1.83)**
R^2	0.80		0.67		0.62		0.68		0.60	
WT	0.55	0.06	0.30	0.24	3.13	2.05	7.92	4.20	0.19	0.39
N	30	30	30	30	30	30	30	30	30	30

Note: WT stands for wthie's test for heteroscedasticity. Heteroscedasticity seems to be absent as x^2_{p-1} is not significant at 10 per cent level, where p is the number of regressors in the regression of e_i^2 on the explanatory varaibles, their square terms and the product terms.

Empirical results are more or less supportive of the hypotheses. A striking feature is, however, relating to the impact of industrialisation on urban poverty. With larger spread of (organised) industry, urban poverty is found to grow as labour demand tends to fall much short of the labour supply growth. As an activity organised industry encourages labour transfer from rural to urban areas, but sluggish employment growth compels them to get residually absorbed in low productivity activities and thus explains a swelling proportion of population living in poverty in the urban areas.

While infrastructure, industrialisation and agricultural productivity show a positive impact on urbanisation, rural poverty tends to reduce it. However, the coefficient of rural poverty does not appear to be statistically significant. From equation (2) empirical results are somewhat supportive of the existence of urbanisation economies. Though per capita income exerts a positive influence on industrialisation, agricultural productivity tends to dampen it. Literacy leads to tertiarisation of the economy rather than industrialisation. Both IND and AGVAPC enhance productivity in rural unorganised manufacturing while AGLAB shows a negative impact on it. The coefficient of urbanisation, however, does not appear to be statistically significant. In the urban areas, unorganised manufacturing productivity is influenced positively by its rural counterpart. IND and ULIT also have a positive impact on UPROD, though INF takes a negative coefficient.

Productivity rise in unorganised manufacturing improves the level of living, though IND, as mentioned above, raises UPOV. Rural male work participation rate slows down urban in-migration which reduces urban poverty. However, the caste factor still plays a role in accessing economic opportunities in the urban areas, which suggests a higher incidence of poverty among the lower castes. But this would also be due to their educational backwardness, which reduces their accessibility to high income jobs.

Elasticity coefficients estimated on the basis of the reduced form coefficient matrix, at mean values of the variables, are reported in Table 8.8. The elasticity of urbanisation with respect to infrastructure is around 0.9, whereas with respect to rural poverty it is almost negligible. The responsiveness of industrialisation to per capita income is quite high (1.38), and so also are the elasticities of both

Table 8.8

Elasticities at Mean Values
Exogenous Variables

Endogenous Variables	*RPOV*	*INF*	*AGVAPL*	*PCI*	*ULIT*	*AGLAB*	*RMWPR*	*USC*
URB	-0.06	0.914	0.04	0.54	-1.18	0.04	-0.90	0.16
IND	0.02	0.38	-0.555	1.38	-1.36	0.145	-1.64	0.038
RPROD	0.005	0.18	0.282	0.93	-0.145	-0.27	-3.35	0.017
UPROD	0.30	-0.13	0.225	1.00	0.118	-0.16	-2.71	-0.204
UPOV	-0.137	0.775	-0.445	0.19	-0.93	0.185	-3.67	0.56

rural and urban unorganised manufacturing productivity with respect to PCI (around 1). The magnitude of impact of literacy on urban poverty is around unity suggesting the effectiveness of education on poverty reduction. Also, the availability of work opportunities in the rural areas subsides urban poverty - the elasticity with respect to RMWPR being -3.67. However, the impact of rural poverty on urban poverty is negligible.

SECTION 5

CONCLUSION

Organised industrial value added growth during the eighties and even during the nineties has been reasonably high despite the deceleration caused by economic reforms in the early-nineties. However, employment growth in organised industry seems to have been sluggish though it improved during the nineties. But the rise was mainly caused by a decline in real wage growth. Besides, the employment elasticity, though calculated for a few years in the nineties, does not seem to be statistically different from that in the eighties. As a result, urbanisation and industrial spread in terms of value added though have been inter-related, the role of industry in reducing poverty through employment generation, does not seem to be significant. On the contrary, it is found to raise urban poverty implying that industrial growth attracts migrants and raises the labour supply, which in the face of sluggish employment opportunities in the industrial sector compels them to get residually absorbed in low productivity activities in the urban areas. Adoption of labour intensive technology without affecting the real earnings adversely can help attain the employment objectives of the industrial policy in India, and strengthen the role of industry in ameliorating poverty. The indirect effects of industrial spread on urban poverty, however, seems interesting. It is found to raise unorganised manufacturing productivity, both in the rural and urban areas, and urban unorganised manufacturing productivity, which is also affected positively by its rural counterpart, reduces urban poverty. Efforts, therefore, need to be made to improve the inter-sectoral linkages within manufacturing across size categories as well as space. Finally, measures for human resource development need to be adopted, as the elasticity of urban poverty with respect to literacy has been reasonably high.

References

Acharya, S. and A. Mitra (2000). *The Potential of Rural Industries and Trade to Provide Decent Work Conditions: A Data Recommaissance in India*, ILO-ARTEP.

Banerjee, B. (1986). *Rural to Urban Migration and the Urban Labour Market: A Case Study of Delhi*, Himalaya Pub. House, Bombay.

Goldar, B.N. (2000). "Employment Growth in Organised Manufacturing in India," *Economic and Political Weekly*, April 1.

Harris, J. and M.P. Todaro (1970). "Migration, Unemployment and Development: A Two Sector Analysis," *The American Economic Review*.

Krishna, K.L. (1977). "A Model of Industrial Cost-Price," in *Towards a Macro Modelling of India*, Mimeo, Delhi School of Economics.

Kuznets, S. (1966). *Modern Economic Growth: Rate, Structure and Spread*, New Haven, Yale University Press.

Lewis, W.A. (1954). *Economic Development with Unlimited Supplies of Labour*, The Manchester School of Economic and Social Studies.

Mills, E.S. (1967). "An Aggregate Model of Resource Allocation in a Metropolitan Area," *American Economic Review*, Vol.57.

Mills. E.S. and Arup Mitra (1997). *Urban Development and Urban Ills*, Commonwealth Publishers, Delhi.

Ministry of Industry (1996). *Hand Book of Industrial Policy and Statistics*, Office of the Economic Advisor, Govt. of India, New Delhi

Ministry of Industry (1997). *Hand Book of Industrial Policy and Statistics*, Office of the Economic Advisor, Govt. of India, New Delhi.

Mitra, Arup (1999). "Agglomeration Economics as Manifested in Technical Efficiency of Firms," *Journal of Urban Economics*, Vol.45. May.

Mitra, Arup (forthcoming). "Urban Labour Market: An Overview," *International Journal of Employment Studies*.

9

Employment Growth in Factory Manufacturing Sector During Pre- and Post-Reform Periods

SURESH D. TENDULKAR

The paper seeks to analyse the employment outcomes resulting from the growth in manufacturing output (in terms of real gross value added) in the factory sector since the reforms in 1991, put them in the perspective of the pre-reform decade and in the process obtain an estimate of elasticity of employment in the factory sector with respect to manufacturing output.

The database is provided by the summary results of the factory sector available in the Annual Survey of Industries (ASI) for various years. The analysis has been carried out for eighteen 2-digit industry groups (for description, *see* Table 9.1) for the period from 1980-81 to 1997-98 which is the latest year for which ASI has been published. It has been divided into two sub-periods: 1980-81 to 1990-91 (1981-91 for short) and 1990-91 to 1997-98 (1991-98). The first sub-period is the decade of the 1980s when hesitant and selective deregulation of industrial and trade policies combined with rising fiscal deficits had resulted in a step-up in output growth compared to 1970s but virtual stagnation in factory sector manufacturing employment. It was widely described as a 'jobless growth' with serious concern for declining employment elasticity. On this background, there had been serious apprehensions when the selective deregulation of the 1980s escalated into wide ranging liberalisation of industrial and trade policies since 1991. Goldar (EPW, April 1-7, 2000) was one of the first to draw on ASI data to point out that, contrary to the apprehensions, the employment growth in the 1990s at 2.69 per cent per annum (pcpa) was higher than virtual stagnation (0.53 pcpa) in the 1980s. He also provides a good survey of earlier writings in this context. This paper extends his analysis. Very briefly we note that numerical differences between his and our comparable results can be attributed to the differences in wholesale price indices at 2-digit level and the growth rates in his calculations being point to point in comparison with exponential trend growth rates presented in this paper.

Table 9.1

Number of Workers in the Factory Sector of Manufacturing Industry at 2-Digit Level

2-Digit Code	Average Number of Workers: 1980-81 to 1982-83 Period I	1988-89 to 1990-91 Period II	1995-96 to 1997-98 Period III	Change Between Periods I and II	Change Between Periods II and III	Percentage Composition of Col (6)
(1)	(2)	(3)	(4)	(5)	(6)	(7)
20-21	1003917	841512	1019154	-162404	177642	15.96
22	389893	440774	532601	50882	91827	8.25
23	920280	729380	736656	-190900	7276	0.65
24	196030	231167	285914	35137	54747	4.92
25	234239	189043	212790	-45195	23747	2.13
26	81383	129342	295523	47959	166182	14.93
27	64027	56768	61643	-7259	4876	0.44
28	221490	207520	251038	-13970	43518	3.91
29	50639	83969	106574	33330	22605	2.03
30	137485	312553	525008	175068	212455	19.09
31	337526	251871	253583	-85655	1711	0.15
32	313039	353578	366623	40539	13046	1.17
33	446511	464682	518163	18171	53481	4.81
34	151701	168529	214906	16828	46377	4.17
35	293754	294784	328251	1030	33467	3.01
36	218543	251101	296148	32558	45048	4.05
37	377624	364991	438183	-12633	73192	6.58
38	51470	66188	107801	14719	41613	3.74
20-38	5489550	5437754	6550562	-51796	1112808	100.00

Source: Annual Survey of Industries, Summary Results for the Factory Sector for Various Years.

Description of the 2-Digit industry code

20-21	food products	22	beverages, tobacco, etc.
23	cotton textiles	24	wool, silk, etc.
25	jute textiles	26	textile products
27	wood, furniture, etc.	28	paper & printing,etc.
29	leather & fur products	30	chemicals, etc.
31	rubber, petroleum, etc.	32	non-metallic products
33	basic metal industries	34	metal products
35	non-electrical	36	electrical machinery
37	transport equipments	38	other manufacturing

To provide a broad perspective, Table 9.1 provides average number of workers in three triennia: 1980-81 to 1982-83 (period I) which provides the initial situation in the 1980s, 1988-89 to 1990-91 (period II) which is the last triennium of the decade and a pre-reform period and finally 1995-96 to 1997-98 (period III), the latest available triennium after the 1991 reforms. Also given is the change in the factory employment during the decade of the 1980s (column (5)) and between the pre- and the post-reform triennia (column (6)) with the percentage composition of the latter given in column (7). The details are given for eighteen 2-digit industry groups and in the aggregate (20-38) in the last line.

The following points may be noted from Table 9.1:

(1) The decade of the 1980s saw a decline in the aggregate factory employment by 52 thousand or about 1 per cent. In contrast, the latest post-reform triennium saw a rise of 1.11 million or 20 per cent in comparison with the last triennium of the 1980s. In the net, over a million workers were added between the first and the last triennium over the 18 year period. In other words, the reform period more than made up for the losses during the 'jobless decade'.

(2) The **prominent losers** in the decade of the 1980s (with percentage share in the first triennium in the brackets) were: **food products** (18), **cotton textiles** (17), **transport equipment** (7) **rubber, petroleum, etc.** (6), **jute textiles and paper and paper printing, etc.** (4 each) and **wood, furniture etc.** (2). These seven industries together accounted for 58 per cent of the factory sector employment in the first triennium and the joblosses over the decade amounted to over 518 thousand. This could not be made up by the job gains to the tune of 175 thousand in **chemicals**, 51 thousand in **beverages, tobacco, etc.**, 48 thousand in **textile products**, 35 thousand in **wood, silk, etc.** and 33 thousand in **leather and fur products**. Clearly, a significant restructuring of the manufacturing employment took place in the 1980s without much globalisation and liberalisation to talk about.

(3) In contrast to the 1980s, there were no net losers between the pre- and the post-reform triennia at the level of 2-digit industry groups. The prominent gainers were **chemicals** (212 thousand on top of 175 thousand in the previous decade), **food products** (178 thousand, more than making up for the earlier losses) **textile products** (166 thousand) and beverages, tobacco, etc. (92 thousand on top of the 52 thousand) and **transport equipment** (73 thousand). These five groups together accounting for 65 per cent of the aggregate increase of 1.11 million. **Wool, silk etc.** and **basic metal industries** added about 54 thousand each. It may be noted that these industries were not prominent in labour absorption in the early-1980s as they accounted for only 36 per cent of the total employment in the first triennium.

Following the changes in the factory sector employment presented in Table 9.1 over the three triennia, Table 9.2 examines (a) whether there was any statistically significant change in the trend growth rate of workers during the post-1991 period and (b) how the share of wage bill in gross output behaved during the post- 1991 period. The motivation for (b) is derived from the interpretation of the share of wage bill in gross output as average (skill-adjusted) wage rate relative to average productivity per worker. At a fairly disaggregated level, it can be taken to be the wage rate (per worker) in efficiency units. However, at the two-digit level of aggregation, it is not warranted. But this interpretation enables us to see that both the average (skill-adjusted) wage rate and the number of workers employed in the industry can go up even with a declining wage share in gross output if the productivity per worker increases more than proportionately. In other words, a declining wage share can be consistent with a rise in both the wage rate and the number of employed workers. A rise in productivity per worker can have several sources: rise in capital intensity, technological change or improved organisational efficiency. Our analysis does not throw light on these sources. In the absence of adequate rise in average productivity per worker, employment and wage rate would obviously move in opposite directions.

Table 9.2

Summary Results for Trend Regressions for Number of Workers and Share of Wages in Value of Gross Output 1980-81 to 1997-98

2-Digit Code	*Number of Workers*			*Share of Wage Bill in Value of Gross Output*		
	t	*D1×t*	$\bar{R}^2$	*t*	*D1×t*	R^2
(1)	(2)	(3)	(4)	(5)	(6)	(7)
20-21	-1.67* (-2.02)	1.88 (3.25)	0.40	D*	D*	0.76
22	2.68 (5.55)		0.64	D		0.61
23	-2.98 (-8.61)	4.25 (5.54)	0.89	D	D	0.91
24	2.21 (9.35)		0.84	D		0.83
25	-2.91 (-2.86)	5.62 (2.48)	0.36	No trend	No trend	-0.03
26	5.52 (6.02)	7.36 (3.61)	0.96	D		0.27
27	-1.61 (-6.11)	4.54 (7.77)	0.81	D		0.67
28	-0.71* (-2.02)	3.16 (4.05)	0.71	D	R	0.93
29	6.06 (9.77)	-3.13 (-2.27)	0.95	D		0.78
30	10.37 (10.38)		0.86	R	D	0.63
31	-4.42 (-2.32)	9.92 (2.34)	0.49	D		0.71
32	1.46 (3.77)	-1.73* (-2.01)	0.58	D	R	0.97
33	0.65 (3.11)		0.34	D	R	0.79
34	1.20* (1.96)	3.49 (2.56)	0.79	D		0.73
35	0.46* (2.10)		0.17	D		0.82
36	1.97 (13.94)		0.92	D		0.74
37	0.68 (2.34)		0.21	D		0.92

Contd. ...

... *Table 9.2 Contd.* ...

2-Digit Code	Number of Workers			Share of Wage Bill in Value of Gross Output		
	t	$D1\times t$	$\bar{R}^2$	t	$D1\times t$	R^2
(1)	(2)	(3)	(4)	(5)	(6)	(7)
38	3.02 (3.28)	4.92 (4.64)	0.97	D	D	0.86
20-38	-0.12 (-0.40)	3.20 (5.02)	0.86	Not calculated		

Notes: 1. t represents time and D1 represents dummy variable defined by D1=1 from 1991-92 to 1997-98 =0 from 1980-81 to 1990-91

2. Results in Columns (2) to (4) for the number of workers are based on semi log trend regression equations whereas those in columns (5) to (7) for the percentage share of wage bill in value of gross output are based on simple linear regression equations. Estimated coefficients in per cent units with corresponding t-values in bracket are reported in columns (2) and (3). For columns (5) and (6) the estimated coefficients being changes in percentage are very small in magnitudes in most cases and hence only the direction (rise(R) and decline(D)) is indicated.

3. Unstarred entries are significant at 5 per cent or lower level.

Starred entries are significant at 10 per cent or lower level but higher than 5 per cent.

No trend is reported when the coefficient of time was not significant even at 10 per cent level.

Adjusted (for degrees of freedom) squared multiple correlation coefficients ($\bar{R}^2$) are reported in columns (4) and (7).

4. Results of trend regression with dummy variable are reported when the coefficient of D1×t was significant at 10 per cent or lower level. Otherwise, results are reported for regression without dummy variable.

Table 9.2 brings out the following salient points:

(1) Wage share has been declining (columns (5) to (7)) in all the 2-digit industry groups except jute textiles (group 25) where there were fluctuations without trend. The decline became faster in the 1990s in four industries: food products (20-21), cotton textiles (23), chemicals (30) and miscellaneous manufacturing (38). It was reversed in the 1990s in two industries: non-metallic products (32) and basic metal industries (33).

(2) Turning to the trend growth in absolute number of workers (columns (2) to (4)), not surprisingly (in view of Table 9.1), all the seven industries where employment was noted to have declined in Table 9.1 with the exception of transport equipment (37) reported significantly negative trend growth rates in the 1980s ranging from 0.7 per cent

per annum (pcpa) for paper and printing etc. (28) to 4.4 per cent per annum for rubber, petroleum etc. (31). In the sole exception of group 37, the positive growth rate of 0.7 pcpa, though significant at 10 per cent was unstable in view of the very low value of $\bar{R}^2$. In all the six industry groups with negative trend growth in the 1980s, the trend was reversed and became positive in the 1990s. Despite this reversal, the share of these six groups in total manufacturing employment declined from 42 per cent in the pre-reform triennium to 39 per cent in the post-reform triennium.

(3) In the remaining twelve industry groups, the trend growth rate was positive in the 1980s ranging between 0.5 pcpa (with considerable instability) for non-electrical machinery (35) to as high as 6 pcpa for leather and leather products (29) which registered a slowdown in the 1990s. The trend growth rate became slightly negative in the 1990s also for non-metallic products (32) where, interestingly, wage share showed a trend increase in the 1990s.

(4) The positive trend growth rate of the 1980s became faster in the 1990s for three industry groups: textile product (26), metal products (34), and miscellaneous manufacturing (38). These three industry groups accounted for nearly 23 per cent of incremental employment between the pre- and the post-reform triennia. Of these, in the miscellaneous manufacturing group, there was a faster decline in the wage share during the 1990s.

How did consumption wage rates (or real wage hereafter) behave across industry groups between the 1980s and the 1990s? Table 9.3 (columns (10) and (11), provides the exponential trend growth rates for the 1981-91 and 1991-98 periods.

The last line indicates that trend growth rates in real wage rate slowed down from 3 pcpa in the 1980s to a more unstable 1.3 pcpa in the 1990s for the aggregate manufacturing sector.

At the industry group level, the biggest gainer in terms of employment, as noted from Table 9.1, was the chemicals industry (30) where (a) real wage rate increased by 4.5 pcpa in the 1980s followed by fluctuations without trend in the 1990s; (b) employment growth slowed down from 9 pcpa in the 1980s to 5 pcpa in the 1990s

Table 9.3

Exponential Growth Rates of Major Industry Characteristics at 2-digit Industry Level 1981-91 and 1991-98

2-Digit Code	Growth Rate of No. of Workers		Growth Rate of Real Value Added		Growth Rate of Product Wage		Elasticity of Wage Bill w.r.t. Value Added		Growth Rate of Real Consumption Wage	
	1981-91	1991-98	1981-91	1991-98	1981-91	1991-98	1981-91	1991-98	1981-91	1991-98
(1)	(2)	(3)	(4)	(5)	(6)	(7)	(8)	(9)	(10)	(11)
20-21	-1.94	2.67	9.61	9.46	9.18	2.47	0.8538	0.7451	7.46	0.92
	(0.30)	(0.89)	(0.87)	(0.90)	(0.87)	(0.62)			(0.90)	(0.27)
22	1.55	2.70	8.26	7.62	3.48	1.53	0.8127	0.7876	4.19	0.81
	(0.15)	(0.69)	(0.77)	(0.92)	(0.52)	(0.56)			(0.71)	(0.45)
23	-2.98	0.65	3.54	0.92	4.92	-3.75	0.8139	0.6774	1.71	-1.27
	(0.86)	(0.22)	(0.57)	(0.048)	(0.89)	(0.89)			(0.81)	(0.66)
24	2.29	3.45	6.04	8.49	1.39	1.62	0.8398	0.7701	1.74	-1.04
	(0.68)	(0.86)	(0.78)	(0.67)	(0.35)	(0.92)			(0.79)	(0.65)
25	-2.91	2.08	-2.05	4.27	2.63	1.43	1.2736	0.9439	2.87	1.40
	(0.54)	(0.18)	(0.13)	(0.63)	(0.15)	(0.082)			(0.65)	(0.37)
26	5.52	12.79	11.28	10.78	1.87	-0.76	0.7967	1.0599	1.45	0.35
	(0.83)	(0.92)	(0.76)	(0.65)	(0.30)	(0.098)			(0.76)	(0.06)
27	-1.61	2.68	4.74	-3.29	5.90	-7.25	0.9546	0.9085	2.76	0.81
	(0.82)	(0.86)	(0.77)	(0.096)	(0.96)	(0.47)			(0.86)	(0.22)
28	-0.71	2.47	6.39	6.38	4.40	3.72	0.7955	0.9869	2.89	1.76
	(0.32)	(0.78)	(0.88)	(0.64)	(0.98)	(0.61)			(0.93)	(0.69)
29	6.06	3.22	9.59	8.65	0.13	4.79	0.805	0.9496	-0.25	-0.24
	(0.91)	(0.67)	(0.87)	(0.72)	(0.0019)	(0.78)			(0.04)	(0.016)
30	9.39	5.19	20.28	11.05	7.57	0.27	0.8699	0.7159	4.52	-0.18
	(0.59)	(0.98)	(0.91)	(0.91)	(0.96)	(0.0201)			(0.92)	(0.02)
31	-4.42	5.26	3.67	8.01	5.34	2.72	0.6821	0.9979	2.04	1.14
	(0.28)	(0.96)	(0.39)	(0.62)	(0.93)	(0.74)			(0.73)	(0.37)

Contd. ...

Contd. ...

(1)	(2)	(3)	(4)	(5)	(6)	(7)	(8)	(9)	(10)	(11)
32	1.46	0.05	10.04	3.84	4.25	3.04	0.7313	0.941	2.04	2.86
	(0.57)	(0.002)	(0.97)	(0.41)	(0.84)	(0.94)			(0.88)	(0.96)
33	0.47	1.66	4.10	11.96	0.73	7.42	0.7877	0.8496	2.02	5.57
	(0.17)	(0.39)	(0.59)	(0.84)	(0.24)	(0.77)			(0.78)	(0.58)
34	1.20	3.99	4.22	11.01	1.82	3.83	0.9079	0.8173	2.30	1.20
	(0.31)	(0.72)	(0.70)	(0.90)	(0.21)	(0.85)			(0.68)	(0.28)
35	-0.04	1.38	4.81	8.74	4.37	4.24	0.9609	0.7969	3.29	1.81
	(0.0015)	(0.28)	(0.84)	(0.81)	(0.96)	(0.79)			(0.92)	(0.56)
36	1.69	2.18	9.00	6.04	4.75	2.42	0.8304	0.8682	2.56	1.15
	(0.75)	(0.83)	(0.91)	(0.77)	(0.89)	(0.46)			(0.89)	(0.15)
37	-0.53	3.22	4.22	13.19	3.98	5.28	0.8891	0.7517	3.09	1.94
	(0.28)	(0.67)	(0.83)	(0.81)	(0.86)	(0.88)			(0.96)	(0.56)
38	3.03	7.70	11.43	15.59	8.12	3.84	0.9793	0.8214	2.40	1.88
	(0.81)	(0.95)	(0.88)	(0.85)	(0.94)	(0.89)			(0.63)	(0.64)
20-38	-0.12	2.92	7.13	9.09	4.48	2.62	0.7981	0.7885	3.02	1.29
	(0.016)	(0.89)	(0.97)	(0.94)	(0.93)	(0.80)			(0.92)	(0.56)

Notes: 1. Growth rates (per cent per annum) (columns (2) to (7) and (10), (11)) are the slope coefficients of semi-log trend regression equations with squared product-moment correlation coefficient (r^2) in brackets. They have been given for the decade of the 1980s (1980-81 to 1990-91) denoted as 1981-91 and the 1990s (1990-91 to 1997-98) denoted as 1991-98.

2. Variable Description:

(i) Real value added is defined as the nominal gross value added deflated by the wholesale price index for the industry group.

(ii) Real product wage is defined by the nominal wage per worker deflated by the wholesale price index for the industry group representing the output price movements for the group.

(iii) Elasticity of nominal wage bill (NWB) with respect to the nominal gross value added (NGVA) is derived by the exponential growth rate of NWB divided by the exponential growth rate of NGVA.

(iv) Real Consumption wage is defined by the nominal wage per worker deflated by consumer price index number for industrial workers.

(v) Aggregate real value added (20-38 in the last row, columns (4) and (5)) is the sum of 2-digit industry specific real gross value defined in (1).

(vi) Deflator for the aggregate real product wage (20-38) in the last two columns (6) and (7) is the implicit deflator for aggregate real value added defined in (v).

Source: Annual Survey of Industries, Summary volumes for the factory sector for various years.

(column (2) and (3) of Table 9.3). This was associated with halving of the trend growth rate in real value added (columns (4) and (5)). Clearly, very high growth rate of real output (20 pcpa) resulted in a trend growth in both employment and real wages in the 1980s. The slowdown in the 1990s resulted in slower growth in employment but a stagnation in real wages.

The second biggest gainer in terms of employment in both periods was textile products (26) which experienced 11 pcpa growth in output in the pre- and post-reform period that was associated with acceleration in employment from 5.5 pcpa to a massive 13 pcpa but very low real wage growth (1.4 pcpa) during 1981-91 followed by virtual stagnation in real wage rate during 1991-98.

The third biggest gainer in terms of employment during the post-reform period was food products group (20-21) with contrasting movements in the 1980s and 1990s. In this case, a respectable 9.6 pcpa growth in output in the 1980s was associated with the highest real wage growth of nearly 7.5 pcpa and a significant decline of 1.9 pcpa in employment. Output growth was about the same during the 1990s but 2.7 pcpa growth in employment and stagnation in real wages. In other words, the same growth rate of real output was associated with real wage growth at the cost of employment loss in the 1980s but employment gain at the cost of stagnation in real wages in the 1990s.

While interested readers may get more out of Tables 9.1 to 9.3, we wish to mention two more cases. The first is wood, furniture, etc. (27) where a three-fold step-up in the trend growth rate of real value added was associated with a much lower and more unstable three-fold rise in growth rate of employment but a much stronger growth in real wages. The next is wood, furniture, etc. (27) where an unstable and negative growth in real value added was associated with positive growth in employment and a virtual stagnation in real wages.

How do we understand the foregoing diversity illustrated from Table 9.3 with respect to growth in employment and real wages? For this purpose, we need to move from real consumption wage which measures the welfare enjoyed by workers to real product wage (or product wage hereafter) which reflects the unit cost of labour in relation to output price to which employers are expected to respond in hiring workers. Trend growth rates of product wage are presented in columns (6) and (7) of Table 9.3. In commenting on the product wage growth, we may mention that the consumer price index for industrial workers (CPIIW) grew at the rate of 8.3 pcpa during the 1980s and 9.1 pcpa in the 1990s. The last line of Table 9.3 (columns (6), (7), (10) and (11)) indicates that in the aggregate, product wage growth exceeded that in real wage so that (implicitly) weighted wholesale price index for manufacturing output grew slower than CPIIW. Other things remaining the same, a faster growth in CPIIW than output price index puts a damper both on real wage growth and (derived) demand for labour by raising the unit labour cost. While this has happened in the aggregate as well as for majority of industry groups in both the periods, the growth in product wage at 4.5 pcpa in the 1980s has distinctly slowed down to 2.6 pcpa in the 1990s in the aggregate as well as for the fourteen out of eighteen 2-digit industry groups. This is expected to favour employment growth in the 1990s in comparison with the 1980s.

The demand for labour being derived from that for output, growth in real value added which was higher at 9 pcpa in the 1990s than 7 pcpa in the 1980s may also be expected to boost *ceteris paribus* demand for labour.

Growth in real value added (or output growth) and in product wage are the two variables that Goldar (2000) uses to explain the cross section variation in growth rates in employment across eighteen 2-digit group industries in the two periods. We add one more variable in repeating the estimation of the Goldar equation, namely, elasticity of wage bill with respect to gross value added (both) at current prices (denoted as a in Table 9.3). This summary indicator of wage bill flexibility is expected to lie between zero and unity (though empirically, it exceeded unity in the 1980s in the jute textile industry (25) *see* columns (8) and (9) in Table 9.3). In the current exercise we postulated this relationship without intercept. (It may be useful to estimate it with intercept from a double log regression). To sort out the expected direction of the coefficient of α in a cross section relationship, α can be shown to be equal to

$$\frac{g_{pw} + g_e + g_{pv}}{g_{pv} + g_v}$$

where

g_{pw} is the growth rate of product wage

g_e is the growth rate of employment

g_{pv} is the growth rate of output price

g_v is the growth rate of real value added.

Holding constant g_{pw}, g_v (the other two explanatory variables in the cross-section regression) g_{pv}, the coefficient of α would reflect the demand for labour and hence positive in magnitude.

Table 9.4 presents the estimated regression equations. Notice that in comparison with Goldar (2000), we introduce an additional variable α and drop the growth rate of man days worked per worker (g_M). The reason for dropping g_M is that we postulate the (derived) demand for labour being in units of number of workers rather than in terms of mandays. Consequently, real consumption and product wage rates are in terms of average wage rate per worker.

The estimated equations help us to get an estimate of employment elasticity defined as percentage change in demand for workers in response to a percentage change in real gross value added.

A widely calculated employment elasticity in the context of the "jobless growth" of the 1980s was the ratio of growth rate of aggregate employment to aggregate real value added. Calculated thus from Table 9.3, it was negative and negligible in the 1980s (the basis of the description of jobless growth) but during the post-reform period, it becomes positive and goes upto 0.32. This implicitly assumes the cross-section relationship to go through the origin. If we permit intercept, equation (1) indicates that the gross employment elasticity (without netting out the influence of other possible variables) in the 1980s, instead of being negative and negligible, was significant and as high as 0.6 and, interestingly declines to 0.3 in the 1990s and significant only at 10 per cent level.

Addition of product wage growth (with expected negative coefficient) in equations (3) and (4) not only improves the fit but also shows that (partial) employment elasticity was higher around 0.75 in both the periods.

Introduction of elasticity of wage bill with respect to value added increases the numerical value of (partial) employment elasticity further to around 0.85 in both the periods.

Our interpretation is that after netting out the negative influence exerted by the growth in product wage and the positive influence of

Table 9.4

Results of Estimated Regression Equations Cross Section of Eighteen 2-digit Industry Groups

Dependent Variable: Exponential Growth Rate (per cent per annum) of the Number of Workers (g_e)

Ser. No.	*Period*	*Constant*	g_{va}	g_{pw}	α	R^2	$\bar{R}^2$
(1)	(2)	(3)	(4)	(5)	(6)	(7)	(8)
1	1981-91	-3.3303 (-3.69)	0.5997 (5.67)			0.6678	0.6470
2	1991-98	1.0761 (0.83)	0.3081 (2.16)			0.2258	0.1774
3	1981-91	-1.3719 (-2.30)	0.7501 (11.77)	-0.7308 (-6.07)		0.9039	0.8911
4	1991-98	-0.7811 (-0.77)	0.7523 (5.15)	-0.8128 (-4.18)		0.6424	0.5948
5	1981-91	-8.9795 (-9.19)	0.8516 (27.96)	-0.8307 (-15.43)	8.4257 (8.07)	0.9830	0.9794
6	1991-98	-15.5298 (16.80)	0.8959 (25.92)	-0.9705 (-21.30)	16.2980 (16.48)	0.9825	0.9787

Notes: 1. Variable description

g_{va}: exponential growth rate of real value added

g_{pw}: exponential growth rate of product wage

α: elasticity of wage bill with respect to gross value added

2. For detailed description of variables, see notes on Table 9.2.
3. t-values in bracket below estimated coefficients.
4. Squared multiple correlation coefficient (R^2) in column (7).
5. Squared multiple correlation coefficient corrected for degrees of freedom in column (8).

Source: Calculated from Table 9.2.

α (holding constant growth rates of output and product wage), employment elasticity of output was not low or negative during the decade of the so-called "jobless growth" of the 1980s but was as high as 0.85. It did not change during the post-reform period either. Quick preliminary covariance tests (to be further verified) suggest that there was no statistically significant difference in the estimated slope coefficients between the decade of the 1980s and the 1990s. In other words, the reform process did not appear to have made a difference to the underlying parameters of the cross-section relationship but possibly contributed to the faster pace of manufacturing growth and slowing down of the growth in product wage in the 1990s in comparison with the previous decade.

In order to analyse the offsetting effects of output growth and product wage growth, Table 9.5 provides the *ceteris paribus* impact of each explanatory variable in generating the predicted value for each 2-digit industry group for the 1981-91 period. The same is presented in Table 9.6 for 1991-98 period.

Table 9.5

Contributions of Explanatory Variables in the Predicted Value of Each Industry Group, 1981-91

(per cent per annum)

2-Digit Group	*Constant*	g_{va}	g_{pw}	α	*Estimated* g_e	*Actual* g_e
(1)	(2)	(3)	(4)	(5)	(6)	(7)
20-21	-8.9795	8.1841	-7.6258	7.1939	-1.23	-1.94
22		7.0342	-2.8908	6.8476	2.01	1.55
23		3.0147	-4.0870	6.8577	-3.19	-2.98
24		5.1437	-1.1547	7.0759	2.09	2.29
25		-1.7458	-2.1847	10.7310	-2.18	-2.91
26		9.6060	-1.5534	6.7128	5.79	5.52
27		4.0366	-4.9011	8.043	-1.80	-1.61
28		5.4417	-3.6551	6.7026	-0.49	-0.71
29		8.1668	-0.1080	6.7827	5.86	6.06
30		17.2704	-6.2883	7.3295	9.33	9.39
31		3.1253	-4.4359	5.7472	-4.54	-4.42
32		8.5500	-3.5305	6.1617	2.20	1.46
33		3.4916	-0.6064	6.6369	0.54	0.47
34		3.5938	-1.5110	7.6497	0.75	1.20
35		4.0962	-3.6302	8.0954	-0.42	-0.04
36		7.6644	-3.9458	6.9975	1.73	1.69
37		3.5938	-3.3062	7.4913	-1.20	-0.53
38		9.7338	-6.7453	8.2513	2.26	3.03
20-38		6.0720	-3.7216	6.7246	0.10	-0.12

Note: Based on equation (5) in Table 9.4.
For variable description, see Table 9.4.

We may start by examining the industry groups where absolute employment losses were noted in Table 9.1 to be significant in the 1980s. Out of the seven industry groups contributing 518 thousand job losses in the 1980s (industry groups 20-21, 23, 25, 27, 28, 31 and

37) all except the food products group (20-21) experienced lower than average output growth in the 1980s (including negative growth in the case of jute textiles (25)) that was almost totally neutralised by the product wage growth of similar magnitude. In the case of the sole exception, namely food products, the industry was marked by 9 pcpa plus growth in output as well as in product wage which was the highest among the eighteen groups.

Table 9.6

Contributions of Explanatory Variables in the Predicted Value of Each Industry Group, 1991-98

(per cent per annum)

2-Digit Group	Constant	g_{va}	g_{pw}	α	Estimated g_e	Actual g_e
(1)	(2)	(3)	(4)	(5)	(6)	(7)
20-21	-15.5298	8.4743	-2.3971	12.1437	2.69	2.67
22		6.8260	-1.4849	12.8364	2.65	2.70
23		0.8241	3.6394	11.0403	-0.03	0.65
24		7.6053	-1.5722	12.5511	3.05	3.45
25		3.8251	-1.3927	15.3837	2.29	2.08
26		9.6570	0.7376	17.2751	12.14	12.79
27		-2.9497	7.0361	14.8068	3.36	2.68
28		5.7152	-3.6103	16.0845	2.66	2.47
29		7.7487	-4.6487	15.4766	3.05	3.22
30		9.8986	-0.2620	11.6678	5.77	5.19
31		7.1754	-2.6398	16.2654	5.27	5.26
32		3.4399	-2.9503	15.3365	0.30	0.05
33		10.7138	-7.2011	13.8468	1.83	1.66
34		9.8628	-3.7170	13.3204	3.94	3.99
35		7.8293	-4.1149	12.9879	1.17	1.38
36		5.4107	-2.3487	14.1500	1.68	2.18
37		11.8156	-5.1242	12.2512	3.41	3.22
38		13.9655	-3.7267	13.3872	8.10	7.70
20-38		8.1428	-2.5427	12.8510	2.92	2.92

Note: Based on equation (6) in Table 9.4.
For variable description, see Table 9.4.

As regards the major gainers in terms of employment in the 1980s, in chemicals (30) the highest output growth (20.3 pcpa) managed to more than neutralise the adverse impact of third highest product wage growth (7.6 pcpa). In the case of other major gainers, namely, beverages, tobacco, etc. (22) and textile products (26), the impact of below average moderate product wage growth could be more than offset by above average output growth.

The contrast between the 1980s and the 1990s could be gauged by comparing Tables 9.5 and 9.6. Focussing on the contribution of product wage growth, six out of eighteen industry groups (29, 33, 34, 35, 37, 38) accounting for 24 per cent of incremental employment where the offsetting effect of product wage is larger in the 1990s than in the 1980s. This was more than neutralised by a stronger output growth in all these cases with the exception of leather and fur products (29). In the remaining twelve industry groups, the output growth effect was stronger in the 1990s than in the 1980s combined with more moderate growth in product wage (which was negative in two cases).

Two overall conclusions may be noted. One, the *ceteris paribus* output elasticity of factory sector employment based on cross section of 2-digit industry groups was as high as 0.85 during the decade of the so-called "jobless growth" of the 1980s when the pace of manufacturing output growth was faster than in the pre-1980-81 period. The elasticity did not change during the post-reform period. Two, the robust growth in employment in the post-reform period was generated by a stronger output growth in the 1990s that was reinforced by a slower product wage growth than in the 1980s.

Our interpretation of the results is that the first generation reforms launched in 1991, by removing/relaxing the entry barriers in the domestic as well as external sectors, unleashed the competitive pressures that resulted in efficiency gains from a reallocation of resources in favour of the relatively more labour using industries. This was reflected in the gains in employment in all the 2-digit level industry groups. This does not rule out employment losses at a more disaggregated level of industries and certainly not at the individual enterprise level. These losses undoubtedly resulted in hardships and dislocation for the affected workers but they constitute unavoidable concomitants of the transition from low-volume, high margin non-competitive industrial structure of the pre-reform period to the high volume, low margin competitive structure that is recognised to be necessary for rapid economic growth. In turn, rapid economic growth is the best available time-tested device for eradication of abject poverty. While there is certainly a need to minimise and alleviate the social costs resulting from unemployment and dislocation of affected workers, protecting and continuing the affected units is not a solution. What is important to underline is that in net terms, there have been significant employment gains in the high productivity organised factory manufacturing sector during the post-reform period, contrary to the apprehensions expressed by the radicals when the process of economic reforms was initiated in 1991.

10

Institutional Environment and Development of Information and Communication Technology in India

K. LAL

SECTION 1
INTRODUCTION

Recent technological development led by information and communication technologies (ICTs) is regarded as revolutionary (Mansell and Wehn, 1998). Its potentials are recognised by both developing and developed nations. In the words of the Secretary General of the United Nations: "Communication and information technologies have enormous potential, especially for developing countries, and in furthering sustainable development" (Annan, 1997).

The applications of ICTs cut across geographical boundaries and types of activities. ICTs are considered to be very pervasive as they can be applied in a wide variety of fields such as agriculture, health, education and training, manufacturing, services, transport, business, and environmental management. In recent years, the manufacturing of ICT products and related services has been a major industry in the US, Japan, and Europe (Dedrick and Kraemer, 1993). Several developing countries have also emerged as major producers of ICT products and services. India too has made significant progress in the development of an IT industry that is capable of producing hardware for the domestic market and software for exports.

It is argued in the literature (Coase, 1992; North, 1991) that the institutional environment created by governments in the form of policies and interventions has a bearing on economic development in developing as well as developed nations. In developed countries, interactions between firms and government may not be very strong, while in developing countries interactions are not only very strong but many times firms require proactive and promotional measures. The economic performance of a country is significantly influenced by the promotional and proactive policies of governments. The emergence of the strong economies of newly industrialised countries (Singapore, South Korea, Taiwan, and Hong Kong) is a case in point. The World Bank (1993) attributed the astonishing success of the East Asian "Tigers" mainly to liberalisation, export orientation, high levels of investment, and education. Despite the pervasiveness of ICTs, the diffusion and development of ICTs in developing countries has been uneven (Mansell and Wehn, 1998). There have been several studies (UNCSTD, 1997; Howkins and Valantin, 1997; Lal, 1999) that analyse the causes and consequences of the adoption of ICTs in developing countries. These studies emphasise the importance of information infrastructure in the diffusion of ICTs. Besides information infrastructure, the UNCSTD (1997) study concluded that governments need to give priority to policies, regulations, education, and training, as also to technology assessment programmes to enhance the capacity for creatively producing or using ICTs. While emphasising the role of creating a conducive institutional environment, the UNCSTD study underlines the necessity of a national ICT strategy.

Lack of information infrastructure is considered to be one of the major impediments in the diffusion of ICT. Information infrastructure includes the development of technological capabilities for use and production of ICTs and can be categorised into three groups: (1) Global Information Infrastructure (GII); (2) National Information Infrastructure (NII); and (3) Local Information Infrastructure (LII). Governments can play a very important role in building a proper information infrastructure. However, models of development of information infrastructure are dependent on the stage of development of an economy and are expected to vary significantly in less developing and least developing countries (Mansell and Wehn, 1998).

There are strong reasons for scepticism about the positive impact of liberalisation. It may lead to the destruction of domestic manufacturers, who cannot compete with low-cost imports. It could also lead to duality in economic development, because the benefits of liberalisation could be grabbed by the elite. Despite these risks, every county that has become a significant player in the global IT industry has employed some form of promotional policies (Evans, 1992; Dedrick and Kraemer, 1993).

There have been several studies (Brunner, 1991 and 1995; Dedrick and Kraemer, 1993) that deal with the development of the ICT industry in India. The studies by Brunner (1991) and by Dedrick and Kraemer used the data of the pre-liberalisation period of the Indian economy, whereas Brunner's 1995 study, though carried out after liberalisation, concentrates on the technological changes in the Indian computer industry. While the earlier studies were undertaken in the era that was dominated by import substitution rather than by an export-oriented policy regime, this study examines the impact of liberalisation on the growth of the IT industry, in India, in an era of privatisation and deregulation, the tenets of the neo-classical approach toward economic development.

The analytical framework that encompasses the interactions among the elements of the network—that is, among government policies, information infrastructure, IT industry, and markets, is depicted in Figure 10.1.

Figure 10.1

Analytical Framework

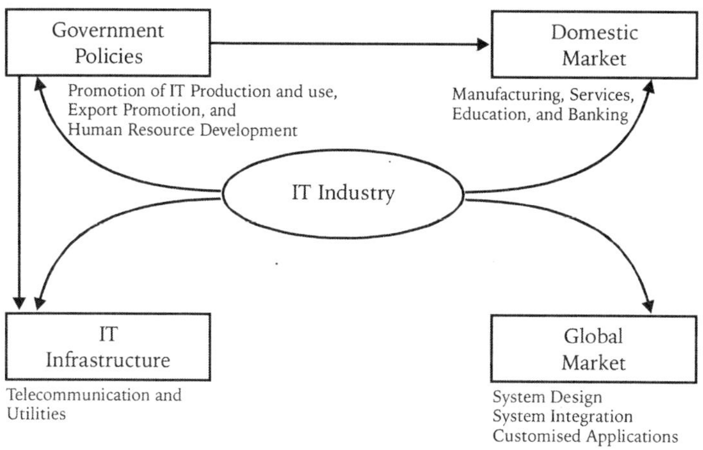

Arrows in Figure 10.1 represent the direction of the influence of one element of the network onto another. As shown in the figure, governments can influence the growth of the IT industry by embarking on economic policies aimed at affecting supply side as well as demand side factors. Supply side factors consist of telecommunications network, power, transport, human resources development, and export-import policies, whereas the demand side factors include encouragement of use of IT in the domestic market. Demand elasticity of IT products in the domestic market can be greatly influenced by proper monetary and fiscal policies. For instance, banks and other financial institutions can provide loans for the purchase of IT products to individuals and corporations, at a competitive rate of interest. Another area, where government intervention is needed to harness the potential benefits of the IT revolution is in human resources development. Liberalisation of export-import policies are equally important for efficient allocation of resources.

The remainder of this paper is organised as follows. The highlights of export-import (EXIM) are presented in Section 2, while Section 3 deals with technological policies. In Section 4 we outline human resources development policies, whereas Section 5 delineates the structure of the Indian ICT industry. Performance of the ICT industry in domestic as well as in international markets is discussed in Section 6. Finally, the findings of the study are summarised in Section 7.

SECTION 2

EXPORT-ORIENTED POLICY REGIME

Past and present policies of the government of India have been responsible, by and large, for the success and failure of the growth of the ICT industry. Until the mid-eighties, India had been following the structuralist approach toward economic development by concentrating on import substitution policies. Inward-looking policies, however, could not achieve rapid economic growth, significant improvement in the living conditions of the people, or self-reliance, for which policies had been justified by successive governments since independence. In 1985, the government started a reform programme aimed at changing import substitution to export-oriented policies. Due to an unstable political environment during

1988-90, the reform process could not maintain its momentum. With a relatively stable government in place in 1991, the liberalisation process was accelerated. Major policy changes in the electronics sector were introduced.[1] In the next sub-section, we present the salient features of the policies that might have contributed in the growth of the IT industry in India.

Export Processing Zones (EPZs)

The concept of EPZs was introduced in 1975 with the establishment of the Santa Cruz Electronics Export Processing Zone (SEEPZ) in Mumbai. Foreign and Indian investors were offered incentives to establish the export base in SEEPZ. The incentives included inexpensive land, tax holidays, duty-free import of inputs, and a single-window clearance process. However, the procedures for acquiring a license to import inputs were very complicated. It was mandatory to get a Not-Manufactured-In-India (NMI) certificate for the import of inputs. This policy, under the general import-substitution policy regime, was aimed at encouraging the use of indigenous inputs as much as possible. Consequently, the success of the establishment of the SEEPZ was limited.

After liberalisation of industrial policies in 1991, the mandatory requirement of the NMI certificate was relaxed on almost all electronic components.[2] The new liberalised import policy resulted in the establishment of several EPZs in other parts of the country. At present, EPZs are located at Mumbai, Kandla, Falta (Calcutta), Chennai, Kochi, Noida, and Vishakhapatnam. Of these, the SEEPZ is primarily meant for the development and promotion of the electronics industry. The salient incentives available to a unit in an EPZ are as follows:[3]

1. Goods supplied to the units in EPZs from the Domestic Tariff Area (DTA) are treated as exports eligible for export incentives.

---

1. Industrial policies are promulgated by the Government of India through legislation published in the *Gazette of India*. Industrial policies witnessed major changes in 1991 and 1998; these policy documents were published in the *Gazette of India* in the respective years.
2. *Monthly Newsletter*, India Investment Centre, April 1992.
3. *Investment Promotional Programmes for Electronic Hardware and Software,* Manufacturers Association of Information Technology (MAIT), 1999.

2. Permission to sell in the DTA up to 40 per cent of the production in case the value addition exceeds 25 per cent, and up to 30 per cent of the production in case the value addition is between 15 per cent and 25 per cent (such sales attract 50 per cent of normal customs duty).
3. Minimum value addition for computer software is 30 per cent.[4]
4. Complete exemption from central taxes on production and sales.
5. Tax holiday for a period of five consecutive years during the first eight years of operation.

Free Trade Zones (FTZs)

Introduction of free trade zones is a very recent development in the liberalisation process. FTZs were expected to be in operation beginning in July 1999.[5] Units in the free trade zones shall be permitted to carry out any manufacturing or trading activities. They shall not be subjected to any predetermined value addition, export obligation, or input-output/wastage norms. They shall be treated as outside the customs territory of the country, and customs officials shall man only entry and exit points. This scheme is expected to further boost export performance, as the minimum value addition of 30 per cent of software items has been relaxed.

Export Promotion Capital Goods (EPCG) Scheme

Capital goods are allowed to be imported at 10 per cent customs duty, with an export undertaking worth 4 times the CIF value of imports over a period of five years. In the amended EXIM policy, the threshold limit for zero-duty import of capital goods for the software sector has been brought down from Rs. 200 million to Rs. 1 million. Software exporters can also import computer hardware under this scheme. Zero-duty import of capital goods in the electronic sector, other than software, has been brought down to Rs. 10 million from Rs. 200 million.

4. Ministry of Information Technology (earlier DOE) Annual Report, 1999.
5. National Association of Software and Services Companies (NASSCOM) Annual Report, 1999.

Duty Exemption and Duty Drawback Schemes

Exporters are eligible for reimbursement of all customs duty paid on imported inputs of an export product. In few cases, a fixed percentage of the export value is paid to facilitate quick reimbursement. Duty-free import of raw material, components, consumables, parts, accessories, mandatory spares, and packing material are permitted against a duty-free license.

Foreign Direct Investment (FDI)

FDI policies provide automatic permission from the Reserve Bank of India for foreign equity up to 51 per cent in almost all areas of electronics and software. Proposals from non-resident Indians (NRIs) and overseas corporate bodies whose predominant owners are NRIs receive automatic approval for up to 100 per cent equity on a repatriable basis. Foreign investment up to 100 per cent is welcome in electronics and software industries that are set up exclusively for exports. The units set up under these programmes are eligible to import their entire requirement of capital goods, raw materials and components, spares, and consumables etc., free of duty. Deemed export benefits are available to suppliers of these goods from the DTA. These units are also entitled to the benefits that are available to EPZ units.

SECTION 3

TECHNOLOGY POLICIES

The success of the IT industry is intertwined with communication technologies. Particularly in the era of networking and distributed computing, communication technologies have taken a pivotal place in the diffusion and production of IT. Thus, while discussing the salient features of IT-related policies, we shall highlight the measures taken for the development of communication technologies.

Information Technology

Market equilibrium is determined by supply and demand factors. *Laissez-faire* market economy may not be the right policy choice for the development of a new industry such as IT. Realising the need for proper policies for the promotion of IT use as well as the encouragement of IT production and related services, the government has initiated various schemes in different policy regimes. We discuss, in this section, the important policy measures that have been taken to promote the IT industry. The entire period of development of IT can be divided into three phases. The first period, before 1991, was dominated by a structuralist approach toward economic development. The second period, from 1991-1997, witnessed outward-looking liberal policies. The third period, after 1998, is expected to have a more liberal policy regime. We shall concentrate on the growth of IT industry in the last two periods.

Although the government encouraged the production of IT in India during the 1980s, it failed to create the competitive environment which is crucial for growth of any industry. High tariff barriers were erected to prevent multinationals from entering in the domestic market. During the 1980s the emphasis was on production of micro- and mini-systems. The computer software sector could not flourish, due to the non-accessibility of mainframe, mini-, and micro-systems. In that period, systems were not based on an open architectural design. Consequently, software packages (system as well as application) used to be system-specific. By the late-1980s, PCs came into the Indian market. These systems were easily accessible to software companies, which began developing software on PCs in an MS-DOS environment. By the early-1990s the IT industry, particularly the software sector, emerged as a sun-rising industry. The government responded positively and came out with several policy measures to boost the development of the IT industry. A brief summary of the reform programmes started during 1991 and 1998, and of the performance of the IT industry, is presented in the next two sub-sections.

First Generation of Reforms: 1991-97

Although programmes to encourage the use of computers started in the mid-eighties, by and large these remained restricted to government-funded institutions. The main hindrance to the penetration of computer use into the private sector was the high price of the systems. This was because of high tariff barriers (180-200 per cent duty on inputs and finished goods). Government institutions, however, were provided separate funds for the computerisation of their activities. The diffusion process gained real momentum in 1992 when the tariffs were brought down substantially and the import of computers and accessories was made much simpler.[6]

Several factors, such as the high price of systems, lack of an information infrastructure, non-availability of customised products, the complexity of the technology, uncertainty about returns on IT investment, the competitive environment, and limited access to financial institutions could be cited as main reasons for the slow diffusion and production of IT. Government policies, such as substantial changes in import duty on inputs and on finished IT products, drastically reduced the prices of IT products in the domestic market. Consequently, PCs came within the reach of small companies and individuals. Reduction in prices due to low tariffs and high competition from multinationals might have resulted in the fast diffusion of IT. Availability of industry- and function-specific IT tools might also have contributed to the rapid adoption of IT. In the last few years, IT firms have launched a larger number of application packages such as inventory management, accounts software, and office automation packages. These function-specific IT tools are expected to play a crucial role in the diffusion of IT.

Diffusion of IT

Massive computerisation programmes were launched to harness the potential benefits of IT in the manufacturing and service sectors. Private sector firms are provided free technical services by the government. For instance, free consultancy services are being provided to the manufacturing sector by Foundations of Innovative Technology Transfer (FITT), an organisation funded and supported by the Indian Institute of Technology, Delhi. Efforts were also made to influence the supply-side factors. Several IT manufacturing firms collaborated with financial institutions for fast diffusion of IT in the domestic market. Under the agreement of IT firms and financial institutions, buyers of IT products manufactured by such firms could get loans on easy terms and conditions from those financial institutions. The unprecedented growth of IT diffusion during 1991-97, in India, may be due to the promotional measures taken by the government. Figure 10.2 shows the growth of IT industry in the domestic market, in value terms.

6. *Monthly Newsletter*, India Investment Centre, April 1992.

Figure 10.2

Diffusion of IT in India

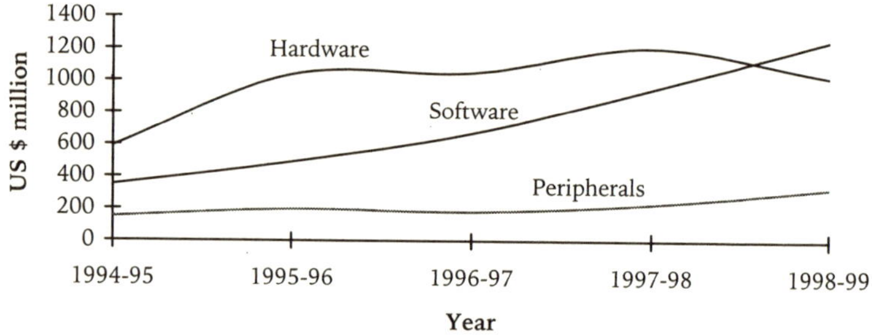

Source: NASSCOM, 1999.

It can be seen, from Figure 10.2, that the use of software is steadily rising. Its CAGR has been growing at 37.8 per cent. Figure 10.2 also shows that growth of hardware sales is negative from 1997-98 to 1998-99. The negative growth rate of hardware in value terms is a result of stiff price competition. Although this is true in value terms, in quantity terms the industry has experienced a positive growth. According to an estimate of NASSCOM during 1998-99, more than 820,000 PCs were sold in India. This took the PC penetration in India to 3.2 PCs per thousand persons by the end of 1998-99. The manufacturing sector has experienced an average growth rate of 28-30 per cent over the last one decade. The hardware sector witnessed an accelerating paradox of increasing unit sales and constrained revenues.

Production of IT

In 1991, the government changed its economic policies and moved along the neo-classical approach to economic development. It opened the Indian market to foreign firms on the one hand, and embarked upon export promotion policies on the other. Major steps taken to augment export intensity included the establishment of Software Technology Parks (STPs) and Electronic Hardware Technology Parks (EHTPs).

The Ministry of Information Technology (then Department of Electronics) created STPs as autonomous institutions to cater to the needs of the IT industry in the fields of export of IT software and services. An STP acts as a single-window solution provider for organisations engaged in export of IT software and services. It provides infrastructural facilities including high-speed data communication services, and solicits all the approval required by this industry with a minimum gestation period. STPs also own gateways for data communication. At present, fifteen STPs are in operation in the country.

The EHTP scheme is not meant only for IT hardware. It has been designed to meet the specific requirement of the electronics sector. The EHTP scheme was launched to enhance the ease of doing business in international markets while making preferential access to the vast domestic market. The salient features of the scheme are: (1) duty-free imports of raw materials, components and other capital materials, and (2) sales into the domestic market from EHTP units are permissible up to 50 per cent of FOB exports and subject to only 50 per cent of customs duties. The growth of IT production is shown in Figure 10.3.

Figure 10.3

Production of IT in India

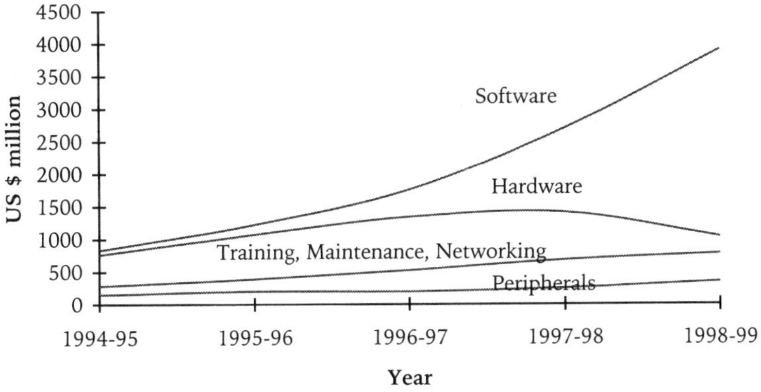

Source: NASSCOM, 1999.

It can be seen, from Figure 10.3, that the performance of the software, services, and peripherals sectors has been steadily increasing since 1994-95. However, despite the EHTP and other promotional measures, IT hardware has not been able to keep pace with IT software. The main hindrance in the growth of the IT hardware sector has been lack of financial resources and procedural delays in importing inputs such as microchips and other accessories that are not manufactured in India. Another reason for decay in the IT hardware sector has been the delays in fulfilling the commitments made to foreign buyers. A high rate of obsolescence and an incapability of Indian IT firms to respond to the changes in product specifications and designs have also contributed to the dismal performance of the Indian IT hardware sector in global markets. The government has taken a few steps to augment IT production in the second phase of reforms.

Front-runner in the Age of Information Revolution: 1998-2002

An ambitious second generation of the economic reforms programme was initiated in a very fluid political environment in 1998. The return of the same political party in 1999 provides reasonable political stability, so the reform process is likely to be accelerated soon. Having noticed the impressive performance of the Indian IT industry in the world market, the government constituted a National Task Force on information technology in 1998 to recommend steps to be taken for removing the bottlenecks and to revise the existing policies in order to make India a superpower in the global IT industry. The salient features of the 108 recommendations of the Task Force aimed at increasing the production and diffusion of IT are discussed in this section.[7] These recommendations became effective in July 1998, and are as follows:

1. For any investment made in IT products and IT software, 100 per cent depreciation shall be allowed in two years for which the Ministry of Finance shall take suitable action.
2. A major promotional programme that includes the development of software in regional languages shall be launched.
3. 1-3 per cent of the budget of every Ministry/Department shall be earmarked for applying IT in that Department.

7. The *Gazette of India*, No. 60, New Delhi, July 25, 1998.

4. Government shall soon launch three schemes for students, teachers, and schools desirous of buying computers under attractive financial packages. These schemes will be supported by initiatives for the donations of computers by IT companies and other business houses, as well as bulk donations by NRI organisations.
5. Computers and the Internet shall be made accessible to schools, polytechnics, colleges, and public hospitals in the country by the year 2003.
6. Out of the 217 items listed in ITA-I, 94 items which were proposed earlier for zero duty by January 1, 2000 shall now be advanced to January 1, 1999. These items include the components that are used to manufacture IT products.
7. The remaining items earlier proposed for zero duty by January 1, 2003/2004/2005 shall now be advanced to January 1, 2002.
8. Duty on capital goods for the manufacture of items covered under zero import duty by 2002, becomes zero by January 1, 2000.

With the implementation of above recommendations, it is expected that the Indian IT industry might achieve an even higher growth rate compared to what it has been experiencing. If second-generation reform programmes succeed, India might achieve its target of a tenfold increase in the penetration rate of PCs by 2008.

Communication Technology

An effective telecommunication network is a crucial element of the IT infrastructure. The government, after realising the importance of this sector, started reforms in 1991. Consequently, telephone density per 1000 persons increased from 5 in 1989 to 12 in 1996 (Mansell and Wehn, 1998). However, the reforms initiated during 1991-1997 were considered insufficient to keep pace with the technological development in IT. Thus, the National Task Force has made several recommendations to remove the bottlenecks to create a powerful telecommunication network. The important recommendations are:

1. Voice and data communication on dedicated or leased circuits is permitted for IT software development and services, but no telephone traffic is permitted.

2. Requests made by STPs or IT promotional organisations approved by the government for release of bandwidth shall be acted upon by Videsh Sanchar Nigam Limited (VSNL) within two weeks of receipt.
3. Providing access to the Internet through authorised cable TV providers shall be permitted to any service provider without additional licensing, subject to applicable cable laws.

The recommendations of Task Force are expected to show their impact on further growth of Indian IT industry after some lag.

SECTION 4

HUMAN RESOURCE DEVELOPMENT

Human capital is a key to success in a high-technology sector such as IT. Skilled workers are needed not only for the production of IT, but also for its successful use. The technological change caused by adoption of IT is regarded as skill-biased technological change (Doms *et al.*, 1997; Lal, 1996).

The private sector, in India, took the first initiative to impart training in computer applications. NIIT and Aptech (earlier Apple Computers) were among the few private firms to start training programmes in the early-eighties. Subsequently, in the late-eighties, public-sector institutions and a few universities also started offering computer courses. Among the public-sector institutions that offer degree and diploma courses in computers are the Electronic Trade & Technology Corporation (ET&TC), the Ministry of Information Technology (MIT), the Computer Maintenance Corporation (CMC), and the UP State Electronic Corporation (UPTRON).

We can group the computer training institutions into four categories: (1) universities; (2) technology institutions; (3) state-owned public-sector institutions; and (4) private institutions. Universities offer courses in computer applications such as Bachelor of Computer Applications (BCA) and Master of Computer Applications (MCA), whereas courses offered by technological institutions concentrate on system software, and system design and architecture. Most of the engineering colleges, the Indian Institute of Technologies (IITs), and the Indian Institute of Science (IISc), are the technological institutions that offer B.Tech. and M.Tech. degrees in Computer Science. State-owned public-sector organisations provide part-time training for in-service persons in applications areas, while private-sector institutions offer all types of courses including networking, Internet, and other applications areas. The training infrastructure of private institutions in some cases is better than that of other organisations. The duration of the courses offered by all institutions varies from six months to five years.

In 1996, the Indira Gandhi National Open University (IGNOU) took the responsibility of providing computer education to people in remote areas. IGNOU started distance education computer courses leading to BCA and MCA degrees. The success of IGNOU's programme can be judged by the increasing number of students in these courses. In 1998-99 the total enrollment was more than 10,000 all over the country. Despite these efforts in human resources development, the National Task Force in information technology has made the following recommendations to meet the growing demand for highly qualified engineers and technologists:

1. All universities, engineering colleges, medical colleges, research and development organisations, and other institutions of higher learning in the country shall be networked for a supplementary programme of distance education for improving the quality of education before the year 2000.
2. The seven national institutions (six IITs, IISc) shall be encouraged to triple their output of students in IT by suitably restructuring the programme.

SECTION 5

INDUSTRY STRUCTURE

Although there are around 135 companies involved in the production of IT, training, and software development, the Indian IT industry may be considered as a fairly concentrated industry in which the top five companies accounted for 64 per cent of the market share in 1989-99. The performance of these five firms is presented in Table 10.1.

Table 10.1

Structure of the IT Industry in India

Company	*Turnover*#	*Annual Growth (Turnover)*	*Profit*#	*Year*
Wipro Corporation	18308.4	28.31	1702.0	1998-99
HCL Infosys	6940.1	8.80	261.3	1998-99
Infosys Technologies	5088.9	97.50	1352.6	1998-99
NIIT	4576.2	·41.10	1083.5	Oct. 97-Sep. 98
Satyam	3781.3	111.85	728.0	1998-99

Note: #= Amount is in Rs. million.

Source: Dataquest, August, 1999.

Almost all of the above firms had collaborations with MNCs. For instance, Wipro's collaboration with Acer lasted for several years. Acer and Wipro are now doing business in India independently. Similarly, HCL's partnership with Hewlett-Packard was broken in 1997. By and large, the above five companies have been maintaining their market share for several years. For a better understanding of the impact of liberalisation on the growth of the IT industry, case studies of the above firms are presented in the next sub-section.[8]

The companies selected for these case studies represent the major activities of the IT industry: software development, hardware manufacturing, human resources development, and internet services provider.

Wipro Corporation

The company is a large conglomerate with operations in agro-based industry, medical equipment, consumer products, financial services, and information technology. In 1994-95, Wipro and Acer (Taiwan) began a joint venture to manufacture and market the entire range of Acer products including desk-tops, laptops, servers, and monitors. The joint venture Wipro Infotech consolidated its position and emerged as one of the leading IT companies in India. Its sales turnover has been highest for the last two consecutive financial years.

8. The data and the descriptive information presented in the case studies have been taken from the Capital Line database. This database is collected, maintained, and distributed by Capital Line. The database contains comprehensive information about more than 8000 Indian companies.

After liberalisation, the company concentrated on software engineering and IC designs for international customers. According to the Chairman of Wipro, Azim Premji, this initiative has changed the mindset of the company from that of a provider of hardware products to a company that is a provider of software services and customised, integrated, high-value, information-technology-based productivity solutions. The new strategy is earning dividends for Wipro. Table 10.1 shows that the profit and sales turnover of Wipro was highest in 1998-99. The company enjoys 30 per cent of the market share of the Indian IT industry.

HCL Infosys

The company was set up by a group of technocrats in April 1986. It was established during the time when a reform process had begun to take form under the dynamic leadership of India's youngest Prime Minister, Rajiv Gandhi. The major thrust of the reform process was a shift from import-substituting inward-looking policies to export-oriented outward-looking policies. The reform programmes included steps to simplify the tax system and shift import control from licensing to tariffs. However, tariff rates were kept high to prop up sick state-owned enterprises. India could not attract foreign investment due to barriers created by the Foreign Exchange Regulation Act. Although the reforms introduced in the mid-eighties were welcome, they were neither sufficient for the IT industry to grow in the domestic market nor were they enough to permit venturing into the international market.

In 1991, the government implemented a broader reform programme. Foreign equity participation was raised from 40 to 51 per cent and restrictions on foreign investment were also eased. HCL Infosys took advantage of these policies and entered into a joint venture with Hewlett-Packard, US, for computer hardware manufacturing, marketing, and servicing. Its range of products included multi-user super-minis and engineering workstations. The technology of these products was being provided by the foreign partner.

Initially, the company was not in the software business. After establishment of STPs by the Government of India, HCL Infosys opened its software subsidiary. In 1998, the collaboration with HP was broken and the company was renamed HCL Infosys. As can be seen from Table 10.1, the growth of its sales turnover has been much less than that of other firms. This may be because the main business of the company is hardware manufacturing. Although India has been successful in building an IT industry that is capable of producing hardware for the domestic market, the export performance of the hardware manufacturing segment has been negligible. In that sense, the market for hardware firms is limited to the domestic market. Moreover, MNCs have also made a dent in the domestic hardware market. Despite the presence of MNCs in the domestic market, HCL Infosys enjoys a very high share (67 per cent) in the domestic corporate market.

Infosys Technolcgies

This is a 100 per cent software company. Although the company was incorporated in 1981, it came into the limelight in 1992. It can take credit for being the only Indian software company to have a joint venture in the US, with Kurt Salmon Associates (KSA). The company has several overseas software centres and is engaged in software development in the areas of distribution, financial services, manufacturing, and communications. The company has been growing at more than 70 per cent since 1992. Infosys is one of the few Indian firms that are listed on the NASDAQ stock exchange. Such an impressive growth rate might be attributed to the export promotion policies of the government.

National Institute of Information Technology (NIIT)

NIIT was incorporated by an Indian Institute of Technology-trained engineer in 1981. The company came into being with the objective of training professionals for the Indian IT industry. It diversified into corporate training and software development in 1984. While focusing on training IT professionals in India and abroad (Jakarta and Bangkok), NIIT started catering to system integration and IT consultancy. It is the largest private training institution in India, having a network of more than 600 centres. At present NIIT has offices in 17 countries including the US, UK, and Japan. The company's performance has been indirectly influenced by liberalisation as its success was linked with the growth of the IT industry. The company has been growing at the same rate (more than 50 per cent of the Indian IT industry) since 1992.

Satyam Computer Services Limited

Satyam Computer Services Limited (SCSL) has been in the software development business for quite a long time. However, the company made its presence felt in the Indian IT industry only in 1991. SCSL became a private limited company in the same year; it is one of the IT firms that took advantage of the liberal economic policies of 1991 to set up four software development centres in four major Indian cities: Chennai, Secunderabad, Bangalore, and Hyderabad. Initially, it was engaged in the development of software for IBM systems, Windows, and Unix platforms. Of late SCSL has emerged as the largest internet-service-providing company, while maintaining its dominance in software exports to France, Sweden, and the US. In 1989-99, the firm was listed in NASDAQ. The company's average annual growth rate has been more than 60 per cent since 1991.

SECTION 6

PERFORMANCE

The performance of the IT industry may partly be attributed to the liberalisation and deregulation programmes that were started in 1991. The IT industry has grown at 31.3 per cent during 1994-95 and 1998-99. While the CAGR of software exports has been 53.8 per cent, the software sector in the domestic market has achieved CAGR 37.8 per cent for the same period. However, the performance of IT hardware has neither been impressive in the domestic market (13.4 per cent growth rate during 1994-99) nor in the export market. In fact, India's hardware exports declined substantially in 1998-99 from the previous year. It may be mentioned here that India has a comparative advantage of a large pool of skilled workers. A comparative advantage of this kind is necessary but not sufficient for the development of IT hardware manufacturing, which is skill- as well as capital-intensive. FDI flows, therefore, are expected to have bearings on the growth of the IT hardware sector. The software sector, on the other hand, is neither capital-intensive nor does it face the problems of procedural delays in fulfilling the commitments of foreign buyers. The ꞏoftware developed for foreign buyers can be transferred instantaneously through the Internet. The software sector, being more skill-intensive and less capital-intensive compared to its twin, is unlikely to be affected by FDI flows. The impressive performance of the software sector may be partly attributed to the characteristics of the sector and the comparative advantages of the country. Stanford University (1997) conducted a survey to examine the comparative advantages of several developing and developed nations; the findings of the survey are presented in Table 10.2.

It can be seen from Table 10.2 that an institutional environment created by the government, in the form of investment policies, specific training programmes, and better communication infrastructure, has been found very conducive for the growth of IT industry. These comparative advantages are not natural, but rather are acquired. India might have been able to acquire them as a result of the first generation of liberalisation. The second generation of reforms may further strengthen them. We now proceed to evaluate the performance of the IT industry in the domestic and international markets.

Domestic Market

We have already discussed the performance of IT hardware and software sectors in Section 3. However, the other features of IT such as internet, intranet, and extranet that started becoming popular in the Indian market in the late-eighties need to be discussed. Initially, access to the Internet was controlled by government institutions, and services were available to select educational and research institutions and government departments. In 1995, access to the Internet was made available to the general public. Since then the number of Internet users has grown exponentially. In the following sub-section, we discuss the growth of the Internet in India.

Internet

The National Informatics Centre (NIC) and the Ministry of Information Technology (MIT) have been providing e-mail and Internet services for a fairly long time. NIC's network (NICNET) became functional in the late-eighties, whereas MIT's Education and Research Network (ERNET) was started in 1992. NIC has been providing Internet facilities to government departments, while MIT

Table 10.2

Comparative Advantages of Selected Developing and Developed Nations

	India	*Russia*	*E. Europe*	*Malaysia*	*Singapore*	*China*	*Japan*	*Israel*	*Ireland*
1. Good general engineering education system	+	+	+	–			+	+	
2. Specific software and system training	+			–			+	+	
3. Large pool of capable programmers	+	+	+	–	–	+	+	–	
4. English language competence	+	–	–			–	–	+	+
5. Government policies on investment	+	–		+	+	–	+	+	+
6. Communication Infrastructure	+	–		+	+		+	+	+
7. Entrepreneurial know-how	+	–			+		+	+	+
8. Foreign corporate investment	+	+			+	+	–		+

Note: + strong positive; - strong negative

Source: Adopted from Stanford University Computer Industry Project, 1997.

has focused on educational and research institutions. It is worth mentioning that NICNET is India's largest satellite-based network, providing connectivity to all districts of the country, the ministries, and the government departments. Although NIC and MIT were actively involved in encouraging the use of the Internet and in remote access of data by government institutions, Internet access was commercially launched for the general public by VSNL only on August 15, 1995. Despite initial bottlenecks in the communications infrastructure, the number of Internet users has been growing exponentially. The growth in numbers of Internet users is shown in Figure 10.4.

Figure 10.4

Growth of the Internet in India

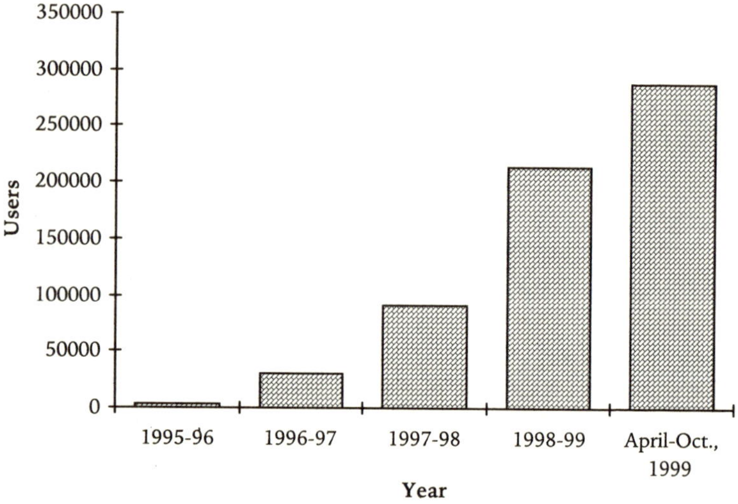

Source: VSNL,[9] 1999.

Figure 10.4 is based on data on Internet users who have access to the Internet through VSNL. The data provided by VSNL may be treated as representative of the total number of Internet users in India, because until recently VSNL was the only Internet Service Provider (ISP) in the country. The domain of VSNL has not been

9. Videsh Sanchar Nigam Limited (VSNL) Annual Report, 1999. The data for April-Oct. 99 were collected through the interview of the VSNL officials.

limited to the general public, however; it has successfully penetrated into government-owned and autonomous institutions. This may be attributed to the state-of-the-art technology provided by VSNL and its virtual monopoly on data communication gateways. Although the government of India, in its 1998-99 telecommunication policy, allowed private companies to set up their own gateways,[10] not a single private company has come forward so far to enter into gateway services.

Internet Service Providers (ISPs)

The Government of India, in its 1998-99 telecommunication policy, also opened the Internet service sector to private- and public-sector companies. This policy became operative in December 1998. State-owned and private companies have responded very positively to the new policy. During the eight months, since the launch of the scheme, 175 companies have obtained licenses to provide Internet services.[11] Mahanagar Telephone Nigam Limited is one of the major state-owned public enterprises to enter into this business, while Satyam Computers Pvt. Ltd. is a very large private company that has begun competing aggressively with other ISPs.

International Market

In the export market, the performance of the IT industry has been better than in the domestic market. The trends in software, hardware, and peripherals exports are shown in Figure 10.5.

Figure 10.5 shows that the export of software has been steadily rising at an annual growth rate of 53.8 per cent. On the other hand, the export intensity of hardware and peripherals has been fluctuating. The exports of peripherals have increased from US $ 6 million in 1994-95 to US $ 19 million in 1997-98 and then declined in 1998-99 to US $ 18 million. There could be three main reasons for such a phenomenal growth rate in the software sector. First, software is a knowledge-intensive industry which requires lesser fixed capital as compared to the hardware sector. Second, there is availability of

10. Ministry of Communications, Guidelines and General Information for Internet Service Providers, No. 845-51/97-VAS, Department of Telecommunication, Government of India.
11. Ministry of Communications, Department of Telecommunication Report 1999, Department of Telecommunication, Government of India.

qualified programmers and system analysts at a reasonable remuneration. Third, archaic procedural delays are not applicable to these sectors. Firms can honour, without any delay, their commitments to foreign buyers. The most important element for the success of software industry is a very reliable and high-speed communication network. Besides offering liberal policies, the major contribution of the government has been in providing communication infrastructure.

Figure 10.5

Export Performance of the IT Industry in India

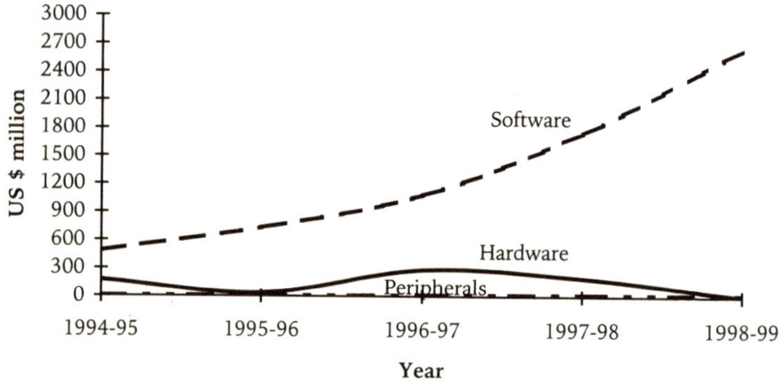

Source: NASSCOM, 1999.

SECTION 7

CONCLUSIONS

This paper examined the effect of institutional environment on the performance of the Indian information technology (IT) industry. Information on reform programs that have been in effect during various policy regimes was collected from the Planning Commission, Ministry of Information Technology, and the Department of Telecommunications. Performance data were collected from the National Association of Software and Services (NASSCOM), the Manufacturers' Association for Information Technology (MAIT), and Videsh Sanchar Nigam Limited (VSNL). The entire development period of IT has been divided into three parts, that is, the pre-liberalisation period (before 1991), the first generation of reforms period (1991-1997), and the second generation of reforms period (after 1997).

The study reveals that the government pursued a structuralist approach toward economic development before the first-generation reforms period, that is, pre-1991. The thrust during this period was to achieve economic development through import-substitution activities rather than export-led development. Although MNCs were permitted to play in the Indian market, the domestic firms were protected by fiscal instruments. Consequently, the Indian IT hardware sector could not become internationally competitive. The IT software firms could not flourish as they did not have easy access to MNCs' computer hardware. Access to their hardware was essential to develop software for systems that were based on proprietary system architecture and designs.

The first generation of reforms was aimed at augmenting the growth of the IT industry in India. Therefore, policy measures were taken for a rapid diffusion of IT in the domestic market, and for boosting the export performance of the IT industry. Customs duty on finished IT hardware product and components was reduced from 200 per cent in the mid-eighties to 25 per cent in 1990 (Dedrick and Kraemer, 1993). The performance of the Indian IT industry in the post-reform period, that is, after 1991, may be partly attributed to the export-oriented policies launched in 1991. The Indian IT industry has achieved a 31 per cent CAGR during 1994-95 and 1998-99, while the CAGR of IT software exports has been 53.8 per cent during the same period. The government succeeded to a great extent in integrating the Indian IT industry with the global IT industry. However, despite several policies for IT manufacturing, the hardware sector has not performed according to expectations. The second generation of reforms launched in 1998 is expected to boost the performance of the hardware sector. However, there are reasons to be sceptical about the success of the hardware sector even after the second generation of reforms.

The IT software sector has increased its share of total exports of the country from 2.4 per cent in 1994-95 to 4.5 per cent in 1998-99. The software sector has followed the Schware (1992) model of export growth—producing for the domestic market gives companies the skills and a strong financial basis for entering export markets. Having recognised the unprecedented success of the IT software industry, the government constituted a National Task Force on information technology in 1998 to recommend policy measures that can be initiated to make India a global IT superpower and a front-runner in the new millennium. The recommendations of the National Task Force emphasise e-commerce and e-governance. The major impediment in e-commerce and e-governance is the legality of electronically transferred documents. The present government has drafted the IT Bill 1999 that not only deals with the legalisation of electronically transferred documents, but has also proposed cyber laws to facilitate electronic communication. The Bill was passed by the Parliament on May 16, 2000, and is likely to greatly stimulate the further diffusion and growth of the IT industry in India.

The impact of liberalisation has perhaps been more noticeable in IT software and services. In fact, the hardware sector is thoroughly demoralised in India. As pointed out by Evans (1992), India needs to have a positive agenda rather than merely adopting a *laissez-faire* policy, at least in IT manufacturing. The government needs to take immediate corrective steps to augment IT hardware manufacturing. One of the steps could be the creation of a stable investment climate. This can be achieved by further liberalising the FDI policies to attract foreign investors. For instance, the facilities available to NRIs in the new FDI policies may be extended to other foreign investors. Another measure could be the removal of bureaucratic delays in hardware exports. The main reason for China being considered a desirable destination for investment is the pro-investment policies of the country. As argued by Dedrick and Kraemer (1993), given India's endowment, the government should provide incentives for MNCs to produce in India or to work with Indian companies in order to promote IT manufacturing.

Despite having so-called liberal FDI policies in place, foreign investors have been India-shy. In 1997, of the 10 most significant investments in China, 5 were in IT totaling up to over \$6 billion, whereas in India, since liberalisation until 1998-99, only \$3 million were invested in IT manufacturing (MAIT, 1999). India must embark on proactive policies to boost IT manufacturing. Failing that, India may witness the exit of the IT hardware manufacturing industry and could become an IT hardware trading country, once WTO recommendations are in place.

References

Annan, K. (1997). Secretary General Stresses International Community's Objective of Harnessing Informatics Revolution for Benefit of Mankind. In *United Nations Commission on Science and Technology for Development "Inter-Agency Project on Universal Access to Basic Communication and Information Services."* Geneva, 12 May, E/CN16/1997/Misc.3.

Brunner, H.P. (1991). "Small-scale Industry in India: The Case of the Computer Industry." *Small Business Economics* 3:121-9.

———. (1995). *Closing the Technological Gap: Technological Change in India's Computer Industry.* New Delhi: Sage Publications.

Coase, Ronald H. (1992). "The Institutional Structure of Production." *American Economic Review* 82:713-19.

Dataquest (A monthly IT Magazine). August, (1999). *Top 20 IT Companies of the Year.* New Delhi: Dataquest.

Dedrick, Jason and Kenneth L. Kraemer (1993). "India's Quest for Self Reliance in Information Technology: Costs and Benefits of Government Interventions." *Asian Survey* 33(5):463-92.

Doms, M., T. Dunne, and K.R. Troske (1997). "Workers, Wages and Technology." *Quarterly Journal of Economics* CXII(1):253-90.

Evans, Peter B. (1992). "Indian Informatics in the 1980s: The Changing Character of State Involvement." *World Development* 20(1):1-18.

Howkins, J. and R. Valantin (1997). *Development and Information Age: Four Global Scenarios for the Future of Information and Communication Technology.* Ottawa: International Development Research Center.

Lal, K. (1996). "Information Technology, International Orientation and Performance: A Case Study of Electrical and Electronic Goods Manufacturing Firms in India." *Information Economics and Policy* 6(3):269-80.

———. (1999). "Determinants of Adoption of Information Technology: A Case Study of Electrical and Electronic Goods Manufacturing Firms in India." *Research Policy* 28(7):267-80.

Manufacturers' Association for Information Technology (MAIT) (1999). *IT Action Plan-II: Breathing Fresh Life into IT Manufacturing.* New Delhi: MAIT.

Mansell, Robin and Uta Wehn (eds.). (1998). *Knowledge Societies: Information Technology for Sustainable Development.* Oxford and New York: Oxford University Press for the United Nations Commission on Science and Technology for Development.

Ministry of Communications, Department of Telecommunications (1997). *Guidelines and General Information for Internet Service Providers,* No. 845-51/97 VAS. New Delhi: Government of India.

Ministry of Communications, Department of Telecommunications (1999). *Department of Telecommunications Report 1999.* New Delhi: Government of India.

National Association of Software and Services Companies (NASSCOM) (1999). *Annual Report: IT Industry in India.* New Delhi: NASSCOM.

North, Douglass (1991). "Institutions." *Journal of Economic Perspective* 5:97-112.

Schware, Robert (1992). "Software Industry Entry Strategies for Developing Countries: A Walking on Two Legs Proposition." *World Development* 20(2):143-64.

Stanford University Computer Industry Project (1997). *Report of the Computer Industry Project.* Stanford: Stanford University Press.

United Nations Commission on Science and Technology for Development (UNCSTD) (1997). *Report of the Working Group on Information and Communication Technologies for Development.* E/CN.16/1997. Geneva: United Nations.

Videsh Sanchar Nigam Limited (VSNL: A Government of India Public Sector Undertaking). 1999. *Annual Report.* New Delhi: VSNL.

World Bank (1993). *The East Asian Miracle: Economic Growth and Public Policy.* A World Bank Policy Research Paper. New York: Oxford University Press.

11

Infrastructure Projects: Estimation and Mitigation of Contingent Fiscal Liabilities

SANJEEVAN KAPSHE

SECTION 1

INTRODUCTION

Now, it is well accepted that governments have not been able to keep pace with the growing demand from their citizens for infrastructure facilities. Increasingly, private parties are being invited to participate in developing infrastructure. However, due to their inherent characteristics infrastructure projects are not among the favoured candidates for commercial financing. In order to make infrastructure projects attractive for private parties governments have offered many sweeteners. The most common among the sweeteners is revenue guarantees in various forms. Such guarantees have resulted in contingent fiscal liabilities for the governments. Often, no explicit attempts are made to measure/estimate these contingent fiscal liabilities. In absence of measurement/estimate of contingent fiscal liabilities, chances of application of appropriate mitigating mechanisms tend to be rather remote. In this paper, we make an attempt to measure/estimate and mitigate contingent fiscal liabilities at project level.

This paper is divided into seven sections. The second section briefly covers the evolution of development policy. The third section mentions key features and basic issues relating to infrastructure projects and financing, with special reference to Build-Operate-Transfer (BOT) contracts as a mechanism for sharing risk between government and private party. The fourth section covers recent discussion relating to contingent fiscal liabilities arising out of various government guarantees to private investors in infrastructure projects. In the fifth section, we describe, in brief, basic financial options and similarity between managerial decisions and financial options. In the sixth section, we propose modifications to typical/ standard BOT contract, in order to address issues brought out in earlier sections, by combining 'option-like' features in a project with 'structured settlement annuities'. The seventh and the last section is about future possibilities in this area.

SECTION 2

EVOLUTION OF DEVELOPMENT POLICY : THE BACKGROUND

The evolution of development policy in post-WWII era, in brief, can be noted as:

- 1960's were the days of 'big plans', primary focus was on long term issues, with a typical planning horizon of twenty to twenty-five years, and management of 'supply',
- 1970's oil crisis forced adoption of 'incremental approach', focus shifted to short term issues, with reduction in planning horizon, typically, to ten to fifteen years, and management of 'demand',
- 1980's were the years of realisation that it is better to keep 'direction' and 'design' of policy separate, and
- 1990's (till date) are the years when the state has taken back seat and asked/permitted market forces to lead the show.

In the Indian context, we can characterise the relationship between government and the market, with respect to the issues relating to infrastructure projects, by noting that:

- The past was captive to 'antagonistic cohabitation',
- The present is about 'selective collaboration', and
- The future is likely to be woven around 'active cooperation'.

SECTION 3

INFRASTRUCTURE PROJECTS

Key Features

As described by Raghuram *et al.*, (1999), the key features, that distinguish infrastructure projects from other projects, are:

- The infrastruture projects are expected to be natural monopolies, working as public utilities in most of the cases. For example, road and rail transport, electricity distribution, water supply, sanitation, etc. However, in certain cases, a competitive situation is also possible. For example, independent electric power production/generation, consumer telecommunication services, educational facilities, running transport services, etc.
- At present, infrastructure projects are expected to work on self-sustaining basis with commercial/business principles.
- In almost all cases, infrastructure projects have a definite impact on the primary and the secondary socio-economic environment. However, for simplification of models, it is often assumed that an infrastructure project has no interaction effects.
- At a broad level, an infrastructure project can be seen as a sequence of design, construction, and operation (with either finite or infinite life). Here, infinite life will mean an operating life going well beyond possible technological obsolescence.
- Another important feature of infrastructure projects is investment lag because of long gestation periods.

Issues Relating to Financing

Traditionally, finances for large infrastructure projects were raised with the help of the central and/or the state government(s) through general revenue collected out of taxes, and/or loans from international financing agencies such as IBRD, ADB, and World Bank. In India, financial institutions like LIC, IDBI, etc. have also played an important role. Recently, attempts have been made to tap capital market for infrastructure projects. However, it is observed that this approach to financing is not adequate to meet huge demand for funds.

Over the years, it is noted that competition is missing in infrastructure sector and efficiency is being neglected. The users accept the quality of services offered as *fait accompli*. Therefore, participation of private sector enterprise in infrastructure projects is necessary to create competition and bring in managerial efficiency. (Mustafa (1999), and Gavieta (1999)). This participation of private sector enterprise can be in the form of financing, ownership, and operation of an infrastructure project.

The planners have attempted to increase role of private investment in infrastructure through various mechanisms. For example, Barnett (1990) suggests – equity, mezzanine finance, bank loans, leasing, taxation at global level and at local level, property development, real estate, air space utilisation, etc. – among many other possibilities.

It is also possible to set up new institutions to make funds available below commercial rates of interest. Alternatively, existing institutions could be asked to evolve new schemes to serve the purpose. Finnerty (1996) presents case-studies relating to financing of infrastructure projects.

In India, some progress has been made on this front and a legal and institutional framework is slowly emerging. For example, Gujarat Infrastructure Development Act, 1999 is a step in this direction.

Build-Operate-Transfer (BOT) Projects

As described by Sharrock (1999), the basic rules – while allocating risk, in general, and in the case of BOT projects, in particular, – are:

- Understanding risk(s) that each party (including government) will have to take to make the project bankable;
- Arranging finances on non-recourse basis; and
- All risk(s) to be recorded unambiguously in a written contract document.

As shown in Figure 11.1, a BOT project is, essentially, a sequence of Promotion, Financing, Building, Operating, and Transfer. However, the core of a BOT project is the 'concession agreement'. This is the part of a BOT contract, in which a counter party agrees to perform certain tasks in a pre-specified manner and, in return, government agrees to provide certain concessions, such as, payment of lease charges, tax benefits, subsidised/free right-of-the-way, explicit sharing of risks, etc.

Estache and Carbajo (1996) discuss experiences from toll-road concessions in Argentina. Ruster (1997) reviews Mexican Toll-road programme during 1989-1994. The issues that clearly emerge are:

Figure 11.1

Phases in Typical BOT Project

- It is important to have simple and transparent criteria for bidding,
- The rules for renegotiating contracts should be spelt out as early and as clearly as possible,
- The institution building (including markets) must be taken seriously, and
- Due diligence exercise to be undertaken by all stakeholders.

In India, National Highway Authority of India (NHAI) has a model concession agreement that has taken into account various problems faced by numerous agencies world over. This model concession agreement also covers a lot of weaknesses observed in previous typical/standard BOT contracts. However, some of the issues that are not addressed by NHAI are reported in *Indian Infrastructure* (Anonymous (1999)), "where the project is undertaken purely on a BOT basis (involving only the private sector's equity), the government should pay some amount on receiving the facility back. There is some merit in the private sector's argument as well and a reasonable solution should have been attempted".

While valuing infrastructure projects, it is always useful to know, in advance, that whether government will or will not step in as the buyer of the last resort. Some of the critical questions at this stage are: 'What is the value that will be assigned by government to an infrastructure project being abandoned?' Or 'How to value risk(s) being assumed by government by providing 'sovereign guarantee' to a project?'. Pyle (1996), and Engle, Fischer, and Galetovic (1997 a, b) argue that the government guarantee valued at Lowest-Possible-Value-of-Revenue (LPVR) is equivalent to a financial put-option on a project.

SECTION 4
CONTINGENT FISCAL LIABILITIES

In this section, we will focus on the issues pertaining to contingent liabilities assumed by governments through sovereign guarantees.

Polackova (1998 a, b) divides the fiscal risk of governments as given in Table 11.1 below:

Table 11.1

Fiscal Risk of Government

Liabilities	*Direct Obligation (in any event)*	*Contingent Obligation (if a particular event occurs)*
Explicit (Government liability is recognised by law or contract)		Sovereign Guarantees to Infrastructure Projects
Implicit (A 'moral' obligation of the government that mainly reflects public expectations and pressures by interest groups)		

Claessens (1993), Lewis and Mody (1997 a, b, c), Mody and Brixi (2000) present a detailed discussion about contingent liabilities taken by governments in the form of guarantees and suggest various approaches to mitigate such risk. Mody and Patro (1996) propose methods for valuation of various government guarantees.

Mody (2000) is of the opinion that the major cause of the East Asian crisis was failure of banking sector, however, except in Korea, failure of infrastructure projects added to fiscal distress.

Thorat and Roy (2001) present a macro-perspective of contingent liabilities in India. They also present state-wise analysis of debt with guarantees, and discuss Reserve Bank of India (RBI) directives on this subject.

In the past years, governments have offered/assumed almost unconditional guarantees to cover various risks associated with numerous infrastructure projects. However, no 'register' is maintained to keep track of quantum of such contingent guarantees.

Whenever such guarantees were 'called-in' the governments' response ranged from attempts to browbeat the counter party, on one end, and to complete and abject surrender to such demands, the other end of the spectrum.

Increasingly, credit rating agencies have started showing their discomfort about limited capacity of government to take contingent liabilities. One finds similar views in Davis (1999), Chew (1999), Ma (2000), and Hemming and Petrie (2000). There is a clear possibility that some of the credit rating agencies might downgrade the central sovereign debt.

Under these circumstances, it is imperative to structure the BOT contracts in such a way that the contingent liabilities assumed by the state and the central governments are not only contained, and mitigated, but also estimated at the beginning of a contract to avoid a fiscal fiasco at a subsequent date.

SECTION 5

OPTIONS CONTRACTS AND MANAGERIAL DECISIONS

In this section, a brief description of various types of financial options contracts and their similarity with managerial decision situations is presented.

Options Contracts (Hull (2000))

In general, an option contract gives its holder a right (but not obligation) to do something to the underlying asset at a pre-fixed price on a pre-fixed date.

There are two basic types of option, namely, *call* and *put*. A call option gives its holder a right to buy an asset on a certain date at a certain price. A put option gives the holder the right to sell an asset by a certain date for a certain price. The specified date is known as the expiration date, the exercise date, the strike date, or the maturity. The specified price is known as the exercise price or strike price.

We can divide the options on the basis of time of exercise. Typical names are: *American* – and option that can be exercised at any time up to and including the expiry date; *Bermudan* – an option that can be exercised only on pre-specified and finite number of instances up to and including the expiry date; and *European* – an option that can be exercised only on the expiry date.

The payoff from the exercise of a call option is *max* (strike price – asset price, 0); and payoff from exercise of a put option is *max* (asset price – strike price, 0). However, one can arrive at various pay-off structures by combining past asset prices, etc. Typically, when asset price used for comparison with the strike price is some 'average' of past asset prices (values that depends on the 'path' followed by a variable) the pay-off is referred as 'asian' pay-off.

Further, by temporal combination of call and put options with American/Bermudan/European exercise and various pay-off structures one can create numerous option contracts. These contracts are commonly referred as exotic/compound/complex options.

Comparison with Managerial Decision Situations

A manager, while facing real life project situations has, typically, the following choices:

- Defer/delay investment
- Time-to-build or staged investment
- Alter scale of operations
  - To expand
  - To contract/reduce
  - To shutdown and restart
- Abandon operations
- Switch output(s) or input(s)
- Invest for growth
- A combination of above mentioned choices.

These choices or 'options' have close similarity with financial call and/or put and/or a combination thereof. (Trigeorgis (1996)). We will be using this similarity in the following sections to modify 'typical' BOT contracts by explicit introduction of options.

SECTION 6

PROPOSED BOT CONTRACT STRUCTURE

The proposed modifications to typical BOT contract – operationalised through a Special Purpose Vehicle (SPV) – lead to a compound/composite/complex option contract. This contract structure comprises of a path-dependent put option (with finite exercise opportunities) resulting in 'structured settlement annuity'.[1] More specifically, the contract is a Bermudan put option with Arithmetic Average Asian pay-off as structured settlement annuity for remaining concession period of the BOT contract.

The Modifications

We propose the following modifications to typical BOT contract in order to address the issues brought out above.

- The promoters to be given a right but not obligation to abandon the operations and return the project to the government during operating/concession period. This situation is equivalent to a financial put option on the underlying asset.
- On exercise of this option, the private party shall be entitled to receive a constant stream of revenue[2] for the remaining duration of concession period based on a pre-specified formula. For example, the annuity could be

---

1. The definition most frequently cited is the one offered by the Supreme Court of Ontario in Yepremium *Versus* Scarborough General Hospital (No. 2): "Structured settlements are a means whereby all or part of the damages are paid to a claimant by means of periodic payments rather than by means of a lump sum."

   Quite simply, structured settlements are an alternative to the conventional lump sum settlement; that is, they replace the traditional single payment with, primarily, a series of periodic payments. This is not to say, however, that structured settlements do not allow for lump sum payments. The term "structure" comes from the idea that a settlement can be shaped to meet the needs of the situation. Structured settlements can be formulated to allow "up-front" lump sum payments, to allow income to be varied from year to year, to allow certain elements of income to be deferred, to allow for lump sum payments at various times in the future and to allow for the escalation of payments in an effort to offset the effects of inflation

   Source: http://www.henderson.on.ca/Hendersonlow/users.htm

2. For simplification, we are assuming annuity to be uniform and constant, however various interesting annuity structures are possible.

calculated as arithmetic average of immediate past five years net revenue. This kind of pay-off that is based on some kind of average of past values of the underlying variable is known as Asian pay-off in finance literature.

- The private party (SPV) will have to meet all obligations relating to various debtors etc. that it had contracted during build and operate phases of the project. The government will not take over any of the liabilities relating to the project.
- The government wants that the private party can abandon the operation of the project only after as pre-specified year from the date of commencement of operation. For example, the abandonment is permitted only after ten years from commencement of operation.
- The private party can be given an additional right but not obligation to augment the capacity, that is, the private party can begin by building 'base capacity' project and at a subsequent date the private party can decide to increase capacity, if the situation so warrants. This additional right but not an obligation is known as a call option on the underlying asset in finance literature. This option will help the promoters in keeping investment made today to the minimum and under favorable conditions they will be able to augment capacity. However, in this paper we are limiting our discussion to European put option alone. [A call-put structure is discussed in Kapshe (2001)].

Options View of Modified BOT Contract

Now, we are in a position to consider the modified BOT contract from option theoretic perspective. For simplification, we will begin by considering availability of a path-dependent put option, that is, European in exercise and Arithmetic Average Asian in pay-off.

Let only European-Asian (Arithmetic Average) Put option be available at the end of *m*th year of operation. (In Figure 11.2, it is year t_3) When this option is exercised it will lead to:

- Transfer of the project and its operation to the government.

- A constant revenue stream paid by the government to the private party for remaining life of the project, i.e., from year *m* to year *n*. (In Figure 11.2, it is from year $\mathbf{t}_3$ to year **T**)

This revenue stream will be arithmetic average of revenues over immediate past *l* years, (In Figure 11.2, it is the 'shaded' region) i.e., arithmetic average of net revenue for the years (*m-l*) to (*m*).

Figure 11.2

Options View of Proposed BOT Contract

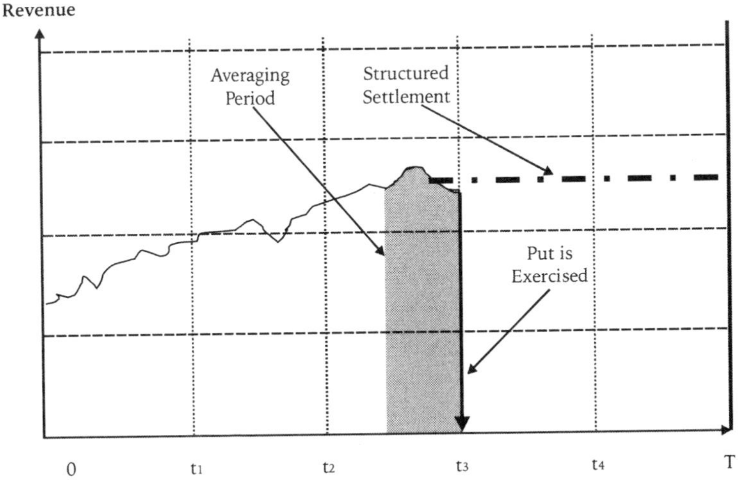

The logic for exercise of put option will be:

If, in year *m*, present value of 'expected future revenue' from operations is strictly less than present value of 'certain revenue' then it is a rational choice to exercise put option and return the bridge to the government.

Here value of option is:

$$\max[\{PV_m(\text{Certain Revenue}) - PV_m(\text{Expected Future Revenue})\}, 0]$$

Further,

$$PV(\text{Expected Future Revenue}) = \sum_{i=m}^{n} \frac{R_i}{(1+r)^{(i-1)}}$$

and

$$PV(\text{Certain Revenue}) = \sum_{i=(m-1)}^{n} \frac{AA_{path}}{(1+r)^{(i-1)}}$$

Where

$$AA_{path} = \frac{1}{1}(R_{m-1} + \ldots + R_m) \equiv \text{Structured Settlement Annuity}$$

In other words,

$$PV(\text{Certain Revenue}) = \text{Structured Settlement Annuity} \times \left[\frac{(1+r)^{n-m} - 1}{r(1+r)^{n-m}}\right]$$

As a logical extension of this contract, with definite increase in computational complexity, Bermudan put option with Asian pay-off can be evaluated.

Estimate of Contingent Fiscal Liability

It is obvious that the value of the option offers a sound estimate of the present value (PV) of contingent fiscal liability assumed by the government through sovereign guarantee. Actually, the option value gives the upper bound on the project specific 'liability'.

Further, once the project is transferred back to the government, it is well within the rights of the government to change some parameters and other related regimes to make the project operational again, earn revenue, and reduce liability. After all, an infrastructure project is not alone socially desirable but essential for economic growth as well.

Mitigating/Sharing Contingent Fiscal Liabilities

The modified BOT contract through an SPV can help in mitigating/sharing 'liability'. As long as the project works in a normal way and put option is not exercised there will not be any problem. However, under such circumstances when future appears to be bleak and SPV finds it attractive to exercise put option, move out of the project operations, and return the assets to the government; either SPV or its next incarnation will take over various obligations relating to the project and become recipient of 'structured settlement annuity'.

Once the option value is estimated, the initial debt can be raised by SPV from various major participants (banks and financial institutions) through some instrument (bond) that offers performance linked (read, net revenue based) returns in addition to some minimum guaranteed returns prior to the exercise of put.

In the event of exercise of put option the return on the instrument can be linked to 'structured settlement annuity' with some minimum guaranteed return.

Further, the major participants can design/offer subsequent/ follow-up instruments to retail market with different returns suiting to various risk-appetite classes.

SECTION 7

CONCLUSION

In this paper, we have demonstrated that by combination of 'structured settlement annuity' and put option(s) it is possible to estimate and mitigate/share contingent fiscal liabilities assumed by government through sovereign guarantee extended to infrastructure projects.

However, the structure suggested in this paper is illustrative in nature. It requires further work on:

- The choice of an appropriate model for revenue 'process',
- Estimation of various parameters of the above mentioned revenue model,
- Regulatory changes, if needed, for introduction of 'structured settlement annuity' in BOT projects.

References

Anonymous (1999). "Model Concession Agreement: Removing the Roadblocks," *Indian Infrastructure*, April 1999, Pages 44-45.

Barnett, M.J.N. (1990). "Finance for Light Rapid Transit," in *Light Transit System: Proceedings of the Symposium on the Potential of Light Transit Systems in British Cities*, B.H. North, (Editor), organised by The Institution of Civil Engineers and held in Nottingham on 14-15 March 1990, Published by Thomas Telford Ltd., Telford House, 1 Heron Quay, London E149XF.

Chew, William H. (1999). "Ratings Enter Infrastructure Market: Reasons for Rating Bank Loans," *Indian Infrastructure*, September 1999, Page 56-57.

Claessens, Stijn (1993). *Risk Management in Developing Countries*, Technical Paper 235, World Bank.

Davis, Henry A. (1999). "Effects of the World Financial Crisis on Project Finance: A Review of the Rating Agency Sourcebooks," *Journal of Project Finance*, Vol. 4, No. 4, Winter 1999, Pages 13-17.

Engel, Eduardo, Ronald Fischer, and Alexander Galetovic (1997a). "Highway Franchising: Pitfalls and Opportunities," *American Economic Review*, Vol. 87, No. 2, May 1997, Pages 68-72.

Engel, Eduardo, Ronald Fischer, and Alexander Galetovic (1997b). "Infrastructure Franchising and Government Guarantees," Conference on *Managing Government Exposure to Private Infrastructure Projects*, at Catagarta, Colombia, May 29-30, 1997.

Estache, Antonio, and Jose Carbajo (1996). "Designing Toll Road Concessions – Lessons from Argentina," *Public Policy for the Private Sector*, Note No. 99, December 1996.

Finnerty, John D. (1996). *Project Financing: Asset-Based Financial Engineering*, John Wiley & Sons.

Gaviets, Rommel C. (1999). "Private Funds, Utility Development, and Government Policy: The Clark Experience," *Journal of Project Finance*, Vol. 4, No. 4, Winter 1999, Pages 51-55.

Hemming, Richard, and Murray Petrie (2000). "A Framework for Assessing Fiscal Vulnerability," *IMF Working Paper*, Fiscal Affairs Department, March 2000.

Hull, John (2000). *Options, Futures, and Other Derivatives*, Third Edition, Prentice Hall India Ltd.

Kapshe, Sanjeevan (2001). *Real Options Approach to Valuation of Transport Infrastructure Projects*, Unpublished dissertation for Fellow Programme in Management (FPM) at Indian Institute of Management Bangalore (IIMB), India.

Lewis, Christopher M., and Ashoka Mody (1997). "The Management of Contingent Liabilities: A Risk Management Framework for National Governments," in *Dealing With Public Risk in Private Infrastructure*, Irwin Timothy, Michael Klein, Guillermo E. Perry, and Mateen Thobain, (Editors), Latin American and Caribbean Studies, World Bank, Washington D.C. Also available at *http://www.amody.com/pdf/lewis.pdf*

————. (1998a). "Contingent Liabilities for Infrastructure Projects: Implementing a Risk Management Framework for Governments," *Public Policy for the Private Sector*, Note No. 148, August 1998.

Lewis, Christopher M, and Ashoka Mody (1998b). "Risk Management Systems for Contingent Infrastructure Liabilities: Applications to Improve Contract Design and Monitoring," *Public Policy for the Private Sector*, Note No. 149, August 1998.

Ma, Jun (2000). *Monitoring Local Fiscal Risks: Selected International Experiences*, Available at *http://www.worldbank.org/wbi/wbiep/adf/papers/ma.pdf*

Mody, Ashoka (2000). "Contingent Liabilities in Infrastructure: Lessons of the East Asian Crisis," in Hana Brixi, Allen Schick, and Sweder van Wijnbergen, eds., *Government at Risk: Contingent Liabilities and Fiscal Risk*, forthcoming Oxford University Press, current version May 2000. Available at *http://www.amody.com/pdf/infrastructure_liabilities.pdf*

Mody, Ashoka, and Hana Brixi (2000). "Priorities for Management of Contingent Liabilities," in Hana Brixi, Allen Schick, and Sweder van Wijnbergen, (editors)., *Government at Risk: Contingent Liabilities and Fiscal Risk,* forthcoming Oxford University Press, current version May 2000. Available at *http://www.amody.com/pdf/Risk_management.pdf*

Mody, Ashoka, and Dilip Patro (1996). "Methods of Loan Guarantee Valuation and Accounting," In Ashoka Mody, (editor)., *Infrastructure Delivery: Private Initiative and the Public Good,* The Economic Development Institute, The World Bank, Washington D.C. Also available at *http://www.amody.com/pdf/methods.pdf*

Mustafa, Amira (1999). "Public-Private Partnership: An Alternative Institutional Model for Implementing the Private Finance Initiative in the Provision of Transport Infrastructure," *Journal of Project Finance,* Vol. 4, No. 2, Summer 1999, Pages 64-79.

Polackova, Hana (1998a). *Topic 12 - Government Contingent Liabilities: A Hidden Risk to Fiscal Stability.* Available at *http://www1.worldbank.org/wbiep/decentralization/Topic12_Intro.htm*

———. (1998b). "Contingent Liabilities - A Threat to Fiscal Stability," *PREM Notes - Economic Policy,* No. 9, November 1998, The World Bank. Available at *http://www1.worldbank.org/publicsector/pe/pnote9.pdf*

Pyle, Thomas H. (1996). "Project Finance in Practice: The Case Studies," in *Infrastructure Delivery: Private Initiative and The Public Good,* (Ed. Ashoka Mody), EDI Development Studies, World Bank

Raghuram, G., Rekha Jain, Sidharth Sinha, Prem Pangotra, Sebastian Morris, (eds.) (1999). *Infrastructure Development and Financing: Toward a Public-Private Partnership,* Macmillan India Limited.

Ruster, Jeff (1997). "A Retrospective on the Mexican Toll Road Program (1989-94)," *Public Policy for the Private Sector,* Note No. 125, September 1997

Sharrock, Judith (1999). "Privately Financed Road Projects: Legal Aspects," *Indian Infrastructure,* February 1999, Pages 34-36.

Thorat Usha, and Sunando Roy (2001). "Contingent Liabilities at the State Level - The Indian Experience," Paper presented in the World Bank Conference *Fiscal policies to Accelerate economic Growth,* May 21-22, 2001, New Delhi. Available at *http://www.fiscalconf.org/papers/usha.pdf*

Trigeorgis, Lenos (1996). *Real Options: Managerial Flexibility and Strategy in Resource Allocation,* The MIT Press,Cambridge, Massachusetts.

World Bank (1994). *Infrastructure for Development: World Development Report 1994,* Oxford University Press, 1994.

Part 3

Trade and Indian Industrialisation

12

Trade Liberalisation and Industrial Performance

A Disaggregated View of Indian Manufacturing in the 1990s

ISHER JUDGE AHLUWALIA

SECTION 1

INTRODUCTION

A major feature of India's economic reforms in the 1990s was the opening up of the Indian economy to foreign trade and foreign investment. After forty years of assiduously building an import substitution regime, 1991 marked a break in policy with the past in that India undertook extensive trade liberalisation from 1991-92 onwards. The decade of the 1980s was mainly devoted to experimental but substantial deregulation of the domestic industrial policy regime, which had become highly restrictive.

The 1991-92 trade policy reforms attempted for the first time to dismantle the import-substitution regime and initiated a gradual but determined process of tariff reduction in the first half of the 1990s although there was some reversal in the second half. With import-weighted tariff at 30 per cent, however, India has more recently, once again, revealed and renewed its determination of the early 1990s to lower tariffs to East Asian levels, and move to only two rates of custom duty, i.e., 10 per cent on intermediate goods and 20 per cent on final goods, by 2004-05. As regards the quantitative restrictions on imports, their removal gathered momentum towards the end of the decade. This was because India found it difficult to justify the retention of non-tariff barriers on balance of payments grounds. Given the GATT provisions which were carried into the WTO and pressure from India's trade partners, the quantitative restrictions on imports into India were finally phased-out in April, 2001.

The reforms in trade policy along with changes in industrial policy and in policy towards foreign investment in the 1990s were aimed at making Indian industry competitive through facilitating technological upgradation, improving operational efficiency and encouraging investment in export-oriented sectors. All this should lead to an improvement in export performance. This paper analyses how far trade liberalisation has succeeded in achieving this objective so far. The layout of the paper is as follows. The theoretical arguments and empirical evidence are outlined in section 2. A brief description of the policy regime in the 1990s is attempted in section 3. Section 4 analyses the industrial performance in India following the reforms in 1990s. The final section concludes the study.

SECTION 2

THEORETICAL ARGUMENTS AND EMPIRICAL EVIDENCE

The role of trade liberalisation in enhancing efficiency and attaining a once-and-for all level effect on output in the economy is well known as is the caveat that market failures and distortions can stand in the way of realising this potential. In a recent article, Srinivasan (2001) has clarified that trade liberalisation also affects the equilibrium growth rate once the underlying growth model assumes a constant positive marginal product of capital, as in the case of the Harrod-Domar model or the Feldman Mahalanobis model. Such models may be more relevant for many labour surplus developing economies. It is only in neoclassical models such as the Solow model that trade liberalisation does not affect the steady state growth rate. This is because these models assume that the marginal product of capital declines towards zero as the capital labour ratio increases. However, as with the level effects, market failures and distortions can also undermine the growth effects of trade policies. In fact, as Bhagwati (1958 and 1968) had shown, in the presence of distortions, free trade could lead to immiserising growth. Similarly, Breacher and Diaz-Alejandro (1977) showed that foreign direct investment in a protected economy could lead to a Pareto-inferior equilirium.

The theoretical argument can be rephrased to state that trade liberalisation allows an economy to exploit its comparative advantage, while opening up to technology can help an economy to benefit from knowledge wherever it is produced. However, to realise the potential offered by these opportunities, the markets, institutions and the political economy of the country concerned have to provide a conducive environment. Before we turn to examine the evidence on the extent of trade liberalisation and other associated policy changes in India in the 1990s and their outcomes, it is useful to review the findings of some recent empirical studies which have tried to explore some elements of the linkage between trade liberalisation and industrial performance in India.

In one of the earliest attempts, Ahluwalia (1991) had found a negative relationship between productivity growth and import substitution in the Indian manufacturing sector over the period 1960–80, thus providing support for the hypothesis that decline in import substitution orientation would lead to an improvement in productivity growth.[1] In a study covering the period 1970-1988 and taking a subgroup of 30 three-digit industry groups, Chand and Sen (2002) observed that a fall in the ratio of domestic to international prices has a statistically significant positive impact on productivity growth. In studies covering more recent periods, Das (2001), and Goldar and Kumari (2002) analyse the impact of trade liberalisation on productivity growth in the organised manufacturing sector in India. Das uses panel data for 72 three-digit industry groups over the period 1980-95, while Goldar and Kumari use panel data at the two digit level of disaggregation for the period 1980-98. Das shows that the reduction in non-tariff barriers as measured by import coverage ratios leads to a rise in total factor productivity, particularly in the case of intermediate goods, while Goldar and Kumari find that a decline in the effective rate of protection has a favourable effect on productivity.

Krishna and Mitra (1998) and Balakrishnan *et al.*, (2000) have attempted to analyse the link between trade liberalisation and productivity growth using firm level data from the Centre for

1. The study used data for 62 three-digit industry groups and used the Chenery measure of import substitution, which uses the difference between actual growth in output during any period and that, which would have been achieved if the import availability ratio had remained constant at its level at the beginning of the period, in a multiple regression framework explaining TFPG.

Monitoring Indian Economy (CMIE), covering the period 1986-93 and 1989-98 respectively, and using dummy variables after 1990-91 to capture the effect of "trade reform." Using dummy variables to measure the impact of trade reforms in this fashion has its limitations, since trade reforms in India have not only been gradual over time but have also proceeded at an uneven pace across sectors. Krishna and Mitra use firm level data for 362 firms for the period 1986-93 for electrical machinery, non-electrical machinery, electronics, and transport equipment. They find strong evidence of increase in competition and some evidence of increase in productivity growth after 1990-91, although their analysis covers only two years after the trade policy reforms were launched. Balakrishnan *et al.*, on the other hand, use a large sample of 2300 firms spanning the period 1989-98. They try to look for evidence of acceleration in productivity growth after 1990-91 and find none.

SECTION 3

THE POLICY REGIME IN THE 1990s

The Indian strategy of industrialisation at the time of independence was formulated around a central role for the public sector, heavy protection from foreign competition and a high degree of domestic regulation of the private sector. Emphasis on heavy industries, extensive use of physical controls and a framework of centralised planning were other important dimensions of the policy regime that need to be kept in mind when analysing the major changes in policies during the 1980s and the 1990s.

The Context

A process of reflection and debate on the need for a change in policies had been set in motion in India in the second half of the 1970s, i.e., about the same time that China was preparing for a major change in policy.[2] It is worth noting that China went ahead with full force towards market orientation and doubled its GDP between 1978 and 1991. By contrast, India used the decade of the 1980s for hesitant experimentation in domestic deregulation, while

2. Among the numerous high-level official committees that were set up were Dagli (1979), Alexander (1978), Tandon (1980), Pande (1980) and Rajadhyaksha (1980).

retaining its highly protectionist trade policy regime and keeping its loss making public sector intact. The reform on the industrial policy front, however, coincided with a sharp deterioration in the fiscal accounts of the government. As the Government of India's policies became increasingly expansionary to support growing levels of current government expenditures on sharply rising interest payments, defence, and subsidies, the gross fiscal deficit of the government increased from 6.2 per cent of GDP in 1980-81 to 8.3 per cent by 1990-91.[3]

While the reorientation of industrial and trade policies evoked a better productivity response and led to substantially higher industrial growth in the 1980s, the deteriorating fiscal position and growing macro-economic imbalances posed a serious challenge to the sustainability of the higher growth of the 1980s. The Gulf War of 1990 provided the trigger, which brought the underlying economic crisis to the force.

The experience of the 1980s had a direct bearing on how the Government of India responded to the crisis of 1990-91. Evidence of faster industrial growth and productivity in the 1980s was clear. Whether it was productivity-led growth or debt-led growth or a bit of both, most policy watchers agreed that the better industrial performance could not be sustained because of the growing macro-economic imbalances during the 1980s. The response to the crisis therefore was twofold – more domestic deregulation and foreign competition and striving to attain macro economic balance. In opening up the economy to foreign trade and foreign investment, the policies represented a more radical break with the past.

As the policy makers turned the crisis into an opportunity for wide ranging reforms, a stabilisation package was put in place in 1991 at the same time that measures were initiated to open the economy to foreign trade and investment in a gradual but determined manner and prepare it for greater market orientation. The year 1991-92 was the year of adjustment to the crisis-driven reform package. Since the process of trade policy reform continued in the following years even though the reform on the macro-economic imbalance front was slowing down, the period from 1991-92 to 1997-98 for which disaggregated data are available for the

3. See Shome P. (2000) for a detailed review of the fiscal trends.

manufacturing sector should enable us to analyse the early impact of trade liberalisation on the industrial sector.

Trade Liberalisation

The Indian experience with respect to trade liberalisation in the 1990s is better understood when analysed in conjunction with the highly protectionist trade policy regime which persisted throughout the 1980s. Replete with quantitative restrictions and very high and differentiated tariff rates, India's trade policy regime in the 1980s was one of the most protectionist in the world. The limited import liberalisation during the 1980s was essentially directed towards attaining technological upgradation for the capital goods industries and enabling easier access to imports of intermediate goods.[4] Agricultural commodities and industrial consumer goods remained subject to import controls. There was very little reduction in the level and dispersion of tariff rates during this decade, while quantitative restriction on imports continued to be dominant.

The anti-export bias generated by the trade policy regime was analysed by Bhagwati and Srinivasan (1975). They computed the effective exchange rate facing exporters and importers to spell out the discrimination against exports which resulted from the import substitution bias of the trade policy regime. The Tandon Committee (1980), which was set up by the Government of India to recommend an export strategy for the 1980s, explicitly recognised the anti-export bias and recommended provision of cash subsidies to exporters to offset the same. As export subsidies were raised through the decade, the resulting budgetary burden became one of the many factors which contributed to the rising fiscal deficits of this period.

The system of import controls in the 1980s had begun to be administered more flexibly and with less discretion, but the restrictive regime was very much in place and the degree of tariff protection was also very high. The crisis of 1990-91 provided an opportunity to begin the task of dismantling the regime by lowering tariffs and removing quantitative restrictions. The import-weighted tariff for the economy as a whole declined from as high as 87 per cent in the pre-reform period of 1990-91 to 25 per cent in 1997-98

4. Technology transfers were also encouraged through the foreign investment regime.

but increased again to 30 per cent by 1999-00 (Table 12.1). The decline was steepest in consumer goods, and among industrial products the rates were the lowest for intermediate goods. Table 12.2 shows how the dispersion in tariff rates for the different categories was also brought down over the 1990s. However, even in 1999-2000, the nominal tariff structure for consumer goods shows a standard deviation of almost 19 per cent. A comparison with selected

Table 12.1

Import Weighted Tariffs

	1990-91	*1992-93*	*1993-94*	*1994-95*	*1995-96*	*1996-97*	*1997-98*	*1998-99*	*1999-2000*
Whole Economy	**87.0**	**64.0**	**47.0**	**33.0**	**27.2**	**24.6**	**25.4**	**29.7**	**30.2**
Agricultural Product	70.0	30.0	25.0	17.0	14.9	14.7	14.0	16.1	17.7
Mining	60.0	34.0	33.0	31.0	27.6	22.0	21.9	19.5	17.7
Consumer Goods	164.0	144.0	33.0	48.0	43.1	39.0	33.8	39.3	32.4
Intermediate Goods	117.0	55.0	40.0	31.0	25.0	21.9	26.1	31.5	31.9
Capital Goods	97.0	76.0	50.0	38.0	28.7	28.8	24.7	30.1	32.2
Peak Rates of Duty	>200.0	110.0	85.0	65.0	50.0	52.0	45.0	45.0	40.0

Source: World Bank.

Table 12.2

Tariff Structure

	1990-91	*1992-93*	*1993-94*	*1994-95*	*1995-96*	*1996-97*	*1997-98*	*1998-99*	*1999-2000*
					Mean				
Whole Economy	128.0	94.0	71.0	55.0	40.8	38.6	34.4	40.2	39.6
Agricultural Product	106.0	59.0	39.0	31.0	25.1	25.6	24.6	29.6	29.2
Mining	n.a	n.a	71.0	48.0	30.0	24.8	24.4	29.4	26.6
Consumer Goods	142.0	92.0	76.0	59.0	45.4	45.4	39.8	45.9	42.9
Intermediate Goods	133.0	104.0	77.0	59.0	43.7	38.8	34.7	40.7	41.2
Capital Goods	109.0	86.0	58.0	42.0	33.1	33.8	29.7	35.5	35.3
					Standard Deviation				
Whole Economy	41.0	34.0	30.0	25.0	19.0	19.0	14.8	15.3	14.0
Agricultural Product	48.0	49.0	39.0	30.0	24.9	21.1	17.7	18.8	16.6
Mining	n.a	n.a	24.0	25.0	15.6	11.9	11.9	12.3	12.1
Consumer Goods	33.0	42.0	36.0	33.0	26.0	27.1	20.5	20.7	18.9
Intermediate Goods	42.0	25.0	22.0	17.0	13.5	13.2	10.3	11.1	10.5
Capital Goods	32.0	26.0	24.0	20.0	12.4	12.2	9.4	10.2	8.2

Source: World Bank.

Table 12.3

Tariff: An International Comparison

Country	Year	Tariff		Import-Weighted
		Mean	s.d.	
India	1990	84.1	39.4	93.6
	1999	34.3	8.0	28.0
China	1992	44.9	33.4	46.5
	1998	17.4	10.8	18.5
Korea	1988	18.6	5.1	17.8
	1999	7.8	2.4	7.0
Indonesia	1989	27.1	23.3	27.4
	1999	11.8	15.3	14.3
Malaysia	1988	17.6	15.6	14.4
	1997	12.0	17.2	9.4
Thailand	1989	41.7	23.6	42.4
	1993	47.3	26.2	43.7
Pakistan	1993-1999	53.0	21.2	N.A
Bangladesh	1989	123.2	89.8	125.5
	1999	22.4	15.0	18.5
Sri Lanka	1990	27.5	24.5	22.2
	1997	19.1	12.6	19.8
Nepal	1998	18.3	15.4	21.0
	1999	13.5	11.5	17.8

Source: World Bank.

countries shows that while India has indeed come a long way in the 1990s, its import-weighted tariff in 1999 was still much higher whether we compare it with China, Korea, Indonesia and Malaysia or indeed with its South Asian neighbours (Table 12.3).

Table 12.4 presents the import-weighted tariff, the effective rates of protection and the coverage ratio of import controls for the two-digit industry groups of manufacturing for two points in time, before and after the reform. Again, clearly, opening up to imports is indicated. For manufactured goods as a whole, the import-weighted tariff declined from 150 per cent to 36 per cent. The highest tariff in 1988-89 and the steepest decline in 1996-97 was in chemical products and basic metal industries. Machinery and transport equipment also experienced significant declines. Printing and publishing remained the industry with the lowest import-weighted tariff, although its effective rate of protection increased. By 1996-97, beverages were the industry group receiving the maximum effective protection. As the last two columns of Table 12.4 show, the quantitative restrictions of imports were all pervasive and remained pretty much so even in 1996-97. Figure 12.1 presents a picture of the change in trade liberalisation between 1988-89 and 1996-97. It was only in the three years ending in April 2001 that the quantitative restrictions were finally removed.

Table 12.4

Indicators of Trade Liberalisation

(Per cent per annum)

	Import Weighted Tariff		*Effective Rate of Protection*		*Coverage Ratio (QR)*	
	1988-89	*1996-97*	*1988-89*	*1996-97*	*1988-89*	*1996-97*
Manufactured Goods	**137.1**	**36.5**	**166.1**	**55.1**	**80.2**	**32.5**
Food	125.0	41.9	233.1	48.9	98.8	82.4
Beverages	150.0	102.0	219.4	173.9	100.0	75.0
Tobacco	150.0	52.0	137.5	60.2	100.0	100.0
Textiles	113.0	51.9	109.8	59.2	98.1	50.8
Footwear	148.0	51.1	160.9	53.4	95.7	92.7
Furniture and Wood Products	108.8	34.6	119.6	38.5	84.7	26.9
Paper and Paper Products	154.0	30.6	172.8	29.7	83.8	42.2
Printing and Publishing	37.5	21.7	7.3	16.3	73.5	56.3
Leather and Fur Products	130.0	42.0	147.1	45.6	56.4	51.3
Rubber Products	143.6	52.0	153.7	69.0	88.2	59.8
Chemicals and Chemicals Products	189.3	39.6	236.5	42.6	77.0	26.2
Petroleum and Coal Products	104.9	31.4	127.5	79.1	81.5	27.5
Non-Metallic Mineral Products	133.7	50.7	139.8	61.0	76.6	61.2
Basic Metal Industries	163.1	31.3	127.8	41.4	81.9	59.1
Metal Products	140.4	36.6	127.8	41.4	81.9	59.1
Non-Electrical Machinery	111.1	31.4	92.0	31.0	71.0	19.0
Electrical Machinery	124.2	38.3	116.2	42.0	72.7	24.4
Transport Equipment	106.1	45.5	96.4	51.0	83.0	36.2

Source: ICRIER.

Figure 12.1

Indicators of Trade Liberalisation 1988-89 and 1996-97

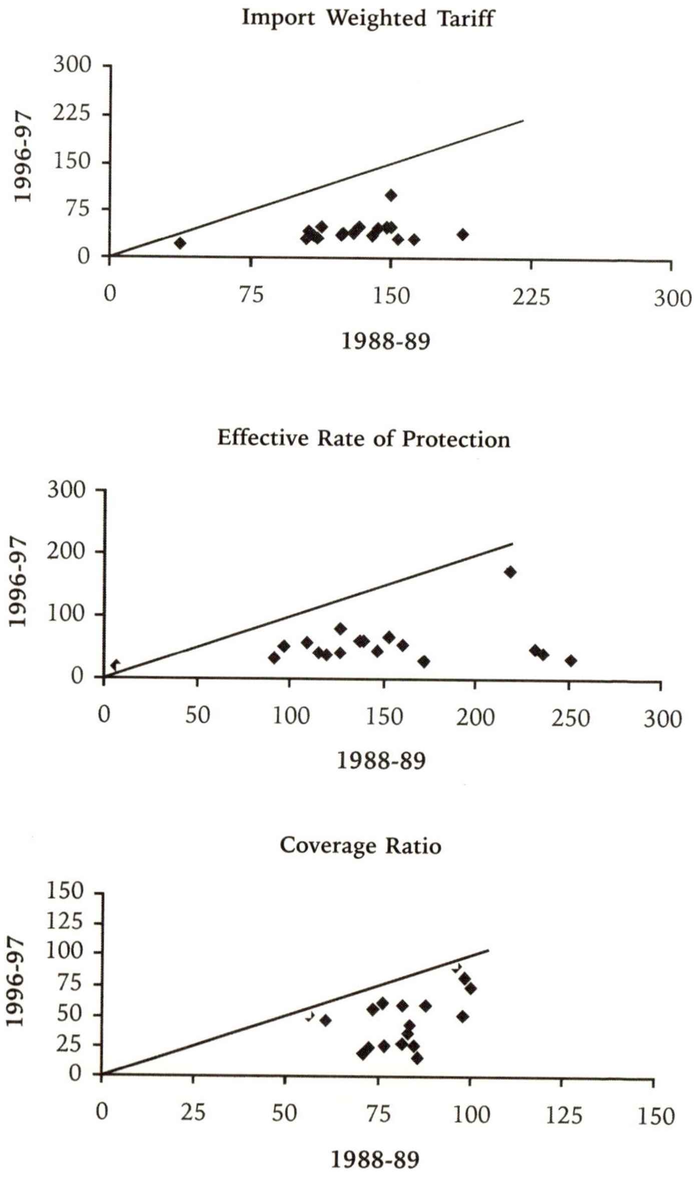

The ten years from 1991 to 2001 therefore, marked a significant transition for the Indian economy from a policy regime with very high rates of protection and all-pervasive quantitative restrictions to moderate rates of protection and removal of quantitative restrictions. The degree of tariff protection, however, was still higher than in most developing economies.

Opening up to Foreign Investment

The reforms of the 1990s marked a significant break with the past in respect of the policy towards foreign investment. From a policy which was restrictive and selective and supported mainly technology transfers, foreign investment policy in the 1990s became more open and more proactive as the rules were liberalised over time with a view not only to gain better access to technology but also to build strategic alliances to penetrate world markets. Besides enlarging the scope for automatic approval over the years, the Foreign Investment Promotion Board was set up to expedite other applications for foreign investment. Specifically, liberal conditions were set up for attracting foreign investment in infrastructure sectors and export-oriented sectors. As of 2001, 100 per cent foreign ownership is allowed in a large number of industries and majority ownership in all but banks, insurance companies, telecommunications and airlines.

Industrial Policy Reforms

As Five Year Plan after Five Year Plan failed to attain the targets set out for industrial growth and other associated objectives, a process of official reflection and policy debate began in the mid-70s on how to correct the course of policy.[5] By the end of that decade, infrastructure constraints had also emerged as a matter of serious concern. Declining public investments in the infrastructure sectors required urgent attention of the policy makers.

Industrial policy changes of the 1980s represented a response to the heavily felt need for domestic deregulation. Experiments with industrial delicensing, weakening of MRTP provisions to provide larger scope for large industrial houses, incentives for modernisation

5. See Chapter 1, Ahluwalia (1991).

of capital stock, policies for major industries such as textiles and sugar, gradual introduction of price decontrol for cement and aluminum, etc., were some of the major steps taken in the direction of domestic deregulation. A move away from physical controls to a system of financial incentives and disincentives and from discretionary to more market-oriented regulation formed the underlying thrust of the industrial policy changes of the 1980s.

A major exception to this thrust was the continuation of the policy of reservation of production for the small-scale sector particularly since it constituted an important hurdle in the way of developing export capability in sectors such as garments, leather products, sports goods, etc., where India has a comparative advantage. Industrial policy in the 1980s also paid little attention to facilitating the restructuring of the industrial sector by removing the numerous barriers to exit. The labour laws, the bankruptcy laws, the laws relating to rent control and urban land ceiling were some of the major legislative barriers which came in the way of moving resources away from the unproductive and economically non-viable sectors to the more vibrant sectors.

Public sector reform and privatisation did not form part of the agenda for industrial policy reform during the 1980s, although some effort was made to arrest the trend of declining public investments in infrastructure, particularly railways. Dominance of the public sector in banking and finance also continued without much discussion of any need for reform, although a process of deregulation of the domestic capital market was initiated during the 1980s.

The industrial policy reforms during the 1990s were bold in doing away with numerous barriers to entry, e.g., removal of industrial licensing for investment, opening up all but a few strategic areas which were earlier reserved for investment only by the pubic sector, preparing to replace the earlier MRTP Act with a new Competition Law which would regulate anti-competitive behaviour. Even on the policy for reservation for the small-scale sector, a beginning was made by dereserving a number of items. However, the absence of institutional and legal reforms creates barriers to exit. Delays in securing numerous permissions from state governments and environmental clearances from the Government of India are also emerging as the new barriers to entry. A recent study by the World Bank (Dollar and Goswami (2002)) has highlighted the impact of these together with that of the availability of infrastructure and the quality of governance in determining the investment climate facing different states in India

Public Sector Reforms, Privatisation and Infrastructure

A major gap in domestic policy reform has been in the area of public sector with maximum adverse effect on the infrastructure sectors with its consequences for the industrial sector as a whole. During the 1980s, while there was disillusionment with respect to the resource generation aspects of the public sector undertakings (PSUs), the objective of the public sector as the guiding spirit for development continued to be at the core of planning. Some effort was made to grant greater autonomy to the PSUs from the control of their administrative ministries, but even at the end of the 1980s there was little improvement in the situation with respect to the operating surpluses of the PSUs.[6]

Public sector reform remained an area of darkness in the 1990s. A significant practical approach was adopted in which the better performing PSUs were given the freedom to access capital markets on the strength of their own performance. They were also given more autonomy in shaping their future. The non-performing PSUs, on the other hand, languished for want of budgetary support or reform.

Privatisation was not pursued as an option in the early phase of reforms. Instead, government policy concentrated on selective disinvestments of public sector equity with a view to finance fiscal deficits rather than address the issue of improving the returns on the capital invested. In 1997, the Government of India set up the Disinvestment Commission. The Commission gave a series of reports analysing the 50 or so cases of PSUs, which were referred to it and made detailed recommendations. Subsequently, the Commission was wound up and a Department of Privatisation was created. While there have been some major privatisations, e.g., BALCO, VSNL, Maruti and IPCL, it remains a highly contentions issue.

There is no getting away form the need for reforming the public sector as the case of power sector makes it amply clear. For example,

---

6. The after-tax profit to net worth ratio of the centrally owned PSUs other than in the petroleum sector was –9.05 per cent in 1990-91.

the pricing policy, which does not cover the cost of producing the infrastructure services is eroding the economic viability of public sector infrastructure and stands in the way of attracting private investment into infrastructure. Since infrastructure services such as electric power, roads, ports, railways and telecommunications are crucial for industrialisation and these services can not be imported, adequate investments (public or private) and efficient use of existing and new investments in these sectors are essential prerequisites for any strategy which seeks to accelerate the pace of economic growth. Unless public sector reforms are undertaken and economic viability of infrastructure operations ensured, private sector investment will not be attracted to these sectors.

Macroeconomic Reforms

The economic crisis of 1990-91 in India had drivehome the importance of a stable macro-economic environment for sustaining high growth rates of GDP. Indeed, an effective stabilisation programme was quickly put in place and the fiscal deficit was brought down from its very high level of 8.3 per cent of GDP in 1990-91 to 5.0 per cent in 1991-92. To some extent, this success generated a sense of complacency. Unlike the industrial and trade policy reforms, which pretty much continued, *albeit* at a gradual pace, through the decade, controlling the fiscal deficit proved to be an elusive target. The lack of buoyancy in tax revenues combined with the government's inability to reduce expenditures meant that fiscal deficit could not be controlled. Ten years after the reforms were launched, in 2000-01, the combined fiscal deficit of the centre and the states was still at 10 per cent of GDP, marginally higher than in the crisis year of 1990-91.

The overview of the policy regime as presented in the preceding five sections is by no means comprehensive. For example, the slow and steady but far from adequate reform of the financial sector, though very important, has not been discussed. However, the discussion of the evolution of the major elements of policy provides a framework within which the economic performance of the industrial sector can be analysed. Admittedly, reform takes time to show its impact and the period of ten years is not long enough to see the impact of the various changes in policy during these years. Keeping these limitations in mind, the following section reviews the performance in the 1990s.

SECTION 4

INDUSTRIAL PERFORMANCE IN 1990s

As is clear from the preceding section, economic reforms of the 1990s had the dual objective of macro-economic stabilisation and enhancing the growth potential of the economy. Policies to promote competition both within the economy and from imports were expected to contribute to cutting costs, improving quality and enhancing competitiveness of Indian industry. A proactive policy of attracting foreign investment was expected not only to ease the resource constraint for investment on account of the deteriorating fiscal situation but also to release critical supply constraints for industry, e.g., in the infrastructure sectors. If the growth of public investment was restrained or at times negative because of the compulsions of macro-economic stabilisation, the expectation was that private investment could fill this void as it would respond to a much improved investment outlook in the economy. The private sector was given more room for greater participation in the process.

What follows is an empirical documentation of the trends in investment, value added and total factor productivity growth for the manufacturing sector and its subsectors. The analysis of exports is presented for the sector as a whole and for a few major groups. The analysis of growth and productivity is carried out at two levels of disaggregation, i.e., use-based sectors and two-digit industry groups.[7] The use-based classification of manufacturing into capital goods, intermediate goods, consumers durables and consumer non-durables allows us to trace the developments in line with the focus of policy in the Indian industrialisation strategy which gave pre-eminence to capital goods, accommodated the demands of the intermediate goods sector and consistently refused to recognise the importance of efficiency and competitiveness for consumer goods. The two-digit level of disaggregation allows us to discern how the major industry groups performed over time and how they were affected by the opening up of the Indian economy and associated reforms.

7. The use based classification has been derived by using the method spelt out in Ahluwalia (1991).

Investment Scenario

As the stabilisation package was put in place in 1991-92 following the crisis of 1990-91, the decline in both public and private investment in that year brought about a decline in the rate of overall investment in the economy from 26.3 per cent in 1990-91 to 22.6 per cent in 1991-92. While the rate of public investment declined and/or stagnated in the rest of the decade, the pick up in private investment materialised only in the first few years; after 1995-96, the rate of private investment also stagnated around 15-16 per cent (Figure 12.2). It would seem therefore that the economic reforms of the 1990s evoked a positive response from private investors in the first few years, but the momentum was lost after 1995-96. Admittedly, reform measures that have been set in motion influence performance with some time lag. It may be too early to gauge the impact of the reforms which are already underway. However, there is no denying that the process of reform needs to be carried forward to elicit better response from investors.

Figure 12.2

Rate of Gross Domestic Capital Formation
(Per cent of GDP)

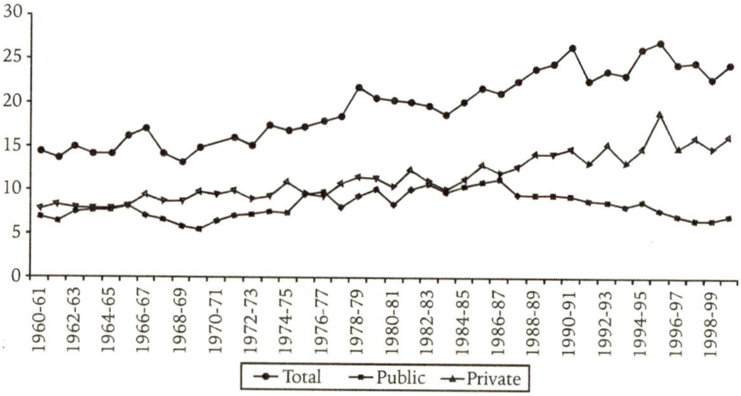

The importance of private foreign investment in releasing the crucial infrastructure bottlenecks was well recognised by policy makers. In fact, fast track mechanisms were put in place to ensure this. In the event, the results were very disappointing. Ahluwalia (1999) provides an appraisal of the complex issues faced in the infrastructure sectors, which leads him to conclude that "The experience of private investors in power and telecommunications provides many examples of problems which could have been avoided if the policy framework had been designed to deal with these difficulties." The high degree of protection of the consumer goods sector also meant that "the tariff jumping variety" of foreign investment was naturally attracted to sectors such as the automotive sector, while the compulsion for private investors in infrastructure to interact with the unreformed public sector acted as a disincentive for private investors to invest in the infrastructure sectors. Foreign investment inflows increased from virtually nothing before 1991 to about 0.5 per cent of GDP by the end of the decade, amounting to $ 2.3 billion in 2000-01. However, this was much below the levels attracted by most other developing economies.

Growth in Value added and Productivity

The performance of growth in value added and productivity in the last two decades is analysed here against the backdrop of a longer-term perspective over the preceding two decades. The relatively poor performance of industrial growth and productivity over the period 1965-1980 and the sharp turnaround in the 1980s has been extensively documented and analysed in the literature.[8] That the better industrial performance of the 1980s, could not be sustained due to the growing macro-economic imbalances during the 1980s has also been extensively discussed. In this section we attempt to analyse the performance with respect to growth of value added, and total factor productivity in the 1990s.

The 1990s have certainly been an eventful period for the industrial economy of India. Crisis, reform, adjustment, recovery, rapid growth and then a downward slide – this decade has seen it all. The collapse from a growth rate of 8.5 per cent in value added of manufacturing in the decade 1981-91 to –2.3 per cent in 1991-92 was followed by a rapid and perhaps unprecedented recovery in such adjustment episodes (Table 12.5). The three years from 1993-94 to

8. Ahluwalia (1991).

1995-96 saw an average growth of 13 per cent per annum (not reported in the table). Even though a major slowdown began in 1996-97, the average growth of value added in the period 1991-92 to 1997-98 was still as high as 9.1 per cent per annum, higher than the rapid growth of the early phase of Indian industrialisation in the first half of the 1960s. However, by 1999-00, the average growth for the decade (not reported in the table) had declined to 8.0 per cent, based on the data for value added in manufacturing from National Accounts, which are available for more recent years.

Table 12.5

Trends in Growth in Value Added Two Digit Industry Groups

(ASI) *(Per cent per annum)*

	Share in Value Added (1990-91)	*1960-61 to 1965-66*	*1965-66 to 1980-81*	*1980-81 to 1990-91*	*1991-92*	*1991-92 to 1997-98*
Manufactured goods (NA)*	**100.0**	**8.3**	**4.1**	**8.5**	**-2.3**	**9.1**
Manufactured goods	**100.0**	**8.9**	**4.5**	**8.2**	**-3.7**	**9.9**
Food	10.7	2.6	2.4	11.2	6.5	8.4
Beverages	1.2	20.0	7.9	10.7	12.4	11.3
Tobacco	2.0	4.0	4.4	13.5	13.2	5.6
Textiles	15.5	5.5	3.8	5.8	-13.3	7.2
Footwear	1.8	15.6	15.3	16.0	17.1	15.7
Furniture and Wood Products	0.4	8.2	4.1	7.0	-3.0	6.1
Paper and Paper Products	3.1	12.0	6.3	8.9	-13.6	4.6
Printing and Publishing	1.6	8.3	2.7	4.1	11.2	8.8
Leather and Fur Products	0.7	5.2	6.3	12.7	23.7	8.4
Rubber Products	2.8	4.5	4.2	16.6	-9.9	12.0
Chemicals and Chemicals Products	18.0	12.0	7.6	10.6	1.6	12.1
Petroleum and Coal Products	5.5	0.4	8.3	26.6	-21.7	6.5
Non-Metallic Mineral Products	6.7	7.0	3.1	12.3	19.6	3.4
Basic Metal Industries	16.4	17.3	4.4	5.6	-23.0	19.5
Metal Products	2.8	13.5	2.1	4.6	11.2	9.6
Non-Electrical Machinery	9.8	20.4	6.4	8.1	0.2	7.9
Electrical Machinery	9.8	12.8	9.5	11.0	-11.6	10.2
Transport Equipment	9.8	11.0	4.5	6.3	-6.2	14.2

Source: Annual Survey of Industries.

* National Accounts.

Among the two-digit industry groups, the fastest growing industries for the period upto 1997-98 were basic metal industries, footwear, chemicals and chemical products, rubber products and transport equipment (Figure 12.3). Growth of value added in textiles at 7.2 per cent per annum in the 1990s was quite a bit higher than in the 1980s but the industry experienced more fluctuations in the 1990s compared to earlier years. Figure 12.4 presents the growth in value added for the major two digit industries from 1965-66 to 1997-98. However, considering India's comparative advantage in textiles, this sector has been an underachiever, even given the constraints of the MFA.

Table 12.6 presents the growth of value added for the use-based sectors. Capital goods emerges as the laggard sector. After its golden period in the first half of the 1960s, the capital goods sector in the Indian economy never really recovered from the setback. A long period of stagnation after the mid-60s was followed by only a modest improvement in the 1980s and some further increase in the growth rate in the 1990s. By contrast, the consumer non-durables sector was a slow growing sector pretty much till the end of the 1980s. The process of domestic deregulation of the 1980s provided a major stimulus to the growth of this sector. The recovery of this sector after 1991-92 was also robust as the sector recorded an average growth of 11 per cent.

Table 12.6

Trends in Growth in Value Added Used-based Sectors

(Per cent per annum)

	Share in Value Added (1990-91)	*1960-61 to 1965-66*	*1965-66 to 1980-81*	*1980-81 to 1990-91*	*1991-92*	*1991-92 to 1997-98*
Manufacturing	100.0	8.5	4.3	7.8	-3.8	9.3
Capital Goods	19.8	15.9	6.7	8.2	1.3	9.2
Intermediate Goods	35.5	10.8	3.9	8.6	-4.3	11.4
Consumer Durables	4.6	11.1	8.1	11.0	5.8	12.9
Consumer Non-durables	40.1	5.1	4.0	10.7	3.9	11.0

Source: Annual Survey of Industries.

Figure 12.3

Index of Growth in Value Added- Two Digit Industry Groups

(X-axis: Year; Y-axis: Per cent per Annum)

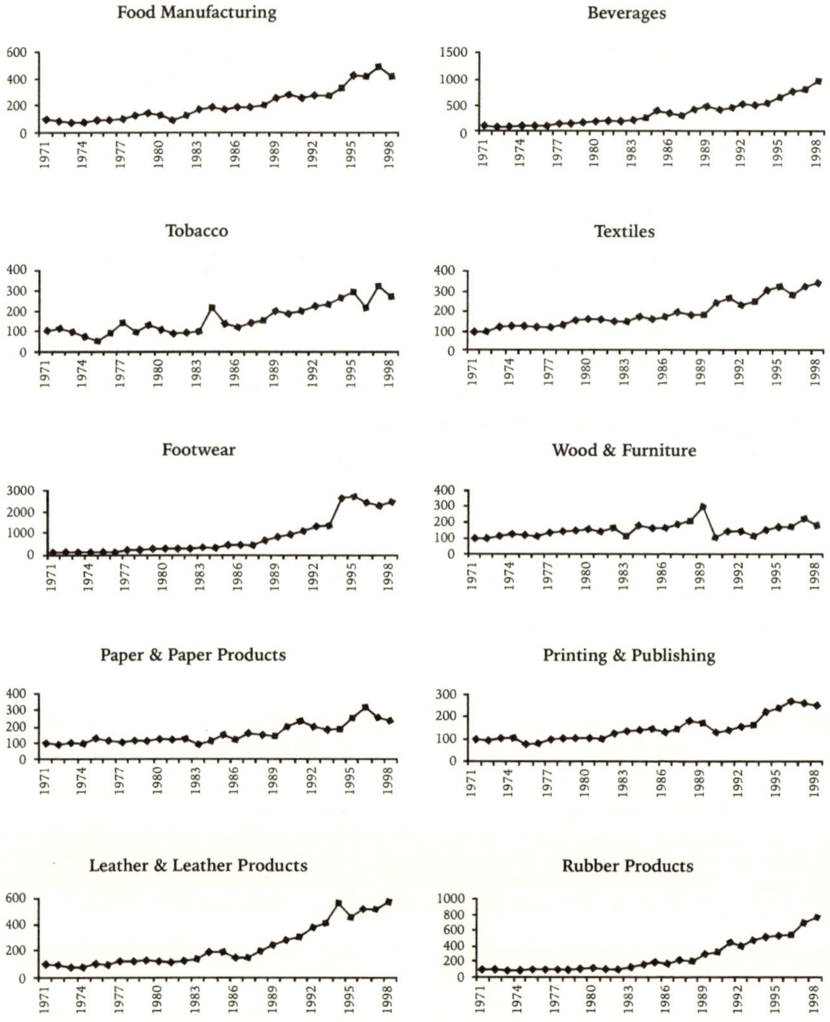

Note: Value added at constant price in 1970-71= 100

Contd. ...

...Contd. ...

Figure 12.3

Index of Growth in Value Added- Two Digit Industry Groups
(X-axis: Year; Y-axis: Per cent per Annum)

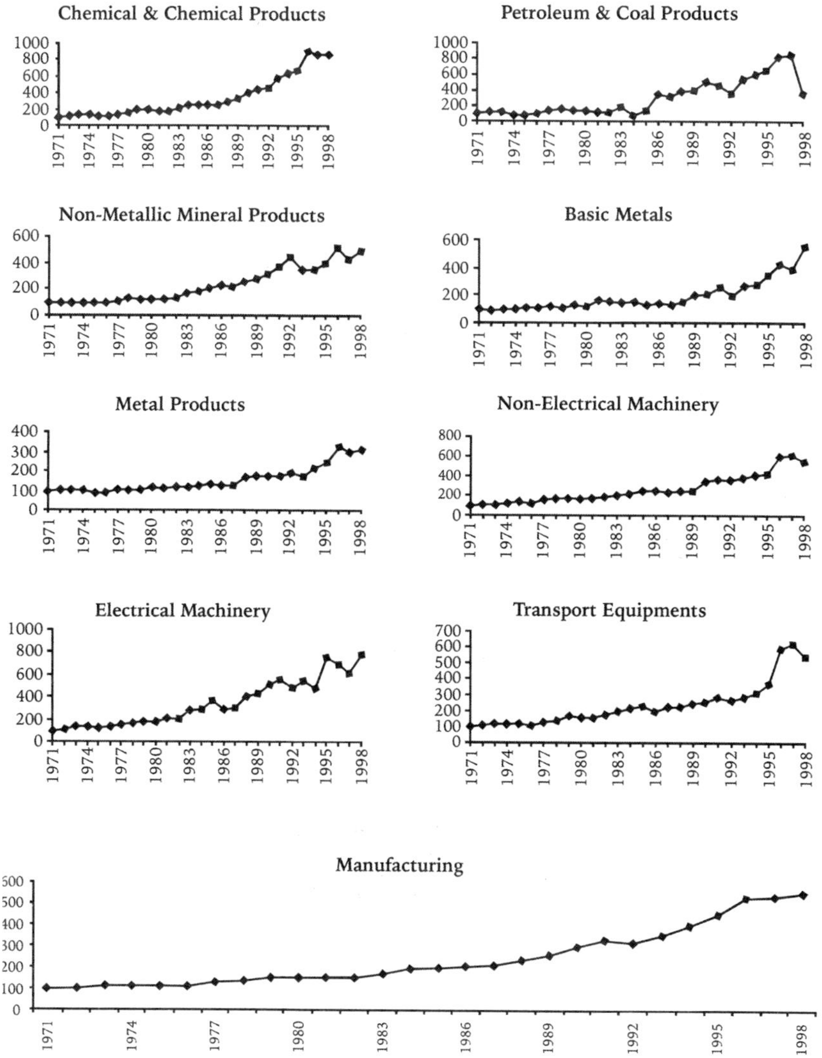

Note: Value added at constant price in 1970-71= 100

Figure 12.4

Growth in Value Added Two Digit Industry Groups

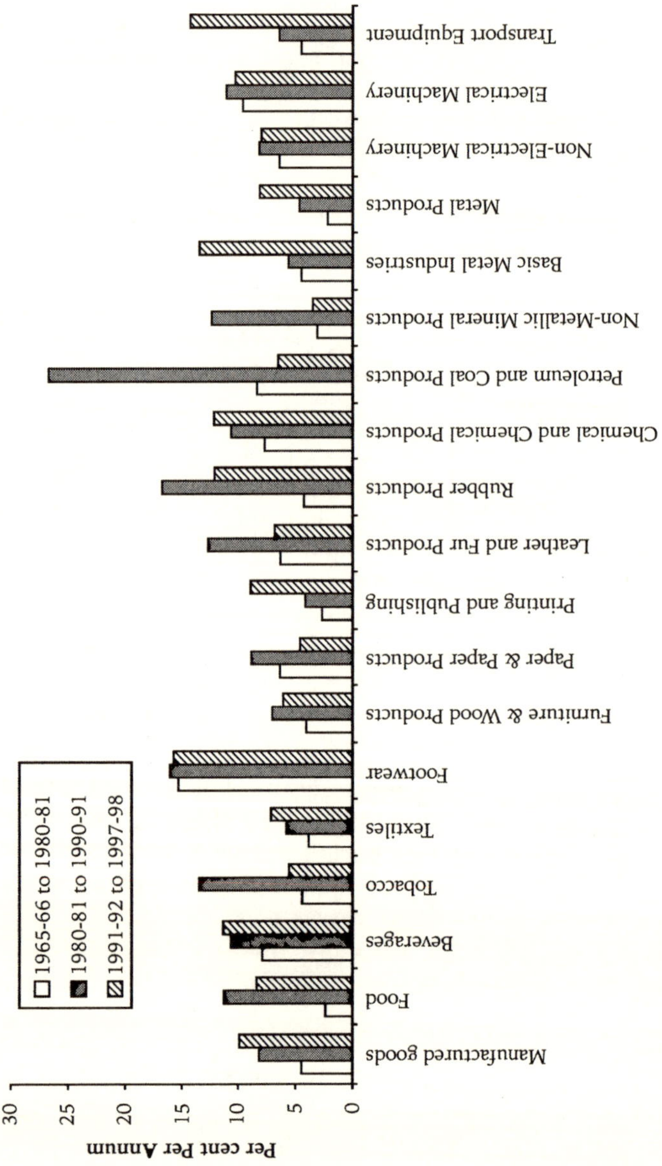

Before turning to the productivity growth trends, it is important to note that the productivity concept used here is total factor productivity (TFP), which measures the efficiency with which labour and capital are combined to generate value added. The growth of TFP is computed as the difference between the rate of growth of value added and the weighted rate of growth of factor inputs, the weights being factor shares on the assumption that the factors are paid the value of their marginal products and the underlying production function is a value added function which relates value added to labour and capital.[9]

Data used for TFP estimation are from the Annual Survey of Industries (Central Statistical Organisation). A careful attempt is made to build the capital stock series at replacement cost at constant prices using perpetual inventory accumulation method.[10] The measure of TFP is directly affected by the accuracy of measurement of capital, labour and value added.[11] If a correct measure of capital is a well-known problem, the importance of skills in the measurement of labour input raises similar problems.

Tables 12.7 and 12.8 present the estimates of TFPG for the two-digit industry groups and the use-based sectors, respectively. Total factor productivity growth for the manufacturing sector during the period 1991-92 to 1997-98 was 3.4 per cent per annum, a little slower than the growth rate of 3.8 per cent per annum in the 1980s. As discussed earlier, a prolonged stagnation in total factor productivity from the mid-60s to the end of the 1970s was followed by a strong turnaround in the 1980s. The policies of

9. Total factor productivity is defined as Δ Log T FP_t = Δ Log V_t – w Δ Log L_t– (1-w) Δ Log K_t where V,L and K denote real value added, labour and capital, respectively, and w stands for the average share of labour in value added averaged for two consecutive years. In some definitions, TFP is derived through a gross output version of the production function which relates gross output to labour, capital and intermediate inputs, so that the intermediate inputs are explicitly taken into account.

10. Ahulwalia (1991).

11. Ideally, a double deflated value added series should be used to arrive at the estimates of TFP growth. For want of accurate deflators for the time-series of intermediate inputs, we use a single-deflation method, the same as used in the National Accounts Series. This has the advantage that the real value added trends for individual sub-sectors of manufacturing are consistent with those reported in the National accounts. Goldar (2000 and 2002) has shown that estimates of TFP growth based on double-deflated value added and gross output specifications are highly sensitive to the base year of the price indices used for deflation.

Table 12.7

Trends in TFPG Two Digit Industry Groups

(ASI) *(Per cent per annum)*

	Share in Value Added (1990-91)	1960-61 to 1965-66	1965-66 to 1980-81	1980-81 to 1990-91	1991-92	1991-92 to 1997-98
Manufactured Goods	**100.0**	**0.1**	**-0.7**	**3.8**	**-7.8**	**3.4**
Food	10.7	-1.9	-3.3	7.4	2.6	2.2
Beverages	1.2	8.6	-1.4	2.2	6.5	1.3
Tobacco	2.0	3.5	-1.9	7.5	9.5	3.1
Textiles	15.5	1.4	0.6	3.6	-15.3	0.3
Footwear	1.8	5.4	2.3	5.4	11.8	8.1
Furniture and Wood Products	0.4	-1.8	0.5	3.9	-11.8	0.9
Paper and Paper Products	3.1	-3.2	-3.6	-1.0	-9.2	-3.6
Printing and Publishing	1.6	-2.4	-0.4	-0.9	-8.4	-3.2
Leather and Fur Products	0.7	3.4	-2.0	5.6	11.8	2.7
Rubber Products	2.8	-4.9	-3.0	7.4	-15.9	6.4
Chemicals and Chemicals Products	18.0	-1.5	-2.3	4.0	-2.7	3.4
Petroleum and Coal Products	5.5	-16.5	0.8	16.4	-26.5	-0.8
Non-Metallic Mineral Products	6.7	1.5	-1.7	4.0	10.4	-2.8
Basic Metal Industries	16.4	-0.4	-1.2	1.4	-25.7	13.0
Metal Products	2.8	1.2	-2.3	-0.6	11.6	1.7
Non-Electrical Machinery	9.8	1.8	0.6	2.5	-3.9	3.1
Electrical Machinery	9.8	-3.2	0.7	5.5	-10.9	2.9
Transport Equipment	9.8	2.1	0.1	4.3	-10.0	8.0

Source: Annual Survey of Industries.

Table 12.8

Trends in Growth in Total Factor Productivity Use-based Sector

(Per cent per annum)

	Share in Value Added (1990-91)	1960-61 to 1965-66	1965-66 to 1980-81	1980-81 to 1990-91	1991-92	1991-92 to 1997-98
Manufacturing	100.0	0.1	-0.7	3.8	-7.8	3.4
Capital Goods	19.8	3.2	0.8	4.2	-3.2	4.0
Intermediate Goods	35.5	-0.9	-1.5	3.5	-8.2	4.4
Consumer Durables	4.6	1.3	0.7	3.1	0.6	3.8
Consumer Non-durables	40.1	0.3	-1.0	5.2	-3.2	3.1

Source: Annual Survey of Industries.

domestic deregulation, market orientation and trade policy simplification, together with some emphasis on better co-ordination among the different infrastructure sectors, e.g., railways and power, and some increase in public investment in these sectors were instrumental in creating conditions for better productivity performance in the manufacturing sector in the 1980s. The slack of unused capacities in the manufacturing sector during the 1980s helped in generating a productivity response. The quick recovery of 1991 and the growth, which followed put further demands on the existing capacities.

Two important considerations need to be kept in mind while analysing the productivity growth performance of the manufacturing sector in the 1990s. First, that in order to sustain a higher growth of value added, infrastructure services are crucial, requiring both expansion in quantity and improvement in quality. This does not necessarily imply larger public investments in infrastructure. In fact, even larger private sector investments are unlikely until much needed policy reforms are undertaken in these sectors. What is needed is accelerated reform of policies to ensure economic viability for the infrastructure sectors. A second consideration relates to the concept of total factor productivity itself. Since the estimate is based on growth of value added at domestic prices, admittedly adjusted for increases in these prices, the measure does not take into account the change in domestic prices relative to international prices. This is specially relevant when comparing the productivity growth estimates for the 1980s and the 1990s because the 1990s was a period in which the Indian manufacturing sector faced much lower levels of protection and domestic prices were much closer to international prices. The estimate of TFPG for the 1990s therefore reflects productivity gains better than that for the 1980s.

As Table 12.7 shows, basic metals, transport equipment, footwear and rubber products are the sectors with the highest TFPG in the 1990s. Figure 12.5 presents the productivity growth profile within the manufacturing sector. These are the sectors, which grew the fastest. Chemicals and chemical products is the only fast growing sector, which shows moderate growth of TFPG of 3.4 per cent per annum in the 1990s (Table 12.7), marginally lower than in the

Figure 12.5

Total Factor Productivity Growth Two-Digit Industry Groups

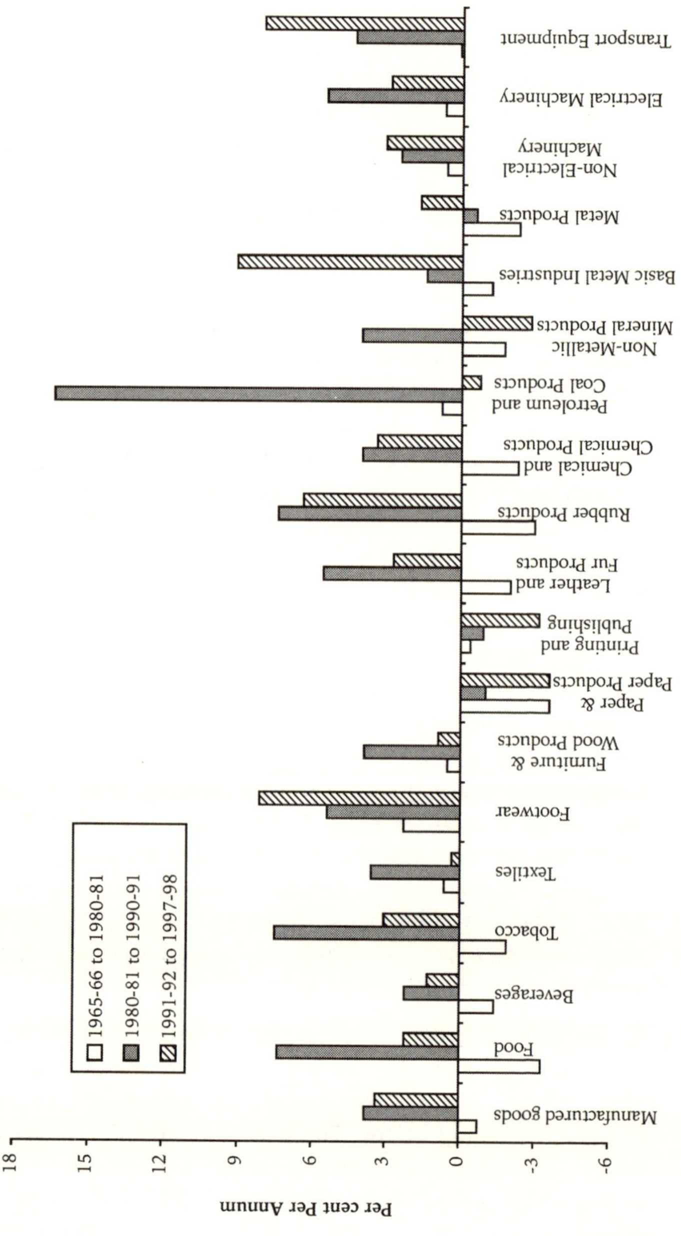

1980s. Pharmaceuticals, a significant component of this industry group also does not show a significant pick up in productivity performance in the 1990s

Table 12.8 provides estimates of TFPG for the use-based sectors. Consumer non-durable goods recorded the fastest TFPG in the 1980s. However, since consumer goods industries remained very highly protected and subject to extensive QRs in the 1980s and the process of tariff reduction for these goods only began in the 1990s, the lower TFPG at 2 per cent for this sector in the 1990s compared with 5 per cent in the 1980s may be reflecting the fact that this sector's domestic prices moved closer to international prices. Capital goods showed a slight deceleration in the growth of total factor productivity. Consumer durables, by contrast, recorded a faster TFPG in the 90s compared with the 80s.

Export Performance

Opening up to competition from imports was a major plank of the economic reforms of the 1990s. The high cost industrial structure of India had eroded the competitiveness of India's exports. Access to cheaper and better quality intermediate inputs and technological upgradation possibilities through liberalised import of capital goods were expected to contribute towards improving the competitiveness of the Indian manufacturing sector. While QRs on consumer goods were removed at the very end of the decade, for capital goods and intermediate goods the process of tariff reduction and QR removal had begun earlier. As Figure 12.6 shows, the period after the mid-1980s was one of steady increase in the ratio of non-oil imports to GDP. Important as it is to analyse the impact of the increased import intensity on the exports of manufactured goods, it is not possible to explore this impact within an econometric framework because of non-availability of consistent time series data on exports at the two-digit level of disaggregation which can be matched with the classification for industry data. Analysis of export performance of the manufacturing sector at a comparable level of disaggregation is hampered not only by the lack of concordance between the classification of trade data and industry data, but also by a break in the time series of the trade data itself at 1986-87. Table 12.9 puts together the available evidence on principal manufactured goods exports, as compiled by the Reserve Bank of India.

Figure 12.6

Total Imports and Non-oil Imports (Per cent of GDP)

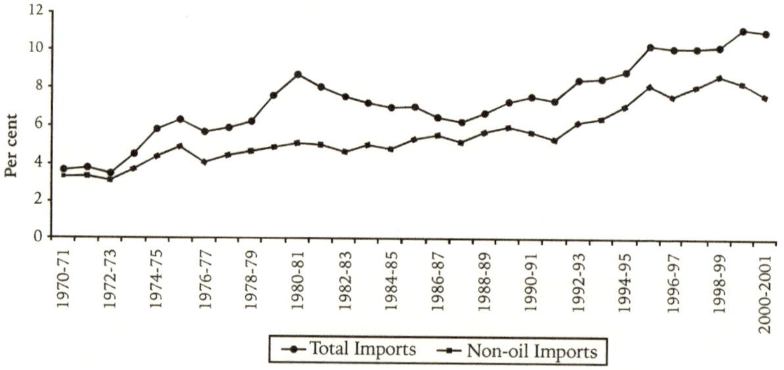

As Table 12.9 shows, the year 1991-92 is excluded from our analysis of export performance in the 1990s. This is because this was the year of adjustment to the macro-economic stabilisation package when the reforms were launched and because this was also the year, which saw the abrupt and significant effect on India because of the break up of the Soviet Union. The growth of manufactured goods exports in the 1990s was marginally higher at 11.8 per cent per annum than in the 1980s. Considering that the second half of the 1980s had shown a strong performance of manufactured goods exports, the opening up of the economy had to build on this strong performance after allowing for the impact of the balance of payments crisis of 1990-91 and the adjustment to the reforms that followed. Except for leather and leather products, all other major categories in Table 12.9 show robust growth in the 1990s. Figure 12.7 presents the indices of total exports and manufactured goods exports in the 1980s ad 1990s. The acceleration in the growth of manufactured goods exports in the 1990s emerges clearly from the data. Figure 12.8 presents the indices for the principal categories of manufactured goods.

Figure 12.7

Exports (US $) Total and Manufactured Goods

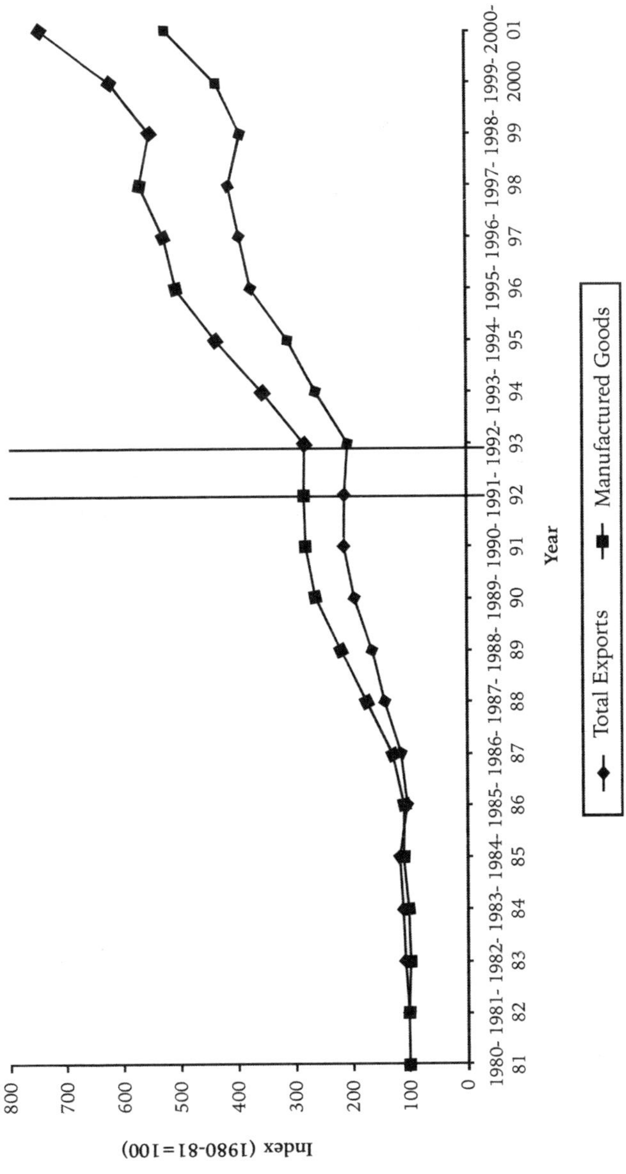

Figure 12.8

Exports (US $): Principal Manufactured Goods

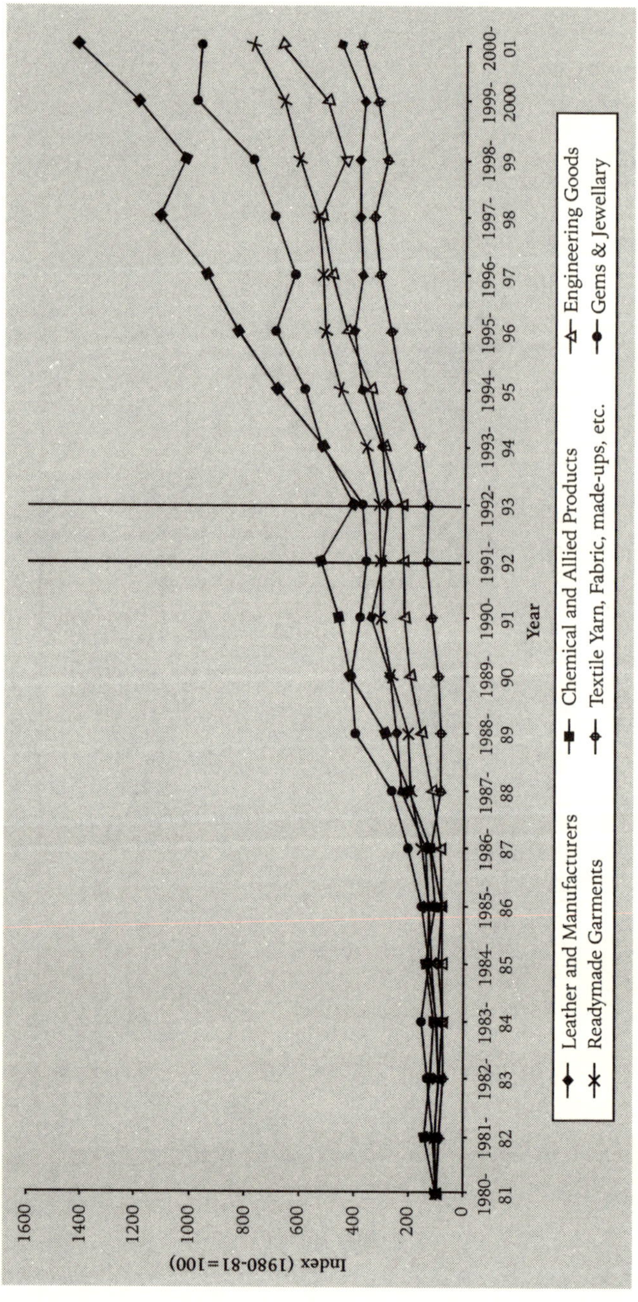

Table 12.9

Growth of Exports: Principal Manufactured Goods (in US $)

(Per cent per annum)

	1980-81 to 1986-87	*1986-87 to 1990-91*	*1980-81 to 1990-91*	*1991-92*	*1991-92 to 1997-98*	*1991-92 to 2001-02*
Total	2.5	16.9	8.3	-0.8	12.2	11.1
Manufacturing Goods*	4.5	21.7	11.4	1.0	12.8	11.8
Leather and Leather Products	5.7	28.2	14.7	-11.8	4.9	5.4
Chemicals and Allied Products	6.1	40.9	20.1	14.0	15.0	13.0
Engineering Goods	-2.5	28.1	9.8	0.9	15.7	14.0
Readymade Garments**	8.1	20.0	12.9	-0.9	10.1	11.1
Textile Yarn, Fabrics, Made-ups, etc.	6.4	1.8	4.6	18.0	16.4	12.7
Gems and Jewellery	13.9	19.1	16.0	-5.7	12.6	12.4

Source: Reserve Bank of India Data Base, and Economic Surveys, Ministry of Finance.*

* Data on Manufactured goods is from Economic Surveys, Ministry of Finance. For the components of manufactured goods, export data on a consistent basis is obtained from the RBI data base in rupees and converted to US $ by using rupee-dollar exchange rate provided by the RBI.

** For years prior to 1998-88, data relates to clothing.

Table 12.10 present India's export shares in the principal manufactured goods over the period from 1970 to 1998. Export shares of total manufactures in world exports of this category increased from 0.4 per cent to 0.5 per cent over the 1980s. The rate of increase appears to have accelerated in the first half of the 90s taking the share to 0.6 per cent in 5 years. Thereafter, however, in the second half of the 90s, the export shares remain the same. Taken as a whole, manufactured exports can be said to have continued to gain competitiveness through the first half of the post-reform period with a loss of momentum in the second half. The most dynamic sector over the longer run is gems and jewellery where India's share of world exports increased from 2.2 per cent in 1970 to 10.7 per cent in 1998. Exports of gems and jewellery from India were affected by the global slump in demand in the late 1990s. After increasing to 11.8 per cent in 1995, India's share of exports in this sector declined to 10.7 per cent in 1998. More generally, India has not been able to make major inroads into the world markets. In leather and leather products, of course, India's share of world exports continued its long term secular decline. This is most likely due to environmental concerns on the part of leather importers. Garment exports also seem to have lost their share marginally in the global slowdown of the late 1990s.

Table 12.10

India's Export Shares in Selected Manufactured Goods

(Per cent per annum)

	1970	*1980*	*1990*	*1995*	*1998*
Manufacturing Goods	–	0.4	0.5	0.6	0.6
Leather and Leather Products	9.1	6.8	6.3	3.3	2.9
Chemicals and Allied Products	0.3	0.4	0.7	0.7	0.8
Engineering Goods	0.4	0.2	0.2	0.2	0.2
Readymade Garments	–	1.8	2.3	2.6	2.3
Textile Yarn, Fabrics, Made-ups, etc.	4.1	2.3	2.1	2.9	3.3
Gems and Jewellery	2.2	3.1	9.8	11.8	10.7

Source: Economic Survey 2000-01.

SECTION 5

CONCLUSION

A disaggregated view of the performance of the manufacturing sector in the 1990s is constrained by data availability only upto 1997-98. This period is dominated by the "good years", 1993-94 to 1995-96, and includes only the beginning of a prolonged slowdown, which has persisted since then. In that sense, the performance tends to be overstated. Even so, what emerges strongly from our empirical detour of growth, productivity and exports at the disaggregated level is a mixed picture. Growth of value added certainly accelerated in the 1990s for most sectors; the most notable exceptions were food products, leather, paper and paper products and non-metallic mineral products, e.g., cement. Growth of total factor productivity in these industry groups, however, was by and large less impressive than in the 1980s. It could well be argued that the domestic prices are more correctly reflecting competitiveness in the 1990s so that the performance in the 90s has to be seen against the TFPG of the 1980s. However, it is also possible that the gaps in the reform effort, particularly those relating to infrastructure, meant that a "productivity response" was more difficult in the 1990s. Finally, on the export front, within the limitations of the data framework, what emerges is a picture where even when Indian exports have done well, they have not done well enough to improve their share in world exports. Gems & jewellery is the only category of exports where India's share in 1998 exceeded 10 per cent of world exports.

At the aggregate level, the available data upto 2000-01 show more clearly both the deceleration in growth of value added and exports. Slowdown in reforms, deteriorating fiscal situation with its impact on the macro-economic management and weakening political will are some factors which could help explain this phenomenon.

References

Ahluwalia, I.J (1991). *Productivity and Growth in Indian Manufacturing*, Oxford University Press, Delhi.

Ahluwalia, M.S. (1998). "Infrastructure Development in India's Reform," in Ahluwalia, I.J and I.M.D. Little (ed.), *India's Economic Reforms and Development: Essays for Manmohan Singh*, Oxford University Press, Delhi.

Alexander, P.C. (1978). Chairman, Report of the Committee on Imports-Exports Policies and Procedures, Ministry of Commerce, Government of India.

Balakrishnan, P., K. Pushpangadan and M. Suresh Babu (2000). "Trade Liberalisation and Productivity Growth In Indian Manufacturing: Evidence from Firm Level Panel Data," *Economic and Political Weekly*, October 7.

Bhagwati, J.N. (1958). "Immiserizing Growth: A Geometric Note," *Review of Economic Studies*, Vol. 25, June

————. (1968). "Distortions and Immiserizing Growth: A Generalisation," *Review of Economic Studies*, Vol. 35.

Bhagwati, J.N. and T.N. Srinivasan (1975). *Foreign Trade Regime and Economic Development: India*, Columbia University Press, New York.

Brecher, R. and C. Diaz-Alexajandro (1977). "Tariffs, Foreign Capital and Immiserizing Growth", *Journal of International Economics*, November.

Chand, S. and K. Sen (2002). "Trade Liberalisation and Productivity Growth: Evidence from Indian Manufacturing", *Review of Development Economics*, Vol. 6, No.1.

Dagli, V. (1979). Chairman, Report of the Committee on Controls and Subsidies, Ministry of Finance, Government of India. New Delhi

Das, D.K. (2001). "Some Aspects of Productivity Growth and Trade in Indian Industry," Unpublished Ph.D. Dissertation, Delhi School of Economics, University of Delhi, Delhi.

Dollar, David and Omkar Goswami *et al.*, (2002). *Productivity of Indian Manufacturing Firms*, CII and World Bank, January.

Goldar, B.N. (2000). "Productivity Growth in Indian Manufacturing in the 1980's and 1990's." Paper Presented at a Conference to Honour Professor K.L Krishna, organised by the Centre for Development. Economics, Delhi School of Economics, Delhi on the theme "Industrialisation in a Reforming Economy: A Quantitative Assessment." Delhi, December.

————. (2002). "TFP Growth in Indian Manufacturing in 1980s", *Economic and Political Weekly*, 37, No 49.

Goldar, B.N. and A. Kumari (2002). "Import Liberalisation and Productivity Growth in Indian Manufacturing Industries in the 1990s." Working Paper # E/219/2002, Institute of Economic Growth, Delhi.

Krishna, P. and D. Mitra (1998). "Trade Liberalisation, Market Discpline and Productivity Growth: New Evidence From India," *Journal of Development Economics*, Vol. 56.

Pande, B.D. (1980). Chairman, Report of the National Transport Policy Committee, Planning Commission, Government of India. New Delhi

Rajadhyaksha, V.G. (1980). Chairman, Report of the Committee on Power, Ministry of Energy & Coal, Government of India. New Delhi

Shome, P. (2000). India: Primary Aspects of a Medium Term Fiscal Strategy, Discussion Paper, Indian Council for Research in International Economic Relations (ICRIER). New Delhi, December.

Srinivasan, T.N. (2001), *Trade, Development and Growth, International Economics Section*, Princeton University, Princeton University, New Jersey.

Tandon, P. (1980). Chairman, Report of the Committee on Export Strategy 1980s, Ministry of Commerce, Government of India.

13

Do Trade Restrictions Distort Domestic Relative-Price Ratio?

HIRANYA MUKHOPADHYAY

SECTION 1

INTRODUCTION

How trade barriers affect growth is still being debated in the literature. However, it has been argued by many that the exact nature in which trade restrictions reduce growth depends on the resource-allocation effect because trade barriers alter the domestic relative-price ratio in favour of the comparatively disadvantaged sector (Rodrik 1995, 2000). In other words, it introduces a wedge between the domestic relative-price ratio and the opportunity costs reflected in relative border prices. This is the so-called static effect of trade restrictions (*see* also Little, Scitovsky and Scot 1970, and Balassa 1971).

How does it work? Perceive a situation where we start with a positive import penetration. Import restrictions increase the market size for domestic producers. Domestic producers, in turn, expand production and raise mark-ups (Roberts and Tybout, 1996; Tybout 2000).[1] The situation is further aggravated when legal and institutional rigidities-very common in developing countries like India- prohibit the entry of new firms despite higher industry profits. There are many studies that support this 'import-discipline' hypothesis (Harrison 1994, Krishna and Mitra 1998, Sen and Chand 1999). For example, Little, Scitovsky and Scot wrote (1970, p.41):

---

1. Of course, a monopolist can sell more and reduce the mark-up. But we are ruling out this possibility for our aim is to explain the changes in the relative-price ratio in favour of import competing industries through higher mark-ups.

"For restraints on imports raise the prices of imports; and the prices of their domestic substitutes usually rise to a par or just below par with the prices of imports. Domestic competition even when deliberately encouraged, often seems insufficient to break this (my emphasis) link between the prices of imports and import substitutes."

Figures in Table 13.1 also corroborate this finding for some sectors in India.

We argue in this paper that the domestic relative-price ratio may not move in favour of the import competing industry (comparatively disadvantaged sector) despite an upward adjustment in the mark-up, provided resulting changes in the price of the comparatively advantaged product in a dual-economy framework are considered. Traditional literature, however, draws its conclusion from a narrow partial framework where this link is absent. In what follows, we present a small theoretical macro model to highlight this point in section 2. We estimate the fundamental relationship of the model in section 3 using Indian data.

Table 13.1

Nominal Rate of Protection and Price-Cost Margin in India: Selected Sectors (per cent)

		1980-81 to 1985-86		*1986-87 to 1990-91*	
		NRP	*PCM*	*NRP*	*PCM*
1.	Weaving and finishing of cotton *khadi*	108.96	13	126.14	12
2.	Thread and nets	133.08	8	130.76	11
3.	Textile, garment and accessories	130.83	7	143.00	14
4.	Consumer goods of leather	114.73	8	124.58	12
5.	Organic and inorganic chemicals	94.02	10	113.34	14
6.	Paints, varnishes and related products	120.89	11	193.00	13
7.	Tyres and tubes	114.98	13	136.34	15
8.	Rubber products, nec.	120.89	1	193.00	11
9.	Refined petro products, nec.	96.37	10	118.02	15
10.	Ferro alloys	92.31	11	110.48	14
11.	Aluminum products	89.12	0.01	109.54	13
12.	Agro machinery and equipment	63.21	10	75.44	16

Note: Price-Cost Margin (PCM) = (Value Added-Total Emoluments)/Gross Output.
Source: Das, 2001.

SECTION 2

THE MODEL

It is assumed that there are two sectors in the economy: a comparatively disadvantaged sector (Y), and a comparatively advantaged sector (F). Let us assume that Y is produced domestically by a monopolist. The entrepreneur decides the price of Y optimally given the demand function of Y and the price of F (P_f). The price of F, in turn, depends on the demand for F and exogenously given net supply of F (excluding own consumption). In the Indian context, Y and F could be classified broadly as industry and foodgrains respectively. It is generally assumed- especially in the Indian context- that the agricultural prices are market clearing type (Rakshit, 1989). The monopolist consumes both Y and F. The model is developed in a static framework where we abstain from studying the impact of changes in the domestic relative-price to resource allocation and consequent changes in outputs. This is beyond the scope of this paper.

Demand for Y is,

$$Y^d = f\left(\frac{P_f}{P_y}, Y, \frac{P_f F}{P_y}, \tau\right); f^1 > 0, f^2 > 0, f^3 > 0, f^4 > 0 \qquad \ldots(1)$$

Where Y is the real income of the monopolist, and τ is a shift factor. τ is the nominal rate of tariff. Given equation (1), the price of Y is optimally derived,

$$P_y = \Psi(P_f, \tau) \qquad \ldots(2)$$

For the sake of simplicity, the focus is on τ and P_f.[2] The sign of the partial derivatives of P_y with respect to τ and P_f depends on whether a rise in τ or P_f raises or lowers the elasticity of demand. If a higher τ shifts the demand function in such a manner so that it lowers the elasticity, then the monopolist will charge a higher price. Similar results holds for P_f. Keeping in view the "import-discipline" hypothesis, we assume Ψ^2 is positive, but the sign of Ψ^1 is assumed to be ambiguous.

A positive Ψ^2 can be demonstrated in the following way. Let it be that the monopolist with a constant average cost of production (c) is

2. We are ignoring cost function parameters and F, though this will be incorporated in the empirical exercise.

facing the demand function: f (P, τ) where $f^1 < 0$ and $f^2 > 0$. The optimum price (P^*) could be derived from the first order condition. It is easy to verify that,

$$\frac{dP^*}{d\tau} = \frac{-(P-c)\frac{\partial^2 f}{\partial P \partial \tau} + \frac{\partial f}{\partial \tau}}{2\frac{\partial f}{\partial P} + (P-c)\frac{\partial^2 f}{\partial P^2}}$$

As a result, dP/dτ could be positive under some plausible parameter configurations.

Using equations (1) and (2), we get the reduced form expression for Y^d,

$$Y^d = \Phi(P_f, \tau);\ \Phi^1 > 0, \Phi^2 > 0 \qquad ...(3)$$

It may be noted that $\Phi^1$and Φ^2 depend on $\Psi^1$and Ψ^2. In other words, the magnitude of Φ^2 is higher if the import-discipline hypothesis does not hold for some reasons (Ψ^2 is zero or negative), and the monopolist does not raise the price despite a shift in the demand function.

The demand for F is,

$$F^d = \left(\frac{P_f}{P_y}\right)^{-a} Y^b;\ a > 0, b > 0 \qquad ...(4)$$

The supply of F is given exogenously. We derive the following expression using the market-clearing equilibrium condition and equation (4).

$$a\frac{d\log P_f}{d\log P_y} = a + b\frac{d\log Y}{d\log P_y} \qquad ...(5)$$

It can be shown using (5) that,

$$\frac{d\left(\frac{P_f}{P_y}\right)}{d\tau} > 0 \text{ iff } \frac{bP_f}{aP_y y}\frac{dy}{d\tau} > 0 \qquad ...(6)$$

$$\frac{dy}{d\tau} = \Phi^1\frac{dP_f}{d\tau} + \Phi^2 \qquad ...(7)$$

Using equations (2), (3) and (4) we derive,

$$\frac{dP_f}{d\tau} = \frac{P_f \Psi^2 ay + P_f bP_y \Phi^2}{P_y ay - P_f ay\Psi^1 - bP_y P_f \Phi^1} \qquad ...(8)$$

Therefore, our final condition is,

$$\frac{d\left(\frac{P_f}{P_y}\right)}{d\tau} > 0 \text{ iff } \frac{bP_f}{aP_y y}\left(\Phi^1 \frac{P_f \Psi^2 ay + P_f bP_y \Phi^2}{P_y ay - P_f ay\Psi^1 - bP_y P_f \Phi^1} + \Phi^2\right) > 0 \qquad ...(9)$$

This condition becomes much weaker if we also assume that $\Psi^1 < 0$. In other words, the producer of Y does not raise his price for a rise in P_f. Let us assume $\Psi^1 < 0$, and define two terms,

$$-\eta_{P_y P_f} = \psi^1 \frac{P_f}{P_y} \text{ and}$$

$$e_{yP_f} = \phi^1 \frac{P_f}{y}$$

Then the R.H.S of (9) is positive if

$$\frac{a}{b} > \frac{e_{yP_f}}{1 + \eta_{P_y P_f}} \qquad ...(10)$$

If $\Psi^1 > 0$, then the condition is,

$$1 > \eta_{P_y P_f} + \frac{b}{a} e_{yP_f} \qquad ...(11)$$

It may also be noted that the effect of a higher F on the domestic relative price ratio is ambiguous. The upshot of the above discussion is that the relationship between the relative-price ratio and the nominal tariff (τ) is not unambiguously negative as argued in the literature. It depends on many crucial parameters. Therefore, we propose to examine the relationship empirically in the next section.

SECTION 3

EMPIRICAL TESTS

The proposal is to test the relationship between relative price (RELPR; defined as P_y/P_f) and the nominal rate of protection (collection rate or nominal average tariff, CR). Our theoretical model, in the previous section, suggests that F (foodgrain production) should also be included in the reduced form. In addition, the unit cost of production (UC) is incorporate to avoid the omitted variable bias. The Figures 13.1 below graph four series. As all the series apparently look like a non-stationary series (Figure 13.1), careful empirical checks must be undertaken.

Figure 13.1

Variable Plots

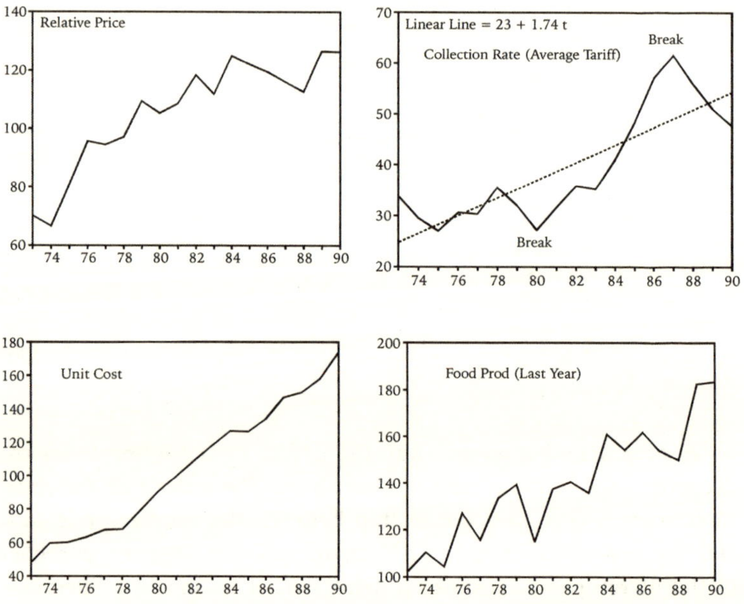

Moreover, there is a need to test whether a non-stationary series is difference stationary (DS) or trend stationary (TS). The graph of

CR suggests two structural breaks during the period 1973-74 to 1990-91.[3]

The test for unit roots is biased in favour of accepting the null hypothesis of unit roots if structural breaks are not explicitly considered (Enders 1995). However, it is not clear at this juncture whether these breaks involve one time change in the level or one time change in the drift of the unit root process or both.

Trends and unit roots in all the series-except CR are tested by using the Augmented Dickey-Fuller methodology. The fundamental regression equation is,

$$\Delta y_t = a_0 + a_1 t + a_2 y_{t-1} + \sum_{i=1}^{k} b_i \Delta y_{t-i} + \varepsilon_t \qquad ...(11)$$

The null hypothesis of unit root is accepted if $a_2=0$. Moreover, the series is trend stationary if the null hypothesis $a=a_2=0$ is rejected. The testing procedure for unit roots in the presence of structural breaks is slightly different. The procedure is as follows. Suppose, we assume that there is a one-time change in the level of the series and also permanent change in the drift.[4] Here, the null hypothesis is

$$H_0 : y_t = a_0 + y_{t-1} + \mu_1 D_P + \mu_2 D_L + \varepsilon_t \qquad ...(12)$$

Where $D_P=1$ for $t=\tau+1$, and 0 otherwise and $D_L=1$ for $t > \tau$, and 0 otherwise. The structural break is assumed to have occurred at t. The appropriate alternative hypothesis in this case is,

$$A_0 = a_0 + a_1 t + \mu_2 D_L + \mu_3 D_T * t + \varepsilon_t \qquad ...(13)$$

Where $D_T=1$ for $t>\tau$, and 0 otherwise. In other words, the alternative hypothesis is that the series is stationary around the trend, and the slope and intercept of the trend line change at $t=\tau+1$.

Perron (1989) suggested a two-step procedure for testing unit roots in the presence of structural break.

Step 1: Detrend the data by estimating the alternative hypothesis and calling the residual y_t^r.

3. We have deliberately truncated the data at 1990-91 because India entered into a completely different regime after 1990-91.

4. Consider the solution of a random walk with drift $y_t = y_0 + a_0 t + \sum_{i=1}^{t} e_i$

Step 2: Estimate the regression $y_t^r = a_2 y_{t-1}^r + \varepsilon_t$

Perron (1989) also suggested critical values for testing $a_2 = 1$ in the presence of one structural break. We assume a break for CR at 1980-81. The characteristic of the structural break is a one-time change in the level of the series and also a permanent change in the drift. As a result, the intercept and slope of the trend line of CR change at 1981-82. $D_L = D_T = 1$ for 1981-82 to 1987-88 and 0 otherwise. It may be noted that this specification takes care of the turnaround in CR during 1987-88 (Figure 13.2).

Figure 13.2

Actual and Predicted CR

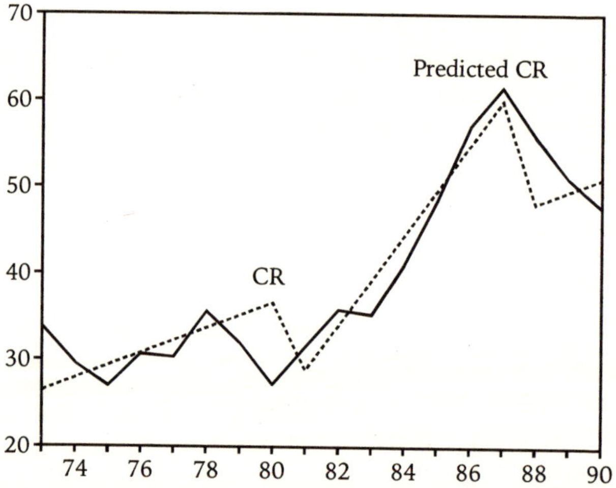

However, it is not appropriate to use the critical values provided in Perron, because the nature of breaks is different. In Perron, unlike our specification, the dummy variable is stretched up to the end of the period (D_T is one for $t>\tau$ to T; and the break occurs at τ). Lumsdaine and Papell (1997) provided critical values for two breaks in the series, but the critical values were obtained for 100 observations with a pre-specified lag length. As a result, we have decided to use the traditional Dickey-Fuller critical values for testing the null hypothesis $a_2 = 0$. Furthermore, it is also proposed that the autocorrelation function of the first-step residual be examined. It can safely be conjectured that CR is a trend stationary process, if the null hypothesis of a unit root is comfortably rejected. The fitted equation with D_L and D_T is,

First Step:

$$CR = \underset{(10.95)}{24.96} + \underset{(6.27)}{1.46\,T} - \underset{(-4.03)}{43.02\,D_L} + \underset{(4.23)}{3.76\,T^*D_T}; \quad R^2=0.86, \ D.W=1.53 \qquad \ldots (14)$$

Let us denote the first-step residual by X.

Figure 13.3

Autocorrelation Functions of X

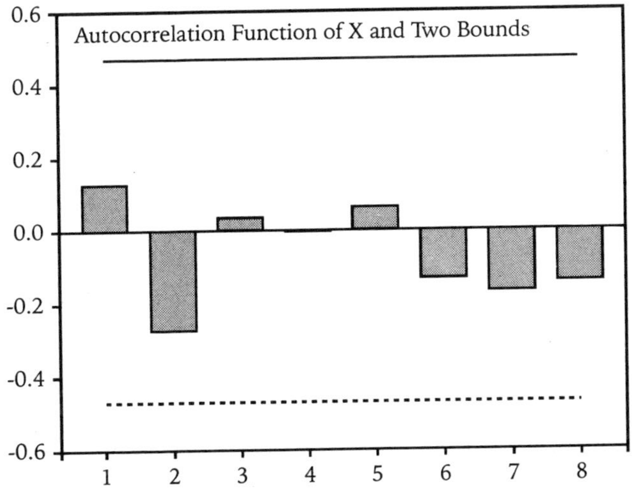

All the autocorrelation functions in Figure 13.3 are not significantly different from zero (within two bounds).[5]

Therefore, it suggests that the series (X) is white-noise. We now apply standard Dickey-Fuller test to check whether or not X is a stationary series.

Second Step:

$\Delta X_t = -0.86\ X_{t-1}$; t-statistic: –3.81 and the D-F critical value for 25 observations: -3.60 (5 per cent with constant and trend). We,

5. Two bounds are $+\frac{2}{\sqrt{T}}$ and $-\frac{2}{\sqrt{T}}$

therefore, conjecture that CR is a trend stationary process. Unit root tests for other variables are summarised in the Table 13.2.

Table 13.2

Unit Root Tests

	Coefficient of y_{t-1}	t-statistic	No. of Lags	Trend	F-statistic (For Joint test)*	Critical Values+	Comments
RELPR	-0.42	-3.31	2	No	5.72	-3.05 (5%)	Stationary
UC	-0.61	-2.79	1	Yes	6.36	Std. Normal	Trend Stationary
FP	-1.26	-4.78	0	Yes	11.49	-4.62 (1%)	Trend Stationary

Note: *Joint test for $a_1=a_2=0$ (equation 11). 10 per cent critical value is 5.91.
+ These are Mackinnon's critical values.

Figure 13.4

Autocorrelation Functions :RELPR

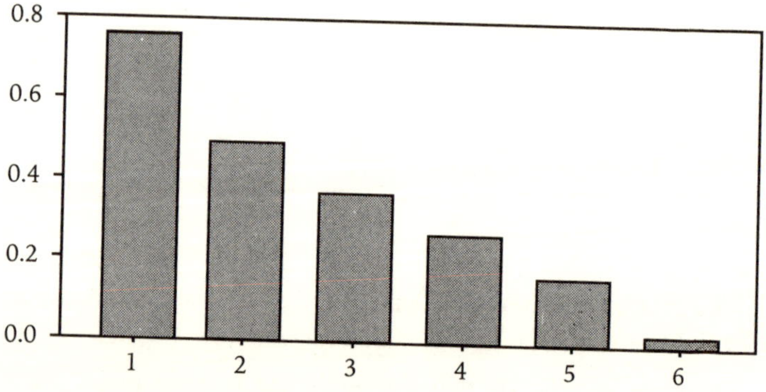

Autocorrelation function of RELPR corroborates our finding that it is a stationary series (Figure 13.4).

The next step is to estimate our main relationship, which is,

$$RELPR = f(UC, CR, FP(-1)) \qquad ...(15)$$

Our theoretical model, suggests that the sign of partial derivatives are ambiguous. Since all three independent variables are trend stationary series and the dependent variable is a stationary variable, therefore, we must include a time trend in the regression equation. The estimated equation is (with t-values in parentheses),

$$\text{RELPR} = \underset{(4.40)}{89.73} - \underset{(-2.48)}{0.73}\ \text{UC} - \underset{(-2.52)}{0.61}\ \text{CR} + \underset{(1.67)}{0.26}\ \text{FP(-1)} + \underset{(3.59)}{8.33}\ \text{T} \quad \text{...(16)}$$

R^2=0.91, D.W=1.33. The D.W statistic belongs to the inconclusive zone, therefore, it is difficult to reject the possibility of first-order positive serial correlation. We shall come back to this problem soon. The graph below plots residuals (Figure 13.5), which reflect some abnormality during the mid-eighties and during 1988 to 1990.

Figure 13.5

Actual, Fitted and Residual from Equation (16)

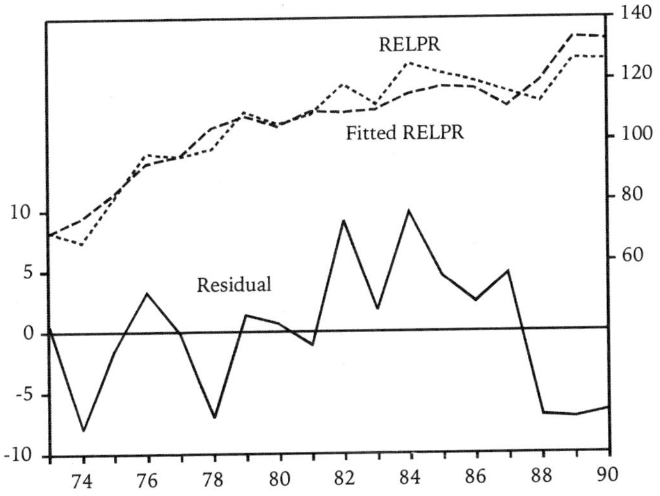

The estimated coefficient of CR clearly demonstrates that the relationship between average nominal protection in Indian industries and the relative price between comparatively disadvantaged sector and the comparatively advantaged sector is negative.

However, given equation (14), equation (16) does not completely eliminate the trend from CR. This could be a reason for a low D.W statistic for equation (16). We therefore, construct a new variable with the help of equation (14), which is,

$$Z = CR\text{-}3.76\ T^{*}D_T \qquad \ldots(17)$$

Z is essentially a transformation of CR, so that it captures one time change in the slope of the trend line during 1981-82 to 1987-88. We shall re-estimate equation (16) after replacing CR by Z. Moreover, the change in the intercept of the trend line during the same period is captured by including D_L in the new equation (*see* equation 14). The estimated equation is,

$$\underset{(5.98)}{RELPR = 95.52} - \underset{(-3.39)}{0.75\ UC} - \underset{(-3.34)}{0.93\ Z} + \underset{(2.54)}{0.30\ FP(-1)} + \underset{(4.76)}{8.36\ T} - \underset{(-2.62)}{32.08\ D_L} \qquad \ldots(18)$$

R^2=0.95, D.W=2.17. D.W statistic accepts the null hypothesis of no positive serial correlation.[6] The qualitative results remain unchanged. The plots of recursive coefficients reveal that there are no structural breaks in parameter estimates (Figure 13.6).

Figure 13.6

Recursive Coefficients

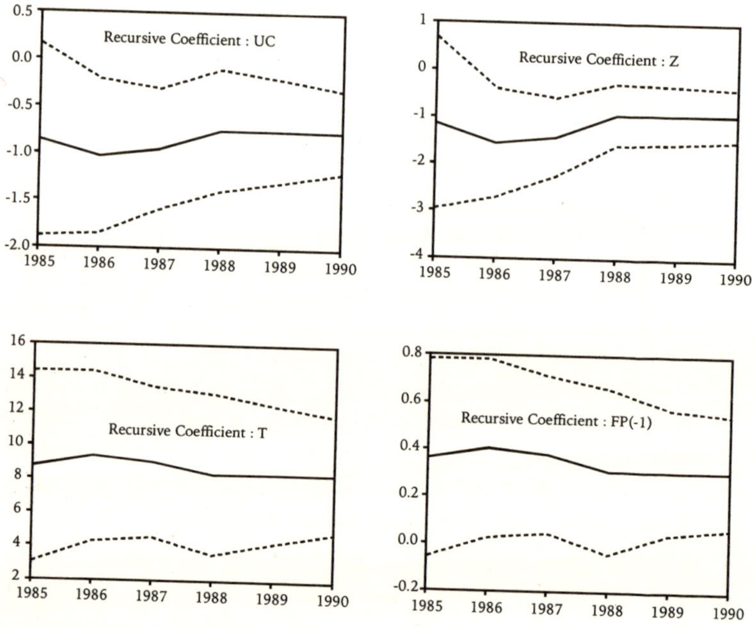

6. For k=5 and n=19, the upper limit (D_u) at the 5 per cent level of significance is 1.90.

Alternatively, we could have defined Z as CR-24.96 + 43.02 $*D_L$-3.76 $T*D_T$, and estimated equation (16) with D_L. The inclusion of D_L is necessary to allow the intercept to change between 1981 and 1987. Autocorrelation problem would emerge if the intercept is not allowed to adjust. However, the results would have remained the same as equation (18)(including the D.W statistic) except the coefficient of D_L and the magnitude of the intercept.

SECTION 5

CONCLUSION

The main objective of this paper was to highlight that trade restrictions may not distort the domestic relative-price ratio in favour of the protected sector. If our empirical results are acceptable, then it must also be accepted that India's restricted trade regime during the seventies and eighties did not distort resource allocation induced by relative price adjustments. However, we do not want to end our paper with the impression that we are, therefore, advocating for a restricted trade regime. The following propositions may still hold good:

1. Resource allocations may still be distorted for other reasons.
2. Restricted trade regime may be a breeding ground for inefficient firms.

A major caveat of this empirical exercise is that the presence of a non-linear relationship between RELPR and CR has not been tested, even while the theoretical model suggests that the relationship between these two variables is essentially non-linear in nature.

DATA APPENDIX

1. Relative Price (RELPR)

RELPR = (Z/W)*100

W = Wholesale price index of foodgrain.

Z = Manufacturing price index, which is derived as (Y_1/IIP_{mnf}.)*100.

Y_1 = Gross value of output (current price).

IIP_{mnf} = Index of industrial production for manufacturing goods (1980-81=100).

Z is known as the Transacted Price in the literature. The advantage of it over the List Price (official Wholesale Price Index) is that it is free from all taxes including import duties. Moreover, it captures the price-shedding behaviour of the entrepreneurs more accurately.

Data Sources

The Handbook of Statistics on Indian Economy, Reserve Bank of India, 1999.

Economic Survey (1990-91), Ministry of Finance, Govt. of India.

National Accounts Statistics, Government of India (various issues).

2. Unit Cost (UC)

It is defined as the weighted sum of wages and input cost.

UC = 0.4 WC + 0.6 IC

WC = Wage cost, which is the ratio of total emoluments to IIP_{mnf}.

IC = Input cost, which is a weighted average of the price indices of non-food articles and fuel, power, light & lubricants (1981-82=100). The weights are being computed from the respective original weights in WPI. Weights of WC and IC are the shares of wages and inputs in total cost in 1973-74 (Chatterjee 1989).

Data Sources

Annual Survey of Industries (summary results for factory sector)-various issues, Central Statistical Organisation, Govt. of India.

Economic Survey (1990-91).

3. Foodgrain Production Index (FP)

Index of foodgrain production (*Economic Survey*, Govt. of India, various issues).

4. Collection Rate (CR)

Total customs revenue divided by the value of imports (*The Handbook of Statistics on Indian Economy*, Reserve Bank of India, 1999).

References

Balassa,B. *et al.*, (1971). *The Structure of Protection in Developing Countries,* Baltimore: John Hopkins University Press.

Chaterjee, R. (1989). *The Behaviour of Industrial Prices in India,* Delhi: Oxford University Press.

Das, D.K. (2001). *Some Aspects of Productivity Growth and Trade in Indian Industries.* Unpublished Ph.D dissertation, Delhi School of Economics.

Enders, W. (1995). *Applied Econometric Time Series,* New York: John Wiley and Sons, INC.

Harrison, Ann (1994). "Productivity, Imperfect Competition and Trade Reform: Theory and Evidence," *Journal of International Economics,* 36, 53-73.

Krishna, Pravin and Devashis Mitra (1998). "Trade Liberalisation, Market Discipline, and Productivity Growth: New Evidences from India," *Journal of Development Economics,* Vol. 56(2), 447-62.

Little, I., Scitovsky, T. and M. Scott (1970). *Industry and Trade in Some Developing Countries,* London: Oxford University Press.

Lumsdaine, R.L. and D.H. Papell (1997). "Multiple Trend Breaks and the Unit-Root Hypothesis," *The Review of Economics and Statistics,* Vol. LXXIV, No. 2, 212-218.

Perron, P. (1989). "The Great Crash,The Oil Shock and the Unit-Root Hypothesis," *Econometrica,* Vol. 57(6), 1361-1401.

Rakshit, M. (eds.) (1989). *Studies in the Macroeconomics of Developing Countries,* Delhi: Oxford University Press.

Roberts, Mark and James Tybout (eds)(1996). *Industrial Evolution in Developing Countries: Micro Patterns of Turnover, Productivity and Market Structure,* New York: Oxford University Press.

Rodriguez, F. and D. Rodrik (1999). *Trade Policy and Economic Growth: A Skeptics Guide to the Cross-National Evidence,* Department of Economics, University of Maryland and John F. Kennedy School of Government, Cambridge, mimeo.

Rodrik, D. (1995). "Trade and Industrial Policy Reform," in J. Behrman and T.N. Srinivasan, eds., *Handbook of Development Economics,* Vol. 3B, 2925-2982.

Sen, K. and S. Chand (1999). "Competitive Pressures from Trade Exposure: Evidence from Indian Manufacturing," *Indian Economic Review,* Vol. XXXIV(2). 113-116.

Tybout, J.R. (2000). "Manufacturing Firms in Developing Countries: How Well Do they Do, and Why?" *Journal of Economic Literature,* Vol. XXXVIII, 11-44.

14

Improving Industrial Productivity: Does Trade Liberalisation Matter?

Evidence from Indian Capital and Intermediate Goods Sectors

DEB KUSUM DAS

SECTION 1

INTRODUCTION

India was largely insulated from the world trading system for most part of the early development phase. The industrial stagnation that marked the period from the mid-1960s to the late-70s led to rethinking on the role of trade-policy in India (Alexander (1977), Hussain (1984) and Narasimham (1984)). The 1980s witnessed a wide array of initiatives aimed at creating a dynamic industrial environment. It was, however, the onset of severe macroeconomics and balance of payments crisis of 1991 that led to a major overhauling of India's economic polices, particularly with reference to trade and industry.

The performance of Indian industry, though moderately encouraging with respect to overall growth and diversification, has been particularly poor when judged in terms of industrial productivity. Studies on India's industrial productivity growth for the post-independence period show that either there has been zero or at most negligible growth in total factor productivity. This has important implications given that during the pre-reform period, producers were severely constrained in their operational and investment decision. There were government controls on location, choice of investment, technology and inputs especially imported inputs. Further, there was hardly any competition in the domestic market due to curbs on imports. Since 1980s however, India has undertaken significant and far-reaching reforms in both trade and industrial policies. Tariff rates, both peak and dispersion has been brought down. Further non-tariff barriers on imports of intermediaries and capital goods have been done away with. These reforms in import policy have been supplemented with substantial changes in industrial licensing, technology imports and FDI rules and regulation aimed at making Indian industries more technically efficient and competitive in the global markets.

The determinants of productivity growth in the industrial sector of India particularly the trade policy regime have received very little attention. Some studies for India drawing upon firm and industry level evidence and using alternative indicators of trade barriers point towards a positive role of trade liberalisation in enhancing productivity growth during the 1980s and 1990s (Krishna and Mitra (1998), Balakrishnan *et al.,* (2000), Chand and Sen (2002), Goldar and Kumari (2002)). The evidence, however, needs to interpret with caution as most studies are faced with shortcomings on several fronts.

This paper addresses the trade liberalisation-productivity growth nexus in the context of India's manufacturing sector. In particular, we explore as to whether trade liberalisation enhances industrial productivity in Indian manufacturing by examining the evidence from the capital and intermediate goods sector. The period of study is guided by considerations that efforts to reduce trade barriers started taking shape from the early-1980s as envisaged in the trade policy documents of the government of India.

The plan of the paper is as follows. Section 2 outlines the conceptual framework and estimation strategy used in the paper. Section 3 presents a description of the data set and the variables used in the estimation. Section 4 details the results from the empirical analysis and compares these with the earlier literature for Indian manufacturing. Section 5 concludes.

SECTION 2

CONCEPTUAL FRAMEWORK AND ESTIMATION ISSUES

Conceptual Framework

The central objective of trade policy reforms is to make markets more competitive and thereby change the performance of the industry by improving its total factor productivity growth.[1] Improved efficiency, in turn, contributes to increased industrial growth. A number of theoretical arguments linking trade liberalisation with higher rate of industrial productivity can be put down. First, those, which help improve productivity growth via the reduction of managerial slackness due to increased competition. Second, those that allow productivity growth via scale benefits associated with trade opening up and finally those that allow imports embodying superior technology to improve productivity.

Trade liberalisation, in India, amongst other things involved (1) lowering of tariff rates both the spread and peak. (2) dismantling of non-tariff barriers, and (3) providing incentives to the exporting sector to compete in the global markets. Lowering of tariff and doing away with non-tariff measures corresponds to the competition effect, whereas the scale effect is realised via incentives that aim at correcting the domestic relative price ratio.

In India, trade reforms have been supplemented by industrial de-regulation. These reforms in industrial policies have aimed at making Indian industries competitive in the external markets and technology efficient. Further, a proper assessment of the impact of trade liberalisation and industrial de-regulations on productivity requires an understanding of the macroeconomic environment in which these reforms take place as an uncertain macroeconomic environment leads to a fall in investment and worsens productivity growth.[2] In India, rising inflation and exchange rate fluctuations have been important macroeconomic issues in the Indian economy in the 1980s and 1990s. Thus, a proper assessment of the impact of trade liberalisation requires an understanding of the macroeconomic environment in which these reforms take place. The arguments put

1. The empirical literature on the impact of trade liberalisation on productivity follows three approaches, one, macro-level cross-country GDP growth regressions associating growth with an aggregate measure of openness to trade. Two, industry level approach considering industries TFP growth on trade policy related variables and finally firm or plant level micro approach using a production function approach. *See* Das (2002a) for an assessment of these studies using alternative approaches.

2. Studies at the World Bank (Michaely *et al.*, (1986)) show that there appears to be extremely strong links between trade liberalisation and accompanying macroeconomic policies. In addition, Thomas and Nash (1991) and Nash (1992) using World Bank data have shown that countries falling under "Significant Reformers" have managed to reduce inflation rate, fiscal deficit within three years of trade reforms.

forward in support of the view that open trade regimes lead to enhancement in productivity growth in Indian manufacturing are summarised in a schematic Figure 14.1.

Figure 14.1

Trade Liberalisation and Productivity Growth: Theoretical Links

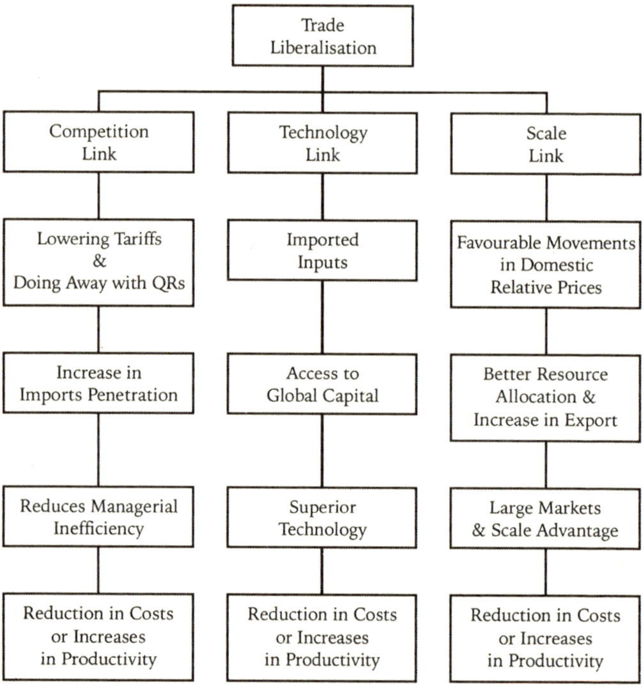

For India, we specify industrial productivity growth as a function of a combination of factors representing trade policy changes, industrial policy reforms and macro environment.[3] That is, total

3. In India, industrial policy reforms were introduced in conjunction with trade liberalisation. The 1980s saw wide ranging changes such as; broad banding, de-licensing of 23 broad categories of industries, relaxation on monopolistic and restrictive trade practices (MRTP) Act, expansion of capacity etc. The 1991-92 economic reforms saw the elimination of MRTP Act, downsizing of the public-sector reservations, abolition of industrial licensing, doing away of phased manufacturing programmes and reforms in regulations concerning foreign technology and investment. Therefore, to assess the impact of trade reforms it is appropriate to conceive a framework which is a combination of industrial and trade policy changes along with the macro environment.

factor productivity growth (TFPG) = f (Changes in Trade Policy, Changes in Industrial Policy and Macroeconomic Environment).

The variables representing trade policy orientation are; change in effective rate of protection (ΔERP), change in import coverage ratio (ΔMCR) and change in export growth (ΔEG). The advocates of a neutral trade regime expect greater improvements in TFP when an outward oriented trade policy is followed than when import substituting trade restrictions are in operation. As suggested by Pack (1988) the specification of correct lag structures is critical, but this aspect has not received much attention. Our review shows that two studies (Weiss (1992) and Iscan (1998)) found evidence for a lagged impact of trade liberalisation on TFP growth. We allow for lagged impact of variables measuring the trade policy changes.[4] To reflect the outcomes of industrial policy reforms, we include three variables, namely; change in the price–cost margins (ΔPCM), change in research and development intensity (ΔR&D) and change in capital intensity (ΔKL). The macroeconomic uncertainty is proxied by the level of inflation ($INFL^u$). We, thus, arrive at a more concrete specification:

$$TFPG_t = f(\Delta ERP_{t-j}, \Delta MCR_{t-j}, \Delta EG_{t-j}, \Delta PCM_t, \Delta R\&D_t, \Delta KL_t \text{ and } INFL_t^u)$$

The algebraic specifications of the model is

$$\begin{aligned} TFPG_{it} = {} & a + \alpha_1 \Delta ERP_{it-1} + \alpha_2 \Delta ERP_{it-2} + \beta_1 \Delta MCR_{it-1} + \beta_2 \Delta MCR_{it-2} + \\ & \gamma_1 \Delta EG_{it-1} + \gamma_2 \Delta EG_{it-2} + \delta_1 OG_{it} + \delta_2 \Delta PCM_{it} + \delta_3 \Delta R\&D_{it} + \\ & \delta_4 \Delta KL_{it} + \theta INFL_{it}^u + \lambda_1 D_1 + \lambda_2 D_2 + \mu_1 D_1 \Delta ERP_{it-1} + \\ & \mu_2 D_1 \Delta ERP_{it-2} + \mu_3 D_2 \Delta ERP_{it-1} + \mu_4 D_2 \Delta ERP_{it-2} + \eta_i + \xi_{it} \end{aligned}$$

We estimate two versions of the above specification from panel data: In model-1, we attempt to capture the impact of trade liberalisation on productivity growth, via lagged changes in effective rate of protection (ΔERP), lagged changes in import coverage ratio (ΔMCR) and lagged changes in export growth (ΔEG). The outcomes of the industrial policy reforms are sought to be captured by using three different indicators; changes in price-cost margins (ΔPCM), changes in research and development intensity (ΔR&D) and changes in capital intensity (ΔKL). In Model-2, we try to capture the outcomes

---

4. In the econometric estimation, the lag length (j) is chosen as 2. *See* the next sub-section on estimation issues for a discussion on the choice of the lag length.

of industrial policy reforms in levels: price-cost margins (PCM), research and development intensity (R&D) and capital intensity (KL). Macro economic uncertainty is captured by the inflation uncertainty variable ($INFL^u$). In both the models, we introduce output growth (OG) as an explanatory variable to verify the Verdoorn's law. We include two period dummies D_1 and D_2 defined in terms of the two phases of trade liberalisation, 1980-85 and 1986-90 respectively to control for any structural breaks in the overall period. Further, to check whether the trade liberalisation impacts are period (phase) specific, we include interactive dummies for effective rate of protection.[5]

Estimation Issues

It is important to consider as to which of the two approaches of panel data modeling (fixed effects (FE) and random effects (RE)) is more appropriate to the examination of the impact of trade liberalisation on productivity growth. We argue that certain institutional factors or characteristics of the data make it inevitable to prefer one to another. The FE or least square dummy variable estimator, though it leads to loss in degrees of freedom, escapes from the omitted variable bias as many industry specific variables which could not be quantified can be taken care of in the fixed effects model.

A major drawback of the literature examining the impact of trade liberalisation on total factor productivity has been the lack of specification of suitable lag structure for the variables representing trade orientation. This assumes importance especially in the light of the evidence that there is a lag between change in trade orientation and change in industrial productivity (Weiss (1992) and Iscan (1998)). Further, there is a dispute over what is the correct specification of a lag structure (Papageriou *et al.*, (1990), Weiss (1992)). We have opted for a lag length of 2 years taking into account two factors. First, the trade policy changes in India were announced on an annual basis for majority of the years 1980-95. Furthermore, the import-export transactions were determined by these yearly policy changes and a 2-year lag seemed appropriate. Second, longer lags mean the reduction in the effective sample size.

5. The interactive dummies with ΔMCR turned out to be collinear.

Both the error component models (FE and RE) assume that the regression disturbances are homoskedastic with the same variances across time and industries. This may be a restrictive assumption when the cross-sectional units, three-digit level manufacturing industries in this case are of varying size and as a result may have unequal disturbance variances. Assuming homoskedastic disturbances when heteroskedasticity is present will still result in consistent estimates of the regression coefficients, but these estimates will not be efficient. Also the standard errors of these estimates will be biased. Correction of the standard errors for the possible presence of heteroskedasticity is desirable. We have computed the Breusch-Pagan statistic to test the null hypothesis of homoskedasticty.

In addition, the classical panel data model assumes that the disturbances ξ_{it} are serially uncorrelated. This may be a restrictive assumption. Ignoring serial correlation when it is present results in consistent but inefficient estimates of the regression coefficients and biased standard errors. We have considered the AR(1) specification $\xi_{it} = \rho\xi_{it-1} + v_{it}$, where v_{it} is assumed to be serially uncorrelated. We have used a modified Durbin-Watson statistic for testing for serial correlation and individual effects.[6]

Finally, the quantification of trade policy changes is not only cumbersome, but also subject to measurement errors.[7] While it is not always possible to counter the effect of measurement errors, it is important to realise what those effects are likely to be in terms of the biases introduced by the measurement errors. Panel data studies in econometrics use the analysis of covariance approach to control various 'individual effects' by estimating coefficients from within dimension of the data. Often, the results are unsatisfactory with low and insignificant coefficients. This is, perhaps, due to errors in measurement of the independent variables. In the presence of the measurement errors, OLS estimates are inconsistent for two separate

6. Baltagi and Li (1995) address the problem of jointly testing for serial correlation and individual effects. *See* chapter 5 of Baltagi (1995) for a detailed discussion on the tests.

7. The import-export data-sets used to measure the trade liberalisation indicators are usually far from accurate and are subject to errors arising from incorrect reporting due to smuggling, weaknesses in the data coverage, coding problems etc. Further, the present study undertakes a mapping of the ITC (R-2)/ITC (HS) product codes with the ASI and errors may creep into the process of aggregating the products to arrive at the industry figures. Therefore, the variables representing trade liberalisation account for measurement errors.

reasons: (1) correlation between the effects and the regressors, and (2) errors in measurement. Further, the presence of measurement errors could make the fixed and random effects estimators even more inconsistent than the OLS estimator.[8] We present the pooled OLS estimates keeping this point in view.[9] However, in the absence of measurement errors, we expect the fixed as well as the random effect models to better estimate the trade productivity impact than the pooled model and therefore, present those estimates as well.

SECTION 3

DATA

Variable Construction

The study attempts to assess the impact of trade liberalisation on industrial productivity in capital and intermediate good sectors respectively. This allows us to trace the trade reforms-productivity growth impact in line with the focus of policy, which gave pre-imminence to these sectors and consistently refused to recognise the importance of efficiency and productivity for consumer goods sector. The data set consists of around 28 and 20 industries at the three-digit NIC category belonging to the capital and intermediate goods industries covering the years 1980-81 to 1994-95. These two sectors constitute around 45 per cent of manufacturing value added and are spread over the following two digit NIC categories: cotton textiles (23); textile products (26); leather and leather products (29); rubber, coal

---

8. Deaton (1997) argues that though the fixed effects estimator suffers from only the attenuation bias, in comparison to the OLS estimator, which has an additional omitted variable bias, but it still does not justify the preference for the fixed effects estimator. The issue, here, is whether the within estimation reduces the variance in the signal relative to the variance of the noise so that the attenuation bias in the within estimation is more severe than the combined attenuation and omitted variable bias in the cross-section regression.[8] However, with time varying measurement errors it may well be that the signal to noise ratio deteriorates so much in the fixed effect case that it rules out a *priori* preference for that estimator over OLS estimator (Griliches and Hausman (1986), Biorn (1996)).
9. To overcome the measurement error we could have used instrument variable (IV) estimation with lagged values as instruments for the fixed and random effects model. We refrain from doing so as our basic model already has two-year lags in the variables capturing trade liberalisation and given that our objective is to capture the impact of trade reforms on TFP, a three or four year lag may not accurately reflect the outcome of trade policy changes.

etc. (30); chemicals (31); metals (33); metal products (34); machinery and electrical machinery (35&36) and transport equipment (37).

The analysis of the impact of trade liberalisation on productivity growth requires data on gross output, labour, capital, intermediate inputs for computing total factor productivity growth rates. In addition, data on export, import, tariffs and import-licensing status are required to construct various indicators of trade liberalisation. The constructions of the variables are discussed below.

Total Factor Productivity Growth

The estimates of total factor productivity (TFP) growth are derived from the growth accounting framework. Following Jorgenson *et al.*, (1987), TFP growth is calculated using the Tornqvist approximation as

$$\text{Ln}\,[TFP\,(t)/TFP\,(t\text{-}1)] = \text{Ln}[O\,(t)/O\,(t\text{-}1)] - \bar{v}_l(t)\,\text{Ln}[L\,(t)/L(t\text{-}1)] - \bar{v}_k(t)\,\text{Ln}\,[K\,(t)/K(t\text{-}1)] - \bar{v}_m(t)\text{Ln}[M(t)/M(t\text{-}1)] - \bar{v}_e(t)\text{Ln}[E(t)/E(t\text{-}1)]$$

Where, $\bar{v}_l(t) = 1/2[v_l(t) + v_l(t\text{-}1)]$, $\bar{v}_k(t) = 1/2[v_k(t) + v_k(t\text{-}1)]$, $\bar{v}_m(t) = 1/2[v_m(t) + v_m(t\text{-}1)]$ and $\bar{v}_e(t) = 1/2[v_e(t) + v_e(t\text{-}1)]$

TFP stands for total factor productivity, O for gross output, L for number of employees, K for fixed capital stock, M for materials used and E for energy used. $\bar{v}_l$, $\bar{v}_k$, $\bar{v}_m$, and $\bar{v}_e$ are the averages of the shares of labour, capital, materials and energy at times (t) and (t-1) and are defined above. The methodology assumes perfect competition and constant returns to scale. Further, the revenue shares of the factor inputs sum to unity. Data used for TFP estimation are from the Annual Survey of Industries. A careful attempt is made to construct the capital stock series using the perpetual inventory method. This enables us to construct a time series of real capital stock using the time series of investment and capital price deflator.[10] To arrive at real intermediate inputs namely, material and energy consumed, we were required to construct the price deflators for the above categories as industry wise material and energy price deflators were not available.[11]

10. *See* Das (2001) for the perpetual inventory method of computing capital stock.

11. *See* Das (2001) for the constructions of material and energy price deflators according to the three-digit industries.

Trade Liberalisation Indicators

We capture the impact of trade liberalisation on productivity growth using three variables: change in effective rate of protection, change in import coverage ratio and change in export growth. The annual survey of industries does not publish any trade-related information by industry groups, thereby making it virtually impossible to analyse trade-industry relationships with such databases. We have established several concordances between trade information at the product level and the industry groups in order to construct our measures of trade liberalisation. First, for computing the effective rate of protection according to industries, we had to establish a concordance between tariff data available at 4-digit ITC (HS) product code and the respective 3-digit industries. Second, to obtain industry wise indicators of non-tariff barriers, we had to establish concordance between import licensing status, 4-digit ITC (HS) product codes and the 3-digit industries according to ASI. And finally, the export figures at 4-digit ITC (HS) product codes were mapped onto 3-digit industry groups to obtain industry-wise export data. The effective rate of protection according to industry groups was constructed according to the Corden measure of ERP. For capturing non-tariff barrier, we used the import weighted coverage ratio (the import coverage ratio). The industry-wise export data was utilised to obtain the export growth rate.[12]

Industrial and Macro Policy Variables

The Annual Survey of Industries provides the information needed to calculate the variables reflecting the outcomes of industrial policy reforms such as price-cost margins (mark-ups) and capital-labour ratio (capital intensity). The data source for the research and development intensity variable (R&D) is the Research and Development Statistics, published by the Department of Science and Technology, Government of India. The price-cost margin is defined as the ratio of value added minus emoluments to the value of output. To compute the above we need time-series data on value-added, emoluments and output according to industries. The information on capital stock and number of employees is needed to calculate

12. *See* Das (2002b) for the methodology and estimates of the quantification of trade barriers by industry groups for the period 1980-95.

industry-wise capital-labour ratio. The R&D intensity is defined as the ratio of R&D expenditures to the value of output. The information on yearly R&D expenditures according to broad industry groups is mapped onto the 3-digit industries to generate the R&D intensity according to our selected industries.

We attempt to capture the macroeconomic environment by considering the uncertainty due to high and rising levels of inflation. We compute a three-year standard deviation of the output price deflator for the different industries to construct our inflation uncertainty index for the industry groups. The output price deflator for each industry is represented by the chosen wholesale price index for that industry.

Descriptive Statistics

Our measures of productivity growth have two in-built assumptions: production functions with constant returns to scale and

Table 14.1

Basic Statistics by Use-based Sectors: Capital and Intermediate Goods Sectors

Variables	*Mean*	*Standard Deviation*	*Minimum Values*	*Maximum Values*
		Capital Goods Sector		
TFPG	1.166	14.596	-85.110	82.91
ΔEG	92.53	1064.90	-100.00	1774.36
ΔMCR	-0.01	0.77	-1.00	11.15
ΔERP	6.94	93.69	-92.99	1450.21
ΔPCM	-44.63	540.04	-8199.03	1209.13
ΔKL	7.56	16.98	-51.15	90.50
ΔRD	25.00	218.53	-100.00	2859.15
$INFL^u$	11.75	8.35	0.80	54.77
		Intermediate Goods Sector		
TFPG	-0.823	15.116	-100	84.68
ΔEG	121.97	617.91	-100.00	7333.93
ΔMCR	0.89	17.99	-1.00	356.14
ΔERP	4.79	77.66	-61.64	903.81
ΔPCM	27.88	780.96	-3121.03	14813.40
ΔKL	11.59	57.39	-79.89	906.88
ΔRD	24.28	358.11	-100	7053.75
$INFL^u$	13.89	11.18	0	86.16

a perfectly competitive market. The mean estimates of productivity growth are larger for capital goods sector. The standard deviations show sharp variations in growth rates across the two sectors. Of the three trade policy variables, the import coverage ratio (MCR) exhibits a very low average of near zero for the two sectors. For each of these measures, the range of variation is very wide as reflected in the maximum and minimum values. The industrial policy variables also reflect sharp inter-industry variations as evident from the standard deviations and values of maximum and minimum. The inflation uncertainty variable is the same across industries and over time

SECTION 4

EMPIRICAL FINDINGS

The model specified in the preceding section is estimated from a panel data for 3-digit manufacturing industries belonging to the capital and intermediate goods sectors covering the period 1980-95. We have allowed for lags up to two years in the trade liberalisation variables to assess whether there is a lagged impact of trade reforms on productivity growth. We have, in addition, included two intercept dummies for the sub-periods 1980-85 and 1986-90. Further, interactive dummies have also been incorporated to assess if the trade liberalisation impact is specific to the trade reform phases.[13] The Pooled OLS, FE and RE estimates of the model are given in the Tables 14.2 and 14.3 respectively. To choose between the FE and RE estimates, we conduct the Hausman test (1978).[14] Our preferred estimate is the FE estimate, considering the fact that several industry specific variables could not be quantified and introduced in the regression equation. The standard errors are corrected for heteroscedasticty and correction for serial-correlation has been attempted wherever necessary. The explanatory power of the regressions as measured by adjusted $\bar{R}^2$ varies between 0.244 to 0.495. However, the $\bar{R}^2$ for pooled OLS, FE and RE regressions are not comparable, because the dependent variable in the three regressions are somewhat different.

13. Multiplicative dummy variables e.g. $D_1\Delta ERP_1$, $D_1\Delta ERP_2$, $D_2\Delta ERP_1$ and $D_2\Delta ERP_2$ are introduced for some of the trade reform specific explanatory-variables. The interactive dummies for the two-year lags of the variable ΔMCR turned out to be collinear. These interactive dummies allow for differences in the coefficients of these variables between the two phases of trade liberalisation.

14. The Hausman statistics as reported in Tables 14.2 and 14.3, however, do not appear to be significant.

Capital Goods Industries

The regression results for the capital goods industry, reported in Table 14.2 , show that without the industry effects, none of the trade liberalisation indicators are significantly associated with productivity growth. Controlling for the industry effects (FE regression), we observe that only the coefficient of the one year lagged change in import coverage ratio (-0.9748) is statistically significant. The negative and significant association between change in import coverage ratio and productivity growth is consistent with the view that lowering of quantitative restrictions on imports introduces competitive pressure which, in turn, cuts cost or increases productivity growth in capital goods industries.

Table 14.2

Panel Data Productivity Growth Regressions: Capital Goods Industries

Version-1	*Dependent Variable: TFP Growth*		
Variables	*Pooled OLS*	*Fixed Effects*	*Random Effects*
Δ EG lag1	-.0005 [.0006]	**-.0006[.0002]***	-.0006 [.0007]
Δ EG lag2	-.0008 [.0007]	**-.0014 [.0004]***	-.0010 [.0007]
Δ MCR lag1	-.7697 [.9211]	**-.9748 [.4573]***	-.8676 [.9492]
Δ MCR lag2	-.0134 [.0425]	-.0496 [.0450]	-.0162 [.0674]
Δ ERP lag1	-.0062 [.0076]	-.0024 [.0035]	-.00782 [.0079]
Δ ERP lag2	-.0167 [.0320]	**.0484 [.0254]***	-.0175 [.0326]
OG	**.4287 [.0310]***	**.4458 [.0670]***	**.4377 [.0317]***
Δ PCM	-.0020 [.0014]	**-.0030 [.0009]***	-.0026 [.0014]
Δ RD	.0022 [.0033]	**.0026 [.0013]***	.00223 [.00337]
Δ KL	.1011 [.0480]	.0920 [.0511]	.09896 [.0493]
IFL[u]	-.0370 [.1123]	-.0791 [.15657]	-.0443 [.1214]
D1	-.0098 [2.507]	.8962 [2.807]	-.1140 [2.586]
D2	1.3159 [2.0195]	1.6304 [2.351]	1.31829 [2.067]
D1*Δ ERP lag1	.0286 [.04382]	-.0767 [.0490]	.03110 [.0442]
D1*Δ ERP lag2	.1686 [.04240]	**-.1705 [.0674]***	.01934 [.0432]
D2*Δ ERP lag1	-.0488 [.0367]	**-.1079 [.4274]***	-.0533 [.0374]
D2*Δ ERP lag2	.2908 [.0405]	**-. 1049[.0389]***	.0018 [.0410]
CONSTANT	-2.902 [2.529]	X	-2.8348 [2.947]
Adjusted R^2	.458	.454	.495

Contd...

...Table 14.2 Contd...

Version-1	*Dependent Variable: TFP Growth*		
Observations	240	240	240
No. of Years	12	12	12
No. of Industries	20	20	20
Hausman Test		5.75	
D-W Test		0.195	
Correction for Serial Correlation	Not Necessary	Not Necessary	Not Necessary
Version-2	*Dependent Variable: TFP Growth*		
Variables	Pooled OLS	Fixed Effects	Random Effects
Δ EG lag1	.0004 [.0066]	-.0003[.0210]	-.0004[.0007]
Δ EG lag2	-.0010 [.0068]	-.0013[.0623]	-.0010[.0007]
Δ MCR lag1	-.9655 [.9759]	-0.9734[23.444]	-.9605[1.008]
Δ MCR lag2	-.0110 [.0444]	.0153[4.785]	-.0083[.0689]
Δ ERP lag1	-.0037 [.0078]	.0006[1.197]	-.0039[.0088]
Δ ERP lag2	-.0089 [.0350]	.0555[12.565]	.0099[.0362]
OG	**.3976 [.0284]***	.4153[1.3730]	**.4050[.0292]***
PCM	**-29.60 [14.12]***	-51.438[354.19]	**-38.879[16.270]***
RD	29.298 [71.54]	-86.942[6221.0]	-8.3064[86.058]
KL	-1.484 [1.268]	-2.592[159.98]	-2.1414[1.8500]
IFL[u]	.0174 [.11262]	.0239[9.769]	.0356[.1233]
D1	-1.422 [2.858]	.3098[557.79]	-1.510[3.1101]
D2	0.519 [2.120]	-.2475[63.866]	0.1173[2.2481]
D1*Δ ERP lag1	.0452 [.045789]	-.0625[29.133]	.0469[.0466]
D1*Δ ERP lag2	.0544 [.047683]	-.1598[55.094]	.0507[.0491]
D2*Δ ERP lag1	-0.6597 [.0380]	-.9899[9.977]	-.0637[.0389]
D2*Δ ERP lag2	-.0327 [.0452]	-.1045[19.674]	-0.0329[.0463]
CONSTANT	3.52603 [3.803]	X	5.92711[4.9311]
Adjusted R^2	.470	.457	.507
Observations	220	220	220
No. of Years	12	12	12
No. of Industries	20	20	20
Hausman Test		8.15	
D-W Test		2.438	
Correction for Serial Correlation	Yes	Yes	Yes

Notes: (1) *Indicates significant at 5 per cent level. (2) White's heteroscedasticty corrected standard errors within parenthesis. (3) If the Durbin-Watson test indicates the presence of serial correlation of order1, the estimates have been corrected using the Cochrane-Orcutt procedure for AR (1).

The relationship between the change in export growth and productivity growth seems to be perverse as evident from the wrong sign and statistical significance. This negative association could be attributed to the effects of omitted variables or aggregation.[15] We have also attempted to ascertain whether the effect of change in ERP on productivity growth is specific to the phases of trade reform by incorporating the following interactive dummies (D_1ERP_1; D_1ERP_2; D_2ERP_1; D_2 ERP_2). The fixed effects estimate shows that the period impacts of change in ERP being significant as reflected in the two year lagged ERP for the years 1980-85. Furthermore, for the period 1986-90, we observe that both the one and two year lags are statistically significant with the magnitude of the coefficient decreasing in case of the two year lag (–.1079) as against the one year lag (–.1705). Thus, it shows that the impact of lowering of ERP on productivity growth is smaller for a two-year lag than for a one-year lag in the second phase of trade reforms. This may reflect the fact that the trade policy changes prior to the 1988 were mostly on a year to year basis and the industries responded with a one year lag.

The variables representing the different aspects of industrial policy changes appear to have a significant impact on productivity growth. The coefficient of the change in price-cost margin (–.0030) is statistically significant with a negative sign. The lowering of markup results in a decline in concentration and an increase in domestic competition, which in turn brings about cost reduction and/ or productivity growth. This could be attributed to the de-licensing and other controls being gradually removed from the mid-1980s, resulting in domestic competition within the machinery sector. Further in the 1990s, the licensing requirement has been done away in all but 15 industries of strategic or environmental concerns. The coefficient of the change in R&D intensity (.0026) is statistically significant at 5 per cent level with the expected positive sign. This indicates that higher R&D intensity tends to improve productivity growth. For the capital goods sector, particularly agricultural machinery industries the real private sector R&D expenditures grew

15. Similar perverse results obtained in a study on Morocco by Haddad *et al.*, (1996). The authors attribute this to the measurement errors that arise from constructing an export growth variable at the industry level from the data at the product level. Our results are also reflective of such a possibility since the export growth variable is constructed from the information at the ITC (HS) product level.

at a rate faster than in the 1980s.[16] Further, Kumar and Aggarwal (2000) confirm that the R&D efforts of the local firms are more towards absorption of knowledge embodied in imported capital goods and is concentrated in industries that offer significant opportunities for product and process adaptations. As with the intermediate goods industry, the variable representing the effect of the macroeconomic environment on productivity growth is of correct sign, though not significant.[17]

Intermediate Goods Industries

The regression estimates for intermediate goods groups of industries are presented in Table 14.3. Looking at the FE estimates, we find that the coefficient of the two-year lagged change in import coverage ratio (-0.1749) is statistically significant at 5 per cent level. A 10 per cent decrease in the import coverage ratio shows approximately 2 per cent point increase in productivity growth with a two year lag. This implies that lowering of quantitative restriction on imports of finished and semi-finished products belonging to various industries brings about competition in the domestic market and helps reduce costs and in turn enhances productivity growth with a time lag. Further, the coefficient of the two year lagged change in import coverage ratio is statistically significant across the three estimators. The one-year lagged change in import coverage ratio, however, does not have any significant impact on the productivity growth.

The coefficient of the one year lagged change in ERP (–.0791) in the FE regression is of correct sign and statistically significant. Our measure of effective rate of protection is based on tariff data and reflects the changes in the levels and dispersion of tariff rates. The decline in the level and dispersion of the tariff rates has implications for productivity enhancement of the industries. In particular, the lowering of protection as evident from the change in ERP is associated with a statistically significant increase in TFP growth. It may be more appropriate to use a price-based measure of the

16. *See* Basant (2000).

17. The results change markedly when we consider the outcomes of industrial policy in levels in model-2. Neither the trade liberalisation indicators nor the industrial policy variables have any statistically significant effect on productivity growth in capital goods industries. *See* lower panel of Table 14.2.

effective rate of protection. However, there are immense difficulties in obtaining reliable and comparable international and domestic prices.[18] The statistically significant impact on productivity growth of both the two-year lagged change in import coverage ratio and the one-year lagged change in ERP highlights the role played by the of reduction in non-tariff and tariff barriers in bringing about competition amongst the domestic industries leading to productivity growth.

Table 14.3

Panel Data Productivity Growth Regressions: Intermediate Goods Industries

Version-1	*Dependent Variable: TFP Growth*		
Variables	Pooled OLS	Fixed Effects	Random Effects
Δ EG lag1	.00003 [.0010]	-.0001 [.0006]	-.0000 [.0010]
Δ EG lag2	-.00125 [.0010]	-.0001 [.0009]	-.0013 [.0010]
Δ MCR lag1	-.00116 [.0345]	.0078 [.0146]	.0008 [.0359]
Δ MCR lag2	**-.1667 [.0580]***	**-.1749 [.0428]***	**-.1687 [.0602]***
Δ ERP lag1	-.0682 [.0524]	**-.0791 [.0349]***	-.0707 [.0541]
Δ ERP lag2	.0019 [.0548]	-.0057 [.0349]	.0001 [.0566]
OG	**.2175 [.01750]***	**.2193 [.0575]***	**.2180 [.0181]***
Δ PCM	.0005 [.0008]	.0007 [.0004]	.0006 [.0008]
Δ RD	.0020 [.0017]	**.0015 [.0004]***	.0019 [.0218]
Δ KL	.0107 [.0184]	.0173 [.0165]	.0122 [.0192]
IFL[u]	-.0335[.0622]	-.0414 [.0434]	-.0349 [.0659]
D1	-1.748 [2.082]	-1.533 [1.658]	-1.696 [2.154]
D2	.0126 [1.723]	.1366 [1.605]	.0438 [1.776]
D1*Δ ERP lag1	.0651 [.0532]	**.0745 [.0348]***	.0673 [.0549]
D1*Δ ERP lag2	-.0844 [.0555]	-.2516 [.0344]	-.0069 [.0573]
D2*Δ ERP lag1	.0432 [.0730]	.0550 [.0518]	.0458 [.0759]
D2*Δ ERP lag2	-.0524 [.0715]	-.0426 [.0482]	.0503 [.0743]

Contd...

18. Hasheem (2001) reports an attempt made to obtain comparable prices for items at the 6-digit level of classification. It was, however, observed that even for a homogenous commodity like iron and steel, there were problems in getting comparable data, as the domestic equivalent of the foreign commodity was not produced in India. Aksoy and Ettori (1992), however, assembled some 500 price-ratios between domestic ex-factory prices and CIF import prices covering the period 1987-89 from BICP reports and World Bank sources. The authors point out that often the nature of the industrial policies make it very difficult to undertake a comparison of international and domestic prices

...*Table 14.3 Contd...*

Version-1	*Dependent Variable: TFP Growth*		
Constant	-1.043 [1.824]	X	-1.063 [1.943]
Adjusted R^2	.343	.305	.376
Observations	336	336	336
No. of Years	12	12	12
No. of Industries	28	28	28
Hausman Test		2.74	
D-W Test		1.834	
Correction for Serial Correlation	Yes	Yes	Yes

Version-2	*Dependent Variable: TFP Growth*		
Variables	Pooled OLS	Fixed Effects	Random Effects
Δ EG lag1	.0002 [.0010]	.0002[.0006]	.0002[.0011]
Δ EG lag2	-.0011 [.0010]	-.0011[.0010]	-.1151[.0011]
Δ MCR lag	1 .0034 [.0351]	.0029[.0113]	.0031[.0369]
Δ MCR lag2	**-.1360 [.0351]***	**-.1370[.0104]***	**-.1364[.00369]***
Δ ERP lag1	-.0693 [.0529]	**-.0696[.0347]***	-.7205[.0550]
Δ ERP lag2	-.0031 [.0556]	-.0075[.0372]	-.5905[.0577]
OG	**.2084 [.0175]***	**.2070[.05983]**	**.2083[.0181]***
PCM	**-25.45 [11.99]***	-38.935[22.143]	**-28.558[13.382]***
RD	-98.76 [286.21]	-858.8[1459.3]	-167.19[367.03]
KL	-.3132 [.18525]	.3825[1.994]	.0091[.2495]
IFL[u]	-.0404 [.0647]	.0012[.0735]	-.0282[.0704]
D1	-3.440 [2.429]	-2.483[3.590]	-3.241[2.539]
D2	-.5879[1.7475]	-0.1250[2.451]	-.473[1.812]
D1*Δ ERP lag1	.06770 [.0538]	**.0684[.0337]***	.0704[.0557]
D1*Δ ERP lag2	-.02702 [.0564]	.0014[.0368]	-.0000[.0584]
D2*Δ ERP lag1	.0440 [.07387]	.0398[.0669]	.0460[.0777]
D2*Δ ERP lag2	-.4742 [.0724]	-.5714[.0842]	-.4710[.0762]
Constant	2.4501 [2.3700]	X	2.5332[2.7437]
Adjusted R^2	.357	.317	.391
Observations	308	308	308
No. of Years	12	12	12
No. of Industries	28	28	28
Hausman Test		4.77	
D-W Test		2.639	
Correction for Serial Correlation	Yes	Yes	Yes

Notes: (1) *Indicates significant at 5 per cent level. (2) White's heteroscedasticty corrected standard errors within parenthesis. (3) If the Durbin-Watson test indicates the presence of serial correlation of order1, the estimates have been corrected using the Cochrane-Orcutt procedure for AR (1).

Amongst the variables reflecting the outcomes of industrial policy changes, we observe that only the change in R&D intensity is significant. This appears to indicate that with easing of restrictions on trade and the availability of imported inputs embodying superior technology, the internal firm efforts towards adaptive R&D helped improve the productivity performance. Our results, corroborate the findings of Basant (2000). His study shows that the R&D expenditure in large number of industries in the private sector grew at around 7 per cent in the 1990s.[19] As expected, the coefficient of output growth (OG) is statistically significant and has a positive sign. This finding is consistent with Verdoorn's law, that economies of scale are a source of productivity growth. Further the result is in line with studies by Goldar (1986) and Ahluwalia (1991), which observed that in Indian manufacturing productivity growth is positively correlated with economies of scale. The variable representing the effect of the macro environment on productivity growth is of correct sign, thereby implying that lowering of inflation uncertainty does lead to an improvement in the productivity growth. The variable, however, is not statistically significant.[20]

19. See Tables 9 and 10 in Basant (2000). For the all-industries sample, the low and negative growth rates of private sector R&D expenditures in the late-1980s /early 1990s in the 3-digit industries, namely cotton textiles, textile products, fertilisers, rubber and transport equipment etc. may have possibly lead to an insignificant effect of R&D intensity on TFP growth.

20. See Figure 14.2 (below) for the trend in inflation uncertainty over the period 1980-95.

Figure 14.2

Trends in Inflation Uncertainty- 1980-81 to 1994-95: Selected Industries

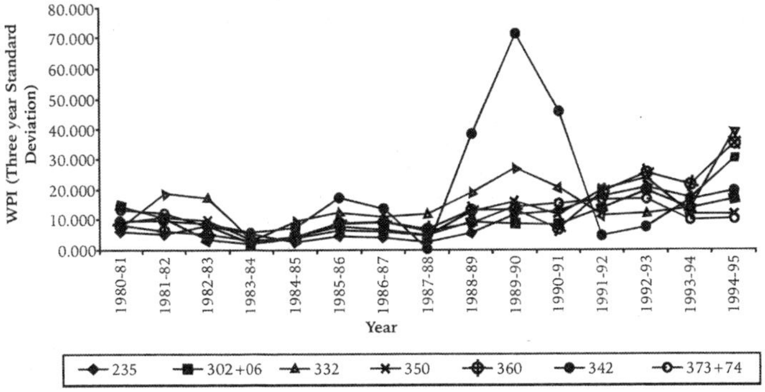

Comparison with Other Studies

As noted in the introduction, policy changes particularly trade as a determinant of industrial productivity growth has received very little attention in the case of Indian manufacturing sector during the past four decades 1950-90. Some studies attempting to document productivity growth for Indian manufacturing sector have partially explored the trade-productivity linkage.[21] Studies on the impact of trade reforms for India have been both at the firm as well as industry level. Krishna and Mitra (1998) and Balakrishnan *et al.*, (2000) incorporate the methodological refinements in the measurement of productivity growth. Both these studies rely on the CMIE database. The periods covered in the two studies overlap. Krishna and Mitra (1998) cover the period 1986-93 for the following industry groups: electrical machinery, non-electrical machinery, electronics and transport equipment and find strong evidence of an increase in competition and some evidence of an increase in productivity growth after reforms In particular, there is evidence of significant reduction in mark-ups in the years following the reforms in three industries. There is also evidence of increases in productivity growth in some industry groups. The study finds that for non-electrical and electronics industry groups, there is evidence of both competition and productivity growth. Balakrishnan *et al.*, (2000), on the other hand show that there is no evidence of increase in productivity since the onset of reforms in 1991-92. Their study covers a much larger sample spanning the period 1989-98. This observed difference between the studies appears to be attributable to differences in the econometric methodology.[22]

Recent studies (Das (2001) , Goldar and Kumari (2002) & Chand and Sen (2002)) have addressed the issue of the trade liberalisation-manufacturing productivity growth linkage with appropriately

---

21. Goldar (1986 a,b) used effective rate of protection and estimates of import substitution as indicators of trade policy, whereas Ahluwalia (1991) used a Chenery measure of import substitution to address the issue of determinants of productivity growth. Both the studies found a negative relationship between productivity growth and indicators of trade policy.

22. The random-effects model is estimated in Krishna and Mitra (1998). The results in Balakrishnan *et al.*, (2000) are based on IV estimation of a fixed-effects model, the time dummy of the intercept indicates no improvement in productivity growth. An important limitation of both the studies is the reliance on dummy variables and the absence of an explicit trade policy indicator to assess the trade liberalisation consequences.

Table 14.4

Trade Liberalisation and Productivity Growth: Evidence for India

Study	*Model Specification*	*Database*	*Methodology*	*Nature of Observed Impact*	*Major Limitations*
Fujita (1994)	TFP growth is a function of Trade Liberalisation (TL)	Cross-section of 3-digit Industries	Inter-Industry Cross-section Regression	TL has a positive impact on TFP growth	Absence of Trade Policy Indicators
Krishna and Mitra (1998)	Production Function Framework Halls Methodology	Panel of Firms	Inter-Firm Panel Regression (Random Effects Model)	TL has a positive impact on TFP growth	Lack of Explicit Trade Policy Indicators
Balakrishnan *et al.*, (2000)	Production Function Framework Halls Methodology	Panel of Firms	Inter-Firm Panel Regression (Fixed Effects Model)	TL has a negative impact on TFP growth	Lack of Explicit Trade Policy Indicators
Hasheem Norouz (2001)	TFP growth is a function of Export Expansion and Import Substitution	Cross-section of Industries	Inter-industry Cross section Regression	TL do not have any significant impact on TFP growth	Lack of Explicit Trade Policy Indicators
Das (2001)	TFP growth is a function of trade, industrial and macro policies	Panel of 3-digit industries	Inter-industry Panel regression (Fixed Effects model)	TL has a positive impact on TFP growth	Time periods of some reform phases too small

Contd...

...Table 14.4 Contd...

Study	*Model Specification*	*Database*	*Methodology*	*Nature of Observed Impact*	*Major Limitations*
Goldar and Kumari (2002)	TFP growth is a function of trade policies and investment	Panel of 2-digit industries	Inter-industry panel regressions (Fixed Effects model)	TL has a positive impact on TFP growth	Lack of any industrial policy variables
Chand and Sen (2002)	Production function framework incorporating intermediate inputs	Panel of 3-digit industries	Inter-industry Panel regression (fixed effects model)	TL has a positive impact on productivity growth.	Lack of any industrial as well as macro policy variables

defined measures of trade policy reforms.[23] These studies use panel data with appropriately defined lag structures for testing the observed relationship. The first one covers the period of 1980s and early-1990s using 72 three-digit industries, the second study extends the period of 1980s up to the late-1990s for 17 two-digit industry groups and the third one covers the period of 1970s till 1988 for around 30 three-digit industry groups. Das (2001) study covers the period 1980-95 and around 72 three-digit industries. Using measures of trade liberalisation such as ERP and NTB, the study attempts to capture the competitive impact of trade policy reforms on manufacturing productivity via lowering of tariff and non-tariff barriers. The results, show that lowering of NTB's have a positive impact on the manufacturing as well as intermediate goods sectors' industrial productivity. The study by Goldar and Kumari (2002) covering the period till 1997-98 shows that a reduction in effective rate of protection to industries appeared to have had a favourable effect on productivity growth in Indian industries. However, the observed fall in productivity in the 1990s may be attributable partly to the gestation lags in investment projects. Sen and Chand (2002) show that a reduction in the price-wedge has a positive impact on productivity growth. Their study, however, covers the much of the period (1973-88) before the onset of major trade liberalisation attempts the impact of trade policy reforms.

SECTION 5

CONCLUSION

Our attempt to explore the impact of trade liberalisation on industrial productivity addresses three important shortcomings in the trade-productivity literature. First, our study has used explicit indicators in terms of tariff and non-tariff barriers to quantify the trade orientation, instead of dummy variables (Krishna and Mitra (1998) and Athukorala and Rajapatirana (2000)). Second, we draw

23. Trade liberalisation indicators for India have either been unsatisfactory (Goldar (1986), Ahluwalia (1991)) or been captured through dummy variables (Krishna and Mitra (1998), Balakrishnan *et al.*, (2000)). The recent studies by Das (2001), Goldar and Kumari (2002) and Chand and Sen (2000) have, however, used various indicators of trade liberalisation to quantify protection and have explored the link using them.

upon the studies by Wiess (1992) and Iscan (1998) for Mexico showing that trade liberalisation has a lagged impact on productivity growth and accordingly, model the trade-productivity relationship with lagged trade liberalisation variables. Finally, to capture the full benefits of trade liberalisation, a supporting set of policies are required (Mussa (1987), Thomas *et al.*, (1991)). These have, however, been missing in majority of the studies trying to assess the impact of trade policy reforms. We control for the influence of policies other than trade policy, especially industrial policy reform and a stable macroeconomic environment.

An examination of the results indicates that the lagged import coverage ratio variable representing the impact of non-tariff barrier is negatively and significantly associated with productivity growth for both capital and intermediate goods sectors. As evident from the coefficient, the lowering of non-tariff barrier leads to an increase in productivity growth. Our other indicators of trade liberalisation namely, the effective rate of protection representing the tariff barrier is also significant in explaining productivity growth for the two sectors.[24] These results are consistent with an increase in competition for the industries following the lowering of protection. The export growth variable intended to capture the scale effect of trade liberalisation turns out to be significant with wrong sign for all the categories of industries. We conjecture that the negative association may be attributable to the measurement errors arising from aggregation.

Our results also indicate that the variables capturing the different aspects of trade liberalisation have different marginal effects on total factor productivity growth. The total effects of changes in tariff and non-tariff barriers are also different across the industry groups. Further, in most cases, the total effects confirm an inverse relationship between changes in import coverage ratio (effective rate of protection) and productivity growth and given that the trade liberalisation variables are weakly correlated amongst the trade policy variables, the results are not vitiated by multi-collinearity.

24. We have incorporated real effective exchange rate (REER) variable in our regression equations to capture the impact of exchange rate overvaluation in assessing the effect of trade liberalisation on productivity. The coefficient turned out to be insignificant and hence was not reported in the regression results.

In conclusion, the results suggest that the trade policy reforms of the 1980s and 90s did contribute to improvements in productivity growth via the lowering of the non-tariff barriers. This holds for the capital as well as the intermediate goods sectors. We find that amongst the trade variables, lowering of non-tariff barriers is consistent with the competitive effect of trade liberalisation. Our results are also in line with those from other studies on South Asia (India-Ahluwalia (1994), Krishna and Mitra (1998), Sri Lanka–Athukorala and Rajapatirana (2000)) and majority of the studies surveyed in the literature.[25] The econometric exercise confirms that trade policy reforms have significant positive impact on productivity change. We may, however, add that the results of the exercise ought to be treated with caution as the study had to confront serious measurement issues connected with the construction of "appropriate" trade liberalisation indicators.

25. Refer footnote1.

References

Ahluwalia, I.J. (1991). *Productivity and Growth in Indian Manufacturing*, Oxford University Press, Delhi.

Aksoy, A. and F.M. Ettori (1992). *"Protection and Industrial Structure in India" Policy Research Working Paper No. 990*, The World Bank, Washington DC.

Alexander, P.C. (1977). *Report on the Committee on Import-Export Policies and Procedures*, Ministry of Commerce, Government of India.

Athukorala, P.C. and S. Rajapatirana (2000). *Liberalisation and Industrial Transformation: Sri Lanka in International Perspective*, Oxford University Press, Delhi.

Balakrishnan, P., K. Pushpangadan and M. Suresh Babu (2000). "Trade Liberalisation and Productivity Growth in Manufacturing: Evidence from Firm Level Panel Data" *Economic and Political Weekly*, October 7, 3679-3682.

Baltagi. B.H. (1995). *Econometric Analysis of Panel Data*, John Wiley & Sons Ltd., England.

Baltagi, B.H. and Q.Li (1995). "Testing AR(1) against MA(1) disturbances in an Error Component Model," *Journal of Econometrics*, 68,133-151.

Basant, R. (2000). "Corporate Response to Economic Reforms" *Economic and Political Weekly*, March 4, 813-822.

Chand, S. and K. Sen (2002). "Trade Liberalisation and Productivity Growth: Evidence from Indian Manufacturing," *Review of Development Economics*, Vol. 6, No. 1, February.

Corbo, V. and J. De-melo (1987). "Lessons from the Southern Cone Policy Reforms," *The World Bank Research Observer*, Vol. 2, No. 2, 111-142.

Das, D.K. (1998). "Trade Liberalisation and Productivity Growth: A Disaggregated Analysis of Indian Manufacturing Sectors," *Working Paper Series No E/200/98*, Institute of Economic Growth, Delhi.

————. (2001). *Some Aspects of Productivity Growth and Trade in Indian Industry*, Unpublished Ph.D. Dissertation, Delhi School of Economics, University of Delhi, November.

————. (2002a). "Trade Liberalisation and Industrial Productivity: An Assessment of Developing Country Experiences" *Working Paper No. 77*, Indian Council for Research on International Economic Relations (ICRIER). April.

————. (2002b). "Quantifying Trade Barriers: Has Protection Declined in Indian Manufacturing," *Mimeo*, Indian Council for Research on International Economic Relations (ICRIER), June.

Deaton. A. (1997). *The Analysis of Household Surveys: A Micro-Econometric Approach to Development Policy*, The John Hopkins University Press, Baltimore and London.

Goldar, B.N. (1986a). *Productivity Growth in Indian Industry*, Allied Publishers, New Delhi.

————. (1986b). "Import Substitution, Industrial Concentration and Productivity Growth in Indian Manufacturing," *Oxford Bulletin of Economics and Statistics*, Vol. 48, No. 2, 143-64.

Goldar, B.N. and A. Kumari (2002). "Import Liberalisation and Productivity Growth in Indian Manufacturing Industries in the 1990s," *Working Paper No. E/219/2002*, Institute of Economic Growth, Delhi.

Griliches, Z. and J.A. Hausman (1986). "Errors in Variables in Panel Data," *Journal of Econometrics*, 31, 93-118.

Hachette, D. (1991). "Chile: Trade Liberalisation Since 1974" in Shepard, G. and C.G. Langoni (eds) *Trade Reform: Lessons from Eighteen Countries*, ICS Press for International Center for Economic Growth, San Francisco.

Haddad, M., J. deMelo, and B. Horton (1996). "Morocco, 1984-89: Trade Liberalisation, Exports and Industrial Performance," Roberts, M. and J.R. Tybout (ed.) *Industrial Evolutions in Developing Countries: Micro Patterns of Turnover, Productivity and Market Structure*, Oxford University Press for The World Bank.

Hasheem, S.N. (2001). *Protection in Indian Manufacturing: An Empirical Study,* Macmillan India Ltd., Delhi.

Hussain, Abid (1984). *Report of the Committee on Trade Policies,* Ministry of Commerce, Government of India.

Iscan, T. (1998). "Trade Liberalisation and Productivity: A Panel Study of the Mexican Manufacturing Industry," *The Journal of Development Studies,* 1, No. 1, 123-148.

Jorgenson, D.W. *et al.,* (1987). *Productivity and US Economic Growth,* Harvard University Press, Cambridge Mass.

Krishna, P. and D. Mitra (1998). "Trade Liberalisation, Market Discipline and Productivity Growth: New Evidence from India," *Journal of Development Economics,* 56, 447-62.

Kumar, N. and A. Aggarwal (2000). "Liberalisation, Outward Orientation and In-house R&D Activity of Multinational and Local Firms: A Quantitative Exploration for Indian Manufacturing," *Discussion Paper No 18,* Institute of Economic Growth, Delhi.

Miachaely M. *et al.,* (1986). "The Phasing of a Trade Liberalisation Policy: Preliminary Evidence," *CPD Discussion Paper No. 1986-42,* Country Policy Department, World Bank.

Mussa, M. (1987). "Macro Economic Policy And Trade Liberalisation: Some Guidelines," *The World Bank Research Observer,* 2, No. 1, 61-77.

Narasimham, M. (1984) *Report of the Committee to Examine the Principles of a Possible Shift from Physical to Financial Controls,* Government of India.

Nash, J. (1992). "An Overview of Trade Policy Reforms, with Implications for Sub-Saharan Africa," in Fontaine, Jean-Marc (ed.) *Foreign Trade Reforms and Development Strategy,* Routledge, London and New York.

Pack, H. (1988). "Industrialisation and Trade" in Chenery, H. and T.N. Srinivasan (ed), *Handbook of Development Economics,* Amsterdam, North Holland.

Pappageorgiou, D., M. Michaely and A.M. Choksi (ed.) (1991). *Liberalising Foreign Trade,* Volumes I-VII, Blackwell, Oxford.

Ravallian, M. M, Heil and J. Jalan (2000). "Carbon Emissions and Income Inequality," *Oxford Economic Papers,* 52, 651-669.

Thomas, V. and J. Nash (1991). "Reform of Trade Policy: Recent Evidence from Theory and Practice," *The World Bank Research Observer,* Vol. 6, No. 2, 219-240.

Thomas, V. *et al.,* (1991). *Best Practices in Trade Policy Reform,* A World Bank and Oxford University Press.

Weiss, J. (1992). "Trade Policy Reform and Performance in Manufacturing: Mexico 1975-88," *The Journal of Development Studies,* 29, No. 1,1-23.

15

Persistence in India's Manufactured Export Performance

SAIKAT SINHA ROY

SECTION 1
INTRODUCTION

The empirical occurrence of persistence in performance is necessarily a long-run phenomenon. Depending on the duration of the process, persistence can be strong or weak. For instance, persistence is strong when the process is prolonged and weak when it is transitory. The inertia to remain in such a state of performance over a long period can result from slow adjustments to either demand and supply shocks,[1] and can have immense implications on developing country performance, especially that relating to exports. A study on persistence in export performance assumes particular importance when developing countries like India are trying to evolve WTO-consistent trade policies so that exports are on a higher growth trajectory.

Even though export growth in India has persisted to remain low to moderate for a long phase during 1960 to 1997, empirical accounting of the phenomenon of persistence in export growth is a rather neglected area of research. A growing literature can be cited on persistence in India's industrial output growth,[2] but the scope of

1. Campbell and Mankiw (1987) define a shock to an economy as persistent if the process continues "for a long time into the future", thus challenging the earlier belief that shocks to output almost dissipate in four to five years. Persistence can even arise from slow adjustment to short term fluctuations, which last for some quarters.

2. A recent debate on this issue of persistence in industrial output can be highlighted, for instance. The studies, Krishnan and Sen (1995), and Dua and Mishra (1999), focus on either weak or strong persistence arising either from the demand or the supply side. While the former study finds weak persistence in index of industrial production, the latter arrives at the finding of strong persistence arising due to supply side shocks.

applied trade models on India is somewhat limited to finding price and income elasticities of tradables. This is very evident from the exhaustive survey by Panchamukhi (1997). Even recent studies on India's export performance, for instance by Joshi and Little (1994), Brahmbhatt *et al.*, (1995), Krishnamurthy and Pandit (1995), Marjit and Ray Chaudhuri (1997) and Srinivasan (1998), do not attempt to account for persistence in performance, even if some of them analyse long run growth behaviour.

In a clear departure from the existing studies on India's export performance, the present study attempts to document persistence in India's manufactured export performance and accounts for the factors contributing to such a long run phenomenon. The study by Mody and Yilmaz (1994) on persistence in developing country export performance can provide some insights on the issue. Mody and Yilmaz (1994) find that manufactured export growth performance in developing countries tends to be persistent. The study finds that correcting for measurement errors, in addition to price and income factors, do not sufficiently explain the long-run phenomenon of persistence in performance. The persistence of developing country export growth is often explained by unobserved factors. The study also provides indirect evidence of varied responses of "insider" and "outsider" suppliers in the world trade for manufactured goods, a condition that tends to perpetuate itself, as an indication to persistence in developing country export performance. Further, the development of transactional infrastructure such as telecommunications network can also explain the phenomenon.[3]

The scheme of the present study is as follows. Section 2 puts forth some empirical evidence on India's manufactured export performance over the long run. While the third section discusses in detail the econometric method used to arrive at the evidence of persistence in performance. Section 4 provides a profile of data used in the study. The fifth section gives econometric evidence on the existence of persistence in performance and the factors contributing to such a phenomenon. Finally, the paper concludes with major findings and their policy implications.

---

3. In particular, a recent study, Kumar (2002), points to the positive impact of availability of quality infrastructure on export orientation of foreign affiliate production in host countries.

SECTION 2

SOME STYLISED FACTS ON INDIA'S EXPORT PERFORMANCE

Manufactured exports, like aggregate exports, have shown an increasing trend over the period 1960-61 to 1997-98. The trends in manufactured export growth show a turn-around and accordingly, the period-wise growth rates, as Table 15.1 shows, point to the evidence of low to moderate export growth in the initial phases till mid-eighties and a phase of high growth thereafter. However, the declining share of India in world's manufactured exports persisted to remain low through till 1997-98.[4] Nonetheless, manufactured exports from India witnessed high rates of growth during trade liberalisation. Further, it is evident from Table 15.1 that growth rates are more stable after the mid-eighties. Despite high average growth during post-reforms, the annual rates of growth in manufactured exports lowered after the mid-nineties, especially in 1997-98 (Figure 15.1). This is indeed indicative of the fact that trade liberalisation is not the sufficient condition for sustaining high export growth.[5] The issue of persistence in performance can, thus, be situated in the context of the above growth profile of manufactured exports.

The long run manufactured export performance can be related to various demand and supply-side factors. In this context, the policy regime becomes the most important factor. In the import-substituting phase of industrialisation, production of manufactures had been primarily for the domestic economy with a limited focus on the external market. With protection during import substitution, as is often stressed in the literature,[6] the exchange rate remained overvalued and resulted in anti-export bias. The changes in policies relating to the external sector, in India, have moved in two directions: the reforms relating to tradeables since the mid-eighties and exchange rate reforms from an earlier period onwards. External sector reforms in, India, have proceeded in terms of reducing price

4. It is well documented in the existing literature that India's share in world trade has been declining since the early-fifties. Though the decline in the share is arrested since the mid-seventies and a turnaround can be observed from the mid-eighties onwards, the share continues to remain low.
5. Sinha Roy (2001 b) has analysed the unsustained pattern of post-reforms export growth in India.
6. *See* Bhagwati and Srinivasan (1975), for instance.

Table 15.1

Growth and Instability of India's Manufactured Exports and Other Associated Variables

(growth rates in per cent)

Period	Manufactured Exports	Total Demand	REER	GDP in Manufacturing
Growth				
1960-73	6.05	8.99	-1.41	4.70
1973-74-1984-85	6.19	4.52	-0.52	6.63
1985-86-1997-98	11.33	7.28	-1.43	7.23
Instability				
1960-61-1972-73	0.96	0.32	4.46	0.85
1973-74-1984-85	1.95	1.56	8.71	0.80
1985-98	0.79	0.35	7.66	0.61

Note: Growth rates are annual average growth rates. Instability is measured in terms of coefficient of variation.

Source: Author's calculation based on different sources.

Figure 15.1

Growth of India's Manufactured Exports and Other Variables

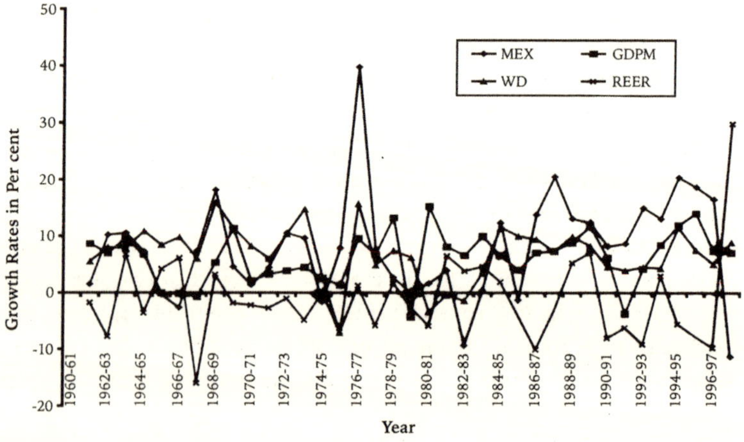

and cost distortions in the economy by eliminating quantitative restrictions and replacing them with tariffs, rationalising the tariff structure and simplifying trade procedures. The trajectory of such trade reforms was incremental between the mid-eighties and the late-nineties. The attempts to liberalise external trade are meant to create export opportunities by allowing competition at the margin apart from providing access to cheap inputs at near-world prices. Thus, reforms in the external sector in a way attempted to make exports responsive to changes in relative prices. In the presence of market imperfections, however, the outcomes of trade liberalisation may be vastly different.[7]

The major thrust of exchange rate reforms, in India, has been towards a depreciating currency for promotion of exports. To that end, the rupee, a managed float by 1985, was devalued in 1991. The depreciation of the currency was carried forward with current account convertibility. In addition, the Reserve Bank of India has often intervened in the foreign exchange market to maintain a depreciating rupee. The real rupee, as Table 15.1 and Figure 15.1 would show, depreciated almost throughout. But, as Figure 15.1 also shows, the devaluation of the currency in 1966 and 1991 did not lead to sustained real rupee depreciation in the following years.[8] The high instability in REER depreciation is indeed indicative of years of real currency appreciation, high rate of appreciation being observed in 1997.

The growth of manufacturing production during different policy regimes, which indicates growth in supply capabilities, can also be an important factor explaining long-run growth of manufactured exports. The growth of manufacturing production provides an expanding base for exports to grow. With changes in policy, not only growing manufacturing production is expected to provide an expanding base for exports, manufacturing production is expected to be more efficient. This would necessarily result in higher export growth. Figure 15.1 shows that manufacturing production grew at high rates in the early-sixties followed by a relative slow down thereafter for about a decade. Growth in manufacturing production revived in the mid-seventies and it continued throughout except for a couple of years during the early-nineties and also in 1979-80. It is, thus,

7. Studies by Bhagwati (1988), Bose (1993), Marjit and Sarkar (1995) and Bhattacharjea (1995) point to this evidence.

8. The rate of depreciation particularly in these years may seem to be high only with respect to real rupee appreciation in the immediate preceding years.

evident that manufacturing production, in India, grew irrespective of the trade regime and it has provided the base for expanding manufactured exports.

In addition to movements in relative prices and growth in manufacturing production, trends in world demand tend to explain export growth in a significant way. At the outset, it needs to be stressed that developed country destinations are the permanent source of demand for India's exports. The emerging destinations, which changed from the Middle-east Asian countries during the seventies to include East and South-east Asia after the mid-eighties, gave rise to additional demand during the period. Total world demand, as is evident from Table 15.1, grew at high rates till the early-seventies, with a somewhat different growth scenario after 1973. This is despite the emergence of new destinations of exports during the period. In the period after the mid-eighties, there is a revival in total demand for India's exports arising due to a revival of demand from permanent destinations together with that from the emerging markets. The lowering of world demand after the mid-nineties is synchronous with declining rates of export growth then.

Overall, most of the above variables are found to have a changing growth path over time. The break in trend can be statistically significant, which can determine the long run behaviour of manufactured exports from India.[9] The significance of the break in trend is ascertained in terms of Chow test.[10] Certainly, high average growth in manufactured exports after the mid-eighties is supported by a significant break in trend in 1985. As Table 15.2 would show, for manufactured exports with breaks in 1976 and 1985, the Chow test F-statistic of 71.66 is significant at 1 per cent level. Individually, however, the break at 1976 gives a Chow test F-statistic significant at 5 per cent level, while that with respect to the break in 1985 is significant at 1 per cent level. Even the variables total world demand and GDP in manufacturing show significant multiple breaks in respective trends. The structural breaks in trend of real effective

9. Though Table 15.1 has adopted a uniform periodisation across variables, it is evident from Figure 15.1 that the break-point in respective trends are not the same.

10. Chow tests or any other structural break test is inconsistent if the time series has unit roots. The Chow test applied in case of these variables is only indicative of the existence of a break in trend.

exchange rate and GDP in manufacturing, however, predate the mid-eighties. Such changing growth pattern for manufactured exports and associated variables is indeed important in determining persistence in performance.

Even if all these factors tend to explain export performance in India over the long run, the issue that remains is whether these necessarily explain the persistence in performance. The short run dynamics assume importance in the context of such long run performance. It is, thus, important to understand whether the changes in relative price or various demand and supply factors contribute to the long run phenomenon. Accordingly, the study has taken into account the market access problem on the demand side and various institutional factors on the supply-side which are persisting over the long run. Even if growth in manufacturing production is an important supply side factor determining long run export performance, provision of services has assumed centre-stage in the context of long run growth. This would require not only transactional infrastructure as discussed by Mody and Yilmaz (1994), but also various transactional services associated with export sale of manufactured goods.

Table 15.2

Structural Break in Different Variables During 1960-97

Variable	*Breakpoint(s)*	*Estimated Chow Test F-Statistic*	*Probability*
Manufactured Exports (MEX)	1976	3.81	0.0322
	1985	35.05	0.0000
	1976-1985	71.66	0.0000
World Demand (WD)	1973	39.46	0.0000
	1982	19.07	0.000003
	1973-1982	42.37	0.0000
Real Effective Exchange Rate (REER)	1983	9.48	0.005
	1984	6.28	0.005
GDP in Manufacturing (GDPM)	1964	6.55	0.0039
	1975	66.47	0.0000
	1964-1975	39.56	0.0000

Source: Author's Calculation.

SECTION 3
THE METHOD

In applied studies, persistence is often measured by estimating distributed lagged model.[11] The phenomenon of persistence in export performance is obscured due to the adoption of *ad-hoc* procedures while estimating export functions. Very often, a lagged independent variable is incorporated as an explanatory variable or a time trend variable is added as an explanatory factor to capture various other determinants into the export equation. Moreover, such estimations are done without taking into account the long run properties of the variables and accordingly, these methods do not serve the purpose of separating out factors that have implications on long run performance. As against these existing methods, the presence of persistence is studied here by testing for unit root in a univariate time series model. Other than unit roots, Campbell and Mankiw (1987) have outlined three methods to observe the phenomenon of persistence in performance.

With unit roots in time series, the OLS estimates cannot be used. The presence of unit roots would require estimation statistic other than that for the classical method. The Augmented Dickey-Fuller statistic is used instead. The Augmented Dickey-Fuller equation involving trend and intercept is:

$$\Delta x_t = \alpha_0 + \alpha_1 t + \alpha_2 x_{t-1} + \sum_{i=1}^{k} \beta_I \Delta x_{t-j} + \varepsilon_t \qquad ...(1)$$

In this model, which includes both a drift term and a deterministic trend, α_2 measures the degree of persistence of deviations of x_t from its mean. In the ADF test, the unit root is the null hypothesis. If $\alpha_2=0$, then the sequence, x_t, has a unit root and the deviations are permanent. In the ADF test, the estimated t-statistic of α_2 is compared with the appropriate critical value of the Dickey-Fuller statistics to validate the null hypothesis. The presence of a unit root implies the predominance of random effects, which have a permanent impact on the stochastic trend. In contrast, for the Mody and Yilmaz (1994) equation involving pooled cross-section and time series data,

11. This is evident from the survey on persistence in profits provided by Martin (1993).

the intercept term was of special interest for identfying persistence. It specifies the effect of country features that remain unobserved, which can be a potential cause of persistence in performance.

However, with the presence of a structural break in the time series, as is often the case with long sequence, usual Augmented Dickey-Fuller equation cannot be applied. This is because the ADF test for unit roots is biased in favour of non-rejection of the unit root (Enders, 1995: 243). The unit root test in the presence of structural break is different from the ADF test. Perron (1989) developed a formal procedure to test for unit roots incorporating structural change. The Perron's procedure, which is primarily based on a modified Augmented Dickey-Fuller equation, is as follow:[12]

$$\Delta x_t = \alpha_0 + \alpha_1 t + \alpha_2 x_{t-1} + \gamma D_L + \sum_{i=1}^{k} \beta_I \Delta x_{t-j} + \varepsilon_t \qquad ...(2)$$

where $D_L = 1$ if $t > \lambda$ and zero otherwise. Here, $a_2 = 1$ is the null hypothesis. Equation (2) can be rewritten with two breaks, as most of the series exhibit so. Despite the existence of statistically significant multiple breaks for many variables, the present unit root exercise is carried out with only one break due to reasons relating to the degrees of freedom. The above equation (2) can be further simplified by testing the null hypothesis of a change in the drift term against the alternative of a change in the slope of the trend. Then, the null hypothesis can be written as:

$$\Delta x_t = \alpha_0 + \alpha_1 x_{t-1} + \gamma D_L + \sum_{i=1}^{k} \beta_I \Delta x_{t-j} + \varepsilon_t \qquad ...(3)$$

However, the null hypothesis can neither be compared to the critical values calculated by Perron (1989), as they are applicable only in large sample cases. The Mackinnon values for testing the null, as used in case of Augmented Dickey-Fuller model, are used instead.[13] Even if the above procedure would help to identify unit roots in individual time series, it would not necessarily lead to conclude the factors causing such persistence.

To arrive at factors determining long-run persistence in manufactured export performance, the following reduced form equation can be estimated:

12. This is adopted from Enders, 1995: 245-248.

13. See Mackinnon, 1991.

$$mex_t = \alpha_0 + \alpha_1 reer_t + \alpha_2 gdpm_t + \alpha_3 wd_t + e_t \qquad ...(4)$$

where 'mex' represents manufactured exports at constant prices, 'reer' represents real effective exchange rate, 'gdpm' is value-added in manufacturing production, 'wd' is world demand and all the variables are in logarithmic form. It would have been ideal to estimate a simultaneous demand-supply equation system for the purpose or even a reduced form equation. The above equation (4) is somewhat similar in structure to a reduced form equation, often termed as an "eclectic" equation in the literature.[14]

The long-run equilibrium condition of equation (4) is estimated using the Engle-Granger two-step procedure.[15] The long run equilibrium relationship between exports and various explanatory factors might even exhibit a structural break. As is often the case with long run time series models, the adjustments are done in the cointegration regression by introducing a dummy variable. In the cointegrating regression, if the break point is known, the adjusted ADF test statistic would test for the null of no cointegration. With an unknown break point, the Gregory-Hansen procedure[16] is applied. Accordingly, the smallest value of the ADF test statistic would specify the time point at which the structural break has taken place while establishing a cointegrated relationship.

The dynamic error correction mechanism (ECM) of the cointegrated variables depicts the short run dynamics towards the achievement of long run equilibrium conditions. The ECM representation of the above equation (4) involving structural break can be as follows:

$$\Delta\, mex_t = \gamma_0 + \gamma_1 \Delta\, reer_t + \gamma_2 \Delta\, gdpm_t + \gamma_3 \Delta\, wd_t + \gamma_4 D_L + \gamma_5 \Delta\, (D_L{}^* \, reer) + \gamma_6 \Delta\, (D_L{}^* \, gdpm) + \gamma_7 \Delta\, (D_L{}^* \, wd) + \gamma_8 e_{t-1} + \mu \qquad ...(5)$$

14. Srinivasan (1998) uses this term while estimating India's export function. It is justified to term the equation "eclectic" in the sense that it accounts for both demand and supply side factors apart from the relative price variable REER, around which there is a sharp division in view points on the factors determining India's export performance.

15. The Johansen (1988) multivariate VAR procedure could have been used instead. But, it would be difficult to identify the exact cointegrating vector from the multiple equations involved in the Johansen method. Thus, given the objective finding the long run determinants of exports and given the simplicity of the method, the Engle-Granger "two step procedure" is used. For an exposition, refer Engle and Granger (1987: 262-4).

16. Gregory and Hansen, 1996: 105-6.

In equation (5), The coefficients γ_i represent the effects of various determinants on manufactured export performance, with $\gamma_1 < 0$, $\gamma_2 > 0$, and $\gamma_3 > 0$. "γ_8" - the coefficient of the error correction term - is indicative of the speed of adjustment and the negative coefficient shows that the errors correct to the equilibrium in the long run. In the ECM representation of the model, often lagged values of variables (dependent and independent) are introduced as explanatory variables.

SECTION 4

THE DATA

The data on different variables used in this paper have been drawn from different sources. Among these variables, while the data on manufactured exports (MEX) and production (GDPM) are used at constant prices, the data on real effective exchange rate (REER) and world demand (WD) are estimated, which needs elaboration. The data on the different variables are detailed as follows.

MEX: The data on India's manufactured exports are collected from the Monthly Statistics of Foreign Trade of India published by the Directorate General of Commercial Intelligence and Statistics (DGCI&S), Calcutta. For constant price estimates, the value of manufactured exports is deflated by Unit Value Index (UVI) of manufactured exports. In fact, unit value index for aggregate manufactured exports is not available. It is estimated based on the UVI of exports of different manufactured items, as provided by the DGCI&S, Calcutta. The DGCI&S quantity index data also provides an estimate of the volume of trade. As value of exports at constant prices and the export volume index have similar trends (Sinha Roy, 2001 a), the latter data could have been used instead.

GDPM: The data on manufacturing value-added are taken from the Government of India, National Accounts Statistics (NAS), various years. The data from this source covers not only production of registered units, but also of unregistered manufacturing units. That is why aggregate manufacturing value-added data used from the NAS source is better than that from the Annual Survey of Industry (ASI) source, which covers only registered manufacturing. The constant prices estimate is arrived at by deflating the current price figure by wholesale price index (WPI) for aggregate manufacturing.

REER: Real effective exchange rate (REER) is generally defined as

$$REER = e.\ (P^*/\ P) \qquad ...(6)$$

where P* and P are price indices of domestic economy and the trading partner economy respectively and "e" is the exchange rate of the domestic economy with respect to the trading partner economies calculated in terms of a numeraire as the SDR. Often WPI, consumer price index (CPI) or implicit GDP deflator are used for the purpose. An alternative way of constructing a proxy for the real exchange rate index is to use the trading partner country's WPI and the domestic country's CPI, where the former is treated as a proxy for prices of tradeables and the latter can be used for price of non-tradaeables. However, for the purpose here, unit value of exports is used relative to the WPI or import unit values of trading partner countries. In this exercise, bilateral real exchange rate is calculated with respect to the most prominent eleven trading partners of India. The multilateral or the real effective exchange rate of the rupee is the weighted average of the bilateral rates, the weights being the 1985 share of India's exports for these eleven trading partner countries. While the above weighting diagram has often been the practice in the literature, there are instances of using contemporaneous weights.[17]

WD: World Demand is represented by a sum total of imports of different countries would necessarily mean aggregate world demand.[18] As realised demand for India's exports are essentially lower than the potential, the aggregation of imports across countries necessitates adjustment. The effective demand is calculated as a weighted sum of imports of individual destination country, the weights being the destination's share in India's total exports in 1985. Such a weighting diagram not only takes into the importance of the individual country, but also takes into account, though indirectly, the structure of imports of individual destination country. The data on value of total imports of different destination countries are obtained from the IMF, International Financial Statistics Yearbook, various years.

17. The real exchange rate series as generated by the RBI and Pradhan use the share of exports for a particular base year as weights, Trivedi (1996) uses contemporaneous weights for the purpose.

18. Muscatelli *et al.*, (1995) use imports of export destination countries as a scale variable as against the practice of using world income, as in Goldstein and Khan (1978).

SECTION 5

THE ECONOMETRIC EVIDENCE

The existence of structural break, often multiple, in different variables led to the use of Perron model in the context of verifying stationarity. For 'mex', while testing for unit roots, 1985 is taken as the only breakpoint even if there are structural breaks at 1976 and 1985. On the other hand, even if the 'reer' series is found to have no significant break in trend, different breakpoints are tried while testing for unit roots. For other variables as well, even if there are multiple breaks, the estimation of the Perron equation took into account a single break only keeping in view the degrees of freedom. In the estimation of unit roots, as elucidated earlier, only level dummy (D_L) is considered. Though none of the variables are found to be level stationary, it is interesting to observe from Table 15.3 that the t-statistic of the coefficient α_1 for all the variables are found to be significant at 1 per cent level. Thus, manufactured exports along with all other variables are found to be integrated of order 1, I (1), after incorporating structural break. The unit root test confirms the existence of persistence in India's manufactured export performance. But, the existence of persistence in performance does not necessarily outline the causes behind such a long run phenomenon. The estimation of the long run equilibrium relationship between

Table 15.3

Unit Root Test for Manufactured Exports and Other Variables

Variable	*Levels/1st Difference*	*Structural Break at*	*t-Statistic*	*Level of Significance*	*Inference*
MEX	1st Difference	1985	-4.443	1%	I (1)
REER	1st Difference	1984	-5.964	1%	I (1)
		1983	-5.910	1%	I (1)
		No break/time	-6.007	1%	I (1)
WD	1st Difference	1973	-5.644	1%	I (1)
		1982	-5.010	1%	I (1)
GDPM	1st Difference	1975	-5.921	1%	I (1)
		1964	-5.439	1%	I (1)

Note: The level of significance is based on Mackinnon's critical values in Mackinnon (1991).

Source: Author's Calculation.

manufactured exports and other variables and the short-run dynamics involved therein would establish the case of persistence in manufactured export growth performance and the causes underlying such a phenomenon.

Since the dependent variable along with all the three independent variables are I (1), they are cointegrated. As all the variables have structural breaks, there is a possibility that the equilibrium relationship also might have a structural break. In identifying the break, it is necessary to view the residual plot of the actual relationship in equation (4). Figure 15.2 plots the actual, fitted and residual plots of equation (4). The figure very clearly shows that the residual plot has breaks at around the mid-seventies and the mid-eighties. This would necessitate a trial and error method of identifying the breakpoint of the cointegrating regression. This would be in terms of the minimum ADF, as required by the Gregory-Hansen (1996) method discussed above.

Figure 15.2

Residual Plot of Equation (4)

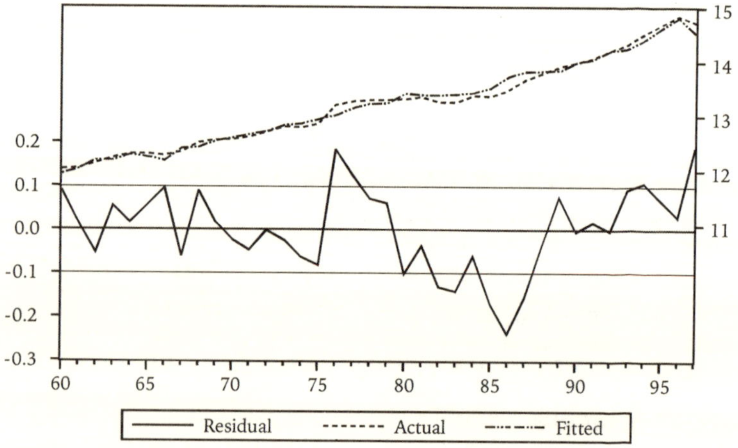

Though more than one break in the residuals can be observed from Figure 15.2, the cointegrating relationship is found out incorporating only one break around the mid-eighties. For the purpose, estimations are carried out with structural breaks at years between 1982 and 1987. Table 15.4 shows that the estimated cointegrating equations with breaks at different years are without lag and the ADF statistic is significant at 1 per cent level for all the years. The lowest ADF for the year 1984 is indicative of a significant structural break in the cointegrating relationship in that year.

Table 15.4

Cointegrating Relationship Involving Structural Break With Unknown Breakpoint

Break at	*No. of Lag(s) in CR*	*Coefficient of CR*	*t-Statistic*	*Level of Significance*
1982	No lag	-0.677	-4.380	1%
1983	No lag	-0.686	-4.363	1%
1984	No lag	-0.738	-4.593	1%
1985	No lag	-0.715	-4.480	1%
1986	No lag	-0.740	-4.589	1%
1987	No lag	-0.684	-4.334	1%

Note: CR means cointegrating regression.
Source: Author's calculation.

By incorporating structural break at 1984, the estimated equation of long term manufactured export performance is as follows:

$$\underset{}{mex_t} = \underset{(3.86)^{\#}}{9.691} - \underset{(-3.87)^{\#}}{1.162\ reer_t} + \underset{(3.94)^{\#}}{0.480\ gdpm_t} + \underset{(2.70)^{\#\#}}{0.285\ wd_t} - \underset{(-2.38)^{\#\#}}{10.236\ d84}$$

$$+ \underset{(0.44)}{1.015\ d84{*}wd_t} + \underset{(1.12)}{0.439\ d84{*}reer_t} + \underset{(0.85)}{0.45\ d84{*}gdpm_t} + e_t \quad \ldots (7)$$

Adj. R^2 = 0.99, d.w. = 1.45, s.e.e. = 0.07.

(Figures in the parentheses denote tabulated t-statistic. (#) denotes significance at 1 per cent, while (##) denotes significance at 5 per cent.)

The results in equation (7) could have been improved by dropping the explanatory variables that are insignificant. But, all the explanatory variables, whether statistically significant or insignificant, are retained as they together determine long run performance of manufactured exports. Figure 15.3 plots the residuals of the above estimated equation (7), which is indeed different from the residual plot shown in Figure 15.2.

Figure 15.3

Time Path of "e_t" With Break at 1984

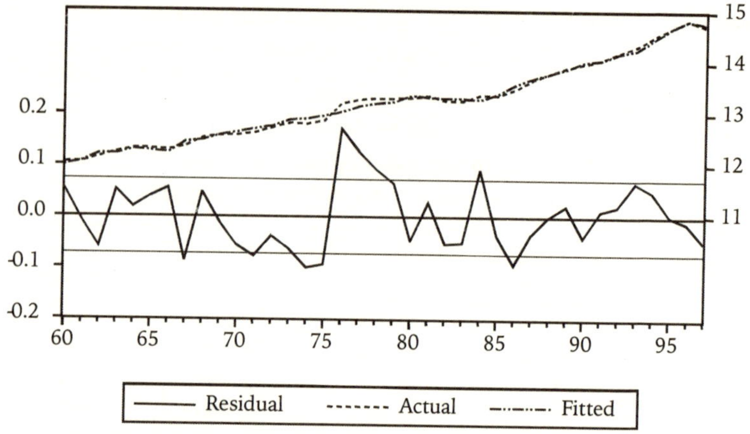

The stationarity test of the residual "e_t", which confirms cointegration with a break at 1984, is as follows:

$$\Delta e_t = -\ 0.738\ e_{t-1} + \varepsilon_t \qquad \text{...(8)}$$
$$(-4.593)^{**}$$

$$\text{Adj. } R^2 = 0.37, \text{ d.w.} = 1.91, \text{ s.e.e.} = 0.06.$$

(Figures in the parenthesis denote tabulated t-statistic, which is significant at 1 per cent against the Mackinnon critical value of -2.626.)

The above estimates in equations (7) and (8) unambiguously confirm that manufactured exports from India and world demand, GDP in manufacturing and real effective exchange have an equilibrium long run relationship. The error correction model would help to understand the short run dynamics and identify the different causal factors leading the long run phenomenon of persistence in performance.

The estimates of the ECM equation (5) are given in Table 15.5. In all the ECM specifications, the coefficient of "e_{t-1}" is significant indicating that the errors correct for the long run equilibrium path. The various factors such as real effective exchange rate, GDP in manufacturing and world demand have impact on correcting short-run disequilibrium and thus, contribute to the existence of persistence in manufactured export performance. However, none of these variables are found to have significant impact after 1984.

Table 15.5 shows the significance of the relative price factor, real effective exchange rate, in the short run dynamics of manufactured export performance. But, the relative price factor is not found to be significant during the post-1984 period when the exchange rate was used as a policy instrument to promote exports. The supply-side scalar factor, GDP in manufacturing, also cause the errors to adjust for the long run equilibrium. The impact of GDP in manufacturing on persistence of manufactured export performance is not as significant as in the case of real effective exchange rate. In fact, in ECM specification III, the variable is not found to be having a significant impact or in ECM specification I, the significance of the coefficient is only at 10 per cent level. Nonetheless, growth of GDP in manufacturing is found to have a relatively better impact on growth in manufactured exports after the mid-eighties.

Apart from the above factors, world demand is found to have significant impact on India's exports of manufactured items. Table 15.5 would show that the impact of this demand side scalar variable is significant at 1 per cent level in certain specifications. Thus, world demand has a predominant effect on persistence in manufactured export performance, in India, over the long run. However, the coefficient for the variable has a negative sign for the post-1984 period, though insignificant. Nonetheless, market access related problems assume importance in this context. Even after liberalisation of world trade in various rounds of multilateral trade negotiations, market access problems for exports from such developing countries as India continue to persist.[19] Elsewhere (Sinha Roy, 2002) it is argued that the market access problems necessarily lead to mismatch between structures of India's exports and world demand. As a result, the perpetuating market access problem provides an upper limit to the realisation of potential world demand and hence, realised world

19. Despite substantial liberalisation of trade in the Uruguay Round of multilateral negotiations, market access problems of developing country exports continue to exist necessarily in terms of tariff peaks, other non-tariff barriers and tariff escalation (UNCTAD, 2000). Mehta and Mohanty (1999) have shown the extent of tariff and non-tariff barriers hindering market access to Indian exports in the post-Uruguay Round scenario.

demand differs from the potential.[20] It is the growth of effective world demand that is of relevance to the growth of manufactured exports over the long run.

Table 15.5

Error Correction Specification of Manufactured Export Growth (Δmex_t) with Structural Break at 1984

Variable	*ECM Specification I*	*ECM Specification II*	*ECM Specification III*	*ECM Specification IV*
$\Delta reer_t$	-0.49 (-2.38)**	-0.42 (-2.06)**	-0.47 (-2.31)**	-0.42 (-2.20)**
Δ $gdpm_t$	0.34 (1.73)***	0.46 (2.52)**	0.29 (1.41)	0.39 (2.06)**
Δ wd_t	0.60 (3.65)*	0.55 (3.31)*	0.49 (2.73)**	0.43 (2.47)**
d 84	0.01 (0.46)	0.01 (0.62)	-0.01 (-0.24)	
Δ (d84* $reer_t$)	-0.18 (-0.71)	-0.28 (-1.08)	-0.24 (-0.91)	-0.30 (-1.35)
Δ (d84* $gdpm_t$)	0.85 (1.81)***	0.12 (1.07)	0.78 (1.66)	0.14 (1.37)
Δ (d84* wd_t)	-0.58 (-1.59)		-0.51 (-1.39)	
Δ mex_{t-1}			0.21 (1.44)	0.22 (1.70)***
e_{t-1}	-0.57 (-3.95)*	-0.56 (-3.76)*	-0.65 (-4.16)*	-0.64 (-4.13)*
Adj. R^2	0.67	0.64	0.60	0.60
Period	1960-97	1960-97	1960-97	1960-97

Source: Author's Calculation.

On the whole, persistence in India's manufactured export performance is explained by such factors as world demand, real effective exchange rate and GDP in manufacturing. However, the short run variations of these explanatory variables do not fully explain yearly changes in manufactured exports. This is evident from the Adjusted R^2 of the different specifications of the ECM model, as

20. Nayyar (1988) have also argued that various barriers to trade have put an upper limit to growth of exports from India.

shown in Table 15.5. Various other supply side factors such as investment or productivity growth, sunk cost, transactional infrastructure and procedural bottlenecks,[21] if taken into account, could have explained the phenomenon of persistence in export performance in a much more robust way.

SECTION 6

SUMMARY AND IMPLICATIONS

The paper confirms the existence of persistence in India's manufactured export performance. This result is consistent with the findings of Mody and Yilmaz (1994). India's manufactured export performance persists despite structural break in 1984. Such persistence in India's manufactured export performance is explained in terms of a large number of demand and supply side factors. Though real effective exchange rate and GDP in manufacturing are significant factors explaining long run behaviour of manufactured exports, their effects are not as significant as that of world demand in determining persistence in manufactured export performance. As relative prices are relatively less significant in explaining persistence in manufactured export performance, they are less effective as an instrument in promoting manufactured exports.

On the demand-side, persistence in performance is largely due to the continuing market access problem in world trade faced by developing countries like India. The perpetuating market access restrictions creates an asymmetry between India's export structure and the pattern of world demand and thus, set an upper limit on the realisation of potential world demand. To a large extent, persistence in manufactured export performance is determined by the resulting effective world demand. This is typically a phenomenon relating to developing countries facing residual world demand. Such persisting market access problem has to be tackled by developing countries adopting a two pronged strategy. Apart from negotiating for a greater market access at the multilateral level, developing countries, and especially India, have to stress on diversifying the export basket

21. Based on a micro theoretic approach, Marjit (1998) has provided evidence on the extent of procedural bottlenecks faced by exporters and the transaction costs involved therein.

towards more value-added and high technology products.[22] This would entail India to move on to a higher value-added growth path.

The relatively less importance of manufacturing GDP as a supply-side determinant of persistence in manufactured export growth shows that the shifts to higher value-added growth would improve the significance of the factor in explaining long run performance. Along with improvements in efficiency, the performance of manufactured exports can also be improved by removing structural impediments in terms of provision of better infrastructure, simplification of trade procedures and focussing on various transactional factors as marketing associated with the sale of manufactures. Further, improvements on the supply side can result from the preparedness of the domestic manufacturing sector to face the challenges and opportunities emerging in the post-MFA scenario. Such developments on the supply side would necessarily result in the diversification of the export basket towards more efficient[23] and higher value-added products. As a result, higher world demand can be realised and larger benefits would accrue to the export sector from every outward shift in world demand.

22. Lall (1999) is of the view that, in contrast to trade in high technology and knowledge intensive products, low skill and technology intensive products are not only low value adding but are also slow moving due to increasing price competition.

23. Das (2001), in terms of a disaggregated analysis, has shown that productivity growth has improved in case of certain manufactures during reforms.

References

Bhagwati, J. (1988). "Export Promoting Protection: Endogenous Monopoly and Price Disparity," *Pakistan Development Review*, 27: 1-5.

Bhagwati, J. and T.N. Srinivasan (1975). *Foreign Trade Regimes and Economic Development: India*, New York: Columbia University Press (for the NBER).

Bhattacharjea, A. (1995). "Protection and Exports," *Economic and Political Weekly*, 30: 2208-10.

Bose, A. (1993). "Liberalisation Debate: Some Careless Mistakes," *Economic and Political Weekly*, 28: 1612-4.

Brahmbhatt, M., T.G. Srinivasan and K. Murrel (1996). "India in the Global Economy," *Policy Research Working Paper No. 1681*, International Economic Analysis and Prospects Division, International Economics Department, Washington D.C.: World Bank, November.

Campbell, J.Y. and N.G. Mankiw (1987). "Permanent and Transitory Components in Macroeconomic Fluctuations," *American Economic Review* (AEA Papers and Proceedings), 77: 111-7.

Das, D.K. (2001). *Some Aspects of Productivity Growth and Trade in Indian Industry*, unpublished Ph.D. Thesis, Delhi School of Economics, Delhi, November.

Dua, P., and T. Mishra (1999). "Presence of Persistence in Industrial Production: The Case of India," *Indian Economic Review*, 34: 23-38.

Enders, W. (1995). *Applied Econometric Time Series*, New York: John Wiley and Sons Inc..

Engle, R.F. and C.W.J. Granger (1987). "Co-integration and Error Correction Representation, Estimation and Testing," *Econometrica*, 55: 251-276.

Goldstein, M. and M.S. Khan (1978). "The Supply and Demand for Exports: A Simultaneous Approach," *Review of Economic and Statistics*, 60: 275-286.

Gregory, A.W., and B.E. Hansen (1996). "Residual Based Tests for Cointegration in Models with Regime Shifts," *Journal of Econometrics*, 71: 99-126.

Joshi, V. and I.M.D. Little (1994). *India: Macroeconomics and Political Economy, 1964-1991*, Delhi: Oxford University Press.

Krishnamurthy, K. and V. Pandit (1995). "India's Trade Flows: Alternative Policy Scenarios: 1995-2000," *Working Paper No.: 32*, Delhi: Centre for Development Economics, Delhi School of Economics.

Krishnan, R. and K. Sen (1995). "Measuring Persistence in Industrial Output: The Indian Case," *Journal of Development Economics*, 48: 25-41.

Kumar, N. (2002). "Infrastructure Availability, Foreign Direct Investment Inflows and their Export-orientation: A Cross-Country Exploration," *RIS-Discussion Paper No. 26*, New Delhi: Research and Information System for the Non-Aligned and Other Developing Countries.

Lall, S. (1999). "India's Manufactured Exports: Comparative Structure and Prospects," *World Development*, 27: 1769-86.

Mackinnon, J. (1991). "Critical Values for Cointegration Tests," in R.F. Engle and C.W.J. Granger (eds.), *Long-Run Economic Relationships: Readings in Cointegration*, Oxford: The University Press.

Marjit, S. (1998). "Transaction Costs of India's Exports: An Analysis," *Occasional Paper No. 64*, Mumbai: Export-Import Bank of India.

Marjit, S., and A. Ray Chaudhuri (1997). *India's Exports*, Delhi: Oxford University Press.

Marjit, S., and A. Sarkar (1995). "Protection and Exports: A Theoretical Note," *Economic and Political Weekly*, 30: 809-10.

Martin, S. (1993). *Advanced Industrial Economics*, Oxford, UK: Blackwell.

Mehta, R., and S.K. Mohanty (1999). *WTO and Industrial Tariffs: An Empirical Analysis for India*, New Delhi: Research and Information System for the Non-Aligned and Other Developing Countries.

Mody, A. and K. Yilmaz (1994). "Is There Persistence in the Growth of Manufactured Exports?: Evidence from Newly Industrialising Countries," *Policy Research Working Paper: 1276*, Trade Policy Division, Washington D.C.: World Bank.

Muscatelli, V.A., A.A. Stevenson and C. Montagna (1995). "Modelling Aggregate Manufactured Exports for Some Asian Newly Industrialized Countries," *Review of Economic and Statistics*, 77: 147-55.

Nayyar, D. (1988). "India's Export Performance: Underlying Factors and Constraints," in R.E.B. Lucas and G.F. Papanek (eds.), *The Indian Economy: Recent Development and Future Prospects*, Delhi: Oxford University Press.

Panchamukhi, V.R. (1997). "Quantitative Methods and their Applications in International Economics," in K.L. Krishna (ed.), *Econometric Applications in India*, Delhi: Oxford University Press.

Perron, P. (1995). "The Great Crash, The Oil Shock, and the Unit Root Hypothesis," *Econometrica*, 57: 1361-1401.

Sinha Roy, S. (2001a). "India's Trade Database: Contours, Inconsistencies and Ways Ahead," *Economic and Political Weekly*, 36: 51-58.

————. (2001b). "Post-reforms Exports Growth in India: An Exploratory Analysis," *RIS-Discussion Paper No. 13*, New Delhi: Research and Information System for the Non-aligned and Other Developing Countries.

————. (2002). *Development Strategy and Macroeconomic Performance: An Enquiry into India's Export Growth During 1960-97*, (mimeo).

Srinivasan, T.N. (1998). "India's Export Performance: A Comparative Analysis" in I.J. Ahluwalia and I.M.D. Little (eds.), *India's Economic Reforms and Development: Essays for Manmohan Singh*, Delhi: Oxford University Press.

Trivedi, P. (1996). "Real Effective Exchange Rate Indices of the Rupee: A Comparison of Selected Alternative Studies," *ArthaVijnana*, 38: 65-94.

UNCTAD (2000). "The Post-Uruguay Round Tariff Environment for Developing Country Exports: Tariff Peaks and Tariff Escalations," *UNCTAD/WTO Joint Study – TD/B/COM.1/14/Rev. 1*, January 28.

Part 4

MNC and Technology Transfer in Indian Industries

16

Foreign Direct Investment, Technology Transfer and Growth

V.N. BALASUBRAMANYAM
DAVID SAPSFORD

SECTION 1

INTRODUCTION

Each and every aspect of foreign direct investment (FDI) has generated a vast literature. Its role in transferring technology and know-how to developing countries is no exception. The debate in the past was centred on the notion that the technologies and products produced by multinational enterprises (MNEs), the principal source of FDI, were inappropriate to the factor endowments and income levels of developing countries. Recent developments in the world economy have steered the debate in new directions. Although the subject continues to be controversial, the opposition to FDI has waned considerably. Indeed, suspicion and distrust of foreign firms seems to have yielded place to a new-found faith in their ability to promote growth and development objectives. A number of factors have influenced this change in attitudes including their increased familiarity with the operations of MNEs, reduced flows of alternative sources of finance such as bank credit and foreign aid and the perception that developing countries in East Asia may owe their growth in part to FDI. Further, the information technology revolution has wrought dramatic changes both with respect to the channels through which technology and know-how is transmitted and its impact on the technology absorptive capacity of host entities. Much less dramatic than the other factors, but nonetheless significant, is the growth in cross border movement of labour. The interrelationships between trade, labour flows and FDI opens up new vistas for research concerning technology and know-how transfer. Further additions to the research menu spring from theoretical developments such as the analysis of convergence and the endogenous growth theory which provide a novel framework for the analysis of FDI, technology transfer and growth.

This brief paper does not attempt to review the vast literature on FDI and technology transfer. Instead its focus is on two interrelated issues of concern to developing countries intent on harnessing FDI to serve their development objectives; factors which influence transborder flows of technology and know-how and the preconditions for the efficient utilisation of imported technology and know-how in the industrialisation process. The paper divides as follows. Section 2 discusses the theoretical literature on the determinants of FDI in developing countries. Section 3 reviews the extant empirical work on determinants. Section 4 discusses the main propositions embedded in the thoeretical literature on trade, FDI and growth. Section 5 discusses the empirical literature on FDI and growth. Section 6 pulls together the main conclusions and identifies areas for further research.

SECTION 2

DETERMINANTS

Why do firms go abroad? Krugman and Obstfeld (2000) argue that there is no specific theory of FDI of the sort we have on trade. Most of what MNEs do trade can do, *albeit* not as well as MNEs do. Shifting of labour-intensive operations from labour scarce to labour rich countries and the export of capital from capital rich to capital scarce countries could be done by trade. Admittedly so. But the main purpose of FDI is to form multinational organisations, which allow for control over operations. An essential attribute of MNEs is that by undertaking FDI they are able to transfer technology and know-how and it is their ability to do so which allows them control over operations.

Much of the received theory on FDI is centred on this notion of control. The origins of the theoretical literature on the issue of control is to be traced to Stephen Hymer's celebrated doctoral thesis (1960) grounded in industrial organisation theory. Although what did Hymer actually say is the subject of a number of studies, his thesis briefly put is that FDI is the preferred route to exploiting the rents inherent in the ownership advantages firms possess. The fruits of R & D, these advantages include patented technology, team specific managerial skills, marketing skills and brand names. trade and licensing agreements are generally inferior to FDI as methods of market penetration because the market for knowledge or advantages possessed by firms tends to be imperfect. In other words they do not permit to exercise control over operations essential for retaining and fully exploiting the advantages firms own. Hymer's insights form the basis for other explanations such as the transactions cost and internalisation theories (Buckley and Casson, 1991), most of which in essence argue that firms internalise operations, forge backward and forward linkages in order to by-pass the market with all its imperfections. Dunning (1973) neatly synthesises these and other explanations in the well-known eclectic paradigm of the MNE. For a firm to successfully invest abroad it needs to own advantages which no other firm possess, it must be capable of internalising operations and the country it wishes to invest in should offer location advantages. Internalisation is synonymous with the ability of firms to exercise control over operations. Such control is essential for the exploitation of the advantages which firms possess and the location advantages which host countries offer.

It is the location advantages emphasised by Dunning, which forms the core of much of the discussion on the determinants of FDI in developing countries. The two other attributes necessary for FDI are taken as given from the perspective of developing countries. Location factors are broadly defined to include factor endowments of the host countries, macro economic characteristics including growth and inflation, foreign trade and industrialisation policies, political stability and regulations governing the operations of foreign enterprises. These and other location specific attributes influence the investment decision process of foreign enterprises including the volume and nature of technology and know-how they transfer abroad. Location factors may also influence the ability of firms to internalise operations. Government regulations on FDI, trade related investment measures (TRIMS), such as local content requirements, stipulations regarding equity ownership and labour laws can constrain the ability of foreign firms to exercise control over operations. Faced with such constraints foreign firms may delimit the volume and quality of FDI they undertake and hence the volume and quality of technology transferred (Greenaway, 1991; Balasubramanyam, 1991). So too can the type of foreign trade regimes in place in the host countries.

It is now an established proposition that outward looking trade policies as opposed to inward looking trade policies attract relatively large volumes of FDI (Bhagwati, 1978; Balasubramnayam and Salisu, 1991). The latter type of regimes, exemplified by the import-substituting trade and industrialisation policies, introduce a variety of factor and product market distortions hardly conducive to the operations of profit maximising firms. The incentives they offer in the form of protection from import competition and in many cases competition from domestic sources also are artificial and transient. It is also an acknowledged proposition that in the absence of genuine location advantages such as stability of policies and an economic environment conducive to the operations of profit maximising firms incentives such as tax holidays and concessions and investment subsidies are unlikely to attract FDI.

The principal concern of foreign firms is the preservation of the monopoly over advantages they enjoy. Widespread dissemination of the technology and know-how would deprive them of the monopoly over advantages they enjoy. This in fact is the basis for internalisation of operations. Acquisition and dissemination of technology and know-how, however, is the objective of the recipients of FDI. The dilemma facing developing countries is how best to maximise the quality and volume of technology foreign firms transfer while at the same time minimising the control over operations they exercise. It is worth noting that there is no guarantee that maximisation of profits by foreign firms will necessarily promote the social objectives of recipients of FDI. In other words, private rates of return to FDI may diverge from social rates of return. Policies, that beget substantial volumes of FDI, may not necessarily promote social objectives such as employment creation and reduction of income disparities. For instance, export processing zones which are ubiquitous in developing countries may attract substantial volumes of FDI but they may not always yield the hoped for social dividends in the form of dissemination of technology and employment creation.

These and other dilemmas facing developing countries in the context of FDI though severe may not be insoluble. Perhaps the one and only policy option which is open to developing countries eager for the technology and know-how which FDI transmits is promotion of competition in the market place. Foreign firms faced with competition from both domestic and international sources would be compelled to act in a manner which promotes the objectives of recipient countries. This in fact is the message which Bhagwati conveys with the proposition that, on balance, given all other factors influencing FDI flows and their efficacy an EP strategy is likely to both attract a higher volume of FDI and promote more efficient utilisation thereof than an IS strategy. In the face of competition foreign firms would have an incentive to restructure and adapt the technologies they transmit. Such technologies and know-how could consist of both tacit knowledge and those embodied in materials and equipment. In the face of competition they may also seek ways and methods of enhancing the range of advantages they possess. One such avenue may be joint ventures. They may seek to enter joint ventures with locally owned firms with a view to obtaining skills including production and marketing skills complementary to the ones they possess. Such genuine joint ventures as opposed to forced ventures dictated by government policy may promote objectives of shared control and dissemination of know-how to locally owned entities. Competition in the market place may also promote externalities i.e. investments which yield social rates of returns in excess of private rates of returns. In the face of competition, cost minimising and profit maximising firms would have an incentive to invest in training of labour and bear the search costs involved in seeking relatively inexpensive and efficient sources of suppliers of materials and equipment in the host countries. Sub-contracting arrangements between locally owned firms and foreign firms for the production of equipment and materials would be one method of knowledge dissemination.

Needless to say promotion of effective competition requires well-designed trade and macro economic policies including exchange rate policies. Competition can thrive only in a stable distortion free macro economic environment. It is worth noting in this context that piecemeal attempts at removing distortions may not yield fruit. For instance, policies designed to liberalise the foreign trade regime which leave factor-market distortions untouched may belong to the realm of the second best. A liberalised trade regime may force competition, it may also allow foreign firms to source their requirements of materials and equipment from the cheapest source. But faced with distortions in the labour market such as restrictions on the hiring and firing of labour and stringent wage legislation, they may opt to service the market from their home base through exports rather than through FDI. India's failure to attract substantial volumes of FDI following the 1991 reforms may be explained in these terms. Trade liberalisation in India has not been matched by removal of distortions in the labour market.

Effective competition in the market place also presupposes the existence of adequate infrastructure facilities and a pool of trainable labour. Empirical studies on the determinants of FDI do capture these elements. There are though very few studies which explicitly identify the impact of competition on the volume of technology and know-how countries receive.

SECTION 3

EMPIRICAL TESTS OF DETERMINANTS

The vast literature on the economics of FDI has spawned, in its wake, a large number of empirical studies. They vary widely in terms of both their level of statistical sophistication and the data sample analysed. Two observations may be in order here. First, the empirical literature has emerged in a somewhat haphazard and piecemeal fashion - with statistical and econometric results of varying degrees of plausibility pertaining to particular theoretical arguments appearing almost before the ink from the theoreticians pen has dried. As a result the econometric literature on FDI lacks a cohesive framework and progression of the sort found in the theoretical literature. Second, there is disturbing tendency for the requirements of statistical technique and dogma to dominate the requirements of the particular problem, with the consequence that at least some recent econometric work has succeeded more in obscuring rather than illuminating our understanding of the FDI phenomenon. Set against this backcloth our objective here is to provide a balanced overview of what we do and do not know about the determinants of FDI in developing countries.

Especially influential in the early literature were two studies undertaken by Dunning (1973, 1981). For an application of Dunning's methodology to the case of FDI in India see Kumar (1990). On the basis of survey evidence gathered from entrepreneurs engaged in trans-national production Dunning (1973) concluded that the magnitude of FDI is determined by three sets of factors; market forces (including market size and growth, as determined by the national income of the recipient country), cost factors (such as labour cost and availability and the domestic inflation situation) and the investment climate (as determined by such considerations as the extent of foreign indebtedness and the state of the balance of payments). Dunning's later work proposed a theory of FDI, based upon elements stemming out of theories of the firm, industrial organisation and location, that places the issue of internalisation at centre stage. This theory, was tested by Dunning (1981) using a statistical approach that some subsequent analysts describe as 'unnecessarily complicated and difficult to interpret' (Schneider and Frey, 1985; p. 165). In this paper Dunning considered the experience of some 67 primarily (although not exclusively) developing countries over the period 1967 to 1978. Dividing this sample into three sub-samples, on the basis of a variant of cluster analysis in which per capita GNP is given prominence and employing stepwise regression, Dunning reports evidence to suggest that flows of investment (in, out and net) are influenced by organisational variables (including human capital stocks, as proxied by skill levels, and research and development expenditures) as well as by internalisation (as proxied by royalties and fees received by local firms as a proportion of those received by foreign affiliates) and locational factors (as represented by such variables as labour earnings, output growth, infrastructure quality and tax burden).[1] Dunning could, however, find no evidence to support the hypothesis that business risk (as proxied by the Business Environment Risk Index, itself a weighted average of a set of survey based indices measuring such factors as political stability, quality of local bureaucracy and the likelihood of nationalisation) influences investment flows.

1. The basis of Schneider and Frey's criticism of Dunning's statistical technique is essentially in the spirit of Leamer's well known point that it is verging on the tautological to use the same statistical information twice, in Dunning's case to form the sub-groups and then to analyse variations within them.

Dunning's (1973, 1981) arguments and analysis proved influential and were pursued further by others. Agarwal (1980) produced a detailed survey of the then existing literature on the determinants of FDI, the findings of which echo many of Dunning's.[2] Widely cited in the early literature is the study of inflows of (non-extractive) investment into 58 developing countries during the period 1966 to 1970, by Root and Ahmed (1979). Sub-dividing the total sample of countries into three groups according to their 'attractiveness' to foreign investment (as gauged by actual per capita inflows of non-extractive FDI over the period) the study examines 38 potentially important discriminators for the country groups, encompassing not only economic, but also social and political factors.[3] Employing multiple discriminant analysis in preference to multiple regression analysis, Root and Ahmed conclude that developing countries, which received the most non-extractive FDI per capita, were those that had substantial urbanisation, coupled with a relatively advanced infrastructure (as measured by the ratio of expenditure on commerce, transport and communication to GDP), comparatively high domestic growth rates and per capita GDP, plus political stability. Notice that the finding regarding the host country's growth rate echoes the findings reported in Dunning (1973 and 1981). On the downside, frequent changes in government seemed to act as a deterrent to non-extractive FDI inflows, although direct governmental involvement in infrastructure and industrialisation programmes did show up as exerting a significant positive influence on investment inflows. Although the study was criticised on the grounds of the particular potential determinants (and proxies thereof) chosen, its strength lies in the impressive array of potential determinants that it was able to consider before arriving at a parsimonious list of significant determinants of FDI flows into developing countries.

In a similar vein, Levis (1979) investigates the determinants of inflows of FDI into a sample of 25 African, Asian and Latin American developing countries over the period 1965 to 67. Although two political variables were included in this study (these being a

2. See also Dunning's (1973) review of empirical studies of FDI.

3. A full listing of these 38 variables may be found in Root and Ahmed's Table 2 (1979, p. 754).

'political competition index' measuring the legitimacy of the prevailing political system, and a measure of the strength of relations between the host country and COMECON countries) Levis interpreted the empirical findings as evidence that a set of economic factors were dominant in explaining variations in FDI. This set comprised per capita GNP (as a measure of 'quality of life'),[4] the balance of payments and the shares of taxes and social services in GNP (seen as a measure of government 'capabilities'). Levis's study has been criticised on the grounds of the presence of some perverse signs (e.g. Schneider and Frey, 1985, p. 164). However, its findings in respect of the roles of per capita income and (if one interprets Levis's tax share variable as capturing, amongst other factors, governmental infrastructural expenditure) infrastructure accord with those of Root and Ahmed (1979) and various subsequent investigators (e.g. Balasubramanyam and Salisu, 1991; Veugelers, 1991). Levis's (1979) finding regarding the significance of the balance of payments is also consistent with the survey evidence reported in Dunning (1973).

In some areas of the literature FDI is seen in the wider macroeconomic context as playing a role in the external adjustment process. From this perspective, Goldsbrough (1979) investigates the extent to which FDI flows are influenced by movements in both the relative competitiveness and real aggregate demand of the host countries. On the basis of some rather rigid assumptions regarding the specific form taken by the distributed lag scheme relating real aggregate demand to the desired capital stock Goldsbrough reports regression results relating to the determinants of inflows and outflows of US, German, UK and Japanese FDI. The study period is 1961 through to mid 1977 for the first two countries and 1964 to mid 1977 for the latter two. In this study relative competitiveness in the host country is proxied by unit labour costs adjusted for movements in the exchange rate, while aggregate demand is proxied by an index of final demand for manufactures in the host country. The results reported by Goldsbrough suggest that the FDI flows were

4. More specifically, Levis (1979) explores the influence on FDI flows of a broader 'quality of life' index, which includes not only per capita GNP but also the number of doctors and hospitals per 1,000 inhabitants and per capita calorie consumption.

significantly related to movements in both real aggregate demand and relative competitiveness. However, as the author acknowledges (Goldsbrough, 1979, p. 751) the estimated parameters relating these two variables to FDI flows vary widely between the countries considered. Although useful, the results of this study need to be approached with caution; firstly because of the rather restrictive nature of the distributed lag schemes that are imposed upon the data and secondly, because of limitations regarding the adequacy of the particular proxies adopted for the theoretically relevant variables. The use of unit labour costs as the sole measure of, in Dunning's terminology, locational cost advantage is questionable as it ignores movements in other variables that feed into production costs; including the cost of raw materials and the costs and productivity of the other co-operating factors of production. Similarly the adequacy of the aggregate demand proxy used may be questioned since it ignores not only variations in real demand for non-manufactured goods but also services; the latter consideration being particularly important in the context of more recent periods. Although reasonably sophisticated by the standards of its day the econometric techniques employed by Goldsbrough (1979) appear rather restrictive (especially in regard to the treatment of distributed lags) by today's standards and it would therefore be a useful exercise to update the study to the more recent experience using today's less restrictive approach to the distributed lag issue, coupled with the use of more adequate proxies for the theoretically relevant variable.

At the risk of over-simplification it may be concluded that the message emanating consistently from these early studies is that FDI flows are related to the following host country characteristics; per capita national income/aggregate demand and its growth, infrastructural quality, state of the balance of payments, the pace of domestic inflation, human capital stocks, and unit labour costs as a component of overall production costs. Although the empirical literature continues to grow unabated both in size and econometric sophistication,[5] its overall message has served to reinforce rather

5. Unfortunately, in this rush towards increased econometric sophistication, many researchers seem to overlook some potentially serious data problems that exist in respect of the FDI flow data, problems that become especially marked when it comes to making comparisons across countries. For detailed discussion see Ramstetter (1992).

than contradict the conclusions of the earlier literature described above.[6,7]

For example, in a study of intra-OECD distribution of foreign affiliates, Veugelers reports that 'sharing the language, being a neighbour, and having a large market are all elements which stimulate the location of foreign affiliates' (1991, p. 371). Langhammer (1991) analyses changes in the destination of Dutch, Japanese, UK, US and German FDI between the 1970s and 1980s and argues that these can in part be accounted for by differentials in overall macro performance as between various Asian and Latin American economies. In a study of the determinants of inward flows of FDI into the US, Roy (1989) concludes that affiliate production is intensive in the use of firm specific human and physical capital and that relative gains in real US growth, along with industry-specific growth, exerted a positive effect on the propensity of foreign firms to invest in the US. Interestingly, evidence is also reported to suggest that inward investments into the US are, whenever possible, timed so as to take advantage of a relatively favourable exchange for the dollar.[8]

It is important to recognise that the 1990s saw the emergence of a number of studies that sought to trace the 'knock-on' effects (particularly labour market effects) of investment abroad on the domestic economy. A number of the findings reported in this literature are relevant to the present discussion. For example, in a comparative study of the US and Swedish cases Blomstrom, Fors and

---

6. Narula and Wakerlin (1998) express a different view, at least as far as developed economies are concerned. On the basis of a study of the determinants of US FDI into the manufacturing sectors of seven industrial countries they conclude that the determinants of FDI vary considerably from one host country to another.

7. Direct investment flows in the 1990s accounted for around twenty five per cent of total international capital flows, having grown since the 1970s relative to other forms of international investment. For detailed discussion, see Lipsey (1999) and Lipsey, Blomstrom and Ramstetter (1995).

8. The relationship between flows of FDI into the US and the (real) exchange rate is explored in more detail by Klein and Rosengren (1994), who argue that the link between these variables is a reflection of wealth effects rather than of relative labour costs, as argued by earlier analysts. However, the findings reported in this paper need to be approached with a degree of caution, not least because the authors appear to base their conclusions on an analysis of relative wages rather than relative unit labour costs (1994, p. 381). It remains to be seen therefore, whether their conclusion is robust to the inclusion into the model of differential movements in labour productivity.

Lipsey (1997) report evidence to suggest that US firms tend to allocate labour-intensive portions of their output, or labour-intensive stages of production, to affiliates in low-wage countries in order to take advantage of lower wage costs; a result consistent with findings reported above in respect of earlier studies.[9,10] Further evidence consistent with this finding is reported by Hatzius (1997a). Using panel data relating to Swedish multinational corporations, estimated labour demand functions indicate that these firms do reallocate employment between the home and overseas market as relative labour costs change. In a subsequent study of German and UK inflows and outflows of FDI Hatzius (1997b) reports evidence indicating that bilateral FDI flows are strongly influenced by movements in relative unit labour costs.[11]

A recurring tension in much of the literature on the determinants of FDI flows is the extent to which they are determined by political as distinct from economic forces. As already noted, a number of early studies included both sorts of variables as possible determinants of FDI flows only to find the general dominance of economic over political factors in explaining variation in FDI flows as the dependent variable. While analysts of different persuasions (e.g. Schneider and Frey, 1985) have debated the adequacy of the various different measures of 'political climate' employed in FDI equations, this debate misses the fundamental point made by Balasubramanyam and Salisu (1991); namely that any attempt to separate the influence of the political climate from those of economic ones may be futile because in the final analysis the former are determined by the latter. At first glance this may perhaps be seen as implying an inevitable problem of multicollinearity between political and economic factors. However, from the econometric viewpoint, the way forward in

9. However, these authors find than in contrast, Swedish multinationals tend, other things equal, to employ more labour at home when they produce more abroad, a result that they interpret as reflecting the need for supervisory and other auxiliary employment within the parent organisation associated with foreign production, especially that located in developing countries

10. In an earlier study Lipsey (1994a) concludes that as far as US multinationals are concerned it is the composition of their employment at home, rather than its size, that is sensitive to overseas production, with a shift towards more managerial and technical employment occurring as overseas production increases.

11. There is also some evidence from the US (Lipsey, 1994b, p. 48) to suggest that an increased presence of foreign operations exerts an upward influence on wage levels in domestic firms.

resolving this debate would appear to lie in the specification and estimation of a simultaneous equation model that explicitly models the determination of the 'political climate' as an endogenous variable.

As already discussed, Bhagwati (1978) has presented a number of arguments that suggest that the volume of FDI flowing into a country will depend on whether it is pursuing an export promoting (EP) or import substituting (IS) strategy in its economic relations with the outside world. Whilst not denying the existence of so-called tariff-jumping FDI, the thrust of Bhagwati's argument is that in the final analysis, the amounts of FDI attracted by countries that pursue the IS strategy will be lower, and less sustained over time, than those attracted by countries taking the EP route. Balasubramanyam and Salisu (1991) tested this hypothesis. It is by no means a straightforward matter to place any given economy in an appropriate position on the spectrum ranging from IS on the one hand to EP on the other. After an evaluation of the relative merits of the various alternative measures of the outward orientation of trade/development policy employed in the literature, Balasubramanyam and Salisu (1991) favour two alternative measures. The first being the share of imports in GDP and the second, the World Bank's well-known 'distortion index'. On the basis of a careful econometric investigation of the determinants of per capita FDI inflows in a sample of some 38 countries over the period 1970 to 1980 these authors (after controlling for variations in such factors as the level and growth of per capita real income, inflows of foreign aid, host country wages and inflation) report strong evidence in support of Bhagwati's hypothesis concerning trade policy and FDI. They find that whenever the orientation of trade policy is included as an explanatory variable in the model (whether proxied by either the import share or the distortion index) it turns out to be both correctly signed and significantly different from zero.

The foregoing review of some of the extant empirical literature on determinants suggests that most of the determinants of FDI are characteristics displayed by countries which are relatively high up in the growth and income league tables. It is not a rich source of funds and know-how which each and every developing country can aspire to seek. Admittedly there are exceptions, China which has attracted substantial volumes of FDI in recent years is a case in point. It should, however, be noted that in some respects, China does offer the sort of location advantages attractive to foreign firms. These include a high literacy rate, a large potential domestic market and relatively low wage costs. It is though arguable whether or not there are also other factors, difficult to identify, at work here. These include the contribution of Chinese Diaspora, much of FDI in China is from the east Asian countries, and what can be termed the *lemming effect* - with MNEs following each other into China lest they be left out of the potential riches the huge market is supposed to offer. It is also worth noting that huge volumes of FDI may not necessarily confer the hoped for benefits. The quality of FDI and its effective utilisation may be much more important in promoting development goals than the absolute volume of investment a country attracts. This is a theme we develop in the following sections.

SECTION 4

EFFICACY

In most cases the preconditions necessary for attracting FDI are also the ones which determine its efficacy, defined to include its impact on growth, dissemination of technology and know-how, employment creation and other development goals. The framework for analysing the efficacy of FDI in promoting development goals is provided by trade theory and growth theory.

Standard models of trade assume that the primary factors of production - labour and capital - are immobile across countries but mobile within countries. They then proceed to demonstrate that specialisation and trade based on comparative advantage confer specialisation and exchange gains on the trading countries. Specialisation gains result from improved allocative efficiency, and exchange gains from the opportunity to trade at a set of prices different from that in autarchy. The assumptions underlying these propositions are well known. Now if factor mobility is introduce, gains from trade essentially hinge on the relationship of factor mobility to trade. Whether or not factor mobility and trade are substitutes for one another is a much-discussed issue, dating back to Mundell's (1957) demonstration that they are substitutes. His proposition though was restricted to demonstrating that factor mobility induced by impediments to trade would result in both commodity and factor price equalisation, much as free trade would do. But there is no suggestion that tariff induced imports of capital would increase the real income of the capital importing country. Indeed, tariff induced capital inflows could reduce the real income of the capital importing country, both because of the tariff induced production distortions and the payments to be made to the capital exporting country. That a tariff jumping type of capital inflow into the capital-intensive importable would necessarily immiserize growth has also been demonstrated (Bhagwati, 1973). Immiserization would occur even under conditions of free trade if the capital inflow were to alter the terms of trade against the capital importing country.

In general, theory suggests that capital inflows, which displace trade, would be immiserizing. However, FDI which enhances the innate comparative advantage which recipient countries possess, will, with exceptions, be of the trade promoting variety. And anything which enhances comparative advantage of countries, is likely to be efficient in promoting industrialisation and other development goals. Hence the debate on whether or not capital inflows complement or substitute for trade. It is now the received wisdom that capital inflows far from displacing trade complement trade (Greenaway and Milner, 1985). Even the tariff jumping variety of capital flows need not displace trade in its entirety. A number of factors support this conclusion. First is the recognition that capital flows imply more than a mere transfer of finance. They consist of FDI with its attendant characteristics of technology transfer and control over operations. Second, FDI is a major determinant of intra-industry trade. Third, the motives for undertaking FDI have changed radically in recent years and the recent vintages of FDI generally promote trade (Dunning, 1993).

Why should trade promoting FDI contribute to development? What are its implications for the volume, quality and price of technology transfer? As said earlier, trade-promoting FDI by definition enhances the comparative advantage of recipient countries. Admittedly even the tariff jumping variety of FDI may generate imports of equipment and machinery which embody technology. But such trade creation hardly promotes the innate comparative advantage of the recipient countries. In fact, most developing countries such as India which in the past had embraced the import-substituting (IS) industrialisation strategy afforded relatively high effective rates of protection to their protected industries. Such a policy encouraged imports of intermediates and equipment. Although such imports may embody technology it is arguable if it was of the appropriate variety and whether or not the technology embedded in them was disseminated within the domestic economy. In most cases the private rates of return to investment in the protected industries were much higher than the social rates of return (Lal, 1975). In other words, the country would have been better off importing the products than making them at home with FDI. The technologies were generally capital-intensive in nature as the tariff jumping variety of FDI was mostly in the capital-intensive import competing industries. These technologies hardly promoted employment or skill formation. Much of import-substituting industrialisation is import-intensive, partly because of the high effective rates of protection afforded to import competing industries and partly because of lack of adequate domestic sources of supply. Admittedly domestic sources of supply can be established and nurtured by foreign firms. Various sorts of sub-contracting arrangements which provide for the transfer of know-how between foreign firms and domestic firms even in import-substituting industries are not unknown. The sub-contracting arrangements for components established by Suzuki the Japanese automobile manufacturer in India for the production of Maruti cars is a case in point. Such cases are infrequent and not all such arrangements promote social goals (Govindan, 1998). In any case, such arrangements should evolve in response to market forces and cannot be forced upon foreign firms. Analysis of the social costs and benefits of trade related investment measures (TRIMS) which include local content requirements suggest as much (Greenaway, 1991; Balasubramanyam, 1991).

It could be argued that the received wisdom concerning the efficacy of FDI in import competing industries is derived from standard trade theories, principally the Heckscher-Ohlin model, which are essentially static constructs. They hardly allow for dynamic gains from trade such as exploitation of scale and scope economies, learning by doing, externalities and X-efficiency. And FDI is a powerful mechanism for the promotion of such dynamic gains. FDI, however, can promote such dynamic comparative advantage only in the presence of an appropriate climate for investment, which is free of factor and product market distortions. In the presence of sheltered markets and factor market distortions profit maximising firms are likely to rest content with tried and tested means of production and envisage little interest in promoting managerial efficiency.

The problem with import-substituting industrialisation is not that it encourages the production of import substitutes *per se*, but that it provides artificial and uncertain incentives for their production. It is thus that Bhagwati advocates a neutral trade policy, which equates the effective exchange rates for import substitution industries with the effective exchange rates for exports. In such a balanced trade regime resource allocation will be guided by market forces and genuine comparative advantage. It is worth noting here that his proposal does not preclude production for the domestic markets. FDI in such a regime may favour production for the domestic market, it all depends on the macro economic environment including market size, exchange rate stability and factor endowments of the recipient countries.

The tariff jumping variety of FDI belongs to the market seeking type of FDI in Dunning's classification of differing types of FDI. As opposed to market seekers there are the resource seekers, efficiency seekers and asset seekers. All of these types of FDI have an impact on trade. Resource seeking FDI by definition is undertaken for acquiring a variety of resources including natural resources such as minerals, relatively cheap labour and in some cases technological capabilities which are either unavailable or much too expensive in the home countries of MNEs. The colonial type of investments were mostly of the natural resource seeking variety, which generally resulted in export enclaves in developing countries. Hans Singer's celebrated analysis of such investments that continues to generate research papers is well known. That which has aroused much controversy is the labour seeking variety of investments, specifically those in the ubiquitous export processing zones in developing countries. These investments located in the zones are for the manufacture and export of mostly components and in some cases finished products. The costs and benefits of such investments are the subject of a number of studies (Balasubramanyam, 1988; Warr,1984). In general export-processing zones are a classic example of the Second Best. They are essentially islands of free trade located in the midst of an otherwise distortion-ridden economy. The benefits they confer on the host economies are at best uncertain. Designed to take advantage of cheap but unskilled labour they are hardly likely to impart technology and know-how to the recipient countries. Admittedly they do create employment and generate foreign exchange earnings. But the social opportunity costs of these gains may be substantial. Apart from the sizeable subsidies of various sorts developing countries provide for firms on the zones, there is the issue of whether or not the jobs they provide and the foreign exchange they generate are net gains. The jobs they provide on the zones for instance could be no more than what the economy could have provided outside the zones if it had pursued a neutral trade regime. The case of the export processing zones serves to illustrate the proposition that each and every type of export is not necessarily conducive to the promotion of development objectives.

The technology and skill seeking type of FDI is though of a different order. An excellent example of such FDI is the foreign investments in India's software sector, which consists of both wholly foreign owned subsidiaries and joint ventures. Here the resource sought by foreign firms is not unskilled labour but skilled labour proficient in the production of software. And for the most part such investments are export oriented. They are designed to exploit the genuine comparative advantage India possess in the production of software. The managerial and marketing skills foreign firms provide assist the country in exploiting its human capital endowments, a result of past investments in education. Apart from the technology embodied in the computer hardware they import, foreign firms also transmit what is termed as tacit knowledge or human skills. The mix of the two depends on their size and market orientation (Siddharthan and Nollen, 2000). Diffusion of such skills in the economy takes place with the frequent movement of software engineers from one company to the other and also when they opt to set up their own companies.

The two other types of FDI identified by Dunning are efficiency seeking and asset seeking investments. The objective of the former is to reap economies of scale and scope by producing in a limited number of locations and servicing a number of markets. Efficiency seeking investments consolidate and rationalise the market and resource seeking investments which companies may have undertaken in the past. Such investments may result in an international division of labour, with capital and human capital intensive production processes and products located in the developed countries and the labour intensive processes and products located in developing countries. Such efficiency seeking FDI in developed countries may be influenced by considerations other than factor endowments. These include the desire to capture scale and scope economies and the desire of consumers for variety. In all these cases FDI generates trade. In the case of FDI in developing countries such trade may involve exports of labour intensive components and parts to locations where the MNEs utilise them in producing final products. It may also generate intra-industry trade between the various subsidiaries of the MNEs. Here again FDI serves to exploit the comparative advantage of countries. Whether or not such efficiency seeking investments transmit technology and know-how of the sort which promote development goals is debatable. The often-heard argument is that such FDI condemns developing countries to specialise in the production of components and they will forever remain suppliers of components and equipment. This is a throw back to the thesis propounded by Hans Singer in the context of colonial investments in natural resources. Present day FDI, however, is in components of manufactured goods, a transition from component supplies to the production of finished final products is possible provided the host countries invest in training and education of labour. The experience of several East Asian countries suggests as much. This sort of a vertical integration across countries is one facet of globalisation and it is not without its problems.

The asset seeking type of FDI is mostly confined to developed countries. Here the objective of the MNEs is to enhance their ownership advantages by acquiring them through acquisitions, mergers and joint ventures across countries. Various strategic considerations such as thwarting competition, acquiring control over distribution channels and exploiting synergies arising from pooled R&D activities influence the asset seeking type of FDI. The trade effects of this sort of FDI are ambiguous. To the extent it enhances the ownership advantages of MNEs and allows them a greater degree of control over operations it may promote intra-firm trade. The technology transmission effects of such FDI are more important than its trade effects. Most strategic asset seeking type of investments can be expected to enhance the size of firms and with it generate scale and scope economies, especially so in R & D. Whether or not such investments also result in diffusion of know-how within the recipient economies is debatable. To the extent such investments enhance internalisation and control over operations by MNEs they delimit diffusion. But in the case of joint ventures forged to capitalise on the complementarity of assets owned by the partners to the venture there could be spillovers of know-how.

The foregoing discussion suggests that FDI which promotes trade based on comparative advantage of recipient countries is generally conducive to the transfer of technology and its diffusion. Trade policy also has implications for both the volume and quality of technologies FDI imparts. Trade and investment regimes which distort factor and product prices away from their true social opportunity cost are likely to induce inflows of technology and production of products which are inappropriate for the factor endowments and markets of recipient countries. Whether or not imported technologies in general are appropriate to developing countries, however, may be a theme of the past. The unskilled labour content of most production process is rapidly declining and most technologies are now intensive in the use of skilled labour and capital. There are though a few sectors and segments of manufacturing (such as clothing, leather products and the assembly of electronic goods) which continue to make use of unskilled labour. But these are far and few between. Resource seeking FDI in these areas is a source of employment, but developing countries seeking such investments have to rest content with the jobs they provide and not expect such investments to transmit technology and know-how.

Endogenous Growth Theory

Trade theory identifies the conditions under which FDI can be an efficient conduit of technology. The insights we gain here, however, are restricted to allocative efficiency and static once and for all gains from trade and FDI. Growth theory is concerned with the impact of factors of production and technical change on long-run growth of output. Here the message of the standard neo-classical growth models is well known. Long run growth is primarily a function of labour force growth and technical change and both of these ingredients of growth are exogenously determined. In the absence of technical change, output growth reaches a steady state given by the exogenous growth rate of labour. The assumptions of constant returns to scale, substitutability of factors of production and flexible factor prices underlying the standard Solow type neo-classical models of growth are well known. Equally well known is the corollary of neo-classical models that with identical technology across countries, poor countries would grow faster than rich countries. This tendency towards convergence of growth rates would occur because capital productivity would be relatively high in poor countries with a low ratio of capital to labour.

FDI can be easily accommodated in this model. Both the capital and technology it provides stimulate growth. The capital contribution moves the economy along the production function whist imports of technology shift the function upwards. The stimulus to growth afforded by FDI in the context of the neo-classical model, however, is not sustained over time. This is because of the assumptions of diminishing returns to capital and the exogenous nature of technical change.

The neo-classical model though elegant is for the most part vacuous. It can neither account for the sustained growth in world incomes and living standards, nor for the observed differences in incomes across countries. Recent developments in growth theory styled endogenous growth theory address these issues. The theory grounded in the economics of industrial organisation questions the basic assumptions of neo-classical models. Imperfect competition and oligopolies and not perfect competition underlie economic activity. Increasing returns to scale and externalities of various sorts are also an observed phenomenon. Incorporating these observed facts new growth theory is able to explain both the sustained growth in world incomes and the observed differences in incomes across countries. There are a variety of models which make up the new growth theory (Romer, 1987, 1990; Lucas, 1988; Helpman and Grossman, 1991), much too numerous to review here. The basic message of the theory, however, is that diminishing returns to capital, the basic tenet of the neo-classical model, would ensue only because the model assumes perfect competition and exogenous technical change. In a world of imperfect competition firms would have an incentive to invest in research and development. They compete with each other on the basis of new cost reducing methods of production and innovations designed to produce new products. Those in the lead would capture the market and retain their market share until imitators of their products and processes appear. But such competition would spur further research and development. In other words, technical change is more than likely to be endogenous - capable of being stimulated by incentives of various kinds including government support. Technological change can be associated not only with physical capital but also human capital. Learning by doing and education can augment human skills and serve to arrest diminishing returns to capital. This idea is captured succinctly in the following model known as the AK model;

$$Y = AK$$

where Y is output growth, A is a given level of technology and K stands for the ratio of capital to labour with capital defined to include human capital, physical capital and non-human capital such as infrastructure.

Now anything which increases the productivity of labour Y/L in the same proportion as K/L would maintain Y/K the capital to output ratio constant. Development of human skills through education and 'learning by doing' can increase labour productivity as capital accumulation proceeds and serve to maintain the productivity of capital constant. Admittedly, some versions of the neo-classical models talk about exogenous technical progress in terms of augmented labour skills. But in the new growth theory technical progress including human capital formation is endogenous, as stated earlier.

Yet another factor which can arrest diminishing returns to capital is spillovers of technology and know-how or broadly put - externalities. Human skills and technical know-how developed by one firm may accrue to others. Technology and know-how are in the nature of non-rivalrous inputs, in the sense that the use of it by one entity does not preclude others from using it. Put differently the marginal cost of replicating knowledge may be zero. It is worth noting that whist increased investments in capital of any kind, including human capital, may result in diminishing returns at the level of an individual firm, it may nonetheless increase productivity of capital at the aggregate level of say the industry. This could be the case if spillovers and externalities are present. This too could arrest diminishing returns to capital at the aggregate economy level. In sum, endogenous growth theory can account for the sustained growth in world incomes.

The implications of endogenous growth theory for FDI and technology transfer are wide ranging. One of the issues is whether or not FDI can shift the growth paths of developing countries on to a new trajectory and thereby promote convergence. Another related issue concerns the sort of policies developing countries should adopt to capture the externalities and human capital that FDI can provide. These issues have figured in the literature but they are yet to be fully explored (de Mello, 1996). As noted earlier the technology FDI provides can shift the production function upwards. But a sustained growth in income over the long-run as opposed to a once and for all shift in the function requires much more than an injection of FDI. The technology and skills MNEs transfer have to be widely diffused in the economy. Here the dilemma is that widespread diffusion of proprietary knowledge or ownership advantages would not be in the interests of profit maximising firms. Indeed, as noted earlier, the motivation for internalisation on the part of MNEs arises from their desire to delimit widespread diffusion of technology they possess. But in the absence of diffusion FDI may not engender sustained growth in the recipient economies. The need is for mechanisms which successfully diffuse the technology and know-how MNEs transmit but at the same time preserve incentives for further production of knowledge. There are several such avenues. Apart from imitation through reverse engineering and commercial piracy, sub-contracting arrangements between MNE's and locally owned suppliers of parts and components would be one such avenue. Another would be joint ventures between MNEs and locally owned firms. In both these cases what is required is a contribution of one sort or another by partners and suppliers of components which enables MNEs to preserve and fully exploit the ownership advantages they possess. In the case of sub-contracting arrangements an assured supply of relatively inexpensive components would provide the MNEs with the incentive to train labour in the locally owned firms. In time, suppliers of components may graduate to the production of final products whist the MNEs may move on to the production of new products and processes. Such a ladder of comparative advantage is a recognised phenomenon in the east Asian countries. Joint-ventures in which the advantages possessed by the foreign firms are complementary to those possessed by local firms can result in diffusion of technology and skills whist allowing foreign firms to fully exploit the advantages they possess.

Spillovers of technology and know-how and externalities have to be induced, they do not materialise from nowhere. Here the issue is not just that the appropriability of rents to existing technologies owned by foreign firms should be preserved but also that foreign firms should be provided with incentives to generate new technologies and knowledge. This can only materialise in the presence of market competition. Any spillovers which occur may in themselves generate such competition. But it can also be engendered through domestic investments in education and research and development and through import competition. It is now an acknowledged fact that for the efficient utilisation of FDI the recipient countries should possess a threshold level of human capital and they must have attained a threshold level of development (Blomstrom, Kokko and Zejan 1994; Balasubramanyam, Salisu and Sapsford 1999). The implications of this proposition are two fold. First, FDI is essentially a catalyst of growth, it is not an initiator of growth. It utilises and augments domestic resources. It complements domestic resources, it does not transfer each and every type of resources required for growth. This is, in fact, what Dunning refers to as the asset seeking FDI discussed earlier. The second implication of the proposition is equally important. Countries which posses a threshold level of human capital and other resources can effectively compete with foreign firms. In the face of such competition foreign firms would be compelled to invest in the generation of new knowledge if only to preserve their market shares. Indeed, the essence of new growth theory, as said earlier, is that imperfect competition and interdependence between firms promotes technical change.

It is worth noting that in the context of endogenous growth theory, convergence is unlikely to occur. Countries endowed with relatively high levels of human capital and resources would be on an entirely different production function from those with low levels of human capital. In any case, in the absence of diminishing returns to capital, convergence would not occur. FDI through transmission of technology and skills may, however, serve to promote convergence. Even so, for the efficient utilisation of FDI certain prerequisites are essential. These include not only threshold levels of human capital but also an economic environment which promotes efficient utilisation of FDI. Such an environment should be free of product and factor market distortions and allow firms to exploit their innate comparative advantage. There is some evidence in support of this proposition. Developing countries following an EP or a neutral development strategy which is free of distortions, as opposed to countries following an IS policy seem to exhibit convergence. In the former group of countries FDI acts as a catalyst and in the latter it is seen to immiserize growth (Silverstradou and Balasubramanyam, 2000).

In sum, endogenous growth theory sheds new light on several of the propositions on FDI in developing countries debated over the years. First, production of new technologies and know-how is endogenous It is endogenous in the sense that investments in R & D are undertaken in response to market forces. Profit maximising firms would be intent on appropriating and preserving for themselves the rents inherent in new knowledge. They would also wish to minimise the costs of transferring and implementing technologies in new investment locations. Much of the suspicion and opposition to the operations of MNEs in developing countries arise from a failure to recognise the commercial orientation of their operations including the generation and transmission of technology. Second, endogenous growth theory emphasises externalities, human capital and returns to scale as the factors which arrest diminishing returns to capital and promote sustained growth. Diffusion of technology and know-how including human skills is central to most models of endogenous growth. But for the most part the theory does not identify the channels and mechanisms of diffusion. We know very little about the mechanisms of diffusion of technology within the recipient countries. Indeed the basic tenet of the internalisation theory of the MNE and FDI is that firms undertake FDI to internalise externalities. The issue then is how best to promote diffusion whilst at the same time preserving the incentives for investments in knowledge production by foreign firms. The one and only solution to the dilemma here is the promotion of market competition as discussed earlier. Third, diffusion of technology by foreign firms is also a function of the ability of locally owned firms to absorb and efficiently utilise the technology and know-how. This too is implicit in the endogenous growth theory. Again as stated earlier, for the efficient utilisation of FDI recipient countries should posses a threshold of human capital and other growth promoting ingredients. A corollary of this proposition is that FDI is a catalyst of growth and not an initiator. And to regard FDI as a panacea for each and every development problem is folly.

SECTION 5

EMPIRICAL STUDIES ON FDI AND GROWTH

Some General Issues

As already discussed, the period since the late-1980s has seen a resurgence of interest in growth economics, with the development of what has subsequently become known as the 'New' or Endogenous Theory of Growth. The early contributions to this literature were framed in terms of the determinants of the rate of growth of income/output per capita in the context of closed economies (see, especially, Romer, 1986; 1987; 1990a; 1990b).[12] Although convenient, the closed economy assumption of the theorist is clearly unrealistic as a description of the real world. As pointed out by Aghion and Howitt (1998)[13] it soon became clear that the introduction into the early endogenous growth models of open-economy considerations revealed the importance not only of international trade in goods but also of international flows and spillovers of knowledge and ideas. Given the role of FDI, discussed above, as a conduit for the transmission of ideas, knowledge and the fruits of research and development both between countries and, via various spillover mechanisms and complementarities, within the host economy, it is no surprise that FDI has emerged in the

12. It is perhaps ironic that this literature has become known as New Growth Theory as little of it is actually new! As Brewer (1991) has observed, the basic ideas of endogenous growth theory can be traced back at least as far as the writings of John Rae (1834).

13. See also Grossman and Helpman (1991) and Young (1991).

second-generation of endogenous growth models as a potent factor in promoting growth.[14] A large empirical literature examining the relationship between FDI flows and economic growth has developed in tandem with the extension of the basic endogenous growth model to the open economy case. Space constraints prevent us from exploring the whole of this empirical literature (see de Mello, 1996 for a comprehensive literature survey); instead we focus our attention upon a restricted range of issues, each of which is of direct relevance to the subject matter of the current paper.

Trade Policy Orientation, FDI and Economic Growth

Evidence supporting Bhagwati's hypothesis regarding the influence that a country's trade policy regime exerts upon the magnitude of the inflows of FDI that it attracts was discussed earlier. The second dimension of Bhagwati's hypothesis relates to the influence that the trade policy regime has upon the growth enhancing effects of the FDI. In formal terms this second dimension to the hypothesis states that, other things equal, the partial derivative of the rate of economic growth with respect to FDI is higher in countries following an EP strategy than in countries following an IS one. Support for this hypothesis is found in the study by Balasubramanyam, Salisu and Sapsford (1996) of the growth enhancing effects of FDI in a cross-section of some 46 developing countries of the period 1970 to 1985. Mention has already been made of the difficulties encountered when classifying countries as either EP or IS in character. In this study a new technique was devised for differentiating between IS and EP cases, involving the application of structural stability analysis to the sample of countries ordered by import shares. This technique broke the total sample into sub-samples consisting of 28 IS countries and 18 EP ones. Support for the hypothesis was found in that the estimated elasticity of growth with respect to FDI was found to be significantly higher for countries in the former category than for those in the latter.[15] The same conclusion was also evident when the

14. For an investigation of possible interaction effects between technology imports and FDI in the context of the export performance of Indian information technology firms see Siddharthan and Nollen (2000).

15. In order to allow for the endogeneity of FDI in the growth equation, the generalised instrumental variable method of estimation was employed. For evidence regarding the existence of bi-directional causality between FDI and economic growth in developing countries see de Mello (1996) and Zhang (2000).

sample was categorised into EP and IS according to the World Bank's alternative classification of countries according to the outwardness of their trade orientation (Greenaway and Nam, 1988).

Empirical support for the proposition that FDI is a more effective engine of growth in EP than in IS economies can also be found elsewhere in the literature.[16] For example, the study of overseas production of US manufacturing multinationals in a sample of 44 countries (almost half of which are industrialised) over the period 1983-1992 by Athukorala and Chand (1998) indicates that other things equal, the productivity gains resulting from international production tend to be greater the more open is the trade policy regime of the host country. The relationship between FDI flows and economic performance in post-reform People's Republic of China has begun to attract considerable interest. Some evidence is beginning to emerge from such studies to suggest the existence of a positive relationship across provinces between openness to trade and economic growth (Berthelemy and Demurger, 2000).

Thresholds and Complementarities in the Growth Process

As noted above the availability (and cost) of skilled labour in the host economy consistently appeared in the early literature as one of the significant determinants of FDI inflows. As we have also seen the quantity and quality of the human capital stock is an issue of pivotal importance in the context of endogenous growth theory. Despite the conceptual simplicity of the human-capital notion there are considerable difficulties in measuring the size of a country's human-capital endowment (for discussion see Balasubramanyam, Salisu and Sapsford, 1999).[17] Notwithstanding these difficulties it has been

16. Evidence reported by Silvestriadou and Balasubramanyam (2000) also suggests that countries that pursue EP policies are more likely to achieve convergence in their per capita incomes than those following IS policies. See Blomstrom and Wolff (1994) for a detailed investigation of the role of foreign owned firms in the Mexican convergence experience.

17. Foremost among the issues involved is whether it is preferable to proxy human-capital by flow type data (e.g. school enrolment rates of the sort available from the World Bank database) or by using stock data relating to educational attainment (which usually means the data contained in the well known Barro-Lee (1993) dataset). Perhaps even more fundamental, however, is the choice between the preceding sorts of measures (which are essentially concerned with inputs into the human-capital accumulation process) and alternative output based measures (e.g. Crafts and Thomas, 1986) based on real wages seen as measures of labour productivity.

argued above that a threshold level of human-capital endowments needs to be achieved before the potential growth enhancing effects of FDI can be unleashed Employing the Barro-Lee (1993) input based measure of human-capital both Borensztein, de Gregorio and Lee (1998) and Xu (2000) report evidence consistent with this notion. Support for the threshold hypothesis is also found by Balasubramanyam, Salisu and Sapsford (1999) who employ the real wage as an output based measure of human-capital. The parameter estimates reported by Borensztein, de Gregorio and Lee (1998, p. 125) suggest that in order to benefit positively in growth terms from FDI, countries need to exceed a threshold of 0.52 years for the average duration of male secondary schooling, while the results reported by Xu (2000) suggest a threshold closer to 1.9 years. Working with the real wage as an output based measure of human-capital endowments in a sample of 46 developing economies, Balasubramanyam, Salisu and Sapsford (1999) report evidence to suggest the existence of a threshold equal to the level of real wage level achieved a little below the second quartile in the sample ranked according to real wages. A similar conclusion is reached by Blomstrom, Lipsey and Zejan (1995, p. 254) who argue on the basis of a study of the determinants of growth in real income per capita in a sample of 78 developing countries over the period 1960 to 1985, that it is only when developing countries exceed a certain threshold level of development that they are able to absorb new technology from investments by foreign firms.

In much the same way that the achievement of a threshold level of host country human capital stock can be important in releasing the potential growth enhancing effects of FDI, so too can the achievement of a threshold in the infrastructure of the other co-operating factors of production. As noted above the importance of host country infrastructure as a determinant of FDI inflows emerged clearly in the early literature and more recently such studies as Helliwell and Chung (1992), Mankiw, Romer and Weil (1992) and Wolff (1991) have illustrated the potential importance in the growth convergence context of achieving a threshold level of infrastructure development. More recently evidence has begun to emerge from the empirical growth literature regarding the importance of infrastructure in releasing the growth enhancing effects of potential of FDI. For example, Balasubramanyam, Salisu and Sapsford (2000) find some evidence to indicate that the quality of a country's road network exerts a significant influence. A recent study of the Chinese post-reform experience by Wu (2000) arrives at a similar conclusion.

Domestic Influences on the Growth Process

Whilst numerous studies (e.g. UNCTAD, 1983; Subrahmanian, 1995) have highlighted the influence of host country market size upon the location decisions of multinational firms, some recent research has focussed on the influence of domestic economic performance and competitive structure upon the growth-FDI relationship. For example, in a detailed study of the activities of US multinationals' affiliates in heavily indebted Latin American countries Blomstrom and Lipsey (1993) demonstrate that affiliates responded to the debt crisis by shifting sales away from the domestic market towards export markets. Further evidence regarding the sensitivity to domestic macroeconomic conditions of FDI flows, seen as one of the determinants of growth performance in Latin America, may be found in studies by Cardoso and Fishlow (1989), Elias (1990) and de Gregorio (1992).

As argued above, the competitive environment in the host country with respect to locally owned firms can play a pivotal role in influencing the efficacy of FDI in promoting growth. It is by no means an easy matter to measure the competitive climate in the relevant markets in developing countries, not least because the relevant data that are necessary to calculate the usual measures of market power (such as concentration ratios) are frequently unavailable. However, some support for the hypothesis that the competitive environment exerts a significant influence of the efficacy of FDI in promoting growth is found by Balasubramanyam, Salisu and Sapsford (1999) who employ the share of manufacturing value added in total value added as a proxy for domestic competition. Using a range of alternative proxies for local competition (including the relative increase in the real capital stock of domestic firms, the percentage increase in the real gross output of domestic firms and the change in the market share of domestic firms, each compiled from unpublished data sources) Blomstrom, Kokko and Zejan (1994) also find empirical support in their study of the Mexican experience for the hypothesis that local competition matters. The results suggest that it matters particularly strongly for consumer goods and intermediates.

In sum the empirical evidence endorses the main proposition that a threshold level of growth and human capital endowments are both essential for the effective utilisation of FDI. Beyond that, effective market competition is essential for both the diffusion and effective utilisation of FDI. In other words, FDI is a ***catalyst*** but rarely, if ever, an initiator of growth.

SECTION 6

CONCLUSIONS

The paper has ranged over a variety of issues relating to the determinants and efficacy of FDI in promoting growth and related development objectives in developing countries. Whilst it does not purport to be an exhaustive survey of the vast literature on FDI, it has attempted to highlight the main propositions the literature yields. The determinants of FDI and factors, which influence its efficacy, seem to be similar if not identical. FDI is a catalyst of growth and rarely an initiator of growth. In the absence of growth promoting ingredients such as human capital endowments, infrastructure facilities and effective market competition, the catalyst is likely to fizzle out. These propositions echo the message of new growth theory. Empirical evidence on these and other propositions is fairly robust.

There are a number of issues which await further research. These include identification of the precise channels and mechanisms through which FDI impacts on growth and development. Econometric evidence available to date suggests causation between FDI and growth but does not illuminate the process by which FDI impacts on growth. Detailed case studies of FDI in differing types of economic environment may be the way forward in this context. Also the quality of FDI as opposed to mere volume may be important in promoting its role as a catalyst. Here again there are complex problems of identifying and measuring quality of FDI. Is it likely that FDI undertaken by the US in say Mexico is much more efficacious than its FDI in comparable industries in China? Is it the case that India because of her institutions, her business culture oriented towards western business practices, including financial and legal norms and practices, is better able to utilise FDI than say China, with the proviso that she embraces a fully liberalised trade regime and distortion free factor and product markets? There are also issues which we have alluded to but not discussed in the paper. These include the impact of the fast growing e-commerce on the volume, patterns and efficacy of FDI. Also relevant for research is the relationship between international flows of skilled labour and FDI. Is it likely labour would increasingly seek capital rather than the observed phenomenon of capital seeking labour? It is our hope that students of Professor Leela Krishna, whose immense contribution to research on trade, investment and industrial economics we are celebrating, will address these issues in the future.

Paper presented at a Conference in honour of Professor Leela Krishna, at the Delhi School of Economics, December 20th to 22nd 2000.

References

Agarwal, J. (1980). "Determinants of Foreign Direct Investment: A Survey," *Weltwirtschaftliches Archiv* 116, 739-773.

Aghion, P. and Howitt, P. (1998). *Endogenous Growth Theory* (Cambridge, Massachusetts and London: MIT Press).

Athukorala, P-C. and Chand, S. (1998). "Trade Orientation and Productivity Gains from International Trade: A Study of Overseas Operations of US Multinationals" (Department of Economics, Research School of Pacific and Asian Studies, Australian National University: mimeo).

Balasubramanyam V.N. (1991). "Putting Trims To Good Use," *World Development*.

————. (1988). "Export Processing Zones" in Greenaway, D. (ed.) *Economic Development and International Trade* (London, Macmillan).

Balasubramanyam, V.N. and Salisu, M. (1991). "Export Promotion, Import Substitution and Direct Foreign Investment in Less Developed Countries" in Koekkoek, A. and Mennes, L. (eds.) *International Trade and Global Development* (London: Routledge).

Balasubramanyam, V.N., Salisu, M. and Sapsford, D. (1996). "Foreign Direct Investment and Growth in EP and IS countries," *Economic Journal* 106, 92-105.

————. (1999). "Foreign Direct Investment as an Engine of Growth," *Journal of International Trade and Economic Development* 8, 27-40.

————. (2000). "Foreign Direct Investment and Economic Growth in LDCs: Some Further Evidence," in Bloch, H. and Kenyon, P. (eds.) *Creating an Internationally Competitive Economy* (London: Macmillan) (forthcoming).

Barro, R. and Lee, J. (1993). "International Comparisons of Educational Attainment" *Journal of Monetary Economics*, 32, 363-94.

Berthelemy, J-C. and Demurger, S., (2000). "Foreign Direct Investment and Economic Growth: Theory and Application to China," *Review of Development Economics* 4, 140-155.

Bhagwati, J.N. (1973). "The Theory of Immizerising Growth; Further Applications," in Connoly, M.B and Swoboda, A.K. (ed.) *International Trade and Money* (Toronto, Toronto University Press).

————. (1978). *Anatomy and Consequences of Exchange Control Regimes*, Vol. 1, *Studies in International Economic Relations*, 10 (New York: National Bureau of Economic Research).

Blomstrom, M., Fors, G., and Lipsey, R.E. (1997). "Foreign Direct Investment and Employment: Home Country Experience in the United States and Sweden" *NBER Working Paper Series* No. 6205 (Cambridge, Massachusetts: National Bureau of Economic Research).

Blomstrom, M., Kokko, A. and Zejan, M. (1994). "Host Country Competition, Labor Skills and Technology Transfer by Multinationals," *Weltwirtschaftliches Archiv* 130, 521-533.

Blomstrom, M. and Lipsey, R.E. (1993). "Foreign Firms and Structural Adjustment in Latin America" in Hansson, G. (ed.) *Trade, Growth and Development* (New York: Routledge).

Blomstrom, M., Lipsey, R.E. and Zejan, M. (1994). "What Explains the Growth of Developing Countries?" in Baumol, W., Nelson, R. and Wolff, E. (eds.) *Convergence of Productivity: Cross-National Studies and Historical Evidence* (New York: Oxford University Press).

Blomstrom, M. and Wolff, E. (1994). "Multinational Corporations and Productivity Convergence in Mexico" in Baumol, W., Nelson, R. and Wolff, E. (eds.) *Convergence of Productivity: Cross-National Studies and Historical Evidence* (New York: Oxford University Press).

Borensztein, E., de Gregorio, J. and Lee, J-W (1998). "How Does Foreign Direct Investment Affect Economic Growth?," *Journal of International Economics* 45, 115-135.

Brewer, A. (1991). "Economic Growth and Technical Change: John Rae's Critique of Adam Smith," *History of Political Economy* 23, 1-11.

Buckley, P.J. and Casson, M. (1991). *The Future of the Multinational Enterprise* (London: Macmillan).

Cardoso, E. and Fishlow, A. (1989). "Latin American Development: 1950-80" *NBER Working Paper Series* No. 3161 (Cambridge, Massachusetts: National Bureau of Economic Research).

Crafts, N. and Thomas, M. (1986). "Comparative Advantage in UK Manufacturing Trade, 1910-1935," *Economic Journal* 96, 629-45.

Dunning, J. (1973). "The Determinants of International Production," *Oxford Economic Papers* 25, 289-336.

————. (1981). "Explaining the International Direct Investment Position of Countries: Towards a Dynamic or Developmental Approach," *Weltwirtschaftliches Archiv*, 117, 30-64.

————. (1993). *Multinational Enterprises and the Global Economy* (Workingham: Addison-Wesley).

Elias, V. (1990). *Sources of Growth: A Study of Seven Latin American Economies* (San Francisco: ICS Press).

Goldsbrough, D. (1979). "The Role of Foreign Direct Investment in the External Adjustment Process," *International Monetary Fund Staff Papers* 26, 725-754.

Greenaway, D., (1991). Why Are we Negotiating on Trims? in Greenaway, D. and R. Hine (ed.) *Global Protectionism* (London: Macmillan).

Greenaway, D. and Nam, C. (1988). "Industrialisation and Macroeconomic Performance in Developing Countries Under Alternative Trade Strategies," *Kyklos* 41, 419-435.

Greenaway, D. and Milner, C. (1986) *The Economics of Intra-Industry Trade* (Oxford, Basil Blackwell)

de Gregorio, J. (1992). "Economic Growth in Latin America" *Journal of Development Economics* 39, 59-84.

Govindan, K. (1998). *Foreign Direct Investment in Malaysia* (unpublished doctoral dissertation, Lancaster University, Department of Economics).

Grossman, G. and Helpman, E. (1991). *Innovation and Growth in the Global Economy* (Cambridge Massachusetts: MIT Press).

Hatzius, J. (1997a). "Domestic Jobs and Foreign Wages: Labour Demand in Swedish Multinationals," *Discussion Paper No. 337* (London: Centre for Economic Performance, London School of Economics and Political Science)..

————. (1997b). "Foreign Direct Investment, Capital Formation and Labour Costs: Evidence from Britain and Germany," *Discussion Paper No. 336* (London: Centre for Economic Performance, London School of Economics and Political Science).

Helpman, E. and Grossman, G. (1991). *Innovation and Growth in the Global Economy* (Cambridge, Mass.: MIT Press).

Helliwell, J. and Chung, A. (1992). "Convergence and Growth Linkages Between North and South," *NBER Working Paper Series No. 3948* (Cambridge, Massachusetts: National Bureau of Economic Research).

Hymer, S.H. (1960). *International Operations of National Firms; A Study of Direct Foreign Investment*. (unpublished doctoral dissertation, MIT).

Klein, M. and Rosengren, E. (1994). "The Real Exchange Rate and Foreign Direct Investment in the United States: Relative Wealth vs. Relative Wage Effects," *Journal of International Economics* 36, 373-389.

Krugman, P. and Obstfeld, M. (2000). *International Economics; Theory and Policy* (Addison-Wesley, Massachsetts).

Kumar, N. (1990). Multinational Enterprises in India (Routledge: London).

Langhammer, R. (1991). "Competition Among Developing Countries for Foreign Investment in the Eighties - Whom Did OECD Investors Prefer?," *Weltwirtschaftliches Archiv*, 127, 390-403.

Lal, D. (1975) *Appraising Foreign Investment in Developing Countries* (London: Heineman).

Levis, M. (1979). "Does Political Instability in Developing Countries Affect Foreign Investment Flows? An Empirical Examination", *Management International Review*, 19.

Lipsey, R.E. (1994a). "Outward Direct Investment and the U.S. Economy" *NBER Working Paper Series* No. 4691 (Cambridge, Massachusetts: National Bureau of Economic Research).

————. (1994b). "Foreign-Owned Firms and U.S. Wages" *NBER Working Paper Series* No. 4927 (Cambridge, Massachusetts: National Bureau of Economic Research).

————. (1999). "The Role of Foreign Direct Investment in International Capital Flows" *NBER Working Paper Series* No. 7094 (Cambridge, Massachusetts: National Bureau of Economic Research).

Lipsey, R.E., Blomstrom, M. and Ramstetter, R. (1995). "Internationalised Production in World Output" *NBER Working Paper Series No. 5385* (Cambridge, Massachusetts: National Bureau of Economic Research).

Lucas, R. (1988). On the Mechanics of Economic Development, *Journal of Monetary Economics*, 22 , 3-42.

Mankiw, N., Romer, D. and Weil, D. (1992) "A Contribution to the Empirics of Economic Growth," *Quarterly Journal of Economics* 107, 407-437.

de Mello, L. (1996). "Foreign Direct Investment in Developing Countries and Growth: A Selective Survey" (Department of Economics, Keynes College, University of Kent, *mimeo*).

Mundell, R. (1957). "International Trade and Factor Mobility," *American Economic Review*, 57.

Narula, R. and Wakerlin, K. (1998). "The Dynamics of Country-Specific Determinants of Foreign Direct Investment," (Economics Department, Nottingham University, England, *mimeo*).

Rae, J. (1834). *Statement of Some New Principles on the Subject of Political Economy* (Boston: Hilliard, Gray and Co.)

Ramstetter, E. (1992). "Data on Foreign Direct Investment and Multinational Firms: Problems and Suggestions for Collection" (Faculty of Economics, Kansai University, Osaka, Japan, *mimeo* dated May 14th).

Romer, P. (1986). "Increasing Returns and Long Run Growth," *Journal of Political Economy* 94, 1002-1037.

————. (1987). "Growth Based on Increasing Returns Due to Specialisation," *American Economic Review Papers and Proceedings* 77, 56-72.

————. (1990a). "Endogenous Technical Change," *Journal of Political Economy* 98, 71-102.

————. (1990b). "Capital Labor and Productivity," *Brookings Papers on Economic Activity, Microeconomics Special Issue*, 337-367.

Root, F. and Ahmed, A. (1979). "Empirical Determinants of Manufacturing Direct Foreign Investment in Developing Countries," *Economic Development and Cultural Change* 27, 751-68.

Roy, E. (1989). "The Determinants of Foreign Direct Investment in the United States, 1979-85" in Feenstra, R. (ed.) *Trade Policies for International Competitiveness* (Chicago: University of Chicago Press for National Bureau of Economic Research).

Schneider, F. and Frey, B. (1985). "Economic and Political Determinants of Foreign Direct Investment," *World Development* 13, 161-174.

Siddharthan, N. and Nollen, S. (2000). "The Contributions of Foreign Collaborations and Technology to Exports of Firms in India" (Institute of Economic Growth, Delhi University, *mimeo*).

Silvestriadou, K. and Balasubramanyam, V.N. (2000). "Trade Policy, Foreign Direct Investment and Convergence," *Review of Development Economics* 4, 279-291.

Subrahmanian, K. (1995). *Economic Reforms, Foreign Firms and Export Performance: A Study of the Large Corporate Sector of India* (Trivandrum, India: Centre for Development Studies).

UNCTAD (1983). *Explaining and Forecasting Regional Flows of FDI* (New York: United Nations).

Veugelers, R. (1991). "Locational Determinants and Ranking of Host Countries: An Empirical Assessment," *Kyklos* 44, 363-382.

Warr, P. (1984). The Jakarta Export Processing Zone; Benefits and Costs, *Bulletin of Indonesian Economic Studies*,19.

Wolff, E. (1991). "Productivity Convergence at the Aggregate Level: A Survey" (Economics Department, New York University, *mimeo*).

Wu, Y. (2000). "Measuring the Performance of Foreign Direct Investment: A Case Study of China," *Economics Letters* 66, 143-50.

Xu, B. (2000). "Multinational Enterprises, Technology Diffusion and Host Country Productivity Growth," *Journal of Development Economics* 62, 477-493.

Young, A. (1991). "Learning by Doing and the Dynamic Effects of International Trade", *Quarterly Journal of Economics* 106, 369-406.

Zhang, K. (2000). "Foreign Direct Investment and Economic Growth in Developing Countries" (Department of Economics, Illinois State University; paper presented at ASSA Annual Conference).

17

Liberalisation, Outward Orientation and In-house R&D Activity of Multinational and Local Firms

A Quantitative Exploration for Indian Manufacturing

NAGESH KUMAR
ARADHNA AGARWAL

SECTION 1

INTRODUCTION

In an increasingly globalising and knowledge-based world economy, the technological capacity is seen as an important influence on a country's international competitiveness and growth prospects in the recent theoretical and empirical literature. Given its critical role for growth and competitiveness, technology has received important attention in economic policy-making in most industrialised and newly industrialising economies. The national and local governments play an important role in the national innovation systems of these economies and aggressively promote innovative activity of national enterprises. These trends have been variously described as technonationalism or technoprotectionism (Kumar and Siddharthan, 1997, for a recent review). As a result, the national R&D expenditure as a proportion of GNP has risen for the world from 1.85 per cent in 1980 to 2.55 per cent in 1990s.

Against that background, the proportion of national resources spent on R&D by India has declined steadily from a peak of 0.98 per cent in 1988 to 0.66 per cent in 1997 (India, DST, 1999). The declining importance attached to R&D in India is a matter of serious concern given the international trend. It threatens to widen the already serious technology gap between India and the world economy.

The bulk of R&D expenditure in India is accounted for by the public funded R&D institutions with industry spending only 28 per cent of national R&D expenditure. Hence, the decline in the proportion of national R&D expenditure may largely be due to budgetary squeeze. However, even the rate of growth of R&D expenditure in industry has declined in the 1990s compared to the 1980s. R&D expenditure in real terms has declined in 12 out of 28 broad industries in the 1990s and even where it has risen, the R&D to sales ratios have either stagnated or declined. (Basant, 2000. Mani and Bhaskar, 1998, have also observed a similar trend).

The decline in the importance attached to R&D by industry has coincided with the progressive liberalisation of Indian economy since 1991 as a part of the package of reforms adopted. It tends to suggest that liberalisation of policy environment has affected the technological activity of enterprises. It is not clear, however, if it has affected just the demand for R&D activity of enterprises because of relatively freer access to technology imports or whether it has affected the technological behaviour of enterprises as well. If latter is the case then different factors would determine the R&D activity of enterprises in the post-reform period compared to pre-reform period. Furthermore, one of the most important aspects of liberalisation is increasing global integration of the Indian economy. This may induce enterprises to become more international in their outlook. The internationalisation of enterprises takes the form of not only diversification in export markets but also by investing in subsidiaries and joint ventures abroad. A number of Indian enterprises have indeed adopted internationalisation as a part of their growth strategy in recent period. The internationalisation of operations is likely to increase the demand for technological inputs by them. Hence, international orientation of enterprises may have a greater bearing on their propensity to do R&D in the post reforms period than in the pre-reform period. Finally, a key aspect of reforms is liberalisation of foreign direct investment (FDI) regime to attract multinational enterprises (MNEs) to invest in the country. Given the captive access that they enjoy to the laboratories of their parents, the R&D behaviour of MNE affiliates may be determined by different factors compared to R&D activity of their local counterparts.

In this context, the present paper analyses the determinants of R&D activity of Indian enterprises using a large unbalanced panel data set consisting of 4209 observations for 840 companies in the manufacturing sector for the period 1992-93 to 1998-99. Given the strategic and rather longer term nature of technology behaviour, the effect of reforms on the R&D behaviour of enterprises may not be spontaneous and is expected to be subject to lags. Hence, comparison of R&D behaviour in early post-reform period (say 1992-93 to 1994-95) and in the subsequent period may give an idea of the nature of liberalisation-induced effects. The coverage of both MNE affiliates and their local counterparts in different manufacturing sectors allows us to observe the differences in their R&D behaviour.

The structure of the paper is as follows: Section 2 describes the data set for the study and discusses the trends and patterns in enterprise level R&D activity in Indian corporate sector. Section 3 discusses the analytical framework for the quantitative analysis and summarises key hypotheses and variable measurements. Section 4 discusses empirical findings from estimations for the full sample and sub-samples. Section 5 concludes the paper with a few remarks on the implications of the findings and inferences.

SECTION 2

TRENDS AND PATTERNS IN ENTERPRISE LEVEL R&D IN INDIAN MANUFACTURING

To examine the trends and patterns in the R&D activity of Indian enterprises over the 1990s, we make use of the on-line Prowess Database (June 2000 Release) of the Centre for Monitoring Indian Economy (CMIE). Prowess covers financial data of over 7000 companies incorporated in India. Most of the companies covered in the Database are listed on stock exchanges. The financial data covered by the Database includes most of the information that incorporated companies are required to disclose in their annual reports *viz.* profit and loss account and a balance sheet along with information contained in the schedules and annexures. The generally accepted disclosure norms under the Indian Companies Act 1956, as amended from time to time, require companies to report all those heads of expenditure which account for more than 1 per cent of their turnover. Because R&D expenditure often accounts for under 1 per cent of turnover, it is up to the management to report it separately or not. A growing number of companies do report R&D expenditure. The lack of a mandatory disclosure of R&D expenditure in accounts, however, causes a source of bias. When a company does not report R&D expenditure, it is not clear if the company does not spend anything on R&D or it does but chooses not to report it because it is less than 1 per cent. Given this situation, we decided to focus on companies reporting R&D activity. All the companies reporting any R&D expenditure, either capital or current, in a year were extracted for the period 1992-93 to 1998-99. That yielded a total of 4723 observations with a varying number of companies reporting R&D expenditure in different years (444 in 1992-93 to a peak of 920 companies in 1996-97 and 668 companies in the terminal year). After excluding non-manufacturing companies out of these 4723 observation, we were left with 4209 observations. These observations were classified into 13 broad branches of manufacturing accounting for the bulk of their activity (including a miscellaneous category that also covers diversified companies that could not be classified in any particular industry). Companies with 25 per cent or more foreign equity by foreign parent (and not foreign equity owned by foreign institutional investors and holders of ADRs/GDRs of Indian companies) were classified as MNE affiliates. Of the 4209 observations 915 belong to MNE affiliates.[1] The sample period was split into two viz. 1992-93 to 1994-95 as the early reform period and 1995-96 to 1998-99 as the late post-reform period. Given the fact that R&D behaviour relates to medium and long term corporate strategies and is subject to a lagged response, the early reform period i.e. 1992-93 to 1994-95 is likely to reflect the tendencies of the pre-reform period only, as the changes brought in the policy as a part of reforms were taking shape during this period. The 1995-96 to 1998-99 period is expected to capture the effect of liberalised regime that resulted from the adoption of reforms in the country. Hence, we will refer to these periods as pre-reform and post-reform respectively for the purposes of this paper.

The patterns in R&D expenditure for the sample companies as a proportion of their turnover are summarised in Table 17.1. The average R&D intensity of the group for the entire period is 0.846 per

1. The information contained in Prowess on foreign equity ownership is not complete. Hence, it had to be supplemented with other sources such as Capital Line, company directories, India, DSIR (1998), among other sources. Similarly, Prowess does not provide for industry classification but only broad industry name. The companies were regrouped in 13 broad industry groups on the basis of the descrfiption provided.

Table 17.1

R&D Intensities of Sample Enterprise Across Industries

(percentages)

Industry	1992-93 to 1994-95			1995-96 to 1998-99			1992-93 to 1998-99		
	Local	MNE Affiliates	Total	Local	MNE Affiliates	Total	Local	MNE Affiliates	Total
Food, Beverages & Tobacco	.34	.28	.33	.43	.30	.40	.406	.296	.38
	(.006)	(.003)	(.006)	(.010)	(.002)	(.009)	(.009)	(.003)	(.008)
	52	18	70	152	32	184	204	50	254
Textiles	.389	.828	.43	.300	.700	.33	.326	.74	.36
	(.009)	(.0124)	(.009)	(.007)	(.008)	(.007)	(.008)	(.009)	(.007)
	89	9	98	208	17	225	297	26	323
Metal and Metal Products	.6	.30	.58	.365	.64	.4	.47	.50	.475
	(.016)	(.002)	(.015)	(.006)	(.009)	(.007)	(.011)	(.007)	(.011)
	125	20	145	188	27	215	313	47	360
Automobile	1.31	.65	1.05	1.33	.872	1.15	1.33	.794	1.12
	(.017)	(.005)	(.0146)	(.0166)	(.008)	(.0142)	(.017)	(.007)	(.0149)
	83	56	139	164	101	265	247	157	404
Machinery	.96	.89	.936	.889	.963	.915	.92	.937	.923
	(.010)	(.007)	(.009)	(.009)	(.010)	(.009)	(.009)	(.008)	(.009)
	82	48	131	136	74	210	219	122	341
Electrical	1.13	.923	1.08	1.13	.88	1.08	1.13	.90	1.08
	(.018)	(.013)	(.017)	(.019)	(.018)	(.019)	(.0189)	(.016)	(.018)
	181	55	236	330	92	422	511	147	658
Drugs and Pharma	1.69	1.06	1.57	1.74	1.12	1.58	1.72	1.10	1.55
	(.023)	(.012)	(.021)	(.021)	(.013)	(.019)	(.022)	(.928)	(.020)
	128	48	176	220	80	300	348	128	476
Personal Care Products	1.43	.53	1.15	2.06	1.06	1.80	1.81	.822	1.54
	(.023)	(.004)	(.019)	(.033)	(.010)	(.029)	(.03)	(.008)	(.026)
	20	9	29	32	11	43	52	20	72
Other Chemicals	.782	.81	.78	.72	1.00	.77	.74	.92	.78
	(.012)	(.007)	(.011)	(.012)	(.009)	(.012)	(.012)	(.008)	(.001)
	206	53	259	408	86	494	614	139	753
Cement and Glass	.87	.34	.77	.67	.47	.628	.73	.43	.60
	(.0187)	(.002)	(.0167)	(.019)	(.005)	(.017)	(.019)	(.004)	(.017)
	50	12	62	122	31	153	172	43	215
Rubber & Rubber Products	.528	.63	.53	.397	.396	.397	.44	.44	.44
	(.067)	(.003)	(.007)	(.004)	(.004)	(.004)	(.005)	(.004)	(.005)
	29	2	31	61	8	69	90	10	100
Paper and Wood	.21	.61	.23	.16	.33	.173	.183	.42	.10
	(.003)	(.005)	(.003)	(.002)	(.002)	(.002)	(.002)	(.003)	(.002)
	43	2	45	29	4	83	122	6	128
Miscellaneous Products and Diversified	.396	.45	.403	.389	.42	.394	.39	.428	.397
	(.0054)	(.0012)	(.005)	(.0058)	(.0027)	(.005)	(.0056)	(.0023)	(.0052)
	36	6	42	69	14	83	105	20	125
Full Sample	.90	.766	.868	.831	.852	.835	.854	.818	.846
	(.015)	(.008)	(.014)	(.015)	(.011)	(.014)	(.015)	(.010)	(.0145)
	1125	338	1463	2169	577	2746	3294	915	4209

Note: Parentheses show S.D.; the bottom figure represents number of observations.

cent. Local firms' average for the period was slightly higher at 0.854 per cent compared to MNE affiliates' 0.818 per cent. In automobiles, electrical machinery and equipment, drugs and pharmaceuticals, cosmetics and toiletries, cement and glass, and in food and beverages, R&D intensity of local companies is higher while in non-electrical machinery, industrial chemicals and chemical products, metals and products, and textiles, MNE affiliates have a higher R&D to sales ratio compared to local firms. In rubber products, R&D intensity of the two groups is equal.

There is also variation over time. Compared to pre-reform period the average R&D intensity has gone down in the post-reform period from 0.868 per cent to 0.835 per cent. However, the bulk of the decline is on account of local firms. MNE affiliates as a group have increased R&D intensity from 0.766 per cent in the pre-reform period to 0.852 per cent in the post-reform period which is slightly higher than local firms' at 0.831 per cent. Therefore, MNE affiliates seem to have shown a greater tendency to do R&D in response to liberalisation measures. The inter-industry pattern of focus of MNE affiliates and local firms has not changed much between the sub-periods. A more detailed analysis of inter-firm, inter-group, inter-industry and inter-temporal patterns is attempted below.

SECTION 3

EXPLAINING THE ENTERPRISE LEVEL R&D BEHAVIOUR: AN ANALYTICAL FRAMEWORK

Enterprise level R&D effort has been examined in a broad framework that associates it with scale of operations, technological opportunities and demand conditions prevailing in the industry in which the firm operates, external technology purchases, internal flow of resources and government policy, among other factors (See Cohen 1995; Kumar & Siddharthan 1997, for recent surveys of literature). Adapting this broad framework to the present context the following explanatory factors are identified.

Firm Size

The firm size has generally been posited as a determinant of innovative activity in the literature in a neo-schumpeterian tradition.

Schumpeter, however, was 'primarily impressed by the qualitative differences between the innovative activities of small, entrepreneurial enterprises and those of large, modern corporations with formal R&D laboratories' (Cohen 1995: 184). Yet the empirical studies have tended to expect a linear continuous relationship between firm size and intensity of innovative activity, attributing it to Schumpeter. Nelson and Winter (1982:349) have justified a positive effect of firm size because larger firms are better able to appropriate returns from their innovative activity. The empirical studies have yielded mixed findings (Cohen 1995; and Kumar and Siddharthan 1997, for recent surveys). Previous Indian studies have generally reported a favourable effect of firm size on R&D (e.g. Lall, 1983; Katrak, 1985; Kumar and Saqib, 1996). A few studies have also reported a U-shaped relationship between firm size and R&D (e.g. Acs and Audretsch, 1988). Siddharthan (1988) reported a U-shaped relationship even for a sample of 166 Indian firms. Some studies have also found evidence of cubic relationship with two thresholds acting on the firm size and R&D intensity relationship (Scherer, 1965; Audretsch and Acs, 1991). In our data set too which covers a very wide range of firm size, the relationship might be characterised by two thresholds. Hence, while postulating a positive relationship between firm size (*SIZE*) and R&D intensity of enterprises, quadratic and cubic terms will be included to capture possible non-linearities.

Technology Imports

In developing countries such as India, import of technology is the most important source of knowledge acquisition by enterprises. Technology imports are likely to affect the propensity to undertake R&D activity. The nature of relationship between technology imports and in-house R&D has been subject to considerable debate in the literature with some studies postulating a complementary relationship between them and others arguing for a substituting one (see Bluementhal, 1979. Kumar and Siddharthan, 1997, provide a recent review). The overwhelming evidence in the case of India has supported the complementarity hypothesis, that is, technology imports are followed up by further technological effort for adaptation and absorption of imported knowledge (see Lall 1983; Katrak 1985; Kumar, 1987; Deolalikar and Evenson 1989; Siddharthan 1988, 1992; Aggarwal 2000, among others). However,

Fikkert (1993) reported an inverse relationship between technology imports and R&D in a framework that treated them jointly determined. Kumar and Saqib (1996) found neither complementarity nor substitution dominating the relationship. Kumar and Siddharthan (1997:133) after reviewing the empirical literature emphasised on the complex nature of the relationship which depends upon interactions with a number of variables. Nevertheless we posit a favourable effect of technology imports on in-house R&D activity. Imports of knowledge in both disembodied (*TECHDISEM*) (such as patents, designs and drawings, process and product licensing) as well as embodied (*TECHEM*) (as incorporated in the plant and machinery) form will be taken into account. This is because embodied knowledge also offers valuable opportunities of absorption and adaptation through reverse engineering.

Outward-Orientation

It is expected that outward-oriented enterprises will have a greater need for in-house R&D than those oriented to domestic markets. That is because of the need for product and process adaptations for the foreign markets in tune with nature of demand, tastes, product standards, availability of raw materials etc. Some evidence corroborates a significant positive effect of export-orientation on R&D intensity (Braga and Willmore 1992, for Brazil; and Kumar and Saqib 1996, and Goldar and Ranganathan 1998, for India). In the current age of globalisation, overseas investments and technology transfers are increasingly important modes of outward orientation. In-house R&D activity may play an important role for supporting the overseas investment and licensing activity of Indian enterprises by providing technological inputs. In this study, we specify the two aspects of outward orientation *viz.* export-orientation (*OUTEX*) and orientation toward overseas investments/licensing etc. (*OUTINV*) postulating their favourable effect on R&D intensity of firms.

Multinational Affiliation

MNE affiliates have a captive and life-long access to their parent's laboratories. On the other hand, local firms importing technology through markets may be anxious to absorb imported knowledge within the term of the licensing contract (Kumar, 1987, 1994). Hence, the propensity of MNE affiliates to undertake R&D could be lower than that of their local counterparts. It is also possible that R&D behaviour of MNE affiliates and national firms also differs and is determined by different factors. Kumar (1991) found R&D intensity of MNE affiliates to be significantly lower than that of local firms in India in univariate tests. The significance of these differences, however, vanished when extraneous influences were controlled for in multivariate tests. The existing literature does not provide any basis for expecting differences in R&D behaviour of the two groups of firms. Yet it is plausible to find a different R&D behaviour in some respects. For instance, outward orientation of MNE affiliates may not be driven by their own R&D activity but by the technology supplied by their parent's laboratories. In view of this we test for differences in both intercepts and slopes of functions explaining the R&D intensity of the two groups of enterprises. The intercept difference will be examined with the help of a dummy separating MNE affiliates (*DMNE*).

Internal Resource Generation and Tax Incentives

The profit margins may affect the propensity to do R&D activity of enterprises in more than one manner. Firms may be unwilling to fund R&D with borrowed funds given the highly uncertain returns from it. High profit margins may indicate internal generation of funds and hence, may favour R&D activity. Furthermore, in order to encourage enterprise level R&D activity the government has extended certain tax breaks. Expenditure on recognised R&D units is offset out of taxable corporate profits. Since 1995-96, a weighted tax deduction is applicable at the rate of 125 per cent of R&D expenditure. The tax breaks, however, encourage R&D activity of only profitable enterprises because those not earning taxable profits are unable to avail of them. Hence, R&D activity may become more attractive for firms with high profit margins as it offsets their tax liability. Goldar and Ranganathan (1998) also find evidence supporting that firms facing a heavier tax burden increase their R&D intensity presumably to reduce their tax liability. The attractiveness of the tax breaks, however, may have gone down over the years with the declining corporate tax rates from about 50 per cent in the early-1990s to 35 per cent since 1996-97.

Opportunities for Adaptations

Scherer (1965) had found that about half of the total inter-industry variation in innovative activity of US manufacturing industries could be explained in terms of 'dynamic supply conditions' dependent upon broad advances of science and technological knowledge, referred to as technological opportunity. Kumar and Saqib (1996) argued that in developing countries like India where the bulk of R&D activity is of an adaptive rather than a creative type, inter-industry differences in opportunities for product and process adaptation are more relevant in determining the R&D strategy of enterprises than technological opportunities. The opportunities for adaptation may vary across industries depending, among other factors, upon the maturity of technology, the gap between the local and global standards, the degree of monopolistic hold over technology and the nature of intellectual property protection, and the need for such adaptation arising from different local conditions. The opportunities for adaptations were expected to be particularly greater in capital goods industries because of the minor design changes needed to adapt them to local conditions, or in chemical industries where the absence of product patents has encouraged the Indian firms to work out alternative processes of known chemical compounds and drug molecules. A similar approach using dummies identifying broad industry groups (*DADAPT*) will be employed to capture the extent of opportunities for adaptations offered by them. The dummy variables, however, may capture the effect of not only the opportunities for adaptations present in a particular industry but also other industry conditions such as market structure, appropriability and returns from innovations etc. This limitation needs to be kept in mind while interpreting the results.

Summarising the above discussion in a functional form:

$$RDS_{it} = \alpha + \beta_1\, SIZE_{it} + \beta_2\, SIZE_{it}^{2} + \beta_3\, SIZE_{it}^{3} + \beta_4\, TECHEM_{it} + \beta_5\, TECHDISEM_{it} + \beta_6\, OUTEX_{it} + \beta_7\, OUTINV_{it} + \beta_8\, PCM_{it} + \beta_9\, DMNE_{i} + \Sigma^{12} t_j\, DADAPT_j + \mu_{it} \quad \ldots(1)$$

Hypotheses

Given the above broad framework, let us now summarise the key hypotheses.

- Given the captive access to parents' research laboratories to satisfy their technological needs, MNE affiliates may have a lower propensity to undertake R&D, holding other factors constant. There may also be differences in R&D behaviour of MNE affiliates and local enterprises, as well. For instance, the propensity to absorb knowledge embodied in plant and machinery would be more pronounced for local enterprises than for MNE affiliates.
- R&D activity of MNE affiliates would be more focused on customisation of product to the local needs and not for absorption and for exploiting the opportunities for process and product adaptations.
- Outward orientation of local enterprises is more likely to be driven by their own R&D than that of MNE affiliates given the captive access of the later to the laboratories of their parents.
- More competitive environment prevailing in the post-reform period would force local enterprises to pay a greater attention to absorption and adaptations of imported knowledge.
- The importance of profit margins as a determinant of R&D activity would decline with the falling rates of corporate tax.

Data-Set and Variable Measurements

The above hypotheses are tested with the data-set consisting of 4209 observations for Indian enterprises in manufacturing for the period 1992-93 to 1998-99 as described in Section 2 above. The variable definitions are as follows:

RDS_{it}: Total R&D expenditure of *i*th firm as a proportion of its sales in *t* th year.

$SIZE_{it}$: Net sales of *i*th firm in *t* th year (transformed into logarithms).

$TECHDISEM_{it}$: Royalties and technical fee paid abroad by *i*th firm as a proportion of its sales in *t* th year.

$TECHEM_{it}$: Imports of capital goods by *i*th firm as a proportion of its sales in *t* th year.

$OUTEX_{it}$: Exports of goods by *i*th firm as a proportion of its sales in *t* th year.

$OUTINV_{it}$: Earnings of foreign exchange by *i*th firm on account of royalties, technical fees, dividends etc. from abroad as a proportion of its sales in *t* th year.

PCM_{it}: Profit margins before tax of *i*th firm as a proportion of its sales in *t* th year.

$DMNE_i$: A dummy variable taking value one for companies with 25 per cent or more foreign ownership by a controlling shareholder.

$DADAPT_j$: Dummies identifying 12 broad branches of manufacturing accounting for at least fifty per cent of *i*th firm's activities.

SECTION 4

EMPIRICAL FINDINGS ON R&D BEHAVIOUR

In what follows we discuss the findings pertaining to various estimations of Model [1] for the full sample and sub-samples and sub-period estimations. Given the panel nature of the data-set, year dummies are included to capture fixed effects of intertemporal shifts. Tests conducted on preliminary estimations revealed presence of heteroskedasticity. Since the form of heteroskedasticity is unknown, co-variance matrices are corrected for heteroskedasticity using the White's estimator in all the estimations. In what follows we summarise the findings pertaining to overall sample and sub-samples and sub-periods.

Full Sample

Table 17.2 summarises the findings of overall estimation for the full period. The explanatory power of the equation is statistically significant in terms of F-test. Although R^2 is rather low at 18 per cent, it is reasonable given the large heterogeneous cross-section of companies covered in the sample. Findings pertaining to the role of different variables are discussed below.

Firm Size: It is apparent that firm size and R&D intensity relationship is characterised by non-linearity for the given sample of Indian industry. A cubic relationship fits well for all the estimations robustly and consistently whether for full sample or different sub-

Table 17.2

Estimations Explaining R&D Behaviour of Indian Enterprises

	Entire Period	*Pre-Reform Period*	*Post–Reform Period*
Variable	Coefficient (t-Statistic)	Coefficient (t-Statistic)	Coefficient (t-Statistic)
Constant	0.027248 (7.692326)	0.031057 (4.271805)	0.025594 (6.959053)
SIZE	-0.012503 (-6.103877)	-0.013949 (-3.174449)	-0.011651 (-5.124802)
SIZE^2	0.002057 (5.062389)	0.002255 (2.571972)	0.001960 (4.290514)
SIZE^3	-0.000110 (-4.331029)	-0.000119 (-2.151646)	-0.000108 (-3.735088)
TECHDISEM	0.075473 (9.190930)	0.08557 (1.271481)	0.075588 (9.445622)
TECHEM	0.005193 (1.541030)	-0.000642 (-0.076297)	0.005803 (1.487973)
OUTEX	0.003239 (2.125906)	0.006145 (1.631995)	0.001819 (1.252860)
OUTINV	0.065976 (2.913496)	0.018102 (0.702767)	0.072856 (3.024669)
PCM	-0.000828 (-1.042563)	0.007403 (2.212792)	-0.001030 (-1.342102)
DMNE	-0.001426 (-3.358346)	-0.001806 (-2.594394)	-0.001271 (-2.351066)
FOOD	-0.000151 (-0.210565)	0.000829 (0.564119)	-0.000706 (-0.707421)
TEXTILES	-0.000536 (-0.785472)	-0.00192 (-1.80583)	-0.001653 (-1.866868)
METALS	3.15E-05 (0.040442)	-0.001697 (-1.478819)	-0.002115 (-2.252708)
AUTO	0.007301 (8.358156)	0.005362 (3.3192)	0.006925 (6.028097)
MACHINERY	0.004853 (6.624043)	0.004335 (2.859183)	0.004128 (4.027653)
ELECTRICAL	0.004922 (6.363450)	0.003898 (2.997757)	0.003994 (3.892131)
PHARMA	0.011293 (10.26427)	0.009399 (5.319228)	0.010891 (7.582932)
PERSONAL-CARE	0.011100 (3.874115)	0.005326 (1.671248)	0.013286 (3.070742)
OTHER-CHEM	0.003006 (4.579941)	0.00176 (1.488733)	0.002353 (2.545982)

Contd...

...*Table 17.2 Contd...*

	Entire Period	*Pre-Reform Period*	*Post –Reform Period*
CEMENT	0.002990 (2.306459)	0.002653 (1.189341)	0.001882 (1.162152)
RUBBER-PROD	0.000512 (0.674859)	-0.000606 (-0.442672)	-0.000588 (-0.611882)
PAPER	-0.001224 (-2.102762)	0.000641 (0.424013)	-0.002243 (-2.761013)
YER4	3.93E-05 (0.041349)	-0.000211 (-0.215831)	
YER5	1.46E-05 (0.016296)	-0.000241 (-0.259876)	
YER6	-0.000570 (-0.665764)		
YER7	4.47E-05 (0.052518)		0.000609 (0.885606)
YER8	-0.000339 (-0.411382)		0.000227 (0.339330)
YER9	0.000246 (0.280574)		0.000764 (1.034727)
R-squared	0.181989	0.13257	0.221072
Adjusted R-squared	0.176706	0.118706	0.214201
F-statistic	34.45103	9.561923	32.17757
N	**4209**	**1463**	**2746**

samples and sub-periods as seen later. This suggests that firm size and R&D intensity relationship is horizontal S-shaped. That is very small firms have very high R&D intensity but R&D intensity of smaller firms declines with firm size up to a threshold level beyond which it rises up to another threshold before falling again with size. A number of earlier studies have also reported S-shaped relationship between firm size and R&D intensity (e.g. Scherer, 1965; Audretsch and Acs, 1991). For Indian industry a U-shaped relationship has been observed by some studies (e.g. Siddharthan, 1988; Kumar and Saqib, 1996).

Technology Imports: TECHDISEM, the variable capturing the extent of imports of disembodied technology by firms comes up with a significant positive effect. This tends to corroborate that imports of knowledge have been followed up by further technological effort by Indian firms in tune with findings of a number of earlier studies (e.g.

Lall 1983; Katrak 1985; Kumar, 1987; Deolalikar and Evenson 1989; Siddharthan 1988, 1992; Basant 1997, Aggarwal 2000, among others). *TECHEM* capturing embodied technology imports comes up with a positive sign and just misses statistical significance in terms of t-test. It tends to suggest that knowledge imports in the form of capital goods may also provide opportunities for technological effort by Indian industry.

Outward Orientation: Both *OUTEX* and *OUTINV* come up with positive and statistically significant effects. It suggests that outward orientation of firms whether in the form of higher proportion of exports in turnover or overseas investments and technology licensing activities significantly increases the need for an in-house R&D effort to support overseas operations.

Profit Margins: PCM comes up with a coefficient that is not significantly different from zero in statistical terms. Hence, profitability of firms does not seem to be affecting the intensity of R&D. However, the effect of profitability on R&D intensity may be sensitive to the period as the tax rates have changed considerably over the period and might have affected the relative attraction of the tax benefits granted by the government to promote enterprise R&D activity. Hence, it is subject to verification later.

Multinational Affiliation: The dummy variable capturing the effect of affiliation with MNEs has a significant negative effect on the R&D intensity. That suggests that MNE affiliates spend less on R&D activity per unit of their income compared to their local counterparts, holding other factors constant. Affiliates of MNEs may feel less need of R&D given their captive access to the R&D laboratories of their parents abroad. This finding, however, is based on a restrictive model where the slope coefficients of R&D behaviour of MNE affiliates and local firms are not allowed to vary. It is possible that even the R&D behaviour of the two groups of firms is determined differently. That is explored later with sub-sample estimations.

Opportunities for Adaptation: Of the 12 sectoral dummy variables employed to capture the variation across industries in the opportunities they offer for adaptations, eight achieve statistical significance, seven with a positive sign and one with a negative sign. This suggests that with respect to the benchmark industry (that is miscellaneous manufacturing), automobiles, non-electrical machinery, electrical equipment, drugs and chemicals, personal care products, other chemicals and products, and cement and glass industries have a higher and paper and paper products has a lower R&D intensity. This finding is consistent with the earlier findings of Kumar and Saqib (1996) who reported a higher tendency of Indian engineering firms to conduct product adaptations and incremental innovations to make their product more appropriate for the local market. They also found Indian chemical and related industry firms doing process adaptations which was facilitated by a soft patent regime. In particular, the coefficients of drugs and pharmaceutical industry and personal care products industries are quite large in relative terms suggesting that Indian enterprises in these industries have been more R&D intensive than others.

Intertemporal Shifts: None of the six time-dummies included in the estimations to capture year-to-year shifts in the intercept with respect to the base year emerges significantly different from zero in statistical terms. Therefore, there is no evidence of a shift in the intercept during the period covered. However, the liberalisation might have affected the R&D behaviour of enterprises. That remains to be verified with sub-period estimations below.

Liberalisation and R&D Behaviour

To examine the possible effect of liberalisation on the R&D behaviour of Indian enterprises, the sample period was split between two sub-periods as discussed in Section 2. F-tests conducted on the basis of pooled estimations for the entire period and the estimations for the sub-periods suggest that the slopes of R&D behaviour have significantly changed between the two sub-periods. The estimation results pertaining to the two sub-period are also presented in Table 17.2 (equations 2 and 3, respectively). Here we confine to a discussion of only the main differences emerging between the two sub-periods to get an idea of the nature of effect of liberalisation on R&D behaviour.

Technology import variables show a change over the sub-periods. In the first period, both the technology import variables remain not significantly different from zero. However, *TECHDISEM* assumes a strong statistical significance with a positive sign in the second period. *TECHEM* also has a positive sign and just misses the statistical significance. It would appear from this that liberalisation of trade, industrial policy and technology import policy in the 1990s has made Indian enterprises more conscious of the need to devote a further technological effort to technology imports. This indeed is a welcome development. One possible explanation of this trend could be increased threat of competition from imports and entry of foreign and local firms and adoption of product-based rivalry by Indian enterprises. More detailed research is indicated to find exact explanations of this trend.

The other major difference observed between the two sub-period estimations is with respect to the performance of outward orientation variables. In the first period, only *OUTEX* has a significant effect (with positive sign) and *OUTINV* remains not significantly different from zero. In the second period, however, *OUTINV* emerges with a robust positive effect although the coefficient of *OUTEX* loses its significance. This is an interesting finding. It tends to suggest that overseas investment has become an important aspect of strategy of Indian enterprises in the post-reform period. That, in turn, has pushed R&D intensity to provide technological back-up to overseas operations. Here again more work is needed before a more definitive statement could be made.

The performance of *PCM* is also affected by the period. In the first period this variable has a significant positive effect while in the second period its coefficient becomes not significantly different from zero. It seems to be on account of declining rates of corporate income tax from 45-50 per cent (depending upon whether the company is closely held or widely held) in the early-1990s to 35 per cent during 1996-97. Lower rates of tax reduce the importance of tax incentives as an inducement of R&D activity. Hence, more profitable companies have lesser incentive to spend on R&D activity compared to the earlier period.

Finally, in terms of industry-dummies representing opportunities for adaptation, there are few changes. The dummies representing other chemical products and personal care products, that were significant in full period estimations do not remain statistically significant in the first period, while cement and glass industry dummy loses its statistical significance in both the periods. Food products industry for the first period and metals and metal products for the second period assume significant negative effect. The broad industry pattern of high R&D intensity being confined to engineering and drugs and pharmaceuticals industry holds good in both the sub-periods.

R&D Behaviour of MNE Affiliates and Local Firms: Is it different?

It was observed above that MNE affiliates spend proportionately less on R&D activity compared to their local counterparts. That model, however, is a restrictive one in that it imposes a condition of similar slopes of the two groups of firms. Given the captive access of the former to their parents' laboratories, it is possible that even R&D behaviour of the two groups of firms is different and hence slope coefficients vary. To verify this proposition the R&D functions of the two groups of firms are estimated separately. F-tests conducted on full sample estimation and sub-sample estimations confirm that both intercept terms and slope coefficients of R&D functions vary significantly. Table 17.3 presents the sub-sample estimations. Here again, we confine ourselves to a discussion of main differences only.

The first difference between the two groups in terms of R&D behaviour is noted with respect to technology import variables. While R&D intensity of both local firms and MNE affiliates is related to imports of disembodied technology, only local firms seem to be following up the imports of embodied knowledge with further effort (as *TECHEM* has a positive and nearly significant (at 12 per cent) effect in their case). It is plausible because in the case of MNE affiliates, knowledge embodied in imported capital goods is likely to be already known to their parents who are generally sources of these imports. Local firms, on the other hand, may be keen to absorb the knowledge contained in imported machinery through reverse engineering for trouble shooting, replication and updation etc. Hence, MNE affiliates use their R&D activity for adaptations of products and processes for the local markets.

The other notable difference is with respect to outward orientation variables. Both of the variables capturing outward orientation exert a significant positive effect in the case of local firms but turn up with negative and not significantly different from zero

Table 17.3

Explaining R&D Behaviour of Local Enterprises and MNE Affiliates

	Local Firms	*MNE Affiliates*
Variable	Coefficient (t-Statistic)	Coefficient (t-Statistic)
Constant	0.025412 (6.454683)	0.041749 (4.886900
SIZE	-0.011301 (-4.995223)	-0.022703 (-4.632602)
SIZE²	0.001781 (3.924118)	0.004211 (4.396182)
SIZE³	-9.18E-05 (-3.191401)	-0.000247 (-4.171678)
TECHDISEM	0.075207 (1.704545)	0.077302 (9.276062)
TECHEM	0.007652 (1.534655)	0.002178 (0.837043)
OUTEX	0.003201 (1.848459)	-0.000995 (-0.438632)
OUTINV	0.080129 (3.555755)	-0.005214 (-1.074570)
PCM	-0.000920 (-1.174208)	0.005052 (2.007195)
FOOD	0.000317 (0.368422)	-0.001637 (-1.012166)
TEXTILES	-0.000511 (-0.689424)	0.003108 (1.259473)
METALS	-3.69E-05 (-0.041433)	0.000278 (0.151676)
AUTO	0.009117 (7.684958)	0.003382 (2.092995)
MACHINERY	0.004736 (5.344217)	0.004029 (2.252208)
ELECTRICAL	0.005491 (5.894557)	0.002321 (1.351341)
PHARMA	0.012723 (9.173271)	0.006863 (3.478140)
PERSONAL-CARE	0.013411 (3.459211)	0.003244 (1.284127)
OTHER-CHEM	0.002523 (3.289478)	0.005221 (3.050651)
CEMENT	0.003862 (2.452046)	-0.000122 (-0.066919)

Contd...

...Table 17.3 Contd...

	Local Firms	*MNE Affiliates*
RUBBER-PROD	0.000914 (1.081481)	0.000182 (0.077083)
PAPER	-0.000934 (-1.427153)	0.000499 (0.239975)
YER4	0.000129 (0.105830)	-0.000317 (-0.298175)
YER5	4.19E-05 (0.037240)	-0.000368 (-0.350709)
YER6	-0.000866 (-0.815550)	0.000838 (0.737051)
YER7	-7.28E-05 (-0.068271)	0.000749 (0.700382)
YER8	-0.000781 (-0.764016)	0.001365 (1.286265)
YER9	0.000243 (0.221829)	0.000406 (0.390071)
R-squared	.179092	0.333048
Adjusted R-squared	.172559	0.314292
F-statistic	27.41303	17.75719
N	3294	915

effect in the case of MNE affiliates. Apparently, local firms use their R&D activity to support their overseas expansion. Overseas expansion of MNE affiliates is likely to be based on their parents' strategy, resources and technology. Outward orientation of MNE affiliates is either home market seeking where they produce intermediate products of given specifications for their principals and affiliates or they receive regional or global product mandates from their parent for serving mandated markets for specific products (see Kumar 1998, for a detailed analysis). In both the cases, their parents are likely to provide the technological backup.

There is also a difference in the role of *PCM* across the two groups. *PCM* has a statistically significant positive effect for MNE affiliates while it remains not significantly different from zero with a negative sign for local firms. It tends to suggest that availability of tax incentives and internal flow of resources are more important considerations for determining the R&D behaviour of MNE affiliates than their local counterparts. R&D activity of local firms seems to be driven more by strengthening their competitive position.

Finally, different sectoral pattern of R&D activity of MNE affiliates and local firms also needs to be explained. R&D activity of local firms is concentrated in the industries that offer significantly more opportunities for product adaptations (as branches of engineering) or process adaptations (as chemical and related industries). Process adaptations in chemicals and pharmaceuticals industries are facilitated by softer patent regime India has adopted that does not recognise product patents in these industries. Introduction of product patents in India by 1-1-2005 as obligated under the Agreement on TRIPs under WTO has the prospect of adversely affecting the process innovative activity of Indian enterprises.

MNE affiliates have concentrated their R&D activity in automotives, machinery, drugs and pharmaceuticals, and other chemicals. Their R&D activity in auto and machinery industries could be attuned to product customisation for the local market. Their R&D activity in drugs and chemicals industries seems to be part of a recent trend of MNEs locating R&D units in India and other such countries in these industries (as in software development), to exploit her advantages such as availability of low cost trained manpower, and to absorb knowledge spillovers from technological activity in the public funded laboratories and innovative activity of leading national enterprises (see Kumar, 1996, 2000, for detailed analyses of determinants of overseas R&D activity of MNEs). This has led to a number of MNEs such as Astra AB of Sweden, Eli Lilly, Du Pont, Abbot Labortaories, Parke Davis, Smith Kline and Beecham all of USA, and Akzo of Netherlands, among others, to set up global R&D centres, enter into R&D joint ventures with Indian companies and contract public funded laboratories for R&D (see Kumar, 1999, for more details). It appears that MNE affiliates in chemicals and pharmaceuticals in our sample are performing R&D activity for their parents as a part of this emerging trend. In the terminology of Kuemmerle (1999) it is a case of 'home base augmenting' R&D activity while the product adaptive R&D of MNE affiliates in engineering industries could be termed as 'home base exploiting' R&D.

Liberalisation and R&D Activity of MNE Affiliates and Local Enterprises

Given the earlier observation that reforms and liberalisation have affected R&D behaviour of Indian enterprises, we now examine how the R&D behaviour of the two groups of firms have been affected by reforms. The estimations for the two groups for the two sub-periods have been summarised in Table 17.4.

Table 17.4

R&D Behaviour of MNE Affiliates and Local Firms in Sub-periods

	Local Firms		*MNE Affiliates*	
	Pre-reform	*Post-reform*	*Pre-reform*	*Post-reform*
Variable	Coefficient (t-Statistic)	Coefficient (t-Statistic)	Coefficient (t-Statistic)	Coefficient (t-Statistic)
Constant	0.028161 (3.482315)	0.023160 (5.910152)	0.045217 (3.196863)	0.042064 (4.710864)
SIZE	-0.011998 (-2.536550)	-0.010821 (-4.377107)	-0.024195 (-2.654290)	-0.020376 (-4.449173)
$SIZE^2$	0.001806 (1.942849)	0.001769 (3.499681)	0.004631 (2.411765)	0.003827 (4.370130)
$SIZE^3$	-8.86E-05 (-1.533288)	-9.53E-05 (-2.930914)	-0.000284 (-2.232962)	-0.000229 (-4.248968)
TECHDISEM	0.064753 (0.874519)	0.091132 (2.055244)	0.182060 (2.327334)	0.073376 (7.993606)
TECHEM	0.001657 (0.175049)	0.009254 (1.548935)	-0.014565 (-1.708814)	0.002817 (0.914604)
OUTEX	0.006467 (1.471903)	0.001498 (0.919320)	0.002842 (0.907236)	-0.001515 (-0.512631)
OUTINV	0.028422 (0.869575)	0.087122 (3.762103)	-0.019184 (-2.348069)	-0.001229 (-0.218234)
PCM	0.006580 (1.766003)	-0.001086 (-1.429005)	0.012159 (2.188597)	0.002346 (0.924322)
FOOD	-0.001536 (-1.077383)	0.000663 (0.644261)	-0.004440 (-3.145545)	-0.005020 (-1.790636)
TEXTILES	-0.000574 (-0.377565)	-0.000759 (-0.948097)	0.000572 (0.139758)	-0.000745 (-0.211154)
METALS	0.001324 (0.772495)	-0.001336 (-1.456353)	-0.003721 (-2.645480)	-0.004668 (-1.590739)
AUTO	0.007325 (3.239028)	0.009451 (6.829034)	-0.000469 (-0.388081)	0.000455 (0.160328)

Contd...

...Table 17.4 Contd...

	Local Firms		*MNE Affiliates*	
	Pre-reform	*Post-reform*	*Pre-reform*	*Post-reform*
MACHINERY	0.004253 (2.561074)	0.004569 (4.417859)	0.000761 (0.527148)	0.001032 (0.334658)
ELECTRICAL	0.004642 (2.426142)	0.005465 (5.099984)	0.001162 (0.838870)	-0.001936 (-0.656160)
PHARMA	0.010379 (4.564456)	0.013444 (8.002537)	0.004275 (2.058368)	0.003374 (1.041670)
PERSONAL-CARE	0.007075 (1.558921)	0.016544 (2.934019)	-0.002336 (-1.193045)	0.001734 (0.407735)
OTHER-CHEM	0.001367 (0.937168)	0.002645 (2.972138)	0.001645 (1.212753)	0.002229 (0.742816)
CEMENT	0.003613 (1.323923)	0.003478 (1.850829)	-0.002642 (-1.964437)	-0.003851 (-1.278057)
RUBBER-PROD	0.000819 (0.478801)	0.000714 (0.771676)	0.000700 (0.363267)	-0.004296 (-1.343017)
PAPER	-0.001741 (-1.424903)	-0.001097 (-1.491587)	0.001696 (0.719684)	-0.004474 (-1.499075)
YER4	-0.000105 (-0.082446)		-0.000348 (-0.330295)	
YER5	-0.000142 (-0.121081)		-0.000307 (-0.283121)	
YER7		0.000818 (1.013312)		-0.000268 (-0.249719)
YER8		0.000106 (0.136459)		0.000385 (0.351499)
YER9		0.001091 (1.254667)		-0.000634 (-0.586670)
R-squared	0.127366	0.220168	0.298464	0.401273
Adjusted R-squared	0.109945	0.211806	0.249467	0.376371
F-statistic	7.311063	26.33012	6.091566	16.11417
N	1125	338	2169	577

Confining to the main changes that emerge from these estimations, one finds that the effect of technology import variables in the case of local firms becomes statistically significant in the second period while it was not significantly different from zero in the first period. Therefore, liberalisation and reforms seem to have pushed the local firms to follow up the technology imports with further technological effort on adaptation and absorption. Earlier studies had found a complementary relationship between technology imports and local R&D intensity for the pre-reform period as well. However, those studies did not separate MNE affiliates and local firms.

OUTINV becomes significant for local firms only in the second period. As observed earlier, reforms seem to have led Indian companies to globalise their operations which has in turn pushed them to pay a greater attention to R&D activity. Finally, *PCM* has statistically significant positive effect in the first period for both MNE affiliates as well as local firms, its significance vanishes in the second period for both the groups of firms. Therefore, the declining rates of corporate tax in the second period seem to have affected the importance of tax incentives for undertaking R&D activity of both groups of firms.

SECTION 5

IMPLICATIONS OF THE FINDINGS AND CONCLUDING REMARKS

In an increasingly globalising and knowledge-based world economy where technological capability of firms and countries determine their competitiveness and growth, declining importance of R&D activity in India is a matter of concern. In that context, this paper has analysed the determinants of R&D behaviour of Indian enterprises to examine, among other issues, if liberalisation as a part of reforms of 1991 has affected the motivation of firms to do R&D and their R&D behaviour and if R&D behaviour of MNE affiliates and local firms is different. The analysis is conducted in a broad analytical framework that has evolved over the years with numerous studies in a neo-Schumpeterian tradition and employs a large panel data-set of Indian enterprises for the 1990s.

Overall trend in the data-set shows a decline in the average R&D intensity of Indian enterprises over the post-reform period. Starting with a relatively lower R&D intensity compared to local firms, MNE affiliates have increased their R&D spending rapidly over the 1990s. R&D intensity of local firms has declined over the same period. However, the quantitative analysis shows that after controlling for extraneous factors such as firm size and profit margins, MNE affiliates have a lower R&D intensity compared to local firms, presumably on account of their captive access to the laboratories of their parent and associated companies.

The analysis also reveals other differences in the nature of R&D activity of MNE affiliates and local firms. For instance, local firms seem to be directing their R&D activity towards absorption of knowledge embodied in imported capital goods, especially in the post-reform period. Technology imports in disembodied form also prompt further technological activity of importing firms. However, their effect has become more pronounced in the post-reform period especially for local firms. R&D activity of local firms seem to be driven by their outward orientation especially through overseas investments in the post-reform period. The reforms seem to have pushed local firms to internationalise their operations and in-house R&D activity is required to provide a technological backup for that process. MNE affiliates' outward expansion, if any, is not related to their in-house R&D activity. R&D activity of local firms is concentrated in industries that offer significant opportunities for product or process adaptations.

That implies that R&D activity of local firms is more directed towards building in-house technological capabilities through absorption of knowledge acquired from external sources and exploiting opportunities for product adaptations (as in engineering industries) and process innovations (as in chemicals and pharmaceutical industries). These capabilities assist them in the process of their internationalisation. Drugs and pharmaceutical industry presents a case in point where facilitated by softer patent regime Indian companies have focused their R&D activity on process innovations or adaptations and have emerged as the cheapest producers of a number of important generic drugs in the world. They are now able to participate in the emerging international division of labour in the generics market. MNE affiliates, on the other hand, either focus on customisation of their parents' technology for local market or on exploiting the advantages of India as a R&D platform for their parents (now referred to as home-base augmenting R&D). Seen from that perspective the R&D activity of local firms has more favourable externalities for the domestic economy in the form of building up of locally anchored technological capability and internationalisation than that of MNE affiliates.

India's obligation under the WTO's TRIPs Agreement to provide product patents by 2005 has the prospect to adversely affect the process innovative activity of Indian chemicals and pharmaceutical enterprises. It is likely to lead to an international division of labour where countries with limited capability for product innovations in these industries such as India will specialise in off-the-patent generic drugs market and more advanced countries on innovation based new drugs. As a step towards preparation for the emerging patent regime, the Indian pharmaceutical enterprises have already started turning the focus of their R&D activity to development of new drug delivery systems.

Over time trends give the impression that although average levels of spending may have gone down, reforms and liberalisation and resulting threat of competition seem to have pushed local firms to rationalise their R&D activity and make it more meaningful, such as by tuning it to the needs of internationalisation and for absorption of imported knowledge. In the pre-reform period a large part of R&D activity of MNE affiliates and local enterprises was driven by availability of tax incentives. The declining rates of taxes seem to have reduced the importance of tax incentives as a factor determining the scale of R&D.

The relationship between firm size and R&D intensity is found to be horizontal S-shaped. Thus, very small specialised firms are highly R&D intensive but until certain threshold is reached R&D intensity declines with firm size. Then it rises with firm size until second threshold is reached beyond which it declines again for very large firms. Therefore, medium sized firms do bulk of the R&D activity. However, the absolute scale of larger firms' R&D activity may be larger. Given the economies of scale (and scope) in R&D activity in many industries, the productivity of their R&D activity may be even higher. Furthermore, it is the R&D activity of larger national champions that can make a visible difference to the national technological capabilities. For instance, Philips representing the electronics capability of the Netherlands and Samsung of Korea, and so on (see Kumar and Siddharthan, 1997, for more detailed analysis). Hence, it might be important to push larger firms to build innovative capacities while encouraging R&D activity of smaller and medium firms.

Now a word on policy implications. The economic reforms seem to have served to rationalise the R&D activity of corporations and make it more meaningful. However, R&D intensities of Indian enterprises are too small compared to global standards to make a significant difference to their competitiveness. The policy framework needs to encourage R&D activity geared to build in-house capability for product and process innovations for competing in the increasingly globalising and knowledge based world economy. The tax incentives as means for promoting R&D activity seem to have lost their relevance. They should be replaced now with more direct incentives such as R&D subsidies that are aggressively used by most of the industrialised and newly industrialising economies to promote international competitiveness of their national champions (see Kumar and Siddharthan, 1997, for evidence). While the WTO regime sanctions most of the subsidies, R&D subsidies up to 50 per cent and for basic research up to 75 per cent are non-actionable. Furthermore, in the case of subsidies it is possible to direct the R&D effort of enterprises in a desirable direction or field. For instance, it may be used to promote capability building for new product or process innovations for local markets or internationalisation rather than customisation of imported technologies and products. It is also possible to achieve other desirable objectives such as promoting industry's linkages with the public funded research laboratories and Universities through more direct subsidies.

Besides promotion through subsidies etc., local technology generation activity also needs some protection to come up like an infant industry. This is because imported technology has several commercial attractions over the locally developed alternatives such as its already proven nature, hence, low risk and uncertainty, availability of financing from suppliers, market power of well known brands and trade marks that come with it, among others (see Kumar, 1990). Given the liberal policy on technology imports, enterprises feel less inclined to invest in a rather uncertain activity like in-house R&D and prefer to meet their technological needs through imports. Technology imports could continue to be governed by liberal policy such as automatic approvals as in force currently, because restricting them also could possibly lead to technological obsolescence. However, the landed cost of technology imports could be increased through levies imposed on technological payments. These levies could be returned to the domestic enterprises conducting R&D. Furthermore, products based on indigenously developed technology could be extended excise concessions (such as those extended to products of small scale industry) and income tax concessions (such as those enjoyed by export turnover) to encourage innovations.

References

Agarwal, Aradhna (2000). "Deregulation, Technology Imports and In-house R&D Efforts: An Analysis of the Indian Experience," *Research Policy* (Forthcoming).

Acs, Z.J. (1988). "Innovation in Large and Small Firms: An Empirical Analysis," *American Economic Review*, 78:678-90.

Audretsch, D.B. and Z.J. Acs (1991). "Innovation and Size at the Firm Level," *Southern Economic Journal* 57(3), 739-744.

Basant, Rakesh (2000). "Corporate Response to Reforms" in Nagesh Kumar (ed.) *Indian Economy under Reforms: An Assessment of Economic and Social Impact*, New Delhi: Bookwell, (in press).

Blumenthal, Tuvia (1979). "A Note on the Relationship between Domestic Research and Development and Imports of Technology," *Economic Development and Cultural Change*, 27: 303-6.

Braga, Helson and Larry Willmore (1991). "Technological Imports and Technological Effort: An Analysis of their Determinants in Brazilian Firms," *The Journal of Industrial Economics*, 39: 421-32.

Cohen, W.M. (1995). "Empirical Studies of Innovative Activity," in Paul Stoneman (ed.), *Handbook of the Economics of Innovation and Technological Change*, Oxford: Blackwell; 182-264.

Goldar, R.N. and V.S. Ranganathan (1998). "Economic Reforms and R&D Expenditure in Industrial Firms in India," *The Indian Economic Journal*, Vol. 46, No. 2, 60-75.

Fikkert, Brian (1993). *"An Open or Closed Technology Policy? The Effects of Technology Licensing, Foreign Direct Investment, and Technology Spillovers on R&D in Indian Industrial Sector Firms,"* unpublished Ph.D. dissertation, New Haven, CT: Yale University.

India, DSIR (1998). *Compendium on In-house R&D Centres* (in two volumes), New Delhi: Department of Scientific and Industrial Research.

India, DST (1999). *Research and Development Statistics 1996-97*, New Delhi: Department of Science and Technology.

Katrak, Homi (1985). "Imported Technology, Enterprise Size and R&D in a Newly Industrialising Country: The Indian Experience," *Oxford Bulletin of Economics and Statistics*, 47: 213-30.

Kuemmerle, Walter (1999). "The Drivers of Foreign Direct Investment into Research and Development: An Empirical Investigation" *Journal of International Business Studies*, 30 (1):1-24.

Kumar, Nagesh (1987). "Technology Imports and Local Research and Development in Indian Manufacturing," *The Developing Economies*, 25:220-33.

————. (1990). "Cost of Imported and Local Technologies: Implications for Technology Policy," *Economic and Political Weekly*, 25(January 13): 103-6.

————. (1991). "Mode of Rivalry and Comparative Behaviour of Multinational and Local Enterprises: The Case of Indian Manufacturing," *Journal of Development Economics*, 35: 38192.

————. (1994). *Multinational Enterprises and Industrial Organisation: The Case of India*, New Delhi, Thousand Oaks and London: Sage Publications.

————. (1996). "Intellectual Property Protection, Market Orientation and Location of Overseas R&D Activities by Multinational Enterprises," *World Development*, 24(4): 673-88.

————. (1998). "Multinational Enterprises, Regional Economic Integration, and Export-Platform Production in the Host Countries: An Empirical Analysis for the US and Japanese," *Weltwirtschaftliches Archiv* (134(3), 450-483.

———. (1999). "Multinational Enterprises, Overseas R&D Activity and Global Technological Order," *RIS Occasional Paper No. #56*, New Delhi: Research and Information System.

———. (2000). "Determinants of Location of Overseas R&D Activity of Multinational Enterprises: The Case of US and Japanese Corporations," *Research Policy*, forthcoming.

Kumar, Nagesh and Mohammed Saqib (1996). "Firm Size, Opportunities for Adaptation, and In-house R&D Activity in Developing Countries: The Case of Indian Manufacturing," *Research Policy*, 25(5): 712-22.

Kumar, Nagesh and N.S. Siddharthan (1997). *Technology, Market Structure and Internationalisation: Issues and Policies for Developing Countries*, Routledge and UNU Press, London and New York.

Lall, Sanjaya (1983). "Determinants of R&D in a LDC: The Indian Engineering Industry," *Economics Letters*, 13:379-83.

Mani, Sunil and M. Vijaya Bhaskar (1998). "A Curmudgeon's Guide to Economic Reforms in India's Manufacturing Sector," *Economic and Political Weekly*, 19 December.

Nelson, R.R. and Sidney G. Winter (1982). *An Evolutionary Theory of Economic Change*, Cambridge and London: Harvard University Press.

Scherer, F.M. (1965). "Firm Size, Market Structure, Opportunity, and the Output of Patented Inventions," *American Economic Review*, 55: 1097-125.

Siddharthan, N.S. (1988). "In-house R&D, Imported Technology and Firm Size: Lessons from Indian Experience," *Developing Economies*, 26:212-21.

———. (1992). "Transaction Costs, Technology Transfer, and In-house R&D: A Study of the Indian Private Corporate Sector," *Journal of Economic Behaviour and Organisation*, 18:265-71.

18

Technology Acquisition and Export Competitiveness

Evidence from Indian Automobile Industry

K. NARAYANAN

SECTION 1

INTRODUCTION

This paper aims at analysing the impact of technology transfer and the import liberalisation, introduced in India during the mid-1980s and early-1990s, on the international competitiveness [defined in terms of export intensity] of Indian automobile firms. Specifically the analysis would attempt to answer the following questions, namely: (1) why do some firms export while others don't, and (2) to what extent the export orientation of firms is guided by the policy regime in which they are operating? The analysis uses firm level data and adopts the evolutionary theoretical framework of the neo-technology theories. A Tobit model is estimated to take into account the fact that some firms in the sample do not export. The role of different modes of technology acquisition, firm size, capital intensity, vertical integration and imports of components in export behaviour is examined under three different policy regimes.

This paper is divided into eight sections. In section 2 the background literature dealing with technology and international competitiveness is reviewed. Section 3 refers to the literature on technology and trade in developing countries and outlines the context in which the analysis is carried out. Descriptive statistics on export intensity of automobile firms under different policy regimes are presented in section 4. While section 5 deals with the construction of the variables and hypotheses in determining exports, section 6 specifies the Tobit model used for empirical analysis.

Section 7 presents the results of the empirical exercise, and the major findings are summarised in section 8.

SECTION 2
THE BACKGROUND ON TECHNOLOGICAL THEORIES OF TRADE

The relationship between technology and international competitiveness has been a major area for both theoretical and empirical analyses.[1] The central focus of these studies is to analyse the role of differences in technological capabilities in determining trade performance. For a general role of technology, the starting point for most of these studies has been Schumpeter's concept of innovation. Posner's (1961) seminal paper opened the way to the development of an alternative paradigm. Starting from a point that a firm which introduced a new product may enjoy an export monopoly from the country of origin, at least until the imitators come into the market, Posner developed a set of concepts which became the basis for various 'technology gap' theories of trade. Posner not only discussed the existence of these technology gaps between nations, but also pointed out that these gaps are maintained by the nations and firms through quality and scale of commitment to R&D, clustering of technical innovations and dynamic economies of scale. Hufbauer (1966) provided an empirical illustration and validation of technology gap theory in his study of international trade in synthetic materials. He found a distinct relationship between trade performance and innovative leadership. Soete (1981) regressed export performance on technology variable for a sample of OECD countries and 40 industrial sectors and found a crucial role of a technology variable in explaining inter-country variation in export performance in majority of the industries. As a result, these new trade theories emphasised the importance of innovative activities within imperfect competition models of trade and growth (Grossman and Helpman 1991). These theories are useful in analysing the net outcome of uneven technological activities of different nations.

---

1. See Fagerberg (1996) and Wakelin (1997) for a more recent and detailed review of the studies linking technology and international competitiveness of a country.

Most of the later empirical examination of the relationship between technology variables and countries' export performance was also undertaken within a "technology-gap" approach (Vernon 1966, Krugman 1979, Fagerberg 1988 and Dosi, *et al.*, 1992). The results indicate robust correlation between national technological capabilities and export performance.

The literature starting with technology gap and product life cycle models of trade (Posner 1961, Hufbauer 1966, Vernon 1966), and the more recent 'new trade' theories (Grossman and Helpman 1991) clearly argue that international technological differences form a fundamental basis for trade. However, it is the evolutionary theoretical approach of Nelson and Winter (1982) which make the firm as the centre of analysis. Dosi (1984) followed it up with his famous sketch of a firm's technological evolution through the example of semi-conductor industry. Dosi *et al.*, (1992) provide a detailed account of how long-term trends in trade performance of each economy are essentially determined by their different degrees of innovativeness and technological dynamism. Posner also considered the results of firm level learning as a possible creator of technology gap. However, it was Dosi (1984) and Pavitt (1984) who chose to discuss the evolution of technological capabilities within a firm and the role of differences in these technological capabilities in explaining inter-firm differences in competitiveness. Dosi *et al.*, (1992) have also discussed the possibility of growth or exit of an individual firm as a function of their relative technological success.

Automobile exports from India until the early-1980s largely consisted of medium and heavy commercial vehicles and four-wheeled utility vehicles (called 'Jeep'). These exports were mostly directed to countries in the middle-east (Saudi Arabia and Kuwait) and neighbouring developing countries in the South Asian region (such as Sri Lanka and Malaysia) and Africa (Tanzania, Kenya, Ghana and Zambia). Similar road and load conditions, driving habits, and hot and humid weather conditions, combined with geographical proximity, seems to have created a demand for Indian commercial and multi-utility vehicles in these countries. In the case of commercial vehicles, these Asian and African developing countries seem to prefer medium sized vehicles because of their narrow roads. Indian road conditions are also similar to these and most of the adaptation requirements of the borrowed Western technology in automobile production began with this. Most of the technological efforts in this industry were addressed to solve the problem of making them suitable to Indian resource and market conditions.

One of the key features of automobile production in India was the protection given to it from both imports and foreign direct investment. Furthermore, stringent industrial licensing requirements ruled out the possibility of new entry. Protection provided under 'infant-industry' argument reduced the capability of most of the Indian automobile firms to compete in global markets. Under these circumstances, technological efforts of selected Indian companies, that too in the form of making the vehicle suit local conditions, could only prompt them to look for markets in other developing countries. This dependence on developing country markets, rendered them unsuitable for much larger markets in both developed and newly industrialising countries. Indian car and light commercial vehicle (LCV) firms were unable to compete in the world market due to high cost of production (because of small scale production) and lack of energy efficiency and technological sophistication. While the small-scale operation was largely due to capacity licensing restrictions, poor efficiency of Indian vehicles was due to inadequate technological efforts.[2]

With a change in the policy framework, during the mid-1980s, the situation was expected to be better. Entry of Maruti in the car segment witnessed introduction of the Japanese style of management (Flexible Management System (FMS) and Just in Time (JIT) delivery. Maruti was set up in India around the time when Japanese firms began to establish assembly operations in North America and Europe. Suzuki Motors, in collaboration with Maruti in India, captured the domestic market by small-sized and fuel-efficient passenger cars. Production of 800cc cars and multi-utility vehicles in India was a transplant of this version of low-end model by Suzuki. Intra-firm trade and exports to other developing country markets

2. Japan also protected its automobile firms from imports and foreign direct investment during the early phase of development. However, within this protected environment, a large number of domestic entrants were attracted to enter the industry and compete vigorously. Ozawa (1997) pointed out that fierce and condensed domestic competition compelled the Japanese firms to develop capabilities to compete in the global markets.

from Maruti enabled India to enter global market in the car segment as well. In the case of commercial vehicles, however, Indian firms started facing setbacks in the global market during this period. The engine power of Indian commercial vehicles lags far behind the international standards in terms of speed and acceleration. Moreover, Indian commercial vehicle manufacturers produce a common chassis and engine for buses and trucks. These chassis weigh very low and, therefore, results in excessive wear and tear of engine components, reduce the life of the engine and cause higher fuel consumption.[3] This had been a major handicap for Indian firms in export markets. Exports of Indian commercial vehicles, therefore, continued its dependence on markets in other less developed countries during this period. The LCV segment, on the other hand, appears to be more flexible to face the global market. During the de-regulation period, maximum entry has been in the LCV sector and most of them were with Japanese equity and/or technical collaboration. These Japanese companies have already been highly competitive in LCVs, and therefore they could make use of their marketing and service networks in foreign markets in order to facilitate exports. In both the cases (car as well as LCV), therefore, entry of Japanese companies appears to have brightened the chances of exports from India. However, since these Japanese companies find the quality of local parts highly unsuitable for their differentiated models, they also encourage their component and parts suppliers to set-up plants in collaboration with local (host country) firms. Ozawa (1997) found that it has taken a considerable amount of time for the Japanese firms to recruit and mould some local suppliers into Japanese-style design-in parts manufacturing and JIT delivery. Gittelman and Dunning (1992) pointed out the difficulties involved for these Japanese car-making firms in replicating their successes internationally in different national cultures. These difficulties arise largely because "the ownership advantages of Japanese firms are not easily internalised in an overseas location; they are in this sense more location bound."[4] With minority equity participation,[5] these difficulties could reduce the speed of local technological efforts of

3. see Shah, S.G. (1996) for the technical details.
4. Gittelman and Dunning (1992) p. 256.
5. Maruti is the only exception in this, because Maruti was a jcint venture between Government of India and Suzuki Motors of Japan with equal [50:50] investment.

new firms in the auto industry in India during this period and the resultant slow rate of progress in exports.

With an across the board liberalisation in industrial and trade policy restrictions, allowing majority equity participation, automobile industry in India witnessed the entry of several global players. Creation of a competitive atmosphere could force many firms (Indian as well as the multinational) to establish certain technological advantages in the product (vehicles) or processes. They may even produce differentiated vehicles to suit the local and export demands separately. The technological efforts could take the form of cost-efficient production as well as fuel-efficient and consumer asthetic design of vehicles. As a result, the role of technological factors in creating international competitive advantage would be much greater than before.

The above mentioned characteristics of Indian automobile industry suggest the importance of technological factors in determining global competitiveness of firms. The discussion also highlights the importance of firm specific niches in accumulating technological capabilities and its possible effects on export performance. As a result, any attempt to explain the determinants of exports of firms in this industry, must take into account the inter-linkages between various technological paradigms and trajectories. To carry out this analysis, this study, therefore, follows the evolutionary theoretical framework of Nelson and Winter (1982) and Dosi *et al.*, (1992). The focus of this analysis would be on the importance of the changing nature of technological efforts of firms in this industry to explain their export performance.

SECTION 3

LITERATURE ON TECHNOLOGY AND TRADE IN DEVELOPING COUNTRIES

While most of these studies discussed above have tested these theoretical specification for developed countries on the basis of inter-industry cross section data, a few studies have examined the role of technology in export performance of developing countries as well (Hirsch and Bijoui 1985, Lall 1986, Kumar 1990, Willmore 1992, Kumar and Siddharthan 1994, Athukorala *et al.*, 1995, Haddad *et al.*, 1996 and Wakelin 1997).

Hirsch and Bijoui (1985) tested the relationship between technology and export performance for 111 firms drawn from Israel. Technology in their analysis was captured by R&D expenditure, while regressing the rate of change in exports during 1979-81 over 1975-77 on R&D expenditure in 1977, and the firm size, they found R&D expenditure playing a significant role in explaining the export intensity of Israeli firms.

Lall (1986) focused on technological variables affecting export performance for data on the 100 largest engineering and the 45 largest chemical firms in India. He considered four variables covering different facets of technology, namely, the value of royalty and licensing fees paid abroad, the percentage of equity held by foreign firms and R&D. The results of his exercise suggest that both foreign share and R&D positively influence the export performance of only the Chemical firms. In the case of engineering firms, R&D turned out to be significant with a negative sign, implying that most of the adaptive R&D that these engineering firms undertake to suit their products to the Indian resource conditions did not enable them to compete internationally. R&D efforts in process technology in chemical industry did not constitute a handicap in terms of product quality and design characteristics and, therefore, has a positive influence on exports.

Kumar (1990) analysed the differences in the export behaviour of domestic and foreign firms belonging to 42 manufacturing industries in India. The results of his empirical examination suggested that the technology factor was not important for Indian manufacturing exports. His analysis also did not bring out any statistically significant differences in export performance of foreign and local enterprises in Indian manufacturing.

Willmore (1992) concentrated on the role of transnational corporations in Brazil's trade performance. He analysed the determinants of both exports as well as imports. The analysis used data for a cross-section of 17,053 industrial firms in Brazil. The study found foreign ownership of Brazilian industry to have a very strong positive effect on both export performance and import propensities. However, R&D expenditures by the firm appeared to have no significant effect on its exports.

Kumar and Siddharthan (1994) analysed the effect of R&D expenditure on the exports for 640 Indian firms for the period 1987-88 to 1989-90. This period signifies partial de-regulation of trade and investment controls in India. They classified the industries into low, medium and high-technology categories and found R&D to be positively influencing the export performance of both low and medium technology firms. Their study suggested that India may not have a comparative advantage to trade in high-technology industries.

Athukorala *et al.*, (1995) attempted to find whether multinational enterprises are more export oriented than the wholly domestic-owned firms for a sample drawn from Sri Lanka. Their results pointed out evidence for multinational affiliation to be an important determinant of whether a firm is an exporter or not. However, they found no significant relationship between multinational affiliation and the degree of export orientation of exporting firms.

Haddad *et al.*, (1996) regressed export share in sales on foreign share in ownership, age of the firm, share of the firm's sales in total sales of three-digit industries, capital-output ratio and the labour-output ratio for a cross section of firms belonging to Morocco. The data for their analysis related to the year 1987, a period of slow but progressive opening to foreign competition and introduction of some incentives to export. They found a positive association between foreign share and exports and pointed out that knowledge gained from foreign markets is an important determinant of export performance.

Wakelin (1997) analysed the role of firm-specific innovative characteristics in influencing trade performance for a sample of 500 UK firms for a period of five years from 1988 to 1992. She included both sector specific (domestic market size and technological opportunity at the sector-level) and firm specific (capital intensity and R&D expenditure) determinants and found that the relative importance of sector and firm characteristics does vary with the type of firm being considered. Moreover, firm-specific characteristics appear to be more important for innovating firms than the non-innovating firms. The results show that there are considerable differences in the reactions of innovating and non-innovating firms, in relation to their export behaviour. This result was further reiterated by the analysis of quoted firms, where firm-level R&D and capital intensity have a positive impact on the exports of the innovating firms.

The present study begins with the premise that firms which posses advantage in terms of technological capabilities do perform better in international trade. This would imply that there is a systematic difference in the characteristics and performance of firms that rely mostly on the domestic markets and those which also sell in foreign markets. The arguments provided here are consistent with the 'evolutionary' micro-foundations, whereby firms with different technologies and organisational traits interact under conditions of persistent disequilibrium in the technology under use.

Consider a growth maximising firm. Its decision to export could arise from (a) the need to achieve economies of scale or (b) restrictions in the domestic market on product diversification. This would mean that there exists a significant difference between the rate at which the firm would like to grow and the actual rate of growth of domestic demand. In this case, the firm chooses to export as an alternative to product diversification.

In the case of automobile manufacturing firms in India, there were numerous restrictions on expansion of capacity and firms were licensed to supply specific products. Although the industry witnessed excess demand conditions, the excess demand was more in the form of unfulfilled demand rather than a high rate of growth in demand. Further, the policy measures toward exports were more in the form of import entitlements rather than export promotion *per se*. There were some incentives for a firm to export. This is because exports were considered to be an important method to earn the most needed foreign exchange. However, firms were operating in a completely protected market, which along with product specific licensing failed to motivate them to be innovative and reap the benefits of scale economies. Foreign collaborations, which could improve export potential, were not allowed for a long time.

De-regulation of industrial and technology policies were brought about in India for the first time during the mid-1980s and major policy reforms were introduced from the year 1991 onwards with a view to make Indian industries internationally competitive. These policy changes resulted in the entry of new firms, shifts in technological paradigms and trajectories and a subsequent change in the domestic market share of individual firms. These policy changes also brought about a change in the external competitiveness of firms. This is especially because of the changes in foreign equity participation, trade restrictions and market determined exchange rates. It is important, therefore, to analyse the impact of these liberalisation measures in the determination of inter-firm variation in export performance.

SECTION 4

EXPORT BEHAVIOUR OF FIRMS UNDER DIFFERENT POLICY REGIMES

Export behaviour of firms considered in the study is presented in Table 18.1. The table reports the mean and coefficient of variation of export intensity (exports as a percentage of annual sales turnover) for each firm during the three policy regimes. The table clearly indicates that the export intensity of automobile firms in India during the liberalisation period is much higher than that experienced during both licensing and de-regulation regimes. Overall export intensity for all firms taken together declined from 3.06 per cent during licensing period to 1.79 in de-regulation period, but increased substantially to 5.96 per cent during the post-liberalisation period. The variability has declined from the first to second and third period. Achieving an export intensity of about 6 per cent is a substantial improvement for this sector when compared to the earlier periods. The import substitution led industrial and trade policies that the Government of India followed for a long period resulted in sheltered markets and high costs. This policy climate in an economy with a large and expanding domestic market rendered inward oriented marketing strategy far more attractive. Government of India did offer various export incentives.[6] Until the liberalisation measures introduced in July 1991, these export incentives consisted of (a) cash compensatory support (CCS) at 20 per cent of the fob (free on board) value, (b) duty drawback (DD) of 4 to 8 per cent of fob value, (c) import replenishment (REP) licenses to provide importable inputs at international prices, and which can be sold in the market at a

6. See Government of India, Hussain Committee Report (1984) Chapter 3 for the details.

Table 18.1

Export Intensity of Indian Automobile Firms [per cent]

Firm	*Policy Regime*					
	Licensing [1980-81 to 1984-85]		*De-regulation [1985-86 to 1990-91]*		*Liberalisation [1991-92 to 1995-96]*	
	Mean	*C.V.*	*Mean*	*C.V.*	*Mean*	*C.V.*
TELCO	6.01	31.66	4.12	26.75	9.31	13.33
MAHINDRA	7.00	32.86	4.00	32.50	3.00	16.67
PREMIER	3.00	2.67	0.40	150.00	0.30	26.67
HMOTOR	2.00	65.00	1.90	26.32	1.80	61.11
ASHLEY	5.00	74.00	2.40	58.33	9.00	21.89
SMOTOR	0.90	128.89	0.36	66.67	0	0
BAJAJ	0.40	100.04	0.50	48.00	1.56	42.31
MARUTI	—	—	1.30	146.15	8.50	27.06
SMAZDA	—	—	0.48	112.50	4.08	97.06
DAEWOO	—	—	1.42	197.18	15.70	43.31
EMOTOR	—	—	1.14	120.17	5.59	56.71
ALL FIRMS	3.06	106.54	1.79	104.47	5.96	88.93

Source: Author's calculation on the basis of data obtained from the balance sheets and annual reports of companies.

premium, and (d) international price reimbursement scheme (IPRS) to cover the difference between domestic and international prices of pig iron, alloy steel, and aluminium. All these incentives meant that the fob price could be 30 to 40 per cent lower than the domestic price. Whether these incentives would necessarily lead to maximisation of exports crucially depend upon the profitability of exports. In a study conducted by ICICI in 1985 comparing profitability of exports and domestic sales, during 1978-79 to 1980-81, gross profit on export sales (with incentives) turned out to be (in the range of 20 to 24 per cent) much higher than on domestic sales (in the range of 9 to 11 per cent) for the commercial vehicle manufacturers. Going by the incentives and the profitability, therefore, it is possible to argue that poor technological standard of Indian vehicles was the most important reason for low export intensity. Making these vehicles suitable to Indian road and weather conditions have only enabled us to export to small developing countries, while reducing the scope for wider direction of trade. While the policy changes introduced during the mid-1980s did make imports - especially for technological upgradation and modernisation - a little more easier and attractive, regulated and overvalued rupee could have made the exports costlier in the international markets. In the post-1991 policy changes, although the scope of product-specific incentives had been reduced substantially with the abolition of the CCS and REP licenses, rupee was devalued and a freer foreign trade regime was sought after and the rupee was also being made convertible on the current account, thereby allowing the market to determine the exchange rate. These policy factors could be the reason why the export intensity of the automobile industry as a whole was very low in the first period, declined during the second and increased substantially during the liberalisation period.

Two leading commercial vehicle manufacturers, Telco and Ashok Leyland, turned highly successful in the international market during the liberalisation period. Telco and Ashok Leyland, along with Mahindra were the major exporters in the Indian automobile sector even during the licensing regime. While Telco and Ashok Leyland were both exporting MHCVs to the developing middle-East, Asian and African countries which have similar road and demand conditions like us, Mahindra emerged very successful in exporting its multi-utility vehicle (Jeep) and, therefore, had the highest export intensity during this period. One major factor that enabled Telco and Ashok Leyland to export was also their ability to provide after-sales service in these destinations. Mahindra also established servicing network for their Jeeps in countries like Sri Lanka and Mauritius. Premier and Hindustan Motors were exporting cars of very old vintage, mostly to the neighbouring countries like Bangladesh, Nepal and Sri Lanka. These two companies had an average of about 3 per cent and 2 per cent export intensity respectively. Hindustan Motors was also exporting Bedford brand medium sized commercial vehicles to Bangladesh. While all these firms experienced a decline in the exports during de-regulation period, Telco and Ashok Leyland were able to recover and improve their international market position very well during the liberalisation period. Telco brought about a paradigm shift and diversified into Light Commercial Vehicles (LCV) sector during the de-regulation period and the car sector during the liberalisation period.

The literature on technology gap models (mentioned above) could be interpreted to state that a change of techno-economic paradigm accentuates certain types of comparative advantage since the leading firm is capable of exporting a wide range of new and improved vehicles. These vehicles have performance characteristics and costs which are generally superior to those of the competitors. On the other hand, firms which lag behind (laggard firms), on the other hand, who are slow to adopt to new paradigm, are geared to a pattern of production and exports which is increasingly obsolete and non-competitive in terms of technology. This phenomenon clearly explains the difference between Telco and Ashok Leyland on the one hand and Mahindra and Premier on the other.

Among the new entrants in both Car and LCV sector, Daewoo Motors and Maruti had higher than industry average export intensity during the de-regulation period itself. While Maruti was the domestic market leader in the Car segment right from the time it came into being, Daewoo Motors (which was DCM Toyota at that time) was trying to establish itself in the Indian markets. The other entrants basically concentrated more on the domestic market only. Both Daewoo and Maruti emerged as leading exporters in the liberalisation period as well, with an average export intensity of about 15.7 and 8.5 per cent respectively. Daewoo's 15.7 per cent average turns out to be nearly three times higher than the industry average of about 5.96 per cent. This is again a case of successful diversification with foreign majority equity participation and change in the paradigm of operations. Other firms with Japanese collaboration, Swaraj Mazda and Eicher Motors, have also improved their export intensity during the liberalisation period. Bajaj is the only firm that has been relying mostly on Indian markets. It exports 'Matadors' (multi-utility vehicle) and a few three-wheeled 'Tempos' (small sized carriers) to neighbouring countries. Bajaj's export intensity remained very low during all the periods. Standard Motors, which used to export LCVs, has gone out of fray since the late-1980s.

Table 18.2 presents the annual average rate of growth in export intensity of Indian automobile firms under different policy regimes. The table indicates a rate of growth of 14.48 per cent during the first, 27.59 per cent in the second and 62.08 per cent during the liberal economic policy regime. It is evident that the growth rate has

Table 18.2

Annual Average Rate of Growth in Export Intensity of Indian Automobile Firms [per cent]

Firm	Policy Regime		
	Licensing	*De-regulation*	*Liberalisation*
TELCO	3.94	0.87	12.30
MAHINDRA	-13.04	3.73	2.59
PREMIER	5.25	113.33	8.54
HMOTOR	15.52	23.96	53.61
ASHLEY	44.99	22.09	16.49
SMOTOR	10.57	0	0
BAJAJ	-32.77	26.70	47.66
MARUTI	—	23.32	32.88
SMAZDA	—	12.84	378.57
DAEWOO	—	75.00	31.77
EMOTOR	—	12.64	36.41
ALL FIRMS	14.48	27.59	62.08

Note: These growth rates represent annual rate of change in export intensity and the table provides average annual growth during the three policy regimes.

nearly doubled over these three policy periods. While much of the growth during the de-regulation period is due to Premier automobiles and Daewoo Motors [it was called DCM Toyota during that period], Swaraj Mazda (another Japanese collaboration), which had a negative growth in exports during the second period, accounted for the maximum increase in growth of exports during the liberalisation period. Indian commercial vehicle manufacturers (MHCV), Telco and Ashok Leyland both experienced a decline in their growth in the second period when compared to the first, but recovered in the third. Telco's ability to diversify into LCV and car sectors resulted in this spurt in its growth of exports. Ashok Leyland brought about substantial improvements in its vehicles to boost exports. However, Bajaj is the only Indian LCV firm which had higher than industry average growth in exports. The ability of Japanese firms to succeed in exports during the liberal economic policy period is well highlighted by the Table 18.2.

In an earlier study (Narayanan 2001a) it was observed that the conduct and performance of firms belonging to the Indian automobiles did vary with respect to the policy regime, and export intensity emerged as the most important discriminant. Narayanan 2001b found that differences in firm level technology acquisition activity explained much of the determination of growth of Indian automobile firms. Panda and Oba (2000) observed that though higher export was not a reason behind higher growth of output of firms, exports did contribute to growth of output of firms, in general, over time. These studies provide valuable input in hypothesising the relationship between import liberalisation, technology transfer and export intensity.

SECTION 5

DETERMINANTS OF EXPORTS: VARIABLES AND HYPOTHESES

On the basis of the literature survey and the empirical knowledge about the automobile firms presented above, the variables to determine inter-firm variation in export intensity and hypotheses concerning them are presented in this section.

Technology Acquisition and Exports

Most of the studies explaining inter-firm variation in exports considered either technology imports or in-house R&D as an explanatory variable. A few studies included foreign equity share also to denote technology content of a firm. This study would consider the role of four forms of technology acquisition: namely IMTECH, FE, IMCAP and RD, along with their interaction factors, in the determination of export intensity. An attempt has been made to compare the differences in the role played by each one of these technology variables in explaining inter-firm variation in export behaviour during all the three periods under study.

From the literature survey explaining export performance of firms drawn from developed and developing countries (presented in sections 2 and 3) and the empirical observations on Indian automobile firms (presented in sections 2 and 4), it emerges that technological capabilities play a much greater role in influencing export competitiveness of firms positively than the price factors. One major difference between the firms operating in a developing country and those in a developed country is the need to complement technology imports with in-house R&D efforts (Kumar & Siddharthan 1994). The need usually arises from the adaptation requirements of the imported technology to suit the developing countries' resource and market conditions. Further, the technological regime in which the firms have been operating also changed drastically during the study period. As stated earlier, technological regime is by and large governed by the economic policy framework in which the firms were operating. A change in the policy in the form of promoting technology transfer and modernisation, brings about a change in the technological regime and as a result the technological variables behave differently in different technological regimes.

Indian automobile firms faced numerous restrictions in terms of indigenisation of the vehicle production/assembly during the pre-1985 regulated regime. Following Lall (1986) one could argue that the substitution of local for imported components may lead to lower product quality. As a result, adaptation of the vehicles to Indian road and other resource conditions may adversely affect the marketability in other countries. Access to foreign technology and in-house R&D efforts directed to accomplish certain technological improvements of the vehicles were the two most important methods of technology acquisition during this period. These two technology variables, therefore, would be determining exports positively. Their interaction term, FE*RD and IMTECH*RD, may not turn out significant or may even end up with a negative sign, because of the local adaptations facilitated by these two interaction variables.

During the de-regulation period, relaxations of restriction on imports of technology, capital goods, components and parts and selective permission for foreign equity participation involving technology transfer facilitated entry of new firms to produce new and technologically superior vehicles, which in turn enabled them to capture the local market. In order to cater to the international market, firms would have to be cost efficient as well. This is especially because of the need to face competition from among others, the technology suppliers to India. In-house R&D efforts are very essential to modify the newly imported technology and accomplish certain technological trajectory shifts. These developments could be in the form of producing cost and fuel-efficient vehicles suited for the road and resource conditions of the targeted markets. Firms could, therefore, use the interaction between technology imports and in-house R&D efforts to facilitate trajectory shifts. Firms which succeed in adapting the imported technology and establishing specific trajectory advantages would be able to build international competitive capabilities. However, the analysis carried out in an earlier study indicated that most of the firms using FE of IMTECH mode of technology transfer attempted to secure local market share during this period (Narayanan 1998). This was largely due to the excess (unfulfilled) demand condition that prevailed in India during this period. Export intensity of most of the firms actually declined. The study, therefore, postulates that the interaction between various modes of technological imports and in-house R&D efforts (IMTECH*RD, FE*RD & IMCAP*RD) may not emerge significant in determining the inter-firm variation in export competitiveness during the de-regulation period. If most of their technology imports and in-house R&D efforts are due to domestic market pressure, and do not give them any advantage for exports, the variables capturing technological efforts (viz., RD, IMTECH, FE, and IMCAP) may also not, individually, emerge significant in the determination of export intensity. On the contrary, if firms invest in R&D and imports of technology more because if they do not they will loose the local market, some of their individual coefficients may even end up with a negative sign.

With an across the board liberalisation and automatic approval for majority foreign equity participation, firms would prefer to use all the three modes of acquisition from abroad. However, a more realistic exchange rate and higher cost of import, would make the firms a bit cautious in using IMTECH and IMCAP. The most preferred mode of technology acquisition would be FE. As pointed out earlier, the Indian automobile sector experienced the maximum number of foreign equity participation from the world auto leaders during the post-1991 period. While a number of them have come to India to cater to the local market, the vehicles assembled/produced from India have also been exported to destinations which do not attract levies for imports from developing countries. Firms like Telco which relied on their in-house R&D efforts, to produce cars and multi utility vehicles, would also gain in exports in the changed circumstances. As a result, two out of four technology variables (FE and RD), independently, would emerge positive and significant in determining competitiveness. IMTECH and IMCAP, as well as their interaction factors (IMTECH*RD and IMCAP*RD) may not emerge significant in determining exports during this period. In the case of foreign firms it is difficult to predict the nature of their R&D in host economies. Some multinationals produce differentiated vehicles for local and export market from their plant in India. Since R&D data is not available at the line of business level, it is difficult to predict an exact sign for FE*RD during this period. If the R&D efforts in Indian plants are directed to suit their vehicles for Indian market, weather and driving conditions, and to develop competitive capabilities in the domestic market (as the results of market share change equation indicate), FE*RD may turn out to be insignificant. This is especially because they are all multi vehicle assembly plants and may not try to export what is being sold in the local market. On the contrary, if they try to export the same vehicles which are sold in the domestic market, FE*RD may even take a negative sign if these local adaptations restrict the possibility of their exports.

Firm Size and Exports

Apart from technology acquisition, size of the firm (SIZE) would also influence its export performance positively. Exporting is a costly and risky activity and smaller firms on their own may be at a disadvantage in gathering information, launching overseas sales promotion campaigns, bearing exchange rate and other risks, and adapting their products to foreign markets (Lall, 1986 and Bannacorsi, 1992). Large firms in this industry also own and operate retail/service outlets. All these factors could enable large sized firms to export more. This paper, therefore, hypothesises a positive role for firm size in the determination of exports during all the three period of analysis. Empirical evidence (Hirsch and Adar 1974; Gleijser *et al.*, 1980; Lall 1986; Kumar 1990; Bannacorsi 1992; Kumar and Siddharthan 1994 and Patibandla 1995) on the relationship between firm size and exports is mixed.

Vertical Integration and Exports

The study also explores the role played by the degree of vertical integration (VI) in the determination of inter-firm differences in export performance. Kathuria (1996) found vertical integration to be a very important factor explaining the observed differences in technological capabilities of firms in the Indian commercial vehicles industry. Commercial vehicle sector in India, which was the major exporter during the first period, is vertically deep in its structure of manufacturing activities (Lall, 1980). In organising and managing such vertical integrated production, this sector has formed an externalised pattern of vertical division of labour. The vertical division of labour could be designed to exploit intra-firm pattern of comparative advantages *vis-a-vis* their rivals. Such a comparative advantage could then be used to competitive advantage for exports. This paper, therefore, postulates a positive role for Vertical Integration in determining export intensity during the licensing regime.

With a change in policy during the mid 1980s firms chose to acquire most of the components and parts through imports or from the market. Degree of Vertical Integration actually declined from about 22 per cent in the licensing period to 14.77 per cent in the second. The second period witnessed entry of Japanese multinationals in the Indian car and LCV sectors. These Japanese firms preferred to develop vendors for their components and parts and, therefore, encouraged parallel transfer of technology from the vendors of their parent plant in Japan to their counterparts in India. With liberalisation and a more realistic market determined exchange rate, although the degree of Vertical Integration increased to about 16.56 per cent, this increase was due largely to the higher cost of imports and absence of quality inputs and parts for the new and technologically sophisticated vehicles that Korean and other multinationals were producing. However, the government policy of draw-back provision for duty-free import of inputs used in the production of goods for exports is also more valuable to a firm relying on outside suppliers, one who is not vertically integrated. As a result, Vertical Integration is expected to have an inverse relationship with exports during the second and third period.

Import of Components and Exports

Import of components (IMCOM) takes place in order to enjoy certain price and quality advantages. During the licensing regime there were numerous restrictions on import of components. Phased indiginisation meant that only new firms were permitted to import components. As a result, imports of components to bring about product quality improvements for exports was uncommon in this industry. Imports of components, therefore, may not significantly determine export intensity during the licensing period. During the de-regulation period, with relaxation of restrictions on imports and favourable exchange rate for rupee, imports of components actually increased many-fold. However, these relaxations on component imports were for a short period and the government policy insisted on phased indigenisation of the vehicles assembled. Most of the firms used these imported components to sell their vehicles in the domestic market. As a result, imports of components may not turn out significant in explaining exports even during this period. But, with an across the board liberalisation, more realistic exchange rate and absence of restrictions on imports, firms are likely to use imports much more judiciously. Imports of components are likely to be meant for product quality improvements rather than guided by favourable exchange rate. As a result, imports would be directed mostly to facilitate exports. Import of components for product quality improvements is, therefore, expected to influence inter-firm variation in exports positively during the liberalisation period.

Capital Intensity and Exports

Capital intensity, following Wakelin (1997), could be expected to embody part innovation as well as influencing the marginal cost of output of the firm. During the licensing regime, where international competitiveness need to be established through cost efficiencies, firms relied heavily on efficient utilisation of their existing capital stock. Capital intensity, therefore, is likely to be inversely related to export competitiveness. Even with de-regulations and permission for expansion of capacity, firms need to compete internationally through cost efficiencies and efficient utilisation of the capital stock. As a result, a negative relationship between capital intensity and exports is hypothesised for this period. With liberalisation, market determined exchange rate and absence of restrictions on capacity, there is an incentive for the firms to make their capital stock embody the learning outcome of the diffusion of new technologies. Most of the new firms are still in the process of capital creation. Although the average capital intensity of the industry has gone down, the exporting ones are those new firms which are yet to stabilise at a certain level of capital stock. Capital intensity, therefore, is likely to have a positive sign in explaining exports during this period.

SECTION 6
THE MODEL

The export behaviour of firms within this industry could be analysed in the framework of the following model:

Let

$$Yi^* = b' ci + ei^* \quad (i = 1,2,....,n) \qquad ...(1)$$

be a regression equation which fulfils all the classical assumptions. Let Y* be an index variable which is not observed for some range. In this situation, instead of observing Y*, we observe Y which is

$$Yi = Yi^* \text{ if } Yi^* > 0 \qquad ...(2)$$
$$= 0 \text{ if } Yi^* < 0$$

Equations (1) and (2) represent Tobit Model. In terms of Y, equation (1) becomes

$$Yi = b' ci + ei \qquad ...(3)$$

The lower tail of the distribution of Yi is cut off at zero and that of ei is cut off at b' ci, and the probabilities are piled up at the cut-off points. It is important to note that the mean of ei is different from that of ei* and the mean of Yi is also different from that of Yi*. This implies that limiting the range of values of dependent variable yields biased and inconsistent estimates if the Ordinary Least Squares (OLS) method is applied to equation (3). The OLS estimates of the slope parameters are biased towards zero. Moreover, the magnitude of the bias being proportional to the probability of the index variable being non-positive. Amemiya has shown that Maximum Likelihood Estimates (MLE) of the model are consistent and asymptotically normal.[7] Since the dependent variable, export intensity is zero for some firms we estimate our Tobit model by the method of maximum Likelihood.

---

7. Refer Green (1993) for more details.

The empirical form of the testable equation is given as:

EX = f (Size, VI, CI, RD, IMTECH, FE, IMCAP, IMCOM, IMTECH*RD, FE*RD, IMCAP*RD)

where EX is the export intensity of a firm measured by exports as a proportion of sales turnover.

SECTION 7
EMPIRICAL ANALYSIS

Sample, Data and Time Period

Data for the statistical analysis is largely drawn from the balance sheets and annual reports of companies. As mentioned earlier, the database contains firm level data for 11 automobile manufacturing companies for the years 1980-81 to 1995-96. There are year to year changes in the sample-set due to the entry and exit of firms. This is especially after the year 1984-85. The data relate to firms assembling/producing cars and other four wheeled vehicles and light, medium and heavy commercial vehicles.

The observations for sixteen years namely 1980-81 to 1995-96 were pooled into three separate groups for the empirical exercise. Government of India took major decision to introduce partial relaxation on restrictions for capacity expansion and trade in Indian industry since 1985-86. The liberalisation measures of 1991 had far reaching implications. In this chapter, analysis of inter-firm differences in export intensity is, therefore, carried out separately for these three different policy regimes.

Empirical Results

The sample consists of exporters as well as non-exporters. The dependent variable, as a result, had a number of zero value observations. As mentioned above, if observations on the dependent variable cluster around zero, the Ordinary Least Squares provide biased estimates of the coefficients. Tobit with Maximum Likelihood method of estimation was chosen in order to overcome this problem. The results of the empirical estimation are presented in Table 18.3.

Table 18.3

M.L. Estimates of Export Intensity Equation [Tobit Model] By Policy Regime: Panel Data

Variable	*Licensing* [1980-81 to 1984-85]	*De-regulation* [1985-86 to 1990-91]	*Liberalisation* [1991-92 to 1995-96]
Constant	**-0.7466**	**-0.0989**	**-0.3229**
	(-4.774)	**(-3.724)**	**(-3.526)**
Size	**0.0632**	**0.0155**	**0.0271**
	(5.498)	**(5.557)**	**(3.687)**
VI	**0.6057**	-0.0282	-0.1356
	(2.598)	(-0.572)	(-0.977)
CI	**-0.0876**	<u>-0.0306</u>	**0.1042**
	(-2.79)	(1.895)	**(3.595)**
RD	1.4261	**-3.5814**	0.9729
	(0.597)	**(2.719)**	(0.504)
IMTECH	2.0433	**-0.8569**	-0.4613
	(1.313)	**(-2.396)**	(-0.415)
FE	**0.0018**	-0.0004	**0.0011**
	(3.341)	(-1.472)	**(2.187)**
IMCAP	-0.0523	**-0.7250**	0.0459
	(-0.188)	**(-2.382)**	(0.103)
IMCOM	0.0428	0.0074	**0.4668**
	(0.416)	(0.331)	**(3.286)**
FE*RD	-0.0502	0.0634	0.0220
	(-0.507)	(1.327)	(0.373)
IMTECH*RD	-239.18	129.23	-33.888
	(-1.274)	(1.349)	(-0.295)
IMCAP*RD	41.59	**121.51**	-53.703
	(1.529)	**(2.388)**	(-0.656)
NOBS	37	60	50
No. of Firms	8	11	10

Notes: (i) Figures in parentheses represent t values. (ii) Coefficients printed in bold are significant at 1 per cent level and those underlined are significant at 5 per cent level by two tailed test.

In thc empirical exercise, since the same export equation was fitted for comparable panel data for three different policy regimes, a Likelihood Ratio [LR] test of homogeneity of the Tobit model for the time periods was conducted.

(i) Homogeneity between licensing and de-regulation periods,

(ii) Homogeneity between de-regulation and liberalisation periods,

(iii) Homogeneity between licensing and liberalisation periods, and

(iv) Homogeneity for all the three periods.

The null hypothesis of homogeneity stood rejected in all the cases.

In general, the results support the hypotheses presented in section 5. The results for all the three periods of analysis highlight the differences in the role played by technology and other firm level strategies in determining inter-firm variation in export competitiveness.

Among the technology variables, foreign equity participation, FE, is the only variable that emerged significant with a positive coefficient for the licensing period. This supports the view that even during product specific capacity licensing and highly inward looking protectionist regime, access to foreign technology enabled the firms to be export oriented. Lall and Mohammad (1983) also found a positive impact of foreign ownership on export performance of largest corporate firms in India during the inward looking policy regime. Two other forms of technology acquisition, IMTECH and RD, though entered the equation with positive coefficients, did not turn out to be significant in determining exports. IMTECH was used by the firms to bring about certain specific incremental changes in technological trajectories and in-house R&D efforts were directed to facilitate the adaptation process. The level of in-house R&D was too low to bring about technological innovation needed for global competitiveness. Further, adaptation to suit the Indian resource conditions may reduce the scope for exports. This inference is drawn from the negative (though insignificant) coefficients of two of the interactive terms, FE*RD and IMTECH*RD. Both imports of capital goods, IMCAP, (with a negative sign) and its interaction term, IMCAP*RD, (with a positive sign) turned out insignificant.

For the de-regulation period of the three technology interaction factors, IMCAP*RD is the only variable which emerged significant with a positive sign. Other interactions like FE*RD and IMTECH*RD also had a positive sign each but did not turn out to be statistically significant. This could be because most of the firms used their technological efforts to capture the domestic market, rather than exports during this period. Further, Telco, Mahindra and Ashok

Leyland continued to be leading exporters, while all the new firms with Japanese collaboration had less than industry average export intensity. Telco, Mahindra and Ashok Leyland also imported technology and were trying to bring about technological paradigm shifts. However, on an average, the values of these interaction terms for the industry as a whole declined during this period. This decline in their average value could be a possible reason for their insignificance. As mentioned earlier, in order to succeed internationally, the Indian auto firms need to establish certain cost or quality advantages to overcome the possible unfavourable exchange rate for exports. However, since firms in this industry seem to have specialised in the domestic market, technology variables individually have turned out significant with a negative coefficient.

During the third period, with liberalisation and entry of world leaders with majority foreign equity holdings, access to foreign technology (FE) emerges as one of the most important factors in explaining export intensity. Exports for these firms could also be in the form of intra-firm trade. In the sample, apart from Telco, firms with a larger foreign equity share (Daewoo Motors, Ashok Leyland, Maruti, Eicher Motors and Swaraj Mazda) were exporting more. Ashok Leyland was an Indian majority holding company until it was taken over by Hinduja Group in 1994. This could also explain the positive and significant coefficient of FE. RD efforts, which increased during this period compared to both first and second period, also turned out to be positive, but with low and insignificant t value. Imports of capital goods (IMCAP) and licensing (IMTECH) were not the preferred mode of technology acquisition during this period to facilitate exports. This could be the reason why they both turned out insignificant. None of the interactive factors appeared to be significant, as hypothesised, although FE*RD emerged with a positive sign, while IMTECH*RD and IMCAP*RD took negative signs. This could indicate that adaptation of borrowed technology (arms' length purchases and import of capital goods) with domestic efforts to suit Indian tastes and preferences may actually inhibit, rather than promote exports. Firms that used intra-firm mode of technology transfer seem to be an exception to this. Foreign firms appear to be spending on R&D activity in India perhaps in the process of diffusion of their technology or to exploit the locally available resources for R&D. Positive sign for FE*RD perhaps confirms Reddy's (1996) findings that during liberal economic policy regime, entry of multinationals has actually enhanced R&D activity in India. Case study of firms that have acquired technology through all these modes and their R&D activity could alone resolve this issue. Such case study is beyond the scope of the present analysis. This study is based largely on published data.

Size of the firm emerged significant with a positive sign for all the periods supporting the view that there are certain threshold requirements to be export oriented. Most of the earlier studies have also found size to have a positive sign in explaining inter-firm variation in export intensity. The average size of firms in this industry in India has increased across the three periods. While a part of this increase could be due to inflation (size is measured by log value of annual sales turnover at current prices), large sized firms, due to their ability to establish technological trajectory advantages, gather information, launch overseas sales promotion campaigns and ability to bear exchange rate and other risks, are in a better position to export than their smaller counterparts. In the sample also, the leading exporters are all large sized firms producing diversified vehicles which could explain positive coefficient for the size variable during all the three periods.

Vertically integrated firms turned out to be more export intensive than the others during the licensing period. Automobile firms did have a high degree of vertical integration during this period, especially due to the possibilities of trading the tacit technological knowledge among themselves. High degree of vertical integration could also enable the firms to produce domestically most of the high quality components and parts, which are essential to trade internationally. Changes in trade policy and possibility of imports reduced the advantages associated with Vertical Integration. Entry of Japanese firms which preferred vendor development and promoted parallel transfer of technology to component manufacturers, could also be a reason for this negative sign. Vertical integration actually declined in both the second as well as the third period. Though the mean value of Vertical Integration increased in the third in comparison to the second period, automobile firms were much less integrated in the third when compared to the first period. The government policy also was more favourable to a firm relying on outside suppliers of components. This could be the reason why Vertical Integration emerged insignificant.

The results of the empirical analysis also confirm a changing role for imports of components during these three periods. As hypothesised, IMCOM did not emerge significant in explaining inter-firm variation in exports during the first and the second period. However, with liberalisation, component imports meant for product quality improvements turned out to be significant with a positive sign in explaining exports. This result confirms the hypothesis that in an era of market determined exchange rates, firms prefer to import components mostly in order to maintain a higher quality of the vehicle for international market. Controls and restrictions, inspite of the regulated favourable exchange rate, is unlikely to attract imports which may be cost and product effective for the firms to trade in the international market.

Another important firm level strategic variable, capital intensity, emerged significant in all the three periods. CI and export intensity were inversely related during the licensing and de-regulated policy regimes, thus supporting the need for efficient capital utilisation in order to be successful in the export market. Lall and Mohammad (1983) and Kumar and Siddharthan (1994) also found capital intensity to be inversely related to exports in the case of Indian firms for the time period 1976-77 to 1977-78 and 1987-88 to 1989-90 respectively. With liberalisation, however, CI turned out to be significant with a positive sign indicating a change in the nature of relationship. The positive coefficient of CI during the third period could also be due to the reason that most of the exporters were new firms and these new firms are still in the process of expanding their capital stock. In the case of already established firms like Telco and Ashok Leyland, capital intensity could also reflect the innovation results of their past technological activity. Wakelin (1997) also found positive coefficient for CI in explaining inter-firm variation in exports for UK firms.

Table 18.4 provides the estimated marginal effects of the different explanatory variables included in the analysis. The estimated parameters obtained from the Tobit model (b‘) are not marginal coefficients. Marginal effect is the 8 partial derivative of the expected value of the dependent variable with respect to the explanatory variable. It is compared at the means of the explanatory variables. Marginal coefficient for a given explanatory variable is derived as:

$$\partial E(Y/X_i) / \partial X_i = \beta_i \, \phi(\beta' X/\sigma)$$

where $i = 1,2,\ldots,n$ are the individual explanatory variables and $\phi(\beta' X/\sigma)$ is the scale factor. The estimated marginal coefficients are proportional to parameter estimates.[8]

Table 18.4

Marginal Effects from the Tobit Model

Variable	*Licensing*	*De-regulation*	*Liberalisation*
Size	**0.0565**	**0.0132**	**0.0259**
VI	**0.5416**	-0.0239	-0.1302
CI	**-0.0783**	-0.0260	**0.1001**
RD	1.275	**-3.045**	0.9341
IMTECH	1.827	**-0.7285**	-0.4429
FE	**0.0016**	-0.0003	**0.0011**
IMCAP	-0.0467	**-0.6164**	0.0440
IMCOM	0.0382	0.0063	**0.4482**
FE*RD	-0.0449	0.0539	0.0211
IMTECH*RD	-213.90	109.8745	-32.5387
IMCAP*RD	37.1964	**103.3099**	-51.5645
NOBS	37	60	50

NOTE: Coefficients in bold represent significance of t values at 1 per cent level and those underlined at 5 per cent level.

From Table 18.4, the difference in the roles of FE, firm size and capital intensity in determining export intensity across the three policy regimes emerges quite distinctly. At the margin, the role of Size declined in the second when compared to the first and increased in the third period. Capital intensity also follows the same pattern. Intra-firm technology transfer, FE, however, shows an increase in its role between licensing and liberalisation periods. These differences in the magnitude of the impact on export intensity clearly are due to the changes in policy environment in which the firms operated over the 1980-81 to 1995-96 period.

8. Refer Greene (1993) and Limdep version 7.0 manual for further details.

SECTION 8

SUMMARY OF FINDINGS

This paper has sought to examine the international competitiveness of firms by analysing determinants of export intensity of the firm, in the evolutionary theoretical framework. It begins with the premise that there is a systematic difference in the characteristics and performance between firms that sell in the foreign market and those which are mostly dependent on the domestic market. The differential ability to acquire technological capabilities through the accomplishment of technological paradigm and trajectory shifts forms the basis for the asymmetry among firms. Accomplishing technological paradigm and trajectory shifts crucially depends upon the policy environment in which a firm operates. Specifically, this paper, therefore, analyses the differences in the role played by technology and other firm specific characteristics like size, degree of vertical integration, capital intensity and imports of components in explaining export intensity of firms across three different policy regimes.

On the whole, the results of the Tobit model estimation presented in this paper, confirm the hypotheses that inter-firm variation in export intensity is broadly explained by the variables representing technology acquisition, firm size, vertical integration, capital intensity and imports of components. One major finding of this paper is the difference in the role played by all these technology and other firm specific characteristics in explaining export intensity across three different policy regimes. This difference in the role of technology variables is largely due to the differences in the technology regime in which the firms have been operating. Specifically, in an inward-looking policy regime, all firms tend to export less, though foreign firms, with monopolistic advantage are better exporters. Indiginisation requirements and restrictions on imports of technology forces the firms to direct their technological activities to suit Indian road, market and resource conditions. These niches allow a firm to explore only those markets that have comparable road and living standards. In a liberal economic policy regime, however, firms that accomplish technological paradigm shifts through either foreign equity participation or in-house R&D efforts tend to be more export-oriented. During the transitory period of de-regulated regime that India witnessed between 1985-86 and 1990-91, firms appear to have been got caught in capturing the domestic market. All technological adaptations made to suit the local market requirements appear to have reduced their international competitive capabilities.

Large sized firms, which not only enjoy scale advantages in production, but also are in a position to take the risk of external markets, emerged more export intensive than their smaller counterparts in all the three periods. Further, the results also highlight the differences in the role played by vertical integration and capital intensity in determining export intensity across the three policy regimes. Vertically integrated firms turned out to be export intensive only during the restrictive policy regime. Advantages of integration appear to have disappeared with de-regulation and liberalisation. Also, efficient utilisers of capital stock turned out to be more successful in exporting during both the licensing and de-regulated regimes. To sum up, the results clearly highlight the differences in the role of technology acquisition and other conduct variables in determining export performance of Indian automobile firms. The nature and direction of the relationship between these explanatory variables and export intensity is, however, governed by the policy framework in which a firm operates. This type of an analysis of the determinants of export intensity over varying policy regimes has not been the focus of attention in the literature so far.

References

Athukorala, Premachandra, Sisira Jayasuriya and Edward Oczkowski (1995). "Multinational firms and export performance in developing countries: Some analytical issues and new empirical evidence," *The Journal of Development Studies,* 46, 109-122.

Banaccorsi, Andrea (1992). "On the Relationship between Firm Size and Export Intensity," *Journal of International Business Studies,* 23 (4), 605-35.

Dosi, Giovanni (1984). *Technical Change and Industrial Transformation,* London: Macmillan.

———. (1988). "Sources, Procedures and Microeconomic Effects of Innovation," *Journal of Economic Literature,* 26 (3), 1120-1171.

———. Keith Pavitt and Luc Soete (1992). *The Economics of Technical Change and International Trade,* Brighton, Harvester-Wheatsheaf.

Fagerberg, J. (1988). "International Competitiveness," *Economic Journal,* 98, 355-374.

———. (1996). "Technology and Competitiveness," *Oxford Review of Economic Policy,* 12 (3), 39-50.

Glejser, H., A. Jacquemin, and J. Petit (1980). "Exports in an Imperfect Competition Framework: An Analysis of 1,446 Exporters," *Quarterly Journal of Economics,* 94, 507-524.

Greene, W. (1993). *Econometric Analysis* 2nd Edition, London: Macmillan.

Grossman, G.M. and E. Helpman (1991). *Innovation and Growth in the Global Economy,* Mass, MIT press.

Haddad, Mona, Jaime De Melo and Brandan Horton (1996). 'Morocco, 1984-89: Trade Liberalisation, Exports and Industrial Performance', in Roberts, Mark J. and James R. Tybout (1996), *Industrial Evolution in Developing Countries,* New York, Oxford University Press.

Hirsch, S. and I. Bijaoui (1985). "R&D Intensity and Export Performance: A Micro View," *Weltsirtschaftliches Archiv,* 121, 138-151.

Hirsch, S. and Z. Adar (1974). "Firm Size and Export Performance," *World Development,* 2 (7), 41-46.

Hufbauer, G.C. (1966). *Synthetic Materials and the Theory of International Trade,* London, Gerald Duckworth.

Kathuria, Sanjay (1996). *Competing Through Technology and Manufacturing Strategy: A Study of the Indian Commercial Vehicles Industry,* New Delhi, Oxford University Press.

Krugman, Paul (1979). "A Model of Innovation, Technology Transfer and the World Distribution of Income," *Journal of Political Economy,* 87,253-266.

Kumar, Nagesh (1990). *Multinational Enterprises in India,* London and New York: Routledge.

———. and N.S. Siddharthan (1994). 'Technology, Firm Size and Export Behaviour in Developing Countries: The Case of Indian Enterprises', *The Journal of Development Studies,* 31 (2), 289-309.

Lall, Sanjaya (1980). "Vertical Inter-firm Linkages in LDCs: An Empirical Study," *Oxford Bulletin of Economics and Statistics,* 42 (3),203-26.

———. (1986). "Technological Development and Export Performance in LDCs: Leading Engineering and Chemical Firms in India," *Weltsirtschaftliches Archiv,* 122 (1), 80-91.

———. and Sharif Mohammad (1983). "Foreign Ownership and Export Performance in the Large Corporate Sector of India," *The Journal of Development Studies,* 20 (1), 56-67.

Lall, Sanjaya and Wolfram Latsch (1998). "Import Liberalisation and Industrial Performance: The Conceptual Underpinnings," *Development and Change,* 29,437-65.

Narayanan, K. (2001c). "Evolution of Automobile Industry in India through Changing Policy Regimes" in Carrillo, Jorge, Yannick Lung and Rob van Tulder (eds.) *Cars, carriers of regionalism?* [Macmillan] – (forthcoming).

————. (2001b). "Technology Transfer and Growth of Firms under Changing Policy Regimes: A Study of the Indian Automobile Sector", Centre for Development Economics, Delhi School of Economics, Delhi India, Working Paper No.93, June.

————. (2001a). "Liberalisation and Differential Conduct and Performance of Firms: The Case of Automobile Sector in India", The Institute of Economic Research, Hitotsubashi University, Tokyo, Japan, *Discussion Paper Series A*, No.414.

————. (1998). "Technology Acquisition, De-regulation and Competitiveness: A Study of the Indian Automobile Industry", *Research Policy*, 27 (2) pp. 215-28.

Nelson, Richard R. and S.G. Winter (1982). *An Evolutionary Theory of Economic Change*, Cambridge MA, Harvard University Press.

Ozawa, Terutomo (1997). '"Managed" Growth, Relocation and Restructuring: The Evolution of Japan's Motor Industry into a Dominant Multinational Player', in Buckley, Peter J. and Jean-Louis Mucchielli (eds.) *Multinational Firms and International Relocation*, Cheltenham (UK) and Brookfield (US), Edward Elgar.

Panda, Hrushikesh and Hiroyuki Oba (2000). "Liberalisation and Strategy of Growth of The Indian Automobile Firms," *Reitaku International Journal of Economic Studies*, 8 (2), 1-22.

Patibandla, Murali (1995). "Firm Size and Export Behaviour: An Indian Case Study," *The Journal of Development Studies*, 31 (6), 868-882.

Pavitt, K. (1984). "Sectoral Patterns of Technical Change: Towards a Taxonomy and a Theory," *Research Policy*, 11, 33-51.

Posner, Michael V. (1961). "International Trade and Technical Change," *Oxford Economic Papers*, 13, 11-37.

Reddy, Prasada (1997). "New Trends in Globalisation of Corporate R&D and Implications for Innovation Capability in Host Countries: A Survey from India," *World Development*, 25 (11), 1821-37.

Shah, S.G. (1996). *Shaping the Indian Automobile Industry*, New Delhi, Association of Indian Automobile Manufacturers.

Siddharthan, N.S. (1998). "Differential Behaviour of the Japanese affiliates in the Indian Automobile Sector," *Japan and the World Economy*, 10 (1), 97-109.

Society of Indian Automobile Manufacturers [SIAM] (1996). *Profile of the Automobile Industry*, New Delhi, SIAM.

Soete, Luc (1981). "General Test of Technological Gap Theory," *Weltwirtschaftliches Archiv*, 117, 638-659.

Vernon, R. (1966). "International Investment and International Trade in the Product Life Cycle," *Quarterly Journal of Economics*, 80, 190-207.

Wakelin, Katharine (1997). *Trade and Innovation: Theory and Evidence*, Cheltenham, and Northamption-MA, Edward Elgar.

Willmore, L. (1992). "Transnationals and Foreign Trade: Evidence from Brazil," *The Journal of Development Studies*, 28 (2), 314-335.

19

R&D, Import of Technology and Trade Intensities

A Simultaneous Equation Micro-level Examination

NEELAM SINGH

SECTION 1

INTRODUCTION

This study examines the firm-level determinants of R&D, import of technology and (merchandise) trade intensities along with their interdependence for a sample of primarily pharmaceutical manufacturing companies operating in India. Export orientation, import substitution and in-house technological effort are closely linked to the development of an industry, subsuming the technological development. Whether the import of technology stimulates or displaces in-house R&D, has been a contentious issue. Given the foreign exchange constraint, also their comparative effects on export and import propensities, and whether the export performance improves significantly with higher import intensity, need to be inquired.

Examining the 'R&D, import of technology, and trade intensities' together and their interconnections, we get a more coherent picture of corporate conduct. The earlier cross-section (usually single equation) studies estimating these relationships have almost invariably overlooked the possible simultaneity. A detailed review of literature is in Section 2. There are few multivariate studies of the determinants and impacts of import intensity in India. Notwithstanding the regulated imports and export-import institutional linkages, imports are not (primarily) pre-determined; there are also global considerations of the MNE.

Our estimated model focuses on the firm-size and foreign ownership related variables among the exogenous ones. Exploring how the size, research intensity, multinationality etc. of the foreign collaborator affect the relative performance of different foreign-owned affiliates - hardly examined so far - yields some interesting findings. The MNE-data are compiled from the Discover Worldscope Industrial Company Profiles. Examining the inter-dependence between R&D and import of technology adds to the few such empirical attempts in the context of the substitutability *Vs.* complementarity debate. The effects of these two types of technology inputs on trade intensities are compared; a related dimension analysed is the influence of the MNE R&D intensity. These issues are important in the context of the ongoing liberalisation of merchandise imports, foreign investment and technology, and industrial (capacity) licensing. This study covers the period financial years (April-March) 1988-89 to 1991-92 when the 'post-1985' technology and merchandise import liberalisation were already under way - though essentially just prior to the post-July 1991 accelerated liberalisation - and further reforms in the similar directions were anticipated.[1,2] Hence the results obtained here are likely to be portends. Section 2 deals with the literature review and model specification. Section 3 is on the sample, data and variables. Section 4 analyses the results. The main findings and concluding remarks are in Section 5.

SECTION 2

REVIEW OF LITERATURE AND THE MODEL SPECIFICATION

The import of technology is defined here broadly, including also the informal elements - possibly a prelude/follow-up to formal agreements - and assistance received to facilitate procuring of crucial imports and the access/exposure to foreign markets.

Inter-relationships Among the Co-determined Variables

We discuss first the likely interactions among the R&D, import of technology, export and import intensities (RDRI, MT, XIG & MIG).

1. My inability to update the MNE-related data - collected earlier from the US libraries - prevents a pre/post-1991 comparison.
2. Lessening of capacity constraints facilitates integration of overseas and domestic sales, and reduces uncertainty of yield from R&D. For the drug industry, price control was relaxed towards the late 1980s and in 1994, expected to improve profits; our study period has much higher trade intensities than immediately before.

Import of Technology and R&D: These means of technological upgradation compete indeed for investible funds and limited (top) managerial resources. In-house R&D improves the ability to assimilate technological development of others, including spillovers (Basant, 1993). Imported know-how may lead to adaptive efforts, and increase the correspondence between R&D expenditure and R&D-based output (Braga and Willmore, 1991; Katrak, 1994). Any strong adverse influence of technology import on the R&D (the substitutability) can lead to the technological dependence (Chaudhuri, 1995), while a complimentarity would enhance the national technological capability (Subrahmanian *et al.*, 1996).

Existing firm-level studies of R&D generally (ignoring the simultaneity) point to a complementarity relationship - usually small and weak (Braga and Willmore, 1991; Evenson and Westphal, 1995; Kumar and Siddharthan, 1997; Subrahmanian *et al.*, 1996). Basant(1993) and Fikkert(1995) take account of the interdependence of technology import and R&D (and numerous zero values) and find these to be weak substitutes (a small negative effect) for firms in India during 1974-75 to 1982-83; only about 10 per cent units have both expenses positive.[3] We estimate the interactions between MT and RDRI; since foreign affiliates unbundle less the imported technology (Pillai and Shah, 1988), the 'MT* foreign ownership dummy' variable is added experimentally in the RDRI equation. Our data is more recent (post-1985 period); even with a wide firm-size range, almost all MT and RDRI values are positive, also due to a broad MT measure and the R&D data being taken from the Directors' Report (see Section 3 below). The 'censoring problem' does not arise. The net effect of in-house R&D on MT may be positive (Siddharthan and Krishna, 1994); the R&D could replace the import of similar technology but require import of some more advanced technology, foreign travel and technical consultancy.

R&D and Export Intensities: Some studies on export behaviour (e.g. Braga and Willmore, 1991) argue a two-way reinforcing relationship between the R&D intensity and export intensity (or success in

---

3. Their R&D expenses data is from the profit-loss statements of company annual reports, often under-reporting these expenses; only if this expense is not mentioned here while the firm was a DST-recognised centre or assigned patents, they use the DST R&D data.

international markets). Export markets have diverse consumer preferences and though relatively more competitive in some ways, may involve overcoming different types of marketing barriers; exports by increasing the market-size and diversity, enhance the potential rents from innovation. In India, greater domestic rivalry since the late-1980s is rendering the improvement of quality/ specifications of products imperative, thereby also enhancing the export competitiveness; with liberal imports, the cost innovation may receive less emphasis. So we expect the total R&D (and quality upgradation) expenses and export intensities to be closely linked. The existing (single-equation) studies evidence for India is mostly not strong though (Kumar and Siddharthan, 1994; Lall, 1983).

The Other Inter-dependencies: The literature discusses extensively the import-intensive bias of foreign technology, and the often accompanying import tie-in clauses; MIG may not affect the MT, except for minor payments of commission for procuring imports and foreign travel. Export-oriented firms require greater technology import to be internationally competitive (Siddharthan and Krishna, 1994), foreign travel and export marketing assistance (included in MT); a higher maximum royalty rate is allowed on 'exports production'. The firm may gain from global marketing network and brandnames of the technical collaborator; but the likely export restrictions cause an anti-exports bias (below-potential exports).

Larger exports might slightly affect the imports through the added requirements. A higher import content enhances the export competitiveness but also the domestic market power (Patibandla, 1992). With import quotas/REP licences somewhat linked to the exports, a firm with relatively large requirements of imports may decide to export more, to lessen the (private costlier) purchase of REP licences etc.

In the short-run the R&D activities require more imports, specially of capital goods (Siddharthan and Safarian, 1995); import licences for R&D purpose are easier to procure, particularly for the DST-recognised R&D centres. However, the medium/long-run effect is likely to be import-substituting, considering the gradual 'indigenisation' policy criteria for import of inputs (Basant, 1993), and the likely adaptation of imported technology to local conditions. So RDRI is expected to have a negative effect on MIG. A greater availability of import licences to a firm, say through personal rapport, may reduce the incentive, or pressure to undertake R&D (Goldar and Ranganathan, 1998); their evidence is weak.

The Model Specification: Equation-wise

The exogenous variables are: the firm-size (LSIZE, LSIZE2); FERA and non-FERA foreign ownership dummies (FERAD, NFERAD); the MNE size, R&D intensity, multinationality and growth rate, and US-MNE dummy (FSF, RDF, MS, SGF, USMNED); the firm growth rate, recentness of equipment, skill, capital intensity, vertical integration, profitability, indebtedness, advertisement intensity, and 1988-89 dummy (RGNS, RRE & RRELD, SKILL, CIR, VERTI, PMAV, LEV, ADI, D88).

The R&D Intensity (RDRI) Equation: Several studies have examined the effect of size (Chaudhuri, 1995; Katrak, 1994; Kumar and Siddharthan, 1997; Nath, 1993), usually as a 'Schumpeterian hypothesis' test. The oft-quoted arguments are: more stable internal funds and diversification of large firms, as against the bureaucratisation, market power and industrial licensing restrictions. The budgetary constraints and a large threshold expense level of many R&D activities may render the nature of technological programmes differ qualitatively between small and large firms, viz. 'minor' ones and 'major' (country and industry-specific). Thus the size-R&D intensity relationship may be U-shaped among those undertaking R&D, as found in some earlier studies.

Operating in 'high quality' segments by accessing the MNE's research findings, foreign affiliates, in general, may not be much enthusiastic about adapting the technology to locally available raw materials, consumer preferences and tropical diseases. (Pillai and Shah, 1988). Some R&D work may be simply preliminary stage testing for a global project, having limited usefulness and benefits-appropriability for the host country. Multivariate studies of R&D intensity usually point to the foreign ownership being an insignificant factor (Chaudhuri 1995; Dunning, 1992; Fikkert, 1995; survey by Kumar and Siddharthan, 1997). Internationalisation of R&D by MNEs (Dunning 1992; Kumar, 1995; Pearce and Singh, 1992) seems somewhat smaller for US-MNEs (specially the drug sector); rises with the multinationality ratio (local adaptation); there is mixed evidence for the size effect; a low share of developing nations. We explore the effects of MNE multinationality and research intensity (MS and RDF). A positive effect of RDF would reflect similar production patterns and corporate practices. However, the access to new technology by 'high RDF' affiliates may reduce R&D by them; 'relatively marketing-oriented MNEs' affiliates may undertake more local R&D to sustain their growth (Pearce and Singh, 1992).

A higher R&D intensity is expected with a relatively high skill of top-level employees (Lall, 1983), capital intensity, recentness of equipment (dynamism of the firm), and vertical integration (a form of diversification; better appropriation of the R&D findings); we find generally insignificant influences of VERTI and CIR.

Higher profits may both drive and facilitate (financing of) R&D; the empirical evidence is somewhat mixed (Braga and Willmore, 1991).[4] Himmelberg and Petersen(1994) argue that given the fluctuating cash flows, the R&D expenses are smoothed to minimise the costs of firing researchers (transmitting information to competitors), or integrating new ones etc.; innovation being inherently risky, the internal finance is extremely important. Accordingly, we employ a 5-year average of profit margin on sales, PMAV, or of the 'internal cash flow to sales ratio'. However, the coefficient is small and never highly significant.[5]

The Import of Technology (MT) Equation: There are few multivariate econometric investigations of the determinants of inter-firm differences of technology import (expenses) intensity in developing countries. In India with the technology import liberalisation since the mid-1980s, the market forces are now more operative. Using the RBI data on large quoted companies for 1987-88 to 1989-90, Siddharthan and Krishna(1994) explain the technology import intensity values (a sizable proportion being zero) employing the Tobit model. The results are mixed and vary across sectors; the market share, skill, capital intensity and recentness of equipment have generally positive impacts. Evenson and Joseph (1999) examine

---

4. Some studies examine the R&D expenditure as one of the co-determined financial decisions; see Himmelberg and Petersen (1994).
5. With the current profit margin, PM instead, the coefficient is sometimes negative; r(PMAV, PM)= +0.6; r(RDRI, PMAV) = +0.18 only.

separately the royalty rate and lumpsum payments; thus it is hard to infer regarding the overall payments.

Like R&D, there may be economies of scale regarding technology import, and the smaller firms generally seeking minor professional and consultancy services and large firms entering into formal technical agreements. We expect a U-shaped relationship between the firm size and MT. Foreign-owned firms spend relatively more on import of technology (Basant, 1993; Pillai and Shah, 1988). There may be greater implicit payments (instead through return on equity) for 'higher foreign ownership' firms.[6] Having a larger global marketing network and technological base to draw upon, affiliates of relatively big or high R&D intensity MNEs (higher FSF or RDF) may have a greater import of technology and marketing assistance.[7] Relatively high advertisement intensity, ADI firms may undertake more foreign travel and seek greater marketing assistance. We also examine the effect of recentness of equipment, RRE (dynamism), possibly different for local and foreign-owned firms.

The Export Intensity (XIG) Equation: Bigger or foreign-owned firms enjoy better export competitiveness due to economies of scale also in marketing and risk-handling, and enormous resources of the MNE (Kumar and Siddharthan, 1997; Singh, 1989). But their export orientation could be less on account of the domestic market power (brandname loyalty), and the MNE-imposed export restrictions (intra-MNE sales inter-dependence). A local (independent) firm may view its exports as (more) strategically linked to the growth and technological advancement of the enterprise. Considering the importance of global marketing and technology networks, the relatively large global size, multinationality and research intensity of the MNE are potentially favourable factors for exports by the affiliate.[8] Faster growing firms being more dynamic are likely to sell proportionately more overseas, also to overcome the domestic demand constraint. Vertical integration affects the product structure.

---

6. Transfer pricing (unique technologies) and costlier transfer to pure licensees affect the foreign ownership coefficients.
7. Japanese firms pay a higher royalty rate (Siddharthan, 1999).
8. However, horizontal integration of more internationalised MNEs could affect it adversely (Kumar, 1998, p. 455). Faster growing MNEs may 'regulate' less their affiliates foreign trade. We find the MS and SGF variables unimportant for XIG.

Earlier studies find usually a weak positive effect of SKILL (export competitiveness). Exports being a relatively risky activity (compared to domestic sales), a high indebtedness of the firm, LEV, acts as a restraining factor.

The Import Intensity (MIG) Equation: Bigger and foreign-owned firms are better equipped to produce import substituting items but they also enjoy an easier availability of import quotas and licences. Providing a market for products of their associates elsewhere/parent MNEs (specially smaller MNEs) and the transfer pricing may lead to a relatively high import propensity of foreign-owned affiliates, as found in several studies for India, mostly for the period upto the mid 1970s (Pillai and Shah, 1988; Singh, 1989). This tendency to import heavily - somewhat curbed by the phased manufacturing programme, PMP policy since the mid-1970s - is probably getting reverted with the import liberalisation since the early-1980s and the Post-1991 PMP discontinuation. Among foreign units, the 'more internationalised MNEs' affiliates perhaps enjoy greater autonomy for procuring the intermediates. Also, the US affiliates may have lower import propensity (large domestic market of the parent unit). The 'MNE R&D intensity' by influencing the sophistication of technology, would increase the import intensity.

With import liberalisation the relatively high RRE, faster-growing (capital-stock) firms might have indulged in heavy imports of capital goods (Siddharthan and Safarian, 1995) and other items. SKILL and CIR may increase the MIG while greater vertical integration enables more of import-substituting production. The preferred specification of the model is as in Table 19.1 later.

SECTION 3

THE SAMPLE, DATA AND THE VARIABLES

Sample

Our sample of 35 large and medium-sized private sector pharmaceutical companies operating in India covering the period 1988-89 to 1991-92, accounted for roughly 45-50 per cent of pharmaceutical formulations output in India. These fairly well-established firms cater primarily to the domestic market. The pooled annual observations are 120 (given some yearly data gaps); trying different sets of year dummies, we retain only the year 1988-89 dummy.[9]

Data Sources

The author collected the firm-specific data from the company annual reports; the R&D data are from an Appendix to the Directors' Reports.[10] The MNE-data for foreign-owned affiliates are compiled from the Discover Worldscope Industrial Company Profiles, various published Vols./CD-Rom by Disclosure Inc., Bethesda, USA.

Variables

Unless stated otherwise, current (price) values are employed. The MNE-specific variables are indicated as such.

ADI advertisement (expenses) intensity (%); ratio to net sales.

CIR capital intensity ratio; ratio of gross total capital employed (book value) to total sales and other revenue.

D88 dummy for year 1988-89.

FERAD, NFERAD FERA (≥ 40%) and non-FERA (25 to <40%) foreign ownership dummies.[11]

---

9. We employed various sets of year dummies. The 1991-92 dummy may capture any (Post-July 1991) structural change within this year (April-March). Its coefficient is expectedly non-significant - the likely lags in the policy implementation and corporate responses. Only the 1988-89 dummy is significant (in XIG equation).

10. This Appendix providing comparable data on R&D expenses has been attached only since around 1988-89. R&D data reported in the profit-loss statements - employed in several earlier studies - seem incomparable and usually grossly understated (Basant, 1993); probably the raw materials and salaries expenses etc. for R&D purpose get clubbed under the respective broad category. The RBI data seem to be understated similarly, e.g. these industry averages of R&D intensity in Siddharthan and Krishna (1994, Table 1) v. the DST/DSIR data for recognised R&D Centres in Basant (2000, Table 10). Some studies use the DST unpublished firm-level R&D data.

11. This distinction is India-specific; activities of FERA firms have been relatively more constrained - through industrial licensing and other policies (FERA Act, 1974). However, MNEs classify their overseas ventures as subsidiaries and minority-owned; 50/75% voting rights are relevant to ordinary/special company resolutions. Post-1991 the majority foreign ownership is being allowed liberally for new and existing alliances. Hence we alternatively employ the minority (25 to below 50%) and majority foreign ownership dummies instead, which yield largely similar results; the main differences are pointed out later.

FSF log of size (global foreign sales) of foreign collaborator; this measure adjusts for the MNE's 'domestic size' variation.

LEV leverage ratio; total borrowings to gross capital employed (%).

LSIZE loge size; size is 'sales revenue + dividends, interest and net misc. receipts' (Rs. crore=10 m.); drugs and medicines WPI price deflator (1981-82 base) is used. LSIZE2=LSIZE*LSIZE.

MIG import intensity; total merchandise direct imports to 'value of (own) output, net of purchase of finished goods for resale' (%).

MS multinationality of sales of foreign collaborator; global foreign sales to total sales (%).

MT import of technology (& marketing elements/assistance); % of value of (own) output.

This measure is based on foreign exchange expenses on 'royalty, lumpsum payments/technical fees, foreign travel and subscription, management, professional and consultancy fees, commission, and misc. expenses'; preferred to 'royalty and technical payments rate'.

PMAV profit margin (averaged); gross operating profits before tax, interest and depreciation to net sales (%); 5-year average (t to t_4).

RDF R&D intensity of foreign collaborator (% of its net sales).

RDRI R&D revenue (current) expenditure intensity; % of value of (own) output. With annual current data, we prefer to exclude the R&D capital expenses due to their lumpiness and lagged effects.

RGNS (relative) growth rate of net sales; deviation (%) from the year's sample average growth rate, as the latter shows large fluctuations and concerns the demand constraint to growth.

RRE relative recentness of equipment; deviation from the year's sample average RE, the ratio of net to gross value of plant and machinery. RRELD=RRE*Local ownership dummy (LD).

SGF (global net) sales growth rate of foreign collaborator (%).

SKILL skill level; 'high' income (≥ Rs. 6000 p.m. for 1988-89 and 1989-90; Rs. 12000 later) employees remuneration to total wages and salaries ratio; % deviation from the sample average for the year.

USMNED US-MNE dummy; 1 for US collaborator.

VERTI vertical integration; gross value added to 'value of (own) output plus purchase of finished goods for resale' (%).

XIG export intensity; total merchandise exports to net sales (%).

For the MNE characteristics, considering the major (if >1) foreign financial (equity) collaborator, the ultimate holding company data are utilised. For the variables MNE's R&D intensity, growth rate and multinationality of sales, % deviation is taken from the respective average value for the year for foreign affiliates in the sample; logarithmic (loge) deviation is taken similarly for the MNE-size.[12] Among foreign affiliates, the standard deviation of FSF, MS, RDF and SGF variables are 0.94. 39.58, 54.21 and 125.34 respectively.

More on the Sample

Of the 120 annual observations all endogenous variables values are positive, except 3 for export and R&D intensity separately (1 firm each); some values are quite small. Average XIG and MIG for the sample are 6.48 and 8.87. Non-merchandise exports being generally negligible, are ignored here. LSIZE ranges from 2.443 to 5.619 (mean=3.735) - to be considered for the firm-size effects. Of the 80 observations on foreign-owned firms, about 3/4th are FERA units and 1/3rd US-affiliates.

For the present sample, the export and import intensities are closely related, as also the skill and R&D intensities. The total technology expense ratio (MT plus R&D intensity) is generally small to moderate. The low sample average R&D intensity, RDRI (0.88%; 1.09% with R&D capital expenses included), however, far exceeds the average import of technology (defined broadly) expenses ratio, MT (0.19%). The r(RDRI, MT) is +0.461. It is similar for the foreign-owned affiliates. Their average in-house R&D intensity (RDRI) at less than 1.0%, falls much short of that for the associated MNEs (8.5%). Further, their r(RDRI, RDF) is notably negative (-0.448). Multinationality of sales of the MNE and its R&D intensity (MS and RDF) are positively associated.

---

12. Thereby the 'base' foreign affiliate for comparison is the 'average' in these regards, and the interpretation of results (of these and foreign ownership coefficients) is facilitated. The effect of foreign ownership is seen through the coefficients of foreign ownership dummies along with that of US-MNE dummy.

SECTION 4

ANALYSIS OF RESULTS

Due to the possible specification bias we prefer the 2sls estimates to a system method like 3sls estimates. The constant term was quite insignificant in the estimated XIG and MT structural equations. The 2sls estimates are reported in Table 19.1; Table 19.2 presents their derived reduced forms (henceforth DRF) and we discuss these

Table 19.1

2sls Estimates of RDRI, MT, XIG and MIG Equations
(Panel Data; 35 firms, 1988-99 – 1991-92)

N = 120

Equation *Explanatory Var.*	*RDRI*	*MT*	*XIG*	*MIG*
Endo. Variables				
RDRI		0.130 (4.380)	2.134 (1.752)	-3.333 (2.116)
MT	1.262 (3.062)			12.105 (2.378)
XIG	0.034 (2.815)	0.008 (2.231)		0.394 (2.664)
MIG	-0.030 (2.390)		0.711 (6.716)	
Exog. Variables				
LSIZE	-2.297 (4.350)		11.368 (5.406)	-2.163 (2.455)
LSIZE2	0.284 (4.193)		-1.367 (4.699)	
NFERAD		0.106 (2.157)		2.848 (1.960)
FERAD		0.061 (1.736)		3.226 (2.866)
USMNED				-5.030 (4.154)
FSF		0.071 (3.021)	0.837 (1.658)	
MS	-0.004 (2.849)			-0.055 (3.119)
RDF			-0.036 (3.190)	0.056 (4.452)

Contd...

...Table 19.1 Contd...

N = 120

Equation / *Explanatory Var.*	*RDRI*	*MT*	*XIG*	*MIG*
SGF/100		-0.026 (1.676)		
RGNS			0.014 (2.298)	
RRE	-0.932 (2.299)	1.245 (8.764)		-11.697 (1.746)
RRELD		-0.810 (3.375)		17.667 (2.198)
SKILL	0.004 (6.354)		-0.019 (2.545)	0.019 (2.108)
CIR				5.801 (2.636)
VERTI			-0.546 (4.943)	-0.323 (1.920)
PMAV	0.021 (1.361)			
LEV			-0.225 (5.247)	
ADI		0.008 (1.124)		
D88			-1.611 (2.056)	
Constant	4.977 (4.824)			16.172 (3.973)
R-sq	0.688	0.631	0.733	0.649
R-bar-sq	0.663	0.604	0.708	0.602
F	26.966	23.694	29.906	13.868

Note: t - values in parentheses.

coefficients as well for the overall effects of important exogenous variables. Some preliminary explorations are mentioned too.

The R&D Intensity (RDRI) Equation

Contrary to the finding of Basant (1993) and Fikkert (1995) who also allow for the simultaneity, we find the technology import and R&D intensities (MT and RDRI) to be complementary. The relationship is positive and significant both ways; the variable

'MT*foreign ownership dummy' in RDRI eq. is highly insignificant. However, there is no significant direct favourable impact of foreign ownership or MNE research intensity on RDRI, implying any intra-MNE trickle-down or spillover effect on the affiliate being feeble. A direct explicit import of technology may induce in-house R&D efforts, for local and foreign-owned firms alike. In-house R&D seems partly driven by the export orientation, both for local and foreign-owned firms; the 'XIG*foreign ownership dummy' coefficient is quite weak. The negative coefficient on MIG reflects the Indian institutional conditions mentioned above. The MT, XIG and MIG effects are all significant and fairly sizable.

This study finds relatively high research intensity of large v. medium-sized firms in the sample, given a consistently prominent U-shaped size-RDRI relationship, as expected; Section 3 reports the sample size range. For the direct effect (Table 19.1) the turning point LSIZE is 4.044, a medium-large size; comparatively, the estimated RDRI(%) of the biggest firm is higher by 0.705. Considering that the sample average R&D intensity is low, this difference is not small, notwithstanding the oligopolistic tendencies and small size of Indian giants relative to international giants (Nath, 1993). The corresponding DRF calculations are 4.013 LSIZE and 0.774 higher RDRI; the smallest firm has a similar higher RDRI.

Foreign ownership does not directly determine the RDRI; the DRF coefficients are slightly positive though. As for the MNE's research intensity, RDF, its coefficient is generally positive but small and insignificant; hence RDF is dropped here. The overall effect of RDF on RDRI (the DRF coefficient) is negative and modest (as also their pair-wise correlation for foreign-owned affiliates), supporting the view that the affiliate may strive harder to gain technological strength on its own when the parent company is less R&D-oriented. Affiliates of more internationalised MNEs are less R&D intensive; MS may partly capture the effect of RDF variable. A larger MNE size increases the RDRI only indirectly and slightly.

The variable gross profit margin, PMAV, is at best only weakly significant with a positive sign. Its coefficient is also small; the 'PMAV* local ownership dummy' term was insignificant too. Thus there is no strong support for the argument that more profitable firms are relatively R&D intensive. A multiple of other factors seem

Table 19.2

Derived Reduced form Coefficients (2sls estimates, Table 19.1)

N = 120

Equation *Explanatory Var.*	*RDRI*	*MT*	*XIG*	*MIG*
LSIZE	-2.4104	-0.2179	11.8386	7.9010
LSIZE2	0.3003	0.0254	-1.6939	-1.3613
NFERAD	0.1867	0.1680	4.7576	6.1346
FERAD	0.1099	0.1107	4.4726	5.9639
USMNED	-0.0087	-0.0451	-5.5022	-7.7169
FSF	0.1732	0.1136	2.4642	1.7693
MS	-0.0056	-0.0013	-0.0674	-0.0780
RDF	-0.0021	-0.0002	0.0033	0.0617
SGF/100	-0.0447	-0.0350	-0.4041	-0.4344
RGNS	0.0008	0.0003	0.0228	0.0097
RRE	0.8661	1.3964	4.8579	4.2353
RRELD	-1.3616	-0.9322	6.7437	13.5790
SKILL	0.0040	0.0005	-0.0025	0.0110
CIR	0.0100	0.0521	6.3457	8.9000
VERTI	-0.0334	-0.0142	-1.2358	-0.8706
PMAV	0.0285	0.0040	0.0386	-0.0313
LEV	-0.0135	-0.0047	-0.3638	-0.1548
ADI	0.0144	0.0113	0.1305	0.1403
D88	-0.0969	-0.0334	-2.6053	-1.1087
Constant	6.7259	1.0864	26.7587	17.4580

more relevant. Overall there is lower R&D by more indebted firms; the direct effect of LEV is weak though. The negative direct impact of RRE (Table 19.1) is unexpected; however, the overall effect is small and negative for local firms (RRE+RRELD coefficients, Table 19.2), while positive for foreign affiliates. Perhaps local firms face more competition for funds between the fixed capital investment and R&D (recurring) expenses, RDRI. The SKILL has a favourable effect. ADI, VERTI and sales growth are uninfluential.

The Import of Technology (MT) Equation

More export-oriented firms and specially high R&D intensive firms have a significantly larger import of technology. Siddharthan and Krishna (1994) find such effects only in a minority number of industries, using, however, the conventional narrow definition of technology import expenses pertaining to formal technical agreements. The MIG variable is expectedly not important. The firm-size has no significant direct influence on MT; the DRF estimates indicate a mild U-shaped relationship. Compared to local firms, both FERA and non-FERA foreign-owned units have higher MT levels, particularly the latter; this tendency appears sharper in the DRF estimates. With minority and majority foreign ownership dummies employed instead, both coefficients are positive but the latter is statistically weak.

The SGF coefficient is surprisingly negative and modest in size; probably affiliates of 'slow-growing MNEs' may engage in greater (arms-length) technical agreements with other parties, also involving more of explicit payments. The 'bigger MNEs' affiliates have considerably higher import of technology. The other MNE-characteristics seem unimportant. As in Siddharthan and Krishna(1994), relatively recent equipment firms spend more on technology import; this is seen here both for local and foreign-owned firms, remarkably so for the latter. The ADI variable has only a weak positive effect.

The Export Intensity (XIG) Equation: The export performance is expectedly superior for high research intensity firms. The RDRI coefficient is almost invariably significant at least at 5 per cent level (one-tailed test). The addition of 'RDRI*foreign ownership dummy' term indicates weakly the favourable effect of RDRI to be larger for local firms, as expected.[13] The technology import does not favour the export intensity directly in this model. The import intensity adds considerably to the export intensity; however, since the MIG coefficient is consistently below unity statistically, the adverse effect of a higher import intensity on the balance-of-trade (BOT) is not fully neutralised; in proportionate terms the BOT is roughly XIG minus MIG.

The effect of firm size is significant and inverted U-shaped. The turning point LSIZE is 4.158 (Table 19.1), for which the estimated XIG exceeds that for the smallest and the largest firms by 4.021 and

13. It renders the RDRI coefficient larger and more significant.

2.918 respectively. The unfavourable effect of large (*vs.* medium or medium-large) size on XIG holds more sharply for the DRF estimates (Table 19.2). Considering the coefficients of NFERAD, FERAD and USMNED together, foreign ownership has only a slight indirect positive effect on XIG. Relatively 'high R&D MNEs' affiliates do not exhibit a superior export performance; the direct effect of RDF is notably negative, though the overall effect is positive but negligible. However, the 'larger MNEs' affiliates have a higher export-sales ratio; the DRF coefficient on FSF is even bigger. A large negative overall effect of USMNED (Table 19.2) is probably through a lower MIG.

A faster growth rate of sales improves modestly the export-sales ratio, corroborating the existing limited evidence. Highly indebted firms have a lower proportion of overseas sales, as expected. The D88 coefficient is negative and large, implying a rise in XIG after 1988-89. The SKILL level has a negative direct influence.

The import intensity (MIG) equation: The (merchandise) import intensity is higher for a larger technology import which is consistent with the existing evidence. In contrast, much lower import intensity accompanies greater own technological effort i.e., R&D is import-substituting. The MIG is higher for a rise in the export intensity.

Bigger firms have substantially lower import intensity; the LSIZE-square term being insignificant, is dropped. The DRF coefficients also point to a negative effect for almost the entire size range. The 'large v. medium size' seems to reduce somewhat more the import intensity than the export intensity, specially as judged by the overall effects, thereby improving slightly the proportionate balance-of-trade. Among foreign-owned firms, the US affiliates have much lower import intensity, apparently similar or slightly smaller than that for local firms; but the non-US affiliates have considerably higher import propensity. Compared to the indigenous firms, on the whole both non-FERA and FERA (or minority and majority) foreign-owned firms have an expected higher import intensity. The DRF estimates point to similar yet stronger tendencies.

Consistent with *a priori* expectations, the import-output ratio is considerably higher for affiliates of high research intensity MNEs, and lower for 'more multinational MNEs' affiliates. Associates of relatively large MNEs do not import less; the DRF coefficients on

FSF (Table 19.2) indicate their higher import propensity - both merchandise and technology import - though exhibiting also a better export performance. The contrasting effects of the three technology-acquisition related variables, namely MT and RDF (related indirectly) v. RDRI, makes an interesting finding. Further, RDRI also influences favourably the XIG. The overall effect on the balance-of-trade appears favourable for RDRI, while unfavourable for MT and RDF and somewhat so for foreign ownership.

Among locally-owned firms, a higher RRE increases the import intensity, as expected. For foreign-owned units, no clear-cut picture emerges; the RRE coefficient is negative in the structural equation while slightly positive in the reduced form. As noted above, the finding that 'relatively recent equipment' firms incur larger expenses on technology import, holds more strongly for foreign affiliates. Perhaps with liberal norms for technology import payments, the MNEs might prefer this direct route of payments for technology transferred to the overpricing of imports.

SECTION 5

MAIN FINDINGS AND CONCLUDING REMARKS

This being a study of micro-level relationships, we confine the concluding remarks largely to those. We find strong inter-dependencies among the endogenous variables of the model. R&D and technology import intensities strengthen each other. Thus even while capturing the simultaneity, the stimulative (consistently positive) effect of import of technology on R&D intensity holds, indicating a complementarity. A high R&D intensity boosts the export-sales ratio, somewhat more for local firms. Considering the large favourable effect of export intensity on R&D intensity, the export assistance policies may indirectly promote in-house R&D. Export intensity increases considerably with the import intensity. As against the import intensive bias of foreign technology and foreign ownership, there is not any superior export performance (directly). The import intensity is sizably higher for a larger technology import or MNE research intensity while a greater in-house technological effort of the enterprise reduces it much.

Compared to medium-sized firms, large firms are more inward-oriented both in terms of export and import intensities. However, they have a conspicuously higher R&D intensity; probably the nature of their R&D activities differs too (Kumar and Siddharthan, 1997). Incidentally, faster growing firms have a higher overseas sales ratio. Profitability has little influence on the R&D intensity. Foreign-owned firms seem to have somewhat higher merchandise and technology import propensities. Even a high degree of foreign ownership (comparing the FERA/Non-FERA, or majority/minority ownerships) improves neither the R&D intensity nor the balance-of-trade. These statistical tendencies are worthy of concern when the FDI inflow is being viewed as a kind of major 'policy target'.

Our explorations regarding the MNE-influences indicate the US affiliates having comparatively lower outward-orientation, particularly the import intensity. The 'bigger MNE' affiliates spend relatively more on superior technology acquisition (directly) through its import only; they export more but have largely matching higher merchandise import intensity. The 'high research intensity MNE' affiliates do not exhibit significantly elevated R&D and export intensity levels; the direct effect on export intensity is actually negative; they have a much higher import intensity. So the financial collaboration with a rather big or highly R&D intensive MNE may not serve better the interests of a developing country.

Now in a stronger patent regime, specially with pharmaceutical product patents, the technology import or 'high R&D intensity MNE' association would further enhance the relative export competitiveness of the enterprise, but probably also the severity of export-restrictive and import tie-in clauses. The patent regime is unimportant for R&D location by MNEs (Kumar, 1995). Among locally-owned firms, at least the large units are likely to strive hard for product development by stepping up their R&D activities. However, the immediate Post-1991 period has observed an overall stagnancy of R&D intensity and the 'quality upgradation through product differentiation' receiving a priority over 'R&D and innovation' (Basant, 2000). In the case of indigenous firms this has been probably a short-term/survival response to the phenomenally growing market control by MNEs, through equity alliances (mostly majority stake) and acquisitions & mergers.

References

Basant, R. (1993). "R&D, Foreign Technology Purchase and Technology Spillovers in Indian Industry: Some Explorations," Working Paper No. 8, August, UNU/INTECH, Netherlands.

————. (2000). "Corporate Response to Economic Reforms," *Economic and Political Weekly* 35(10): 813-22.

Braga, H. and L. Willmore (1991). "Technological Imports and Technological Effort: An Analysis of Their Determinants in Brazilian Firms," *Journal of Industrial Economics* 39(2): 421-32.

Chaudhuri, D. (1995). "Technological Capability in Indian Electronics Industry under Economic Liberalisation," *Economic and Political Weekly* 30(Feb. 18-25): M-13 to M-18.

Dunning, J. (1992). "Multinational Enterprises and the Global Economy," Addison-Wesley, England.

Evenson, R. and K. Joseph (1999). "Foreign Technology Licensing in Indian Industry: An Econometric Analysis of the Choice of Partners, Terms of Contracts and the Effect on Licensees," *Economic and Political Weekly* 34(27): 1801-09.

Evenson, R. and L. Westphal (1995). "Technological Change and Technology Strategy," in J. Behrman and T. Srinivasan (eds.). *Handbook of Development Economics*, Vol. 3A, Handbooks in Economics, North Holland, Amsterdam.

Fikkert, B. (1995). "An Open or Closed Technology Policy? The Effects of Technology Licenses, Foreign Direct Investment, and Domestic and International Spillovers on R&D in Indian Firms," March, Unpublished Paper, University of Maryland.

Goldar, B. and V. Ranganathan (1998). "Economic Reforms and R&D Expenditure in Industrial Firms in India," *Indian Economic Journal*, 46(2): 60-75.

Himmelberg, C. and B. Petersen (1994). "R&D and Internal Finance: A Panel Study of Small Firms in High-Tech Industries," Review of Economics and Statistics 76(1): 38-51.

Katrak, H. (1994). "Imports of Technology, Enterprise Size and R&D-Based Production in a Newly Industrialising Country: The Evidence from Indian Enterprises," World Development 22(10): 1599-1608.

Kumar, N. (1995). "Industrialisation, Liberalisation and Two Way Flows of Foreign Direct Investments: Case of India," *Economic and Political Weekly* 30(Dec. 16): 3228-37.

————. (1998). "Multinational Enterprises, Regional Economic Integration, and Export-Platform Production in the Host Countries: An Empirical Analysis for the U.S. and Japanese Corporations," Review of World Economics 134(3): 450-83.

Kumar, N. and N. Siddharthan (1994). "Technology, Firm Size and Export Behavior in Developing Countries: The Case of Indian Enterprises," *Journal of Development Studies* 31(2): 289-309.

————. (1997). "Technology, Market Structure and Internationalisation: Issues and Policies for Developing Countries," Routledge, London.

Lall, S. (1983). "Determinants of R&D in an LDC: The Indian Engineering Industry," Economic Letters 13(4): 379-83.

Nath, P. (1993). "Firm Size and In-House R&D: The Indian Experience Revisited," The Developing Economies 31(3): 329-44.

Patibandla, M. (1992). "Scale Economies and Export Promotion in a Import Substituting Regime: Some Observations for Indian Industry," *Economic and Political Weekly* 27(Feb. 29): M24-30.

Pearce, R. and S. Singh (1992). "Globalising Research and Development," Macmillan, London.

Pillai, P. and J. Shah (1988). "Multinational Corporations and National Technological Capability," Sardar Patel Institute of Economic and Social Research, Ahmedabad, Monograph Series 13.

Siddharthan, N. (1999). "European And Japanese Affiliates in India: Differences in Conduct and Performance," *Economic and Political Weekly* 34(22): M-61 to M-65.

Siddharthan, N. and K.L. Krishna (1994). "Determinants of Technology Imports: Evidence for Indian Firms," Working Paper No. E/161/94, Institute of Economic Growth, Delhi.

Siddharthan, N. and A. Safarian (1995). "Technology Transfer and Import of Capital Goods: Recent Indian Experience, in Canada-India Institutional Linkage Program Workshop, Trade, Innovation and Industrial Performance," Institute of Economic Growth, Delhi, Feb. 19-20.

Subrahmanian, K., Sastry, D., Pattanaik, S. and S. Hajra (1996). "Foreign Collaboration under Liberalisation Policy: Patterns of Collaboration and Technology-transfer in Indian Industry since 1991," August, RBI, Mumbai.

20

Inter-source FDI Differences in Technology Transfer Behaviour

A Comparison of US and Japanese FDI in Indian Manufacturing

K.U. UMAKRISHNAN

INTRODUCTION

FDI inflows has been encouraged and competed for in the recent times because of the belief that it is not only a source of non-debt creating foreign exchange but a conduit for the state-of-the-art technology for the developing countries. However, this view is not an un-debated one, and has triggered much discussions and empirical investigations on the impact of FDI on the host economy (See Saggi and Pack, 1999 for a survey). Past studies, however most often fail to take into account the heterogeneity of FDI and the differences in their nature and behaviour across sources. This paper is an attempt in the direction of trying to bring out the inter-source differences in the technology transfer behaviour of FDI in the context of Indian manufacturing.

The paper is divided into six sections. We shall look at the increasing relevance of FDI in India and the technology policy environment of the country in the first section to provide the background of the study context. Following it, we shall make a case for the need to compare the technology transfer behaviour of US and Japanese FDI. The role of ownership control in determining is brought out in section 3. Data set and empirical analysis make up the section 4 and 5 respectively. Conclusion brings up the 6th and final section of the paper.

SECTION I

CHANGING MACRO ENVIRONMENT IN INDIA

Increasing Importance of FDI in India

The role of FDI in Indian economy has undergone a perceptible shift since independence in 1947, and yet again with liberalisation in 1991.

The bulk of the foreign investments in the pre-independent India was undertaken by the United Kingdom. This was only natural considering that the political power was wielded by them and therefore they could receive maximum incentives and operate under conducive policies in India. However in the decades following independence, the socialist pattern of development envisaged did not encourage FDI. It was not until the late-eighties and more specifically since 1991, when the country was opened up, that FDI began to play an important role. The increasing significance of FDI in India in recent years is reflected in the jump in FDI to Gross Fixed Capital Formation ratio from 0.3 per cent in 1992 to 3.6 per cent in 1995.

Table 20.1

Share of Each Source Country in Total Outstanding FDI (in per cent)

	UK	*USA*	*Japan*	*Germany*	*Sweden*	*Switzerland*	*Total (in Rs. crore)*
1965	75.13	15.18	0.21	1.73	1.29	2.45	611.9
1975	58.57	22.60	0.44	4.22	1.70	4.18	973.3
1986	52.72	18.88	3.27	8.47	3.01	3.72	1557
1995	27.9	24.10	7.55	8.94	1.28	5.54	9416

Source: RBI Bulletins, various issues.

Although UK continues to dominate in the share of outstanding FDI, the Table 20.1 indicates that its share has been steadily decreasing while that of the US has steadily increased and has reached at par of UK. Other countries especially Germany and Japan has substantially increased their stronghold. It is to be noted that in recent years it is the Japanese flows that have experienced the highest growth. Outstanding liabilities from Sweden and Switzerland are seen to be stagnating in recent years and Sweden seem to be losing the importance it had gained in the late-seventies.

With the change in the source of flows, a change in the sector to which they flow can be discerned (Table 20.2). Plantations no longer account for the major chunk of inflows. The share of manufactures has shown quantum leap and within it too a change in the alignments can be noticed.

Table 20.2

Share of Outstanding FDI in Each Industry Within Manufacturing

Industry	*1960*	*1975*	*1986*	*1995*
Food, Beverages	21.60	7.42	7.4	6.87
textile Products	8.48	4.35	6.4	2.86
Transport Equip.	3.97	5.19	11.7	14.91
Machinery & Machine Tools	2.69	7.42	13.7	16.85
Metal & Metal Prod.	9.49	13.87	5.7	5.46
Electrical Goods & Machinery	11.24	11.61	13.4	14.96
Chemical & Allied Prod.	21.74	33.56	34.5	28.3
Miscellaneous	20.79	16.57	6.89	9.75
Total	**100**	**100**	**100**	**100**

Source: RBI Bulletins, various issues.

Over the period 1950 to 1980, the increase in the share of the Manufacturing sector seem to be due to the increasing flows into chemical and allied production followed by machinery and machine goods as well as metal and metal production. The industries that have lost out are food and beverages, textiles, and building materials. This is the period when UK investments were being replaced by investments from other sources especially US. This indicates the concentration of US investments in chemical and allied production. In the period since 1980, when Japan increased its flows into India, we see a substantial increase in the share of transport industry. The industry-wise flow of various sources of investment clearly indicate that Japanese investments are concentrated in the transport sector.

Sweden on the other hand has concentrated its investment in the machinery and machine tools industry. German investments on the other hand is not seen as concentrated in any particular industry.

Table 20.3

Outstanding FDI (Country and Industry-wise)
March-end 1995 (per cent)

	UK	US	Japan	Germany	Sweden
Plantations	16.76	0.04	0.00	0.00	0.00
Mining	0.91	0.00	0.00	0.00	0.00
Petroleum	6.19	1.10	0.00	0.00	0.00
Manufacturing of which:	71.85	91.72	88.47	96.20	85.95
Food & Beverages	17.29	4.61	3.34	0.25	0.96
Textiles	6.24	0.38	0.48	5.31	0.00
Transport Equip.	9.84	5.28	60.57	22.22	0.00
Machinery & Machine Tools	8.36	15.90	1.43	18.89	64.42
Metal and Metal Products	5.18	1.78	0.95	3.46	5.77
Electrical Goods	3.01	15.61	13.67	18.27	17.31
Chemical & Allied	41.78	30.55	8.27	21.98	3.85
Others	7.88	25.89	11.29	9.63	7.69
Trading	1.86	0.93	2.81	1.19	0.00
Construction	0.72	0.53	0.70	0.36	0.00
Transport	0.04	0.00	0.00	0.00	0.00
Utilities	0.00	0.48	0.00	0.00	0.00
Financial	0.80	1.63	6.19	0.00	0.00
Others	1.18	3.57	1.83	2.26	14.05
Total	**100**	**100**	**100**	**100**	**100**

Source: RBI Bulletins, various issues.

However the increasingly dominant presence of FDI in Indian manufacturing in itself does not entail the acquisition of technology. The technology policy of the host country has a strong influence on it and it becomes imperative to look into this aspect of Indian economy.

Technology Policy Context in India

The single-most emphasised objective of India's industrial strategy since the 1950s has been the attainment of growth with self-reliance. Although the objective of industrial growth cannot be said to be attained, marked by declining industrial growth rates in the 1960s and 70s (Ahluwalia, 1985), India did have the lowest relative reliance on foreign technology among all the NICs in the period (Lall,1985). This was attained by a conscious policy of regulating various forms of technology transfer like foreign direct investment, foreign turnkey projects and use of foreign consultants, foreign licensing etc. Among these various modes of technology transfer, the latter was the favoured means of obtaining technology that was not domestically available.

A continuation of this broad policy can be seen in the technology Policy of 1983 which envisaged a selective import of technology where domestic capabilities have not been fully developed. In contrast to this, the Statement of Industrial Policy tabled by the Govt. of India on July 24, 1991 substantially liberalised the provisions and simplified the procedures governing Foreign Technology agreements. As per the Foreign Technology Policy (as contained in the New Industrial Policy 1991), there is a great need for promoting an industrial environment where the acquisition of technological capability receives priority. It was realised that the relationship between technology suppliers and users as a continuos one which becomes difficult to achieve when constant approval of the government is required on a case to case basis. With liberalising technology imports, the state has considerably withdrawn from direct R&D efforts, its share in total R&D falling from 87 per cent in 1989 to 82 per cent in 1996 leaving the technology transfer and acquisition to the free hands of the market (See Mani for further details).

This is on the assumption that FDI will bring in technology; however this is being done without ensuring the demand side factors. In an economy with little competition and pressure to innovate and change, merely opening up the economy to direct investments need not necessarily bring in technology transfer. This is indicated by the fact the FDI firms are not seen to conduct greater R&D *vis-à-vis* their counterparts in public and private domestic sector (Table 20.4).

Table 20.4

Expenditure on R & D as per cent of Sales by Industry Groups for Public and Private Sector Industries

	Public Sector Firms (as per cent STO)	Private Sector Firms (as per cent STO)	FDI Firms (as per cent STO)
Electric & Electronics	.59	0.78	0.46
Transportation	.14	1.09	0.47
Chemicals	.55	0.65	0.67
Food	.23	1.20	0.16
Textiles	.25	0.26	0.11
Engineering	2.02	0.43	0.23
Metals	.37	0.33	0.24

Source: For Public and Private Sector: Department of Science and Technology, 'R&D Statistics', and own estimation for FDI firms based on the sample.

STO: Sales Turn Over.

With the increasingly important role attributed to FDI as a medium of technology transfer, it will be interesting and imperative to understand the FDI behaviour keeping in mind the heterogeneity in the nature and characteristics of FDI.

SECTION 2

NEED FOR AN INTER-SOURCE FDI COMPARISON OF TECHNOLOGY TRANSFER BEHAVIOUR

Apart from being the two largest and growing sources of outward investments (Table 20.5), US and Japanese FDI presents an interesting case of comparison. The need for an inter-FDI source technology transfer behaviour is made out by three points of differences:

First, the nature and characteristics of the FDI source;

Two, the nature of technology policy; and

Three, the nature or mode of technology transfer.

Nature and Characteristics of US and Japanese FDI

Based on the nature and direction of direct foreign investment, Kojima (1978) has distinguished two types of FDI. FDI that is released from a comparatively disadvantageous industry in the

Table 20.5

Outward Stock by Parent Country (as Per cent of Total)

	1980	*1985*	*1990*	*1994*
Total Outward Stock	100	100	100	100
Developed Eco.	98.78	96.89	95.87	93.02
UK	15.66	14.63	13.71	11.66
Germany	8.39	8.74	9.00	8.28
France	4.59	5.41	65.32	7.60
Sweden	1.09	1.81	2.94	2.12
US	42.86	36.62	25.84	25.29
Other Developed Eco.	5.48	8.72	14.64	13.99
Japan	3.67	6.46	12.15	11.78
Developing Eco.	1.20	3.10	4.12	6.94

Source: UNCTAD, "World Investment Report" various years.

Table 20.6

Outward Direct Investment Stake of US & Japan by Main Manufacturing Sectors (Per cent)

	US			*Japan*		
	1975	*1985*	*1997*	*1975*	*1985*	*1997*
More Technologically Intensive Sectors	69.2	62.82	61.5	39.4	73.46	77.91
Chemicals and Allied	22.6	21.41	25.5	15.3	9.33	7.63
Mechanical & Instrument Engineering	20.2	20.05	11.6	7.4	16.45	6.94
Electrical Engineering	11.4	8.99	11.7	10.3	25.93	32.07
Transport Equipment	15.1	12.37	12.6	6.3	21.76	29.57
Precision Instruments						1.70
Less Technologically Intensive Sectors	30.8	37.18	38.5	60.6	26.54	22.09
Food, Drink and Tobacco	8.5	9.77	13.3	5.6	3.34	3.50
Textiles, Leather, Clothing & Footwear	1.7			22.2	1.66	2.68
Paper, Printing & Publishing	5.9			10.2	1.50	0.88
Primary & Fabricated Metals	6.6	5.29	5.1	15.4	8.62	6.10
Other Manufacturing	8.1	22.11	20.1	7.2	11.43	8.93
All Manufacturing	**100**	**100**	**100**	**100**	**100**	**100**

Source: US Dept. of Commerce "Survey of Current Business", various issues and JETRO, Japan "White Paper on Japanese Investments Abroad."

investing country into the industry with overt or potential comparative advantage in the host country, would develop into a new export industry in the host country. The author finds the Japanese investment to be of this kind and hence terms it "Japanese type FDI". Conversely he notices a tendency in some investing countries (like the US), to invest abroad starting from industry in which it has the comparative advantage (computer for example). In this case the consequence would be the reverse. He names this kind of FDI as the "American-type FDI".

Japanese investment till the early-70s was mostly directed towards natural resource development in which Japanese economy is comparatively disadvantaged.[1] Even investments in manufacturing has been confined to such industries' textiles, clothing and processing of steel in which Japan has been losing comparative advantage, or the assembly of motor vehicles, production of parts and components of watches and radios and other electronic gadgets in which cheaper skilled labour are necessary. This increases exports by the Japanese affiliates of items in which Japan has lost its comparative advantage and also enables the restructuring of the Japanese economy according to its comparative advantage. This demonstrates the need for step by step transfer of manufacturing industries from advanced to developing countries.

Kojima also notes that Japanese FDI in manufacturing is undertaken by small and medium sized firms on a smaller scale than investments by American firms and transferred technology suitable to local factor proportions with larger employment and training effects than those with 'enclave' characteristics. Japanese investments thus seem to be in keeping with the H-O theorem of comparative advantage which propounds that only less capital and knowledge intensive industry profitably invests abroad. Moreover, Japanese investments are seen to prefer joint ventures to wholly owned subsidiaries.

---

1. According to a MITI report, in an accumulated total foreign investment of $3596 million between 1951 and 1970, mining accounts for 31.4 per cent while manufacturing accounts for 26.9 per cent, and commerce for 10.3 per cent and others including agriculture, fishing, forestry, construction etc. for 31.4 per cent.

American FDI, on the other hand cannot be explained in the comparative advantage paradigm as relatively new industries of the capital and knowledge intensive type move abroad through foreign investment from America. Vernon (1966) and Hymer (1976) have tried to explain this phenomenon.

Vernon describes through his product-cycle hypothesis how a new product is invented and FDI is used to manufacture on a large scale in leading industrial countries once the product is standardised and explains how US FDI has come about mainly in the kinds of industries (like chemical industries, the machinery industries, transportation industries and the scientific instruments industries) which are associated with innovation and oligopoly.

Hymer in his seminal doctoral thesis noted the association of MNCs with a few large firms with oligopolistic characteristics like heavy industry rather than light i.e. in industries characterised by large firms, high capital intensity, advanced technology, differentiated products etc. These theories, which characterise US-type FDI are however, cannot be used to characterise the Japanese FDI.

Table 20.7

Industry Distribution of Japanese FDI, Across Region (in Per cent)

	Developed Countries		*Latin America*		*Asia*	
	1951-80	*1986-90*	*1951-80*	*1986-90*	*1951-80*	*1986-90*
Less Technology Intensive	50.28	34.31	52.66	32.74	60.45	39.13
Food	7.47	4.11	4.75	4.54	3.15	8.24
Textiles	9.79	2.76	11.31	0.00	20.17	6.07
Lumber & Pulp	10.24	3.42	6.76	0.48	3.11	3.01
Iron, Non-Ferrous Metals	16.20	8.09	27.04	24.57	22.66	9.99
Others	6.57	15.93	2.81	3.14	11.38	11.82
Technology Intensive	49.72	65.69	47.34	65.29	39.55	60.87
Chemicals	10.66	12.44	18.14	12.71	15.84	11.94
Machinery	10.41	11.09	9.19	4.10	5.98	9.63
Electric & Electronics	24.10	29.86	7.70	19.21	11.88	30.21
Transport Equipment	4.56	12.30	12.31	29.27	5.85	9.09
Total	**100**	**100**	**100**	**100**	**100**	**100**

Source: Same as Table 20.6.

The American economy has a dualistic structure: a) innovative and oligopolistic industries, or, in brief, new industries; and b) traditional industries (textiles, steel, agriculture etc.) which are price competitive and stagnant. The US foreign investment successively takes place only from within the first group i.e. new industries of the capital and knowledge intensive type move abroad through US FDI before they are standardised. FDI from these new industries which rank at the top of US comparative advantage are anti-trade oriented or involve FDI which work against the structure of comparative advantage.

Table 20.8

Industrial Distribution of US FDI, Across Regions

	Developed Countries		*Latin America*		*Asia*	
	1985	*1996*	*1985*	*1996*	*1985*	*1996*
Less Technology Intensive	36.12	36.59	46.94	50.35	17.43	28.97
Food & Kindred Products	9.30	10.42	13.93	22.66	4.17	8.68
Primary & Fabricated Metals	5.11	5.58	5.77	4.67	2.87	3.19
Other Manufacturing	21.71	20.59	27.24	23.02	10.40	17.11
Technology Intensive	63.88	63.40	53.07	49.65	82.57	71.03
Chemicals	21.07	28.48	21.22	23.38	27.77	20.46
Machinery	22.35	13.11	11.12	4.67	12.05	11.42
Electrical & Electronics	7.82	8.43	7.03	7.74	38.96	33.31
Transportation	12.65	13.38	13.70	13.86	3.79	5.84
Total	**100**	**100**	**100**	**100**	**100**	**100**

Source: Same as Table 20.6.

Differences in the nature of FDI from US and Japan not only reflects on the trade of the host and home countries but also on the technology transfer that takes place through FDI. Heavy US investments are usually made in the extracting sectors with only two-thirds of FDI going to the manufacturing sector. However, manufacturing FDI is seen to be the fastest growing in recent years. American FDI in manufacturing is seen to usually undertake investments in the most technologically sophisticated industries with not yet standardised products that are more capital than labour intensive and rank on the top of the comparative advantage of the home economy. This implies a large gap between the existing technology of the host developing country and that transferred through the US FDI which leads to the creation of 'enclaves' and makes spillovers of the transfer of technology to the domestic firms difficult. Kojima calls this 'reverse-order' transfer of technology.

On the other and, the unique characteristics of Japan's transfer of technology is characterised as an orderly transfer of technology of standardised production which begins in those industries where technological gap between the providing and receiving countries is the lowest and therefore, making transfer of technology easier and its spread effects larger.

Determinants of the Japanese and US FDI also are seen to be different for the developing countries. While the latter are found to be the market entry propagated kind, the former is more to exploit the comparative advantage of the region.

Further in the specific case of India, the concentration of US FDI in chemical and pharmaceutical industries which involves process technology makes their technology less susceptible to reverse engineering or imitation unlike the transportation equipment and electronic technology which is the stronghold of Japanese FDI in India.

Significant inter-source differences can also be noticed in the mode of entry. Although both US and Japanese are seen to be increasing their financial to technical collaboration ratio, the ratio is still less than one in the case of Japan. This implies that Japanese being relatively new entrants to the Indian economy are less willing to enter financial equity participation. Those who do, tend to prefer joint ventures/minority ownership to fully/majority owned subsidiaries.

Unlike the Western MNCs, the Japanese were more willing to enter into minority ownership joint ventures in relatively low technology industrial products in South, South-East and Latin America unlike the US who are seen to enter mostly majority ownership relation. Hence the national origin of FDI can differ. Lan (1996) also concludes that the role of FDI varies with the national origin of FDI. While US and other Western investors are seen with high capability and willingness to transfer technology and Japanese investors as possessing but unwilling to transfer high technology.

Table 20.9

Countrywide Distribution of Financial Collaborations Approvals in Various Equity Ranges in India -1996 (No. of Collaborations Including NRI Equity and Percentage in Parentheses)

Country	0-25	26-39	40-49	50-59	60-74	>74	Total
Japan	14(18.4)	14(18.4)	20(26.3)	12(15.8)	4(5.3)	12(15.8)	76
USA	30(8.8)	25(8.8)	62(12.9)	36(12.8)	16(5.7)	113(40.1)	282

Source: Ministry of Science and Technology, India (1998) "Foreign Collaboration Approvals".

Table 20.10

Proportion of Majority-Owned Affiliates in Total Number of Affiliates (Per cent)

	US		Japan
All countries	88	All countries	71
Canada	94	US	85
Europe	93	Europe	84
Latin America	86	Latin America	71
Asia & Pacific	79	Asia	63

Source: Same as Table 20.6.

These differentiating characteristics of the two FDI sources, makes the Japanese FDI more susceptible to spillovers or leakage's to their overseas competitors. This forces them to adopt a technology strategic that is more centering around parent firm and less globalised.

Technology Transfer Policy

More recently Kumar empirically points to inter-source difference in technology transfers at the country level. He has noted that Japan while accounting for 17-18 per cent of global R&D expenditure and US patents, it receives only 7 per cent of the global technological receipts. The technological effort of the Japanese corporations seems to be geared towards obtaining competitiveness of their products in domestic and export markets more than supporting transfer of technology and production. He however does not make an attempt at giving an explanation for this. Another limitation is that no attempt has been made to include embodied technology in the definition of technology transfer. It is accepted with increasing importance of soft technology in terms of production organisation, management and skill imbibed in human capital, technology receipts may be a narrow way of looking at things. It is accepted that Japanese employ a higher share of expatriate human capital and points to an under estimation of technology transferred through this means.

Table 20.11

Technology Generation and Transfer Activities of US and Japan

Countries	*R&D Expenditure 1993*		*US Patents taken, 1977-96*		*Technology Fees Received, 1993*	
	(billion PPP $)	*Per cent in Total*	*In '000*	*Per cent in Total*	*Billion $*	*Per cent in Total*
USA	166.3	39	985.3	57	20.4	40
Japan	74.4	17	307.6	18	3.6	7
World	428.58	100	1732	100	51	100

Source: Kumar 1997.

Figures on globalisation of R and D activity also points to the fact that there is very little diffusion of research activity among the biggest firms of the world (Table 20.12). There is however much source-wise difference evident. UK and Germany seem to have diffused their R and D effort considerably, while France and Sweden seem to have diffused their R&D to some extent. Japanese firms especially seem to follow a strategy of concentrating their R&D activities in the parent country itself leading to extremely low share of innovations taking place in host economies.

Table 20.12

The Share of US Patents of the Largest Firms Attributable to Research in Foreign Locations (Outside the Home Country of the Parent Company Organised by Nationality of Parent Firms, 1969-90 in Per cent)

	1969-72	*1973-77*	*1978-82*	*1983-86*	*1987-90*
USA	4.96	5.93	6.47	7.61	7.96
Japan	2.62	1.88	1.22	1.26	0.93
Germany	12.76	11.04	12.07	14.17	17.05
UK	45.37	43.93	41.08	47.86	49.18
France	8.19	7.74	7.19	9.2	15.87
Sweden	18.01	19.51	25.19	28.82	28.34

Note: Excluding companies registered in Panama.

Source: Howells and Michelle (1993).

Nature of Technology

Furthermore the nature of technology transfer also starkly differs between Japan and US. It is oft quoted that Japanese production model draws its strength from the human related dimension of engineering technologies, workplace practices and corporate culture more than through in-house R&D or technology imports through capital goods or in other disembodied technology imports. Organisational innovation and management practices have in recent times come to be accepted as one of the major aspects of technological development for enhancing productivity and growth. The principle components of Japanese Management Techniques (JMT) involve;

Transfer of technology and techniques like Just-in-time delivery (in the place of the usual Just-in-case delivery) where the philosophy is to produce to order rather than to stock up. This necessitates the downsizing production and multi-skilled workforce in keeping with the nature of order. This results in constant restructuring of production layout, absence of job specifications as well as horizontal mobility of workers and job rotation. Also, the absence of inventories and nature of demand-driven system requires total Quality Control (TQC), quality Circles (QC) to ensure zero defects

Japanese management and production systems have attracted attention because they offer techniques and methods of production that out-perform existing US or European engineering technologies. Studies analysing the differences in the management techniques of the Japanese and non-Japanese firms include Dore 1973, Aoki 1990 and others who examine the impact of these techniques on the performance of the firms.

No systematic data are as yet available to document the extent of such technology transfer and the expatriate employment in foreign affiliates may be taken as a proxy for the same. Japanese affiliates have a higher proportion of home country citizens in total employment as compared to US affiliates indicating the greater importance the former attributes to technology transfer through human related dimension of engineering technologies.

Table 20.13

Percentage Share of Expatriate Employment in Total Employment of Foreign Affiliates

Sector	*United States*		*Japan*	
	1982	*1989*	*1982*	*1989*
All Industries	0.8	0.4	2.0	3.0
Mining	5.3	2.6	1.2	2.5
Manufacturing	1.9	0.2	1.0	1.7
Services	1.3	0.5	..	..
Wholesale	0.6	0.4	10.2	8.8
Other services	1.7	0.6	5.4	5.1

Source: World Investment Report (1992).

Seen in this backdrop of differeing attributes, US and Japanese FDI can be expected to differ in their technology transfer behaviour.

SECTION 3

TECHNOLOGY TRANSFER, OWNERSHIP CONTROL AND APPROPRIATION OF RETURNS

The rate at which technology is diffused worldwide depends heavily on resource costs of transfer—both transmittal and absorption costs—and the magnitude of the economic rents obtained by the seller. The resource cost depends on the characteristics of the transmitter, the receiver the technology being transferred, and the institutional mode chosen for transfer. (Teece 1998).

The cost are lower the greater the similarities in the experience of the transmitting and receiving units, for greater the similarities, the easier it is to transfer technology in codified form such as blueprints, formulas or compute languages. Uncodified or tacit knowledge, on the other hand is slow and costly to transmit. Ambiguities abound and can be overcome only when communications take place in face to face situations. This takes up the resource cost of transfer i.e. the costs of labour and capital that must be employed to effect transfer.

Technology transfer behaviour is examined here in the framework of ownership control as it best incorporates the various aspects of differences in the nature of FDI and the technology transfer policy.

By Ownership control here we mean, the level of control of the parent technology supplier over the FDI firm. This determines the cost of transfer and the risk involved (Wang and Blomstrom 1992). Level of control of the parent company over the host firm is usually determined by the share of equity stake of the technology supplier in the FDI firm and can be divided as fully or majority-owned subsidiaries (51 to 100 per cent foreign equity), and joint ventures or minority ownerships (25-50 per cent foreign equity). These channels reflect different functions and characteristics in transferring technology.

Wholly or majority owned Subsidiaries are firms where the technology suppliers enjoy full control over the decision-making process. For this, and the reason of minimising transaction costs through internal mode of transfer, it has been found that technology suppliers are most willing to supply the latest and/or least matured technology to their affiliates. Technology supply is usually in a complete package form with associated supply of capital goods and secret and unpatented know-how, technical, marketing, management and organisational training etc. (UNCTC 1987). However, because of the complete control of the subsidiary by the parent firm and the 'internalised mode' of transfer, the scope for technology diffusion to the local firms is limited.

Earlier studies (Dunning 1981, Marton 1986) indicate such intra-firm transactions as concentrated in the high or medium research intensive sectors like electrical and non-electrical machinery, transport equipment, chemical and pharmaceuticals industries as they enjoyed a better bargaining power, the government of the host countries having little choice in the matter. However, with the changing attitude of the developing countries and competition between them to attract FDI, parent to subsidiary internal mode of technology transfer is attaining greater proportions.

Joint Ventures/Minority Ownership on the other hand, are firms involving equity participation by a foreign firm as well as a dominant local partner, offers greater scope for the effective diffusion of technology to the host economy. Other than learning by watching, local partners can comprehend the technology through learning by doing, learning by sharing and learning by training (UNCTC 1985, 1987, UNCTAD 1990). However, the surveys of UNCTC 1985 technology supplied under the arrangement is very often matured and standardised, less firm specific and not changing very much. Hoyle (1990) in his study of Russia found that technology transferred through joint ventures to be sufficiently attractive to the host country but not enough to increase the international competitiveness and hence the exporting capacity of the firm. This is because the sharing of technology with partners in developing countries has been viewed as potentially eroding the proprietary know-how of MNCs and more threatening than investment and licensing arrangements in this regard (Marton, 1986). However, when joint venture remains the only open mode of entry to some of the largest markets and raw material sources, the MNCs resort to it, however taking measures to ensure its global profitability and secrecy of its technology and know-how. The Indian experience till the late-1980s seems to be in similar lines though it was also part of a conscious strategy of import substitution rather than export-oriented growth.

This ensures less degree of control by the technology supplier and hence stands the danger of know-how dissemination. Together with the limited scope for appropriating returns from the exploitation of such technology, MNCs usually resist transferring the latest and unstandardised technology under this arrangement. Therefore the technical assistance provided under this framework is expected to be more limited than joint ventures or wholly/majority owned subsidiaries. The technology supplied is expected to be limited and not enough to enhance the export competitiveness although it might be sufficient for domestic production.

Table 20.14

Mean and Standard Deviation of No. of Years Between Tehnology's Transfer Overseas and Its Initial Introduction in the US, for 65 Technologies

Channel of Technology Transfer	*Mean (years)*	*Standard Deviation(years)*	*No. of Cases*
Overseas Subsidiary in DC	5.8	5.5	27
Overseas Subsidiary in Developing Countries	9.8	8.4	12
Licensing or Joint Venture	13.1	13.4	26

Source: Edwin Mansfield and Anthony Romeo (1979).

The study argues that the technology supplier will be willing to undertake greater risks only given greater scope for returns. Given our assumption that the technology supplier to the FDI firms is the parent firm, the latter can maximise benefits the greater its equity stake. A foreign controlled firm's decision hence will depend on the foreign equity stake, which is the determinant of its ability to appropriate the benefits.

The higher the foreign equity stakes of the supplier firm in the technology purchasing firm, greater the formers ability to appropriate returns not only by way of royalty but also by way of dividends and profit repatriation. At lower levels of foreign equity the supplier would be faced with a risk-return mismatch and hence would prefer embodied technology transfer.

The Assumptions made in this frame work are:

1. All technology transfers are intra-firm, implying that the parent firm is the dominant supplier of technology, be it embodied or in disembodied form.
2. The objective of the supplier firm is maximising returns and minimising the risk of dissemination of technology.

And the emerging hypothesis are:

1. Higher levels of ownership Control accompanies greater technology transferability.
2. Japanese FDI involves less transfers of technology controlling for the ownership factor.

SECTION 4

DATA SET

The empirical evidence presented here is based on a sample of 197 Indian manufacturing companies participating in foreign collaboration. Financial collaboration has been defined for the study as foreign equity participation of 10 per cent or more (meeting the World Investment Report definition of FDI) from various sources. The source-wise distribution of companies and their share in the total sample is given in Table 20.15.

Table 20.15

Distribution of Sample Companies: Number and Proportion in Total Sample

Country	*No. of Firms*	*Proportion*
USA	68	66.1
Japan	35	33.9
Total	**103**	**100**

Source: CMIE: Prowess data base.

The number of companies collaborating with various sources are in proportion to their existing distribution in the economy.

Table 20.16

Industrial Distribution as Proportion of the Various FDI Sources (Per cent)

Industry	*FDI Source*	
	USA	Japan
Electric & Electronics	30	26
Transport Equipment	3	23
Chemicals	30	14
Food	6	0
Textiles	6	8.5
Engineering	11	13
Paper & Glass Products	6	8.5
Others	8	7
Total	**100**	**100**

Source: Same as Table 20.15.

The industrial distribution of the sample reflects the concentration seen in the economy. Concentration of US and Germany in the Chemical and allied industries, Japanese in the electrical and electronics and automobile industry, Swedish in the Engineering industry etc. can be noted from Table 20.16.

Sixty nine per cent of the 197 companies engaged in foreign financial collaboration were minority owned by the foreign source i.e., with foreign equity participation of less than 50 per cent; while the remaining 31 per cent had greater than 50 per cent foreign equity i.e., the foreign interest had a majority ownership. Since one of the objectives of this paper is to understand the influence of equity levels in determining the technology diffusion behaviour, it will be fruitful to comprehend the levels of equity participation of various FDI sources (Table 20.17).

Table 20.17

Source and Level of Foreign Equity Participation (as proportion of total)

Country	Minority Owned	Majority Owned	Total
US	70	30	68
Japan	86	14	35

Source: Same as for Table 20.15.

Eighty six per cent of companies with Japanese FDI is observed to be minority owned by foreign interests and only 14 per cent of them is majority owned. This is the lowest among the various sources considered here indicating that literature pointing to this tendency of Japanese firms to prefer minority ownerships is not without truth. The other sources of FDI seem to prefer majority ownerships more; even though companies with minority equity stake are seen to exceed the majority equity ownerships.

The very differing pictures portrayed by the various sources of FDI underlines the need to proceed further and analyse the behavioral differences brought about by differences in the structure of ownership of companies.

Our analysis is based on the Centre for Monitoring Indian Economy data set used in the analysis of the technology generation activities of the FDI-firms from various sources.

SECTION 5

EMPIRICAL ANALYSIS

In this section we undertake both bivariate statistical and multivariate econometric analysis to check our hypothesis.

Bivariate Analysis

The hypothesis that Japanese FDI involves less technology transfer is validated by the wilcoxen signed rank test. In fact, the international scenario is mirrored in the Indian context too with Japanese FDI conducting lower R&D *vis-a-vis* their US counterparts irrespective of the nature of industry. The significant results for both the in-house R&D and technology imports indicate that US FDI undertakes significantly more of these activities.

Table 20.18

Industry and Source-wise Average R&D and Royalty Expenditure as Percentage of Net Sales (1992-1996 average)

	R&D		*Tech Imports*	
	US	*Japan*	*US*	*Japan*
Electric & Electronics	.58	.17	.85	.46
Automobiles	.46	.24	.41	.45
Chemicals	.48	.17	.44	.14
Textiles	.20	.07	.32	.22
Engineering	.18	.09	.28	.90
Others	.42	.09	.62	.46
Wilcoxen Signed Ranks Test				
		Z test		Significance
R&D		-2.201		0.028
Technology Imports		-1.99		0.046

All the industries mark Japanese having a lower R&D ratio. Only in the case of engineering industries can the technology imports of Japanese seen to be greater than US FDI firms.

Table 20.19

Distribution of US and Japanese FDI Firms According to Their R&D Activities and Parental Ownership Control

	US		*Japan*	
	Minority	*Majority*	*Minority*	*Majority*
No R&D	43.1	6.3	39.3	0
0<R&D<0.5%	33.3	75	60.7	100
R&D>0.5%	22	19	0	0

Bringing in the concept of ownership control, the distribution of firms according to their R&D levels is enlightening. No Japanese firm, minority or majority owned, is seen to undertake R&D more than 0.5 per cent of their total sales. However more important points are brought out by the technology imports distribution, the majority owned Japanese FDI seems to import technology substantially greater than their minority ownership counterparts.

Table 20.20

Distribution of FDI Firms According to Their Technology Imports and Parental Ownership Control

	US		*Japan*	
	Minority	*Majority*	*Minority*	*Majority*
No TM	37.3	6.3	28.6	0
0<TM<1%	49	75	60.7	40
TM >1%	13.9	18.8	10.7	60

This prompts us to look at the importance of ownership levels in determining the technology and trade behaviour of US and Japanese firms. The Wilcoxen signed ranks test establishes that the Japanese Majority ownership firm behaved significantly different from their minority ownership counterparts. This however could not be said to be true of US firms where the minority and majority ownership firms were not found to differ significantly in their behaviour.

Table 20.21

Mean Values of TT and Trade According to Parental Ownership Control

	US			*Japan*		
	Minority	*Majority*	*Total*	*Minority*	*Majority*	*Total*
R&D	0.305	0.315	0.307	0.175	0.196	0.178
TM	0.445	0.451	0.447	0.352	1.067	0.461
Exports	9.5	8.4	9.2	6.18	10.54	6.86
Net Exports	-9.37	-9	-9.2	-8.67	-1.07	-7.31

Wilcoxen Signed Ranks Test

	Z test	Significance
US	-0.405	0.686
Japan	-2.023	0.043

Multivariate Analysis

In this section we undertake a multivariate analysis to establish the role of ownership in determining the technology transfer behaviour and bring out the inter-source FDI differences.

Determinants of Level of R&D Activities

The R & D activities of FDI firms is determined by the larger R&D strategy of the parent firms. The existing literature has focused attention on the determinants of inter-industry (Lall, 1979; Hirschey and Caves,1981; and Pearce, 1989) or inter-firm variation (Mansfield, Teece and Romeo, 1979) in the propensity to internationalise R&D and to the analysis of factors that determine the location of overseas R&D (Hakanson, 1992; Kumar 1996) by MNEs based on the Parent firm data. The latter group of studies is propelled by the noticeable concentration of overseas R&D in the developed countries.

Studies on the inter-industry variation in globalisation of R&D have identified a positive relationship between overseas R&D and the extent of multinationality of the industry as well as the R&D intensity of the industry. The latter was explained in terms of the higher pressure to locate R&D abroad on cost saving reasons. Hirschey and Caves found the economies of scale in R&D discouraging overseas R&D. The tendency to centralise production for foreign markets at a few overseas locations favoured overseas R&D. The relative cost of doing R&D in the parent country was also found to be positively related to overseas R&D. The industries producing durable goods were undertaking more overseas R&D because of the need to adapt their products to local conditions. Natural resource based industries showed a weaker tendency to place R&D operations overseas compared to other industries.

Mansfield *et al.*, (1979), in a study covering a sample of 55 US and middle Atlantic firms, found the proportion of overseas R&D to be positively related to the proportion of subsidiary sales, negatively related to exports, and positively related to firm size. Drug industry firms revealed a higher propensity to locate R&D abroad than other firms to avoid the more strict regulations at home country.

The host country characteristics like the size of the market, per capita income, level of development and scientific resources available were found to be significant determinants of location of overseas R&D. The physical and cultural distance between the parent and affiliates and overseas R&D was found to be negative. In addition Kumar (1996) identifies policy environment of the host country in terms of their intellectual property protection to be an important determinant of overseas R&D based in industrialised countries though it was not relevant in the context of developing countries.

The above studies have limited their analysis to single source of multinational activity (mainly US, Japan and Sweden). Moreover, the studies have invariably based on the data provided of overseas R&D behaviour of parent firms or source industries. A need for the comparison of the determinants of overseas R&D across various sources is brought out in the previous section highlighting the variation in globalisation of R&D not only between various locations but also between various sources. While location factors are called upon usually to explain the variation in the global distribution of overseas R&D, much attention does not seem to have been directed to bring out the determinants of inter source variation in internationalisation between various sources. The present attempt is in determining the causes for the differences in this behaviour more closely by taking up the issue from a different angle namely; from the affiliate perspective. This will enable us to standardise for the location factors as we concentrate on the source behaviour variation within one host country.

Studies of the industrial characteristics of Indian firms include Goldar and Renganathan (1997) which concentrates on the impact of liberalisation on the in-house R&D activities brings out that contrary to expectations there has not been a growth in the R&D activities of the firm in the post-liberalised scenario. The analysis also highlights the size and the foreign ownership as important determinants of R&D intensity of Indian industrial firms.

Hypothesis and Model for Estimation

Internationalisation of R&D is commonly understood to be dependent on the cost and benefits of MNEs in undertaking overseas R&D. Costs include compromising on the scale economies by concentrating R&D activities at home location, risks of dissipation of trade secrets etc. while benefits include, better adaptation to local market conditions, reduction in cost of R&D and appropriation of local knowledge. Given the industry one cannot expect much variation in the level of overseas R&D within a single host country considering only the above cost and benefit aspects. It is the hypothesis of this paper that there are basic differences in the nature of overseas investment undertaken by various sources which contribute to the source variation in the levels of globalisation of R&D as reflected in the R&D activities of the FDI firms.

The share of foreign equity investments determine the rates at which the foreign investors are thought to be able to appropriate the benefits of investments. The case is true also for the R&D investments undertaken, and it follows that the foreign investor can be expected to invest more in R&D only when sure of appropriating the benefits of it fully. Thus a positive relation can be thought to exist between the level foreign equity and R&D activity of the firm.

The intensity of technology import also determine the intensity of in-house R&D depending on the nature of import. The nature of the relationship will determine the sign of the coefficient. R&D undertaken to adapt and complement the imported technology to local conditions can be expected to have a positive relation. On the other hand, technology may be imported to substitute in-house R&D in which case a negative relation can exist between the variables. Hence the nature of technology import undertaken by the various FDI sources becomes relevant. Technology imports (sum of capital goods imports and royalty payments) to value of output ratio has been included in the model to incorporate the impact of the nature of technology imports on R&D activity. Further, it also captures the technology intensity of the firm.

The nature of manufacturing activity undertaken also determines the level of R&D activity. A unit merely assembling imported parts cannot be expected to undertake much independent R&D. Thus the level of value addition is an important positive determinant of R&D activity. Higher value additions also point to greater scales of production making independent R&D viable. The variable used for the purpose of capturing this effect is the gross value added to total value of output ratio. The ratio also captures the extent of vertical integration of the firm and greater vertically integrated firms are expected to conduct R&D.

R&D activity is also determined by the market orientation of the production. Production for the local market necessitates adaptation to the local condition which is best done through decentralised R&D activity. At the same time, production for third markets through exports indicate concentration of production at the location making R&D necessary to adapt and support production for international markets. This is however not true for exports to parent country as the overseas firm need only to produce as per the designs supplied by the parent firm without much adaptations. The variable used to capture the dynamics is the value of exports to total sales ratio. As in the present data set, it has not been possible to differentiate between exports to parent country and the third markets, the sign of the coefficient is expected to differ given the direction of exports. On the other hand, it can be expected that a firms' diversification into IN markets is affected by the quality of the product that may in turn be determined by the product improving R&D undertaken; in which case a direct relation may be expected between the exports and R&D activity.

The competitive pressures within the host country is thought to influence the level of technology activity of a firm increasing the propensity to innovate with increasing competition. In other words, the high profitability (reflecting the absence of competition) and R&D activity are negatively related as per the neo-Schumpeterian logic. On the other hand, high profits implies the availability of internal funds to set apart for R&D activity. Here there is the danger of simultaneity bias because R&D investments can lead to innovations resulting in higher profits. However, past studies (Sidharthan and Dasgupta 1983, Kumar 1990) show that in the Indian context this may not be serious.

Market concentration reflects the competition faced by the firm. A firm in a highly competitive market is thought to undertake more

R&D in order to gain mileage over its rivals. Hence a negative relation is expected between the level of market concentration and R&D activities of a firm.

Firms which begin production fully dependent on imported or traditional technology, accumulate knowledge and capacity to modify, improve and innovate through years of learning-by-doing. Thus the R&D activity of a firm can be expected to increase with experience. The year of incorporation of the firm, deducted from 2000 has been used as the proxy to capture the accumulated learning effect in undertaking R&D.

R&D activities in India are more of the adaptive kind rather than that oriented to scientific and technical advances. The need and opportunities for adaptation may vary across industries influencing the local R&D undertaken. Thus industry-wise variation may be expected in the globalisation of R&D activity. This is captured in the model using dummies. As nine industry categories (*viz.*, electrical and electronics, transport machinery, chemical and allied, food and beverages, textiles, machinery, glass and ceramics, paper and wood, and miscellaneous industries) have been considered, eight dummies have been used in the model to capture the industry variation.

lgrd = f(experience, export propensity, foreign share,
(+) (+/-) (+)
profit rates, market concentration, technology imports,
(+) (-) (+/-)
value added, labour-capital ratio, product dummies)[2]
(+) (-)

Estimation

The model specified above was estimated using the logit function as well as Panel data estimation for the period 1991-1996. In the case of the former, the dependent variable used was binary in nature

---

2. Product
1: electrical and electronics industry,
2: transportation equipment industry,
3: chemical industry,
4: food and beverages industry,
5: textiles industry, and
6: engineering industry.

with R&D dummy taking value 0 for firms not undertaking R&D and R&D dummy taking value 1 for firms undertaking R&D. Logit is used to comprehend the role of the factors in the model in the decision making of the firm to conduct R&D activity or not. Given the decision to undertake R&D, panel data estimation model determines the role of the factors in determining the level of R&D undertaken.

The logit results indicate that, vertically integrated firms with higher levels of foreign financial participation had a higher probability to undertake R&D.

Table 20.22

Multivariate Analysis Results

Variable	*Logit Results*		*Panel Data Estimation*	
	US	*JAP*	*US*	*JAP*
exp	0.0035	0.02	0.0002	-0.078
expsal	0.1795	0.03	0.0003	-0.011
fshar	0.426	0.80***	0.0001	0.006*
pbt	0.52***	0.04	0.070**	-0.014
tecimp	0.120	0.034	0.010*	0.002
valad	0.48	-0.85	0.00006*	0.052
Scale	0.499***	0.76***	0.042**	0.075*
mktshare	1.71**	4.39**	0.114	1.5*
wagecap	-0.023	-0.052	0.0220	0.078
prod1	-0.3217	-0.95	0.165	0.004
prod2	0.759	-0.39**	0.381**	0.061
prod4	-0.486		0.0460	
prod5	-2.34**	4.9	0.1602	0.159
prod6	-1.02	2.4**	0.0325	0.318
constant	-6.61	-10.59	0.2218	-0.843
chi-sq	88.8*	81.8*	42.2*	25.3*
n	268	158	268	158

Product 1: electrical and electronics industry,
2: transportation equipment industry,
3: chemical industry,
4: food and beverages industry,
5: textiles industry, and
6: engineering industry.

Both the Logit model as well as the random effects model accepted through the Hausman's statistic validates our bivariate analysis conclusions. The importance of the ownership level both in the decision to conduct R&D as well as in determining the level of R&D is brought out in the case of Japanese FDI firms. The other determining factors vertical integration, scale of production, and market share are seen to be common for both the sources of FDI.

Determinants of the Technology Import Strategy

My analysis on the technology imports behaviour of US and Japanese FDI also corroborates the earlier findings. The model used is a panel data model with the cost of technology imports (proxies as an aggregate of royalty payments and licensing fees). This is because technology imports need not be a continuos phenomenon undertaken every year. An OLS model is estimated:

Technology imports = f(Foreign Equity, Capital Intensity,
(+) (+)
Vertical Integration, Scale of Operation,
(+) (+)
Export Propensity, Domestic Marketshare,
(+) (+)
Experience)
(-)

Studies have found that FDI firms in general tend to import more technology in relation to domestic firms (Emmanuel 1999). These studies treat the issue of foreign control using a dummy variable in the econometric exercises identifying the determinants. This is on the assumption of homogeneity of the class of FDI-firms. However, earlier look at the characteristic point to significant intra-group differences in behavior within FDI firms and points to the necessity of a more in-depth look at the various techno-economic aspects that determine an FDI-firm's decision to import technology.

While most of the theory on the determinants of technology imports can be thought to be extended to apply to the FDI firms, our argument regarding the importance of the level of foreign equity share is an additional variable to be considered in this context. As explained in the earlier section, a positive and significant relationship is expected between the foreign equity stake and the ratio of disembodied to embodied technology transfer considering the risks and return trade-off of the foreign technology supplier.

Export Propensity: firms producing for the international markets have to keep up with the international standards and such a firm may be thought to import technology on a more priority basis than those producing for the domestic market. Hence, a positive sign is expected for this variable.

The capital intensity of the firm is expected to have a positive relationship as the technology intensity of the firm is expected to be positively related to the capital/labour ratio of the firm.

Degree of vertical integration of the firm indicates the scope for greater technology absorption *vis-a-vis* mere assembling units. Hence this variable is expected to have a positive relation to the technology imports.

Experience of the firm is expected to have a negative impact on the technology imports. This is because as a firm accumulates knowledge by learning by doing, its need to import technology is thought to decrease.

Scale of operation is expected to have a positive impact because imported technology is usually optimal for large scale production. Downsizing of technology is necessitated in the event of small firm importing technology for optimal utilisation of capacity by smaller firms.

A large market player is more capable of finding the incentive matched by resources to import and constantly upgrade technology. Hence a positive relationship is expected between the market share of the firm and its technology imports.

These are variables that have been included in the literature on determinants of technology import behaviour of firms. However, our objective is to understand the differences in the US and Japanese firm behaviour in this context. Hence independent estimates are obtained for the firms of the two sources of FDI and results compared.

The results bring out much the similar differences between the sources as seen in the R&D behaviour.

Table 20.23

OLS Results: Determinants of Technology Import Behaviour

Variable	*US*	*Japan*
Fshare	1.69E-02	4.95***
K/L	0.904***	-7.04E-02
VI	-9.06E-03	-0.105***
Export	-0.944	0.469
Scale	-1.05E-04	-1.829E-04
Experience	1.32E-03	-0.109***
Marketsh	3.277*	5.863***
Constant	1.605*	5.47***
R2	0.34	0.56
F	3.94***	8.55***

The importance of ownership control in determining the direct technology transfer through technology imports is underlined by the multivariate analysis in the case of Japanese firms. This factor however does not seem to be exerting any significant influence on the US firms.

SECTION 6
CONCLUSION

It is to be understood that FDI *per se* does not lead to technology transfer. To make FDI serve the role of the conduit of technology transfer, it is necessary to put in place certain policy conditions and environment that would provide an incentive for the same.

With all the limitations of a secondary data study of the technology transfer behaviour of firms, the major contribution of this paper has been in emphasising the heterogeneity of FDI flows and the inter-source differences that have to be kept in mind in any anaylsis of the technology transfe impact of FDI on host economies. This has been accomplished studying the behaviour of US and Japanese FDI in the world and more specifically in the Indian economy.

The Japanese FDI was found more wary of transfer of technology to the host economy *vis-a-vis* their US counterparts. The level of ownership control was found a crucial factor in determining the

Japanese technology transfer behaviour with the majority owned Japanese affiliates transferring significantly more than the minority owned Japanese FDI firms. This is indeed the direct effect of FDI but determines the level of indirect spillover effects on the domestic firms. This can hence be said to be a critique of the industry level empirical estimates that consider the FDI homogenous and estimate the spillover effect as a function of share of FDI firms in the industry. However the need for in-depth case studies cannot be over-emphasised in order to capture the finer nuances of FDI behaviour and impact.

References

Ahluwalia I.J. (1985). "Industrial Growth in India: Stagnation Since Mid-sixties" Oxford University Press.

Aitken and Harrison (1993). "Does Proximity to Foreign Firms Induce Technology Spillovers?" PRD Working Paper, World Bank.

Aoki M. and Ronald Dore (1994). "The Japanese Firm: The Sources of Competitive Strength" Oxford University Press.

Blomstorm M., Ari Kokko and M. Zejan (1994). "Host Country Competition and Technology Transfer by Multinationals," *WeltwirscaftlichesArchives* 130:521-533.

Blomstrom and Frank Sjoholm (1998). *"Technology Transfer and Spillovers: Does Local Participation with Multinationals Matter?"* NBER Working Paper 6816.

Blomstrom M. and Wolff E.N. (1994). "Multinational Corporations and Productivity Convergence in Mexico," in Baumol, W.J., Nelson R.N. and Wolff, E.N., Des *Convergence of Productivity: Cross National Studies and Historical Evidence*, New York: OUP 263-84.

Buckley and Casson (1992). "Multinational Enterprises in the World Economy, Essays in Honour of John Dunning" Edward Elgar, England.

Cantwell (1989). "Technological Innovation and Multinational Corporations, Oxford: Basil Blackwell.

Caves (1996). "Multinational Enterprise and Economic Analysis, Second Edition, Cambridge; Cambridge University Press.

Contractor Frank J. (1990). *Do Government Policies Toward Foreign Investment Matter* Newark, NJ: Rutgers University (GSM Working Paper No. 90-15).

Dore Ronald (1973). "British Factory- Japanese Factory, the Emergence of National Diversity in Industrial Relations" University of California Press.

Dunning (1981). "International Production and Multinational Enterprises," London: Allen & Unwin.

Dunning H. (1994). "Multinational Policy and Globalisation of Innovatory Capacity," *Research Policy*," Vol. 23, No. 1pp.67-88.

Dunning (1993). "Multinational Enterprise and the Global Economy" Workingham.

Emmanuel (1999). "Determinants of Technology Import Behaviour," Unpublished M. Phil. Thesis, Jawaharlal Nehru University 1999.

Findlay (1978). "Relative Backwardness, Direct Foreign Investment and the Transfer of Technology: A Simple Dynamic Model," *Quarterly Journal of Economics* 92(1) February.

Gershenberg, Irving (1987). "The Training and Spread of Managerial Know-how: A Comparative Analysis of Multinational and Other Firms in Kenya," *World Development* 15:931-939.

Globerman S. (1979). "Foreign Direct Investment and 'Spillover' Efficiency Benefits in Canadian Manufacturing Industries," *Canadian Journal of Economics*, 12, 42-56.

Goldar and Renganathan (1997). "Economic Reforms and R&D Expenditure in Industrial Firms in India" National Institute of Public Finance and Policy, New Delhi.

Haddad and Harrison (1993). "Are There Positive Spillovers from Foreign Direct Investment? Evidence from Panel Data for Morocco," *Journal of Development Economics*, October.

Hirschey and Caves (1981). "Research and Transfer of Technology by Multinational Enterprises" *Oxford Bulletin of Economics and Statistics* Vol. 43, 115-130.

Howells J. and Michelle Wood (1993). "The Globalisation of Production and Technology," Belhaven Press, London.

Hymer S. (1976). "The International Operations of National Firms: A Study of Direct Foreign Investment, Ph.D. Dissertation (MIT 1960), Cambridge, Mass: MIT Press.

Kojima (1978). "Direct Foreign Investment" Croomhelm London.

Kokko A. (1994). "Technology, Market Characteristics and Spillovers," *Journal of Development Economics*, 43:279-293.

————. (1996). "Foreign Direct Investments and Technology Transfers in Development: A Perspective n Recent Literature" UNU-INTECH Discussion Paper 9606.

————. (1997). "Technology Generation and Technology Transfers in the World Economy: Recent Trends and Implications for Developing Countries" UNU-INTECH Discussion Paper 9702.

————. (1998). "Globalisation, Foreign Direct Investment and Technology Transfers" Routledge.

————. (1990). "Internalisation of Technology Transfer by US Multinationals: A Transactions Cost Perspective," Paper Presented at the Annual Meeting of the Academy of International Business, Toronto, October.

Kumar Nagesh (1996). "Intellectual Property Protection, Market Orientation and Location of Overseas R&D Activities by Multinational Enterprises" *World Development Vol. 24*, No.4, 673-688.

Lall, S. (1980). "Vertical Inter-firm Linkages in LDCs: An Empirical Study," Oxford University Press.

————. (1985). "Learning to Industrialise: The Acquisition of Technological Capability by India" Macmillan Press.

Lan Ping (1996). "Technology Transfer to China through Foreign Direct Investment" Avebury, England.

Mani Sunil "The Indian Industrial R&D System: A Rudderless Model" in his book "Models of Organising Industrial R&D" unpublished.

Mansfield and Anthony Romeo (1979). "Technology Transfer to Overseas Subsidiaries by US-based Firms," Research Paper, University of Pennsylvania.

Mansfield Edwin *et al.*, (1982). "Technology Transfer, Productivity and Economic Policy," W.W. Norton and Co., NewYork.

Marton K. (1986). "Multinationals, Technology and Industrialisation: Implications and Impact in the Third World Countries," Lexington, Massachusetts.

Pack and Saggi, (1997). "Inflows of Foreign Technology and Indigenous Technological Development" *Review of Development Economics*1(1):81-98.

Pearce, R. (1989). "The Internationalisation of Research and Development by Multinational Enterprises," Macmillan Press.

Romer (1990). "Endogenous Technological Change" *Journal of Political Economy*, Vol. 98.

Saggi and Pack (1999). "Foreign Direct Investment and International Technology: A Survey" Working Paper, Southern Methodist University.

Saggi (1996). "Entry Into a Foreign Market: Foreign Direct Investment *Versus* Licensing" *Review of International Economics*, 106:531-346.

Subrahmaniam K.K. *et al.*, (1996). "Foreign Collaboration Under Liberalisation Policy: Patterns of FDI and Technology Transfer in Indian Industry Since 1991" Dept. of Economic Analysis and Policy, RBI, Mumbai.

Teece David (1977). "Technology Transfer by Multinational Firms: The Resource Cost of Transferring Technological Know-how" *The Economic Journal*, June, 87, 242-261.

————. (1998). "The Mkt. for Know-how and the Efficient International, Transfer of Technology" in David J Teece ed. "Strategy, Technology and Public Policy," Edward Elgar, UK.

UNCTAD (1992). "World Investment Report: Transnational Corportations as Engines of Growth" United Nations, New York.

————. (1990). "Joint Ventures as a Channel for the Transfer of Technology" United Nations, New York.

UNCTC (1988). "Trasnational Corporations and World Development," United Nations, New York.

UNCTAD (1996). "Transnational Corporations and World Development" Published by the ITBP Division on Transnational Companies and Investment.

Vernon. R. (1966). "International Investment and International Trade in Product Cycles" *Quarterly Journal of Economics*. 80, pp. 190-207.

Wang and Blomstrom (1992). "Foreign Investment and Technology Transfer: A Simple Model," *European Economic Review*, 36, 137-155.

Part 5

Indian Industry and Environment

21

Policy Options for Prevention and Control of Industrial Pollution in India

U. SANKAR

SECTION 1

INTRODUCTION

This paper explores various cost-effective options for prevention and control of industrial pollution in India. Section 2 reviews the existing command and control type of policy regime for industrial pollution control, identifies its weakness and stresses the need for adopting a mix of regulatory and market based instruments (MBIs). Section 3 considers some issues in the design of MBIs and their application to large industrial units and suggests a menu of possible options based on the nature of pollution and certain criteria. Section 4 deals with small scale industries where the information base for design and enforcement of environmental policy is weak and the costs of pollution prevention and control are high compared with large industries, but consideration of the trade-off between development and environment requires a different type of policy intervention. Case studies of two highly polluting small-scale industries viz. tanneries and textile bleaching and dyeing units are used to recommend cost-effective policy options. Section 5 contains some concluding remarks.

SECTION 2

PRESENT POLICY REGIME FOR INDUSTRIAL POLLUTION CONTROL

Legal Framework

The Indian Penal Code 1860 and various legislations enacted till 1974, including the Factories Act, 1948 contain provisions relating to discharge of untreated effluents, gases and fumes into the environment. However, the first major environmental legislation relating to industry is the Water (Prevention and Control of Pollution) Act 1974. It paved the way for the creation of Central Pollution Control Board (CPCB) and State Pollution Control Boards (SPCBs). This Act was followed by the Air (Prevention and Control of Pollution) Act, 1981, the comprehensive Environment (Protection) Act, 1986, the Public Liability Insurance Act 1991 and the National Environment Appellate Authority Act, 1997. These Acts and the rules and notifications issued under these Acts provide the legal framework for prevention and control of pollution in India.

Section 3.2 of the Environment (Protection) Act gives the following regulatory powers to the central government:

i. laying down standards for the quality of environment in various aspects;

ii. laying down standards for emission or discharge of environmental pollutants from various sources whatever;

iii. restriction of areas in which any industries, operations or processes or class of industries, shall not be carried out or shall be carried out subject to certain safeguards;

iv. laying down proceedures and safeguards for the prevention of accidents which may cause environmental pollution and remedial measures for such accidents;

v. laying down proceedures and safeguards for the handling of hazardous substances;

vi. examination of such manufacturing processes, materials and substances as are likely to cause environmental pollution; and

vii. inspection of any premises, plant, equipment, machinery, manufacturing or other processes, materials or substances and giving, by order, of such directions to such authorities, officers or persons as it may consider necessary to take steps for the prevention, control and abatement of environmental pollution.

Section 3.3 of the Act empowers the central government to constitute an authority or authorities to deal with specific environmental matters. The Courts have used this provision to direct the central government to constitute separate authorities in certain cases.

Under the Environment (Protection) Rules, 1986, both industry-specific standards (Schedule I) and general standards (Schedule VI) have been prescribed. The effluent standards for 40 pollution parameters differ depending on the medium of discharge viz, in land, surface water, public sewers, land for irrigation and marine coastal areas. Wastewater generation standards have been prescribed for 11 industries and load-based standards for two industries. As for the emission standards, there are concentration based standards, equipment based standards for dispersal of sulphur dioxide, and load, mass-based standards.

The Rules allow the CPCB or the SPCBs to "specify more stringent standards from those prescribed in respect of any specific industry, operation or process depending upon the quality of the recipient system and after recording reasons therefor in writing." New industrial units or existing units planning modernisation/ expansion are required to comply with procedures and obtain clearances from the authorities where necessary. For particulars regarding projects requiring site selection, site clearance, and environmental clearance see CII (1999) pp 73-76.

Under the Water Act, it is necessary for an industrial unit to obtain "consent to establish," prior to taking any steps to establish any industry, operation or process or any treatment and disposal system which is likely to discharge effluents. "Consent to operate" permission is necessary before commencing operations of any industry or any treatment and disposal system which is likely to discharge effluents. The "consent to operate" must be renewed before the expiry of the validity period. The Air Act 1981 requires an industrial unit to obtain similar consents if it operates in an air pollution control area. All units coming under consent under the Water Act/Air Act and the Hazardous Wastes (Management and Handling) Rules are required to submit an environmental statement in a prescribed form every year. Section 8 of the Environment (Protection) Act, 1986, requires that, where the discharge of any environmental pollutant in excess of the prescribed standards occurs or is apprehended to occur due to any accident or unforeseen act or event; the person responsible for such discharge and the person in charge of the place at which such discharge occurs or is apprehended to occur shall be bound to prevent or mitigate the environmental pollution caused as a result of discharge and shall also forthwith intimate the fact of such occurrence or apprehension of such occurrence; and be bound, if called upon, to render all such assistance.

The Public Liability Insurance Act, 1991 was passed to provide for mandatory public liability insurance for installations handling hazardous substances to provide minimum relief to the victims based on no fault liability. Due to the reluctance of insurance companies to give insurance policies for unlimited liability of the owners, the Act was amended in 1992 to limit the liability of the insurance companies to the amount of insurance policy and also create an environmental relief fund with the additional money collected from the owners to meet the requirement of providing immediate relief to the victims.

The Acts give the central government power to issue directions including (a) closure, prohibition or regulation of any industry, operation or process or (b) stoppage or regulation of the supply of electricity or water or any other service. The Acts also provide penalties for contravention for various offences and failures to comply with the directions. The penalties are in the form of imprisonment or fine, or with both and in case the failure or contravention continues with additional fines and imprisonment for a longer period.

Weakness and Need for Change

The industrial pollution control regime comes under the category standards and regulation approach. A major weakness of this regime is absence of mechanisms for the revelation of the private information available with polluters regarding the sources of pollution, options for pollution prevention and control and the likely impact of the regulations on costs, prices, production, exports etc. Very often the laws have been enacted and the standards set without ascertaining the behavioural responses of the affected parties. See Sankar (1998). This criticism is also valid for other laws and regulations introduced in the seventies but continuation of this practice is not desirable when the government favours liberalisation and globalisation as means of achieving higher growth rate in GDP.

There is some justification for relying on regulations when the damage function is very steep or there are irreversible externalities. Here the precautionary principle is valid. In all other cases, there is a strong case for undertaking cost-benefit analysis of laws and regulations so that a transparent and conscious assessment of the trade-off between environment and development is possible. With over 30 per cent of the people living below the poverty line and persisting unemployment and under employment, intra-generational equity is perhaps more important than inter-generational equity for a country like India. Hence the policy objective should be, except in cases where the precautionary principle is applicable, to achieve environmental protection at least possible social cost.

It is well known that when the marginal pollution abatement cost functions vary among the sources, imposition of uniform standards for all sources will not result in minimisation of aggregate compliance costs. Therefore, in case of purely public bads where only aggregate pollution matters, imposition of uniform source-specific standards is not desirable. In case of local bads the standards need to be differentiated based on the assimilative capacity of each region and other location-specific factors. But in India, even though the Water Act and Air Act allow the government to tighten the standards based on regional considerations, the preferred option seems to be physical restrictions on location of new units/expansion of old units than on imposition of differential standards. For example, under the Air Act each state can identify and declare regions as air pollution control areas, but most states have declared the entire state as air pollution control areas.

Even under a source-specific standard regime, the polluting units have some choices with regard to the methods of pollution control, but technology based standards, restrictions on water usages, and norms for some inputs reduce the options available to the polluters in searching for cost minimising solutions for pollution control. In general, the source-specific standards direct the firm's activities to end-of-pipe treatment rather than pollution prevention. In case of concentration based standards the firm can achieve the standards by increasing the volume of effluent. There is also no incentive for the polluter to abate beyond the prescribed standards.

Mehta, Mundle and Sankar (1993/1997) find that ambient standards of air and water pollution continue to be routinely exceeded and in some places quality has distinctly deteriorated. They attribute this "among other things to a certain hiatus between the macro goals of our environmental policy and the micro nature of operational provisions for enforcement of the policy. Hence, though standards have been laid down for ambient air and water quality, actual enforcement relates mostly to source standards laid down for individual polluters, factories, transport vehicles and so on. Furthermore, the ambient and source-standards are laid down independently, unrelated in terms of the volume of pollution generating activities. Hence, it is quite conceivable that the quality of the environment could continue to deteriorate inspite of high degree of compliance among individual polluters. It is also possible, of course, that the degree of compliance itself is poor, adding to the adverse effects of the policy hiatus" (pp 1-2).

Enforcement of environmental legislations and rules are affected by various factors. The SPCBs depend mainly on the water cess and consent fees as revenue source. They do not have adequate manpower and technical skills to monitor and enforce the laws and standards. In most industries discharges of effluents and emissions are continuous and they require continuous monitoring. In the absence of meters capable of measuring volume of and concentrations of pollutants in the effluents, the enforcement authorities often rely on indirect methods such as capacities of the firm for compliance with the standards, as for example, the technology/process adopted or control devices for emissions or erection of effluent treatment plants. The SPCBs gather these information from the consent to establish and consent to operate forms and annual environmental statements. Fiscal concessions such as customs and excise duties rebates on pollution control equipment, accelerated depreciated allowance and soft loans lower the capital costs and thereby encourage the polluting units to undertake these investments. Such investment meets "initial compliance" but there is no guarantee that the units will operate these control devices or effluent treatment plants unless their net operating costs are negative.

The Acts prescribe the sampling procedure for collection of effluents with the approval of the firm and their testing by approved environmental laboratories. Stochastic variations in effluent quality and the requirement that the sample is taken in the presence of the victim make the burden of proof difficult. Even if the polluter is prosecuted it may take long time for the courts to deliver judgement. Poor compliance with environmental regulations can arise even under perfect monitoring when the penalties are unrelated to the costs of compliance with the standards. As the fines are not indexed, the real values of fines decrease over time. In a lax and corrupt enforcement regime there is ample scope for engaging in bribe and other illegal activities.

There is a remedy available to public-spirited individuals or societies to go the Court under Article 32 for the enforcement of the fundamental right to life (including clean air and water) contained in Article 21. The banner of public interest litigation (PIL) has resulted in judicial activism in the form of court directions to government to create authorities under the Environment (Protection) Act 1986, to polluting firms to face closure or comply with standards, and sometime payment of compensation to victims and for restoration of the affected areas. The Courts have also endorsed the polluter pays principle and the precautionary principle. But most of the PIL cases are time-consuming because of the lack of evidences on valuation of damages and costs of compliance with the standards. Unfortunately, the information generated via consent certificates and various reporting requirements are not effectively utilised either for the litigation or bargaining between polluters and pollutees or bringing market and community pressures on firms not complying with the regulations.

The government has attempted a few incentive based schemes. The Water (Prevention and Control of Pollution) Cess Act, 1977 provides for the levy and collection of a cess on water consumed by persons carrying on certain industries and by local authorities. It also provides a rebate of 25 per cent of the amount collected for a unit provided its water consumption is less than the maximum prescribed quantity and it complies with the provisions of the Water Act. The cess is very low compared with the cost of water and its main objective is to augment the resources of the CPCB and SPCBs. The fiscal concessions given for setting up pollution control devices or/ and effluent treatment plant, as noted earlier, meets only initial compliance and not continuing compliance. The Task Force Report (NIPFP (1997)) recommended discontinuation of such fiscal concessions. Other supportive measures include schemes such as promotion of common effluent treatment plants for small polluting units in industrial clusters, programme for adoption of clean technologies by small manufacutures enterprises, trade in environment services & technologies programme, eco-labelling scheme. See CII (1999) for details. Some of the schemes could achieve only limited success.

Thus, the present regime exhibits many inefficiencies both in the design of the policies and their enforcement.

SECTION 3

INDUSTRIAL POLLUTION FROM LARGE UNITS

An ideal pollution control policy for large industrial units must take into consideration (a) whether or not the pollution is continuous or occasional/random, (b) the type of pollution, e.g. emissions, effluents, solid wastes or noise, and (c) shape of the marginal damage function. When the marginal damage function is very steep there is a case for using quantitative restriction on the magnitude of pollution generated. When the pollution damage is occasional and the probability of the occurrence of the damage and the extent of damage can be lowered by preventive measures, a well designed public liability insurance scheme or a performance bond executed by the polluting unit before it commences its operation provides a simple mechanism for internalising the negative externality. In addition, such units should get the consent to establish and consent to operate certificates and send periodical environmental statements as per the laws and rules to the SPCBs. The SPCBs main tasks are to ensure that the firm has taken the necessary precautionary measures for prevention of damages and that, in the event damages occur, the insurance amount or the bond value is sufficient to cover the compensations to the victims and necessary remediation expenses. There is no need for continuos monitoring by the SPCBs.

For emissions discharged into the atmosphere, the United States prefers markets for tradable permits whereas most European countries prefer emission charges. This choice is partly a reflection of different governments' faith in the efficient functioning of markets and partly of their desire to raise revenues to cover part of the costs of environmental programmes. Weitzman (1974) has shown that the choice between a quantity based instrument (marketable pollution permit) and a price like instrument (pollution charge) under uncertainty depends largely on the relative slopes of the marginal abatement cost and marginal damage functions. Quantity-based instrument is preferred to a price-like instrument when the marginal damage function is steeper relative to the marginal abatement cost function. When the marginal damage function it relatively flatter, price-like instrument is preferred.

These considerations help in making a choice between standards and permits approach and standards and charges approach advocated by Baumol and Oates (1987). In the standards and permits approach there are two cases - emission permit system (EPS) and ambient permit system (APS). EPS is desirable when a society's concern is on the aggregate emission in a region or air shed. This is the case when a pollutant is uniformly distributed, that is, it is a pure public bad. In such a situation the regulator's tasks are (a) to conduct a baseline survey of emissions from various sources, (b) to determine the desired level of aggregate pollution, (c) to allocate the permits among the sources by grandfathering or auctioning, and (d) to create markets for tradable permits, certify the surplus permits, and facilitate transactions in surplus credits for future use and exchange among existing and new firms, and (e) to monitor that the aggregate emissions do not exceed the permissible levels. The main advantages of EPS are that (a) it makes use of the private information with sources in finding least cost solutions for pollution control, (b) it achieves environmental effectiveness, (c) the permit price is determined by market forces and can vary over time with market conditions. However, EPS presupposes a good data base, measurement and monitoring system and fairly large markets to prevent monopoly or monopsonist practices or strategic policies on the part of incumbent firms to prevent entry.

Theoretically APS is preferred when the pollution is not a public bad. Regional variations in dispersion pattern of pollutants and assimilative capacities may require subdivisions of the markets. If there are m sources and n monitoring points, then the m x n dispersion matrix summarises dispersions of emissions from m sources to n the receptors. Every source may require a portfolio of pollution permits depending on the dispersion pattern of its emissions. Further the exchange of permits is not on one to one basis. Design and operation of APS require reliable information base and expertise on the part of certifying and monitoring authorities. In view of the divisions of the markets the number of trades in any time period in any particular market may be small and the exchange of permits is made complex because the trade is not on one to one basis and of the search costs.

In the Indian context, experimentation with intra firm/plant trading is worth while. This can be done by replacing the same emission standard for each vent/chimney in a large plant/firm by an aggregate emission standard for the plant/firm as a whole. This will give an opportunity to the management to undertake greater abatement activity where it is cheaper and thereby achieve cost minimisation subject to the ceiling on aggregate emission. See Pandey (2000) for an estimate of cost saving in case of an integrated steel plant. It is also worth conducting pilot studies for introduction of EPS for a few selected uniformly dispersed pollutants, restricting the coverage initially to a few major polluting industries.

The standards and charges approach provides a framework for the design of pollution charges and determination of penalty rates for non-compliance with the standards. In the text book version, with a single pollutant, the marginal abatement cost (MAC) increases with the level of abatement. The recommended pollution charge is equal to the MAC corresponding to the standard. When such a tax is designed and enforced, the polluter has an incentive to abate upto the point where his MAC is equal to the tax rate. When the abatement level falls short of the standard, he has to pay tax on the excess amount (difference between pollution concentration in the effluent and the standard).

There are many conceptual, measurement and econometric problems in the estimation of MAC function for each pollutant.

There are also problems in the transition from determination of MACs to the design of pollution charges. Mehta, Mundle, Sankar (1993/1997), James and Murty (1999), Murty and Kumar (2000), Pandey (1998), Roy and Ganguly (1997) and Goldar, Misra and Mukherjee (1999) consider problems in specification, estimation and applications of MAC functions with data for Indian industries. Even though these studies differ with respect to model specification, data base and estimation proceedure, all the studies show that (a) there are significant economies of scale with respect to the volume of effluent treated, and (b) the MAC increases with the level of abatement.

Economic theory suggests that the abatement cost function depends on the volume of effluent, concentrations of pollutants before treatment and concentrations of pollutants after treatment, prices of inputs used in the abatement activity and firm-specific characteristics. Even though all the studies use either cross-section or panel data, none of them introduces firm-specific or even location-specific variables. Firm-specific characteristics such as age of the plant, process used, product-mix would affect the abatement costs. The responses of the firms regarding the extent of compliance with the standards will, in general, depend on the firm-specific characteristics. For a firm with an individual effluent treatment plant, there is also an incentive to reduce waste generation in the main plant and thereby achieve overall cost savings. Thus we observe large variations among firms regarding the extent of compliance with the standards, from zero compliance to full compliance.

The MAC curve is with respect to reduction in the concentration of a pollutant. In India, the general standards are concentration based standards. Therefore, for designing pollution charges we need MACs for each major pollution parameter corresponding to the prescribed standard. Most empirical studied deal with only one pollution parameter, BOD or COD. The MAC depends on the parameter values in the influent and effluent. In Mehta Mundle and Sankar these values appear as separate values, in James and Murty in ratio form and in Goldar, Misra and Mukherjee as pollution reduction and value in the effluent. Goldar, Misra and Mukherjee view reduction in the pollution load, namely, volume times the difference between concentration in the influent and the effluent as output of the abatement activity. There are two problems. First, under the concentration based standard, a polluter can reduce the concentration in the effluent by increasing water quantity and thereby comply with the standard. Second, the cost elasticities with respect to the volume and pollution reduction need not be identical; in fact the former value is likely to be less than one and the latter value more than one.

The estimates of parameter values are subject to unknown biases because of the omission of firm-specific variables, and failure to include other pollution concentration measures. Discussions with pollution abatement experts reveal that BOD or COD cannot be treated as a proxy for all pollutants. In fact the treatment process is in three stages: primary, secondary and tertiary. Further, most effluent treatment plants have been designed for pollution abatement with respect to only a few parameters. For example, in highly polluting industries such as tanneries and textile bleaching and dying totally dissolved solids (TDS) reduction is a difficult and costly matter. The point is that researchers must probe into these issues and, based on technical and statistical considerations, show that the econometric estimates are not biased and robust.

As the MAC for even one pollutant depends on the volume of effluent treated and on the level of concentration in the influent, the obvious question is which of the MACs are to be used for designing the pollution charge. In our concentration-based system, if the tax is set equal to the MAC corresponding to the standard for a case with lowest volume and highest concentration in the influent, then the tax rate will be very high.

Reviews of the system of effluent charges prevailing in Europe, USA and some developing countries, see for example, Anderson, Lohof and Carlin (1997), OECD (1994), NIPFP (1997) and O' Conner (1998) show that (a) the charge system is based on the volume of effluent discharged and concentration levels of a few parameters/or an index of toxity in the effluent, (b) the charges are far below the MACs in many European countries and in the United States, (c) the polluters are given time to adjust to the system, and (d) in a few countries the polluters are told the standards would be tightened over time or/and the charges would be revised at periodical intervals. It appears that no country has designed its charge system on the basis of econometric analysis of cost functions.

The pertinent question is that how can environmental effectiveness criterion be satisfied when the charges are below the respective MACs. First, consider the case of effective enforcement. Even then, under the standards and charges approach, a firm has an incentive to abate only upto the point where its MAC is below the tax rate. Some low cost abators would achieve the standards but the high cost abators would undertake either no abatement or abatement upto certain levels where their MACs are below the tax rate. By paying charges for the excess pollution in the effluents they can meet their legal obligations, but the overall environmental target will not be met. It is possible that a firm's expectation that the charges will be increased in the future or/and its compliance with the standards will improve its public image and growth prospects may induce it to achieve full compliance. Porter and Linde (1995) stress the dynamic efficiency gains from over compliance. Such a firm can also signal the need for tightening the standards to the regulators and thereby gain market advantage.

The major problem in India and in many developing countries is lax enforcement. Even in a developed country where the regulator has limited budget for enforcement, Harrington (1988) argues that by categorising the polluters into two or more groups on the basis of their past compliance status and signalling them that increases in the number of violation will result in transfer of their names to groups with higher probabilities of inspection will ensure better compliance. He calls this "enforcement leverage".

Becker's Model (1968) suggests that the probability of conviction and the amount of fine, when convicted, do influence a criminal's behaviour. See Cohen (1998) for a survey on monitoring and enforcement of environmental policy. In the Indian context, the probability of conviction is low because of (a) the limited budget of the SPCBs, (b) the burden of proof of violation due to absence of meters at the discharge points and cumbersome proceedure for sampling and testing of effluents, (c) difficulty in prosecution because of political interference or/and corruption, and (d) long delays in court decisions. As mentioned earlier, the fines are fixed at the time when the law is enacted and there is no indexing for inflation; the fines are unrelated to the compliance costs. Only in case of serious damages and widespread public protest the decision is closure of unit.

Against this background, the recent experiences of Colombia, Indonesia, Philippines and a few other countries in finding cost-effective solutions based on public disclosure/environmental rating of firms and use of market forces and community support deserve consideration for replication/adaptation in India. See World Bank (2000). The essential features of the new paradigm can be explained using the MAC and marginal expected penalty (MEP) curves. In the Figure 21.1 horizontal axis measures pollution generated per unit of output and the vertical axis measures MAC and MEP. As the level of abatement (pollution reduction) activity increases, MAC increases. As the level of pollution generation increases, the MEP will also increase. The increase in MEP is due to both higher probability of inspection in case of large deviations from the standards and also community protest. The initial equilibrium is at the point e_0. The regulator can use instruments such as environmental ratings of firms and public disclosure of the extent of non-compliance by firms and

Figure 21.1

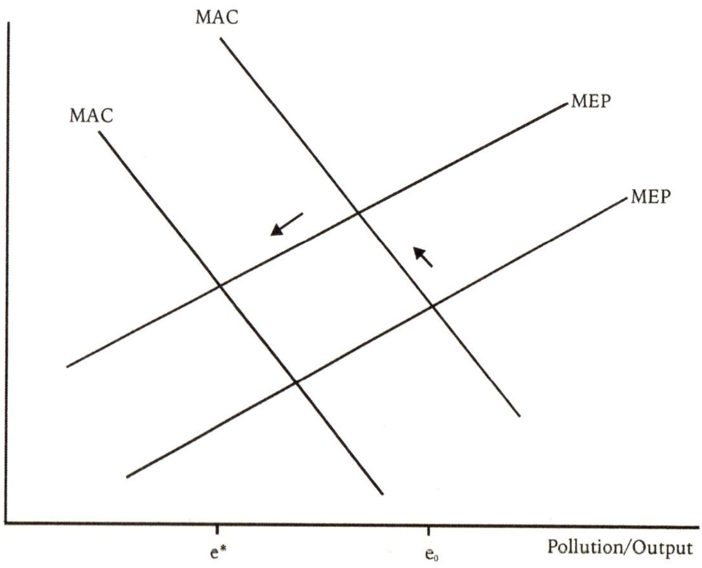

Source: The New Model: Greening the Industry, World Bank (2000).

make the information available in the public domain. Poor environmental rating can affect the expected net present value of the polluting firm. If the market signals work, then the firms share prices will fall, its cost of raising money via equity or debt will increase because of the higher perceived environmental risks, and loss in sales because of consumers' boycot. The ratings and public disclosures can provide valuable information to the affected parties or their agents to take the polluters to the Court under the public litigation banner or/and to put pressures on the SPCBs to take necessary action against the culprits. Thus these policies will shift the MEP to the left.

Adverse environmental ratings and public disclosure may turn the attention of the top management to environmental problems facing the firms and take steps for waste minimisation, end of pipe treatment and recovery and use of products from the wastes generated. Supportive measures by government such as facilitating access to information about clean technologies and low cost end-of-pipe treatments, transfer of environmentally sustainable technologies, creation of markets for wastes and subsidies for recovery and recycling of valuable resources can also shift the MAC downward. Thus, it is possible to reach a new equilibrium at e^*.

Environmental ratings and public disclosure based on scientific evidence and endorsed by independent and reputed certifying agencies can also facilitate bargaining between the polluting firm and the affected parties to arrive at mutually, agreed-upon solution with low transaction costs. The Centre for Science and Environment, an NGO, is in the process of developing environmental rating of firms in India. The Court's interpretation of the peoples right to clean environment as on integral part of right to life under Article 21 of the Constitution and judicial activism in case of environmental cases resulting in closure of units and payment of compensation to victims for past damages on the one hand, and the high transaction costs of reaching settlement via Courts on the other hand, create an opportunity for the polluters and victims to search for non-litigatory low cost dispute settlement mechanisms.

SECTION 4

INDUSTRIAL POLLUTION FROM SMALL-SCALE INDUSTRIES

Since independence, the government has nurtured the growth of small-scale industries by exempting them from the ambit of many laws, reservation of products and providing many incentives. The rationale for this policy is employment generation and dispersed industrial development.

The pollution intensities in small scale industries are generally higher than those in the corresponding large scale industries. Their MACs are higher compared with larger units, because of small size, lack of information about pollution prevention and control, and managerial and financial constraints. The costs of enforcing environmental laws are relatively high because most units do not maintain even data on inputs and outputs and the units are widely dispersed. Due to reasons of loss in output and employment, the authorities had been reluctant to enforce the laws for a long period. The continued discharge of untreated pollutants on land and water bodies adversely affected the quality of water, agricultural productivity and human health in many areas. Public interest litigation by the affected parties and judicial activism culminating in the threat of closure for non-compliance with the standards alerted the authorities and the affected industries on the need for compliance with the regulations.

The empirical literature on pollution control in small-scale industries in India is scanty. The studies by Sankar (1998/2000), Misra (1998), Murty and Prasad (1999), and Pandey and Deb (1999) provide justification for common effluent treatment plants (CETPs). Misra (1998), and Goldar, Misra and Mukherjee (1999) provide estimates of abatement cost functions for industrial units in Nandesari Industrial Estate in Gujarat, but these functions are based on data for primary treatment for units connected to a CETP. Pandey and Deb present case study of a CETP at Jagmau in Kanpur where combined treatment of industrial and domestic sewage is undertaken.

In this paper we report pollution abatement cost estimates for firms with individual effluent treatment plants (IETPs) and for CETPs in two highly polluting industries, namely tanneries and textile bleaching and dyeing units. These cost estimates are based on an economic costing exercise and relate to both the costs incurred and the expenditure required for full compliance with the standards. These case studies help in analysing the trade off between development and environment.

India has comparative advantage in production of leather and textile products. This comparative advantage arises from the strong raw material base, long and rich tradition of craftsmanship and availability of cheap but skilled labour. Our commercial policy exploited this opportunity. The compound annual rate of growth of total leather exports increased from 5.5 per cent during 1951-52 – 1971-72 to 15 per cent during 1971-72 – 1981-82 and further to 19 per cent during 1981-82 – 1991-92. The share of readymade garments of all textile materials in total exports increased from 0.15 per cent in 1960-61 to 11.56 per cent in 1995-96. The prospects for exports of textile garments in the new WTO trade regime are brighter with the phasing out of the textile quota under the multifibre agreement. But these two industries face now both internal and external problems. As per the Supreme Court orders the tanneries and textile bleaching and dyeing units have only four options - (a) erect IETP, (b) become member of CETP, (c) relocation or (d) closure. As they are intermediate segments, the environmental costs will affect the costs and prices of their upstream industries and exports. Externally, they (a) face keen competition from China and South-East Asian countries, and (b) fear loss of export markets in developed countries as environmental considerations are being brought into the world trade agenda.

CETP is a cost-effective option for compliance with the standards because of economies of scale in effluent treatment. The following cost function is based on estimates of capital costs for 28 CETPs planned in Tamil Nadu;

$$\text{LnC} = \underset{(0.3831)}{0.9923} + \underset{(0.0835)}{0.5100}\ \ln E + \underset{(0.0912)}{0.2528}\ \ln N$$

where C=capital cost, E=volume of effluent and N=number of units. It shows that the elasticity of capital cost with respect to the volume of effluent is only 0.51. It also shows that the elasticity of capital cost will respect to number of beneficiaries is positive because of the incremental cost in the conveyance system. CETP as an institutional mechanism offers many benefits to its members and society. The members are eligible for subsidy on the capital cost of CETP. The central government and state government provide subsidy upto 25 per cent the project cost each, subject to a ceiling of Rs. 50 lakh each. There is also a financial package through financial institutions. Jointly the members can seek technical expertise in designing and erecting CETPs. The society can achieve cost saving if monitoring and enforcement can be done at the CETP level rather than at the unit level; the members can be also free from inspections and harassment by the regulators.

The Court orders refer to only initial compliance. People in affected areas want full compliance with the standards. The export prospects also depend on full compliance. What are the compliance costs? How do they differ under the two alternative institutional arrangements, namely CETPs and IETPs? What are the opportunities for making CETPs as instruments of incentive-based and cost effective options for pollution prevention and control? We give briefly the results based on case studies of tanneries in Ranipet and Vaniyambadi and textile bleaching and dyeing units in Tirupur in Tamil Nadu. For details, the readers are referred to Sankar (1998/2000).

Tanneries

The tanning process from raw to finish stage requires 34 to 40 litres of water per kg of hides and skins processed. About three-fourth of the weight of hides and skins processed and four-fifth of the water applied become waste products. The process uses many chemicals. The concentrations in waste water in vegetable tanning process are in the following ranges: BOD 2300-2650 mg/l, COD 5320-7160 mg/l, SS 3000-5600 mg/l, and TDS 8500-19680 mg/l. The concentration ranges in waste water in chrome tanning process are in the ranges: BOD 1200-2500 mg/l, COD 3000-6000 mg/l, SS 3500-4500 mg/l, and TDS 14000-20500 mg/l and total chromium 80-250 mg/l. The standards prescribed for discharge into surface are 30 mg/l for BOD 250 mg/l, for COD 100 mg/l, for SS 2100 mg/l for TDS and 2 mg/l for total chromium. Thus the need for effluent treatment is obvious.

Tamil Nadu accounts for two-third of tanneries in India. Ranipet and Vaniyambadi located in Palar river basin in Vellore district are important tannery towns. The BOD pollution load in untreated effluents from tanneries in Ranipet town in 1995-96 was 5.44 times the load generated from the town sewage; the corresponding figure for Vaniyambadi was 3.85 times. If all the tanneries had complied with the BOD standard of 30 mg/l, then the ratio would decrease from 5.44 to 0.058 in Ranipet and 3.85 to 0.058 in Vaniyambadi.

When the survey was conducted in 1996-97 there were 5 functioning CETPs in the Study Area. Some characteristics of the CETPs are given in Table 21.1. The share of conveyance and pumping cost varies from 8.80 per cent in Udayendram, the smallest CETP in terms of number of beneficiaries to 32.64 per cent in Valayampet, the largest CETP. The capital costs were converted to 1995-96 prices. Then the annualised capital costs were computed based on the assumptions of 20 years plant life, 15 per cent discount rate and full utilisation of CETPs. The economic cost (excluding government subsidy) per KLD of effluent treated varies from Rs. 16.30 in the CETP with the largest designed capacity to Rs. 40.28 in the CETP with the smallest designed capacity, providing evidence of economies of scale in the waste water treatment.

Table 21.1

CETPs For Tannery Effluents in Ranipet and Vaniyambadi: Characteristics

Name	*Beneficiaries No.*	*Process Capacity KGD*	*Effluent Volume*		*Length of Sewer KM*	*Capital Cost*	
			Design KL	*Actual KL*		*Rs. Lakh*	*Subsidy Per cent*
Ranitec	76	134000	4000	3000	7.60	607.1	39.9
Valayampet	110	83600	2850	2400	8.00	440.5	31.4
Sidco Phase 1	81	117500	2500	1300	6.86	312.0	32.1
Visharam	22	82450	3375	1200	1.50	407.7	24.1
Udayendram	10	8000	200	200	2.20	84.0	34.2

Notes: 15 beneficiaries to be added at visharam and 6 at Sidco Phase 1 Capital cost at 1995-96 prices.
KGD: Kilogram of hides and skins per day.
KL : Kilo litres.

All the CETPs comply with the standards for pH, sulphide and total chromium. For all CETPs the TDS values in the effluents are far above the standard of 2100 mg/l; in CETPs 1 and 2 more than 7 times, in CETP 4 nearly 4 times and in CETP 5 about 2.5 times. In

CETP 3, the value was only 3690 mg/l because all members undertake only processing from semi-finished to final stage. CETP 3 violates the standards for BOD, COD, SS and TSS. CETPs 3 and 4 violate the standard for COD and CETP 2 violates the standard for SS. Based on National Environmental Engineering Research Institute (NEERI) site survey conducted in 1997 we revised the cost estimates for compliance for all parameters except TDS and they are given in the last column of Table 21.2.

Table 21.2

CETPs for Tannery Effluents in Ranipet and Vaniyambadi: Costs of Effluent Treatment (Rs.)

Name	*Cost per KLD Treated*			
	Capital Cost	*Operating Cost*	*Total*	*Total**
Ranitec	9.30	7.00	16.30	16.30
Valayampet	12.96	8.18	21.14	23.24
Sidco Phase 1	11.59	13.18	24.77	26.67
Visharam	14.85	15.00	29.85	32.25
Udayendram	20.28	20.00	40.28	43.58

Note: Total* includes additional expenditures needed for compliance with standards for BOD, COD, PH and TSS.

There are two technical options for TDS reduction – membrane separation (reverse osmosis (RO) process) and high rate transpiration system HRTS. As there are some uncertainties about the sustainability of the HRTS, here we consider only the RO process. The RO process is desirable when the value of water recovered is high as it is in most areas of Tamil Nadu. The add-on costs per KLD increase rapidly as the size of the CETP decreases. The abatement cost per kg of hides and skins processed and the share of abatement cost in sales for members of the smallest CETP are above 1.5 times the figures for members of the largest CETP.

We could obtain data only for 13 tanning units with IETPs. The characteristics of the IETPs and treatment cost per KLD are given in Table 21.4. Even though there are wide variations in design capacity and actual volume of KL, we observe no systematic relationship between capacity/volume and either capital cost or O & M cost. The units are heterogeneous in many respects. IETPs 4,7,8 and 9 engage from semifinish to finish processing stage. Their extent of compliance vary. IETPs 3,5,10 and 13 do not meet the COD standard. IETP 3 does not even meet the pH and BOD standards. Hence, omitting these 4 IETPs, we calculate the add-on compliance costs for the remaining 9 IETPs. The total abatement cost (full compliance cost) per KLD varies from Rs.74 to Rs.127. The full compliance cost as per cent of sales varies from 0.56 to 2.71.

Comparing the full compliance cost data for CETPs (Table 21.3) with the data for IETPs (Table 21.5) it is obvious that the cost per KLD for the IETPs are all above the costs for the CETPs; if we take the subsidy for CETPs into account, the CETP costs are still lower. It is interesting to note that the share of abatement cost in sales is lower for IETP 1 than the CETPs 3 and 4. The lower cost for IETP 1 compared with CETP 4 can be explained in terms its higher designed capacity and larger volume of effluent treatment. The lower cost for IETP 1 compared with CETP 3 may be due to economies of scope in having main plant and IETP under the same management, cost savings by avoiding expenditures on conveyance and pumping, and absence of coordination costs.

Table 21.3

CETPs for Tannery Effluents in Ranipet and Vaniyambadi: Add-on Costs and Pollution Abatement Costs for Full Compliance with the Standards

(Rs.)

Name	Add-On Costs per KLD					Total Cost per KLD**	Abatement Cost	
	RO Process			Total	Sludge Treatment Cost			
	Capital Cost	Operating Cost						
		Gross	Net*				Per Kg Rs.	Share in Sales %
Ranitec	16.27	12	-12	4.27	0.19	20.76	0.65	0.33
Valayampet	16.27	12	-12	4.27	0.15	27.66	0.95	0.48
Visharam	16.27	16	-8	8.27	0.11	38.63	1.18	0.60
Udayendram	18.45	28	4	22.45	0.15	66.18	1.66	0.85

Notes: Sidco phase 1 is omitted as it processes effluents generated from semifinished to finished stage.

Total cost includes cost of compliance with conventional parameters as given in the last column of Table 21.2.

* Gross operating cost less value of water recovered. The opportunity cost of water is taken at Rs. 30 per KL. 80 per cent is recovered in the RO process.

** Including the compliance costs for other pollutants.

Table 21.4

IETPs for Tannery Effluents in Ranipet and Vaniyambadi: Characteristics and Treatment Costs

IETP	Process Capacity KGD	Effluent Design KL	Volume Actual KL	Capital Cost Rs. Lakh*	Cost per KLD Treated		
					Capital Cost Rs.	Operation & Maintenance Cost Rs.	Total Cost Rs.
1.	10000	800	400	85.00	9.29	26.58	35.87
2.	10000	300	130	51.67	17.37	26.86	44.33
3.	5000	200	200	22.00	4.81	7.56	12.36
4.	4000	60	60	20.26	14.75	33.33	48.08
5.	3000	100	80	17.01	9.29	18.33	27.62
6.	2500	45	38	14.17	16.30	32.45	48.75
7.	2000	35	30	10.19	14.84	49.66	65.96
8.	1600	45	42	7.50	7.81	16.67	24.48
9.	1500	50	30	4.13	6.01	36.66	42.67
10.	1500	50	50	9.50	8.30	23.67	31.97
11.	1500	35	35	7.50	9.37	37.14	46.51
12.	1000	35	23	4.67	8.87	30.43	39.30
13.	1000	59	59	12.92	9.57	20.95	30.52

Notes: KGD: Kilogram of hides and skins per day. * At 1995-96 prices.

Table 21.5

IETPs For Tannery Effluents in Ranipet and Vaniyambadi: Add - On Costs and Pollution Abatement Costs for Full Compliance With the Standards

IETP	RO Costs per KLD (Rs.)				Sludge Treatment	Total Abatement Cost**	
	Capital Cost	Operating Cost		Total			
		Gross	Net*			Per KLD	Per cent of Sales
1.	27.19	35	11	38.19	0.19	74.25	0.56
2.	29.01	40	16	45.01	0.19	89.53	1.28
4.	34.48	45	21	55.48	0.05	103.61	2.71
6.	38.12	45	21	59.12	0.19	108.06	NA
7.	39.94	45	21	60.94	0.05	126.95	1.62
8.	38.12	45	21	59.12	0.05	83.65	1.68
9.	39.94	45	21	60.94	0.05	103.66	2.25
11.	40.00	45	21	61.00	0.19	107.70	NA
12.	**41.76**	**45**	**21**	**62.76**	**0.19**	**102.25**	**1.18**

Notes: * Gross operating cost less value of water recovered. The opportunity cost of water is taken at Rs. 30 per KL. 80 per cent is recovered in the RO process.

** This is the sum of the compliance costs for other pollutants and RO and sludge treatment costs.

Textile Bleaching and Dyeing Units

For the costing exercise we have chosen Tirupur town area. Tirupur is being cited as a model of decentralised and self-generating industrial development based largely on private initiative. It is a classic example of an export-led industrial growth centre. The hosiery town accounted for about 50 per cent of the value of India's cotton hosiery exports in 1996.

The water requirement for processing 1 KG of grey cloth to bleached cloth is in the range 40-48 l. The water requirement per KG of dyeing bleached cloth is around 87 l for light and medium shade, around 111 l for dark shade and around 150 l for very dark shade. The concentrations of pollutants in the untreated waste water show wide variations depending on the process adopted and the shade chosen: BOD 90-360 mg/l, COD 410-1940 mg/l, SS 75-1800 mg/l, TDS 4720-13000 mg/l, chlorides 1400-5200 mg/l and sulphide 58-814 mg/l. Compared with tannery untreated effluents, the BOD, COD, SS, and TDS ranges are lower for bleaching and dyeing units; but chlorine is an important pollutant in bleaching and dyeing process.

As on 1, January 1998 there were 8 CETPs in Tirupur area but none of them was operational. We could get information about characteristics and capital costs for 6 CETPs. The estimates of operating costs and add-on costs are based on discussions with pollution abatement experts.

The characteristics of the CETPs are given in Table 21.6. There are wide variations in number of beneficiaries, process capacity and design capacity. The economic cost of water treated ranges from Rs.6.77 KLD to Rs.8.71 KLD. These costs are below the costs for CETPs in tanneries reported in Table 21.2. The abatement costs (including add-on costs) are also lower compared with tanneries; these costs are in the range Rs.6.30 to Rs.14.19 KLD. We observe an inverse relation between CETP size and the compliance cost.

Similar data for 12 IETPs in textile bleaching and dyeing units are furnished in Table 21.9. All the 12 units were functioning at the time of the survey. For all the IETPs, 53 per cent of the capital cost was on civil work, 26 per cent was on land and 21 per cent on machinery and equipment. In IETPs, 6 and 11 land cost accounted for more than

50 per cent of the project costs. We do not observe strong inverse relationship between cost per KLD of effluent treated and actual effluent volume because of variations among units in terms of process adopted, shades of dyeing and share of land prices in the project costs.

Table 21.6

CETPs for Textile Bleaching and Dyeing Effluents in Tirupur: Characteristics

Sl. No	Name	Beneficiaries No.	Process Capacity KGD	Effluent Volume		Length of Sewer KM	Capital Cost	
				Design KL	Actual KL		Rs. in Lakh	Subsidy Per cent
1.	Veerapandi	75	87000	10000	9790	3.17	675	14.8
2.	Angeripalayam	90	51062	8500	8487	3.50	720	13.9
3.	Chinnakarai	31	30500	5000	4880	2.50	280	35.7
4.	Andipalayam	21	24300	5000	4250	1.00	263	38.0
5.	Mamarai	32	35250	4250	4149	1.00	242	41.3
6.	M.Pudur	11	11150	1600	1600	1.00	140	46.4

Notes: Capital cost at 1997-98 prices.
KGD: Kilogram of cloth bleached and dyed per day; KL: Kilolitre.

Table 21.7

CETPs for Textile Bleaching and Dyeing Effluents in Tirupur: Cost of Effluent Treatment

(Rs.)

Sl. No	Name	Cost per KLD			Cost per KG of Cloth	
		Capital Cost	Operation & Maintenance Cost	Total	Economic	Actual
1.	Veerapandi	3.02	4.17	7.19	0.83	0.99
2.	Angeripalayam	3.71	4.23	7.93	1.32	2.15
3.	Chinnakarai	2.51	4.27	6.77	1.11	1.30
4.	Andipalayam	2.70	4.41	7.12	1.46	1.44
5.	Mamarai	2.55	4.38	6.93	0.83	0.92
6.	M.Pudur	3.82	4.88	8.71	1.25	1.44

Table 21.8

CETPs for Textile Bleaching and Dyeing Effluents in Tirupur: Add - On Costs and Pollution Abatement Costs for Full Compliance With the Standards

(Rs.)

Sl. No	Name	Add - on Costs per KLD				Abatement Costs**	
		Capital Cost	Operating Cost		Total	Per KLD	Per KG of Cloth
			Gross	Net*			
1.	Veerapandi	13.11	10.00	-14.00	-0.89	6.30	0.72
2.	Angeripalayam	13.11	10.00	-14.00	-0.89	7.04	1.17
3.	Chinnakarai	15.30	11.00	-13.00	2.30	9.07	1.49
4.	Andipalayam	15.30	11.00	-13.00	2.30	9.42	1.94
5.	Mamarai	15.30	11.00	-13.00	2.30	9.23	1.10
6.	**M.Pudur**	**17.48**	**12.00**	**-12.00**	**5.48**	**14.19**	**2.04**

Notes: * Gross operating cost less value of water recovered. The opportunity cost of water is taken at Rs. 30 per KL. 80 per cent is recovered in the RO process.

** Includes the compliance costs for other pollutants.

All the IETPs met the standards for pH, SS and COD. 3 IETPs did not meet the BOD standard, but the extent of violation was only 10 mg/l or less. All violated the standards for TDS, chloride and sulphide. The add-on costs for full compliance with the standards, and the full abatement costs are given in Table 21.10. Comparison of the full compliance costs for CETPs (Table 21.8) with the costs for IETPs (Table 21.10) shows that the full compliance costs for IETPs are several times above the costs for the CETPs. For the IETPs the abatement burden, measured as full abatement cost as per cent of sales, is below 10 per cent only in 3 cases, and above 50 per cent in 3 cases. The new Tirupur Water Project promoted by Infrastructure Leasing and Financial Services and Tamil Nadu Government is a 30 year project on build-own-operate-transfer basis. Under this project industrial consumers have to pay Rs.50 per KL instead of Rs.30. At this price, the net operating cost is positive only for IETP 12.

CETPs: Incentive Structure for Dynamic Efficiency Gains

Our comparative study of CETPs and IETPs in two highly polluting industries shows that CETP is a low cost institutional

Table 21.9

IETPs in Tirupur: Characteristics

IETP	Process Capacity KGD	*Effluent Volume* Design KLD	Actual KLD	Capital Cost Rs. lakh	*Cost per KLD in Rs.* Capital Cost	Operation & Maintenance Cost	Total	Share in sales %
1.	2000	400	400	14.20	1.55	4.94	6.49	0.87
2.	2500	350	350	25.00	3.12	2.79	5.91	0.48
3.	3500	300	300	12.25	1.78	3.11	4.89	1.75
4.	4000	500	200	13.25	2.90	3.26	6.16	2.96
5.	2000	200	200	12.00	2.62	1.51	4.13	1.78
6.	2000	300	200	25.00	5.46	3.89	9.35	2.69
7.	1500	300	170	10.00	2.57	5.53	8.10	5.06
8.	2000	200	135	6.26	2.03	3.29	5.32	0.38
9.	1000	200	100	9.25	4.04	4.46	8.50	5.67
10.	700	200	100	8.25	3.61	4.44	8.05	7.73
11.	350	100	50	14.00	6.12	2.82	8.94	8.53
12.	**1000**	**100**	**70**	**3.45**	**3.02**	**4.00**	**7.02**	**8.04**

Notes: KLD: Kilolitre per day, Capital cost at 1997-98 prices.

mechanism for achieving full compliance with the standards. The CETPs have been registered under section 25 of the Companies Act 1956. The members of the CETPs are the polluting units and they were under pressure to cooperate because of Court orders and fear of loss of overseas markets. They all come from small geographically contiguous region. They know each other and communicate with each other. They can revise policies as and when the circumstances dictate. There is ample scope for making the CETPs as fair, efficient and stable institutions for achieving growth while ensuring compliance with the standards. We indicate such opportunities below. For details see Sankar (2000).

The major weakness of the institutional arrangement is the absence of an incentive based cost-sharing formula. The basis for allocation of equity and monthly contribution in the tannery CETPs is on the basis of installed capacity (e.g. KG of hides and skins processed or number of pieces), equal amount for every member or volume of estimated effluent. In the present system there is no incentive for a member unit to reduce the volume or concentrations of pollutants in the effluents, as the payments are independent of these values; further these values are not monitored.

Table 21.10

IETPs in Tirupur: Add - On Costs and Pollution Abatement Costs for Full Compliance With the Standards

IETP No	*Add - on Costs per KLD (Rs.)*				*Abatement Costs***	
	Capital Cost	*Operating Cost*		*Total*	*Per KLD (Rs.)*	*Share in Sales Per cent*
		Gross	*Net**			
1.	27.19	35.00	11.00	38.19	44.68	5.98
2.	27.19	35.00	11.00	38.19	44.10	3.59
3.	27.19	35.00	11.00	38.19	43.08	15.42
4.	29.01	37.00	13.00	42.01	48.17	23.11
5.	29.01	37.00	13.00	42.01	46.14	20.06
6.	29.01	37.00	13.00	42.01	51.36	14.81
7.	29.01	37.00	13.00	42.01	50.11	31.31
8.	29.01	37.00	13.00	42.01	47.33	3.43
9.	30.83	40.00	16.00	46.83	55.33	36.90
10.	30.83	40.00	16.00	46.83	54.88	52.71
11.	30.83	40.00	16.00	46.83	55.77	53.17
12.	34.48	45.00	21.00	55.48	62.50	71.50

Notes: * Gross operating cost less value of water recovered. The opportunity cost of water is taken at Rs.30 per KL. 80 per cent is recovered in the RO process.
** Includes the compliance costs for other pollutants.

Creation of an environmental management information system (EMIS) is needed for effective governance of the CETPs. A necessary first step for establishing the EMIS is installation of meters at the outlets of the member units. The meters should record both the volumes of and concentrations of pollutants in the waste water discharged into the conveyance system. The meters must be tamper proof and be connected to the CETPs. The EMIS will generate good data base on the volume of and concentrations of pollutants in the effluents on real time basis, make the monitoring feasible, and facilitate introduction of EIs for pollution prevention and control.

It will be possible to introduce a three part tariff. The first part will cover capital related cost. The second part will be in the form of user charges based both on the volume of and concentrations of pollutants in the effluent. The third part will be customer related cost. The tariff revision can be made once a year. If a member can achieve reduction in the volume of or/and concentration of pollutants in the effluent, the member must be given rebates on the charges. If, on the other hand, a member increases the volume or the concentration levels, he should pay, in addition to the user charges, penalties on the excess loads. The cost sharing arrangement should be incentive compatible in the sense that each member's contribution should be between his incremental cost to the CETP and his stand alone cost.

There is scope for pollution prevention. Ramasami (1999) reports that in tanneries by adoption of in plant control measures, net reductions of 30-35 per cent in the levels of BOD and COD, 50-60 per cent in sulphide, 98-99 per cent in chromium and 20-25 per cent in dissolved solids are feasible. Such opportunities do exit in bleaching and dyeing units. In Tirupur, discussions with pollution experts reveal that measures such as installation and operation of water softening plant, substitution of alternate chemicals for toxic chemicals and segregation of dyeing bath effluent for separate treatment can result in waste minimisation. Adoption of such measures will enable the members to achieve growth while containing the aggregate volume of effluent.

It is worth experimenting a tradable permit system among members of each CETP. The firms' abilities in reducing pollution loads via adoption of pollution prevention measures on primary treatment differ because they are heterogeneous in terms of size, vintage, raw materials processed and process adopted. A tradable permit scheme of EPS type based both on volume of and concentrations of pollutants in the effluent will provide an incentive to each unit to search for least cost options for reduction of pollution loads. If a member unit reduces the volume of or concentrations of pollutants in the effluent, it can use the surplus permit for its capacity expansion or sell it to another member.

CETP as a large organisation can seek technical assistance from universities, institutions and international agencies on pollution abatement, recovery and reuse of water and chemicals, and safe disposal of wastes.

Small IETPs and Isolated Units

We have shown that for IETPs with designed capacities below 200 KL the cost of full compliance with the standards are high. The RO process is capital intensive and its capital costs for some units are even higher than the costs of the main plants. Implementation of HRTS requires large land area for cultivation of trees which can withstand salinity. If TDS and chlorine standard are enforced, many IETPs may not be viable. For units with small IETPs and isolated small units we suggest two options – (a) transportation of effluents by truck to nearby CETP or a large IETP, if there exists excess capacity, or discharge in a public sewer, if it exists, for combined treatment of industrial and municipal wastes, and (b) relocation of such units in industrial estates with CETP facilities.

In case of large companies whose shares are listed in stock exchanges and which go to the primary market for equity and loans and whose products have brand equity, internalisation of externalities by means of market signals and upward shift of MEP is feasible. In case of small scale units MAC cost can be lowered via the CETP option. Government should as a facilitator in creating access to cost-effective end-of-pipe technologies, clean technologies and information about wastes minimisation. There is no rationale for fixing a ceiling on government subsidy for CETPs. Subsidies for investments in recovery of materials from wastes and reuse of water, and installation of meters at discharge points of CETP member units serve a social purpose. The regulator can save monitoring and enforcement costs by making CETPs responsible for compliance with the standards, and involving affected persons and local bodies in monitoring compliance by CETPs.

SECTION 5

CONCLUDING REMARKS

India's new economic policy envisages 7 per cent GDP growth. There have been many changes in industrial fiscal, monetary and financial sector policies during the last decade, but so far no serious attempts have been made to initiate environmental policy reforms in India. We still rely largely on command and control (CAC) policies for environmental protection. Developed countries also started with CAC policies but now they rely heavily on MBIs. The regulatory process has become open and transparent providing an opportunity to different economic agents to air their views and facilitating flow of information among the regulators, regulated units, the experts and the general public. Many countries, including U.S.A., have made cost-benefit analysis mandatory before introducing laws and regulations which have significant impact on production, employment, prices and export competitiveness.

Use of MBIs while lightening government's administrative burden and some time raising revenue, provides flexibility to economic agents in finding least-cost solutions for compliance with environmental regulations. Markets can also be used along with NGOs and local communities in enforcing environmental regulations. Markets can do the signalling function efficiently only when the resource prices reflect their social scarcity values. Therefore, there is a strong case for setting prices of resources such as water and energy right. Government has also an important role in providing access to environmentally sustainable technologies, information about wastes minimisation and recovery of resources from wastes, and technical and institutional support especially to small-scale industries. The role of government in environmental protection must change from that of a regulator – administrator to that of a facilitator – mediator.

References

Anderson, R.C., A.Q. Lohof and A. Carlin (1997). "The United States Experience with Economic Incentives in Environmental Pollution Control Policy," Washington D.C.: Environmental Law Institute.

Baumol, W. and W.E. Oates (1988). *The Theory of Environment Policy*, Cambridge, Cambridge University Press.

Becker, G.S. (1968). "Crime and Punishment: An Economic Approach," *Journal of Political Economy*, 76, 169-217.

Cohen, M.A. (1998). "Monitoring and Enforcement of Environmental Policy," mark.cohen @owen.vanderbilt.edu

Confederation of Indian Industry (1999). Environmental Legislation in India, (ed.) S. Shrivastava, Delhi: Confederation of Indian Industry.

Goldar, B., S. Misra and B. Mukherji (1999). "Water Pollution Abatement Cost Function: Methodological Issues and an Application to Small-Scale Factories in an Industrial Estate in India," *Environment and Development Economics* (forthcoming).

Harrington, W. (1988). "Enforcement Leverage When Penalties are Restricted," *Journal of Public Economics*, 37, 29-53.

James, A.J., and M.N. Murty (1999). "Water Pollution Abatement: A Taxes-Standards Approach for Indian Industry," in M.N. Murty, A.J. James and S.Misra, *Economics of Water Pollution The Indian Experience*, Oxford University Press.

Mehta, S., S. Mundle and U. Sankar (1993/1997). "Controlling Pollution: Incentives and Regulation," NIPFP Report 1993, Delhi: Sage Publications.

Misra, S. (1998). "Economies of Scale in Water Pollution Abatement: A Case Study of Small-Scale Factories in an Industrial Estate in India," Working Paper No.57, Delhi: Centre for Development Economics.

Murty, M.N., and S. Kumar (2000). "Measuring Cost of Environmentally Sustainable Industrial Development in India: A Distance Function Approach," presented at the Second International Conference on Environment and Development; Stockholm, September 6-8.

Murty, M.N. and U.R. Prasad (1999). "Collective Action for Pollution Control in Practice: Experiences of Some Industrial Estates in South Asia," in M.N. Murty, A.J. James and S.Misra, *Economics of Water Pollution*, Delhi: Oxford University Press.

National Institute of Public Finance and Policy (1997). Report of the Task Force to Evaluate Market Based Instruments for Industrial Pollution Abatement, New Delhi.

O'Connor, D. (1998). "Applying Economic Instruments in Developing Countries from Theory to Implementation," *Environment and Development Economics*, 4, 91-110.

OECD (1994). "Managing the Environment: The Role of Economic Instruments," Paris: OECD.

Pandey, R. and G. Bharadwaj (2000). "Tradable Permits for Intra-firm Trading," presented at the Second International Conference on Environment and Development; Stockholm, September 6-8.

Pandey, R. and S. Deb (1999). "CETPs and Pollution Abatement in SSIs," Delhi: National Institute of Public Finance and Policy.

Porter, M.E., and C.V.der Linde (1995). "Towards a New Conception of Environment – Competitiveness Relationship," *Journal of Economic Perspectives*, 9, 97-118.

Ramasami, T. (1999). "Upgradation of Technology and Environment in Leather Sector: A Call for Technology Policy Dialogue," presented at International Consultation Meeting on Technology and Environmental Upgradation in Leather Sector, New Delhi, November 29-30.

Roy, J. and S. Ganguli (1997). "Evaluation of Pollution Abatement Policy for Paper Industry in India – Standards vs Tax," Mimeo, Jadavpur University.

Sankar, U. (1998). "Laws and Institutions Relating to Environmental Protection in India," presented at the Conference on The Role of Law and Legal Institutions in Asian Economic Development, Erasmus University, 1-4, November.

———. (1998/2000). "Economic Analysis of Environmental Problems in Tanneries and Textile Bleaching and Dyeing Industries," UNDP Project Report 1998, Delhi, Allied Publishers (2000).

———. (2000). "Common Effluent Treatment Plants: An Institutional Arrangement for Pollution Control in Small Scale Tanneries in India," presented at the International Conference on Environment and Development; Stockholm, September 6-8.

Weitzman, M.L. (1974). "Prices vs Quantities," *Review of Economic Studies*, 41(4), 477-491.

World Bank (2000). *Greening the Industry*, New York: Oxford University Press.

22

Measuring Productivity of Natural Capital

M.N. MURTY
SURENDER KUMAR

SECTION 1

INTRODUCTION

Natural resources supply environmental services to the industry apart from supplying material inputs. If the quality of water resources and atmosphere are kept at their natural regenerative level, they provide sustainable supply of waste disposal services to the industry. The conventional theory of production does not consider environmental services as inputs in explaining the technology of firms. In the absence of environmental regulation, a firm takes environmental services as free goods and therefore does not find it necessary to treat them as inputs in making production decisions. The regulatory instruments like pollution taxes and marketable pollution permits will make the firm to take into account the cost of pollution abatement in making profit calculations. Once the firm complies with the standards, it is taken that it is not creating any demand for environmental services since the complying with the standards by all the firms normally means that the quality of natural resource is kept at the natural regenerative level. However, environmental resources still provide inputs to the industry in this case, because they are taking pollution loads from the industry permitted by the standards. Therefore, irrespective of presence or absence of environmental regulation, industries receive waste disposal services as inputs from the environmental media.

One of the objectives of this paper is to deal with the problem of measurement of productivity of natural capital, the water resources, in the industry. The water resources provide the important environmental inputs to the industry, the waste disposal services. It is useful to know the productivity of the environmental inputs along with the productivity of conventional inputs in the industry. In the generalised structure of production for the industry, man made capital, natural capital and labour are taken as primary factors of production and the value added in industry is attributed to all these factors. It is important to know the share of natural capital in the value added by the industry and how the value added and the natural capital's share in it are affected with the degradation of natural capital. Also, it is natural to look for the estimates of generalised structure of production for the industry with natural capital as one of the inputs for estimating the green GDP.

The estimates of efficiency measures of firms (technical, allocative and overall) with the incompletely specified production structures will be misleading. It is, therefore, interesting to see whether the estimates of efficiency of firms based on generalised production structures considering natural capital as input will be different from the estimates based on the conventional production structures.

In some recent studies, the technology of firms using environmental resources is described as one of joint production of good and bad outputs, the bad output being the pollution load generated by the firm. The output distance function with the assumption of weak disposability is used to describe this technology. These studies provide estimates of shadow prices of pollutants, scale economies, and technical efficiency for the firms. There are some limitations on the estimates of shadow prices of positive and negative outputs and technical efficiency of firms based on the output distance function. The estimation of output shadow prices requires the assumption that the market price of one of the outputs is its shadow price. The weak disposability assumption implies that free disposal of bad output is not possible and the production of one of the positive outputs has to be reduced to reduce the production of bad output. However, one advantage of this method is that it provides the estimates of shadow prices of outputs at the observed levels of production which are useful for evaluating pollution control programmes.

Ideally, the technology of environmental resource using firm may be described as one of jointly producing at least two good outputs, the main product and the pollution reduction. It is natural to interpret the reduction in pollution load by the firm as a positive output. Reduction of pollution by the firm results in the benefits for the rest of society. In the case of a pollution tax, a firm will get benefit from the reduced tax liability.[1] The technical and allocative efficiency of polluting firms can be estimated using input distance function describing this type of technology.

The paper is organised as follows: Section 2 discusses the methodology. It describes the methods of measuring productivity of natural capital. In this context, the conventional production frontier approach, and the concepts of output and input distance functions are discussed. It also discusses the methods of measuring productive efficiency of firms using environmental inputs. Section 3 deals with the estimation of productivity of inputs including natural capital using frontier production function. Section 4 describes the estimation of productive efficiency of firms using input distance functions. Estimates of technical and allocative efficiency for the firms using environmental inputs are provided. Section 5 provides conclusions.

SECTION 2
METHODOLOGY

Measuring Productivity of Natural Capital

Estimation of productivity of natural capital requires the description of technology of firms as one of using natural capital along with man made capital and other inputs. Suppose that a firm employs a vector of inputs $x \in \Re^N_+$ to produce a vector of outputs $y \in \Re^M_+$, where $\Re^N_+$, $\Re^M_+$, are non-negative N- and M-dimensional Euclidean spaces, respectively. Let $P(x) \subseteq Y$ is the feasible output set for the given input vector x and L(y) is the input requirement set for a given output vector y. Now the technology set is defined as

$$T = \{(y, x) \in \Re^{M+N}_+ \; |x \text{ can produce } y|\} \qquad ...(1)$$

We assume that the technology satisfies the following axioms:[2]

1. $0 \notin L(y),\ y \neq 0$
2. $x \geq y \in L(y) \Rightarrow x \in L(y)$

1. The pollution tax is levied such that the rate of tax is higher than the marginal cost of pollution abatement so long as the firm has not reduced pollution load to meet the desired pollution standards. Therefore, the firm has incentive to abate pollution rather than paying the tax (Baumol and Oates, 1981).
2. For a detailed description of these axioms see Fare, 1988.

3. L(y) is convex
4. L(y) has a closed graph
5. $L(\theta y) \subseteq L(y)$, $\theta \geq 1$

In the generalised technology description, the input vector x also includes environmental services as inputs. The production function defines the maximum output that can be produced from an exogeneously given input vector while the cost function defines the minimum cost to produce the exogeneously given output. The productivity of environmental inputs in the firms producing different outputs can be estimated by estimating the generalised production function defined with conventional and environmental inputs. The generalised production function may be defined as

$$Y = F(X_1, X_2, X_3, X_4, X_5) \qquad ...(2)$$

where Y, X_1, X_2, X_3, X_4, and X_5 respectively represent output, labour, capital, material, power and environmental inputs. The factor productivities and the technical efficiency of firms using environmental inputs can be estimated by considering stochastic frontier production function described in equation (3).[3]

$$Y = F(X_1, X_2, X_3, X_4, X_5, \alpha, \beta) + v + \mu \qquad ...(3)$$

where α, and β are vectors of parameters and v and μ respectively represent random error and a measure of inefficiency. After having estimated (3), $E[\mu/(\mu+v)]$ can be computed for each plant from which plant specific efficiency measures are calculated. The marginal productivity of environmental inputs can be computed by simply having the partial derivatives of the production function with respect to environmental input.

In some recent studies, the technology of firms creating demand on environmental resources is described as one of joint production of good and bad outputs, the bad output being the pollution generated by the firm (Fare *et al.*, 1993; Hetemaki, 1996, Kumar, 1999, Murty and Kumar, 2000). The technical efficiency of firms and the shadow prices of outputs are estimated using output distance function[4] with the assumption of weak disposability. Using the

3. See Aigner, Lovell and Schmidt (1977) for the details about the formulation and estimation of stochastic frontier models.
4. Shephard (1953) has introduced the distance function in the theory of production.

definition of technology set in equation (1) the output distance function is defined as

$$D_0(x,y) = \min\{\theta > 0 : (y/\theta) \in P(x)\} \ \forall x \in \Re^N_+ \qquad \text{...(4)}$$

The output distance function in equation (4) describes "how far" an output vector is from the boundary of the representative output set, given the fixed input vector. It characterises the output possibility set by the maximum equi-proportional expansion of all outputs consistent with the technology set (1). The stochastic output distance function for estimation is given as follows:

$$D_0 = f(x, y, \alpha, \beta) + \varepsilon, \qquad \text{...(5)}$$

where D_0 is the distance measure, f (.) is the production technology, x is a vector of inputs, y is a vector of outputs, α, β are vectors of parameters to be estimated, and ε is the additive error term.

The basic problem with distance functions that concerns econometric estimation is that one does not observe (have data on) the dependent variable. Further, if one sets the distance function equal to its efficient (frontier) value, $D_0 = 1$, the left-hand side of the distance function is invariant, an intercept cannot be estimated, and OLS parameter estimates will be biased. Further, if the distance function is expressed in logarithms, the left-hand side of the distance function will be zero for all observations (i.e., $\ln D_0 = \ln(1) = 0$). In order to avoid the above problems, Lovell *et al.*, (1990), Grosskopf *et al.*, (1996), Coelli and Perelman (1996) and Kumar (1999) utilise the property that the output distance function is homogeneous of degree one in outputs (see also Grosskopf and Hayes 1993). Thus, for each observation to be used in estimating the distance function, a value that is unique to that observation can be used to multiply all output values on the right hand-side and the value of the distance function on the left-hand side. Thus, for an output distance function the following relationship (ignoring the error term) holds:

$$D_0(x, \lambda y) = \lambda D_0(x,y), \text{ for any } \lambda > 0 \qquad \text{...(6)}$$

In the literature, typically one of the outputs is chosen arbitrarily as a scaling variable (Lovell *et al.*, 1990, Grosskopf *et al.*, 1996, Coelli and Perelman 1996 and Kumar 1999). For example, if we chose the M-th output, and set $\lambda = 1/y_M$, equation (6) may be written as,

$$D_0\ (x,\ y/y_M\ ) = D_0\ (x,y)/y_M. \qquad ...(7)$$

Now assume that we impose some logarithmic functional form on the output distance function, in accordance with most of the empirical literature. Then, equation (7) becomes

$$l\ n\ (D_0/y_M) = f(x,\ y/y_M,\ \alpha,\ \beta), \qquad ...(8)$$

where f denotes some logarithmic functional form, such as translog and α, β the parameters. Alternatively, equation (9) may be expressed as,

$$\ln(D_0\ ) - \text{In}(y_M) = f(x,y/y_M,\ \alpha,\ \beta), \qquad ...(9)$$

or

$$- \ln(y_M) = f(x,y/y_M,\ \alpha,\ \beta) - \ln(D_0). \qquad ...(10)$$

Given the data, the parameters in equation (10) can be estimated in various ways, depending on the estimation criteria chosen. Basically, the objective for the estimation method is to generate parameter estimates that fit the data as closely as possible while maintaining the requirement that $0< D_0 \leq 1$, which in the logarithmic case implies $-\infty<\ln D_0 \leq 0$.

Similar to the stochastic frontier production function described above, the stochastic frontier distance function includes the composed error term in which a symmetric error term accounts for noise and an asymmetric error term accounts for production inefficiency. For the inefficiency component of the error term, one assumes a functional form and simultaneously estimates all the technology parameters and the parameter(s) of the distribution of the inefficiency term. Adding a symmetric error term, *v*, to equation (10), and denoting the distance to frontier term, - *ln* (D_0), by μ, we obtain the stochastic frontier output distance function

$$- \ln(y_M) = f(x,y/y_M,\ \alpha,\ \beta)+v+\mu. \qquad ...(11)$$

Typically, in the literature it has been assumed that v is distributed - $N(0,\sigma^2_v)$ and independently from μ, while μ is assumed to be either half-normal, truncated normal, exponential, or gamma distributed (see Greene 1993 a,b). It appears that the most popular choice for application has been the half-normal distribution and ML estimation (Coelli 1995). After having estimated (11), $E(\mu/\mu+v)$ is computed for each plant from which plant specific efficiency measures are calculated as

$$D_o(x, y) = \text{Exp}\{-E(\mu/\mu+v)\}. \qquad ...(12)$$

Productive Efficiency of Firms Using Environmental Services

Farrell's (1957) has introduced the concept of productive efficiency as a product of technical efficiency and allocative efficiency. Subsequent literature has addressed a number of questions raised by him and generalised his analysis. For example, the assumption that the production function exhibits constant returns to scale has been relaxed, as has that of homotheticity. Fare and Lovell (1978) set out a number of desirable properties that should be possessed by efficiency measure and they argued that Farrell's measure possesses them only under very restrictive assumptions. They then suggested an alternative measure that has desirable characteristics under more general assumptions regarding technology than those employed by Farrell. A useful and comprehensive discussion of these measures can be found in Fare, Grosskopf and Lovell (1985). The presentation made here is heavily based on Fare and Grosskopf (1990) and Fare, Grosskopf and Nelson (1990).

The productive efficiency of firms can be estimated from the estimation of cost or profit functions in the conventional theory of production. Alternatively the productive efficiency of the firm can be measured using the input distance function which is defined as follows:

$$D_1(x, y) = \max\{\lambda > 0 : (x/\lambda) \in L(y)\} \ \forall y \in \Re^M{+} \qquad ...(13)$$

The input distance function has the properties: $x \in L(y)$ if and only if $D_I(x, y) \geq 1$, and that the distance function is homogeneous of degree +1 in the inputs. The input distance function described in equation (13) shows how far is the input vector from the input vector corresponding to the least cost for producing a given vector of outputs. It characterises the maximum equi-proportional contraction of all inputs consistent with the technology set (1).

The input distance function has several advantages over more traditional means of representing technology such as the cost function.

First, it completely describes technology and is scalar valued as is the traditional functions. In contrast to the traditional functions, the distance function models joint production of multiple outputs.

Second, the input distance function is the reciprocal of Debreu-Farrell input based measure of technical efficiency. The isoquant for any level of y can be written as

$$\text{Isoq}(y) = \{x : D_I(x, y) = 1\} \qquad \ldots(14)$$

The input based measure of technical efficiency introduced by Debreu and Farrell can thus be interpreted as

$$DF_I(y, x) = \min\{\lambda : \lambda x \in \text{Isoq}(y)\} \qquad \ldots(15)$$

which is less than or equal to one and further, is the reciprocal of the input distance function. That is

$$DF_I(y, x) = 1/D_I(x, y) \qquad \ldots(16)$$

Third, the duality between the input distance function and the cost function allows us to retrieve the shadow prices, which are needed to measure the price (allocative) efficiency of a firm.

Fare, Grosskopf and Lovell (1985) has defined three components of efficiency technical, allocative and productive efficiency as follows:

$$TE = 1/[D_I(y, x)]$$

$$AE = C^s(y, p^s)/ C^0(y, p^0)$$

$$PE = TE * AE$$

where p^s and p^0 represent shadow prices and observed prices of inputs and $C^s(y,p^s)$ and $C^0(y,p^0)$ are shadow cost and cost at observed input prices to produce a given level of output vector y.

SECTION 3

ESTIMATION OF PRODUCTIVITY OF NATURAL CAPITAL

Estimation of productivity of water resources, an important natural capital, in the Indian manufacturing industry is attempted in this section. Also, the estimates of technical efficiency for the industries using water as an environmental resource are made for alternative specification of production structure of industry. The alternative production structures considered are two types of production functions, one without environmental inputs and another with environmental inputs and the output distance function with a firm producing good and bad outputs jointly. The bad output being pollution. The estimate of production function with environmental services as inputs enables one to obtain marginal products of environmental inputs while the estimates of output distance function can be used to estimate the shadow prices of pollutants or marginal cost of pollution abatement.

The waste disposal services in terms of BOD, COD and SS loads received by the water resources are the important environmental inputs to the industry. In equation (3), instead of one environmental input, X_5 there are now three environmental inputs, X_5, X_6, and X_7, representing BOD, COD and SS loads disposed by industries to the water resources.

For the estimation of production frontiers defined in equations (2) and (3), the maximum likelihood (Coelli 1995) method is adopted. This stochastic method was first used by Aigner *et al.*, (1977). The approach is based on the composed error term idea, in which a symmetric error term accounts for noise and an asymmetric error term accounts for production inefficiency. For the inefficiency component of error term, a translog functional form is assumed and all the technology parameters and the parameters of the inefficiency term are simultaneously estimated. Typically in the literature it is assumed that the systematic error term v is distributed $-N(0, \sigma^2_v)$ and independently from μ, while μ is assumed to be either half-normal, truncated normal, exponential, or gamma distributed (Greene 1993a,b). It is assumed that μ is distributed half normal. After having estimated the production frontier, the $E[\mu/(\mu+v)]$ is computed for each plant from which the plant specific efficiency measures are calculated as $Exp\{-E[\mu/(\mu+v)]\}$.

The data used in this paper is from a recent survey of water polluting industries in India.[5] This survey data provide information about the plant characteristics. The plant characteristics include sales value, capital stock, wage bill, fuel cost and other material input cost for the main plant. For the effluent treatment plant they constitute waste water volume, influent and effluent quality for BOD (bio oxygen demand), COD (chemical oxygen demand) and SS (suspended solids), capital stock, wage bill, fuel and material inputs. The data are given for a sample of 66 firms. These firms in the sample belong to chemicals, fertilisers, pharmaceuticals, drugs, iron and steel,

5. A Survey of Water Polluting Industries in India, Research Project, 'Fiscal Instruments for Water Pollution Abatement in India', Institute of Economic Growth, Delhi.

thermal power, refining and others. For estimating the output distance function, the technology of each plant is described by joint outputs: sales value (good output) and COD, BOD and SS (bad outputs) and inputs: capital, labour, fuel and materials.

The water polluting firms in the Indian industry are supposed to meet the standards set for the pollutants (30mg/l for BOD, 250mg/l for COD, and mgl/l for SSP) by the Central Pollution Control Board. Command and Control regulatory instruments are used to make the firms realise the standards. All 66 firms in the sample have effluent treatment plants and in addition some firms are using process changes in production to achieve the effluent standards. However, there is a large variation in the degree of compliance among the firms measured in terms of ratio of standard to effluent quality. The large variation in the degree of compliance by the firms can be explained by the laxity of formal environmental regulation by the government. The use of command and control instruments which may not provide incentives to the firms for choosing least cost abatement technologies, and the absence of informal regulation[6] by the communities in the neighbourhood of firms contribute to the non-compliance by industries.

Table 22.1 provides the descriptive statistics of variables used in the estimation. The input output ratios for an average firm using water resources as environmental input for all the seven conventional and water based environmental inputs considered are as follows: For the conventional inputs, capital, wages, power, and material inputs they are respectively 3.10, 0.06, 0.60, and 0.10 while for the environmental inputs, BOD, COD, and SS they are respectively, 85.83, 686.04, and 1203.45 tonnes for every million rupees worth of sales. The estimate of value added for an average firm is Rs. 377.64 million.

Tables (22.2) and (22.3) provide respectively the estimates of parametric values of conventional production frontier and the generalised production frontier with environmental inputs. Table 22.4 provides estimates of mean level of technical efficiency for the Indian industry. The estimate of technical efficiency based on the conventional input production frontier is 0.777 while the estimate of

6. For empirical evidence about informal regulation by the local communities see Murty *et al.*, (1999) and Greening Industry Report, World Bank, 2000.

Table 22.1

Descriptive Statistics of Variables Used in Estimation

Variable	*Maximum*	*Minimum*	*Mean*	*Standard Deviation*
1. Sales	24197.40	6.32	1239.75	3205.20
2. BOD	1368203.00	59.13	106405.57	226137.46
3. COD	10005560.00	269.37	850515.03	1881510.70
4. SS	15658500.00	613.2	1491981.00	2707672.00
5. Capital	66288.70	11.10	3848.97	11059.36
6. Wage Bill	1341.90	0.05	78.48	183.47
7. Power Cost	16150.00	2.58	738.75	2392.90
8. Material Cost	892.50	0.13	123.36	200.69

Note: Sales, wage bill, power cost, material cost and capital are in Rs. Million and BOD, COD and SS are in tonnes.

Table 22.2

Parameter Estimates of Conventional Production Frontier

Variable	*Coefficient*	*t-Statistics*
Constant	0.0201	3.69
X1	-0.166	-0.555
X2	0.899	2.92
X3	0.264	1.067
X4	0.26	0.86
SX1	0.0066	0.178
SX2	0.068	1.27
SX3	0.004	0.08
SX4	0.057	0.87
X1X2	-0.111	-2.09
X1X3	0.116	1.83
X1X4	-0.027	-0.43
X2X3	-0.11	-1.68
X2X4	0.038	0.483
X3X4	-0.069	-0.93
σ	0.166	3.06
γ	0.738	3.88
Log likelihood Function	-12.52	

Table 22.3

Parameter Estimates of Production Frontier with Environmental Services as Inputs

Variable	*Coefficient*	*t-Statistics*
Constant	9.88	9.88
X1	-0.343	-0.343
X2	1.354	1.354
X3	-1.561	-1.561
X4	2.171	2.171
X5	-0.976	-0.976
X6	0.521	0.521
X7	-0.839	-0.839
SX1	0.001	0.001
SX2	0.138	0.138
SX3	0.083	0.083
SX4	0.225	0.225
SX5	-0.635	-0.635
SX6	-0.150	-0.150
SX7	0.021	0.021
X1X2	-0.133	-0.133
X1X3	0.164	0.164
X1X4	-0.036	-0.036
X2X3	-0.159	-0.159
X2X4	0.0025	0.0025
X3X4	-0.346	-0.346
X5X6	0.212	0.212
X5X7	0.004	0.004
X6X7	0.025	0.025
X1X5	0.112	0.112
X1X6	-0.834	-0.834
X1X7	0.0031	0.0031
X2X5	-0.025	-0.025
X2X6	0.023	0.023
X2X7	-0.028	-0.028
X3X5	-0.082	-0.082
X3X6	0.134	0.134
X3X7	0.078	0.078
X4X5	-0.14	-0.14
X4X6	0.065	0.065
X4X7	-0.07	-0.07
σ^2	0.057	0.057
γ	0.05	0.05
Log likelihood Function	2.11	

technical efficiency based on generalised production frontier is 0.959. This result, a measure of technical efficiency increase when environmental inputs are accounted in the production process, is important in many respects. First, a correct measure of productive efficiency of the industry can be obtained only when environmental inputs are accounted in the production process. Secondly, it highlights the importance of green accounting by the firms. Thirdly, it underscores the estimation of environmentally corrected GDP for India.

Table 22.4

Mean Level of Production Frontier Technical Efficiency

Production Frontier	*Technical Efficiency*
Conventional Production Frontier	0.777
Generalised Production Frontier	0.959

Table 22.5

Mean Level of Marginal Productivity of Environmental Inputs

Pollutant (tonnes)	*Marginal Productivity(Rs. Million)*
BOD	0.581
COD	1.421
SS	2.122

Table 22.5 provides the estimates of productivity of environmental inputs based on the estimate of generalised production frontier. The marginal productivity of a tonne of BOD, COD and SS are respectively given as Rs. 0.581, Rs. 1.421 and Rs. 2.122 million.

Alternative specification of production structure of industries may result in different estimates of technical efficiency. Murty and Kumar (2000) report the estimate of technical efficiency based on stochastic output distance function as 0.899 while the one based on generalised frontier production function is 0.959. As could be seen from Section-2, both the specifications of production processes account for environmental services to the industries, but they differ in the method of accounting. In the generalised production frontier, environmental services are taken as inputs to the industry while in the output distance function, pollution is taken as negative output of the industry.

Murty and Kumar (2000) also report output distance function based estimates of shadow prices or marginal cost of abatement of pollutants BOD, COD and SS for the Indian industry. The average shadow prices for water polluting industries are Rs. 0.437, Rs. 0.068 and Rs. 0.0 million per tonne respectively for BOD, COD and SS.[7] These shadow prices may be interpreted as cost to the industry to meet the pollution standards or to keep the quality of water resources at their natural regenerated level. The estimated marginal products of environmental inputs based on the generalised frontier production function reported above are benefits to the industry from keeping the quality of environmental resources at their natural regenerative level. However, the estimates of costs of pollution abatement and marginal products of environmental inputs reported above are not comparable because they are based on different specifications of production structure of industry.

SECTION 4

ESTIMATING PRODUCTIVE EFFICIENCY OF WATER RESOURCE USING INDUSTRIES

In this section, the methodology of input distance function is used to estimate the production efficiency of industries. As already mentioned in the introduction, the assumption of joint production of good and bad outputs in the definition of output and input distance functions will create problem for the interpretation of technical efficiency of the firm. Therefore, the input distance function defined with the assumption of joint production of all good outputs with reduction in pollution load considered as a good output by the firm is used here.

In order to estimate the shadow prices of inputs and technical and allocative efficiency for the Indian water polluting industry, the parameters of input distance function have to be estimated. The

7. The zero shadow price for SS may imply that in the process of reducing BOD and COD, the SS is jointly reduced so that the additional cost of reducing SS is zero to the industry.

translog functional form is chosen for estimating the input distance function for the Indian water polluting industries which is given as follows:

$$\ln D_I(x, y) = \alpha_0 + \Sigma\beta_n \ln x_n + \Sigma \alpha_m \ln y_m + 1/2\Sigma \Sigma \beta_{nn'} (\ln x_n) (\ln x_{n'}) + 1/2 \Sigma \Sigma \alpha_{mm'} (\ln y_m)(\ln y_{m'}) + \Sigma \Sigma \gamma_{nm} (\ln x_n) (\ln y_m)$$

where x and y are respectively, Nx1 and Mx1 vectors of inputs and outputs.

In this section, a linear programming technique is used to estimate the parameters of a deterministic translog input distance function (Aigner and Chu 1968). This is accomplished by solving the problem,

$\min \Sigma [\ln D_I (x , y) - \ln 1]$,

subject to

(i) $\ln D_I (x, y) \geq 0$

(ii) $\Sigma \beta_n = 1$

$\Sigma \beta_{nn'} = \Sigma\gamma_{nm} = 0$

(iii) $\beta_{nn'} = \beta_{n'n}$

$\alpha_{mm'} = \alpha_{m'm}$

The first output y is the main product of the firm while the remaining (M-1) outputs are also good outputs which are pollution load reductions obtained by the firm. The objective function minimises the sum of the deviations of individual observations from the frontier of technology. Since the distance function takes a value of greater than or equal to one, the natural logarithm of the distance function is greater than or equal to zero. The first set of constraints, i.e. (i) restricts the individual observations to be on or 'above' the frontier of the technology. The constraints in (ii) impose homogeneity of degree +1 in inputs. The final set of constraints in (iii) imposes symmetry.

Table 22.6 provides the estimates of parameters of input distance function for the Indian water polluting industries. Using these parameter estimates, the shadow prices of inputs, and the measures of allocative and technical efficiency for the Indian industry are estimated. Given the estimates of technical and allocative efficiency, the productive efficiency (which is defined as the product of technical and allocative efficiency) is also estimated. Table 22.7 reports these estimates.

Table 22.6

Programming Input Distance Function with Pollution Reduction as Good Output

Parameter	Value	Parameter	Value
α0	3.159	β44	0.04
α1	-0.910	β12	-0.003
α2	-0.109	β13	-0.010
α3	-0.092	β14	0.019
α4	-0.06	β23	-0.061
β1	0.224	β24	0.012
β2	0.026	β34	0.020
β3	0.114	γ11	-0.016
β4	0.63	γ12	0.099
α11	-0.020	γ13	0.099
α22	-0.003	γ14	-0.13
α33	-0.006	γ21	0.014
α44	0.0006	γ22	0.008
α12	-0.027	γ23	0.021
α13	0.057	γ24	-0.01
α14	0.010	γ31	-0.012
α23	0.01	γ32	-0.014
α24	0.002	γ33	-0.033
α34	0.003	γ34	0.00
β11	0.003	γ41	-0.008
β22	-0.020	γ42	-0.002
β33	-0.028	γ43	0.004
		γ44	-0.00

Table 22.7

Estimates of Input Technical Efficiency, Price Efficiency and Productive Efficiency of Water Polluting Industries in India Based on Input Distance Function

Variable	Mean	Standard Deviation
Technical	0.992	0.014
Allocative	0.545	0.466
Overall	0.542	0.465

SECTION 5
CONCLUSION

Estimates of productivity of water resources as a natural capital in the Indian manufacturing industries are obtained by making use of generalised frontier production function methodology. These estimates can be interpreted as benefits that the Indian industry gets by keeping the quality of water resources at their natural regenerative level. However, the industry has to incur cost to maintain the quality of water resources. The shadow prices or marginal costs of pollution abatement estimated for the industry using the methodology of output distance function can be interpreted as the cost the industry has to incur in this context. These cost and benefit estimates given in the paper are not comparable because they are estimated using different specifications of production technology of firms.

Estimates of technical efficiency are obtained for different specifications of production technology for the Indian industry. They are production frontier with conventional inputs, production frontier with conventional and environmental inputs, output distance function with the joint production of good and bad outputs by the firm, and the input distance function with the joint production of main products and pollution reduction as good outputs. The estimate of technical efficiency increases when environmental inputs are taken in the production function. This result underscores the importance of environmental resource accounting for the firm and for estimating the environmentally corrected GDP.

Estimate of technical efficiency is also found sensitive to the specification of production technology of firms, the estimate using the generalised frontier production function being higher than the estimate using the output distance function. There is criticism about using output distance function for measuring technical efficiency in the case of a firm producing good output and pollution jointly saying that this method underestimates the efficiency. The result mentioned above reinforces this criticism.

APPENDIX

Derivation of Shadow Prices of Inputs Using Input Distance Function

Shephard (1953, 1970) has shown that input distance function and cost function are dual to each other.

$$C(y, p^s) = \min_x[\ p^s x : D_I(x, y) \geq 1] \qquad \text{A.1a}$$

$$D_I(x, y) = \min_p[p^s x : C(\ y, p^s\ ) \geq 1] \qquad \text{A.1b}$$

To make use of the duality in finding shadow prices of inputs, it is assumed that cost and distance functions are differentiable and consider the Langrange problem

$$\min \Lambda = p^s x - \lambda[D_I(x, y) - 1] \qquad \text{A.2}$$

The first order conditions for input choices are

$$p^s = \lambda(y, x)\nabla_x D_I(x, y) \qquad \text{A.3}$$

where p^s and $\nabla_x D_I(x, y)$ are of dimensions (NX1) and is a scalar. Shephard (1970) demonstrated that $\lambda(y, x) = C(y, p)$ at the optimum. Thus

$$p = C(y, p)\nabla_x D_I(x, y) \qquad \text{A.4}$$

The relationship between the gradient vector $\nabla_x D_I(x, y)$ and the shadow prices can be established by making use of second part of the duality theorem, namely

$$D_I(x, y) = p^s(x, y)x \qquad \text{A.5}$$

where $p^s(x, y)$ denotes the cost minimising input price vector. Shephard's dual lemma can be applied to yield the desired relationship

$$\nabla_x D_I(x, y) = p^s(x, y) \qquad \text{A.6}$$

substitution of (6) into (4) yields

$$p = C(y, p)p^s(x, y) \qquad \text{A.7}$$

Thus $p^s(x, y)$ derived from Shephard's dual lemma may be interpreted as a vector of normalised or cost deflated input price vector. The formulation in A.7 shows that undeflated shadow price p can be computed when minimum cost C(y, p) is known. However, C(y, p) depends on p, which is the vector of shadow prices, the value of which have to found. Therefore, in order to obtain C(y, p), one has to assume that one observed input price equals its absolute shadow price.

Suppose, the observed price of the nth input p_n^o equals its absolute shadow price p_n^s. Then, whenever, x and y are known, we can compute minimum cost from A.7 as

$$C = p_n^o / p_n^s(x, y) \qquad \text{A.8}$$

For all n'≠n absolute shadow prices $p_{n'}^s$ are given by

$$p_{n'}^s = C.p_{n'}^s(x, y) = C.[\partial D_I(x, y)/\partial x_{n'}]$$

$$= p_{n'}^o \frac{\partial D_1(x,y)/\partial x_{n'}}{\partial D_1(x,y)/\partial x_n} \qquad \text{A.9}$$

References

Aigner, D. and S. Chu (1968). "On Estimating the Industry Production Function," *American Economic Review* 58, 826-839.

Aigner, D.J, C.A.K. Lovell and P.J. Schmidt (1977). "Formulation and Estimation of Stochastic Frontier Models," *Journal of Econometrics*, 6, 21-37.

Baumol, W.J. and W. Oates (1988). *The Theory of Environmental Policy*, Second Edition, Cambridge: Cambridge University Press.

Fare, R. (1988). *Fundamental of Production Theory* (Heidelberg, Springer-Verlag).

Fare, R. and C.A.K. Lovell (1978). "Measuring the Technical Efficiency of Production," *Journal of Economic Theory* 19, 150-162.

Fare, R., S. Grosskopf and C.A. K. Lovell (1985). *The Measurement of Efficiency of Production* (Kluwer Nijhoff, Boston).

Fare, R., S. Grosskopf and J. Nelson (1990). "On Price Efficiency," *International Economic Review* 31,709-720.

Fare, R., S. Grosskopf, C.A.K. Lovell, and S. Yaisawarng (1993). "Derivation of Shadow Prices for Undesirable Outputs: A Distance Function Approach." *Review of Economics and Statistics*, 75, 375-80.

Farrell, M.J. (1957). "The Measurement of Productive Efficiency," *The Journal of Royal Statistical Society* 120, series. A, 253-281.

Kumar, Surender (1999). "Economic Evaluation of Development Projects: The Case Analysis of Environmental-health Implications of Thermal Power Sector in India," A Ph. D. thesis submitted to the Jawaharlal Nehru University, New Delhi.

Lovell, C.A.K. and P. Schmidt (1988). "A Comparison of Alternative Approaches to the Measurement of Productive Efficiency," in: A. Dogramaci and R. Fare, eds., *Applications of modern production theory: Efficiency and productivity* (Kluwer Nijhoff, Boston), 3-32.

Murty, M.N, A.J. James and Smita Misra (1999). *Economics of water pollution: The Indian experience* (Oxford University Press, New Delhi).

Murty, M.N, and Sureder Kumar (2000). "Measuring Cost of Environmentally Sustainable Industrial Development in India: A Distance Function Approach," Working Paper No. E/208/2000, Institute of Economic Growth, University Enclave, Delhi-110007.

Shephard, R.W. (1953). *Cost and Production Functions* (Princeton University Press, Princeton).

———. (1970). *Theory of Cost and Production Functions* (Princeton University Press, Princeton).

World Bank (2000). *Greening Industry: New Roles to Communities, Markets, and Governments*, Oxford University Press, New York.

This paper forms part of the work of ongoing research project on 'Accounting and Valuation of Industrial Pollution: Environmentally Corrected GDP for India'. We are grateful to Dr Adi Bhavani for providing useful comments on an earlier draft of this paper.

23

Economies of Scale in Water Pollution Abatement

A Case of Small-Scale Factories in an Industrial Estate in India[1]

SMITA MISRA

SECTION 1

INTRODUCTION

The potential benefits from industrial water pollution abatement at Nandesari Industrial Estate comprising 250 small-scale factories has been estimated for six villages and for the city of Vadodara using the contingent valuation method (Misra, 1997). As a next step, it is important to estimate the cost to factories for complying with State Pollution Control Board standards. The cost of industrial pollution abatement continues to worry policy makers as hardly any empirical evidence is available in this area. As far as small-scale factories are concerned, there is in fact *no empirical evidence* on the costs of meeting standards and this study is an attempt to bridge that gap. Information about abatement costs would be extremely useful for designing cost-effective regulation since small-scale factories continue to be a major source of water pollution in India. This study examines in detail the effluent control behaviour of small-scale factories and the costs they have to bear for water pollution abatement.

The case of Nandesari Industrial Estate is interesting to study because effluent treatment is at two stages: a primary treatment within the factory premises mainly for controlling chemical oxygen demand, dissolved solids and suspended solids and a secondary treatment with the help of a Common Effluent Treatment Plant

1. This paper is a part of my doctoral dissertation.

(CETP) for controlling biological oxygen demand. This *two-step treatment method* is an illustration of how small-scale factories can benefit from economies of scale in water pollution abatement technology.

The cost of effluent control at Nandesari Industrial Estate is estimated for the following: (a) a primary abatement cost for effluent control at the level of each factory to treat effluents in accordance with the technological requirements of the CETP and (b) a secondary cost of effluent control for treatment at the CETP to meet the State Pollution Control Board (SPCB) norms. In addition, (c) a total abatement cost function has been estimated for complete effluent control at the level of each factory to meet the SPCB norms in the absence of a CETP.

This paper shows that there are benefits in treating factory effluents jointly, which arise from considerable economies of scale associated with the provision of wastewater treatment services. Increased flow from industrial enterprises to the CETP made possible by large scale participation reduces the average treatment costs. This provides incentives for small-scale factories to engage in joint treatment facilities or common effluent treatment plants. Nandesari Industrial Estate plays a role model in this respect.

The paper is organised as follows: Section 2 discusses briefly the industrial pollution and control in India; Section 3 deals with some conceptual and methodological issues in the estimation of cost function; Section 4 discusses the data and variables used in this study; Section 5 presents estimates of the primary abatement cost function; Section 6 presents estimates of the total abatement cost function; Section 7 gives the estimated price elasticities and the elasticities of cost with respect to wastewater volume and post-treatment pollution concentration level; Section 8 deals with the average and marginal costs of treatment; Section 9 discusses the costs of abatement under alternate institutional arrangements and Section 10 presents the conclusions.

SECTION 2

INDUSTRIAL POLLUTION CONTROL IN INDIA

Growing industrialisation and accompanying urbanisation have placed increasingly competitive demands on the nation's common property resources such as water. During the past decade, there has been increasing concern about misallocation of resources and environmental degradation. Various environmental regulations provide the necessary support for and are a reflection of a national concern about the levels of environmental degradation. The Water (Prevention and Control of Pollution), Act, 1974, amended in 1986; the Water (Prevention and Control of Pollution) Cess Act, 1977, amended in 1988; the Environment Protection Act, 1986 are the most important laws pertaining to industrial pollution abatement in India. These laws set national goals for eliminating the practice of discharging pollutants into rivers without providing the required treatment and there are specific guidelines for effluent discharges from all sources. Although there have been various legislations in India empowering Central and State governments to implement these regulations, these attempts have not been successful. Strict laws have been enacted, but it is common knowledge that the administrative machinery has not been able to enforce the regulation (Murty 1995, Gupta 1996). Murty (1995) shows that industry and bureaucracy have incentives to collude for sharing the costs saved from non-compliance of environmental standards by the industry. Gupta (1996) argues that the division of environmental functions between the central, state and local levels reflect the underlying tension over the distribution of power and the institutional framework dealing with environmental issues is of fairly recent origin and is still very weak.

Welfare economics suggests government intervention as the only solution to deal with situations of market failure (Pigou, 1932, Baumol, 1972). However, direct regulation on effluent discharge cannot work for small-scale factories since they are afflicted with problems of resource, space and technology (Misra and Murty, 1995). Hence command and control regulations in India have not proved very effective for controlling water pollution in small-scale factories. Infact they have failed! The result of a strict application of command and control regulations in the case of small-scale factories could be either (1) small-scale factories incur pollution abatement at a very high cost, or (2) they continue to pollute because compliance with the legislation imposes large abatement costs. Rather than bearing the costs imposed by a heavy environmental regulation which substantially erodes their profitability, the small-scale factories find it is easier to bribe the regulatory authority and thus continue environmental degradation. Hence the failure of government in dealing with water pollution problem relating to small-scale factories is mainly due to (a) high cost of abatement, (b) non-benevolent behaviour of the government and (c) prohibitively high policing costs.

It is, therefore, imperative to investigate how externalities maybe internalised for a cluster of small-scale factories. The Nandesari case does not show how market mechanism can be revived. *It basically shows that without the institution of CETP, internalisation of the externalities is not possible.* The existing technology of water pollution abatement suggests that there are increasing returns to scale with respect to pollution loads. Some empirical studies about the cost of technological processes for water pollution abatement confirm the presence of increasing returns to scale (Dasgupta and Murty 1985; Batstone and others 1989; Mehta, Mundle and Sankar, 1993; James and Murty 1996). James and Murty have estimated a water pollution abatement cost function using data for an all India sample of 131 factories drawn from 17 highly water polluting industries. They have found decreasing marginal cost with respect to volume of wastewater for the given levels of concentration of Chemical Oxygen Demand (COD) and Biological Oxygen Demand (BOD).

SECTION 3

CONCEPTUAL ISSUES

A Critical Review of Some Recent Studies

There have been several studies on the cost of pollution abatement for industries in India in which the cost behaviour has been analysed with the help of an estimated abatement cost function. Some of these studies have used a Cobb-Douglas function while some others have made an attempt to use the translog functional specification (the results have, however, not been satisfactory). A careful examination of the methodologies adopted in these studies reveals certain serious inadequacies and for this study a different approach has therefore been taken. Before explaining the methodology adopted, the inadequacies of the earlier studies may be discussed briefly.

Some of the earlier studies in this area e.g. Rossi, Young and Epp (1979), Fraas and Munley (1984) have several problems of interpretation with the framework they use (Goldar and Mukerji, 1998). Problems of interpretation arise because what constitutes the output of the abatement activity is not clearly defined. Also, there are certain inadequacies in the functional specifications used in some of these studies.

Rossi, Young and Epp (1979) specify the production function associated with water pollution abatement as:

$$O = f(N, I) \quad \text{...(1)}$$

where O is the vector of flow and quality characteristics of effluent stream, N is the vector of flow and quality characteristics of influent stream and I is the vector of factors of production. The corresponding cost function would be:

$$C = g(O, N, P) \quad \text{...(2)}$$

where C is the cost and P is the vector of prices of factors of production.

There are several problems of interpretation with (1) and (2). N cannot be treated as an input in the same way as I (Goldar and Mukerji, 1998) as labour and capital cannot substitute the volume and characteristics of influent stream. Also, volume and characteristics of the effluent stream cannot be taken as the output of the production function. There are problems in interpreting the partial derivatives of O with respect to I and N. Another problem is that, given I and N, the vector O is not unique since the abatement activity may be directed more at one pollutant rather than another. This is specially true for a cluster of small-scale factories where pollution abatement could be at two stages, primary treatment at the factory level and a secondary treatment at the CETP level.

Other problems arise with respect to the kind of specifications used. For Indian industries, James and Murty (1996) have used the following cost function specification:

$$\ln C = a + \alpha \ln V + \beta \ln (qi / qe) + \Sigma\, bj \ln pj \quad \text{...(3)}$$

whereas Roy and Ganguli (1997) and Goldar and Pandey (1997) have used the following:

$$\ln C = a + \alpha \ln V + \beta \ln qi + \mu \ln qe + \Sigma bj \ln pj \quad \text{...(4)}$$

where C is the total cost of abatement, V is the volume of water treated, qi is the level of a particular pollutant 'i' is the influent stream, qe is the level of the pollutant in the effluent stream and pj are the input prices of labour, capital, energy, materials etc.

There are several problems with the above specifications:

(i) A measure of output (Y) corresponding to Goldar-Pandey specification (equation 4) is

$$Y = AV^{\alpha}\ qi^{\beta}\ qe^{\mu} \qquad ...(5)$$

The interpretation of this expression is not clear with respect to the work done by the abatement plant. This problem arises because the output of the abatement activity is not clearly defined and the form of the cost function has not been deduced from a production function.

(ii) Corresponding to the James-Murty cost function the output definition should be

$$Y = AV^{\alpha}\ (qi/qe)^{\beta} \qquad ...(6)$$

Again, the meaning of this expression is not clear. Further, one may ask: What is the unit of measurement of output in (5) and (6)?

(iii) The derivation of the cost function from the production function requires that the prices of all inputs be taken as arguments in the cost function. This has, however not been done in studies on abatement cost function for Indian industries. Some studies have not taken prices of inputs at all (Mehta, Mundle and Sanker, 1993) while other studies have taken prices of some but not all inputs (James and Murty, 1996; Goldar and Pandey, 1997). The main problem these studies faced in including input prices in cost function was that they used cross-section data and hence there was absence of inter-factory variation in prices of some inputs.

(iv) The variables qi and qe have the same coefficient in the James-Murty (1996) model which involves a restrictive assumption. This can be tested and the results of Goldar-Pandey (1997) for distilleries indicate that this assumption is not justified.

(v) Even if qi=qe (for James-Murty and Goldar-Pandey model), the abatement cost does not go to zero, with the consequence that the estimated cost function will overstate the cost of abatement at low levels of abatement. This affects the estimates of marginal abatement cost.

(vi) Due to high intercorrelation among BOD, COD etc., cost function has been estimated separately for each. However, then one does not get the proper marginal costs.[2]

(vii) In the James- Murty model, cost of abatement is determined by the percentage reduction in pollutant concentration level. But, the cost of reduction of BOD level from 1000 to 500 mg/litre is likely to be different from that of reducing BOD level from 500 to 250 mg/litre. It is important, therefore, that in the estimated cost function, the initial or the post-treatment level of pollutant concentration be included as an additional variable.

(viii) Elasticity of cost with respect to qe is a constant in all the studies mentioned above. This is clearly a restrictive assumption.

(ix) Although data from diverse industries are pooled in some of the above studies, dummy variables are not used to take into account inter-industry differences.

Methodology

The methodology adopted for deriving the cost function in this study is presented below. First, the approach taken is discussed, followed by details of the methodology.

Generally in econometric studies on cost function, cost is taken as a function of output of the activity and prices of inputs. The same approach needs to be taken for the abatement cost function. Thus the output of the abatement plant can be specified as

$$Y = Y\ (O,\ N) \qquad \ldots(7)$$

2. Given a variety of pollutants like Biological Oxygen Demand (BOD), Chemical Oxygen Demand (COD), Suspended Solids (SS), Dissolved Solids (DS) etc, there is problem of multicollinearity as these pollutants are found to be highly correlated with each other. This problem has important implications for evaluating the marginal cost of abatement. The marginal cost cannot be computed separately for each pollutant unless they are all included in the estimated regression (Goldar and Mukerji, 1998).

where Y is the output of the abatement plant, O is the vector of flow and quality characteristics of effluent stream and N is the vector of flow and quality characteristics of influent stream.

The production function corresponding to this definition of output is

$$Y = f(I) \qquad ...(8)$$

where I is the vector of factors of production. Given the production function in equation (8), the cost function is

$$C = g(Y, P) \qquad ...(9)$$

where P is the vector of input prices.

The above formulation of production function and cost function avoids the problems of interpretation arising in earlier studies. The production of the abatement plant is viewed as a *'service activity'* or *'work done'* to reduce the level of pollution. The output of the abatement plant is the extent of pollution reduction achieved for each pollutant for a given volume of wastewater treated. Given a fixed volume of water treated (V), typically for estimating abatement cost functions from *time-series data* for a firm whose production level and wastewater discharge level does not change over time, the output of the abatement plant could be written as:

$$Y = y\,V \qquad ...(10)$$

and

$$y = (qi - qe) \qquad ...(10a)$$

where qi is the level of a particular pollutant in the influent stream, qe is the level of the pollutant in the effluent stream and y measures the output of the abatement plant in terms of a reduction in pollution load per litre of wastewater treated. The term qi-qe implies a reduction in the pollution concentration level (milligrams per litre). The advantage of this specification is that it takes care of the problems discussed above with respect to qi and qe. The initial level of pollution concentration, qi may be taken as given. Thus, a higher level of qe implies a lower output and a lower level of qe implies a higher output. Hence the output is negatively related with qe.

For a Cobb-Douglas functional specification, assuming there are only two inputs, labour and capital, the production function is:

$$Y = AL^{\alpha}K^{\beta} \qquad ...(11)$$

where L and K denote labour and capital input for treatment of wastewater. Let w be the wage rate and r the rental of capital, then the cost of treatment of wastewater is given by:

$$C = wL + rK \qquad ...(12)$$

Assuming that the factory minimises the cost of treatment, given prices of inputs and volume of wastewater, the corresponding cost function could be derived as:[3]

$$C = B\, w^{\gamma}\, r^{1-\gamma}\, y^{\delta} \qquad ...(12a)$$

and it can be shown that,

$$\gamma = \alpha/(\alpha+\beta) \text{ and } \delta = 1/(\alpha+\beta) \qquad ...(13)$$

The Cobb-Douglas specification requires that α, β and γ should be positive. The exponents of w and r must add up to unity since the cost function is homogeneous of degree one in input prices. In order to achieve lower levels of qe, the inputs required also increases and after a point further reductions in qe are increasingly difficult, requiring more than proportionate increase in inputs reflected as diseconomies of scale in the production function. Hence, $\alpha + \beta$ should be less than 1 and δ should be greater than 1. The functional form given above can be easily extended to more than two inputs. Also, one may use the translog functional form instead of the Cobb-Douglas functional form used above.

In the cost function specification above, only one pollutant has been considered. A useful extension of the cost specification could be a multi-output cost specification. A multi-output cost function will have various outputs as its arguments.

$$C = f\,(Y_{COD}, Y_{BOD}, Y_{SS}, Y_{DS}, pl, pk, pm, pe), \qquad ...(14)$$

where, C is the cost of abatement, BOD, COD, DS, SS are different pollutants, pl is the price of labour, pk is the price of capital, pm is the price of materials and pe is the price of energy. However, experience gained in empirical research bring out that there is a high correlation among the extent of reduction of different pollutants making it difficult empirically to estimate the cost implications of the different components of output. It may be necessary therefore to

3. The derivation of the cost function is in Goldar and Mukerji, 1998.

use one of the pollutant as an overall indicator of the pollution level and the extent of abatement done.

The cost of abatement is expected to vary in a dissimilar manner with respect to volume of wastewater treated and the extent of abatement (Figure 23.1). As the volume of water treated increases, the cost of abatement will increase less than proportionately due to economies of scale in treating a larger volume of water but as the extent of abatement increases, the marginal cost will increase as further reduction in the pollution level becomes more and more difficult. Also, economies of scale need not be prevalent for all pollutants. There may be economies of scale in treatment of BOD but no such economies of scale in treatment of COD, SS or DS. This is very true for a cluster of small-scale factories. For Nandesari Industrial Estate, some reduction in the levels of COD, SS and DS are made during primary treatment at the factory whereas BOD and COD are reduced to meet SPCB standards at the CETP. This is indicative of economies of scale in treating larger volumes of water for BOD and COD but no such economies for SS and DS.

Figure 23.1

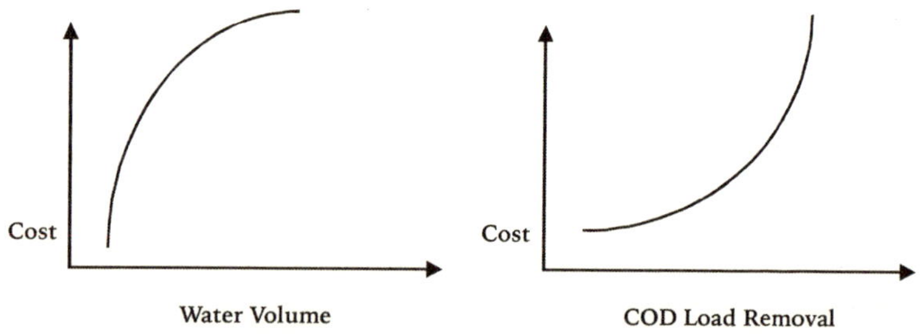

Economies of scale in treatment of wastewater should be checked by analysing variation in abatement costs across firms of different size. For estimating the cost function given in equation (12) above from cross-section data, some modification becomes necessary. The volume of water treated will have an influence on cost of treatment per litre. Also, the post-treatment pollution concentration level has to be included in the cost function.[4] Accordingly, the cost function is specified as:

$$C = A\ w^{\gamma}\ r^{1-\gamma}\ (qi - qe)^{\delta}\ V^{\epsilon}\ (qe)^{\mu} \qquad \text{...(15 a)}$$

In the discussion above, a two-input production function has been assumed for ease of exposition. For this study, a three-input model has been used taking labour (l), capital (k) and materials plus energy (me) as three inputs. Accordingly, the cost function using the Cobb-Douglas functional form in (15 a) has been specified as:

$$\ln C = A + \delta \ln (q_i - q_e) + \epsilon \ln V + \mu \ln (q_e) + \alpha_l \ln p_l + \alpha_k \ln p_k + \alpha_{me} \ln p_{me} \qquad \text{...(15 b)}$$

where pl = price of labour; pk = price of capital; and pme = price of materials plus energy.

Since the cost function must be linear homogeneous in input prices, α_l , α_k and α_{me} must add to one.

A serious limitation of Cobb-Douglas (CD) functional form is that the elasticity of substitution is unity between each pair of inputs. This format assumes substitution possibilities to be the same and does not allow complimentarity between any pair of inputs. One way of getting over this problem is to use a Transcendental Logarithmic (translog) functional format. The translog specification is a more general specification than the Cobb-Douglas specification. It allows the possibility of testing whether Cobb-Douglas can be taken as the right specification for cost functions. The translog functional format is linear in its parameters and provides second order approximation in input prices to an arbitrary continuously differentiable cost function. Also, it is known from Shepherd's duality theorem that the econometric estimation of the parameters of a cost function is equivalent to estimating the parameters of the underlying production function, provided producers behave competitively in the factor markets.

Using the translog specification, the cost function may be written as:

4. The need for including V and qe as additional variables in the cost function has been discussed by Goldar and Mukerji (1998). They point out that one may use qi or qe to take into account inter-firm differences in initial and post-treatment levels of pollution concentration level, but advance argument in favour of inclusion of qe as an explanatory variable in the cost function.

$$\ln C = A + \delta \ln (q_i - q_e) + \in \ln V + \mu \ln (q_e) + \Sigma \alpha_j \ln p_j + 1/2 \; \Sigma \Sigma \beta_{zj} \ln p_z \ln p_j + \Sigma \gamma_j \ln V \ln p_j + \Sigma \varphi_j \ln (q_i - q_e) \ln p_j + \Sigma \lambda_j \ln q_e \ln p_j \quad \text{...(16 a)}$$

where,

$$\beta_{zj} = \beta_{jz}$$

The conditions necessary for the translog form to be linearly homogeneous in input prices are:

$$\sum_j \alpha_j = 1, \quad \sum \beta_{zj} = 0, \quad \text{for } z = 1, k, me$$

$$\Sigma \gamma_j = 0, \; \Sigma \varphi_j = 0 \text{ and } \Sigma \lambda_j = 0, \text{ for } j = 1, k, me$$

For this study, translog cost function has been estimated along with cost share equations using the LIMDEP software. The seemingly unrelated regression estimates (SURE) procedure is used. While estimating the parameters of the cost function and cost share equation, appropriate restrictions on parameter estimates are imposed both within equations and across equations. Thus the parameter estimates are obtained such that the conditions of linear homogeneity are satisfied.

A truncated version of the above model has also been estimated in which the interaction terms involving ln V, ln (qi-qe) and ln qe are dropped, i.e. one assumes,

$\gamma_j = \varphi_j = \lambda_j = 0$ for j = l, k and me. Thus equation 16a reduces to

$$\ln C = A + \delta \ln (q_i - q_e) + \in \ln V + \mu \ln (q_e) + \Sigma \alpha_j \ln p_j + 1/2 \; \Sigma \Sigma \beta_{zj} \ln p_z \ln p_j \quad \text{...(16 b)}$$

We shall be referring to this model as truncated translog model (and the model in equation 16a as the full translog model). The truncated translog model has relatively fewer parameters and is therefore easier to estimate, but the full translog model provides greater flexibility and is obviously superior in terms of functional specification. The full translog has a flexible functional format and has been successfully used in this study to estimate the cost of abatement at Nandesari.[5] The cost share equations can be derived as

$$Sj = pj\, Xj/C = \partial \ln C/\partial \ln pj \qquad j = 1, k, me \qquad \text{...(17)}$$

5. To the best of the author's knowledge, there is no study on abatement cost function in the Indian context in which a full translog specification has been used.

The cost share equations for labour, capital and materials-energy for the full translog model are as follows:

$$Sl = \alpha_l + \beta_{ll} \ln p_l + \beta_{lk} \ln p_k + \beta_{lme} \ln p_{me} + \gamma_l \ln V + \varphi_l \ln (q_i - q_e) + .\lambda_l \ln q_e \quad \text{...(17 a)}$$

$$Sk = \alpha_k + \beta_{lk} \ln p_l + \beta_{kk} \ln p_k + \beta_{kme} \ln p_{me} + \gamma_k \ln V + \varphi_k \ln (q_i - q_e) + \lambda_k \ln q_e \quad \text{...(17 b)}$$

$$Sme = \alpha_{me} + \beta_{lme} \ln p_l + \beta_{kme} \ln p_k + \beta_{meme} \ln p_{me} + \gamma_{me} \ln V + \varphi_{me} \ln (q_i - q_e) + \lambda_{me} \ln q_e \quad \text{...(17 c)}$$

where Sl = share of labour, Sk = share of capital, Sme = share of materials plus energy.

Since three inputs have been considered, cost shares for any two inputs have to be used along with the cost function. In this study, cost share equations for (i) labour and (ii) materials plus energy inputs have been chosen for estimation.

SECTION 4

DATA AND VARIABLES

Time series primary data (for the years 1993-94 to 1995-96) were collected for a sample of 45 factories from Nandesari Industrial Estate comprising 250 small-scale factories producing different kinds of organic and inorganic chemicals and pharmaceuticals. A questionnaire was designed to collect information about costs of abatement from the sample factories providing primary treatment during 1993-94 to 1995-96. Detailed information was collected about the labour costs, capital costs, material costs and energy (fuel and power) costs over the three years using stratified random sampling method for factories producing organic, inorganic and pharmaceutical products. The data on the volume and characteristics of influent wastewater and effluent wastewater were collected from the records maintained by the factory owners for Nandesari Association as well as SPCB.

This study uses pooled data for 38 factories for a period of three years, 1993-94, 1994-95 and 1995-96. Sample data of seven factories were excluded because of incomplete reporting. Besides data on abatement activity, data were collected on the revenue of the production unit (factory), and detailed data on the input costs. The data set used for this study includes the wage bill, number of workers, fuel and energy prices and expenditure, price and quantity of materials used and the expenditure on capital equipment for the three years both for the main production plant and for the effluent treatment plant (ETP). The advantage of using a pooled data set (with intertemporal variations in prices) is that prices of all inputs can be used in estimating the abatement cost function. This is a considerable improvement over the earlier attempts at estimating abatement cost functions.

This study uses a three input model. Capital is taken as one input, labour as another. Materials and energy are taken together as one input. Cost of abatement is obtained as the sum total of costs with respect to these three inputs. For estimating the cost function, prices of inputs are needed. Standard procedure was adopted to calculate the price of capital services. Price of capital service is obtained as:

$$pk = pi\ (r + d), \qquad \text{...(18)}$$

where pk = price of capital input (service), pi = price index of capital goods, r = rate of return on capital and d = rate of depreciation.

For computing the price index of capital goods pi, the wholesale price index of machinery was taken for the three years as reported in *Economic Survey,* 1997. A measure of stock of capital goods was formed by expressing the value of capital assets in the three years at 1996 prices. The rate of return on capital, r was obtained as follows:

Value Added by capital = Total Revenue - Wage Bill (Main Plant + ETP) -Materials and Energy Cost (Main Plant + ETP)

Rate of return on capital = Value Added by capital / (Value of assets in Main Plant + Value of assets in ETP)

The reported rate of depreciation was used for each factory. From r, d and pi, the price of capital pk was computed. This multiplied by the quantity measure of capital stock yielded the annual cost of capital input for the abatement which as pointed out above is a component of the total abatement cost.

The price of labour was calculated as the wage bill divided by the number of labourers used for the ETP. Earlier studies on abatement cost function for Indian industries have also used this method to derive the price of labour input.

A weighted price index was constructed for raw materials used in the ETP. Generally, four types of materials are used for primary treatment at ETPs in Nandesari Industrial Estate. These are ferrous sulphate, hydrated lime, soda ash and caustic soda. For 3 million litres of wastewater, about 4000 kg ferrous sulphate, 500 kg hydrated lime, 550 kg soda ash and 500 kg caustic soda are needed. The Table 23.1 shows the weighted price index of raw materials used in the ETP for the three years.

Table 23.1

Price Index of Raw Materials (1995-96=100)

	Hydrated Lime	*Soda Ash*	*Caustic Soda*	*Ferrous Sulphate*	*Weighted Average*
1993-94	66.66	86.36	66.66	70.00	71.76
1994-95	83.33	90.90	133.33	80.00	96.77
1995-56	100.00	100.00	100.00	100.00	100.00

Note: weights are the share of the raw material in the total cost of raw materials.

A price index of energy and fuel (e) used for ETP was computed for the three years. A combined weighted price index of materials and energy (me) was then computed, the respective weights being the relative share of materials and energy in the total cost of materials plus energy used in the ETP.

In this way the price of labour, price of capital and a combined price of materials and energy used in the ETP was obtained with intertemporal as well as inter-factory variations.[6]

Besides collecting data on abatement cost for the sample factories, such data were collected for the CETP. Another questionnaire was designed for this purpose to collect similar data from CETP for providing a joint secondary level treatment to meet the SPCB norms.

6. There are intertemporal variations in prices of labour and capital services over the three year period and inter-factory variations for each year. The price index for materials and price index for energy vary over the three year period but are the same for each factory observation in each year. These indices have been combined to get a weighted price index of materials plus energy using factory specific expenditure on materials and energy for abatement activity in each year. This introduces inter-factory variation in price of materials plus energy in each year.

The data for capital costs and operation and maintenance costs of the CETP were obtained for 1995-96 and 1996-97.

One important question investigated in this study is how far small-scale units can save the cost of wastewater treatment by setting up CETP. It was necessary, therefore, to find out what cost the factories will have to bear if they have to undertake complete treatment. Accordingly, a separate part of the questionnaire for factories collected information about additional costs of abatement the factories will have to incur to meet SPCB standards in the absence of a CETP. This part requested factory owners to give an estimate of additional abatement costs necessary to meet the SPCB standards if total abatement was undertaken at the factory level. The factory owners provided information about the additional cost for labour, materials, energy and fuels and the additional investment in capital assets.

The sample information gives the mean price of labour as Rs. 24,257 per annum (s.d. = Rs 18,240). The mean price index of capital services is 1.11 (s.d. = 0.91) and mean price index of materials plus energy is 87.10 (s.d. = 12.9). The average volume of wastewater discharged is 7.3 million litres per annum. It ranges from 0.1 million litres per annum to 69 million litres per annum. The initial level of COD concentration ranges from 100 mg per litre to 10,000 mg per litre. On an average, the initial level of COD concentration is 3450 mg per litre. The reduction of COD concentration during primary treatment, on an average is 2615 mg per litre. The cost of primary water pollution treatment on an average per factory is Rs. 1.5 million per annum. It ranges from Rs. 0.04 million to Rs. 13.9 million per annum. If the factory has to undertake total water pollution abatement at the factory level (complying with SPCB standards), the average *additional* cost burden per factory is Rs. 1.4 million per annum, ranging from Rs. 60,000 to Rs. 8 million per annum.

SECTION 5

PRIMARY COST OF WATER POLLUTION ABATEMENT

The estimation of the primary abatement cost function has been based on factories' reported direct costs of installing and operating water pollution control equipment.[7] The translog specification has been used to estimate the costs of abatement. The estimates of translog cost function parameters are presented in Table 23.2. The notation for variables is as follows:

V = volume

dci = (qi - qe) influent concentration of COD - effluent concentration of COD

qe = effluent concentration of COD

pl = price of labour

pk = price of capital services

pme = price index of materials and energy

From Table 23.2, which gives the estimates of primary abatement cost functions using both full and truncated translog specifications, it is seen that the models fit the data well as indicated by the values of R^2. Most coefficients are found to be statistically significant. The coefficient of V in full translog is less than 1 showing there are economies of scale in industrial water pollution abatement for small-scale factories. The coefficient of variable dci is positive showing that the greater is the difference between the influent concentration and effluent concentration of COD, the greater is the primary cost of abatement. The coefficient of qe is negative showing that the lower is the concentration of COD effluent to be achieved, the higher will be the primary cost of abatement. Price of capital and labour are highly significant in explaining the primary cost of abatement.

Restrictions on parameters reduce the full translog model to the restricted translog model and further to the Cobb-Douglas model. In cost function studies, these alternative specifications are commonly tested with 'likelihood ratio test' (Greene 1993). In this case, the likelihood ratio statistic is 273.46 (d.f. = 9) for the restrictions that reduce the full-translog model to Cobb-Douglas and 41.26 (d.f. = 6) for the restrictions that reduce the full translog model to the

7. Given the multicollinearity problem between BOD, COD, SS and DS pollutants, one of them has to be chosen as the measure of pollution level. The CETP at Nandesari has a technological requirement for the COD concentration level to be reduced in the range of 250 - 1500 mg per litre at the factory level. The Nandesari Association regularly monitors the COD effluent from factories to enable the proper functioning of the CETP. Hence COD is the obvious choice for a measure of pollution level in this study.

truncated translog model. Both are statistically significant at one per cent level and therefore both the truncated translog and Cobb-Douglas model are rejected. Also, R^2 and Adjusted R^2 are distinctly better in the full translog model as compared to the truncated translog model for the estimates of the cost share equations.[8] Therefore, the full translog model is superior to the truncated version and had been used for the estimation of primary water pollution abatement costs for Nandesari Industrial Estate.

The condition of monotonicity for a well-behaved translog function requires that

$\partial C / \partial pj > 0$ for j = l, k and me. This condition implies that the share of factor inputs should be positive. This has been checked and it is found that the estimated share equations in the full translog model satisfy this condition.

SECTION 6

TOTAL COST OF WATER POLLUTION ABATEMENT

The estimate of primary abatement cost function presented in the previous section was based on data relating to actual cost of wastewater treatment in factories. Since the factories are doing only primary treatment, the estimated cost function can be used to get estimates of primary treatment costs. It is reasonable to argue that the cost function estimates presented above may not give the right estimates of abatement cost, if the factories have to undertake total abatement. To get over this problem, this study estimates the abatement cost function from an enlarged data set in which the additional abatement cost to undertake total abatement at the factory level is provided by the 38 factories.

Hence, this part of the study uses the *additional* abatement cost data provided by 38 factories if they have to undertake total abatement at the factory level (in the absence of a CETP) to meet the SPCB norms. The factories were asked to give details of the *additional*

8.

	Truncated Translog		*Full Translog*	
	Sl	*Sme*	*Sl*	*Sme*
R^2	0.43	0.21	0.46	0.42
Adjusted R^2	0.42	0.19	0.43	0.39

Note: Sl= share of labour; Sme = share of materials and energy.

costs they will have to incur in order to meet SPCB standards in the absence of a CETP.[9] The additional cost for total abatement was added to the actual costs for primary abatement to get an estimate of the total cost of abatement at the level of each factory. The functional specifications and the method of estimation used are the same as in the previous section.

Table 23.2 also presents the results of the translog specifications for estimating the total abatement costs for Nandesari. Both full and truncated translog forms have been used. The results are similar to the estimation of primary abatement cost. The coefficient of V is less than 1 indicating the presence of economies of scale in industrial water pollution abatement for small-scale factories. The variable dci has a positive coefficient showing that the greater is the difference between the influent concentration and effluent concentration of COD, the greater is the total cost of abatement; the coefficient of qe is negative which is the correct sign showing, the lower is the concentration of COD effluent to be achieved, the higher will be the total cost of abatement. Price of capital and labour are very significant in explaining the total cost of abatement.

The likelihood ratio test statistic is 388.2 (d.f.= 9) for the restrictions that reduce the full-translog model to Cobb-Douglas and 46.58 (d.f. = 6) for the restrictions that reduce the full translog model to the truncated translog model. Both are statistically significant at one per cent level and therefore both the truncated translog and Cobb-Douglas model are rejected. Also, the R^2 and Adjusted R^2 are higher for the full translog model as compared with the truncated translog model for the estimates of the cost share equations.[10] Thus, the full translog model is preferable to the

9. It should be pointed out that while making estimate of cost function based on cost of primary treatment data, three observations (for the three years, 1993-94, 1994-95 and 1995-96) were used for each factory giving a total of 114 observations. After adding the additional cost of abatement we get one more observation for each factory. Thus a panel of four observations for each of the 38 factories giving a total of 152 observations was used for the estimates presented in this section.

10.

	Truncated Translog		*Full Translog*	
	Sl	*Sme*	*Sl*	*Sme*
R^2	0.49	0.21	0.51	0.38
Adjusted R^2	0.48	0.19	0.49	0.36

Note: Sl= share of labour; Sme = share of materials and energy.

Table 23.2

Estimates of Cost Function for Water Pollution Abatement at Nandesari Industrial Estate

Dependent Variable ln C

	Primary Cost of Abatement		*Total Cost of Abatement*	
Explanatory Variables	*Truncated Translog*	*Full Translog*	*Truncated Translog*	*Full Translog*
ln V	0.337 (6.555)***	0.602 (5.977)***	0.320 (7.200)***	0.564 (6.474)***
ln dci	0.297 (6.571)***	0.391 (4.555)***	0.297 (7.924)***	0.435 (6.073)***
ln qe	-0.253 (-3.083)***	-0.047 (-0.307)	-0.282 (-4.560)***	-0.193 (-1.662)*
ln pk	1.907 (17.652)***	1.454 (7.787)***	1.906 (23.072)***	1.523 (10.571)***
lnpk*lnpk	0.166 (13.419)***	0.152 (11.696)***	0.163 (17.123)***	0.153 (15.089)***
ln pl	-0.927 (-7.120)***	-0.502 (-2.727)***	-0.937 (-9.176)***	-0.650 (-4.584)***
lnpl*ln pl	0.123 (6.836)***	0.133 (7.845)***	0.122 (8.390)***	0.131 (9.423)***
ln pme	0.0206 (0.199)	0.049 (0.354)	0.031 (0.370)	0.128 (1.143)
lnpme*ln pme	0.085 (4.209)***	0.100 (5.116)***	0.078 (4.559)***	0.087 (5.041)***
ln pl*lnpk	-0.102 (-9.267)***	0.152 (11.696)***	-0.103 (-12.136)***	-0.098 (-10.941)***
ln pl*ln pme	-0.0208 (-1.248)	-0.041 (-2.633)***	-0.019 (-1.346)	-0.033 (-2.432)***
ln pk*ln pme	-0.0638 (-5.911)***	-0.060 (-5.657)***	-0.060 (-6.744)***	-0.054 (-6.160)***
ln v*ln pl		-0.036 (-3.645)***		-0.030 (-3.777)***
ln v*ln pk		0.011 (1.117)		0.011 (1.374)
ln v*ln pme		0.025 (3.131)***		0.019 (2.820)***
ln dci*ln pl		0.009 (1.031)		0.004 (0.543)
ln dci*ln pk		0.025 (2.937)***		0.026 (3.807)***

Contd. ...

...Table 23.2 Contd. ...

	Primary Cost of Abatement		*Total Cost of Abatement*	
Explanatory Variables	*Truncated Translog*	*Full Translog*	*Truncated Translog*	*Full Translog*
ln dci*ln pme		-0.034 (-5.188)***		-0.029 (-5.457)***
ln qe*ln pl		-0.027 (-1.736)*		-0.011 (-0.969)
lnqe*ln pk		0.011 (0.710)		0.006 (0.522)
lnqe*lnpme		0.016 (1.264)		0.005 (0.517)
constant	13.002 (15.870)***	8.479 (5.981)***	13.421 (20.311)***	9.689 (8.442)***
number of observations	114	114	152	152
R^2	0.65	0.66	0.65	0.66
Adjusted R^2	0.61	0.58	0.62	0.61

Note: t-ratios are in parenthesis; *** significant at 1 per cent ; ** significant at 5 per cent; * significant at 10 per cent.

truncated translog model and has been used for estimating the total cost for water pollution abatement at Nandesari Industrial Estate.

The condition of monotonicity for a well-behaved translog function requires that $\partial C / \partial pj > 0$ for j = l, k and me. This condition implies that the share of factor inputs should be positive. The estimated share equations in the full translog model satisfy this condition.

SECTION 7

PRICE ELASTICITIES AND COST FLEXIBILITY

The advantage of the translog specification is that it does not assume the elasticity of substitution between factors of production to be constant. Hence, the elasticity of substitution and the price elasticity can be computed using the translog specification[11] for labour (L), materials-energy (M) and capital (K). These elasticities

11. The own elasticity of substitution can be estimated for labour as, (σll) = (βll + (Sl)(Sl-1))/(Sl*Sl), where Sl = share of labour in total cost; price elasticity of labour (ηl) = (σll) * Sl and cross elasticity of substitution of labour for capital, (σlk) = (βlk + (Sl)(Sk))/(Sl*Sk), where Sk = share of capital in total cost. From cross elasticities of substitution, cross price elasticities can be derived.

have been computed from the estimated full translog model for both primary cost and total cost function. Table 23.3 shows (as expected) that the own price elasticities are negative. Also, labour, capital and materials-energy are substitutes as the elasticity of substitution are positive for them. Since for both models, price elasticities are low, it may be inferred that the substitution possibilities among labour, capital and materials-energy are limited.

Table 23.3

Elasticities

	Primary Cost Model	*Total Cost Model*
Own Price Elasticity		
LL	-0.20	-0.19
MM	-0.33	-0.37
KK	-0.17	-0.17
Cross Price Elasticity		
KL	0.07	0.04
LK	0.17	0.11
ML	0.05	0.08
LM	0.05	0.08
MK	0.29	0.33
KM	0.11	0.13
Cross Elasticity of Substitution (Allen)		
LK	0.30	0.19
LM	0.21	0.38
KM	0.51	0.59

Elasticities of substitution and price elasticities (own and cross) are parameters of interest that can be derived from an estimated cost function. Another parameter of interest is the effect of volume of wastewater treated on the cost of treatment. Similarly, the effect of lowering post-treatment pollution concentration level on treatment cost would be important to estimate. These require that the total effect of V and qe on C be computed.[12] In the translog specification, due to the existence of various interaction terms, the total effect of a variable, say V cannot be directly read from the estimated equation.

12. In the cost function literature, the elasticity of cost with respect to output is called cost flexibility. The elasticities of C with respect to V and qe computed here are akin to the concept of cost flexibility, since V and qe are connected with the output of abatement activity.

However, the total effect can be computed at the sample mean by differentiating the estimated cost function and setting the various explanatory variables at the sample mean.

Table 23.4

Cost Flexibility

	$\partial \ln C/\partial \ln V$	$\partial \ln C/\partial \ln qe$
Primary Treatment	0.35	-0.50
Total Abatement	0.35	-0.43

The *total effect* of volume of wastewater treated on the cost of abatement (i.e., $\partial lnC / \partial lnV$) has been computed by this method for the estimated primary and total cost functions. The computed elasticities gives the returns to scale in wastewater treatment. Table 23.4 shows there are considerable economies of scale in wastewater treatment as $\partial lnC/\partial ln V = 0.35$ both for primary as well as total costs of abatement (which implies that a 10 per cent increase in water volume leads to 3.5 per cent increase in treatment cost). Also, the total effect of effluent characteristic of COD on the cost of abatement (i.e. $\partial lnC/\partial lnqe$) has been computed from the estimated equations. Table 23.4 shows that for a one per cent reduction in qe, there is a 0.5 per cent increase in primary cost of abatement and a 0.4 per cent increase in total costs of abatement.

SECTION 8

AVERAGE AND MARGINAL COSTS OF TREATMENT

The estimated cost functions for primary treatment and total abatement (without CETP) can be used to derive the average costs and marginal costs of water pollution abatement, thus providing important policy implications for regulation of industrial water pollution in the case of small-scale factories. The full translog specification has been used to estimate the cost of abatement per kilolitre of wastewater treated, keeping input prices, qi and qe at their mean values and varying the quantity of wastewater. Table 23.5 and Figure 23.2 show the average costs of treatment with respect to quantity of wastewater.

Table 23.5

Quantity of Wastewater (Kilolitres per annum)	*Average Cost of Treatment (Rs. per kilolitre)*	
	Primary Treatment Cost Function	*Total Treatment Cost Function*
900	370	516
1200	310	428
1500	260	369
1800	230	328
2100	210	296
2400	190	272
2700	180	251
3000	170	235
3300	160	220
3600	150	208
3900	140	198
4200	130	188
4500	130	180
4800	120	172
5100	120	166
5400	110	160
5700	110	154
6000	110	149

Figure 23.2

Average Cost of Treatment

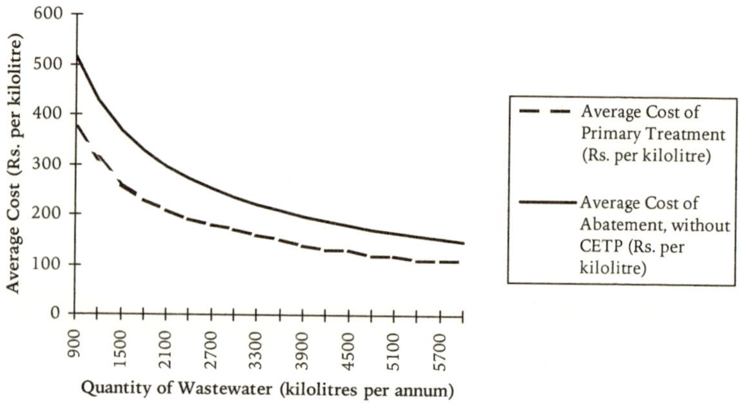

Table 23.5 and Figure 23.2 clearly show that the average cost of treatment falls sharply as the volume of wastewater treated increases, both for primary treatment and total abatement without CETP. Average cost for primary treatment is very high at Rs. 370 per kilolitre when the quantity of wastewater treated is only 900 kilolitres. Due to economies of scale, the average cost falls sharply as the volume treated goes up. At the level of 6000 kilolitres of wastewater, the average cost is Rs. 110 per kilolitre.[13] This shows that a small factory at a level of 6000 kilolitres of wastewater will have a much lower burden of water pollution abatement cost compared to a factory at the level of 900 kilolitres. The respective cost burden is much higher for the total cost of abatement. Hence smaller factories will have a greater cost advantage to join CETP for internalising the externalities.

The full translog specification has been used to estimate the marginal cost of treatment. For these computations, input prices, V and qi are kept at their mean values; qe and hence the pollution load of COD effluent are varied. The pollution load is the product of COD effluent concentration and the volume of wastewater. Table 23.6 and Figure 23.3 show the marginal cost of abatement per unit of pollution load. The graph shows an inverse relationship between marginal cost and the COD effluent concentration. It is seen that at

Table 23.6

COD Effluent (mg/litre)	*Marginal Cost (Rs. per 1000 mg)*	
	Primary Treatment Cost Function	*Total Treatment Cost Function*
200	0.7	0.8
300	0.4	0.5
400	0.3	0.3
500	0.2	0.3
600	0.2	0.2
700	0.2	0.2
800	0.2	0.2
900	0.2	0.3
1000	0.3	0.3

13. The Goldar-Pandey (1997) study finds that abatement cost of wastewater treatment in distilleries (where the average per day wastewater volume is much larger), is in the range of Rs. 20-30 per kilolitre. One must bear in mind that the nature of effluents is very different and simple cost comparisons between two studies cannot be made.

COD concentration level of 600 mg/litre, the marginal abatement cost is Rs 0.2 per gram of COD load. At COD concentration level of 200 mg/litre, the marginal abatement cost is Rs 0.7 per gram of COD load (higher in the estimate based on total abatement cost function).

Figure 23.3

Marginal Abatement Costs

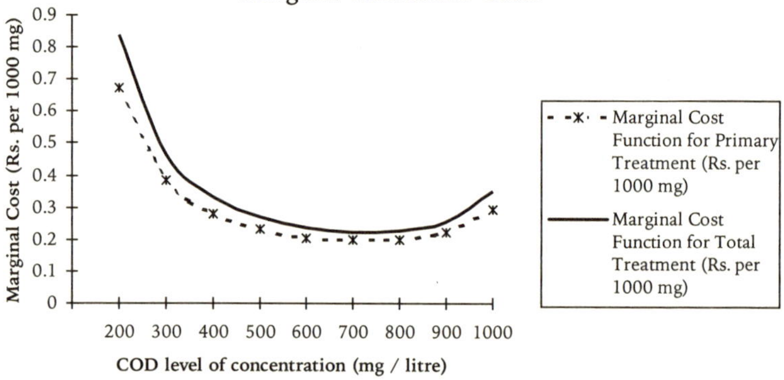

From Table 23.6 it can be seen that a water pollution tax on factories necessary for bringing about a complete abatement (SPCB requirements of COD = 250 mg per litre) should be around Rs. 0.65 per gram of COD.[14] This is a very high rate of tax for internalising the water pollution externalities to small-scale factories and clearly shows why such an instrument cannot be used.

SECTION 9

COSTS OF ABATEMENT UNDER ALTERNATE INSTITUTIONAL ARRANGEMENTS

Having estimated the costs of water pollution abatement, it is necessary to determine the institutional arrangements which will efficiently internalise the externalities for the cluster of small-scale factories at Nandesari. This study compares the costs of abatement

14. According to James-Murty paper, the tax liability should be Rs. 0.32 per 100 grams of COD in the case of large firms. Goldar-Pandey (1997) paper finds that at a tax rate of Rs. 30 per 100 grams of BOD, the distillery will bring down the BOD concentration level to 30 mg/litre which is the present specified standard. One must bear in mind that the nature of effluents is very different and simple cost comparisons between two studies cannot be made.

under (a) command and control regime, (b) market based solutions and (c) CETP arrangements.

(a) Command and Control Regime

Threats of closure of a polluting activity and penalties and imprisonment for the offending parties as envisaged in various legislations are 'command and control' type of regulatory measures. It is widely known that command and control measures do not provide the necessary incentives to the polluters for the choice of least cost methods of pollution control (Cropper and Oates, 1992).

The cost of water pollution abatement for Nandesari Industrial Estate has been computed for a command and control regime. The estimated equation of total cost of abatement (without CETP) was used to find the actual costs for each factory to meet the SPCB requirement of COD = 250 mg/litre and the cost for the entire industrial estate was estimated. The cost of water pollution abatement under a command and control regime (without a CETP) works out to Rs. 419 million. It reduces to Rs. 331 million if the SPCB requirement relaxes to COD = 500 mg/litre. The command and control institution of abatement is highly inefficient because the factories are all abating to the same extent (SPCB requirements) but their marginal costs differ due to differences in size, pre-treatment level of pollution concentration etc.

(b) Market Based Solution

An efficient solution would arise if factories are allowed to trade the extent of water pollution abatement among themselves (meeting the SPCB standards for the entire industrial estate) and are not required to abate to the same extent individually. Such a solution could be brought about with the use of economic instruments (marketable pollution permits are used in USA) which in this study we shall call the 'market based solution'. A 'market based solution' cost of water pollution abatement has been obtained using a cost minimisation model for this study. The total cost of water pollution abatement and water pollution load for the nth factory can be defined as follows:

$$TC(n) = f\,(V(n),\ dci(n),\ qe(n),\ pl(n),\ pk(n),\ pme(n)),$$

$$LD(n) = V(n) * qe(n),$$

$$\text{and } \sum_{n=1}^{38} LD(n) = LD$$

where

TC(n) = total cost of water pollution abatement for nth factory,

pl(n) = price of labour for nth factory,

pk(n) = price of capital for nth factory,

pme(n) = price index of materials and energy for nth factory,

dci(n) = qi(n) - qe(n) = difference between the influent and effluent concentration of the COD pollutant for nth factory,

qe(n) = effluent concentration of COD pollutant for nth factory,

V(n) = quantity of wastewater used for treatment in nth factory,

LD(n) = water pollution load for nth factory,

LD = total water pollution load for the sample factories.

The cost minimisation model is as follows:

$$\text{Minimise } Z = \sum_{n=1}^{38} TC(n)$$

subject to

$\sum_{n=1}^{38} LD(n) = LD \leq LD^*$ (which is some targeted level of water pollution load to be achieved).

and $qe(n) \geq 0$.

Choice variables are qe(n) for n = 1,....38.

Since TC(n) is a non-linear function of qe(n), we get a non-linear programming problem.[15]

LD* has been specified at two levels, for COD at 250 mg/litre and COD at 500 mg/litre.

15. Excel Solver (programme) has been used for generating qe(n) for the sample factories.

Having thus obtained qe(n), the corresponding cost of water pollution abatement for each factory and for the entire industrial estate has been estimated using the translog cost function.

For a requirement of COD = 250 mg/litre, the least cost market solution generated a water pollution abatement cost of Rs. 382 million i.e there is a saving of about Rs. 37 million annually (or about 10 per cent efficiency gains over command and control regime). The implication of this exercise is interesting because *each* factory need not abate to the level COD = 250 mg/litre. The *overall water pollution load* of Nandesari Industrial Area will meet the SPCB requirements of COD = 250 mg/litre. This is analogous to the market permit system already well established in USA. For a requirement of COD = 500 mg/litre, the least cost market based solution generated an abatement cost of Rs. 260 million. In this case, the cost saving was even greater.

(c) Common Effluent Treatment Plant

As an alternative to the two institutional set-ups considered above, this study estimates water pollution abatement cost under a third institutional arrangement which is actually operating in Nandesari, namely a two step set-up based on primary treatment and a joint abatement at the CETP. In order to estimate the full cost of water pollution abatement (i.e. primary + CETP), the annualised cost of CETP is added to the annual primary treatment cost. This is the joint cost of water pollution abatement as a result of the institution of collective action (Misra 1995).

The capital cost of the CETP at 1996 prices is Rs. 37.3 millions. Taking 18 per cent as the opportunity cost and 10 per cent as depreciation, the annualised value of the CETP capital cost is Rs. 10.4 million. The operations and maintenance cost is reported as Rs. 1 million per month. Thus the total CETP cost per annum is Rs. 22.4 million. The total primary treatment cost incurred by the Nandesari Industrial Estate is estimated as Rs. 100 million using the primary treatment cost function. Hence the total cost of water pollution abatement (i.e. primary +CETP) is Rs. 122 million to meet the SPCB requirement of 250 mg/litre. This is the most efficient institution for water pollution abatement as can be seen from the Figure 23.4. The cost reduces to Rs. 114 million if the SPCB relaxes the statutory requirement to COD= 500 mg/litre.

Table 23.7 and Figure 23.4 show the relationship between the three institutional arrangements, CC (Command and Control), MS (Market Based Solution) and PCETP (Primary with CETP). The institutional arrangement of the PCETP is most economical. The user and non-user benefits estimated for six villages and the urban city of Vadodara have been estimated as Rs. 330 million (Misra 1997) using the contingent valuation method. Figure 23.4 shows large potential benefits can be generated using a CETP for water pollution abatement at Nandesari Industrial Estate. This study shows that collective action and a joint abatement is the ideal solution for internalising the water pollution externalities to small-scale factories.

Table 23.7

Rs. (millions)

	Institutional Arrangements		
	CC	*MS*	*PCETP*
COD=250 mg/litre	419	382	122
COD=500mg/litre	331	260	114
BENEFITS=Rs. 330 million	330	330	330

Figure 23.4

Costs of Water Pollution Abatement under Alternate Institutional Arrangements

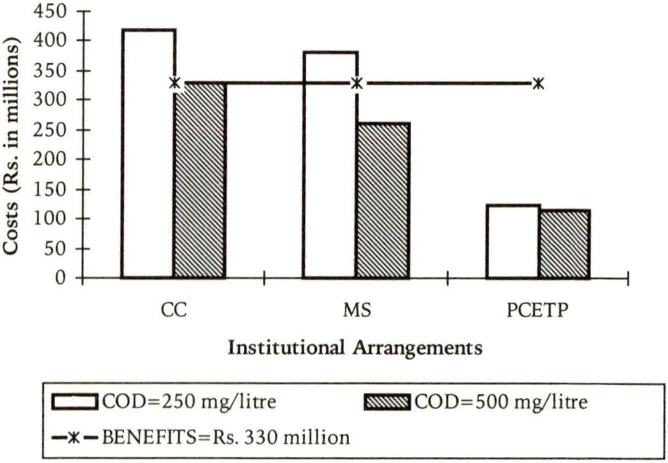

SECTION 10

CONCLUSIONS

There has been no economic analysis of water pollution control decisions affecting operation and regulation of *small-scale* factories and this study is an attempt to bridge this gap, providing empirical evidence on costs of meeting standards for a cluster of 250 small-scale factories in Nandesari Industrial Estate of Gujarat in India. There have been several studies estimating the cost of pollution abatement for large industries. But there are serious inadequacies in the methodologies and problems of interpretation in these studies. While correcting for these inadequacies, this study estimates the costs related to water pollution abatement activity. The production of the abatement plant is viewed as a *service activity* or work done to reduce the level of pollution. The output of the abatement plant is the extent of pollution reduction achieved for each pollutant for a given volume of wastewater treated. Hence, the cost function used in this study has been derived from the related production activity.

The water pollution abatement activity at Nandesari is interesting since the abatement takes place at two stages. There is a primary treatment plant at the factory level to reduce the COD concentration level in the wastewater discharges. A secondary water pollution abatement takes place at the Common Effluent Treatment Plant mainly treating the joint effluents for BOD and COD concentrations to meet the standards of the State Pollution Control Board. The other important objective is to make an estimate of the cost of water pollution abatement to these small-scale factories in the absence of the CETP arrangements. For this purpose, the factory owners were asked to give details of the additional costs they would bear for a total abatement at the factory level. Using data collected from a sample of factories, this study estimates the costs of total abatement (in the absence of a CETP) in addition to the costs of primary treatment (with CETP).

The likelihood ratio test strongly rejected the Cobb-Douglas and truncated translog specifications in favour of the full translog specification of the cost function. Hence a full translog specification has been used to estimate the cost function. The present study is an improvement over the earlier studies in which the translog form could not be used for various reasons. The translog function results show that labour, capital and materials-energy are substitutes as the elasticities of substitution are positive for them. However, since price elasticities are low, the substitution possibilities between the inputs are limited for both primary treatment and total abatement.

This study provides empirical evidence of economies of scale in water pollution abatement activity. The results show that the average cost of treatment falls sharply as the volume of wastewater treated increases, both for primary treatment and total abatement (without CETP). Average cost for primary treatment is very high at Rs. 370 per kilolitre for 900 kilolitres of wastewater treated. The average cost is Rs. 110 per kilolitre for 6000 kilolitres of wastewater treated. This shows that the burden of water pollution abatement is higher for a smaller factory compared to a bigger one. The respective cost burden is much higher for the total cost of abatement. Hence smaller factories will have a greater cost advantage to join CETP. Also the results show an inverse relationship between marginal cost and the COD effluent concentration. A water pollution tax necessary for bringing about total abatement inorder to meet the SPCB requirement (COD = 250 mg per litre) should be around Rs. 0.65 per gram of COD which is very high and clearly shows that this instrument will not work in the case of small-scale factories.

Alternate institutional arrangements have been considered for water pollution abatement activity at Nandesari. This study considers command and control, market based solutions and common effluent treatment as alternative scenarios. The costs of meeting SPCB standards is Rs. 419 million for command and control regime; Rs. 382 million for a market based solution and Rs. 122 million for primary and common effluent treatment. The market solution cannot take advantage of a common treatment and hence is not as economical as the CETP arrangement. The potential benefits from water pollution abatement activities at Nandesari Industrial Estate have been estimated as Rs. 330 million in an earlier study (Misra, 1997) for six villages surrounding Nandesari and the urban city of Vadodara, using the contingent valuation method. This study clearly shows that the institutional arrangement of the CETP is necessary to internalise the water pollution externalities in the case of small-scale factories and that large potential welfare gains can be generated.

References

Batstone, R. *et al.*, (edited), (1989). "The Safe Disposal of Hazardous Wastes," Volume II, *World Bank Technical Paper* No. 93.

Baumol, W.J. (1972). "On Taxation and Control of Externalities," *American Economic Review*, Vol. 42, No. 3, 1972, pp 307-322.

Cropper, M.L. and Oates, W.E (1992). "Environmental Economics: A Survey," *Journal of Economic Literature*, 30, pp 1-44.

Dasgupta, A.K. and M.N. Murty (1985). "Economic Evaluation of Water Pollution Abatement: A Case Study of Paper and Pulp Industry in India," *Indian Economic Review*, Vol. 20, No.2, 1985, pp 231-267.

Frass, A.G. and Munley, V.G. (1984). "Municipal Waste Water Treatment Cost," *Journal of Environmental Economics and Management* 11, pp 28-38.

Goldar B. and R. Pandey (1997). "Fiscal Instruments for Pollution Abatement: A Study of Distilleries in India." Paper presented at the 53rd Congress of the International Institute of Public Finance, Kyoto, August 25-28.

Goldar B. and B. Mukerji (1998). "Pollution Abatement Cost Functions: Methodological and Estimation Issues, C.D.E.," Working Paper No. 56., Delhi School of Economics, University of Delhi, Delhi.

Greene, W.H. (1993). "Econometric Analysis, *Macmillan Publishing Company*," *New York*, pp 135.

Gupta, S. (1996). "Environmental Policy and Federalism in India," National Institute of Public Finance and Policy, New Delhi.

James A.J. and M.N. Murty (1996). "Water Pollution Abatement: A Taxes-and-Standards Approach for Indian Industry," Working Paper No. E/177/96, Institute of Economic Growth.

Mehta S., Sudipto Mundle and U. Sankar (1993). "Incentives and Regulations for Pollution Control with an Application to Waste Water Treatment," National Institute of Public Finance and Policy, New Delhi.

Misra, S. and M.N. Murty (1995). Collective Action in Industrial Water Pollution Abatement: Some Conceptual Issues," Working Paper No.E/166/95, Institute of Economic Growth, Delhi.

Misra, S. (1996). "Accounting for Costs of Water Pollution Abatement: A Case Study of Nandesari Industrial Area," Working Paper No.E/179/96, Institute of Economic Growth, Delhi.

————. (1997). "Measuring Benefits from Industrial Water Pollution Abatement : Use of Contingent Valuation Method in Nandesari Industrial Area of Gujarat in India," Working Paper No.E/185/97, Institute of Economic Growth, Delhi.

Murty, M.N. (1995). "Collective Action: A Deterrant on Colluding Industry and Corrupt Bureaucracy in the Water Pollution Abatement," Working Paper Series, No. E/165/95, Institute of Economic Growth, Delhi.

Pigou, A.C. (1932). The Economics of Welfare, 4th edition, London.

Roy, J. and S. Ganguli (1997). "Evaluation of Pollution Abatement Policy for Paper Industries in India—Standard vs Tax," (Mimeograph Paper) Jadavpur University, Calcutta.

Rossi, D., C.E. Young and D.J. Epp (1979). "The Impact of Joint Treatment of Domestic and Poultry Processing Wastewaters," Land Economics.

24

Prospects of Market for Water Pollution in India

A Study Based on Selected Dirty Industries

SARMILA BANERJEE
SIMANTI BANERJEE

SECTION 1

INTRODUCTION

Indian environmental protection policies are mainly based on Command and Control. Standards are set for pollutants and wastes, non-compliance of which leads to closing down of industrial units by legal orders imposing high social and economic costs. Both the environmental economists and the regulators are convinced about the high enforcement costs involved in this approach.

Restoring allocative efficiency through the adoption of incentive-based policies is a better option in many ways. Two major alternatives here are pollution taxes and the tradable pollution permits. In case of emissions trading, the pollution externality is internalised through free initial distribution of permits followed by a provision for further possible cost saving reallocation by exchange of permits among the polluters. For a specified environmental standard, to attain efficient allocation of pollution abatement, emissions trading approach is theoretically proved to be the least cost one (Montgomery 1972). It is equally efficient as pollution taxes and, if properly designed, is definitely easier to implement.

In case of tax-based pollution control policies, the primary problem faced by the regulatory authority is the information asymmetry regarding the marginal abatement costs of the polluters. This typical revelation problem can be successfully overcome by an emissions trading scheme. Here, the individual unit has to know its marginal abatement cost and the permit price prevailing in the market. If the price exceeds its marginal abatement cost the firm will go for abatement and sell the permit whereas in the opposite case, it would be a net buyer of permits. The scheme has an in-built incentive to tackle the moral hazard problem arising out of asymmetric information.

Like any trading process, the gains from trade in pollution permits is a function of the difference in the marginal abatement costs of the industrial units involved in the mechanism. The process will ultimately ensure allocative efficiency, as the marginal abatement costs would be equalised across firms, value of which will emerge as the equilibrium price of a permit.

The present paper is based on some preliminary set of simple regressions with small datasets to investigate the possibilities of pollution trading in India. This study particularly aims to explore how an internal market for Biological Oxygen Demand (BOD) can be developed to control industrial water pollution in India.

One possible source of inter industry differences in emission control behavior is the difference in abatement cost structures. The main findings of our analysis suggest that in India, there exist differences in the marginal cost functions for wastewater treatment across industries, even though they employ the same technique for pollution control. Also, the pollutant specific Minimum National Standards (MINAS) set by the Central Pollution Control Board sometimes vary across industries. These differences can be successfully utilised to formulate emissions trading policies between industries. Since there is a dimension of location attached to such a policy, we need to specify a particular region for which the scheme can be applied. As a first move towards this new policy, we can conceive of a hypothetical industrial estate where the proposed market for water pollution can be set up

To explore the possibilities of emissions trading among the Indian industries we have concentrated on a few 'dirty' industries and have collected information on their wastewater treatment from the Comprehensive Industry Documents (COINDS) published by the Central Pollution Control Board (CPCB). The analysis will be focused to address the following questions:

(a) Corresponding to the tolerable limits specified by MINAS (Minimum National Standard) for each pollutant, whether there exist any industry-level difference in the cost of treating wastewater.

(b) If the MACs are different, what could be a viable trading scheme to ensure efficiency? (Given uniform MINAS, difference in MAC is sufficient for trading but not necessary. When MACs are identical, difference in MINAS or difference in initial conditions may form the basis of trading. For both the cases, physical proximity of the units is an important requirement).

With information on these two dimensions, we would be in a position to suggest the pattern of trade that can efficiently control water pollution in a particular area. In this context, we can also comment on the choice of industries for any industrial area in India where efficient permit trading could be arranged in future to ensure impersonal implementation of pollution control policies. The analysis would be organised as follows: Section 2 will review the available studies on the estimation of abatement cost function both at the aggregate industry-level and for a few specific industries in India and abroad to have an overview of the methodologies of abatement cost estimation existing in the literature. Section 3 will present a description of the database. Here we have reviewed the data on water pollution available in the form of COINDS documents for nine dirty industries published by CPCB. After analysing the existing data for these nine industries we have chosen three industries for which adequate firm-level data (which can be utilised for a valid econometric analysis) are available. The model used for our estimation is also spelt out in this section. Section 4 reports the major regression results whereas marginal costs are estimated in Section 5. In Section 6, the design of a viable trading scheme is suggested for an industrial area where the problem of pollution is acute. Some limitations of the analysis are indicated in Section 7. The direction for future research is discussed in the concluding section.

SECTION 2

REVIEW OF EXISTING STUDIES

In this section, we will give a brief survey of the literature on estimation of abatement cost function, with particular attention to the functional form chosen in each case. The references covered for the analysis share a common objective; all of them attempt to fit a cost function for wastewater treatment, either for the industry as a sector, or for a particular industry, in an economy. The marginal cost functions are then derived to prescribe some important policy parameters.

The earliest work to treat abatement cost as a function of performance levels (i.e. how much of the influent is being treated) is by Fraas and Munley (1984). Before that, the EPA in the US used the volume of wastewater as the only independent variable. Fraas and Munley takes the specific form as:

$$C = K\, F^{\alpha}\, I^{\beta}\, E^{\gamma}\, U^{\delta}$$

Where

F = Flow of wastewater;

I = Influent concentration;

E = Effluent concentration;

U = Avg. capacity utilisation.

Economists in their works have used different variations of this functional form. Two of them, Mehta, Mundle and Sankar (1993) and Roy and Ganguly, (1997) uses this form for estimating the abatement cost function for the paper and pulp industry in India. The capacity utilisation variable is not required for their purpose. So this variable was dropped. Mehta, Mundle and Sankar tried another functional form, which included the effluent concentration multiplied by a constant as a power of e. Goldar and Pandey (1997) takes Fraas and Munley's form to estimate the cost for distilleries in India whereas Pandey (1998) uses this form to estimate the pollution abatement cost function for India in general.

Another form specifying the functional relationship between cost and performance of a pollution abatement programme incorporates the influent-effluent ratio for the pollutants involved as the independent variables, along with the wastewater flow and plant characteristics. The function can be written as:

$$C = KF^{\alpha} \prod_{j=1}^{m} \left[\frac{E_j}{I_j}\right]^{\beta_j} \qquad j = \text{index for a pollutant.}$$

C, F, E, I having the same meanings as before.

Two articles, which use this form, need special mention. The first one is by Dasgupta *et al.*, (1996) which attempts to estimate the abatement cost function for the Chinese Industry as a whole taking one variable each for suspended solids (SS), biological oxygen demand (BOD) and chemical oxygen demand (COD) and one variable denoting other pollutants, as the independent variables. The other paper, by James and Murthy (1996), estimates the abatement cost of wastewater treatment for the Indian industrial sector as a whole taking the same pollutants. The dataset for both the papers consist of different industries clubbed together.

Goldar, Mishra and Mukherjee (1999) uses a new form of cost function, which incorporates the difference between the absolute levels of influent and effluent of a pollutant as a variable, along with the effluent concentration and volume of wastewater. The form can be explicitly written as:

$C = K F^{\alpha} (I\text{-}E)^{\beta} E^{\gamma}$ the notations having the same meanings.

All the variations of Cobb Doughlus form have been tried with translog specification also. Since the constant elasticity form is easier to handle for policy prescriptions, it is more widely used. Most of the previous studies have derived the pollutant specific marginal cost functions after estimating the cost function and calculated the optimal tax rate for polluting activities in the economy. Some of them have calculated the order of savings in cost for alternative policy regimes.

The main purpose of the present study is to empirically verify whether there exist differences in the abatement cost functions across industries in India. On the basis of these differences, we would also propose the possibility of emissions trading between industries, which can bring efficiency in the system.

SECTION 3

DATASET AND MODEL

In this section we will first attempt to analyse the data related to wastewater treatment by different industries published so far by the Central Pollution Control Board in their Comprehensive Industry Document Series (COINDS). In order to collect information on each type of industry in the country in respect of number of units, their location, capacity, type of product, process adopted, raw materials used, wastewater treatment presently adopted and other aspects of pollution, the COINDS series was started. The primary objective of the series is to evolve standards, which are not specific to location. After a detailed study of the data, we choose three industries for which the data is adequate for estimating abatement cost functions industry wise. In what follows we will attempt an analysis of the data available from COINDS chronologically. The choice of industries and also the pollutants will become evident from our analysis of the data.

Man-Made Fibre

The first in the COINDS series is the Man-Made Fibre industry. The document was published in 1979-80. It gives detailed classification of 28 among the total of 29 operating units in India in terms of different types of man-made fibre, the number of units operating for each category, their location (statewide and river-basin wise), their installed capacity, and future expansion plans. Wastewater discharge and capacity of production data are given for five units. BOD, COD and suspended solids are the most important water-pollutants for this industry. Physico-chemical characteristics of different parts of the rivers, into which the wastes are disposed off, like Ganga, Chambal, Hoogly, Periyar, etc, are also given. Chapters 13 and 14 of this document are the most important chapters for our purpose. The first deals with effluent treatment processes and the second with the cost of effluent treatment. They have recorded average effluent figures product wise and also by the methods used to treat them. For synthetic fibre the effluent normally would contain BOD in the upper range of about 100mg/litre. The average COD of effluents is around 400mg/litre. For the treatment of effluent from synthetic fibre industry, extended aeration by oxidation pond is suggested. This method removes nearly 85-90 per cent of the BOD and COD contents of the effluent. For the viscose rayon product, the most harmful element in the effluent apart from BOD, COD and SS is the zinc content. The harmful effects of the toxicity of zinc are tried to be kept within the tolerable limits by different zinc removal methods like chemical precipitation, ion exchange, absorption through vegetable media, insoluble starch xanthate method and sulfex process. The most practical and economical is the method of chemical precipitation by the adjustment of the pH. The capital cost data for five synthetic fibre plants and 12 cellulosic plants employing different effluent treatment methods are given. But the operating cost figures are only given for one hypothetical firm each for synthetic fibre and viscose rayon with a particular capacity for each, viz. 12 tonne/day and 10 tonne/day respectively.

Oil Refinery

The document on Oil Refineries was published in 1980-81. At that time there were 22 oil refineries operating in India and three were in advanced stage of commissioning. Two classifications of the oil refineries are given. The first one is on the basis of the refining capacities, viz., small, medium, and large and the other one is according to the principal refining processes. The figures for refining capacity per day of these 11 units and the river to which each is disposing off the waste are also given. A field survey was carried out for eight units to collect data on existing wastewater treatment. The treatment facility in a refinery has three principal stages viz. primary oil separation, secondary oil separation including sulphide removal, and biological treatment. Wastewater volume and characteristics at each stage of treatment are given for the sampled firms. The pollutants concerned are BOD, pH, oil and grease, phenol, sulphide and in some cases COD. From the data it is clear that the refineries that have comprehensive wastewater treatment plants are able to achieve the median values of removal of oil and grease by 99.3 per cent, phenol by 65.18 per cent, sulphide by 99.66 per cent and BOD by 83.33 per cent. Loss of oil in the treatment processes and its recovery plays an important role in the cost determination of the treatment processes because a considerable amount of oil gets wasted in the process. Cost figures are given for each stage as percentages of the total treatment costs. The share of primary oil separation is 20 per cent, that of secondary oil separation is 35 per cent, whereas biological treatment costs about 45 per cent of the total cost. Average costs of wastewater treatment are also given for one standard unit.

Sugar

The document for Sugar published in 1980-81 contains firm-level data for 112 factories out of 299 factories of Sugar. The sugar mills are classified according to crushing capacity. But the classes are not the same for all variables, e.g. for wastewater volume, they have given three classes viz. Upto 1500, 1500-3000, 3000 and above (Figures are in Tonnes/day unit). For the treatment cost figures, they have classified the data under four heads of crushing capacity viz. 800-1250, 2000-2500, 3000-3500, and 5000-5500. However, proper caution has been taken to generate a series of data from such unevenly classified figures so that it can best represent the classes. Cost and volume of wastewater series are generated in this way. The influent values of the parameters BOD and SS were given for each firm. The effluent figures were not given. We took the 'MINAS' for each pollutant as the effluent value. Altogether, we chose 21 firms. Out of these, 11 firms underwent only primary treatment, the data for which we had to generate, after consulting experts, by taking primary treatment expenditure as 1-5 per cent of the total treatment expenditure (viz. primary and secondary) for the respective capacities of firms. Since the total treatment cost of different capacities were given, it was not a problem. We estimated two sets of regression one with 21 firms which includes some units with complete treatment and some with only primary treatment, and the other with 10 firms which underwent complete treatment.

Fermentation

The document on Fermentation industry was published in 1981-82. The document includes maltry, brewery and distillery under the heading of fermentation for the analysis. Location and licensed capacity are recorded for most of the units. Wastewater characteristics for model cases for maltry, brewery and distilleries as sectors with particular capacities are given. The most important pollutants are BOD and suspended solids. Capital outlay and operating costs of these sectors are given separately. Costs of a few alternatives like anaerobic lagooning, anaerobic digestion, and potash recovery are also given. The annual burden to turnover ratio for the fermentation industry as a whole is calculated to be 0.15 per cent.

Iron and Steel

The next document we study is the COINDS on Iron and Steel industry. The document was published in 1988-89. Seven integrated iron and steel plants in India are surveyed in this document. Different stages of production are considered and wastewater characteristics of each stage are given. The important pollutants include BOD, COD, suspended solids, phenol, oil and grease, etc. Wastewater discharge data is given for five firms. For each of the major water pollutants the sources and methods for removal are discussed. The document does not deal with cost of treatment.

Large Pulp and Paper

The next is the Large Pulp and Paper industry. This document was published in 1991. There are 40 plants belonging to the large category defined as those having chemical recovery system, with a total installed capacity of 2.03 million tonnes per annum. Water requirements are in the range of 250-440cu.m/tonne of product depending upon quality of paper made and the extent of recycle. Combined wastewater from large mills ranges between 167-281 cu. m/tonne. The pollution load contributed in terms of suspended solids, BOD and COD are in the ranges of 109-280, 54-179, and 160-488 kg/tonne respectively. Performance evaluation of wastewater treatment plants in six mills provides information on design criteria used for different stages of treatment. Suspended solids, COD, BOD removals in primary clarifiers are observed at 80 per cent, 50 per cent, and 30 per cent respectively. Cost incurred for wastewater treatment with three alternatives viz. aerated lagoon, activated sludge and colour removal followed by aerated lagoon are also recorded.

Pesticides

The document for Pesticide industry was published in 1992-93. It gives detailed wastewater characteristic data for 37 firms. For our analysis, data for 18 firms are found to be suitable. Out of these 18 firms, for five firms, we have figures for treatment cost expressed as percentages of total turnover of the respective firms. In order to convert these percentages into Rupees-Crore figures, we had to get the annual turnover data for these firms from the PROWESS database published by CMIE and Capitaline database. Here we take BOD and SS as the pollutants.

Fertilisers

The document on Fertiliser industry was published in 1994-95. It concentrates on the general production and pollution prevention options available to the industry. 48 existing plants and five plants under installation are all taken as the sample of study. Information on 33 plants is available. But very few firms have data on all the variables recorded. Different categories of fertiliser plants are studied. The main water pollutants are BOD, SS and oil and grease. Detailed costs of treatment, split into capital and operating costs, and also as percentages of total turnover are given only for two units.

Textile

The next industry for our analysis is the Textile industry which has the most comprehensive document in the COINDS series.. The COINDS for textile was published in April 2000 and gives firm-level data of wastewater characteristic for 24 firms including 10 composite and 14 processing units. Out of these, data for 13 units are found to be suitable for our analysis. Since the MINAS for liquid effluents do not differ between composite and processing industry, we can attempt an analysis for the textile industry as a whole. The pollutants taken here are BOD, COD, and Suspended Solids.

After going through the data on the above nine industries we find that for only three industries, viz. Sugar, Pesticide and Textile, firm level data for wastewater characteristics and costs exist. The data set for these three industries are also not large enough to represent their share in the economy very well, but each of them is sufficient to tell a story behind an econometric exercise which can initiate a discussion on the said topic and can question the validity of some policy prescriptions.

Model

We fit a constant elasticity model for all the industries.

$$C_i = e^{\alpha_i} v^{\beta_i} \prod_{j=1}^{m} \left[\frac{I_j}{E_j} \right]^{\gamma_j} \qquad \ldots(1)$$

I=industry code;

j= pollutant code;

v=wastewater volume;

I, E, C having the same meaning as before.

MC can be calculated as:

$$\frac{\partial C_i}{\partial E_j} = e^{\alpha} v^{\beta} \gamma_j \frac{1}{E_j} \prod_{j=1}^{m} \left[\frac{I_j}{E_j} \right]^{\gamma_j} \qquad \ldots(2)$$

SECTION 4

REGRESSION ESTIMATES

Let us discuss the results of the estimation exercise in this section. We start with the textile industry. Table A-24.1 in Appendix 1 summarises the results of the first set of regression with annual burden (ab) of the firms as the dependent variable, and, volume, and influent-effluent ratio of each pollutant as the independent variables.

The constant is significant for most of the cases except for equations (3) and (8). Volume is significant in all the equations and the coefficients carry the expected positive sign and the magnitude is less than one, which implies that economies of scale exist in the abatement technology. The BOD ratio is weakly significant in all the equations except for equation (7). The level of significance is around 15-20 per cent. For equation (7), the level of significance is 5 per cent. COD ratio is significant in all the equations and except for equation (1), the level of significance is 1 per cent or 5 per cent. SS ratio is significant for equations (6) and (7), one at 5 per cent level and the other at 15 per cent level.

From the above observations, we can conclude that COD ratio and volume are the most important factors explaining cost followed by BOD ratio. SS ratio can be dropped from the relationship. Finally, equation (9) can be chosen as the estimated equation with $R^2 = 0.82$ and adjusted R^2 is as high as 0.75.

Cost function for textile industry can be given as:

$C^{TEXT} = e^{-9.18}\ v^{0.76}\ br^{0.57}\ cr^{1.42}$

Next to textiles, let us analyse the results for the pesticide industry. For this industry, our dependent variable for the regression remains the same as the first set of regressions done for textiles, i.e. annual burden of the firms, whereas the set of independent variables contains one pollutant less than those taken for textiles. COD is not relevant for our purpose here. We run the regression first with 17 firms and then with 11 firms after dropping some of the observations, which we doubt, carry ambiguous information. The second set of regressions could not improve the results. So Table A-24.2 in Appendix 1 gives only the results for the first set of regressions.

As we can see, volume is not found to be significant in any of the equations. sr is relatively more important though not statistically significant at less than 10 per cent level. In all the equations, BOD is significant at less than 1 per cent level.

Analysis of the results leads us to choose equation (2) as our reference equation as here adjusted R^2 is the maximum (0.28). We use this equation for further calculation of marginal abatement cost. Though equation (1) has the highest R^2, adjusted R^2 is 0.22 and therefore we have preferred equation (2) over equation (1).

Let us write the cost function explicitly:

$C^{PEST} = e^{-0.9}\, br^{0.8}$

The third industry for our analysis is Sugar. The variables, both dependent and independent, are the same as they are for the Pesticide industry. Two sets of regressions are run, the first with 21 observations and the second with 10 observations. The results are summarised in Tables A-24.3a and A-24.3b in Appendix 1 respectively.

The constant is significant for all the equations in both sets, the level of significance being very high in set (b). Volume is also significant in all the equations in both the sets, the level of significance being particularly high in set (b). The BOD ratio is only significant for equation 4(b) at 20 per cent but carries a negative sign which is unusual. SS is weakly significant in both the sets but carries a positive sign for set (b).

Though we cannot get robust estimates from the regression results, we can choose equation 3 of Table A-24.3b for our purpose with R^2 as high as 83 per cent and adjusted R^2 as high as 78 per cent.

The cost function is given by: $C^{SUGAR} = e^{-11.28}\, v^{0.87}\, sr^{0.03}$.

SECTION 5

ESTIMATION OF MARGINAL COSTS

In the previous section, we have derived the cost functions for the three dirty industries we have chosen for our purpose. After omitting the irrelevant variables, we found that in two out of three cases, BOD ratio is one of the important determinants of cost. This supports the fact that it is the most basic water pollutant. Thus, in our marginal cost calculations, we have taken BOD as the relevant variable.

Let us write the cost function for the three industries once again:

$$C^{TEXT} = e^{-9.18}\, v^{0.76}\, br^{0.57}\, cr^{1.42}$$

$$C^{PEST} = e^{-0.9}\, br^{0.8}$$

$$C^{SUGAR} = e^{-11.28}\, v^{0.87}\, sr^{0.03}$$

We are convinced that the abatement cost function is different across the sample of industries we have chosen. We can derive the marginal cost functions of BOD removal for textiles and pesticide industries using equation (2). Let us not take Sugar for our analysis here, as the cost function for sugar does not contain BOD as an explanatory variable.

The marginal cost functions can be written as:

$$MC^{TEXT} = -0.57\, e^{-9.18}\, v^{0.76}\, c_r^{1.42}\, b_I^{0.57}\, b_E^{-1.57}$$

$$MC^{PEST} = -0.8\, e^{-0.9}\, b_I^{0.8}\, b_E^{-1.8}$$

For different levels of volume and influent concentrations, we can generate the marginal cost schedule for each industry. Instead of taking all the values, the marginal costs at the minimum, maximum and MINAS levels of effluent concentrations are shown in Table A-24.4, taking average levels of volume and influent concentration. The figures show that the marginal costs are increasing with the level of abatements.

The common practice in the literature so far has been to calculate the marginal cost at the MINAS level and set the tax rate equal to the marginal cost. For that purpose, a single cost function has to be estimated for industry as a sector.

The purpose of our paper is to use the difference in the cost function between industries, to suggest some new policy prescriptions. We propose that a suitable trading scheme between industries can be formulated for a particular pollutant in a particular region that will lead to savings in the costs of pollution for an economy. As we can see from the Table, marginal costs are different for different effluent levels and also the MINAS across industries for the same pollutant is not always the same. Emissions trading can prove to be more successful than other instruments.

SECTION 6

ENVIRONMENTAL SUSTAINABILITY OF AN INDUSTRIAL ESTATE: A PROPOSAL

We are here to explore the possibility of inter-industry pollution trading with the implicit assumption of uniform abatement technology within an industry. From our estimations, it is apparent that the possibility of pollution trading is the highest in the context of BOD. Here, Textiles has a higher MAC to conform to MINAS compared to Pesticides. So, if located within a reasonable proximity, Textile may be interested in buying permits from Pesticides.[1] As Pesticide will abate more and more to sell permit to textile, its MAC will keep on rising and the trading will stop at a point where for both industries the MAC for the last unit of abatement would be equal.

If a new industrial township is to be developed keeping in mind the issues of sustainability, a careful choice of location for the industries is to be carried out so that those with mutually compatible abatement cost functions can appropriate the benefits of collective emission trading. In fact, there exists a list of possible alternatives from which the industrial estate has to choose its firms. This list contains relevant factors like the availability of raw materials, technology, marketing channel, etc. From within this feasible menu, the planner has to select a viable core which would be both ecologically and geologically sustainable even in the long run. In selecting this core, one may take into account the possibility of emission trading to minimise the environmental impact of the project. In past, when industrial townships were developed in Durgapur, Kalyani and other places, even with initial economic success, they could not be sustained environmentally in the long run as the planners did not place much weight on the environmental management aspect.

SECTION 7

SOME LIMITATIONS

Let us state the limitations of the analysis in brief. First of all the available data is not adequate to carry out an accurate estimation.

1. Since we have cost estimation only for Textiles and Pesticides, our hypothetical example suggests a permit trading between these two without any reference to the practicability of this suggestion.

There are many missing observations in the original document which had to be omitted. This can lead to a sample selection bias.

Secondly, the quality of the data can be questioned because there exist incentives on the part of the firms to misreport. This can lead to measurement error problem.

In order to check the sensitivity of the results, we have carried out a second set of regression with a ratio of annual burden and annual turnover (abat) as the dependent variable for textile industry. The data for abat for the firms are available from the document. Since these are fractions with very little variation, out of fifteen regressions run, only three equations were found to have desired statistical properties. In order to add some variation in the data set without losing its true nature, we multiply the ratios by 100 and then re-run the same regressions. Results improve, and in this case, we can choose at least 11 equations, which help us to understand how the wastewater characteristics of a firm affect abat.

When abat is taken as the dependent variable, const and sr is significant in all the three equations; br and cr are significant in equations (3) and (2) respectively. Volume is nowhere significant. When (abat$\times$100) is taken as the dependent variable, volume is not significant in any of the equations. br is significant in equations (4) and (10), cr is significant in (6), (7), and (8), and sr is significant in all the equations. The constant is nowhere significant. We can see that results are sensitive to the choice of the dependent variable. A different cost schedule can be generated using this estimation.

SECTION 8

CONCLUSION

The main findings of the above study suggest that there exist differences in the marginal abatement cost functions across industries, even though they employ the same technique for pollution control. Also, the pollutant specific standards (MINAS) set by CPCB, sometimes vary across industries. These differences can be successfully used to formulate a policy which allows trading in emissions across industries. Since there is a dimension of location attached to such a policy, we need to specify a particular region for which the scheme can be applied. As a first move towards this new policy, we can conceive of a hypothetical industrial estate where the proposed market for water pollution can be set up.

We have only spelt out the possibility of successful trading. We conceive of a situation where the government distributes pollutant specific permits, free of cost, to the firms in an industrial estate. The total amount of pollution permitted in that area must be equal to the standards specified. The firms are allowed to exchange permits at a price developed through the interaction of demand and supply.

Once it is established that emissions trading through a market for pollution can help industrial estates to develop sustainably, we can propose that among the other considerations taken into account while setting up a new industrial estate, the choice of industries should be made in such a way that their marginal cost functions differ significantly from each other. This will ensure the efficiency of the trading scheme which can be proposed for the new industrial estate to tackle the problem of pollution control.

Glossary of Notations Used in the Text

F or ‘v’. = flow of waste water

I = influent

E = effluent

‘b_I’ = influent BOD

‘b_E’= effluent BOD

‘c_I’ = influent COD

‘c_E’= effluent COD

‘s_I’ = influent SS

‘s_E’ = effluent SS

‘b_r’ = ratio of influent to effluent BOD (b_I/b_E)

‘c_r’ = ratio of influent to effluent COD (c_I/c_E)

‘s_r’ = ratio of influent to effluent SS (s_I/s_E)

References

Banerjee Sarmila and S. Banerjee (2000). "Permit-Trading and Industrial Water Pollution: A Prospect Study Based on Selected Indian Industries," Seminar Paper No. 5, University of Calcutta.

Dasgupta, S., M. Huq, D. Wheeler and C. Zhang (1996). "Water Pollution Abatement by Chinese Industry: Cost Estimates and Policy Implications," *Policy Research Department Woking Paper No. 1630*, World Bank, Washington D.C.

Fraas, A.G. and V.G. Munley (1984). "Municipal Waste Water Treatment Cost," *Journal of Environmental Economics and Management* 11: 28-38.

Goldar, B., S. Misra and B. Mukherji (2001). "Water Pollution Abatement Cost Function: Methodological Issues and An Application to Small Scale Factories in an Industrial Estate in India,": *Environment and Development Economics* 6(1): 103-122.

Goldar, B. and R. Pandey (1997). "Fiscal Instruments for Pollution Abatement: A Study of Distilleries in India," Paper presented at the 53rd Congress of the International Institute of Public Finance, Kyoto, August 25-28.

James, A.G. and M.N. Murty (1996). "Water Pollution Abatement: A Taxes and Standards Approach for Indian Industry," Working Paper No. E/177/1996, Institute of Economic Growth, Delhi; Published in M.N. Murty, A.G. James and S. Misra (eds): Economics of Industrial Pollution Abatement: Theory and Empirical Evidence from the Indian Experience, OUP, New Delhi, 1999.

Mehta, S., S. Mundle and U. Sankar (1993). "Incentive and Regulation for Pollution Abatement with an Application to Waste Water Treatment," Report: National Institute of Public Finance and Policy, New Delhi.

Montgomery W.D. (1972). "Markets in Licenses and Efficient Pollution Control Programs," *Journal of Economic Theory*.

Pandey, R. (1998). "Pollution Taxes and Industrial Water Pollution Control," Report: National Institute of Public Finance and Policy, New Delhi.

Roy, J. and S. Ganguly (1997). "Evaluation of Pollution Abatement Policy for Paper Industry in India – Standard Vs. Tax," *mimeo*, Jadavpur University, Calcutta.

The authors would like to thank the Central Pollution Control Board, New Delhi and Calcutta (zonal office) for the co-operation and support extended during data collection. The authors would also like to thank Snigdha Chakraborty, B.N. Goldar, Dhrubajyoti Ghosh, Ananya Ghosh Dastidar, Jeeta Mohanty, S.K. Nigam, Mohit Roy, Rita Saha, R.P. Sengupta for useful comments and suggestions. The help offered by Murali K. and Arindam Banerjee for making the Prowess and Capitaline data accessible is greatfully acknowledged. Preliminary versions of the paper were presented at the conference organised in the honour of Prof. K.L. Krishna at Delhi School of Economics, 1999 and Annual Conference of Jadavpur University, Calcutta in 2000. The authors would like to thank the participants of both the Conferences. Special thanks to Kavita Ayenger for her useful comments and suggestions as the discussant of the paper at the conference organised in the honour of Prof. K.L. Krishna at Delhi School of Economics.

APPENDIX 1

Table A-24.1

Regression Results for Textile Industry Dependent Variable: Ln (Ab)

VARIABLES → EQUATIONS ↓	CONST	Ln v	Ln b_r	Ln c_r	Ln s_r	R^2	ADJR^2	DF
1	-9.25 (3.5)	.72 (3.2)	.87 (1.4)	.94 (1,08)	.48 (.73)	.84	.73	6
2	-5.25 (-1.9)	.62 (2.72)				.30	.26	17
3	.57 (.75)			1.67 (2.4)		.36	.30	10
4	-5.5 (-1.6)	.28 (1.8)	.83 (1.62)			.40	.30	11
5	-9.1 (-3.6)	.82 (3.9)		1.7 (3.89)		.76	.71	9
6	-6.14 (-1.7)	.6 (2.02)			.96 (1.57)	.40	.29	11
7	-1.46 (-1.46)		1.18 (2.3)		1.26 (2.04)	.45	.34	10
8	.056 (.55)			1.82 (2.07)	.22 (.28)	.40	.30	8
9	-9.18 (-3.6)	.76 (3.62)	.57 (1.2)	1.42 (2.4)		.82	.75	7

Table A-24.1a

Regression Results for Textile Industry
Dependent Variable : Ln (Abat)

VARIABLES → EQUATIONS ↓	CONST	Ln b_r	Ln c_r	Ln s_r	R^2	ADJR^2	DF
1	-2.8 (-3.3)			2.17 (3.2)	.48	.43	11
2	-4.17 (-6.02)		1.25 (2.13)	2.18 (4.02)	.83	.79	7
3	-4.64 (-3.97)	.85 (1.8)		2.56 (4.5)	.70	.64	9

Table A-24.1b

Regression Results for Textile Industry
Dependent Variable: Ln (Abat X 100)

VARIABLES → EQUATIONS ↓	CONST	Ln v	Ln b_r	Ln c_r	Ln s_r	R^2	ADJR^2	DF
1	5.37 (1.06)	-.34 (-.86)	.57 (.74)	.3 (.24)	1.5 (2.09)	.69	.48	11
2	2.72 (2.29)		79 (1.13)			.1	.02	13
3	2.45 (3.34)				1.6 (2.67)	.41	.35	12
4	.93 (.94)		1.03 (1.99)		1.55 (2.94)	.59	.50	12
5	6.28 (1.4)	-.31 (-.86)			1.59 (2.61)	.46	.34	12
6	1.52 (2.02)			1.28 (1.63)	1.2 (1.92)	.63	.54	11
7	2.04 (1.94)		-.0002 (.0002)	2.1 (2.09)		.46	.33	11
8	2.6 (.46)	.04 (.106)		2.05 (2.36)		.46	.33	11
9	1.11 (1.08)			.84 (.78)	1.34 (1.95)	.65	.50	11
10	4.06 (.97)				1.54 (2.05)	.62	.48	12
11	5.22 (1.06)	-.29 (-.76)		.92 (.98)	1.37 (2.02)	.66	.52	11

Table A-24.2

Regression Results for Pesticide Industry
Dependent Variable: Ln (Ab)

VARIABLES → EQUATIONS ↓	CONST	Ln v	Ln b_r	Ln s_r	R^2	ADJR^2	DF
1	-2.81 (-.62)	.16 (.42)	.76 (2.22)	-.67 (-1.1)	.41	.22	9
2	-.9 (-1.23)		.8 (2.52)	-.69 (-1.2)	.40	.28	10
3	-2.86 (.66)	.15 (.4)	.58 (1.88)		.30	.17	11
4	-1.12 (-1.88)		.62 (2.21)		.29	.23	12
5	-4.59 (-1.31)	.36 (1.17)			.07	.02	16

Table A-24.3a

Regression Results for Sugar Industry
Dependent Variable: Ln (Ab) (21 Observations)

VARIABLES → EQUATIONS ↓	CONST	Ln v	Ln b_r	Ln s_r	R^2	ADJR^2	DF
1	-29.89 (-1.42)	2.24 (1.3)	.12 (.13)	-.74 (-1.15)	.14	.007	17
2	-29.12 (-1.48)	2.18 (1.34)		.68 (-1.39)	.14	.05	18

Table A-24.3b

Regression Results For Sugar Industry
Dependent Variable: Ln (Ab) (10 Observations)

VARIABLES → EQUATIONS ↓	CONST	Ln v	Ln b_r	Ln s_r	R^2	ADJR^2	DF
1	-10.95 (-5.08)	.85 (4.8)	.02 (-.46)	.042 (1.26)	.83	.75	6
2	-10.2 (-4.7)	.79 (4.5)	.009 (.19)		.79	.73	7
3	-11.28 (-5.87)	.87 (5.49)		.03 (1.26)	.83	.78	7
4	-.61 (-5.5)		.104 (-1.4)		.19	.10	8
5	-10.02 (-5.9)	.77 (5.46)			.79	.76	8

Table A-24.4

Marginal Abatement Costs of Textile and Pesticide Industries

Industry→		*Textile*			*Pesticide*	
Wastewater Volume (cu.m/year)		292280.76			Not Relevant	
b_I (mg/l)		334.27			17503.83	
c_r		2.896			Not Relevant	
b_E(mg/l)	$b_E^{MAX}=360$	$b_E^{MIN}=28$	$b_E^{MINAS}=30$	$b_E^{MAX}=5532$	$b_E^{MIN}=2.3$	$b_E^{MINAS}=100$
MC(RS.)	$MC(b_E^{MAX})=.009$	$MC(b_E^{MIN})=.54$	$MC(b_E^{MINAS})=.48$	$MC(b_E^{MAX})=.0001$	$MC(b_E^{MIN})=179.6$	$MC(b_E^{MINAS})=.20$

EDITORS

Suresh D Tendulkar
Centre for Development Economics
Delhi School of Economics, Delhi

Arup Mitra
Institute of Economic Growth, Delhi

K Narayanan
Indian Institute of Technology-Bombay (Mumbai)

Deb Kusum Das
Ramjas College,
University of Delhi, Delhi